W9-BJT-183

ALSO BY

CARLETON S. COON

THE STORY OF MAN
(1954, 1962)

THE SEVEN CAVES
(1957)

with Edward E. Hunt, Jr.
THE LIVING RACES OF MAN
(1965)

These are BORZOI BOOKS
published by ALFRED A. KNOPF *in New York*

THE ORIGIN OF RACES

THE ORIGIN OF RACES

by CARLETON S. COON

19  71

NEW YORK : ALFRED·A·KNOPF

L. C. catalog card number: 62–14761

THIS IS A BORZOI BOOK,
PUBLISHED BY ALFRED A. KNOPF, INC.

PUBLISHED OCTOBER 15, 1962
REPRINTED SIX TIMES
EIGHTH PRINTING, JANUARY 1971

TO

FRANZ WEIDENREICH

IN MEMORIAM

INTRODUCTION

In 1933 I was invited to rewrite Professor W. Z. Ripley's classic *The Races of Europe* (New York: Appleton & Co.; 1899). My completely new version of the book was published by The Macmillan Company in 1939. At that time I decided eventually to write a *Races of the World*. For twenty years, in peace and war, at home and on expeditions, I collected material with this task in mind. Finally, in 1956, thanks to an Air Force contract, I was able to make a seven months' trip around the world, visiting countries I had never before seen and conferring with fellow physical anthropologists on the way. From the end of that trip to the present I have been engaged almost exclusively in the preparation of the book at hand.

But this book is only half of what I set out to write. By 1959 it was clear to me that I must write two books, one on the living, as originally planned, and an introductory one on the ancestry of the living races of man. By then I could see that the visible and invisible differences between living races could be explained only in terms of history. Each major race had followed a pathway of its own through the labyrinth of time. Each had been molded in a different fashion to meet the needs of different environments, and each had reached its own level on the evolutionary scale.

What became the first book, the one presented here, may turn out to have been the harder to write, or so it seems now that I have finished it and before I have allowed myself to become immersed in the other. It was difficult because I had spent less time on fossil men than on the living. Also, in 1959 I decided that the framework for the study of fossil man should be built in two di mensions, time and space. Most other writers had stressed only time, and had ignored or neglected geography.

A notable exception was Franz Weidenreich. While I was writing *The Races of Europe* in Cambridge, Massachusetts, he was busy in New York, studying the Sinanthropus remains. At that time he concluded that the peculiarities that made Sinanthropus distinct from other fossil men were of two kinds, evolutionary and racial. From the evolutionary point of view, Sinanthropus was more primitive than any known living population. Racially he was Mongoloid.

Like other premature comets of science, Weidenreich's idea flashed across the sky and was gone, obscured by the clouds of incredulity released by his fellow scientists. Most of them believed, as many still do, that the living races of man could have become differentiated from a common ancestor only after the stage of *Homo sapiens* had been reached. Because *Homo sapiens* was believed to have first appeared only 30,000 years ago, in the guise of Crô-Magnon man, the living races could be only that old. Sinanthropus was not *Homo sapiens*. Therefore he could not have belonged to a modern race, the Mongoloid. Q.E.D. Or so the incredulous thought.

To me there was something very pat, dogmatic, and wrong about the anti-Weidenreich point of view. For years I mulled it over in my mind, and then I decided to collect every scrap of existing information about every single fossil-man bone and tooth in the world. Once I had acquired as much information as I could, I concentrated on the dimension of space and tried to see how many racial lines, including the Mongoloid, could be traced back to the first instance that any kind of man had appeared on the earth. In the end I succeeded in tracing back five, each as old as man himself.

Realizing the enormity of my discovery in terms of its divergence from accepted dogma, I knew that I must provide a theoretical foundation for the facts I had unearthed. The possibility that races can be older than species had to be explored. I soon found, by reading and through conversations with Mayr, Simpson, and other biologists, that what I had thought a revolutionary concept was so common an event in nature that others rarely both-ered to mention it; to wit, that a species which is divided into geographical races can evolve into a daughter species while retaining the same geographical races.

With this matter settled more easily than I had expected, I needed to know what forces exerted pressure on that plastic primate, man, to make him evolve from a lesser to a more *sapient* state. To satisfy this need, I delved into zoogeography, primate behavior, physiology, and social anthropology. At the same time I kept in touch with physiologists studying the mechanisms of adaptation to heat, cold, and altitude, and went with some of them on a field trip to southern Chile.

Because my study made it apparent that the human races had evolved in parallel fashion, I made a brief excursion into the history, anatomy, and physiology of primates, and found many striking examples to back my theory. Meanwhile, the exciting new discoveries regarding fossil apes and Australopithecines drew the prehuman relatives of man forward in time past the very date of the earliest human skull, closing a temporal if not an evolutionary gap. These discoveries opened the possibility that the races of man are even older than the known specimens of *Homo*, a possibility that remains unexplored.

In the introduction to *The Races of Europe* I stated that I would avoid discussion of two subjects, blood groups and racial differences in intelligence. W. C. Boyd was about to publish his massive compilation of blood groups.[1] And I knew next to nothing about racial intelligence and could not see that it would be very useful when applied to regional populations of a single major race, the Caucasoid.

The sequel to *The Origin of Races* promises to be full of talk about blood and brains, but in this present book I have little to say about these subjects—for different reasons than in 1939. Despite claims to the contrary, the blood groups of fossil bones cannot be determined. Nor can dead men take intelligence tests. However, it is a fair inference that fossil men now extinct were less gifted than their descendants who have larger brains, that the subspecies which crossed the evolutionary threshold into the cate-

---

[1] W. C. Boyd: "Blood Groups," *Tabulae Biologicae,* Vol. 17 (1939), pp. 113-240.

gory of *Homo sapiens* the earliest have evolved the most, and that the obvious correlation between the length of time a subspecies has been in the *sapiens* state and the levels of civilization attained by some of its populations may be related phenomena.

Yet every major race, however advanced in civilization some of its component populations have become, also contains remnant bands of simple hunters and gatherers to remind us whence we all came. The monkey-hunters of the forested slopes of Central India are as Caucasoid as Charles de Gaulle, and the Ghosts of the Yellow Leaves, who haunt the hillsides of Upper Siam and Laos, as Mongoloid as the Mikado.

These, however, are not the main points of the book. This is a work of history, the history of a primate genus, and in it science is only a set of tools used to discover the pathways of human evolution—pathways that have led us from a time of obscurity to a moment of bright sunlight, with no man knows what fate lying ahead.

CARLETON S. COON

Devon, Pennsylvania
January 23, 1962

Addendum: Since the first printing of this book I have been criticized for having omitted, in this introduction, what I said in the body of the text, notably on pages 16 and 28–30, that the passage of all but the first of the several subspecies of *Homo* from the *erectus* to the *sapiens* species may well have been the result of peripheral matings between members of neighboring populations rather than of two, three, or four other mutations. For the sake of those who read only the introductions and conclusions of books, I add it here.

West Gloucester, Massachusetts
June 19, 1963

ACKNOWLEDGMENTS

IN THE COMPILATION and preparation of data for this volume I have received financial aid from one private and two governmental institutions, as follows. In 1955 the Wenner-Gren Foundation paid my way to and from the Third Panafrican Congress at Livingstone, Northern Rhodesia, where Mrs. Coon and I were the guests of the Rhodesian government for several weeks. Since then the Wenner-Gren Foundation has given me two other grants. In 1956–7 we went around the world on Contract AF33(616)–6306 with ADTIC (Arctic-Desert-Tropics-Information Center) of the Montgomery, Alabama, U.S. Air Force Base. Thanks are extended to Dr. Paul H. Nesbitt, chief of the ADTIC, and his staff for their helpful suggestions and courtesies. In 1957 I received a two-year grant from the National Science Foundation (NSF 03921). In 1959 I went to Wellington Island, Chile, as a member of an expedition led by T. H. Hammel of the University of Pennsylvania Medical School and financed by the Biomedical Laboratory of the U.S. Air Force at the Wright-Patterson Air Force Base, Ohio.

I am also deeply indebted to those who make decisions in the University of Pennsylvania, and particularly to Froelich G. Rainey, Director of the University Museum, to Alfred Kidder II, Associate Director, and to the Museum's Board of Trustees, headed by Percy C. Madeira, Jr., for allowing me ample writing time, granting me free use of the Museum's facilities, and, even more important, giving me encouragement in the pursuit of what must have been, from the point of view of the Museum, a materially unrewarding subject. I hope that this book will justify their confidence.

To many persons we owe debts of gratitude for fine hospitality on our travels, particularly to Dr. and Mrs. Neil Ransford, M.D., in Bulawayo, to the Gordon Brownes in Siam, to the Gordon Bowles in Japan, to Arthur Prager and the Robert Lindquists in Formosa, to the late B. S. Guha in India, to the Arthur Gardiners in Pakistan, to Colonel and Mrs. W. A. Eddy and Aramco, Saudi Arabia, to the late Baron and the Baroness A. C. Blanc in Rome, to Lidio Cipriani in Florence, to M. and Mme François Trives in Paris, and to our son C. S. Coon, Jr., and his wife and children, in many places.

My wife, Lisa Dougherty Coon, went with me everywhere mentioned except Chile, and where she went she kept me in good health. She also created all but six and a half of the line drawings in this book.

No one can write a book of this scope without friends. Reprint swapping, informal correspondence, and conversations at academic meetings and elsewhere are as important as library research, which itself is greatly facilitated by the interest and good will of librarians.

Below are listed the names, without rank or title, of some of those who have helped me, in one way or other, in terms of principal categories of assistance. Most heartily I thank them one and all.

FIELD TRIPS

Gordon T. Bowles	Tokyo, Johns Hopkins
A. C. Blanc †	Rome
J. Desmond Clark	Livingstone, Berkeley
B. S. Guha †	Ranchi
H. T. Hammel	U. of Pennsylvania, Yale
Louis Leakey	Nairobi
HRH Peter	Prince of Greece and Denmark
Roger Summers	Bulawayo

TAXONOMY

F. Clark Howell	Chicago
Wm. W. Howells	Harvard
Ernst Mayr	Harvard

Brian Patterson   Harvard
Alfred S. Romer   Harvard
George G. Simpson   Harvard
Wm. L. Straus, Jr.   Johns Hopkins

GENETICS

Richard H. Post   University of Michigan

CHROMOSOMES

M. A. Bender   Oak Ridge
John Buettner-Janusch   Yale
E. H. Y. Chu   Oak Ridge
David Hungerford   Institute for Cancer Research,
                         Fox Chase, Philadelphia

CHRONOLOGY

Bruce Howe   Harvard
G. H. R. von Koenigswald Utrecht
Charles E. Stearns   Tufts
Elisabeth K. Ralph   University of Pennsylvania
Kenneth P. Oakley   British Museum (Nat. Hist.)

SKELETAL MATERIAL AND CASTS

Don Brothwell   British Museum (Nat. Hist.)
Georgi Debetz   Academy of Science, Moscow
Paul Deraniyagala   Colombo Museum
A. C. Hoffman   Bloemfontein
S. Kodama   Sapporo
Louis Leakey   Nairobi
P. N. Mitra   Calcutta
Emily Pettinos   University Museum, Philadelphia

Ronald Singer   Capetown, Chicago
John T. Robinson   Pretoria
Wm. L. Straus, Jr.   Johns Hopkins
H. Suzuki   Tokyo
Philip T. Tobias   Johannesburg

GENERAL HELP, PARTICULARLY IN THE SUMMER OF 1958

Edward E. Hunt, Jr.   Harvard and Forsythe
                                   (Boston)

MAKING FLESH RECONSTRUCTIONS OF FOSSIL MEN

Maurice P. Coon   Cambridge, Massachusetts

INFORMATION ABOUT THE TIWI, CHAPTER 3

Jane C. Goodale   University Museum,
                                   Bryn Mawr

RESEARCH: LIBRARIANS

Margaret Currier   Peabody Museum, Harvard
Cynthia Griffin   University Museum, University
                                   of Pennsylvania
Margaret Palmer   Dental School, University of
                                   Pennsylvania

BIBLIOGRAPHY

Janet M. Kliment   University Museum, University
                                   of Pennsylvania

GLOSSARY SELECTION

Mary S. Huhn   Devon, Pennsylvania

WORK ON PHOTOGRAPHS

David Crownover   University Museum
Caroline Dosker   University Museum
Jane C. Goodale   University Museum,
                                   Bryn Mawr
Doris Nicholas   University Museum

But this is not all. Books need publishers as well as authors. I am deeply indebted to Alfred A. Knopf for the privilege of having had Harold Strauss as editor of this volume, with the valuable assistance of Howard Fertig, Sophie Wilkins, and Carmen Gomezplata, and for splendid treatment at the hands of William Koshland.

I am also very happy that my British publisher, Jonathan Cape Ltd., which has stood by me for thirty years, will publish this book in England.

CONTENTS

ANIMALS; THE SEXUAL BEHAVIOR OF PRIMATES, INCLUD-
ING HOMO SAPIENS; THE BEGINNINGS OF HUMAN SOCIETY;
SEXUAL SELECTION AMONG HIGHER PRIMATES; SPEECH,
HUNTING, AND SOCIAL STRUCTURE; RITUAL, LANGUAGE,
AND THE RITES OF PASSAGE; THE DISCOVERY OF FIRE AND
THE CONVERSION OF ENERGY INTO SOCIAL STRUCTURE;
THE EVIDENCE OF LIVING FOOD-GATHERING SOCIETIES: THE
AUSTRALIAN ABORIGINES; THE ARCHAIC SOCIETY OF THE
TIWI; ON COMPARING THE CULTURES OF LIVING FOOD
GATHERERS AND THOSE OF FOSSIL MEN; POPULATION SIZE
AMONG FOOD GATHERERS; SYSTEMS OF MATING AMONG
FOOD GATHERERS; THE LONGEVITY OF FOSSIL MEN; THE
ROLE OF ISOLATING MECHANISMS IN HUMAN EVOLUTION;
ADAPTATION TO CROWDING: A NEW THEORY OF EVOLU-
TION BY SUCCESSION; DWARFING AS A SOLUTION TO THE
PROBLEM OF CROWDING; THE ENDOCRINES AND TEMPERA-
MENT; PARALLELS BETWEEN ANIMAL DOMESTICATION
AND SOCIAL ADAPTATION; THE UNIQUE ADAPTATIONS OF
THE GENUS HOMO

4. THE ORDER OF PRIMATES 119

PRIMATE STUDIES AND THE CLASSIFICATION OF HUMAN
RACES; THE CLASSIFICATION OF PRIMATES; THE PROSIM-
IANS; THE TREE SHREWS; THE LEMURS; THE LORISES;
THE TARSIERS; THE LIVING PLATYRRHINES: THE SOUTH
AMERICAN MONKEYS; THE LIVING CERCOPITHECIDAE: OLD
WORLD MONKEYS; THE LEAF-EATING COLOBINAE; THE
CERCOPITHECINAE; THE ANTHROPOID APES; THE GIBBONS:
SYMPHALANGUS AND HYLOBATES; THE ORANGUTAN
(PONGO); THE CHIMPANZEE (PAN); THE GORILLA (GO-
RILLA); THE HOMINIDAE (HOMO)

5. MAN'S PLACE AMONG THE PRIMATES 151

THE BEARING OF PRIMATE STUDIES ON RACIAL ORIGINS; TO
BRACHIATE OR NOT TO BRACHIATE; THE BEARING OF
HOMINID TEETH ON THE ERECT POSTURE; A FEW DETAILS
OF THE POSTURE STORY; THE EVIDENCE OF TEETH; THE
EVIDENCE OF EMBRYOLOGY; DIFFERENCES IN POSTNATAL
GROWTH; BIOCHEMICAL CLUES TO OUR RELATIONSHIPS
WITH OTHER PRIMATES; PARASITES AND PRIMATES; THE

10. SINANTHROPUS AND THE MONGOLOIDS

11. THE CAUCASOIDS

THE CAUCASOID HOME; POSSIBLE CONTACTS BETWEEN SUB-
SPECIES AND CAUCASOID EVOLUTION; CONTINUITY AND
CHANGE IN THE CAUCASOID QUADRANT; THE MAUER MAN-
DIBLE, OR HEIDELBERG JAW; THE STEINHEIM CRANIUM;
THE SWANSCOMBE CRANIAL BONES; EUROPEAN FOSSIL
MEN OF THE EARLY UPPER PLEISTOCENE; FONTÉCHEVADE;
SACCOPASTORE; THE EHRINGSDORF REMAINS; THE STONE
BRAIN FROM GÁNOVCE, CZECHOSLOVAKIA; THE ROUND-
HEADED PEOPLE OF KRAPINA; THE MANDIBLES OF THE
EUROPEANS OF THE LAST INTERGLACIAL PERIOD; THE
TEETH OF THE EUROPEANS OF THE LAST INTERGLACIAL;
POSTCRANIAL BONES OF THE LAST INTERGLACIAL: THE
EVIDENCE FROM KRAPINA; THE "NEANDERTHALS" OF EU-
ROPE; THE NUMBERS AND DISTRIBUTION OF THE NEANDER-
THALS; THE WESTERN NEANDERTHALS; THE WESTERN
NEANDERTHAL CRANIA; THE WESTERN NEANDERTHAL
MANDIBLES; THE TEETH OF THE WESTERN NEANDERTHALS;
THE POSTCRANIAL SKELETONS OF THE WESTERN NEANDER-
THALS; THE HEIGHT AND BUILD OF THE WESTERN NEAN-
DERTHALS; THE FATE OF THE WESTERN NEANDERTHALS;
THE CENTRAL EUROPEAN NEANDERTHALS; THE THREE
MANDIBLES; THE POSTCRANIAL BONES FROM SUBALYUK;
THE SUBALYUK CHILD'S SKELETON; THE RUMANIAN NEAN-
DERTHAL TOE BONE; THE SIGNIFICANCE OF THE NEANDER-
THAL REMAINS FROM CENTRAL EUROPE; NEANDERTHAL
REMAINS FROM THE SOVIET UNION; THE KIIK-KOBA TOOTH
AND LIMB BONES; THE INFANT SKELETON OF STAROSEL'E;
THE YOUTHFUL NEANDERTHAL OF TESHIK-TASH; THE EAST-
ERN NEANDERTHALS OF SHANIDAR; THE INHABITANTS OF
PALESTINE DURING WÜRM I; TABUN AND GALILEE; THE
SKHUL SKULLS: NO. 4 AND HIS GROUP; THE SKULL OF
SKHUL 5; THE MOUNT CARMEL TEETH; THE POSTCRANIAL
SKELETONS OF THE SKHUL POPULATION; THE MEANING OF
THE MOUNT CARMEL SKELETONS; EGBERT, THE BOY FROM
KSAR 'AKIL; MORE ABOUT NEANDERTHAL ORIGINS; THE UP-
PER PALEOLITHIC PEOPLE AND THEIR CULTURE; UPPER
PALEOLITHIC SITES IN SPACE AND TIME; THE RACIAL
CHARACTERISTICS OF THE UPPER PALEOLITHIC EUROPEANS;

PLATES

DRAWINGS

MAPS

DRAWN BY RAFAEL PALACIOS

TABLES

APPENDIX

PERIODICALS
AND THEIR ABBREVIATIONS

AA	*American Anthropologist*, Washington
AAE	*Archivio per l'Antropologia e la Etnologia*, Florence
AANz	*Anthropologischer Anzeiger*, Stuttgart
AB	*Archaeological Bulletin*, New York
ActG	*Acta Genetica et Statistica Medica*, Basel
AE	*Annals of Eugenics*, London
AEB	*Abhandlungen zur exakten Biologie*, Berlin
Africa	*Journal of the International Institute of African Languages and Cultures*, London
AGMG	*Acta Geneticae Medicae et Gemellologiae*, Rome
AIPH	*Archives de l'Institut de Paléontologie Humaine*, Paris
AJAn	*American Journal of Anatomy*, Philadelphia
AJHG	*American Journal of Human Genetics*, Baltimore
AJPA	*American Journal of Physical Anthropology*, Philadelphia
AJSc	*American Journal of Science*, New Haven
AK	*Animal Kingdom*, New York
AMN	*American Museum Novitates*, New York
AMNH	*Annals and Magazine of Natural History*, London
AN	*American Naturalist*, Lancaster, Pa.
Anatolia	*Revue annuelle de l'Institut d'Archaeologie de l'Université d'Ankara*, Ankara
Antiquity	Cambridge, England (formerly Newbury, Berkshire)
ANYA	*Annals of the New York Academy of Sciences*, New York
AP	*Asian Perspectives*, Hong Kong
APa	*Annales de paléontologie*, Paris

APAM   *Anthropological Papers of the American Museum of Natural History*, New York
AQ   *Anthropological Quarterly*, Washington, D.C.
AR   *Anatomical Record*, Philadelphia
ARSI   *Annual Report of the Smithsonian Institution*, Washington, D.C.
AS   *Archives des sciences physiques et naturelles*, Geneva
ASAG   *Archives suisses d'Anthropologie générale*, Geneva
ASAM   *Annals of the South African Museum*, Cape Town
ASPR   American School of Prehistoric Research, Cambridge, Mass.
ATM   *Annals of the Transvaal Museum*, Pretoria
AuS   *The Australian Scientist*, Sydney

BAM   *Bulletin d'Archéologie Marocaine*, Rabat
BAMN   *Bulletin of the American Museum of Natural History*, New York
BASP   *Bulletin of the American School of Prehistoric Research*, Cambridge, Mass. (formerly New Haven)
BBMNH   *Bulletin of the British Museum of Natural History*, London
BELLETEN   *Belleten Türk Taríha Kurumu Basimeví*, Ankara
BGI   *Bollettino della Società geologica italiana*, Rome
BGSC   *Bulletin of the Geological Society of China*, Peking
BIAF   *Bulletin d l'Institut français d'Afrique Noire*, Paris
BIOMETRIKA London
BMFM   *British Museum Fossil Mammals of Africa*, London
BMSA   *Bulletins et Mémoires de la Société d'Anthropologie*, Paris
BPGO   *Beiträge zur Paläontologie und Geologie Oesterreich-Ungarns und des Orients*, Vienna
BRCI   *Bulletin of the Research Council of Israel*, Jerusalem
BS   *Bulletin Scientifique, Conseil des Académies de la RPF de Yugoslavie*, Zagreb.
BSA   *Bulletin de la Société d'Anthropologie de Paris*, Paris
BSGI   *Bulletin du Service Géologique de l'Indochine*, Hanoi
BSPC   *Boletim da Sociedade Portuguesa de Sciências Naturais*, Coimbra
BSPF   *Bulletin de la Société Préhistorique Française*, Paris
BUM   *Bulletin of the University Museum*, University of Pennsylvania, Philadelphia

CA	*Current Anthropology,* Chicago
CH	*Collection Hespéris,* Paris
CHM	*Cahiers d'Histoire Mondiale,* Paris
CIRCULATION	New York
CIWP	*Carnegie Institution of Washington Publications,* Washington, D.C.
CMES	*Ceylon Museum Ethnographic Series,* Colombo
CMJ	*Chinese Medical Journal,* Shanghai
CNHS	*Ceylon National Museums Natural History Series,* Colombo
CRAS	*Comptes-rendus Hebdomadaires des Séances de l'Académie des Sciences,* Paris
CSHS	*Cold Spring Harbor Symposia on Quantitative Biology,* Cold Spring Harbor, New York
CYTOLOGIA	Tokyo
DAKM	*Deutsches Archiv für klinische Medizin,* Leipzig
DIOGENES	Chicago
DR	*The Dental Record,* London
ENDOCRINOLOGY	Los Angeles
ER	*Eugenics Review,* London
EVOLUTION	Hempstead, New York
EXPEDITION	Philadelphia
EXPERIENTIA	Basel
FICA	*Fifth International Congress of Anthropological and Ethnological Science,* 1956, Philadelphia
GHSP	*Geologica Hungarica, Series Paleontologica,* Budapest
GS	*Göttinger Studien,* Göttinger
HAS	*Harvard African Studies,* Cambridge, Mass.
HB	*Human Biology,* Detroit
IGC	*International Geological Congress,* London, 1948
IJNS	*Indonesian Journal for Natural Science,* Jakarta
ILN	*Illustrated London News,* London
IVPM	*Institute of Vertebrate Paleontology Memoirs,* Peking

JANAT	*Journal of Anatomy*, London
JAP	*Journal of Applied Physiology*, Washington, D.C.
JCPP	*Journal of Comparative and Physiological Psychology*, Baltimore
JEAN	*Journal of the East Africa Natural History Society*, Nairobi, Kenya
JFS	*Journal of Forensic Sciences*, Chicago
JGEN	*Journal of Genetics*, Cambridge, England
JJP	*Japanese Journal of Physiology*, Nagoya
JMBR	*Journal of the Malayan Branch of the Royal Asiatic Society*, Singapore
JPH	*Journal of Physiology*, London
JPLS	*Journal of the Proceedings of the Linnaean Society of London*, London
JPSI	*Journal of the Paleontological Society of India*, Lucknow
JRAI	*Journal of the Royal Anthropological Institute of Great Britain and Ireland*, London
JRAS	*Journal of the Royal Asiatic Society of Great Britain and Ireland, Ceylon Branch, Colombo*
L'ANTH	*L'Anthropologie*, Paris
MAN	London
MANKIND	Sydney, Australia
MB	*Monographiae Biologicae*, The Hague
MJA	*Medical Journal of Australia*, Sydney, Australia
MKNA	*Mededelingen Koninklijke Akademie van Wetenschappen*, Amsterdam
MNGB	*Mitteilungen der Naturforschenden Gesellschaft in Bern*, Bern
MNMM	*Memoires of the National Museum of Melbourne*, Victoria, Australia
MOG	*Medelelser om Grønland*, Copenhagen
MRSE	*Memorias Real Sociedad Española de Historia Natural*, Madrid
NATURE	London
NC	*Neanderthal Centenary*, Utrecht
NG	*National Geographic Magazine*, Washington, D.C.
NH	*Natural History*, New York

NMRI	*Naval Medical Research Institute Lecture and Review Series*, Bethesda, Md.
NYT	*The New York Times*
OCEANIA	Sydney, Australia
OJS	*Ohio Journal of Science*, Columbus
PAf	*Paleontologia Africana*, Johannesburg
PAPS	*Proceedings of the American Philosophical Society*, Philadelphia
PASA	*Proceedings of the Academy of Science of Amsterdam*, Amsterdam
PBM	*Perspectives in Biology and Medicine*, Chicago
PKAW	*Proceedings: Koninklijke nederlandse akademie van Wetenschappen*, Amsterdam
PKSF	*Publications under the Keith Sheridan Foundation for Medical Research*, Adelaide, S. Australia
PLSL	*Proceedings of the Linnaean Society of London*
PMP	*Peabody Museum Papers*, Cambridge, Mass.
PNAS	*Proceedings of the National Academy of Science*, Washington, D.C.
PNHB	*Peking Natural History Bulletin*, Peking
PPS	*Proceedings of the Prehistoric Society*, Cambridge
PRSM	*Proceedings of the Royal Society of Medicine*, London
PS—D	*Paleontologia Sinica, Series D*, Peking
PS—NS—D	*Paleontologia Sinica, New Series D*, Peking
PTCPFA	*Proceedings of the Third Congress on the Prehistory of the Far East*, 1938
PTPA	*Proceedings of the Third Pan-African Congress on Prehistory* held in N. Rhodesia, Livingstone, 1955, pub. London, 1957
PYMP	*Postilla Yale Peabody Museum*, New Haven, Conn.
QJGS	*Quarterly Journal of Geological Sciences*, London
QRB	*Quarterly Review of Biology*, Washington, D.C.
QUARTÄR	Bonn
QUATERNARIA	Rome
RA	*Rivista di Antropologia*, Rome
RBMO	*Research Bulletin*, University of Missouri, College of Agriculture, Agricultural Research Station, Columbia, Mo.

RGA	*Revista Geográfica Americana*, Buenos Aires
RM	*Richerche di Morfologia*, Rome
RQS	*La Revue des Questions Scientifiques*, Louvain
RR	*Radical Review*, New Bedford, Mass.
RSAM	*Records of the South Australian Museum*, Adelaide, S. Australia
SA	*Scientific American*, New York
SAAB	*South African Archaeological Bulletin*, Cape Town
SAJS	*South African Journal of Science*, Johannesburg
SCIENCE	Washington, D.C.
SD	*Science Digest*, Chicago
SE	*Sovetskaia Etnografiia*, Moscow
SlAr	*Slovenska archeologia*, Brno
SM	*Säugetierkundliche Mitteilungen*, Stuttgart
SMC	*Smithsonian Miscellaneous Collections*, Washington, D.C.
SMJ	*Sarawak Museum Journal*, Kuching, Borneo
SNNM	*Soölogiese naborsing nasionale Museum*, Bloemfontein, S. Africa
SRP	*Smithsonian Report, Publication*, Washington, D.C.
SSF-CB	*Societas Scientiarum Fennica, Commentationes Biologicae*, Helsinki
SUMER	Baghdad
SVFZ	*Schweizerische Vierteljahrsschrift für Zahnheilkunde*, Zürich
SWJA	*Southwestern Journal of Anthropology*, Albuquerque, N.M.
SZC	*Spolia Zeylanica*, Colombo
TB	*Tabulae Biologicae*, The Hague
THE LEECH	Johannesburg, S. Africa
TI	*The Interamerican*, Denton, Texas
TIBS	*Trabajos del Instituto "Bernadino de Sahagun" de Antropología y Etnología*, Madrid
TLAB	*Travaux du Laboratoire d'Anthropologie et d'Archéologie Préhistoriques du Musée du Bardo*, Algiers
TMM	*Transvaal Museum Memoires*, Pretoria
TNYA	*Transactions of the New York Academy of Sciences*, New York
TRIANGLE	Basel

TRSL	*Transactions of the Royal Society of London,* London
TRSS	*Transactions of the Royal Society of South Africa,* Cape Town
UMM	*University Museum Memoirs,* University of Pennsylvania, Philadelphia
VGB	*Verhandlungen der Geologischen Bundesanstalt,* Vienna
VGPA	*Verhandlungen der Gesellschaft für physische Anthropologie,* Stuttgart
VP	*Vertebrata Paleasiatica,* Peking
WADD	*Wright Air Development Center Technical Reports,* Wright-Patterson Air Force Base, Ohio
WMDM	*Wetenschappelijke Mededelingen Dienst van de Mijnbouw,* Bandoeng
YAPS	*Yearbook of the American Philosophical Society,* Philadelphia
ZA	*Zoologischer Anzeiger,* Leipzig
ZｆE	*Zeitschrift für Ethnologie,* Berlin
ZｆMｕA	*Zeitschrift für Morphologie und Anthropologie,* Stuttgart
ZｆNF	*Zeitschrift für Naturforschung,* Tübingen
ZｆRK	*Zeitschrift für Rassenkunde,* Stuttgart
Zoologica	New York
ZV	*Zoologische Verhandelingen,* Leyden
ZZ	*Zinruigaku Zassu,* Journal of the Anthropological Society of Nippon, Tokyo University

THE ORIGIN OF RACES

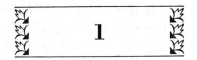

THE PROBLEM
OF RACIAL ORIGINS

On the Antiquity of Races

A T T H E   D A W N of history, which is another way of saying "beginning with Herodotus," literate people of the ancient world were well aware that mankind was divided into a number of clearly differentiated races. Even before that, racial differentiation can be traced back to at least 3,000 B.C., as evidenced in Egyptian records, particularly the artistic representations. We also have pictures of white people on the walls of western European caves which are as much as 20,000 years older.

How many kinds of people there were in the world was not really known until after the voyages of discovery that tore the veil from the Americas, the Pacific islands, and Australia. Even then the problem of classifying the races remained, and it has not been settled to this day.

For present purposes I am using a conservative and tentative classification of the living peoples of the world into five basically geographical groups: the Caucasoid, Mongoloid, Australoid, Congoid, and Capoid. The first includes Europeans and their overseas kinsmen, the Middle Eastern Whites from Morocco to West Pakistan, and most of the peoples of India, as well as the Ainu of Japan. The second includes most of the East Asiatics, Indonesians, Polynesians, Micronesians, American Indians, and Eskimo. In the third category fall the Australian aborigines, Melanesians, Papuans, some of the tribal folk of India, and the various Negritos of South Asia and Oceania. The fourth comprises the Negroes and

Pygmies of Africa. I have named it *Congoid* after a region (not a specific nation) which contains both kinds of people. The term *Negroid* has been deliberately omitted to avoid confusion. It has been. applied both to Africans and to spiral-haired peoples of southern Asia and Oceania who are not genetically related to each other, as far as we know.[1] *Negroid* will be used in this book to denote a condition, not a geographical subspecies. The fifth group includes the Bushmen and Hottentots and other relict tribes, like the Sandawe of Tanganyika. It is called *Capoid* after the Cape of Good Hope. As this subspecies once occupied Morocco (see Postscript, Chapter 13), the cape can be thought of as Cape Spartel.

My aim in this book is to see how far back in prehistoric antiquity these human racial groups can be traced. Did they all branch off a common stem recently, that is, within a few tens of thousands of years, after mankind had evolved as a single unit to the evolutionary state of the most primitive living peoples? Or did their moment of separation lie lower down on the time scale, when long-extinct types like the so-called ape men of Java and China were still alive? If the second is true, the evolution of the existing races may have taken place to a large extent independently over hundreds of thousands of years, with enough intermittent gene flow to preserve the unity of the species but not enough to eliminate subspecies. The first hypothesis is the one more commonly held, but it presents some impressive stumbling blocks.[2]

If all races had a recent common origin, why were the Tasmanians and many of the Australian aborigines still living during the nineteenth century in a manner comparable to that of Europeans of over 100,000 years ago? Either the common ancestors of the Tasmanians, Australians, and Europeans parted company in remote Pleistocene antiquity, or else the Australians and Tasmanians have done some rapid cultural backsliding, which archaeological evidence disproves.

If the ancestors of the living races of mankind were a single

[1] They differ completely in blood-group patterns, particularly in the Rhesus genes.

[2] See W. W. Howells, Jr.: *Mankind in the Making* (New York: Doubleday and Company; 1959), especially p. 236; and C. S. Coon's review of same in *Science*, Vol. 130, No. 3386 (1959), pp. 1399–1400.

people a few thousands of years ago and they all spoke a single language, how does it happen that the world contains thousands of languages, hundreds of which are unrelated to each other, and some of which even use such odd sounds as clicks? Some languages are tonal and others are not, and the difference between a fully tonal and a nontonal language is profound. Eskimo and Aleut, which are closely related languages, have been separated for about two thousand years. It takes at least twenty thousand years for two sister languages to lose all semblance of relationship.[3] If, therefore, all languages are derived from a single mother tongue, the original separation must go back many times that figure. The only alternative is that more than one line of ancestral man discovered speech independently. Even so, the number of languages spoken by a single subspecies, the Mongoloid, is great enough to imply a vast antiquity.

All the evidence available from comparative ethnology, linguistics, and prehistoric archaeology indicates a long separation of the principal races of man. This is contrary to the current idea that *Homo sapiens* arose in Europe or western Asia about 35,000 B.C., fully formed as from the brow of Zeus, and spread over the world at that time, while the archaic species of men who had preceded him became conveniently extinct. Actually, the *homines sapientes* in question were morphologically the same as living Europeans. To derive an Australian aborigine or a Congo Pygmy from European ancestors of modern type would be biologically impossible.

The current idea is based on the study of comparative anatomy without reference to evolution, and a misunderstanding of paleontology. One anatomist, Morant,[4] found by means of a number of measurements taken on less than ten Neanderthal skulls that this ancient population differed in mean measurements from a number of modern populations more than the modern skulls differ from each other. The differences reflected mainly the fact that Nean-

---

[3] D. H. Hymes: "Lexicostatistics So Far," *CA*, Vol. 1, No. 1 (1960), p. 3–44. The 20,000-year calculation, a conservative figure, is my own, based on Hymes's data.

[4] G. M. Morant: "Studies of Paleolithic Man, II, A Biometric Study of Neanderthaloid Skulls and of Their Relationships to Modern Racial Types," *Biometrika*, Vol. 2 (1927), pp. 318–80.

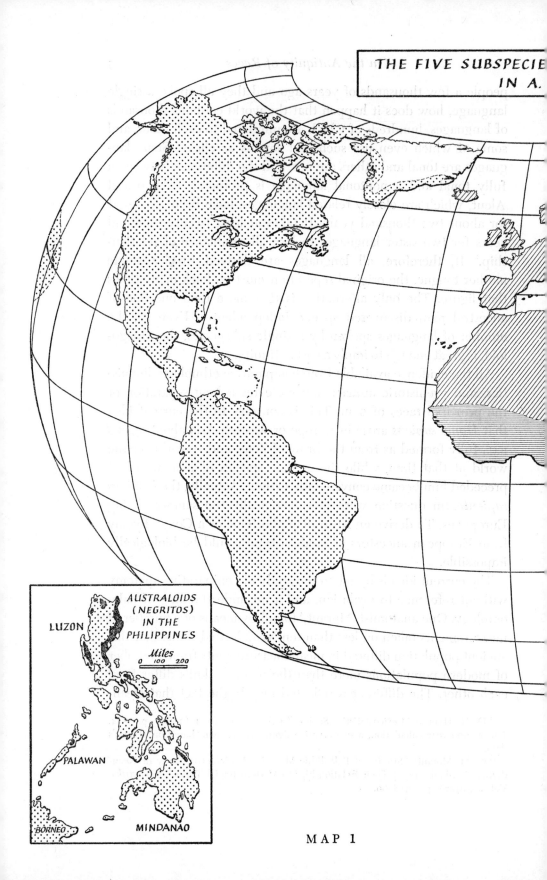

THE FIVE SUBSPECIE
IN A.

AUSTRALOIDS
(NEGRITOS)
IN THE
PHILIPPINES

LUZON

Miles
0   100   200

PALAWAN

BORNEO

MINDANAO

MAP 1

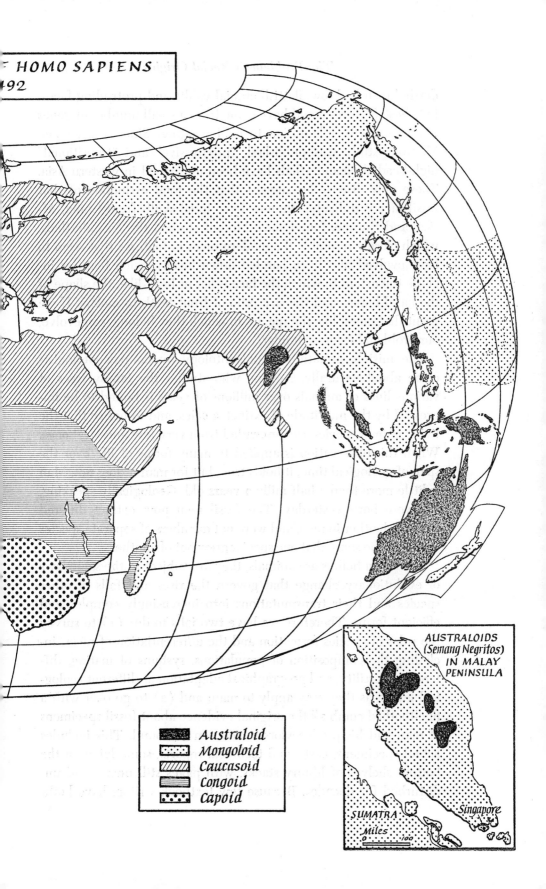

Australoid
Mongoloid
Caucasoid
Congoid
Capoid

AUSTRALOIDS
(Semang Negritos)
IN MALAY
PENINSULA

SUMATRA

Singapore

Miles
0   100

derthal men had low, flattish cranial vaults and protruding faces; but these features could have come from a small number of genes concerned with adaptation to cold weather. Since 1927, when Morant's study was published, "progressive" and "transitional" high-headed Neanderthals have been unearthed in western Asia. These new discoveries suggest that the total extinction of that fossil race is unlikely. We now have fossil skulls from China, Africa, and Europe, found since Morant studied the Neanderthals, which closely resemble the modern races in features that seem to have evolved and been handed down locally. Such features include the extent to which the face is flat or beak-like, the shape of the nasal bones, and the size ratio of front teeth to molars. If we grant that races, like the species to which they belong, can evolve, our problem becomes simpler.

The misinterpretation of paleontology by nonpaleontologists came about naturally. Anyone who studies the family trees of various lines of animals over millions of years is bound to be impressed by the multitude of extinct species, and to notice that the living animal species are descended from very few ancestral ones. When this observation is applied to many forms of life over the span of geological time, it holds true; but for man it does not. Man is little more than a half million years old. Geologically speaking, we were born yesterday. The fossil men now extinct differed from each other in race, and were not members of separate species except in the sense that one species grew out of another.

As human beings are animals, they are subject to the same laws of evolutionary change that govern the rises and falls of other species and their transmutations into increasingly complex and efficient forms. Therefore we have two jobs to do: (1) to survey the rules of species formation and the differentiation of races, including the composition of populations, systems of mating, differential fertility, and geographical adaptation at different ecological levels, as they may apply to man; and (2) to go over with a fine-toothed comb all the original evidence about fossil specimens of man and his predecessors which can be found. This includes actual specimens, casts, and technical reports, some lying on the bottom shelves of library stacks, with pages still uncut, and undisturbed for decades. Because few textbook writers have both-ered to consult these primary sources, few new ideas about the evolution of races have reached the public for a long time.

The Problems of Human Taxonomy: the Genus

O v e r two hundred years ago Linnaeus, the father of *taxonomy*,[5] or *systematics* as he called it, initiated the practice of giving each species in nature an italicized double name, or *binominal*, one of which was *Homo sapiens.* The first word is the name of the genus and the second that of the species itself. In the species *Homo sapiens* he included all living peoples. At that time no fossil men had been discovered, and the genus *Homo* had therefore but a single species.

Linnaeus used only one word to designate biological units smaller than the species: *variety.* At that time the concept had not yet arisen that the unit of inheritance and evolution is the *population* to which an individual belongs rather than the individual himself, and the exact meaning of *variety* was not clear. In recent years taxonomists, in reviewing the nomenclature of species, have found that many units given specific rank in the past were *subspecies,* or geographical races, of larger units, and that what had been called varieties were races of one magnitude or another, or even individual variants.

In order to obtain material for classification, zoologists were kept busy collecting skins and skulls of many kinds of animals, and paleontologists removing bones, teeth, claws, and shells of ancient animals from the ground. Rarely did the paleontologists have whole skeletons to work with; and even when they did, characteristics studied by zoologists, such as hair form and color, skin structure, and the number of mammary glands, could not be determined except in a very few cases, as when mammoths were found frozen in the ground.

Whereas zoologists could collect large numbers of contemporary specimens, paleontologists sometimes possessed only unique

[5] For a lucid introduction to this subject, see G. G. Simpson: *Principles of Animal Taxonomy* (New York: Columbia University Press; 1961) and "The Principles of Classification and a Classification of Mammals," *BAMN,* Vol. 85 (1945).

specimens, which had to be related to others from different times and different places. Often the time gap between apparently related specimens was so great that it was unlikely that they could have belonged to a single species. Being cautious men, most paleontologists considered it more conservative to give separate generic names to unique or rare fossils of different periods than to assume their identity, particularly when in living animals such as the sheep and goat, which belong to different genera, the only difference visible in the skeleton is the relative lengths of the segments of the forelimb. Paleontologists therefore formed the habit of giving new and unique specimens separate generic names, setting aside the finer classification of related species until more bones had been found.

When, in the second half of the nineteenth century, paleontologists and archaeologists began turning up the bones of fossil men, some of them applied this practice to the much more limited field of anthropology, and we find such designations as *Pithecanthropus erectus, Sinanthropus pekinensis,* and more recently, *Atlanthropus mauretanicus* tagged to specimens some of which differ from one another no more than do individuals in the living species.

Homo sapiens

THE FINAL difficulty with this type of taxonomy is that it cannot be reconciled with our time scale. Simpson, Kurtén, and others have shown that, within the geological periods with which we are concerned, a genus of mammals requires about eight million years to establish itself, and it usually makes no difference whether the animals are large or small, or fast or slow to mature.[6]

The oldest fossil-man remains that are definitely and indubitably *Homo* may be no more than 700,000 years old. If there really were, during the last 700,000 years, four genera of fossil men, including *Homo, Pithecanthropus, Sinanthropus,* and *Atlan-*

[6] Simpson: *The Major Features of Evolution* (New York: Columbia University Press; 1953).

B. Kurtén: "Rates of Evolution in Fossil Mammals," *CSHS,* Vol. 24 (1959), pp. 205–15.

thropus, then these genera must have parted company early in the Pliocene, and we have neither manlike bones nor tools from this period.

Later on, after tools had appeared, we find that both *Atlanthropus* in North Africa and *Homo* in Europe were making stylistically similar stone implements. Although a great many claims can be made for parallel evolution, it is inconceivable that men of two distinct genera could have made similar tools.

The concept that the fossil men so far found, who lived during the last half million years, belonged to more than one genus is impossible both anatomically and in terms of behavior, as revealed by archaeology. This concept must be abandoned, and indeed many zoologists and anthropologists have already discarded it. Of the names proposed for our genus, *Homo* has two centuries of priority, and *Homo* is what we are, what our known ancestors were, and what our unknown ancestors could have been for as long as eight million years.

The Species Concept

I N T H E whole field of taxonomy no identification is as important as that of the species of an animal. Higher categories, such as the genus, family, order, and so on, are subject to argument and revision, and lower categories, the subspecies and local race, are also more difficult to establish. The species, however, is the pivot of the entire structure because it is the unit of evolutionary change.

In the early days of taxonomy, a collector would shoot a bird or animal, keep its skin and skull, compare it with others in existing collections to determine whether it was something new, and if it was, he would write up a detailed description, giving the bird or animal a new name. It thus became the type specimen, or *holotype,* of its species, and future collectors would compare their discoveries with it. This practice was applied to the anthropological field. Blumenbach, whose classification of mankind in a fivefold skin-color system was recently used in some school geography books, selected a particularly handsome skull from a European collection as the type specimen of the white race, and as it had belonged in life to a native of the Caucasus Mountains, white people came to be called Caucasians, or Caucasoids, and still are. As late as 1912 Boule selected the skeleton of La Chapelle aux Saints as the type specimen of Neanderthal man, which he compared to the skeletons of one Frenchman and three anthropoid apes.

As early as Darwin, however, it was recognized that a species is not just the specimen that happened to be killed or unearthed first, and others later found to resemble it, but a population. Indeed, Darwin based his theory of natural selection on his observation that individuals of a species are variable, and that one need not be more typical than another. As time went on, it became clear that a species is a breeding unit or population, which has a gene pool of its own, and not just a collection of individuals, and that each population is a separate entity, living in two related states of dynamic equilibrium. The first regulates the balance between the individuals that compose the population. The second governs its relations with the other species in its environment.

Another early observation was that members of different species do not interbreed, at least in a state of nature. It was first thought that this was not for lack of trying but simply because each species was incapable of fertility with any other. However, early in the twentieth century the rising science of genetics made it clear that some animals of different species could produce fertile offspring if they could be made to come together. Sterile hybrids like the mule were known from antiquity, and tiger-lion mixtures have been produced in zoos, but hybridization, it was found, is not a common or important mechanism of evolutionary change in the higher animals, as it is in plants. Furthermore, as each species is in genetic equilibrium with its environment, the addition of new genes from an animal with a different kind of equilibrium could be expected to produce offspring less viable than either parent.

The important distinction is that members of potentially interfertile species do not ordinarily interbreed either because their breeding periods fall at different seasons or because they simply do not attract each other: they do not recognize each other's mating symbols—visual, olfactory, auditory, or whatever.

In any case, whether or not unconfined animals of different populations interbreed when given the opportunity is the critical test of a zoological species. Paleontologists, of course, cannot use this test, which may be another reason why they prefer to deal in the more readily identified unit of the genus. In the case of living human populations, we can confirm Linnaeus's decision that all men belong to the same species, not only because all races are interfertile but also because some individuals among them interbreed, although others oppose mixture. In the case of early human populations unearthed by archaeologists, we cannot be sure whether interbreeding has or has not taken place; and at only one site, the Mt. Carmel caves of Palestine, is there any evidence—a high degree of individual variability combined with a mingling of tool forms—to suggest that the races were mixing, but even that is inconclusive. Therefore, the statements commonly made that Pithecanthropus, Sinanthropus, Neanderthal man, or a member of any other ancient population was unable to interbreed with his neighbors, if he had any, is speculative and cannot be demonstrated.

These statements are based on the old idea that if in some characteristic the ranges of variability of two populations fail to overlap, then these populations are different species. If this were true, then the Pygmies and Watusi of Ruanda-Urundi in Central Africa, who live near each other, would be different species on the basis of stature, and the black-skinned and white-skinned races of the world would also be different species.

This obsolete concept of single-character taxonomy has long since been abandoned. Zoologists now base their decisions on all the characteristics they can identify and measure, characteristics which together give the animal its essential nature, its (to borrow a psychological term) *gestalt*. The determination of species cannot be made by feeding figures into a computer. It is in a sense an art, practiced by men of experience who know, first of all, how species are formed.

The Spatial Requirements of Species and Their Geographical Differentiation

Z o o l o g i s t s recognize two kinds of species, *monotypic* and *polytypic*.[7] A monotypic species contains a single pattern of genetic composition, usually because it is a single population that occupies a single, environmentally unified *lebensraum* in which interbreeding is easy from one end of its territory to the other. Monotypic species are in the minority. A polytypic species, on the other hand, is broken up into a number of separate populations, each occupying its own territory. Usually these territories adjoin each other but are partially separated by environmental barriers. Gene flow across the barriers is infrequent enough to permit the development of separate genetic patterns but frequent enough to prevent the different populations from becoming individual species. When these barriers become absolute, local speciation can occur. Once a new species has arisen, it is likely to expand into a number of territories, where adaptation to new conditions will be rapid. This is undoubtedly what happened to our ancestors once they had acquired the erect posture and begun to use their hands for something beside locomotion and their mouths for something other than feeding and biting.

Regional populations of a polytypic species, once it has become established and has spread, are normally *allopatric*, a term which means simply "occupying different territories." If they were not allopatric, they would compete with each other for food, and one would drive out or absorb the other. Normally the one longest *in situ* has the advantage over newcomers because it has adapted itself to its new environment by favorable genetic changes, unless a geographical principle is involved, as in the case of isolated populations like those that arise on islands. Because they evolved without competition, such populations are usually vulnerable when

---

[7] This term should not be confused with the word *polymorphic*, which means, in the language of geneticists, that inside a given population more than one gene is available for a given position on a chromosome; the father may carry one, the mother another. The best-known example is the possibility of having a gene for A, B, or O on a single chromosome in the ABO blood-group system.

their territories are invaded by newcomers which evolved on large continental areas where competition is keen.

Related species, however, can be *sympatric*, which is zoologese for saying that they can occupy a single territory without interfering with each other, just as zebras, wildebeeste, and giraffes feed together on an African plain. Sympatric occupation is the rule for animals that belong to different genera, families, orders, and even higher categories of classification, which is why we have regional faunas. It is not very common among closely related species because they usually compete for food.

Whether or not related species are sympatric or allopatric depends to a large extent on their eating habits. If a species specializes in a narrow dietary range, it can coexist with another that specializes in a different range. The Australian koala lives essentially on the leaves of a few kinds of eucalyptus, the presence of which limits its range but allows it to coexist with other species of marsupials on the ground below; the giant panda of western China subsists largely on bamboo shoots whereas the smaller red panda eats a variety of foods.

Animal species that specialize in food are called *stenophagous*, the Greek term for narrow-feeding. Those that eat many kinds of food are called *euryphagous*, or wide-feeders. Like any other specialty, stenophagy permits a rapid expansion in a narrow milieu, but it is not the road to evolutionary success. Euryphagy involves an animal in heavy competition, but if it survives, it has a better chance of expanding over areas with differing food supplies, and of undergoing further speciation.

In the case of man, he is euryphagous and always has been. Man can eat roots, succulent leaves, fruits, berries, eggs, and flesh. Except for grass, he can eat virtually everything that other animals eat, and this puts him in competition with many other species and with other populations of his own and related species.

The Subspecies

THE NEXT taxonomic division below that of species is the *subspecies*. A subspecies is a regional population of a polytypic species (a species with a number of separate populations) which meets two tests: (1) *it occupies a distinct geographical territory;* (2) *it differs from other subspecies of the same species in measurable characteristics to a considerable degree* (to be specified shortly).

Subspecies must by definition be allopatric: if several subspecies were to inhabit a single region, they would breed together and the differences between them would be obliterated. Within its own geographical territory, which has an environmental character of its own, the subspecies has achieved, or is in the process of achieving, an adjustment to its local food supply, to the local climate, and to the behavior patterns of other animal species with which it shares its domain. After each subspecies has worked out a balance with all other elements in its local environment, it is not likely to change very much until its situation changes: natural selection will prune off unfavorable mutations that arise locally and keep the favored gene ratio constant.

Over the border, which may be a natural barrier such as a range of mountains or a patch of desert, or even a critical isotherm, may be found another subspecies of the same species, equally well established in a state of equilibrium with its environment. As the two environments differ in certain details, so do the genetic structures of its occupants. What is good for A is less advantageous for B, and vice versa. In each territory, natural selection keeps the gene structure of the local subspecies constant by also eliminating unfavorable genes that flow over the border. However, genes which are unfavorable in both environments may be eliminated in both populations, so that A and B may evolve together into a new polytypic species that retains its original set of subspecies. This is what we think happened when a number of human subspecies passed the threshold from *Homo erectus* to *Homo sapiens.*

Taxonomists have set up an arbitrary procedure to determine whether two or more populations within a species are morphologically different enough to qualify as subspecies. It is called the *overlap test* and is applied both to visible criteria, such as tooth size, and to invisible ones, such as blood groups. If in any well-defined, presumably heritable morphological character, a representative sample of population A differs from a representative sample of population B to or beyond a critical degree, then we are dealing with subspecies. The critical degree is 75 per cent. If 75 per cent or more individuals of A are different from 100 per cent of B, then the two are probably subspecies.[8]

This method was devised for use on large samples of living animal populations and it can be applied to modern anthropometric series, but it is rarely if ever useful in the study of fossil man because we have few samples large enough for analysis by probability statistics. When applied to modern human populations, this test shows that *Homo sapiens* is at present a polymorphic species divided into a number of clearly differentiated subspecies, each centered in its own territory.

The concept of subspecies is essentially zoological and is used almost entirely to describe regional variations in animal species. However, paleontologists also use it occasionally, to describe steps in a single evolutionary line which they consider too small to merit the rank of separate species. Such units may be called *successional subspecies*, or *waagenons*—named for a mid-nineteenth-century paleontologist, W. Waagen.[9] In order to keep confusion to a minimum I shall not use the word subspecies in this book to designate such successive units. When successive species must be split, I shall do it in terms of the evolutionary levels or grades through which they have passed.

Mosaics, Clines, Local Races, and Racial Types

B E L O W the taxonomic level of the subspecies, zoologists find a sometimes bewildering array of local racial variations of a minor nature, which exist because subspecies as well as species can be polytypic. This is as true of men as it is of mice, for man is the

---

[8] E. Mayr, E. G. Linsley, and R. L. Usinger: *Methods and Principles of Systematic Zoology* (New York: McGraw-Hill Book Company; 1953), p. 146. When biometric statistical constants are available, this test can be performed without plotting frequency curves by using the formula C.D. $= \dfrac{M_1 - M_2}{\sigma_1 + \sigma_2}$ in which C.D. equals Coefficient of Difference, M_1 and M_2 the means of two series, and σ_1 and σ_2 their standard deviations. If the C.D. is 1.28 or higher, subspecific rank is indicated. Attributes expressed in percentile values rather than means may be compared directly.

[9] Simpson: *Principles of Animal Taxonomy*, pp. 175–6.

most mobile of mammals. He walks the land, flies the skies, and rides the oceans.

Part of the racial complexity of *Homo sapiens* disappears if we disregard for the moment the distribution of modern peoples like white and Negroid Americans, Latin Americans, South Africans, and white Australians and New Zealanders, whose ancestors reached their homes by ocean-going ships in recent times. Before then each of the five subspecies recognized in this book was firmly and uniquely installed in its geographical center. Between the nuclei of these five centers lie intermediate regions of two kinds.

One of them is the *mosaic*, which contains relict populations living as enclaves in refuge areas. For example, in India at least two forms of Australoids, classified as "tribal peoples," dwell in the hills, surrounded by Caucasoids whose home is the plains. Such a mosaic pattern is the product of earlier, but not geologically ancient, migrations that have not had time to fuse. As will be shown in the next chapter, it is typical of the tropics of the Old World.

The other is a region of racial transition, a frontier-in-depth within which a subspecies grades into another through intermediate forms. It may be called a *clinal zone* because in it the population of the species intergrades in one or more measurable characters. In each heritable feature, the gradient is called a *cline*.[1] For example, the living Europeans grade from a high frequency of blue eyes in the northwest, particularly in Ireland and Scandinavia, to a high frequency of brown eyes in the southeastern part of the continent. This eye-color gradient is a cline.

Whole complexes of related clines are found in clinal zones. For example, in central Asia north of the Himalayas Caucasoids merge into Mongoloids through the persons of several Turkic-speaking peoples like the Kirghiz, Uzbeks, and Turkomans. This clinal zone is a broad one. On the southern face of the Himalayan wall a similar but narrow clinal zone stretches through a steep intermediate altitude zone, in northern India, Nepal, Sikkim, Bhutan, and NEFA (Northeast Frontier Agency). As can be seen by

---

[1] J. S. Huxley: "Clines: An Auxiliary Taxonomic Principle," *Nature*, Vol. 142 (1938), p. 219. See also Simpson: *Principles of Animal Taxonomy*, pp. 178–80.

these examples, the sharper the environmental barrier the narrower the clinal zone between subspecies.

Not only in relict enclaves and clinal zones, but also within the nuclear territories of subspecies, regional populations of minor rank may be found which differ from each other in perceptible ways short of the requirements of subspecies. These are known as *local races*. As they rise and disappear rapidly, they receive little attention from zoologists and usually none from paleontologists. In man they are considered important by people without a biological background, usually because such groups may be identified to a certain extent with social, political, or religious units.

How many local races could be identified and counted among living men is difficult to say, and different anthropologists might each find a different number. Such details are of no importance in this book, but it is important for us to know that local races exist and are formed by the same biological mechanisms that have fostered larger taxonomic units in the past.

Races like the Nordic, Alpine, Mediterranean, East Baltic, and Dinaric, which loom large in the Europe-centered literature of anthropology, are neither subspecies nor, in a strict sense, local races, although some local races may be defined in these terms. These words have also been used in the sense of *types*, which can be picked out of local populations. One may find a Spaniard who is typically Nordic in the midst of a population of Mediterraneans, including his own brothers. In a sense the situation is genetically comparable to finding a man of blood group B whose father's group was A. Types selected in this fashion are interesting to observe, and we notice them every day. Whether or not they reflect the origins of a population in one way or another, we must remember that from the taxonomic point of view such types are not races but simply the visible expressions of the genetic variability of the intermarrying groups to which they belong.

However, if we return to the first test of subspecies, geographical integrity, we are at first sight on shakier ground. Whites, Negroes, and American Indians occupy the United States sympatrically. Hindus, Fijians, and Europeans similarly occupy the Fiji Islands, and many other examples might be cited. As we study each instance, we find that this situation is a recent one, as time is measured biologically, and it is always associated with the expansion of peoples who have left the food-gathering stage of subsistence far behind.

Let us omit, for the moment, the agricultural peoples of the world and the colonists, and consider only the peoples who still are, or until recently were, food gatherers. These hunters and collectors are drawn from all five geographical races listed on page 3. Each race is confined to a single territory without overlap except in two regions: India, and southeast Asia plus Indonesia. Owing to a lack of skeletal material, we do not know when the ancestors of the various food gatherers moved into India, nor indeed which race was earliest there. In southeast Asia and Indonesia we know, as will be explained in Chapter 10, that Mongoloids began replacing Australoids about 10,000 years ago, after the invention of the bow and the domestication of the dog had made some hunters more efficient than others.

This southward movement was a trickle compared to what happened in many other places 4,000 years later. By or after 6,000 B.C. a number of local populations began to advance from the ecological niche of hunters and gatherers to that of food producers, and territorial expansions followed. These movements started no more than four hundred generations ago, counting twenty-five years to a generation. The colonial movements that brought Europeans to America, South Africa, Australia, and New Zealand took place less than twenty-five generations ago; only about twelve generations separate most descendants of passengers on the Mayflower from their celebrated forebears.

These various movements have greatly restricted the territories of aboriginal food gatherers, but gatherers are still present in reduced numbers. Many more have been absorbed into the new food-producing populations or have borrowed the techniques of food production from newcomers to their territories. Since the beginning of agriculture no new subspecies have arisen; the principal changes that have taken place have been vast increases in the numbers of some populations and decreases to the threshold of extinction in others. All this points to one conclusion: the living subspecies of man are ancient. The origins of races of subspecific rank go back into geological antiquity, and at least one of them is as old, by definition, as our species.

The Differentiation of Species

SPECIES FORMATION is believed to be the product of four principal factors: *mutation, recombination, selection,* and *isolation.*[2] A *mutation* is a heritable, spontaneous, and within certain limits random change in the chemical composition of a molecular segment of a chromosome known as a gene or gene locus.[3] These changes take place normally in all organisms at individual frequency rates that can be predicted. As most mutations produce unfavorable effects, relatively few are passed on or participate in species formation. The same mutation, favorable or otherwise, can appear time after time, at its own rate, in individuals of different races. Yet mutation is the primary element in evolution. The other three are secondary.

Recombination is the process which so mixes the genes that it is practically impossible for two individuals other than one-egg twins to be genetically identical. In ovaries and testes, the egg and sperm chromosomes split in a process called *meiosis.* Fertilization brings the halves of the parental chromosomes together. But the pairs do not always merge regularly. In rare instances, chromosomes cross over each other at various loci and trade strings of genes. Others break up and the fragments attach themselves to other chromosomes or get lost. These new arrangements can also cause changes in the resultant organism.[4]

Selection is the well-known pruning process by which the environment determines which novelty produced by mutation or re-

[2] E. Mayr: "Change of Genetic Environment and Evolution," in J. Huxley, A. C. Hardy, and E. B. Ford, eds.: *Evolution as a Process* (London: George Allen and Unwin; 1954), pp. 157–80.

[3] More technically, it is a change in the sequence of nucleotides within a DNA (dexoribonucleic acid) molecule of a single chromosome. See P. Alexander: "Radiation-Imitating Chemicals," SA, Vol. 202, No. 1 (1960), pp. 99–108. According to Demarec, there are about 10 to 15 genes to each DNA molecule, or 20 to 30 to a pair of molecules. M. Demarec: "The Nature of the Gene," *AJHG,* Vol. 13, No. 1 (1961), pp. 122–7.

[4] For present purposes this second process is not also called a mutation. See Simpson: *The Major Features of Evolution,* pp. 82–3.

combination shall gradually spread through the group because of its superiority to the old trait it replaces, and which novelty shall be eliminated because it is unfavorable. As most mutations are unfavorable, when a species is not perceptibly changing, selection serves almost entirely to preserve the status quo. However, the process of replacement is characteristically slow. Old genes have a habit of hanging on as minorities, and if the environment changes back once more, they may re-emerge as majorities, in new combinations.

Isolation, the fourth factor, is necessary for the rise of new species because, unless a breeding population is self-contained, natural selection may be unable to eliminate old, unfavorable genes from its pool. A constant gene flow from neighboring populations may renew the old genes as fast as they are being lost. In a monotypic species such gene flow is impossible by definition. But in a polytypic species only those genes can be eliminated which are unfavorable to all its component units. When this happens, the species evolves as a whole, whereas its component populations may retain their local differences.

Balanced Polymorphism

S O M E T I M E S it is disadvantageous for a population to eliminate its old genes completely. An old gene may possess the ability to meet an old crisis, if that crisis should return. Furthermore, the old gene and the new one with which it shares, as an alternate, its position on the chromosomes of certain individuals may do things together that neither could do alone.

In genetic shorthand, AB may be better under some conditions than either AA or BB. The best-known example of this effect in man is probably the so-called sickling trait common among West African Negroes. This is expressed by the letters S and s. S means that you have the trait, s that you don't. The S gene curls the red corpuscles in the blood, impeding oxygen flow; the s gene has no known effect. The S gene alone resists malignant malaria, which kills many children. But an SS child may die of oxygen starvation, and an ss child of malaria, whereas an Ss child is likely to survive both diseases. The population profits by the retention of both genes, each of which has a disadvantage in that particular environment.

The example just cited may explain the presence of genetic variability in many populations even though we don't yet understand why it is there in each case. It may also in part explain the re-emergence of "types."

On the Timing of the Individual Growth Cycle

I N A D D I T I O N to mutation, recombination, selection, and isolation, biologists have discovered a fifth evolutionary process which is tertiary because it depends on combinations of the other four, only one of which, mutation, is primary. This is a heritable change in the time of appearance of different characters in the growth cycle of the individual.

Each organism passes through three principal stages of development. It starts as an embryo, a fertilized egg in the process of cell division which has not yet reached the point where an embryologist can tell its species. In man this condition lasts about nine weeks. Then in mammals it becomes a fetus, in birds a chick, and in insects a larva.[5] After it has been born, pecked its way out of its shell, or left its cocoon, it starts on the road to adult life in different stages of preparation, depending on the class of animal it belongs to.

Both in fetal and postnatal life, the individual must be adjusted to its environment, or it will perish. Certain traits that are necessary to the fetus and useless to an adult appear in fetal life and then disappear. Other traits appear as they are needed. Incidentally, it is not true that every individual recapitulates the forms of all its ancestors from the beginning of life on earth. We do, however, recapitulate many of the *fetal* traits of our ancestors, but not all of them, and not all in the original order. Nevertheless, the fetus possesses a vast store of transient genetic characteristics that could be used in adult life under different circumstances.

One of the features that all animals inherit is a built-in timing

[5] G. R. de Beer: *Embryos and Ancestors*, 2nd. ed., (New York: Oxford University Press; 1951).

schedule which regulates the order of appearance and the duration of growth of different bodily systems. This schedule can be upset through standard genetic mechanisms, such as mutation and recombination. The survival of fetal traits into adult life occasioned by such a change is called *neoteny*.

The classic example of neoteny is the life cycle of an amphibian of the salamander group, the axolotl. This animal arrives at sexual maturity during its tadpole stage and never leaves the water to become an air breather like other salamanders, frogs, and toads, but reproduces and dies in its original medium. Other examples are found among certain birds that have lost the power of flight. They retain throughout life the down that covers the chick before it breaks out of its shell. Ostriches, emus, cassowaries, and penguins have all acquired this neotenous change independently.

In man's ancestors neoteny may have been at play before the appearance of *Homo erectus*. The position of the head on the neck at right angles to the axis of the vertebral column is neotenous; it is found in the fetuses of all the primates and indeed in those of other mammals. In the fetuses of primates in general the thumb is relatively long in proportion to the length of the other fingers. Among many monkeys and all apes the adult animals have short thumbs, which in man remain neotenously long throughout life.

In insects, which are born fully grown and completely adult, all changes in timing have to be neotenous. In mammals, which are small when born and dependent on their mothers for food and protection, the infantile form differs markedly from the adult in many ways. A baby mammal has to grow mightily and in most species rapidly, and in the higher species it has much to learn. As growth is largely controlled by the endocrines, any shift in endocrine balance can cause radical changes in the form and appearance of the adult animal.

In man some races appear infantile in certain respects throughout life, whereas the children of other races look like miniature adults. In some races the color of the hair never changes during an individual's lifetime, except among persons who reach advanced senility. In others the hair may start out blond, become brown at puberty, and turn white by the age of thirty.

The classbook issued to the members of the Harvard class of

1925 at our twenty-fifth anniversary contains two portraits of each man who was still alive in 1950 and who could be reached. One portrait was taken at graduation, the other twenty-five years later. In some individuals almost no change can be detected; others had changed so much that they were unrecognizable. Yet nearly all these men were of the same racial origin. Age changes, then, vary within populations as well as between them. Not one of my classmates, however, looked like a Pygmy or a Bushman.

Races that retain a number of infantile features throughout life are called *pedomorphic;* those in which mature features appear early are called *gerontomorphic,* after the Greek words *pais,* a child, and *geron,* an old man. Pedomorphism and gerontomorphism are most conspicuous in external, visible anatomy, but they can also affect the nervous system, the vocal cords, other covert systems and structures, and behavior. Most fossil men that we know were gerontomorphic, as witness their heavy brow ridges and long faces. *Homo sapiens* as a whole seems to be relatively pedomorphic, although variable in this respect both racially and individually.

On Size and Form: Allometry

W E   M U S T   be careful, in seeking for relationships between different races, not to confuse pedomorphy and gerontomorphy with normal variations that take place when animals of the same or related species grow smaller or larger. A mouse has a larger brain, in proportion to its body size, than a rat does. A Great Dane's eyeballs are proportionately smaller, although absolutely larger, than those of a terrier.

Animals that are otherwise genetically similar vary in proportions according to size, the small ones being more compact, the larger ones more attenuated. The principle governing these differences is called *allometry.* Zoologists not only recognize this rule but express it in formulas. For example, in the horse family face length equals .3 times skull length, to the 1.2 power.[6] A big horse

[6] de Beer: op. cit., p. 27.

A classic work on this subject is D'A. W. Thompson's *Growth and Form* (New York: The Macmillan Company; 1945).

has a longer face, both absolutely and relatively, in proportion to his skull length, than a small horse does. By the same token, an average African Pygmy has relatively shorter legs and a relatively larger head than does an average African Negro.

On Sexual Dimorphism

A N O T H E R factor to be considered in comparing races and species is the degree of differentiation between adult males and females in a population. This is called *sexual dimorphism.* It varies greatly both in mammals and birds. Male and female cardinals have feathers of different colors; yet it is difficult for a nonornithologist to tell a male from a female robin. Among the primates, a male gorilla may be twice as large as any member of his harem, whereas the only visible difference in gibbons in the wild is the protrusion, through the fur, of nipples in the female that has borne offspring.

Sexual dimorphism serves two principal purposes. First, it may be part of the selective process in mating, as when male birds strut their plumage in the nuptial ceremony, and as when stags lock their horns in mortal combat in competition for a doe. Second, among some animals that inhabit distinct territories, as for example lions, or baboons living in a forest, the exaggerated size and fighting equipment of the males permit them to serve the function of a border patrol in human communities. The male keeps rivals off his feeding ground and away from his wife or wives. Neither the male lion nor the male baboon is any better at obtaining food than his womenfolk; in fact, among lions the female excels at hunting. These animals expend their biological capital for territorial defense, just as we spend the bulk of our tax money for atomic submarines and missiles.

In fossil man there is evidence of sexual dimorphism, but it is clouded by the paucity of material available for study. In living races a great variability can be seen. Australian aborigines and western Europeans are highly variable; Mongoloids little. As Tibetans dress and wear their hair alike, it is sometimes difficult to tell whether any one person is a man or a woman. This does not mean that sexual dimorphism is the same as pedomorphy, for some populations with little sexual dimorphism are in certain ways gerontomorphic. No one could call a Plains Indian infantile, and his women can be huge and craggy. It is difficult, then, to decide whether certain racial traits, like the absence of a beard in many Mongoloid males, are the result of pedomorphy, of a lack of sexual dimorphism, or of some other aspect of the endocrine story yet to be discovered.

In any case, the presence or absence of marked sexual dimorphism is an inherited racial trait that distinguishes some living populations from others. This trait may date back to remote antiquity since it was not involved in the complex of evolutionary changes that led from *Homo erectus* to *Homo sapiens*. Of this we may be fairly confident because the two races that have achieved the greatest cultural advancement, the Caucasoid and the Mongoloid, stand at opposite poles in this respect. At the other end of the cultural scale, so do the Australian aborigines, who show marked sexual dimorphism, and the African Bushmen, who show little of it.

How Species Have Evolved

LIKE ALL MEN, all species must eventually die. Just as some men perish with neither issue nor close kin and others achieve partial immortality through the transmission of some of their genes to their offspring, or more remotely, by the survival and reproduction of their brothers and sisters—so some species become utterly extinct whereas others live on, in a shadowy way, through one or both of two evolutionary mechanisms, *succession* and *branching*. Succession is also called *phyletic evolution* or *anagenesis;* the technical word for *branching* is *kladogenesis.*

Evolution through succession occurs when a genetically isolated population acquires a new and favorable hereditary trait that is controlled by a single gene or by a complex of genes operating in concert. Then the new trait gradually replaces the old one through natural selection.

Evolution through branching occurs when two or more geographically separate populations of a single, polytypic species become genetically isolated from one another and then evolve into species of their own.

Succession tends to favor a process known as *general adaptation* whereas branching works rather through *special adaptation,* but the two are not mutually exclusive.

General adaptation involves the acquisition of a new trait or trait complex that is useful in more than one environment and under various different circumstances. Warm-bloodedness in birds and mammals is one example. Another is an increasing intelligence, which many forms of animal life have developed throughout geological history. A more limited example is the power of speech, which is useful to all men.

Special adaptation involves the acquisition of a new trait or trait complex that is useful in a single environment under special circumstances. It is the process which enables an animal to resist heat, cold, or bright light, to see well in dim light, to run faster or to swim better than its fellows, or to live without water in deserts, and which gives it many other such specializations. Special adaptation led the ancestors of the whales from the land back into the sea, and general adaptation gave them the intelligence needed to communicate with one another, by a system similar to sonar, and to survive, as mammalian populations, in their aqueous medium.

General adaptation tends to lead a species into evolution by succession because most species are polytypic, and a polytypic species includes several populations living in different environments. Each of these populations becomes adapted to its special environment to a certain degree, but it cannot speciate by branching as long as it remains in genetic contact with its sister populations, since new traits involved in local specialization cannot completely replace old ones while genes continue to flow back and forth. If, however, in one or more populations a new trait appears which is equally favorable to all the populations and in all the environments occupied by the species, then the existing gene flow will help the new trait replace its predecessor in all the component populations, including that or those in which it started. By this process the old species evolves as a unit into a new species. At the same time speciation need not prevent the component populations from carrying their old, partial specializations, such as to heat and cold, from one species into another.

If, however, a single population of a polytypic species becomes physically isolated from its fellows, so that gene flow is completely interrupted, then that population can evolve by branching. Now special traits that have no general value can completely replace the old ones that used to flow in over the border. If such a popula-

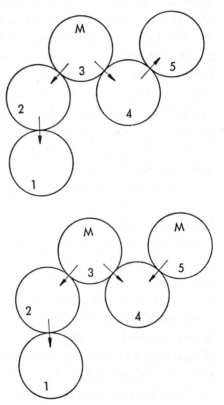

FIG. 1 How One Polytypic Species Can Evolve Into Another. *Above:* Five subspecies, in peripheral contact with each other, are illustrated by five circles, numbered 1 through 5. A mutation favorable to all five arises in No. 3. It spreads to Nos. 2 and 4, and is carried by further peripheral gene flow to Nos. 1 and 5. When all five subspecies have it, the species has begun to evolve into a new one by anagenesis—evolution through succession. *Below:* In this example the favorable mutation arises independently in Nos. 3 and 5, and, except for the direction of gene flow between Nos. 4 and 5, speciation takes place as in the first example.

tion happens to be confined to a small space, such as an island, and has no natural enemies, it can become a monotypic species as specialized as the dodo, the classic example of this process.

Although the component populations of a polytypic species evolve as a unit, they cannot do so simultaneously since it takes time for a mutation to spread from one population to another. If we measure time on the broad scale of tens of millions of years used by paleontologists, these changes may appear simultaneous, but if we measure it on the geologically microscopic scale of the last 700,000 years, which is the age of man, we will see that related populations, which in our case are subspecies, passed from species A, which is *Homo erectus,* to species B, *Homo sapiens,* at different times, and the time at which each one crossed the line depended on who got the new trait first, who lived next to whom, and the rates of gene flow between neighboring populations.

Whether a new species is polytypic or monotypic, whenever it arises the evolutionary process is essentially the same. The new, critical trait responsible for speciation first appears in a few individuals, and its presence makes little difference to the population in which it arises. It may even appear and disappear several times before it takes hold. But after it has begun to spread, a point is reached when those who have it begin to outnumber those who don't. This point is marked by a rapid growth in population. The particular population has gained an advantage over competing species in its own *lebensraum,* and in the process it has become a new species of its own.

It need not, however, have completely lost the gene or genes for the old trait that is on the way out. After the new species has established itself, become stable in numbers, and reached a new equilibrium with the other species of plants and animals in its environment, the old trait may completely disappear. At that point a second and final threshold of speciation has been crossed. One may say that a new species has come into existence when it has acquired a new and more favorable ecological position, and that it has reached maturity when the traits responsible for these changes have completely replaced their predecessors. By the time the second threshold has been crossed, as likely as not a new species-forming mutation shall have begun to appear, and the cycle has started over again.

It is easy to understand, then, why some populations within any polytypic species have come closer, at any given time, to the second threshold of speciation than other populations. In man some groups of people alive today have preserved archaic traits, diagnostic of *Homo erectus,* in a higher percentage of individuals than other populations. For example, more natives of New Caledonia have big teeth and heavy brow ridges than a corresponding percentage of Japanese.

This and similar disparities can be explained in two ways. (1) The more archaic population acquired the new trait complex that led to speciation later than the more modern population did. (2) After crossing the first threshold of speciation, the more archaic population has been discarding its old traits at a slower rate than the more modern population.

Both explanations can be true at the same time. There is no necessary correlation between the time at which a threshold was crossed and the rate of change that follows the crossing. In either case, the critical mutation may have been original to the population concerned, or it may have been acquired by gene flow from a neighboring population. The older the trait the more likely that it was original; the younger the trait the more likely that it was derived from outside.

In any event, once a species has come into being, the old species from which it evolved is extinct. There are several kinds of extinction: utter extinction without issue, which is commonest among monotypic species; extinction through absorption, by which a subspecies ceases to exist as a separate entity when its remaining members are taken into the body of another; and extinction through successive evolution, which is the process we have just described.[7]

In the case of man, only the second and the third kinds of extinction can be traced. The Tasmanian aborigines who died out in the nineteenth century have living survivors among the racially mixed inhabitants of the islands between Tasmania and Australia, and the Fuegian Indians of South America are disappearing into the mixed population of that continent. But neither Tasmanians nor Fuegians were whole subspecies. The Australoid and Mongoloid divisions of man to which they belong survive in large numbers elsewhere. There are also, in a sense, degrees of extinction, for it takes a long time, on our human time scale, for one

---

[7] E. H. Colbert: "Some Paleontological Principles Significant in Human Evolution," in W. W. Howells, ed.: *Early Man in the Far East* (Philadelphia: Am. Assn. Phys. Anth.; 1949), pp. 103–47.

species to replace another completely, and in that sense some human races are more nearly extinct than others.

On the Life Spans of Mammalian Species [8]

ALTHOUGH the antiquity of *Homo sapiens* will be the subject of detailed study in later chapters, we may here profit from a consideration of the life spans of our fellow mammals during the Pleistocene and Recent (or post-Pleistocene) periods, the only periods in which man or any of his close kin are known to have lived. By international agreement the beginning of the Pleistocene has been established at the point when modern genera of elephants, horses, oxen, deer, and some other large mammals were first seen on the continents of the Old World, excluding Australia. The movement that brought them in, mostly from the New World, took place about one million years ago.

Before that stretched the vast temporal expanse of the Tertiary —Paleocene, Eocene, Oligocene, Miocene, and Pliocene—comprising some 77 million years, the Pliocene alone taking up some 12 million. During this long span individual species were born, flowered, and died at what seems to us a leisurely pace. The life expectancy of a mammalian species was then anywhere from one to eight million years.

During the first 300,000 or 400,000 years of the Pleistocene this pace continued, but it was suddenly quickened in various parts of the Old World, particularly its northern portions, by geological events. The planet's crust wrinkled more rapidly than before, raising the toothed edges of mountain ranges and creating great contrasts of climate, both regional and seasonal. First mountain glaciers, then continental icecaps crawled forth and melted away, blowing, like pairs of bellows, alternately cold and warm. In large tropical land masses, as in much of Africa, the bellows blew wet and dry.

[8] This section is based on many sources, including books by G. G. Simpson. However, specific facts and figures come principally from two works of Björn Kurtén: "Rates of Evolution in Fossil Mammals," *CSHS*, Vol. 24 (1959), pp. 205–15, and "Chronology and Faunal Evolution of the Earlier European Glaciations," *SSF-CB*, Vol. 31, No. 5 (1960) pp. 1–62.

In response to these changes, new species evolved rapidly. Many became extinct, but others survived. The life expectancy of a species now dropped to a mere 360,000 years. At a point in time pegged at 300,000 years ago, all or nearly all the living mammals of the European and neighboring fauna, which were fox-sized or larger, had come into existence. The species which have since appeared are bats, insectivores, and rodents, all small animals. During the last 75,000 years, no new mammalian species seem to have evolved at all. Three hundred thousand years ago the evolution of new species of medium-sized and large mammals came to a halt. The heyday of speciation was over.

The oldest known *Homo erectus* is believed to be 700,000 years old. He appeared during the period of frenzied mammalian speciation mentioned above, and seems to have lasted until less than 100,000 years ago in remote parts of the Old World. His known life span as a species, about 600,000 years, was within the normal range for a mammal of his size and vintage. As I shall show in Chapter 11, *Homo sapiens* appeared about 250,000 years ago in an archaic form. Completely modern forms of our species appeared at least 35,000 years ago. Unless our species is a curious exception to the rules by which the game of speciation is played, *Homo sapiens* should go back to 360,000 or 300,000 years ago. This figure would place *Homo sapiens* in the fauna to which he belonged, and would give *Homo erectus*, who appeared exactly when he should have, ample time for speciation by succession.

So much for the actuarial statistics of Pleistocene and Recent species. With subspecies the reckoning is more difficult because subspecies are not easy to sort out when found among fossils. We have no satisfactory information except that subspecies of the ibex have been traced back at least 230,000 years.[9] In the case of man, the subspecies of *Homo sapiens* are probably of different ages, depending on the times at which regional populations of *Homo erectus*, in one way or another, crossed the *sapiens* threshold. But all of them did this before the end of the Pleistocene.

In modern times we have seen whole tribes and peoples disappear after their lands had been invaded by Europeans and other

[9] F. Zeuner: *Dating the Past* (London: Methuen & Co.; 1952), pp. 383–4.

culturally dominant strangers. The native Tasmanians are gone, and so are the Indians of Lower California. The Andamanese of the main islands, the Fuegians, and many others are on their way out. These sad cases of ethnic oblivion give us a feeling that human history is a long record of utter extinctions, but this is not true.

All species are destined to become extinct, but, except as they are parts of species, subspecies need not follow this rule. By definition, species do not ordinarily interbreed, but subspecies do. The Tasmanians were absorbed by the Caucasoids who replaced them on their island. A mixed Tasmanian-European population survives today. If the Indians of Lower California left no mixed descendants—which is unlikely—other Indians very much like them are still alive. When subspecies disappear, they usually, if not always, do so by absorption. Their genes linger on polymorphously with those of their conquerors, to re-emerge, now and then, when needed. The principle is that when a population has been invaded by members of another race the genes that give it its special adaptation to its local environment retain their selective advantage and eventually come to characterize the mixed population through the process of natural selection. For example, central Europe was invaded from the East many times from the Neolithic through the Iron Age, but central Europeans still look more like the hunters of the Mesolithic than like the invaders.[1] Without the concepts of absorption and re-emergence it would be difficult for us to explain the physical diversity and geographical distribution of the living human races.

Part of this diversity may be relatively new. I refer here especially to the reduction in body size that has affected many species of mammals since the end of the Pleistocene, some 10,000 years ago. As will be explained in Chapter 3, extreme cases of size reduction in plants and animals take the form of dwarfing, which means that an irreversible genetic change has taken place. Our species includes a dozen or more populations of dwarfs, living in Africa, southern Asia, and Indonesia. As far as we know, all human dwarf populations are geologically recent.

[1] C. S. Coon: *The Races of Europe* (New York: The Macmillan Co.; 1939).

Genetic Principles and the Origins of Races

IN RECENT DECADES the pursuit of anthropometry has declined, except for applied anthropology. Instead of measuring the bodies of the last remnants of aboriginal populations, anthropometrists measure military personnel and civilians in order to design railroad and airplane seats and space suits. Doctors of Philosophy have become tailors to the new age of science. On the other hand, the pursuit of human genetics has become popular, particularly the study of the frequency in populations of blood-group genes, taste thresholds, mid-digital hair, and hairy ears.

In tracking down the lines of descent of fossil men, none of these characteristics is useful. Thieme and others have shown that it is impossible, using present techniques, to determine the blood type of samples of bone, for they all tend to absorb a group A substance from the ground.[2] Dead men cannot taste noxious chemicals, and the hair on their fingers and ears has long since decayed. What could be done, however, is to work out the relationships between fossil specimens and populations in terms of details of tooth structure, for teeth do not change with age except to be worn down. Molar cusp-numbers, the presence or absence of a kind of curvature of the incisors known as shoveling, and many other features that are preserved in the fossil record are just as useful for genetic studies as blood groups are among the living, and paleontologists have long relied on teeth. Although much work has been done on human teeth, no one has yet produced a work of synthesis covering all fossil specimens by means of which they could be compared with living populations.

Limited as the direct application of genetics is in the study of fossil man, the theoretical aspects of that science have helped us greatly. They have taught us that the unit of inheritance is neither the individual nor the arbitrarily chosen type, often identified with an individual, like Nordic, Dinaric, Neanderthal, and Crô-Magnon, but the population, and that each population has its pool

[2] F. P. Thieme and C. M. Otten: "The Unreliability of Blood Typing Ancient Bone," *AJPA*, Vol. 15, No. 3 (1957), pp. 387–97.

of genes with several possible alternates, known as *alleles*, from many if not all loci. We also know that because individual mutations recur at characteristic rates, resemblances between populations of the same species do not necessarily imply recent common descent. All curly-haired populations do not have to be descended from a common curly-haired ancestor. Pockets of blondism found among nonwhites need not be explained by Viking invasions, nor all Pygmies be considered as having derived from a single tribe.

An acquaintance with the principles of genetics may also help us solve the central problem of this book—that is, to discover how long ago the ancestors of the human subspecies parted company. We have learned, for example, that evolution consists of cumulative changes from one generation to another, over long periods of time, in the frequencies of hereditary variations. If parallel mutations have been occuring in two populations, we cannot expect a large number of identical changes to have taken place at once in each group. Changes in the skeletons of fossil men from period to period in each major area seem to have involved very few factors, not many of them visible below the neck.

Brains have grown larger and brow ridges smaller. Jaws have sprouted chins and teeth have grown smaller in various degrees. Whole sets of these changes can be linked together as common products of one or more shifts in endocrine balance, shifts advantageous in an increasingly group-oriented society in which self-control comes to be more conducive to survival than a hot temper. Other changes may simply reflect a reduction in chewing, especially after the invention of cooking. If in each of several related populations, living in its own territory, changes like these took place not all at once but in sequence, it is possible that each single, parallel mutation prepared the ground for the selective advantage of the one that followed it.

On the other hand, if these sequences of genetic change were initiated in some of the populations by sexual contacts with people from other regions (peripheral gene flow), it would be difficult for us to detect this outside influence from an examination of the skeletons of the resulting mixed population because other genes transferred by the same contact might be disadvantageous in that particular area and would have been eliminated by natural selection.

Although we cannot hope to settle the question of parallel evolution versus peripheral gene flow in the evolution of each race by examining fossil bones and nothing else, such a study may show us how far back in time the various geographical races go. Some of our subspecies are characterized by traits that seem to have had little relation to either climate or culture during the known history of man, and whatever selective advantages or disadvantages they may have must have been acquired long ago. Among these traits are the architecture of the teeth, the shape of the nasal bones, and the degree of flatness of the face. If various combinations of these traits can be seen to have persisted in their special geographical regions despite other changes of a more clearly phyletic evolutionary nature, then the antiquity of individual races may be established. In any case, no form of evidence is unwelcome and only by a close study of detail can we hope to solve this and related problems.

Note: Had I read Bernhard Rensch's book, *Evolution above the Species Level* (New York: Columbia University Press; 1960), before writing my own, I would have found support for my idea that the profound evolutionary changes which a single gene mutation affecting the pituitary can cause may indeed have initiated the *erectus-sapiens* transition. Such a minor genetic change could hardly have hampered interfertility between the haves and the have-nots. As it might conceivably arise as often as once in a hundred thousand persons per generation, statistical probability does not exclude the possibility of more than one independent threshold-crossing. And the long time gaps between crossings in certain races might also be explained on the theoretical basis of more than one such mutation.

Rensch further states that racial adaptations to different environments, each of which involved a number of genes, would have required tens of thousands of generations, or, in man, quarters of millions of years, to become fully established. In other words, the races of man differ more from each other in a quantitative genetic sense than *Homo erectus* and *Homo sapiens* did, and our races are older than our species.

2

EVOLUTION THROUGH
ENVIRONMENTAL ADAPTATION

I N T H I S C H A P T E R we shall discuss the effects of size, space, numbers, and climate on the direction and rate of evolution. Other principles of change will be examined, in addition to those mentioned in the first chapter. By comparing man with other animals we shall see, in particular, how adaptation to the external, nonhuman environment helped shape the living races of man into their present forms.

Body Size, Food, Space, and Climate

A T S O M E turning point in the evolution of our ancestors men became hunters. Instead of relying on roots, fruits, and small, slow-moving animals for their food, they began to compete successfully with the great carnivores and could feed themselves and their families wherever meat was to be found.

Among other carnivores a natural relationship exists between the size of the predator and that of his prey. A fox cannot kill a zebra, but a zebra is the favorite food of lions. Properly armed, however, a man can kill an animal of any size. As he began to do so, it was probably advantageous, all else being equal, for him to be large as well as muscular. At any rate, we have indirect evidence that our ancestors grew larger at about that time. This placed them in the elite company of large land mammals and subjected them to some of the special evolutionary rules that govern such species.

One is that they are few. At present there may not be more than sixty other species of our size or larger,[1] out of 3,500 species in the class of mammals. A second is that most of these have only one species to a genus. This ratio is characteristic of the other large primates—the orang, the chimpanzee, and the gorilla—as well as of the elephant, the hippopotamus, the rhinoceros, and the bear. The larger these animals the more likely that they will be the only species in their genus, at least at any one time. In his utilization of terrain man is in a class with the largest mammals of all; primitive hunters destroy more forest by burning than elephants do by uprooting trees. If, after the beginning of hunting, the genus *Homo* ever consisted of more than one species at a time, not counting species in the act of transition, as from *Homo erectus* to *Homo sapiens*, he would have constituted a curious exception to a well-established rule.[2]

A third rule is that individual animals of large size take up disproportionately more room than small animals, and that the relationship between the sizes of their ranges is believed to be logarithmic.[3] A large animal needs a great deal of space not only for feeding and drinking but also for concealment in the heat of the day and for sleeping and reproduction.

From the time that man became a hunter, if not before, he was a social animal living in groups of families with an optimum population somewhere between twenty and forty persons.[4] As the area required per person must be multiplied by the total in the group, the territory of a feeding unit of this size had to be considerable. Once the ability to eat meat had extended the potential range of man as a species to the limits of the continental land masses of the Old and New Worlds, nothing could stop him from filling these

[1] The uncertainty is due mainly to a lack of agreement on the classification of the Bovidae—cattle, sheep, goats, antelope, etc.

[2] E. Mayr: "Taxonomic Categories in Fossil Hominids," *CSHS*, Vol. 15 (1951), pp. 109–18.

[3] G. E. Hutchinson and R. H. MacArthur: "A Theoretical Ecological Model of Size Distributions among Species of Mammals," *AN*, Vol. 93, No. 869 (1959), pp. 117–25.

[4] The basis of this calculation will be stated later.

spaces except natural barriers, such as glaciated mountains, bodies of water, empty deserts, and extremes of environment to which he was not accustomed, such as great cold, heat, drought, and high altitude.

Some of these extremes he overcame by cultural means, particularly after he had acquired fire. His ability to invent and make adequate housing, clothing, and containers as well as effective weapons must have placed a premium on the kind of intelligence that governs these capacities. In every region where, in addition to hunting, environmental problems had to be mastered by technology, parallel evolution in the direction of higher intelligence must have been in operation.

Once man's inventive genius had made it possible for him to live in extreme environments previously barred to him, a new burden was placed on his physiology because he could not, with his incipient skills, overcome all climatic obstacles. We must expect to see the results of genetic responses, through natural selection, to differences in environment, and we must know how to interpret them, for the patterns they take will tell us much about the early history of our genus and species.

If such differences occur and the subspecies of man turn out to be clearly divided on this basis, so that one is adapted for wet heat, another for dry heat, a third for cold, a fourth for high altitude, and so on, then it will be likely that at the time of the dispersal of the subspecies the ancestors of all of them belonged to a single, monotypic population. If, on the other hand, the existing subspecies do not entirely fit this scheme, and if in addition certain subspecies include regional populations adapted for different climates, then it will appear that *Homo* has been polytypic for a very long time and that the dispersal of our ancestors into different regions took place very early, before the beginning of man's career as a hunter and before he possessed the cultural means to invade and inhabit the regions of the earth's surface previously unavailable to him.

In pursuing this inquiry we shall not be exploring virgin territory. Zoologists have been faced with similar problems for over a hundred years. What happened to human beings once they had come to live in diverse environments had happened to other animal species many times before. The study of animal evolution through environmental adaptation is a part of zoogeography,[5] a well-documented scientific discipline more than a hundred years old. By reviewing its major principles and studying some of the data it has uncovered we may determine what to look for in man.

The Face of the Earth

AS OUR TELESCOPES improve and we learn more and more about the surfaces of other planets—most of which are excessively hot or cold, or vary from one extreme to the other between night and day, and lack the friendly mists and rain that water our woods and fields—the more we appreciate the infinite variety and manifold advantages, to creatures like us, of the face of the earth, our home.

Far from being simply a playground to run about, sleep, feed, and breed in, the skin of our planet, with its myriad variations, has been a major determinant in the evolutionary process. Evolution, itself a product of variability and change, has been cumulative, keeping pace through geological time with the ever increasing rate of differentiation of the surface features of the earth. The planet's crust has wrinkled faster, in cooling, than wind, rain, snow, ice, and all the other forces of erosion have been able to wash away, grind down, flatten, and otherwise homogenize it. The same forces have made the products of evolution increasingly complex and heterogeneous, increasingly sensitive, and increasingly aware of themselves and of their surroundings.

Eight factors have affected the face of the earth from the zoogeographic point of view: the clockwise rotation of our planet, which creates westerly winds; the zonal differentiation of the earth, which makes some latitudes cold and others warm; the tilt of the earth's axis, which creates seasons; the relative sizes of land masses, which emphasize or diffuse seasonal change and give populations breeding grounds of different magnitudes; the rise of

---

[5] The study of plant distribution is called phytogeography. Phytogeography + zoogeography = biogeography, the study of the distribution of living things. Biogeography is a unit; its two components are interdependent.

mountain ranges, which permit altitude to substitute for latitude as a climate maker; the bodies of salt water, which prevent terrestrial animals from crossing from one land mass to another; and the land bridges and strings of islands, which allow certain qualified animals to filter through. The eighth factor is time, particularly the last million years, which have seen the icecaps of the world alternately crawl forth and shrink back three times, with consequent stress and displacement of many forms of animal life, including that far-ranging genus, *Homo.*

Land Masses [6]

A C C O R D I N G to standard school geographies, the world contains seven continents, but for present purposes these will be considered as five. Antarctica can be disregarded because it is uninhabited. Europe is not a real continent; the Greeks distinguished their own peninsula from Asia, which lay on the other side of the Aegean, and this split has since been carried north past the Caspian Sea barrier onto the steppes of Russia. Europe is a highly favored peninsula of Asia. We shall call the combination Eurasia, as do most geographers.

Of the five continents remaining—Eurasia, Africa, North America, South America, and Australia—the first four are strung together in one fashion or another. The Isthmus of Suez ties Africa to Eurasia as it has done for a long time. Both the Bab el Mandeb and the Straits of Gibraltar are deep but narrow saltwater channels, and both were open and ice-free throughout the Pleistocene. Eurasia, the greater and more varied of the two segments, is nearly twice as large as Africa, with 21 to the latter's 12 million square miles, and it contains bits and pieces of all the climates of the world, whereas Africa lacks mid-latitude forests, boreal forests, and taiga.[7]

[6] In this and the following two sections of Chapter 2, I am drawing heavily on P. J. Darlington, Jr.: *Zoogeography* (New York: John Wiley & Sons; 1957).

For the Pleistocene, the best source is J. K. Charlesworth: *The Quaternary Era,* 2 vols. (London: Edward Arnold; 1957).

[7] These terms are taken from Preston James's *Outline of Geography* (Boston: Ginn and Co.; 1935).

Eurasia and Africa are tied together at a latitude of 30° N., and as Suez is normally frost-free, it is not too cold at sea level for most forms of terrestrial life to traverse. Africa is mostly a plateau bent around a cup of low-lying equatorial rain forest; and from the edge of the Sahara to the Cape of Good Hope there stretches an essentially homogeneous environment of grasslands, savannas, and seasonal forests high enough so that temperatures vary little from one latitude to another and grazed throughout by more or less the same kinds of animal herds. By contrast, Eurasia is built like a tent with a pole in the middle and drooping sides. The lofty land mass of Tibet brings an approximation of arctic conditions to a large area partly located in the same latitude zone as Suez. It also partitions off much of southern Asia. The line of mountains reaching diagonally across the map from the Tian Shan to the Bering Strait cuts the northern half of the continent into a northwestern and a far-eastern segment.

The erstwhile land bridge across the Bering Strait, which connected Eurasia with North America, was a broad, flat, ice-free highway that appeared during periods of glaciation whenever the ocean level was lowered by the immobilization of water in the form of ice at the poles. The land bridge last appeared probably between 70,000 and 8,000 B.C., either during this entire period or in parts of it. Although it lay at an altitude of 66° N., the southern shore of the bridge may have had mild winters at this time, being protected from the arctic waters and tempered by the westward flow of the Japanese current. Animals able to live through a moderately cold winter could have crossed the bridge in either direction, and many of them did.

North America, with 8.3 million square miles, is smaller than Eurasia or Africa and differs from both in land formation. Whereas Africa is predominantly a plateau and Eurasia a ring of subcontinents with most of its mountains running east and west, in North America the western and eastern ranges run north and south, leaving a wide trough in the middle which creates extremes of climate at many widely separated points, so that one can shiver in Houston in winter and swelter in summer in Saskatoon.

South America, with 6.8 million square miles, has been connected to North America by the Isthmus of Panama since the beginning of the Pleistocene a million years ago, but during the entire 60 million years of the preceding Tertiary it was isolated by salt water. Like Africa, it has a plateau running across the equator, and this plateau is as high as the Tibetan one although its surrounding peaks are a little lower. But it is narrower, and the equatorial rain forest it shelters is, at the present geological moment, the world's largest.

However, if we return in time to the last glacial advance, and in space to southeast Asia (see Map 2), we see that a vast area of some 800,000 to a million square miles, known as the Sunda Shelf, was then incorporated, as geologists believe, onto Indochina, Malaya, and the islands of Indonesia west of the Bali and Macassar Straits. If, as may be presumed, this lowland was largely covered with rain forest—for it was a wet period—it may well have been as large as the South American rain forest, or even larger. A rain forest of this size is a fertile breeding ground.

Five hundred miles to the south and east lay a continental area of nearly four million square miles, including the present Australia (3 million square miles), Tasmania, New Guinea (300,000 square miles), and some of the Melanesian Islands, joined by another now-submerged stretch of lowland, the so-called Sahul Shelf (over 580,000 square miles). When the sea rose at the end of the Pleistocene, this land mass was split into its present components.

Zoologically these now separated regions are still a unit. Anthropologically we can likewise consider New Guinea, Tasmania, and some of the Melanesian Islands as recently separated peripheries of a fair-sized continent the center of which is the Australian desert. More specifically, woolly hair is characteristic of the Papuans, Tasmanians, and a few of the coastal Australian aborigines. Most of the Australians have straight or wavy hair. Woolly hair, therefore, is geographically peripheral to straight hair in what is left of the former, larger continent.

The significance of the Sunda and Sahul shelves is clear. In no part of the world other than southeast Asia, Indonesia, and Australia are the seas so shallow that vast interconnecting land masses could have been created when the icecaps of the polar regions trapped enough water to lower the sea levels in many parts of

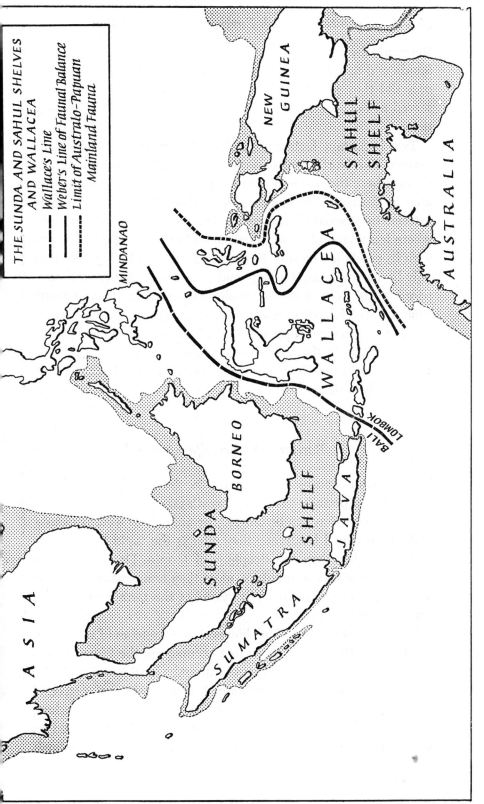

THE SUNDA AND SAHUL SHELVES
AND WALLACEA

    Wallace's Line
    Weber's Line of Faunal Balance
    Limit of Australo-Papuan
        Mainland Fauna

ASIA

MINDANAO

BORNEO

SUNDA

SHELF

SUMATRA

JAVA

BALI

LOMBOK

WALLACEA

NEW
GUINEA

SAHUL
SHELF

AUSTRALIA

MAP 2

the world by forty fathoms below their present shorelines. The Sunda and Sahul shelves are the only real "lost continents." Not only did they join lands now separate, but they may also have served as bellows to suck in and blow out early human populations.

Two important facts emerge from this survey of global land masses. The Northern Hemisphere is the land hemisphere, and the Southern the realm of ocean. Therefore the land masses situated in the north are more continental in climate, that is, more extreme in seasonal change, and stormier than the southern lands, where less meteorological change is taking place. The Old World with its combined mass of Eurasia and Africa, which are divided only by narrow seas, is a huge and varied breeding ground compared to the New with its smaller masses of North and South America, which meet effectively at a single point only. One would expect more to have happened biologically to land animals in the Northern than in the Southern Hemisphere, and also in the Old World than in the New. These expectations have been fulfilled, particularly in the case of man.

Barriers and Breeding Areas

THE MOST conspicuous barriers in the world are probably mountains, especially such lofty breath-takers as the Himalayas, but even their rims can be crossed, by animals as well as people, and the principal hindrance they offer is the rapid temperature gradient rather than the steepness of terrain. Deserts, too, are barriers; there lack of moisture, more than temperature, does the screening, and except in sandy stretches the terrain itself offers little impediment to travel.

The greatest barriers of all, however, are stretches of salt water. That is why the Azores, when first occupied in the fifteenth century, had no land animals except birds and a local lizard, and why the Australian continent contained aboriginally no placental mammals except man, the rat and dog, which went with him, and the air-borne bat. That is why South America contained an almost unique vertebrate fauna when the North American animals began infiltrating over the newly formed Panama bridge at the end of the Pliocene. Lesser barriers such as mountains and deserts serve as screens rather than as roadblocks. While holding back most species, they let dominant ones through to take over new territories. In the case of subspecies, especially qualified individuals can get from one breeding ground to another and spread their genes in the new population.

It is a general rule that relatively numerous populations living in large breeding grounds tend to be dominant over others that have lived in smaller areas. The larger the number of animals in a population, the greater the mathematical chance they have of undergoing a rare, favorable mutation that can spread throughout the group by means of natural selection. Since in small, isolated populations there are fewer individuals there are also fewer mutations, too few in some cases to include any of the uncommon, favorable ones. At the same time, owing to lack of competition in a sheltered environment, some of the commoner, unfavorable mutations can spread unhindered through such a small, sheltered population and eventually bring about deterioration or even extinction. That is why islands are being constantly repopulated by stray sets of dominant species that happen to drift or be blown in from continental land masses.

Genetic Drift

NEVERTHELESS, all mutations need not be perceptibly or measurably favorable or unfavorable in any given situation. In Europe, for example, it can make no conceivable difference to a man's chances of survival and reproduction whether his hair is straight or slightly wavy. In a large population, a neutral or indifferent mutation will not ordinarily spread rapidly, nor will it necessarily be lost. It can be expected, all else being equal, to maintain a low frequency in a large gene pool. In a small population, on the other hand, it can easily be lost through sheer chance —if, for example, the three persons out of ten who have it are eaten by a tiger. The mutation could also spread through the same small breeding unit if the tiger ate the people who did not have it instead of the others. Gene frequencies, then, change more rapidly in small than in large populations. The process by which such fortuitous changes become major characteristics of populations is called *genetic drift,* or the *Sewall Wright effect,* after its discoverer.[8]

Once genetic drift has taken place, the chances are that the population in which it has occured will become extinct, because: (1) the reduction in population which permitted the drift may also have reduced the total number of breeding individuals below the safety level needed for survival; and (2) few genes chosen by chance are likely to be superior to their alternate alleles from the standpoint of survival.

If the population survives and multiplies, this may be because the genetic characteristic or characteristics chosen by drift were favorable for survival in the first place, and the drift merely sped up the process of selection. In the long run, the frequency of this gene or of these genes in the pool would have risen to an optimum level in any case, without danger of extinction.

Genetic drift is often invoked to explain differences between species and subspecies in characteristics that are of no detectable value in natural selection. As our knowledge of genetic processes grows and as our ability to detect selective values increases, we need this theory less and less.

The Dominance of Groups

Dominance has two meanings in zoology: the dominance of individuals in social groups, as shown by the peck order and the like, and the dominance of one kind of animal over another. We are concerned here with the second meaning only.

Groups of dominant animals may range in diversity from whole orders to families to genera and even to species. Examples are the carps (family *Cyprinidae*); the common frogs (genus *Rana*); the common snakes (family *Colubridae*); the perching birds

[8] S. Wright: "On the Role of Directed and Random Changes in Gene Frequency in the Genetics of Populations," *Evolution,* Vol. 2, No. 4, (1948), pp. 279–94.

(order *Passeres*); the rats and mice (family *Muridae*); and the human species (*Homo sapiens*). Even within a species such as ours, certain subspecies and races may show dominance over others. This is part of the evolutionary process.

Dominant groups result from a combination of factors that render them particularly successful in withstanding climatic stress, especially cold; in finding and utilizing food; and in reproducing efficiently under varying circumstances. The perching birds, for example, achieve these ends partly by migration; the rats and mice by storing food and by burrowing underground to escape predators and the rigors of the weather. In the case of man, he is capable not only of using fire and tools intelligently in organized social units but also of undergoing a certain amount of physical adaptation to certain environments.

As a rule, the breeding grounds of dominant animal groups are situated in the centers of the land masses they occupy, with the result that the animals are forced into competition for their ecological niches by rivals from all sides. If in addition to being centrally located, the breeding grounds are in cool regions, then the species living there will produce more offspring than the same or corresponding species in the tropics,[9] not because of greater fertility, but because in warm regions many fetuses are lost through the failure of sufficient pituitary hormone ACTH to reach the embryo from the mother. As this hormone normally balances the adrenal cortisone, which has no difficulty getting through, an excess of cortisone causes the resorptions.[1]

This and other observations partially explain why the cooler portions of the Old World had fewer species, but larger populations, than its tropical regions, and why some of these populations reinvaded the tropics, with varied success.

Zoogeography can also explain many instances in which groups

[9] B. Rensch: "Some Problems of Geographical Variation and Species Formation," *PLSL*, 149th session (1936–7), pp. 275–85. Also *Homo Sapiens, vom Tier zum Halbgott* (Göttingen: Vandenhoeck and Ruprecht; 1959).

[1] W. V. Macfarlane, P. R. Pennycuik, and E. Thrift: "Resorption and Loss of Fetuses in Rats Living at 35° C.," *J. Physiol.*, Vol. 135, No. 3 (1957), pp. 451–9. Also S. Brody, A. C. Ragsdale, R. G. Yeck, and D. Worstell: "Milk Production, Feed and Water Consumption, and Body Weight of Jersey and Holstein Cows in Relation to Several Diurnal Temperature Rhythms," *RBMO*, Vol. 578 (1955), pp. 1–26.

failed to acquire dominance. Animals that inhabit peripheral shores or small islands lead sheltered lives and may develop local peculiarities without facing the pruning effect of rivalry. That is why early mariners found dodo birds strutting around Mauritius and giant tortoises ambling over the glades of the Galapagos. These facts, incidentally, were not lost on the youthful Darwin who voyaged on the *Beagle*. That is also why rabbits and foxes, when let loose in Australia, raised such havoc with the local fauna, and why, in another sense but following the same principle, the white settlers have replaced the aborigines in the wetter sections of the same continent.

The Six Faunal Regions

AS LONG AGO AS 1857, two years before the appearance of Darwin's *The Origin of Species,* an ornithologist named Sclater published a paper [2] in which he divided the world into six faunal regions: Ethiopian, Indian, Palearctic, Nearctic, Neotropical, and Australian. In 1876 Wallace [3] confirmed this division but changed the name of the "Indian" region to "Oriental"; this change has persisted in the corresponding literature. Although a century has passed since Sclater's work was published, zoologists still divide the world in this fashion. The faunal regions, which designate the distribution of the terrestrial and land-locked vertebrates—the fresh-water fishes, amphibians, reptiles, birds, and mammals—proved to have been actual divisions during most of the Cenozoic, or Age of Mammals, except that some of their boundaries shifted during the glacial and interglacial stages of the Pleistocene epoch. In earlier times, of course, the surface of the world was divided differently, but these earlier differences do not concern us in this book.

Matthew, an influential zoogeographer writing in 1915,[4] indicated that the region of primary evolutionary change was the

[2] P. L. Sclater: "On the General Distribution of the Class Aves," *JPLS-Zool.,* Vol. 2 (1857), pp. 130–45.

[3] A. R. Wallace: *The Geographical Distribution of Animals* (London: Macmillan & Co.; 1876).

[4] W. D. Matthew: "Climate and Evolution," *ANYA,* Vol. 24 (1915–1939), pp. 171–318.

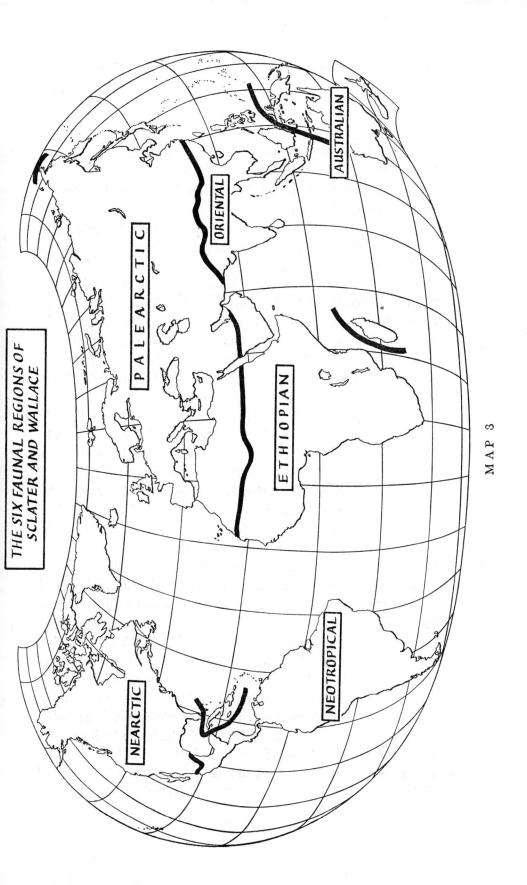

THE SIX FAUNAL REGIONS OF
SCLATER AND WALLACE

PALEARCTIC

ORIENTAL

AUSTRALIAN

ETHIOPIAN

NEARCTIC

NEOTROPICAL

MAP 3

Holarctic, a term combining the Palearctic and Nearctic, and indeed those regions were active centers of change during the first glacial advances of the Pleistocene, when many species of mammals were becoming adapted to cold. However, Darlington now believes that the tropical regions of the Old World, the Ethiopian and particularly the Oriental, have been the principal centers of speciation over a longer period.

The Ethiopian region consists of Africa south of the middle of the Sahara, which in times of drought acts as a barrier to the movements of many animals, and the southwestern corner of Arabia south and west of the Arabian desert. But until the end of the Pleistocene North Africa had an Ethiopian fauna; about ten or twelve thousand years ago it was invaded by Palearctic mammals, including Caucasoid men. Madagascar, with an extremely specialized and archaic fauna, is a special province of its own and was not inhabited by human beings until about the time of Christ. South Africa, which lies as far from the equator as South Carolina, has a Mediterranean climate, but as there is no barrier to separate it from the main part of Africa it has not been isolated enough to have developed a special fauna of its own. The fresh-water fishes, amphibia, and reptiles of the Ethiopian region resemble those of both the Nearctic and the Oriental regions; the birds, as might be expected, have world-wide relationships, though they are particularly linked to the Oriental region; and the mammals can be divided into certain widely distributed families, some related to the Oriental region, some purely local, and a few with other connections. However, for the mammals as for the other classes of land vertebrates, the greatest ties are to be found with the Oriental fauna.

The Oriental region consists of tropical Asia with its fringing islands, including Ceylon, the Andamans, Sumatra, Java, Borneo, Formosa, and in certain respects the Philippines. On the east it encompasses southern China north to Hong Kong, and on the west it runs a few degrees north of the tropics in northern India. There is heavy rain forest in much of Indochina, the Malay peninsula, Siam, and western Indonesia, and patches of it in the Cardamon Hills (Kadar country) of southern India and in the Khasi plateaus of Assam, which is the wettest place in the world.

Oriental fresh-water fishes form a rich and dominant assemblage lacking archaic groups; Oriental amphibia and reptiles are partly similar to and partly unlike the Ethiopian ones; and whereas Africa has more species of lizards, the Oriental region is particularly rich in snakes. Both its birds and mammals are strongly related to the Ethiopian groups, as for example its elephant, its rhinoceros, and the lion, but the Oriental fauna is less sealed off than the Ethiopian. It is also related to the Palearctic, in common with which it has bears and tigers. Both of these are lacking in the Ethiopian region. This relatively open character is reflected in the fact that the Oriental region has fewer purely local (endemic) groups of vertebrates than any other tropical area. Darlington says: "Either it has been a center from which vertebrates have tended to spread into other regions, or it has been a main crossroads in dispersal, or both." [5] Within the Oriental region the fauna can be divided into four regional assemblages. The richest and most varied is in the northeastern part, including southeast China, Indochina, Siam, and Burma; the poorest is in the principal, drier part of India.

Furthermore, the boundary between the Oriental and Palearctic regions which verges on the richest subarea—the south Chinese border—is wide open. Nothing except a very gradual climatic cline stands in the way of free passage northward by Oriental animals, and vice versa. The width of this frontier is greatly extended by a series of cool mountain ridges stretching like fingers from the Chinese highlands southward between the rivers of southeast Asia. *In no other place in the world does an open border exist between a tropical and a temperate faunal region.* As we shall presently discover, this has been significant for man as well as for other animals.

On the western side of the Oriental region the mountain barriers are formidable, but there are passes, particularly the Khyber and Shibar passes, into Palearctic territory, and during certain warm interglacial periods the Mediterranean and western Europe had Oriental faunas. The road to the Ethiopian region now runs along the barren Makran coast of Baluchistan and the connecting piece of the south Persian coast, then either across a small salt-

[5] Darlington: op. cit., p. 436.

water gap or around the head of the Persian Gulf, and down into the Green Mountain of Oman, and finally along the southern coast of Arabia, where only one undessicated pocket, the Dhofar region, remains. During the times when the main movements of animal groups took place between Africa and India, this whole route must have been much wetter than now and easier to cross.

The Palearctic region includes the nontropical parts of Eurasia and the Barbary states. Climatically speaking, it ranges from arctic to Mediterranean conditions, but in all or nearly all of it there is winter frost, which means that all the animals who live in it achieved some kind of adaptation to cold. This fauna is consequently far less rich in species than the Oriental or the Ethiopian. As the principal flow of animal groups has been from southeast Asia to China and thence to points north and west, it is not surprising that the land vertebrate fauna of China is the most varied of the whole Palearctic region, whereas that of the British Isles is quite poor. Furthermore, the animals differ more from east to west than they do from north to south. This is of special interest to anthropologists, because the same thing is true of human sub-species. A Norwegian and a Berber resemble each other far more than either resembles a Chinese, and many a Tibetan could pass for a Chukchi of northeastern Siberia. The diagonal mountain barrier running from the Tian Shan range to the Bering Strait, which partially separates the Caucasoid and Mongoloid realms, has had its effect on other animals as well.

The Nearctic fauna, which occupies all of North America north of the tropical part of Mexico, is relatively poor in species, most of which are derived from the Palearctic, although a few have moved up from tropical Middle and South America. Greenland is part of this area, and contains American mammals only, although some of its birds are European.

South and Central America, the tropical lowland of Mexico, and Trinidad comprise the Neotropical region. The other islands of the West Indies have a greatly reduced fauna, which is transitional in a minor way. On the whole, the Neotropical fauna is a mixture of old forms that developed locally during the Tertiary, and new ones, including man, which came in from North America during the Pleistocene. A few of its mammals, notably the armadillo and the opossum, have migrated northward.

The Australian faunal region encompasses Australia itself, Tasmania, New Guinea, and some of the fringing islands off New Guinea. That this region has been cut off from the rest of the world for a very long time is evidenced by the fact that it is very poor in fresh-water fishes and amphibia, and that its mammals are composed of monotremes (the platypus and echidna) and of six exclusive families of marsupials. Its closest relationships are with the almost equally residual fauna of South America, and it has very little in common with the neighboring Oriental region.

Wallacea

THE REGION between the Oriental and the Australian realms is named Wallacea. Across it the world's richest and poorest continental vertebrate faunas face each other. In 1860 Wallace drew his famous deep-water line between Bali and Lombok, Borneo and Celebes, and Mindanao and the islands of Sangi and Talaud. Although Bali and Lombok are only 15 miles apart, the Oriental fauna is cut off at that point almost as though with a knife. This line is the western frontier of Wallacea; the eastern is close to the so-called bird-head, a peninsula of western New Guniea. The island of Kei is inside Wallacea; and Misol, Waigeo, Batanta, and Salawati go with New Guinea in the Australian region. A third line, known as Weber's, runs down the middle; it is called the line of faunal balance.

Very few land mammals have crossed Wallace's Line, and those that have done so live almost exclusively in the northern part of Wallacea. Celebes was reached by shrews, tarsiers, macaques, squirrels, four genera of weasels, several kinds of pigs, including the endemic Babirussa deer, and an endemic breed of cattle known as the anoa. During the Pleistocene Celebes also harbored a pygmy elephant. Some of these animals reached the Moluccas, but they did not go south. In the Lesser Sundas, east of Bali, porcupines, shrews, crab-eating monkeys, pigs, and deer all reach as far as Timor. All these animals may have been introduced by man, who probably brought them along as pets, food, or both.[6] On the other side, a few Australian marsupials have penetrated into Wallacea as well. There is a bandicoot on Ceram, and phalangers live on Halmahera, Timor, and Celebes.

Wallacea is unique in the world as a barrier-filter. It is of great anthropological significance because it isolated the Australian aboriginal population virtually unchanged since its arrival from the southeastern Oriental region during the late Pleistocene. Even today the population of these small islands is racially intermediate between the more recently arrived Mongoloid peoples of western Indonesia and the natives of New Guinea. As the ancient barrier between the erstwhile Sahul and Sunda shelves, it must be taken into account in any attempt to unravel the complex racial distributions in southeast Asia and Oceania.

The Faunal Regions and Human Origins and Movements

M A N, it is becoming increasingly clear, must have originated in some form in one of the two realms of tropical fauna in the Old World, or in an erstwhile extension of one of them into what is now the Palearctic during a period warmer than the present. Whereas the exchange of animals between Africa and south Asia was intermittent and mutual during the Tertiary and Pleistocene, the Oriental region supplied most of the vertebrate groups to the Palearctic. One principle of the movements of animals may help us decide which way the animals moved. When older, less dominant forms are replaced by spreading dominant forms, the dominant ones do not push the others to the peripheries ahead of them; rather, they overrun them, leaving small, disconnected refugee pockets in their wake.

The Oriental region contains many such small, marginal populations of Australoids, Asiatic Negritos, and primitive, food-gathering Caucasoids, which indicates that these races inhabited that zoogeographic region before its invasion by Mongoloids and modern kinds of Caucasoids from the north. In the Ethiopian re-

[6] Darlington: op. cit., pp. 466–7.

gion the distribution of Pygmies follows a similar refugee pattern, and in East Africa pockets of Bushmen indicate the earlier distribution of Capoids to the north of their historic home. The only comparable relict population in the Palearctic or Nearctic is that of the Ainu, and both their antiquity in northern Japan and their origin are questionable.

Returning to straight zoology, we find that, as many Palearctic genera originated in south Asia, greater dominance was required for some of them to move northward through the eastern part of the Palearctic region and then into Europe and the Americas than for others to reach the Ethiopian realm, particularly in a period of greater moisture than the present. Furthermore, as Rensch [7] points out, more evolution has been taking place in the Northern Hemisphere than in the Southern since the end of Tertiary times, or in other words, since the beginning of the Pleistocene. As a great deal of human evolution occurred during the Pleistocene, the Oriental region, being the more northerly, is a better candidate than the Ethiopian as a possible place of dispersal of the remote ancestors of the living races of man.

Certain complications, however, qualify this interpretation. In the Palearctic region the diagonal mountain barrier that crosses central and northeastern Asia imposes a bar sinister of cold climate between the eastern and western halves of this faunal region. Animals that enter the eastern half from the Oriental region do not all cross it. During parts of the Pleistocene this barrier was glaciated. Also, during the Early Pleistocene and the interglacials of the Middle Pleistocene southern and western Europe were tropical regions, connected by the Near Eastern land bridge to both the Oriental and the Ethiopian regions. Asiatic species were commoner in Europe at these times than African ones, although both were present.

Therefore, if man did not originate in Europe, which we can almost take for granted, he could have arrived there from either southwest Asia or Africa, or from both. It is very unlikely that initially he came across the mountains of central Asia from China. At any rate, once Europe had been populated, alternate periods of glacial and warm or temperate climates gave Europeans more

[7] Rensch: op. cit., pp. 275–85.

than one chance to adapt themselves to new conditions and, like other members of their faunas, to reinvade the tropics.

In sum, the rules of zoogeography apply to man as they do to other animals. They offer us probabilities as to where the genus *Homo* evolved and over what paths different groups of men moved to found regional populations. They also help explain the dominance of some populations over others.

These rules can be applied in another way as well. Animals of many species have become adapted morphologically and physiologically to the exigencies of different climates. As members of a species that inhabits all climates, some of the races of man may have undergone selection for extremes of climate.

Environmental Adaptation and Early Man

ZOOGEOGRAPHY leads by tiny steps into ecology, which deals with the ways different plant and animal species get along together in various environments, and ecology in turn carries us into the study of environmental adaptation. How the polar bear can sit on a cake of ice without melting it, and how desert rodents live without water, are fascinating subjects discussed in an extensive literature. The adaptations of living races of men to climatic extremes have also been studied, to a lesser extent. But for present purposes, since we are concerned only with the history of fossil human races, only two aspects of this subject need be explored here.

(1)   We need to know whether the fragmentary remains of our fossil ancestors contain any telltale indications of adaptation to climatic extremes, in order to determine whether such adaptations are characteristic of subspecies, and to keep ourselves from confusing them with general, evolutionary characters.

(2)   We need to determine what extremes of climate our ancestors could have tolerated with a minimum of cultural equipment—and we can do this by studying and comparing the physiology of living primitive peoples.

The results of both these investigations may help us determine how old the existing subspecies are, and whither and whence they could have migrated during the Pleistocene.

Simply by observing the geographical distribution of living peoples, we can see that no single subspecies is limited to a single climate. Caucasoids live all the way from Norway to India. The aborigines of Tasmania, who were spiral-haired Australoids, went about nearly naked in a climate as cold as England's. Mongoloids may be found from the Arctic to the wet tropics, and both the Australian aborigines and the South African Bushmen, whose ranges are more limited, live through broiling heat and freezing weather at different seasons, with a minimum of cultural assistance. Given time, a population derived from any human subspecies could probably adjust itself to most local conditions. Adaptations to climate, therefore, could occur independently in more than one subspecies and need not be interpreted as evidence of genetic relationship.

In only three kinds of environment are land mammals rigorously selected for their abilities to resist stress: arctic and other cold areas, deserts, and high mountains. The first entails heat regulation; the second both heat regulation and water conservation; and the third oxygen consumption, particularly oxygen transfer from the mother to the fetus. Physiologists have done a great deal of work to explain how the caribou can live in the snow, why the camel can go for days in the summer heat without drinking, and how the llama can bear its young in the thin air of the Andean plateau.

The Rules of Bergmann and Allen

THESE ADAPTATIONS found among living mammals involve fur, skin, blood vessels, interstitial fluids, and blood corpuscles, i.e., soft parts, which ordinarily disappear after death. If geologically ancient human beings also had such adaptations, very few details of these can be detected among the bones at our disposal. Yet certain uniformities which reflect relationships between the bodies of animals and climate may show in the skeleton as a whole. These are the old, nineteenth-century rules. Bergmann's rule,[8] for example, states that in a given species the warm-

[8] Carl Bergmann: "Über die Verhältnisse der Wärmeökonomie der Thiere zu ihrer Grösse," *Göttinger Studien*, No. 8 (1848).

blooded animals which live in cold places tend to have greater body bulk than those which live in hot regions. Allen's rule[9] further states that in a given species animals living in cold areas tend to have shorter extremities than those in warm climates. This does not mean that in cold places animals' ears, legs, or tails become too short to function, only that within functional limits they will become shorter than they might have been had cold stress been absent.

Both these rules concern the physics of heat loss from a warm body to a usually cooler surrounding atmosphere. As a body has three dimensions and its surface only two, the bigger the body, all else being equal, the less the heat loss per unit of volume (Bergmann). Furthermore, the nearer the body comes to being a perfect sphere, the smaller is its surface area per unit of volume (Allen). Each species of animal usually has its own system of conserving and losing heat, so that these rules cannot be used in interspecific comparisons.

In recent years these venerable rules have been criticized by physiologists, some of whom were unaware that the rules apply only to single species; and they have been defended by taxonomists and physical anthropologists.[1] As they represent results rather than processes, they are naturally less useful in studying adaptation than physiological experiments are, but they can be applied to much larger population samples than physiologists can test. As a supplement to physiological experiments, they can be applied to living men, particularly to old, long-established food-gathering populations.

Peoples who live in cold regions are generally heavier than the

[9] J. A. Allen: "The Influence of Physical Conditions in the Genesis of Species," *RR*, Vol. 1 (1877), pp. 108–40. (Reprinted in *ARSI* for 1905 [1906], pp. 375–402.)

[1] For this controversy see:

P. F. Scholander: "Evolution of Climatic Adaptation in Homeotherms," *Evolution*, Vol. 9, No. 1 (1955), pp. 15–26.

Scholander: "Climatic Rules," *Evolution*, Vol. 10, No. 3 (1956), pp. 339–40.

Mayr: "Geographical Character Gradients and Climatic Adaptation," *Evolution*, Vol. 10, No. 3 (1956) pp. 105–8.

M. T. Newman: "Adaptation of Man to Cold Climates," *Evolution*, Vol. 10, No. 3 (1956), pp. 101–5.

C. G. Wilber: "Physiological Regulations and the Origins of Human Types," *HB*, Vol. 29, No. 4 (1957), pp. 329–36.

inhabitants of the tropics, and the ratio of trunk length to leg length is greater in the peoples who dwell in cold areas, who weigh more per unit of stature.[2] As expected, these regional differences are found in all subspecies that encompass wide ranges of climate.

For our present purpose of detecting climatic adaptation in fossil men these rules are rarely useful, with a few exceptions. Several nearly complete skeletons of European Neanderthals have bones so short and heavy that their body weights must have been great per unit of stature, as with living peoples of the Arctic. With these exceptions, we rarely have enough bones from a single individual to calculate both stature and relative trunk height; indeed, stature is usually calculated from the limb bones alone, which defeats our purpose. Also, there is no formula for calculating body weight from the skeleton.

Now and then we find the cervical vertebrae, which tell us whether necks were long or short. This is useful because peoples in cold climates tend to have short necks. We can also estimate the amount of warm arterial blood that flows into the cheeks through the infraorbital foramen (a hole in the zygomatic bone just under the eye socket) by the diameter of that opening. A strong flow of blood through that hole helps keep the cheeks of the Greenland Eskimo warm.[3] Similarly, the size of the mental foramen (mental means *chin* in this case), a comparable hole in the lower jaw, affects the amount of warm blood that reaches the chin.

The shape of the foot is also significant, for people who go barefoot in cold water or snow tend to have short broad feet with short toes. In a few sites whole feet of fossil men have been recovered; in others footprints have been found.

Among living peoples who dwell near or above the Arctic Circle, whether they are Caucasoid or Mongoloid, there is a tendency for the tympanic plate, a bony structure below the ear

[2] D. F. Roberts: "Body Weight, Race, and Climate," *AJPA*, Vol. 11, No. 4 (1953), pp. 553–8.

Newman: "The Application of Ecological Rules to the Racial Anthropology of the Aboriginal New World," *AA*, Vol. 55, No. 3 (1953), pp. 311–27.

[3] W. S. Laughlin and J. B. Jørgensen: "Isolate Variation in Greenlandic Eskimo Crania," *ActG*, Vol. 6 (1956), pp. 3–12.

hole, to become thickened—why we do not know. This thickening has also been observed among the Moriori, the original Polynesian inhabitants of the Chatham Islands, who lived in a cool climate.

Nose Form and Climate

A FURTHER adaptation concerns the nose. In places where the air is dry the nasal aperture tends to be narrow; where it is damp, the openings may be broader. This adaptation involves the function of the nasal passages in moistening inhaled air. Noses also tend to be narrower in cold than in hot climates, because of the heat exchange between the lungs and the inhaled air, but the protection of the lungs from frost is not as critical as the humidifying function.[4]

Ridges and surface irregularities on the skull and mandible indicate how much and how hard a prehistoric individual chewed. This can also be determined, in mature specimens, from the amount of tooth wear. In the earliest fossil hominid remains, particularly those from periods and places without fire, powerful jaws and large, heavily worn teeth reflect a coarse diet without cleaning, cooking, or other effete ways of demineralizing or softening food. Later on, in advanced prehistoric populations living in cold places, jaw muscles (as indicated by the effects they left on bone) again became massive and teeth excessively worn. Like the Eskimo, these people used their teeth in preparing skins for clothing.

Physiological Adaptation to Cold

THESE imperishable details of skull morphology tell us much less about adaptation to climate than the soft parts would have done had they been preserved, as those of mammoths were. Climatic adaptation is physiological, and the physiology of heat and cold adaptation is mostly a matter of oxygen consumption, blood flow, and details of muscles, fat, skin, and nervous tissue. Because

[4] A. Thomson and D. Buxton: "Man's Nasal Index in Relation to Certain Climatic Conditions," *JRAI*, Vol. 53 (1923), pp. 53–92.

J. S. Weiner: "Nose Shape and Climate," *AJPA*, Vol. 12, No. 4 (1954), pp. 1–4.

differences in physiology are racial, and racial differences are as old as *Homo sapiens,* we may venture to project physiological differences in living races backward into the time of fossil men. Many such differences, long suspected, have recently been established.

During the 1940's the global nature of modern warfare stimulated the interest of several nations in man's ability to live in all climates, particularly the arctic. It soon became clear to some researchers that living races differ in their tolerance of heat and cold. Although much work remains to be done, at least seventeen experimental studies published between 1950 and 1960 reported tests of this nature on all five subspecies of *Homo sapiens.*[5]

These tests have shown that Mongoloids are adapted to sleeping and working in the cold as a result of one kind of physiological adaptation; that Australoids and one group of Caucasoids, the Lapps, are cold-adapted in an entirely different way; that Negroes are both adapted to wet heat and sensitive to cold; and that most European Caucasoids and all Bushmen studied lack special adaptations to either heat or cold.

In the Arctic, fur keeps the bodies of most mammals warm. The same furs, tailored into clothing, keep people warm out of doors. But despite the use of warm clothing, blankets, and campfires, Alaskan Indians sleep under conditions of moderate cold while camping out on their trapping routes in the winter. Their bodies, however, compensate for the incurred heat loss by an increased basal metabolism. By burning extra oxygen and calories they are able to sleep without discomfort at temperatures that keep white men tossing and waking.[6] This physiological capacity, which is inherited, is not a seasonal phenomenon. It keeps them warm, with little cover, on chilly summer nights as well as in winter.[7]

[5] Europeans were used as controls in all these experiments except that given in footnote 3, page 65, the Japanese tests. Thus Caucasoid Europeans, other than Lapps, who were tested separately, constitute the norms.

[6] L. Irving, K. L. Anderson, A. Bolstad, R. Elsner, J. A. Hildes, Y. Løyning, J. D. Nelms, L. J. Peyton, and R. D. Whaley: "Metabolism and Temperature of Arctic Indian Men During a Cold Night," *JAP,* Vol. 15, No. 4 (1960), pp. 635–44.

[7] R. W. Elsner, K. L. Anderson, and L. Hermanssen: "Thermal and Metabolic Responses of Arctic Indians to Moderate Cold Exposure at the End of Winter," *JAP,* Vol. 15, No. 4 (1960), pp. 659–66.

A far more spectacular and much better known example of cold adaptation is that of the Canoe Indians of Tierra del Fuego and adjacent South American shores and islands. In 1959 Hammel, Scholander, and others, including myself, went to the islands and glaciers of the southern Chilean archipelago to study the cold adaptation of the Alakaluf,[8] the only one of the four original Fuegian tribes still numerous enough and unmixed enough to warrant investigation.

When first discovered by Magellan, these Indians were going about in canoes in freezing weather with no clothing except an occasional sea-otter skin cape, and with their bodies smeared with sea-mammal fat and ocher. At night they usually slept in small, domed huts covered with skins and heated by fires of *Nothofagus,* an evergreen tree closely related to the beech. This wood throws off great heat and burns nearly all night.

Except for the early morning hours, these Indians were as warm indoors as we are. Out of doors they exposed themselves unclothed to heavy winds and pelting sleet and snow. Furthermore, they walked and swam in the icy water, and dived for shellfish. The work of Hammel and his associates shows that the Fuegians, taking the Alakaluf as an example, were able to survive freezing temperatures without clothing by burning off a large quantity of calories, much more than the Alaskan Indians needed to keep warm at night. The Alakaluf live mostly on shellfish and the flesh of sea mammals, and they eat heartily. Their basal metabolism is 160 per cent higher than the norm for whites of the same weight and stature.

Returning for a moment to arctic mammals, and also to arctic birds, we observe that no matter how warm their fur and down keep their bodies, certain extremities, like seals' flippers, caribou's lower legs, and birds' beaks, remain relatively unprotected. In some species, as for example the fur seal with its exposed flippers, warmth is provided to these extremities by a massive flow of arterial blood close below the surface. This flow of blood burns up many calories, thus enabling the seal to swim in comfort.

On anatomical evidence alone, we have already inferred that

[8] H. T. Hammel: *Thermal and Metabolic Responses of the Alacaluf Indians to Moderate Cold Exposure,* WADD Technical Report 60–633, December 1960.

the cheeks of the Greenland Eskimo receive an extra flow of blood which keeps them warm, but as far as I know this has not yet been tested physiologically. The Eskimo's hands, however, have been tested for the same phenomenon, and they show an increased flow of blood when held in cold water.[9]

The hands of Alaskan Indians respond in the same fashion, producing twice as much blood flow as those of white men tested under the same conditions.[1] The same response was obtained from the hands of Alakaluf women,[2] who collect shellfish by hand in cold water. In Manchuria four groups of Mongoloids were tested by the Japanese for this same phenomenon,[3] and a gradation, or cline, was found which corresponds to the climates of the regions inhabited by the peoples studied. The Orochons, a nomadic, reindeer breeding and hunting tribe of northern Manchuria, had the most adaptation; the Mongols and north Chinese came next (the two were the same); and the Japanese had the least response.

Similar tests performed on the hands of Lapp reindeer herders, who have been living since prehistoric times under the same conditions as the Orochons, showed no cold adaptation in the hands.[4] White Norwegian fishermen living above the Arctic Circle, men whose hands are constantly in cold water, came out the same as the Lapps, and as the white men in the control group, who were mostly scientists.[5]

The experiments reported above indicate that cold adaptation

[9] G. M. Brown and J. Page: "The Effect of Chronic Exposure to Cold on Temperature and Blood Flow of the Hand," *JAP*, Vol. 5, No. 5 (1953), pp. 221–7.

[1] Elsner, Nelms, and Irving: "Circulation of Heat to the Hands of Arctic Indians," *JAP*, Vol. 15, No. 4, pp. 662–6.

[2] H. T. Hammel: "Thermal and Metabolic Responses. . . ."

[3] H. Yoshimura and T. Iida: "Studies on the Reactivity of Skin Vessels to Extreme Cold. Part II: Factors Governing the Individual Difference of the Reactivity, or the Resistance Against Frostbite," *JJP*, Vol. 1 (1950–51), pp. 177–85.

[4] J. Krog, B. Folkow, R. H. Fox, and Andersen: "Hand Circulation in the Cold of Lapps and North Norwegian Fisherman," *JAP*, Vol. 15, No. 4 (1960), pp. 654–8.

B. Hellström and Andersen: "Heat Output in the Cold from Hands of Arctic Fishermen," *JAP*, Vol. 15, No. 5 (1960), pp. 771–5.

[5] Ibid.

Andersen, Løyning, Nelms, D. Wilson, Fox, and A. Bolstad: "Metabolic and Thermal Response to a Moderate Cold Exposure in Nomadic Lapps," *JAP*, Vol. 15, No. (1960), pp. 649–53.

through increased basal metabolism and increased peripheral blood flow is confined to the Mongoloid subspecies, at least as far as we know. They also indicate that the Lapps are Caucasoids, as most physical anthropologists now believe, and not Mongoloid, as was frequently stated in the past by writers who had not seen them.

The second kind of cold adaptation requires no increase in caloric expenditure or in peripheral blood flow. It involves instead an insulation in depth of the body core; the limbs and the surfaces of the trunk serve to insulate the more vulnerable internal organs. This effect is found in domestic swine reared in Alaska, and in hair seals, which have no more fur than the swine do. It is also characteristic of the legs of caribou and of arctic birds. Like the Mongoloid adaptation, this type involves both the body as a whole and the extremities.

In man, cold adaptation through insulation was first observed in Australia, among the aborigines. In west-central Australia the members of the Pitjendjera tribe live naked in the desert. During the day the air is hot, but at night the temperature can go down to freezing or a little lower. Ordinarily the aborigines sleep naked on the ground between rows of small, smudgelike fires, but when the wind is blowing the fires are useless. Scholander, Hammel, and others found that, while sleeping in light sleeping bags without fires at 32° F, the Pitjendjera men maintain an almost normal internal body temperature, as shown by rectal readings, whereas their limbs become chilled. The temperature of their feet read as low as 54° to 59° F.

In the morning these men get up and stamp around, and by the time the sun is up they are as fit as ever. White volunteers who took the same tests lost internal body heat before morning, because the surfaces of their arms and legs threw it off into the atmosphere. The aborigines slept comfortably, but their Caucasoid counterparts spent a miserable night.[6] Later on, these experiments were repeated in midsummer at Darwin, North Australia, on other aborigines from several different tribes. Cold condi-

[6] P. F. Scholander, Hammel, J. S. Hart, D. H. LeMessurier, and J. Steen: "Cold Adaptation in Australian Aborigines," *JAP*, Vol. 13, No. 2 (1958), pp. 211–18.

tions were created by having them sleep in a refrigerated meat van. The physiological response was the same as that of the first group, tested in winter, thereby confirming the fact that the cold adaptation of the Australian aborigines is not seasonal but permanent, and apparently both genetic and anatomical.[7]

In human beings each of the principal arteries of the arm and lower leg—brachial, radial, ulnar, tibial, and peroneal—is accompanied, as a rule in the same sheath, by a pair of companion veins called *venae comites*. At various places, particularly near elbows and other joints, neighboring arteries are connected by short blood vessels, so that under certain circumstances one can replace the other and an exchange of blood can take place. The networks formed by such connections are called *anastomoses*. The economy of engineering that placed the arteries and their pairs of veins together, and the emergency arrangement of connecting arteries at anastomoses, have also provided a mechanism by which under certain circumstances heat can be transferred between the two kinds of blood vessels.

Among the Pitjendjera apparently such a transfer is made during sleep. The outgoing arterial blood warms the incoming venous blood, so that the hands and feet are cool and heat is saved. In a desert where food is scarce, heat conservation is important for survival. Why the whites tested in these experiments failed to transfer heat from arteries to veins in the same way is not known, but without doubt a program of comparative dissection could help determine the answer. Arteries are notoriously variable, and racial differences in their branching patterns have been established between Europeans and Japanese. For other populations, available data are inadequate.[8]

Surprisingly enough, the Australoid type of cold adaptation through insulation has been found in only one other population so far tested, the nomadic Lapps. This evidence, when added to their failure to respond to the cold-water hand test, places the Lapps far from the Mongoloid subspecies. Also, the settled village

---

[7] Hammel, Elsner, D. H. LeMessurier, Andersen, and F. A. Milan: "Thermal and Metabolic Responses of the Australian Aborigine Exposed to Moderate Cold in Summer," *JAP*, Vol. 14, No. 4 (1959), pp. 605–15.

[8] E. Loth: *L'Anthropologie des Parties Molles* (Warsaw and Paris: Masson et Cie; 1931), pp. 348–82.

Lapps, who are more mixed with Finns and Norwegians, show the insulative cold adaptation less than do the reindeer herders, who are less mixed. One is tempted to suspect that this type of cold adaptation was prevalent in Europe during the latter part of the Würm glacial epoch.

Returning to the Southern Hemisphere, where physiologists have found the world's most striking examples of cold adaptation —among the Fuegians and Australian aborigines—we approach the Bushmen of the Kalahari Desert with some hope. The Bushmen, who are also primitive hunters and gatherers, are faced with the same alternate stresses of heat and cold that confront the Australian aborigines. These hopes have not been realized, however. Three separate expeditions [9] have failed to find any differences, in basal metabolism or in any other physiological attribute, between the Bushmen and the whites used as controls. This evidence suggests what has been suspected on other grounds, that the Bushmen have not lived in the desert very long. It also confirms my belief that the Bushmen and the Negroes, although they share a continent, are not closely related.

Heat Adaptation

S O FAR, only the Negroes have been shown to possess heat adaptation. American Negroes can tolerate moist heat better than American whites of the same age and economic background.[1] But as far as I know this difference has not yet been demonstrated in Africa.[2] American Negroes are unable to tolerate cold as well as

[9] C. H. Wyndham and J. F. Morrisson: "Heat Regulation of MaSarwa" (Bushmen), *Nature*, Vol. 178, No. 4538 (1956), pp. 869–70.

Wyndham and Morrisson: "Adjustment to Cold of Bushmen in the Kalahari Desert," *JAP*, Vol. 13, No. 2 (1958), pp. 219–25.

J. S. Ward, G. A. C. Bredell, and H. G. Wenzel: "Responses of Bushmen and Europeans on Exposure to Winter Night Temperatures in the Kalahari," *JAP*, Vol. 15, No. 4 (1960), pp. 667–70.

[1] P. T. Baker: "Racial Differences in Heat Tolerance," *AJPA*, Vol. 16 (1958), pp. 287–305.

T. Adams and B. G. Covino: "Racial Variations to a Standardized Cold Stress," *JAP*, Vol. 12, No. 1 (1957), pp. 9–12.

[2] A study conducted in West Africa by N. A. Barnicot yielded negative results, possibly because he apparently failed to allow for differences in height,

American whites; this is true even when the individuals of both races who are tested have the same amount of subcutaneous fat.[3] This final observation indicates that the difference in thermal adaptation between Negroes and European Caucasoids is not due to insulation alone. Probably a whole complex of physiological processes is involved, particularly those concerned with the deposition of melanin in the skin by the action of three hormones.[4]

The Significance of Adaptation to Heat and Cold

S E V E R A L conclusions can be drawn from this review of human adaptation to heat and cold. One is that the subspecies of man as defined in Chapter 1 tend to sort themselves out on this basis. The Mongoloids are the most distinctive in thermal adaptation as in so many other features, and the Negroes stand at the opposite extreme.

A second is that because these adaptations are both genetic and linked to climate they may have been acquired by the several subspecies of *Homo erectus* at the time of their dispersal into different environmental regions.

A third conclusion is suggested by the Alakaluf study. It indicates that ill-clad human beings carrying fire and the crudest of tools (the Alakaluf cutting tool was a quahaug shell) could have entered North America over the Bering Strait at any time when the sea level was low enough to permit passage. At such times, with the flow of arctic water cut off and the Japanese current swinging along the southern shoreline, the climate could have been no colder than it is in modern Tierra del Fuego.

The two kinds of cold adaptation recently discovered allow

---

weight, and bodily components between the Negroes and Europeans tested. N. A. Barnicot: "Climatic Factors in the Evolution of Human Populations," *CSHS*, Vol. 24 (1959), pp. 115–29.

[3] Baker: "American Negro-White Differences in Thermal Insulative Aspects of Body Fat," *HB*, Vol. 31 (1958), pp. 287–305.

[4] Melanin is deposited by the combined action of one hormone from the pineal gland and two from the pituitary. The melanocytes in which the pigment is formed have their embryonic origin in nerve cells. Thus, skin pigment is basically a neuroendocrinological product. A. B. Lerner: "Hormones and Skin Color," *SA*, Vol. 205, No. 1 (1961), pp. 98–108.

human beings to live at temperatures near the freezing point with little or no environmental protection when out of doors, but they would not allow anyone, however well adapted genetically, to hunt out of doors in the winter temperatures found today in Lapland and Greenland without a combination of good clothing and good housing, both made with good tools by skilled hands directed by a fully evolved modern brain. As far as the fossil record tells us, only *Homo sapiens* has ever lived in such climates.

Adaptation to Altitude

A N D as far as we know only *Homo sapiens* has ever lived at altitudes of over 10,000 feet. Only two plateaus of this height which are large enough to be human breeding grounds exist. They are Tibet and the Andean *altiplano*. Both are inhabited by Mongoloids. Careful physiological and anthropometric work has shown that the Andean Indians have large chests, large lungs, large hearts, and blood that contains a high ratio of red corpuscles. Although each red corpuscle carries less oxygen than it would at sea level, the total amount of oxygen borne by the blood far exceeds that supplied by the arteries of outsiders who have moved into the highlands. Such outsiders may survive, but they have difficulty reproducing because the mother cannot transfer enough oxygen to her embryo to ensure its live birth.[5] That is one reason why the highlands of Ecuador, Peru, and Bolivia are still Indian country four and a half centuries after Pizarro. As far as I have been able to determine, the adaptation of Tibetans to high altitudes has not yet been studied.

On the opposite extreme, Negroes, whose blood carries the sickling trait polymorphically (Ss) and bears with it even less oxygen than that of Caucasoids, may be seen along the Andean coast but not on the plateau. In the Himalayan region the clinal zone between Mongoloids and all others is extremely steep, and in some places it is only a few miles wide.

The fact that adaptations favoring or counteracting excesses of oxygen in the blood stream cannot be demonstrated in fossil man

[5] Newman: "Man and the Heights," *NH*, Vol. 67, No. 1 (1958), pp. 9–19.

does not mean that they did not exist, because such adaptations are found only in perishable fluids and tissues.

In this chapter we have surveyed the principles of geography as they may be applied to the distribution of animals and the development of species and subspecies. We have situated the subspecies of man in their ancient homes, and examined the evidence for climatic adaptation in fossil and living men. We have found that human subspecies differ considerably in climatic adaptation, which has played a part in the ability of human beings to invade and inhabit regions too cold or too dry for other primates. The historic distribution of races, in fact, may partly be explained on the basis of these adaptations.

But we have found no extreme forms of adaptation comparable to those of desert rodents that live without drinking water, or of polar bears that sleep naked on ice floes. The principal adaptations of human beings to climate are technological. Skill at technology, and particularly the inventive genius that makes technical advances possible, requires the possession of a top-grade brain, which our ancestors began to acquire long ago, and which is still useful in an increasingly technological society.

3

EVOLUTION THROUGH SOCIAL ADAPTATION

Leadership, Communication, and Brain Growth

A TOP-GRADE brain is needed not only to master, by technical means, cold, drought, and other environmental difficulties beyond the physiological capacities of the human body, but also to manage human relations skillfully. Natural selection in favor of this second kind of skill has been a prime factor in human phyletic evolution—the rise of a more intelligent species from one that is more primitive intellectually. In this chapter I shall try to show how this kind of natural selection may have operated.

I am particularly concerned with the surviving societies of primitive hunters and gatherers because they serve, to a certain extent, as a window into the distant past, but more advanced systems should not be neglected since all societies are governed by the same natural rules.

In all the historic societies whose structural details are well known, the greatest tangible rewards have rarely gone to the geniuses of technology or to outstandingly skilled craftsmen, however important their work has been for the preservation of human life and to social evolution. The men who have reaped the highest rewards are the geniuses, artists, and skilled craftsmen whose material is not clay, flint, or metal, but other people. They are the "operators," the artificers of human relations. The leader who can keep the peace among his followers, organize his men for war, regulate the distribution of food and other wealth in such a way that everyone will be taken care of, particularly himself—such a man is well paid. He lives in the finest structure, be it hut or palace, eats the best food, and in many societies has the most women. Whatever genes he has that others lack have a better than average chance to multiply in the local pool.

Also well rewarded in esteem, if not in material goods, is the priest, shaman, or medicine man whose artistry allays fears and eases people individually and as groups over the emotional hurdles of crisis and trouble. In many societies his personality is an odd one. As he ministers to both sexes, he is sometimes celibate. What makes him an artist does not necessarily give him more women than the others; a society in which everyone is a shaman would soon fall to pieces. A few of his special genes in the pool will go a long way. Like popes, he can pass on his heritage through nephews.

Under the umbrella of law and order, ritual sanction, and emotional security that both chief and shaman spread, the craftsman can do his work, and every man can get food for his family. As there must be leaders, there must also be followers—men and women who can live together under guidance without disruptive quarreling. During the long stretch of human evolutionary history the sizes and complexities of groups have grown, and the ability of group members to live together peacefully, while presenting a united front against outsiders, has been of great importance for survival. In many structurally simple societies the troublemaker is killed one dark night by his fellows, or driven away, and so the genes which may have contributed to his antisocial behavior are thus, in a sense, fished out of the pool. Social adaptation, which is the capacity for living together in groups, has been as influential in human evolution, if not more so, as environmental adaptation through technology. But the relative importance of these two facets of adaptation is hard to evaluate as they are parts of a single picture.

Both these categories of adaptation depend primarily on an ancient revolution in communication made possible by the invention of speech. Like tool-making and the use of fire, speech, we know, was a human invention. It must be learned, not quickly like some of the semi-instinctive habit patterns of other mammals but slowly and with great effort, and it requires the co-ordination, within the brain, of several different organs that are not used in concert by any other primate. If speech did not have to be learned, the peoples of the world would not speak hundreds of different languages; they would all make the same noises, like sea gulls.[1]

Before speech could be invented, the ancestral primate organism had to undergo certain anatomical changes.[2] These involve the following organs of speech (and, of course, their nerves): the thoracic muscles, which expel air from the lungs; the larynx, which contains the so-called vocal chords and their controlling muscles; the pharynx, which is essentially the valve that opens and shuts the intersection of the air and food passages of the throat, both below and above the meeting point; and the muscles that control the movements of the jaws, lips, tongue, and soft palate.

The principal change was in the pharynx. In primates that walk on all fours, the air tube is continuous from pharynx to nasal passages except when the animal is swallowing or crying out; it takes effort to expel breath through the mouth. In man the valve of the pharynx is habitually open, and breath will come out of the mouth whenever the lips are open and the lungs are exhaling, unless an effort is made to block its passage with the tongue.

The cause of this change was, apparently, the assumption of the erect posture by our ancestors. DuBrul has shown by a series of dissections of the heads and necks of tree shrews, lemurs, tarsiers, Old World monkeys, and apes that the opening of the pharynx in man was only the last step in a series of changes caused by an increasing postural shift from the horizontal to the vertical plane. In the most primitive primates the air passages form almost a straight line from lungs to lips. In man they are

[1] For a thorough discussion of the origin of speech and its role in cultural evolution, see:

A. I. Hallowell: "Self, Society, and Culture," in S. Tax: *Evolution After Darwin* (University of Chicago Press; 1960), pp. 309–71.

C. F. Hockett: "The Origin of Speech," *SA*, Vol. 203, No. 3 (1960), pp. 88–96.

[2] E. L. DuBrul: *Evolution of the Speech Apparatus* (Springfield, Ill.: Charles C Thomas; 1958); and "Structural Evidence in the Brain for a Theory of the Evolution of Behavior," *PBM*, Vol. 1, No. 4 (1960), pp. 40–57.

bent, in the pharyngeal section, into a 45° angle. It was this bending that opened the valve.

Once the pharynx was open, air was free to move between larynx and lips, whether the flap of the soft palate had closed off the nasal passages or left them open. Now it was possible to utter a wide variety of sounds, the formation of which depended on a combination of many factors: the degree of tension of the vocal cords, which could either be tightened so as to vibrate and thus

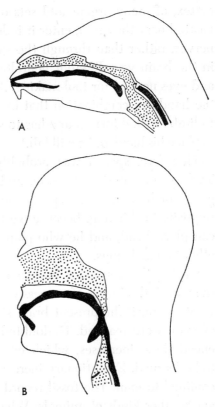

Dots = breathing tube
Solid = feeding tube

Fig. 2 The Speech Organs of Primates. A. *Lemur rufifrons.* The soft palate overlaps the epiglottis, and the corniculate cartilage of the pharynx is hooked to hold its grip over the rear rim of the palatal additus. Air passages are normally open and food passages closed except in swallowing. B. *Homo sapiens.* The larynx has slid far down the neck. Both the front and rear valves are normally open, permitting free air to flow into the oral cavity, while the back flap of the soft palate can close off the nasal passages in speaking. (Drawings after DuBrul, 1958.)

emit voiced sounds, or left slack so as to permit the formation of unvoiced sounds which, if continuous, became whispering; the opening and closing of the nasal passages, which produce nasal sounds if left open; the positions taken by the tongue and lips; and the sequences of all these elements in the formation of words. The number of possible sounds is nearly infinite, but the number used in any one language is limited by the number that can be easily recognized.

To be understood, language must be heard, both by the speaker and by the person addressed. The vocal vibrations of speech pass into the outer environment and return to the brain through the ears. If successful communication is achieved, they also hit the eardrums of a second person, whose answers strike the eardrums of the originator of the conversation.

Speech requires the neural co-ordination, in the brain stem and cortex, of many organs and sets of muscles, all of which, being located near the brain, enter it independently, as do the auditory nerves, rather than through the spinal cord. Their co-ordination in the brain was different neurologically from that of the hands and eyes needed for tool-making. Also, it was acquired later than the hand-eye combination that brachiation (swinging from limb to limb) called for: an ape has to see where he is going, in order to place his hand, or he will fall.[3]

Therefore, speech was probably invented after tool-making. Tools made hunting possible, and the social requirements of a group of hunters made speech necessary. Speech is also a prerequisite to thinking, because we think in words. He who thinks can plan ahead, and he who plans ahead can learn to deal with other human beings.

During the course of human evolution, in different parts of the world, the brains of successive fossil men grew larger as time went on, until the present brain sizes, typical of the living races of man, were reached. Undoubtedly, talking and thinking influenced these increases, which occurred as more and more had to be learned. Evolutionary increases in brain size have not been confined to man. The fossil record shows comparable changes in many other kinds of animals. What is unusual about man is not that his brain grew, but that it grew as much as it did.[4] By and

[3] The other primates lack the extensive pharyngeal plexus needed for speech which is found in man. J. M. Sprague: "The Innervation of the Pharynx in the Rhesus Monkey and the Formation of the Pharyngeal Plexus in Primates," *AR*, Vol. 90, No. 3 (1944), pp. 197–208.

[4] For the problem of brain size vs. body size in animals, see:

B. Rensch: "The Relation Between the Evolution of Central Nervous Func-

large, in response to the needs of communication, the growth of the human brain may be considered primarily a social adaptation and, in addition, an example of evolution through succession.

This increase in brain size probably started with the erect posture. In any evolutionary line of mammals any entirely new kind of locomotion must be learned. Baby seals, for example, must be taught to swim, and baby birds must be pushed out of their nests before they will fly. Each of us, as a baby, must be taught to walk, or we would go on all fours. Learning a new method of locomotion fosters, and indeed requires, a concomitant increase in intelligence and, by the same token, in brain size. An animal bright enough to learn to walk erect might also be bright enough to begin making tools, and so on to hunting and speech.

But brain growth has disadvantages that had to be outweighed by the greater advantages of an increasing intelligence. In the fossil record of our zoological family, brain size increased only gradually; our brain is an expensive organ that grew as man became increasingly able to support it. The brain requires a large skull that must be carried about by the bones, tendons, and muscles of the neck, trunk, and legs. Being very sensitive to changes in temperature, it must be kept warm in cold weather and cool in hot weather. Only the visceral organs, which are much better insulated by the body mass, require such a narrow thermal range. As the brain lies close to the surface of the head, its large size taxes the body's capacity for maintaining thermal equilibrium.

It is also a gluttonous organ, requiring an even blood flow ranging from about 765 cc. a minute when at rest to about 1300 cc. a minute when hard at work. At rest it monopolizes about 12 per cent of the body's blood supply, although it comprises only about

tions and the Body Size of Animals," in J. Huxley, ed.: *Evolution as a Process* (London: Allen & Unwin; 1954), pp. 181–200.

H. J. Jerison: "Brain to Body Size Ratios and the Evolution of Intelligence," *Science*, Vol. 121, No. 3144 (1955), pp. 447–9.

Rensch: "Trends Towards Progress of Brains and Sense Organs," *CSHS*, Vol. 24 (1959), pp. 291–303.

For the functioning of the brain, particularly in speech, see W. Penfield and L. Roberts: *Speech and Brain Mechanisms* (Princeton: Princeton University Press; 1959).

2 per cent of the body's bulk. It burns up a correspondingly great amount of oxygen and sugar, which have to be fed to it constantly.[5]

If the brain is an expensive superstructure for an adult to carry around, it is even more of a burden for infants and children, who have to be protected and fed longer than the young of other animals. At birth it has already reached 24 per cent of its adult mass, whereas the whole infant body is only 5 per cent of its adult body weight. At the age of three, the brain has attained 82 per cent of its adult weight and the body only 10 per cent. When the child is ten years old, shortly before puberty, the brain has attained 95 per cent of its adult volume, and from there on it gains very slowly and very little, whereas the body grows rapidly.[6]

In order to justify its carrying charges, any oversized and overfed organ has to have a selective advantage in the reproductive life of the animal burdened with it, or its frequency will be kept down by natural selection. This has been shown many times in studies of other animals, the most conspicuous example, perhaps, being that of antler size in the deer family. Putting it very simply, there must have been a point in human history at which brains came to be more effective than brawn in acquiring women. Otherwise the brain sizes of various lines of fossil men would not have increased during the Pleistocene. Just how the brainier men won out is not known, except through analogy with living peoples. Clever planning, self-control at the right moments, persuasive talking, the exercise of leadership through language—these are obvious possibilities.

The importance of brain size in relation to more complex social behavior is suggested by comparisons with certain animals. Of all the mammals, only the whales have larger and more complex brains than man. The porpoise *Tursiops truncatus*, which is a small and very bright species of whale, has a very complex brain one third larger than ours, and a highly developed social life. In

[5] C. F. Schmidt: *The Cerebral Circulation in Health and Disease* (Springfield, Ill.: Charles C Thomas; 1950).

[6] J. H. Scott: "The Growth of the Human Face," *PRSM*, Vol. 47, No. 2 (1954), pp. 91–100.

it can be observed clear dominance relationships, and also altruism. Care, anxiety, and friendship between individuals have been seen in the behavior of porpoises (as well as in that of chimpanzees and some other primates).[7] Furthermore, the porpoises have possibly the most elaborate system of vocal communication of all the nonhuman mammals.

On the Antiquity of a Human Type of Society:
the Beginning of Hunting

B E F O R E we can assume that the progressive increases in brain size seen in the fossil record constituted, at least in part, an adaptation to the requirements of living together in a human society, we must establish the antiquity of our basic social system, which consists of a number of families living together and sharing food. We can never do this absolutely—social structure is not a material object that can be fossilized—but we can try to zero in on the point at which it may have begun by following several lines of evidence, including archaeological sequences, comparative animal behavior, and the social systems of living primitive peoples. Let us begin with archaeology.

As previously stated, we may assume that the sharing of food must certainly, because of the nature of the beasts eaten, have begun with hunting, if indeed it had not already been practiced earlier among food gatherers. We can gain some idea of when hunting began by examining the camping sites at which fossil men, or other manlike primates, lived, or at least made their tools and ate.

The two oldest seem to be Bed I at Olduvai Gorge, Tanganyika,[8] and Tell Ubeidiya in the Middle Jordan Valley just south of Lake

---

[7] A. F. McBride: "Meet Mr. Porpoise," *NH*, Vol. 45, No. 1 (1940), pp. 16–29.
McBride and D. O. Hebb: "Behavior of the Captive Bottle-nose Dolphin *Tursiops truncatus*," *JCPP*, Vol. 41, No. 2 (1948), pp. 111–23.
W. R. Thompson: "Social Behavior," in A. Roe and G. G. Simpson: *Behavior and Evolution* (New Haven: Yale University Press; 1958), pp. 291–310.
[8] L. S. B Leakey: "A New Fossil Skull from Olduvai," *Nature*, Vol. 184, No. 4685, pp. 491–3; and "Recent Discoveries at Olduvai Gorge," *Nature*, Vol. 188, No. 4755, pp. 1050–2.

Tiberias in Israel.[9] Both are Lower Pleistocene, and both were discovered in 1959. The Olduvai camp contained a fossil manlike primate which its finder, L. S. B. Leakey, named *Zinjanthropus*, and a second one, the so-called Olduvai child, both of which will be described in Chapter 7. What is important here is that crude stone implements as well as bones which showed signs of being the remains of animals eaten on the spot were scattered there. The tools were sharp enough to enable the hominid who used them to cut skin, which he could not tear with his blunt teeth nor soften with fire, which he lacked. But the bones suggest that he had only begun to hunt: most of his quarry consisted of small, slow-moving animals, like rats, lizards, snakes, and tortoises, which can be caught by women and children. Anthropologists call this category of animals *slow game*.

Leakey also found a few bones of the newborn and suckling animals of large species of ungulates (hoofed mammals). Whether this evidence places the Olduvai creature on the threshold of life as a hunter is not certain; baboons have been seen, by S. L. Washburn and others, to eat the newly born fawns of impala. Eating newborn ungulates is hardly hunting, but it is a gastronomic exercise that gives an animal a taste for fresh meat.

The Jordan Valley site contains tools, very fragmentary human or humanlike remains yet to be described, and animal bones that not only had been broken but also had been scratched with stone tools. Most of the animals eaten seem to have been slow game, as at Olduvai, but some appear to have been adult ungulates. All the geologically later habitation sites we know of, in the higher levels of Olduvai Gorge itself, in North Africa, China, and Europe, indicate full-scale hunting.

Present evidence therefore suggests that true hunting, as opposed to the collection of slow game and baby animals, began, as a way of life, sometime during the Lower Pleistocene, and we are sure that in the Middle Pleistocene it was in progress. Speech probably began with full-scale hunting, and a human kind of social organization must have begun with speech.

[9] M. Stekelis, L. Picard, N. Schulman, and G. Haas: "Villafranchian Deposits Near Ubeidiya in the Central Jordan Valley (Preliminary Report)," *BRCI*, Vol. 9-G, No. 4 (1960), pp. 175–84.

The Mating Systems of Other Animals

WHETHER or not the members of an animal species enjoy tools and speech, the social structure of the species is linked to its mating system, which is further linked to factors of body size, terrain, feeding habits, and climate, including seasonal change. Small animals, like the familiar chipmunks, often live alone in solitary burrows no more than 200 to 300 feet apart, individuals of each species populating a neighborhood and dividing the feeding grounds among them.

Each such animal has a *home*, in which it sleeps, and a *home range*, in which it feeds or collects food.[1] It will defend its home against intruders of the same species, but its home range overlaps those of other individuals, whose presence it tolerates in the common marginal areas. In these shadily defined territories infrequent and seasonal sexual contact takes place. As the offspring are reared by the mothers alone, no elaborate social structure arises and evolution through social adaptation is virtually non-existent.

Larger animals, particularly hoofed and horned browsers and grazers, tend to congregate in herds wherever grass and leaves are abundant enough to feed many animals at once. Among such animals which live on bulky foods, sexual activity consumes much time, energy, and attention. In many species the sexes are separated during most of the year, there being no reason, in the economics of animal life, for them to be together. At breeding time, which in many species comes but once a year, in a favorable season, the males and females come together and the males compete for sexual rights. This period is necessarily brief because, being preoccupied with sex, the animals are especially vulnerable to carnivores. Most if not all females are covered, but some males are left out. Those that impregnate the most does pass on their genetic peculiarities, which consist largely of the traits essential to success in courtship, such as larger antlers and stronger neck

[1] F. Bourlière: *The Natural History of Mammals* (New York: Alfred A. Knopf; 1956), pp. 98, 220 f.

muscles. This kind of selection enhances sexual dimorphism but has little effect on other social capacities.

Yet another kind of mating behavior is found among mammals that inhabit tropical forests, the special domain of primates. Here no major seasonal change of climate or of food supply makes any particular part of the year more favorable either for birth or, by extension, for copulation. As man is a primate, other primates will provide the most desirable comparative material for study. In common with some of these primates, to be described in the following chapter, man retains a very primitive sexual cycle common to some of the simplest mammals, including marsupials and insectivores. This sexual cycle is basic to our human social structure. We have made the most, in this inherited trait as well as in some others, of our lack of specialization.

The Sexual Behavior of Primates, Including Homo Sapiens

M E M B E R S of most species of primates breed around the calendar in roughly monthly cycles, which in the female include the crises of ovulation and menstruation. Among the primates the male is always ready for sexual activity whereas the female's interest is variable.

Two sets of physiological changes can affect her: differences in libido during stages of the oestrual cycle, and the presence or absence of temporary genital swelling. Among some species the female feels an irrepressible urge for sexual attention at the time of ovulation, pinpointing the proper moment for conception. During the rest of the monthly cycle she is either indifferent to sex, or even resistant. Among other species the female feels equally receptive at all times. In some of the species marked by a powerful urge on the part of the female during ovulation, she presents an added stimulus. At this time her genitals puff and swell and turn bright red, creating a conspicuous target that no male can fail to recognize for the signal it is. Among other species that go through the same cycle the aggressive behavior of the female at this time is unaccompanied by such a display. In no case do we find swelling without a marked increase of libido at ovulation.

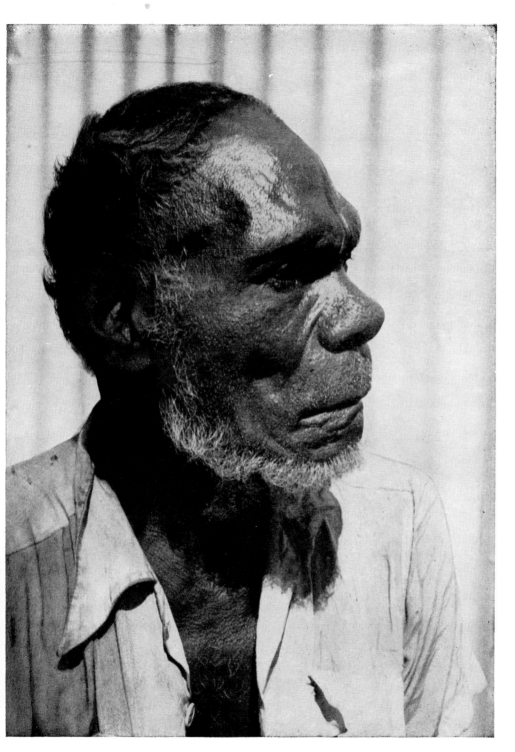

Australoid subspecies: a Tiwi from Melville Island.

Mongoloid subspecies: a Formosan aborigine of the Bunun tribe.

Caucasoid subspecies: a Pathan from the Northwest Frontier.

Congoid subspecies: a Shilluk from the Sudan.

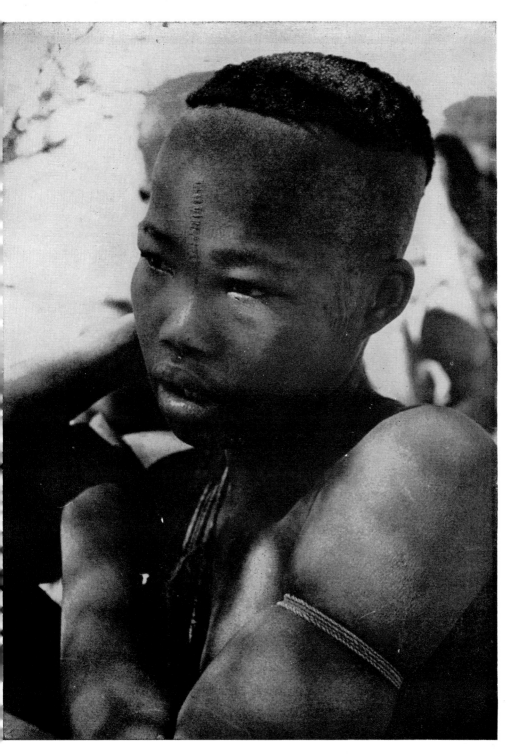

Capoid subspecies: a Bushman woman from the Kalahari.

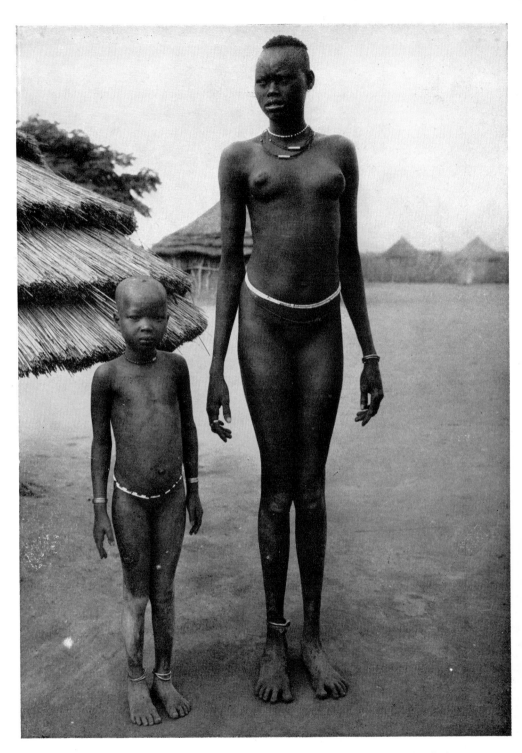

Environmental adaptation: Allen's Rule. Two Dinka girls from the Sudan.

A Norwegian physiologist studying the cold tolerance of an
Alakaluf Indian's foot: Dr. Kristian Lange-Andersen and
Lucho.

The social importance of fire: Bushmen of the Kalahari.

Leadership in operation at a Tiwi funeral: the man on the pole is directing dancers.

a. Common lemur

b. Ring-tailed lemur

c. Slender loris

d. Tarsius

Prosimians

a. Marmoset

b. Capuchin

c. Ornate spider monkey

New World monkeys

a. Pig-tailed macaque

b. Brazza monkey

c. Red-capped mangabey

d. Patas monkey

Old World monkeys

a. Mandrill

b. Proboscis monkey

Old World monkeys

a. Gibbon

b. Siamang

Apes

Orangutan

Chimpanzee

Mountain Gorilla

The first kind of female behavior, the markedly variable, with or without genital swelling, leads to a social structure in which one male, whose libido is constant, serves a number of females in succession. Either he does this as a harem master, brooking no rivals, or as a member of a mutually tolerant team of males that take turns with female after female as their moments of high excitement arise. The result is a choice of two social systems, a harem or a club.

The second or relatively invariable kind of female behavior creates the habitual association of one adult male, who is interested in sex every day, with one generally receptive female. The result then is a third kind of social system, the monogamous family.

According to Kinsey and his associates,[2] 59 per cent of American women interviewed reported that they enjoyed sexual intercourse more at certain points of the oestrual cycle than at others. Of these, only 11 per cent, or 6.5 per cent of the entire sample, preferred it during the middle of the cycle, near ovulation. The other 89 per cent, or 52.5 per cent of the whole, found it most rewarding just before or after menstrual flow, or both. To what extent American women are typical of the human female of all races and cultures is impossible to say. However, in primates in general these characteristics are specific. Women of different races are probably basically alike in this respect.

Although the human population of the world is growing at an alarming rate, and we are having what is called a population explosion, nevertheless, of a good sample of the very women responsible for this explosion, only 6.5 per cent seem to have felt more passion during intercourse at a time useful for conception than at other times. Also, the nonproductive added urge of half of the women before and/or after menses helps them insure attention from their husbands before and after a period of isolation, thus re-enforcing a relationship between marital partners.

As far as reproduction is concerned, all the sexual activity that

---

[2] A. C. Kinsey, W. B. Pomeroy, C. E. Martin, and P. H. Gebhard: *Sexual Behavior in the American Female* (Philadelphia: W. B. Saunders Company; 1953), p. 608. Libido was measured objectively, by observing the amount of vaginal secretion, as well as subjectively, by having questions answered.

takes place among human beings, except at ovulation, is a waste of time, energy, and attention. In addition, many human females enjoy sex long after menopause. Nature is never wasteful, though, and in fact the sexual behavior of the human female is oriented more toward the maintenance of the social structure than toward reproduction. It tends to create a family, an economic unit built around the feeding, care, and education of children, and to secure the continued interest of husbands. What is wasted in one sense is gained in another. As we shall see in more detail later, this pattern is also typical of the other primates whose females resemble ours in this aspect of physiology.

The Beginnings of Human Society

AMONG ANIMALS that do not share food, and man is the only higher primate that does, the function of the family, if any, is to bring up the young ones to the time, or point of development, at which they can fend for themselves. In different species the age of parting from the mother varies. Among the apes the youths are driven out of the family band at about the time of puberty, not so much because they could not feed themselves earlier, but because at that time they begin to arouse jealousy, in the well-known Oedipus fashion, in their parents. The daughter antagonizes her mother because of her father's attentions and the son antagonizes the father because of his advances toward his own mother, or of the mother's toward the son.[3] So both son and daughter are expelled, one at a time rather than simultaneously since, as most primates have single births, the sons and daughters will arrive at puberty at different times. This staggering of expulsions normally prevents mating between brothers and sisters and encourages the mating of individuals of like ages simultaneously expelled from different familes.

At the time of expulsion the offspring, at first singly and then paired, are strong enough and aggressive enough to block out sleeping and feeding territories of their own and to defend them against other family groups, including their parental households.

---

[3] In a family of the harem type the "mother" can be any one of the wives.

The motivation behind the parents' behavior is primarily social, but it has an economic side as well. Each newly weaned infant will naturally stay with its parents as long as it can since finding food where they do is easier for it than discovering new feeding places in unfamiliar territory. But if all the offspring borne by the couple were to remain with their parents indefinitely, there would soon be a food crisis. The daily traveling range would have to be widely extended, or some animals would go hungry. The balance between territorial size and the number of mouths fed can be maintained only by expulsion.

This composite picture of a prehuman primate society can serve as a model for our ancestors before they became organized into groups of mutually dependent families, either at or before the onset of hunting. Whether or not it is a true picture depends basically on how ancient the characteristic behavior of the human female is—that is, how long she has been, as she is now, sexually receptive at all times except during menses and not much more aggressive at one time than at another.

A clue to this problem comes from the birth sex-ratio. Other primates with our type of sexual behavior have a ratio of births of about one male to one female. Those that live in harems or clubs have more nearly three females to each male. But unfortunately we do not know the birth sex-ratios of fossil men. We have not found enough specimens of any population more ancient than Sinanthropus, and even with Sinanthropus we cannot be sure of the sex of each individual, usually fragmentary, specimen.

The chances are, however, that the ratio has been the same as long as our record extends, for physiological matters of this kind are conservative. This does not necessarily mean that all peoples have always been monogamous, only that in most societies most individual men are. In most societies exceptional men are polygamous.

Sexual Selection Among Higher Primates

AMONG several species of higher primates a minority of males seem to go through life without sexual experience, living as solitary outcasts, or as neuters on the fringes of family groups. Among the majority some have more success in mating than others, and the females, at least among chimpanzees, show marked preferences for individual males. Even though females also manifest personality differences, however, all females normally receive sexual attention. Among primates it is easier to be a female than to acquire one.

Sexual selection, therefore, works particularly on males, and whatever genes make a male a more successful lover than his fellows can be expected to remain at a high level in the primate pool. This may be why, among gorillas, males are twice as big as females and it may help explain the extreme aggressiveness of the males in many primate species.

Loving and intelligence do not necessarily go together, in apes or men. But in the human evolutionary line, from the beginning of hunting on, being bright has been an asset to a man in securing the favors of women. He who brings in the most meat feeds the most people, and they give him their daughters in order to insure continued favors. He who handles weapons most skillfully against wild beasts can turn them most lethally against his rivals in the camp. An effective leader who can persuade others to work for him can also outmaneuver his less well organized if more muscular rivals in the game of love.

Speech, Hunting, and Social Structure

LEADERSHIP and persuasion require thinking and talking, and so do clever schemes. The threshold of becoming human which our ancestors once crossed was largely the barrier between communication by grunts, screams, facial grimaces, postures, nudges, and bites on one side of the line, and articulate speech on the other. Language not only made communication easier and clearer, but it also increased its volume. We talk more than we act, and, if we are wise, we think even more than we talk.

The study of speech is a whole world in itself, elaborate and detailed, involving physiology, which we have discussed, as well as psychology, history, and many other disciplines. It mirrors all other subjects that concern man and his behavior. It is difficult to imagine a world without speech, because this kind of imagination requires it. We think in words. Words are what culture is made of, and man alone creates and wields words and has culture. Despite the importance of speech we know little about its beginnings, for it was invented in the dim time about which only specialists in human paleontology and flint archaeology know, and it leaves no imperishable remains.

Whenever it started, once our ancestors had begun hunting, speech was necessary. A hunter needs weapons. Weapons must be made with tools, tools have to be made, and tool-making must be taught. Beyond a certain level of technical skill, teaching requires language. Hunting also requires planning, and planning calls for speech elaborate enough to permit a group of men to talk over, in the evening, what they intend to do the next day. This is a much more advanced type of communication than the common primate practice of uttering imperatives to signal immediate action,[4] which is all that the apes and monkeys can manage.

The social consequences of hunting need language too, even more so than the planning and organization of the chase itself. Except in big, usually annual communal hunts, in which women and children beat the bush and drive game into the center of a circle for the men to kill, hunting separates men from their women. For two or three days and nights a married woman must remain in or near the camp, exposed to the possibility of advances from the old men and perhaps cripples left behind, and from the boys too young to go hunting but old enough to be interested in women. If the hunt is to be successful, if all are to eat meat, and if the band is to retain its composition and integrity, these males must leave her alone, and if any one of them should make the mistake of approaching her, she must refuse him.

If this were not so, her husband would not go out at all, or if he did, he would be so preoccupied when all his attention should be concentrated on his task of finding, following, stalking, and killing animals that he might fail. Even if his hunt were successful, after his return to camp he would have discovered his wife's

---

[4] A. S. Diamond: *The History and Origin of Language* (New York: Philosophical Library; 1959). Also C. F. Hockett: op. cit.

infidelity and there would have been a fight. The survival of any group of hunters depends on the existence of rules governing the behavior of women during their husbands' absences, and on the enforcement of these rules. Such rules cannot be formulated or enforced without language.

In comparing human behavior with that of other primates we must remember that a man can cover more ground in a day than a monkey or ape, that he can carry food and water, that with a stick he can dig roots that lie too deep for the fingers of monkeys, and that he can feed off a larger territory. All else being equal, more human individuals can live together in societies than can other large primates, including those that have our kind of female sexual physiology.

When, therefore, people began sharing food, it was no longer economically necessary to expel both the boys and the girls from the group at puberty. A much more effective system was for either the boys or the girls to leave the parental domain, marry into other households, and live with their in-laws. Such an arrangement tended to foster peaceful relations between neighboring bands, under cover of which gene-flow could extend over a wide area within natural boundaries.

Within individual households, the older men need no longer be killed, driven off, or reduced to a servile state once their strength had begun to ebb. With the power of speech and a long period of dominance behind them, they could persuade the young men to feed them, and might even bluff them into allowing them to have the most desirable women. When the band grew too big for the territory it inhabited, it could simply split under individual leaders, and the pioneer half could set out to find and exploit a new territory of its own. If, on the other hand, a band grew too small for efficient operation, it could combine with a neighboring and related group.

Ritual, Language, and the Rites of Passage

THE ASSOCIATION of several families in a band brought a dozen or more children together. Now they could play games in groups large enough to permit them to sort themselves out into leaders and followers and to learn co-operation. Also, the older children then had a chance to teach the younger ones. By the time a child reached puberty, he or she would have learned more than could have been possible had the families lived apart, and in particular the children would have begun to learn how to get along in groups.

But once the children came to puberty, changes in endocrine balance exposed them to new and violent stresses, which required a special schedule of indoctrination, if order was to be maintained in the camp. The young men had to be segregated in classes, usually recruited from several neighboring bands. They had to be sent out into the wilderness to fend for themselves, with restrictions on certain foods to make the apprenticeship harder than real life; taught obedience by the shock method through the appearance of old men disguised as supernatural creatures; and carefully instructed in the proper behavior toward women. When this "probationary" period was over, they were readmitted into the company of their parents and other relatives as partial or full-scale adults.

Without a puberty ceremony it is difficult to see how the transition from expulsion to incorporation of the young could have been managed. And without language such a ceremony would be impossible. We can be confident, therefore, that language goes back at least as far as this major change in human social organization.

With the awareness of natural processes that language brought, along with a keen observation of every phase of plant and animal life on which human life itself depended, came a full realization of the inevitability of death. People began to generalize and to reason, using the materials at their command as symbols, and building up imaginary worlds of spirits that controlled plants and animals, and of spirits of dead people. These elaborate structures were necessary by-products of man's growing intelligence. He needed them to allay the fears that his new knowledge of the world of the senses brought him, including the inevitability of death. With spirits to help him and an afterlife to look forward to, he could tolerate fear, and create ceremonies for other crises beside puberty, including the crises of birth, of death, of changes in the food supply brought by the cycle of seasons, and of changes in the routine of interpersonal relations consequent on shifts in the seasonal round of activities.

Homo was becoming a more and more sensitive animal, increasingly vulnerable to social disturbance as he came more and more to perceive and use the forces of nature. Individuals who could learn to speak easily had an advantage over those who could not speak at all. Once the use of language had begun, selection in favor of facile talkers must have been an important factor in the stages of human evolution that followed.

The Discovery of Fire and the Conversion of Energy into Social Structure

T H R E E innovations that had to be learned—walking erect, toolmaking, and speaking—prepared our ancestors to organize themselves into bands of families that hunted, shared food, and conducted ceremonies together, but it is highly questionable that these three were enough to make a human social structure possible. One more ingredient was needed. That was the use of fire.

As I have pointed out elsewhere,[5] *human beings convert energy drawn from outside their own bodies into social structure, and the greater the amount of energy consumed, all else being equal, the more complex the social structure.* Such a use of energy increases the physical efficiency of people, individually and as groups, to such an extent that the time spent in obtaining, processing, and eating food is reduced. At the same time, economic activities are shared and divided among the members of the group. The division of labor based on sex, age, and kind of activity which is thus made possible fosters further efficiency. The new relationships between individuals and groups so created acquire more and more social complexity.

Fire has four basic uses: frightening off predators, keeping people warm and dry, cooking food, and providing a spatial nucleus or center for the home territory of a group of people. Here they can sit at night, warm and secure, seeing one another's faces in the

[5] C. S. Coon: *The Story of Man,* p. 64.

firelight, talking over what they did during the day while they were separated, acting out scenes of the hunt, planning for the next day's adventures, discussing matrimonial prospects, and generally getting to know one another so well that friction can be kept at a minimum. They may also dance by firelight, and conduct ceremonies. It is difficult to see how, without fire, human society could have risen much above the level of that of baboons.

If we ignore the Australopithecines, who were probably not full-scale hunters but collectors of slow game, we may state that fire is as old as the oldest undisturbed sites of the genus *Homo* who lived in chilly climates. The oldest men in the Far East, the Sinanthropus population of Choukoutien, had it 360,000 years ago. Evidence of fire has been found at Swanscombe, England, in the same level as the Swanscombe skull, which is over 250,000 years old. The only older specimen in Europe, the Heidelberg or Mauer jaw, was taken from a secondary deposit in a gravel pit. None of the early remains from Java were found in habitation sites. The oldest found to date in Africa south of the Sahara is only 59,000 years old. Despite the careful excavation of several older undisturbed habitation sites in East Africa, no earlier trace of fire has been found there.

The Evidence of Living Food-Gathering Societies— the Australian Aborigines

T u c k e d   a w a y in odd corners of the earth are several hundred tribes and other population units of people who still live by hunting and gathering. Technologically they represent every level of competence discovered by archaeologists. A few make and use stone chopping tools, others manufacture simple flakes, and so on up through the chronological list of archaeological implements to the threshold of metal. Their housing ranges from simple leaf windbreaks to elaborate wooden buildings, and their clothing from complete nudity to the world's most efficient arctic suits.

From our present point of view, food gathering is not a single way of life. The Indians of the northwest coast who harvested salmon and hunted whales attained a high cultural status without

agriculture; and the circumpolar peoples, from Lapland to Greenland, were able to live in an otherwise uninhabitable world only
by the exercise of great ingenuity. Neither of these groups represents the stage of cultural evolution we are seeking. To find it we
must turn to the marginal refuges of the Southern Hemisphere, to
the forest recesses of the Oriental and Ethiopian regions, and
particularly to Australia.

Australia contains the world's most archaic mammalian fauna,
and it also harbors the world's largest assemblage of archaic human beings. However, neither man nor his prey has been there
very long. The monotremes, unique to that continent and New
Guinea, are unknown before the Pleistocene. The marsupials appeared in the Pliocene, and man toward the end of the Pleistocene, about 11,000 years ago, or a little earlier.[6]

The monotremes apparently evolved locally from reptilian ancestors. The marsupials entered the Australian faunal region over
an unknown path from the New World, and Australoid people
arrived from Indonesia by island hopping while the seas were still
low, crossing Wallacea from the Sunda to the Sahul shelf, probably on flimsy rafts and canoes of types still made in modern
times. Linguistic theory (see Chapter 1, p. 5) supports both a
late date of under 20,000 years ago and an invasion or series of
invasions from a single source, because all Australian languages
belong to a single family.

Many studies have been made of Australian social systems but
most are too specialized for our purpose, nor are they organized
from a biological viewpoint. They overconcentrate on theoretical
marriage regulations and give too few case histories and statistics.
In general, they tell us that Australian aborigines live in households of a few families, each in its own hunting territory, and that
from time to time a number of related households meet to conduct
ceremonies jointly. These may include the initiation of a new class

[6] N. B. Tindale: "Ecology of Primitive Aboriginal Man in Australia," in A.
Keast, R. L. Crocker, and C. S. Christian: "Biogeography and Ecology in Australia," *MB*, Vol. 8 (1959), pp. 36–51. Tindale gives a Carbon-14 date of 8,700 ± 120
years ago (about 6,750 B.C.) for a site at Cape Martin, southern Australia, containing the Tartangan culture, which was preceded by the Kartan culture. The Kartan
antedated the rise of the sea level at the end of the Pleistocene, about 10,000
years ago. The laboratory number of the date given above is NZ-69. For an explanation of this symbol, see note on page 311.

of boys and marriage negotiations. In these meetings the older men play a dominant role, just as they do in most other human societies.

The collection of households that meets on such occasions is, in effect, a breeding isolate in the zoological sense. Within its confines rules of various degrees of complexity specify which men are eligible to marry which women, because of their membership in certain segments of the total population. They acquire this membership by descent. Usually a man can marry only women from a group more distantly related to him than others. Thus only a fraction of the women are theoretically available to him, never more than half, and sometimes as few as one thirty-second. Within these limits he can have one or more wives. If no spouse is available at all, the rules can sometimes be stretched to include some other women almost equally distant in kinship. These rules serve to split up the breeding population into a number of smaller isolates that rarely intermarry.

As a man can impregnate many women in the time it takes one woman to bear a child, a man can have more children than a woman can, and he can spread his genes more widely in the local pool. At first glance it would seem that disparity in reproduction among males would have no evolutionary value, being based on accidents of the birth ratio, but this is not the case. A dominant male can manage to have one or more wives by manipulating the marriage system, and a less aggressive, less clever, or less competent male may be left out. As the traits of personality that give some men more women than others are inherited, selection in favor of these traits must occur. On the other hand, women are the prizes of masculine competition and, although some scheming among women also takes place, no woman is sexually neglected who is still able to bear children.

In surveying the literature on Australian social systems, we are soon struck by the great differences in age between husbands and wives. An old man may be married to two teen-age girls, and a younger man to a withered crone. As they can rarely count to ten and have no measure of the passage of years they do not know how old they are, and are in effect as young as they look and feel.

If a man has to wait twenty years for a wife, it is not twenty years to him, but simply a long time.

The Archaic Society of the Tiwi

AN AUSTRALIAN tribe that has been intensively studied recently is the Tiwi, who inhabit Melville and Bathurst Islands.[7] They number about 1,000 persons concentrated near three white settlements, with 600 at a Catholic mission on Bathurst, 50 outside (but not part of) a government half-caste station at Garden Point on Melville, and 150 at a government station at Snake Bay on Melville, in addition to 150 who are working at Darwin.

Within the lifetimes of the older Tiwi, their islands were divided into ten "countries," each occupied by a number of households consisting of one or more families, each in its own hunting and food-collecting territory. As families grew, split, shrank, or combined, so did both the territories and the countries. But the surface of the islands, comprising about 3,000 square miles, was open to all of them when they met to take part in ceremonies, particularly funerals. They spoke one language and were in a very loose sense a people.[8]

The Tiwi went naked and built flimsy shelters to serve as sunshades and as protection from heavy rain. Their only cutting tools were an all-purpose clam shell and a flaked stone ax, poorly hafted and reminiscent of a chopping tool.[9] A few crude stone flakes were used solely for gashing foreheads at funerals.

Melville and Bathurst Islands are well forested and rich in both

[7] C. P. Mountfort: *The Tiwi, Their Art, Myth, and Ceremony* (London: Phoenix House; 1958).

J. C. Goodale: "Alonga Bush, a Tiwi Hunt," *BUM*, Vol. 21, No. 3 (1957), pp. 3–36.

Goodale: "The Tiwi Dance for the Dead," *Expedition*, Vol. 2, No. 1 (1959), pp. 3–13.

Goodale: *The Tiwi Women of Melville Island, North Australia* (Philadelphia: University of Pennsylvania Ph.D. dissertation; 1959).

C. W. M. Hart and A. R. Pilling: *The Tiwi of North Australia* (New York: Henry Holt & Co.; 1960).

[8] Although the Tiwi still practice many of the customs summarized here, they have abandoned others. I am using the past tense only for continuity.

[9] However, better axes with pecked and ground surfaces were found on the beach at Snake Bay. Their age is unknown.

animal and vegetable foods. Wild yams, wallabies, and opossums can still be had on land and shellfish are always available at low tide. The surrounding sea and its estuaries contain turtles, crocodiles, and fish, and fresh-water swamps at the heads of creeks provide food for wild geese. Every year the Tiwi burned over the landscape to keep down the undergrowth which impedes hunting.

All vegetable foods belonged to the women, who dug and collected them. Animal life above the ground, particularly wallabies and opossums, belonged to both men and women and both hunted it. Both could also collect shellfish. The beasts of the sea, including fish, and the fowl of the air belonged to the men alone.

A young man who was a poor or indifferent hunter, and lacked a pleasing personality, could kill enough marsupials to feed himself, but he could not bring in the quantities of meat obtainable by killing sea turtles, crocodiles, and geese. All these animals were hunted by teams, and a boy had to be invited to join such a team. To catch sea turtles and crocodiles, the men traveled by canoe. Usually the owner of the craft paddled in the stern, a boy bailed amidships, and another man stood in the bow with his spear. Only one man made the kill, but all three shared in the meat. Sometimes geese were killed by solitary hunters, but usually men teamed up to cover a greater area. The hunters would spread out along the bank, evenly spaced, to await the geese, which flew over in small flocks. Usually only one man was in range, and no one knew which man this would be.

There was an element of danger in going out in canoes, for the men could drown or be eaten by crocodiles. In goose hunting the accent was on good marksmanship and reliability. The brave, skillful, obedient young man accepted by his elders as a hunting partner was able to feed several persons with his share of the meat. Thus he had a *quid pro quo* for obtaining wives, one which held both economic value and prestige. The indifferent hunter who was not wanted as a teammate was no more useful as a food provider than an indifferent woman.

Good hunting and good partnership, however, were not the only roads to popularity and prestige. The Tiwi put great store in aesthetic achievement. A poet who could compose and sing a new and popular song, a dancer who could create a novel routine, and an artist who could paint stimulating designs on their ultramod-ernistic-looking funeral poles also rose to the top of the Tiwi social ladder and to the intimate companionship of those who dispensed matrimonial largesse.

Once the superior young man—who had to be bright to be superior—had passed the age of thirty and had secured several wives of various ages, he could leave the provision of staple foods, yams, and marsupial flesh to them and could concentrate on sup-plying the prestige foods from the sea and air to a wider circle as he connived at a game of competitive prestige to become more uxorious than ever. When he had finally become too old to hunt, he would have had plenty of people to feed him. In Tiwi society, therefore, a combination of hunting skills, good teamwork, cour-age, and artistic and political competence gave superior men the greatest procreative opportunities, and some men were sloughed off from the gene pool through incompetence on any or all of these counts.

Although greatly condensed, this sketch of Tiwi society is ac-curate enough to demonstrate the reality of social selection. A little detail may further clarify the point. When a boy arrives at puberty, he is usually promised the future daughter of a girl his own age who herself has been spoken for since before her birth. This girl, the boy's future mother-in-law, now becomes the wife of a man at least thirty years old who has been waiting for her all her short life, and who has been a food provider and a constant visitor to her parental household. The future husband of her as yet unconceived daughter, whom she may or may not bear, now also becomes a food contributor and visitor to this growing house-hold. This boy now busies himself providing his future mother-in-law with meat while her husband is still feeding her mother. The better the boy is at obtaining meat the more he pleases other men whose daughters he might also be able to support on the same promissory basis. Such older men will be likely to invite him to go hunting with them.

However, even the most successful man cannot contract for just any unborn girl. Tiwi society is divided into four phratries,[1] sub-

---

[1] A generation ago one of these split into two, making a total of five, but this is unimportant for present purposes.

divided into a total of twenty-one clans, with up to six clans to a phratry. Ordinarily, men of phratry A take their wives from any clan of phratry B, and vice versa; C and D similarly exchange wives.[2] This produces in effect two breeding isolates in Tiwi society and limits the choice of wives to one out of every four girls.

In Tiwi as in other societies, men tend to die younger than women, and because of the age differential at marriage, Tiwi husbands often die long before their wives, leaving one or more widows. These women, including also young girls still living with their parents and others yet to be born, have to be remarried or reassigned. Often the older widows go to the men of thirty or so who might otherwise have to wait ten or twenty years or even longer for their assigned brides to be born and to reach puberty. At this point, through their connections with their elderly wives' offspring, they can sometimes wangle promises of other young brides or pick up young widows. Cleverness in manipulating marriages was as important as skill in hunting sea animals and waterfowl; indeed they were often related.

According to Hart and Pilling, some Tiwi men had over twenty wives. They cite one man who at about age thirty started with two elderly widows and at sixty-six had had six widows and fifteen young wives, of which total three widows and five young wives had died. His youngest wife, not yet nubile, was still with her father. This left him twelve wives in residence at one time.

Those were the good old days. In the pallid present, ridden with white men, things have changed. In the Snake Bay colony sixty men have sixty-six wives, and no man has more than three. Out of fifteen young men between twenty and twenty-nine, seven are already married. In the old days they would still be waiting. Five men between fifty and seventy are still bachelors and probably always will be. Four are the conventional marital failures specified above. The fifth is an excellent hunter of solitary temperament who never wanted to be married, and wasn't.

According to local opinion three of a total of nine men of the senior age group, in their sixties and over, are "big operators," at the top of the pile. In the next age grade, from about forty to sixty,

[2] The rules are far more complex than this. I have simply summarized what happens biologically.

five of twenty-five are the social elite. These eight dominant men out of the thirty-four adult males of their combined age group, or 13 per cent, have sixteen of the thirty-six wives in the group, or 44 per cent; and twenty-eight of its forty-eight children, or 58 per cent. No doubt others coming along nicely in the age group under forty will do equally well later, if Tiwi culture persists.

Tiwi society does not conform to any other primate model, and there is no reason why it should. In some ways it resembles the monogamous, small territory system; in others, the harem system. Like other primates, the Tiwi quarrel over women, particularly when the young, libidinous men become impatient waiting for wives. Young women, bored with their ancient husbands, seek amours outside, and these affairs sometimes lead to blows; eyes are knocked out and flesh wounds are inflicted with throwing sticks and spears. Ordinarily a young man being punished for sexual encroachment will let himself be wounded rather than kill the venerable elder whom he has cuckolded. One man in his fifties, the husband of three young wives, is kept busy fighting off their paramours. As he has punished some of them more than their offenses seemed to warrant, he has lost face and several times has been exiled from Snake Bay by his peers. Their civilized attitude is a far cry from the simpler reaction of harem masters among our lower primate kin. The struggle over sex is still present in Tiwi society, but it is in a new balance. Men who can create fine poetry, dances that rival the ballet, and art that fills the moderns with admiration do as well in the marriage game as bullies, if not better.

Tiwi society is undeniably archaic. The Tiwi lie on the fringe of a marginal continent; they are the most marginal of marginals. They have never had spear throwers, stone-tipped spears, boomerangs, circumcision, or other elements of "advanced" Australian aboriginal culture. Physically they are also archaic full-sized human beings with a plethora of heavy brow ridges and big teeth, and brains of only moderate size. They have had the fortune to be preserved in a geographical paradise in which an early and agreeable form of human life can be led by healthy people without too much effort, and they have the sophistication of participants in a culture that has long since "arrived." Having no sense of inferiority to the white man, they look on us busy overdressed people with an air of amused and kindly tolerance.

As with other peoples, natural selection is still taking place among the Tiwi. Its function is to keep them human, to maintain the ratio of genes that contribute to a civilized life in a stable environment and to keep down the ratio of genes that lead to antisocial or solitary behavior. The population meanwhile remains stable as a result of the mating of old men with young girls, which is relatively unproductive; abortion practiced on the young women to space their children; and probably through other biological forces of which we are not yet fully aware.

Had the Tiwi become extinct several centuries ago, there would be nothing much—in the physical and cultural remains archaeologists might unearth—to indicate the heights of art this people had reached, the fun they had had, or the sophistication of their way of life. *Caveat excavator.* When we come to talk about the Neanderthals and other early folk, let this be borne in mind.

On Comparing the Cultures of Living Food Gatherers and Those of Fossil Men

T H E T I W I are, of course, only one of several hundred surviving food-gathering peoples, but they are particularly useful for present purposes because, with most of the other Australian aborigines, they represent the survival, with little change that we can detect, of a cultural level found elsewhere 70,000 to 100,000 years ago. Most of the other food gatherers that we know about, outside of Australia, either are dwarfs, like the Negritos, Andamanese, and African Pygmies; or they are pedomorphic, like the Bushmen; or they live in an advanced Mesolithic type of culture, like the California Indians; or, like the Veddas of Ceylon, they have long been trading with food-producing neighbors. Some are both dwarfs and traders.

Each of these qualifications weakens comparisons that we may try to make between such living food gathers and fossil men. We have no fossil dwarfs or pedomorphs. The Mesolithic began a mere ten or twelve thousand years ago, long after the time we are interested in. Trading relationships between peoples of different cultural levels constitute a cultural form of the biological process known as symbiosis, and symbiosis is usually accompanied by loss. In a parasitic animal whole organs may be lost. In a parasitic culture whole procedures, such as tool-making, and certain rituals may be lost, and the marriage system may be affected. Also, when food gathers trade with villagers, exchanging forest products for tools and luxuries, some of the more adventurous among the young food gatherers may leave home to join the culturally more advanced population, and this drainage, through selection, can genetically impoverish those left behind.[3]

Population Size Among Food Gatherers

T H E T I W I population of about 1,000 persons is relatively large for Australia. Birdsell[4] finds an average of about 530 persons per breeding unit at the time of their first encounter with whites. This unit, called *tribe* by Australian anthropologists, is the group of related bands and households that come together at least once a year in time of plenty for ceremonies, initiations, matchmaking, and merrymaking. Krzywicki[5] has divided 123 Australian tribes into size groups, as follows. Seventy, or 57 per cent, had under 500 persons; 37, or 30 per cent, had between 500 and 1,000; 12, or 10 per cent, between 1,000 and 2,500; and only four, which were probably confederacies and not breeding units at all, had over 2,500.

In the Andaman Islands the breeding unit was about 350 persons;[6] among the root-gathering Kadars of the Cardamon Hills in India it is 566;[7] and among the /Kung Bushmen[8] of the Kalahari

[3] J. Emperaire and A. Laming: "The Last Fuegians," *Diogenes*, No. 8 (1954), pp. 37–68.

[4] J. B. Birdsell: "Some Environmental and Cultural Factors Influencing the Structuring of Australian Aboriginal Populations," *AN*, Vol. 87, No. 834 (1953), pp. 171–207.

[5] L. Krzywicki: *Primitive Society and Its Vital Statistics* (London: Macmillan & Co.; 1934), pp. 171–207.

[6] A. R. Brown: *The Andaman Islanders* (Cambridge: The University Press; 1922).

[7] U. R. Ehrenfels: *Kadar of Cochin* (Madras: University of Madras; 1952).

[8] The symbol / as used here indicates a Bushman click.

around 750.[9] In north America Krzywicki tabulated 232 food-gathering tribal populations. One hundred tribes, or 43 per cent, were under 500 persons; 63, or 27 per cent, were between 500 and 1,000; and 69, or 30 per cent, were over 1,000. These last were all from the northwest and included many technologically advanced people who harvested annually migrating fish and mammals. Many were confederations, each including several biological populations.

This statistical exercise shows that the ecology of food gathering is the same nearly everywhere. The requirements of hunting and collecting keep the number of people who live near enough to one another to breed as a unit within about 500 or 600 individuals. We may suggest, but we cannot prove, that most of the fossil men whom we shall presently study lived in populations of this size or even smaller. There is no logical reason why their populations should have been larger, at least in the earlier periods.

In any group of 550 persons, if the children, the aged, and the infertile adults are excluded, there would be less than 200 breeders, of whom less than 100 would be males. As most of the living food gatherers observe some kind of marriage regulation comparable to that of the Tiwi, which splits them up into subgroups, the actual breeding units of some of the early populations may have been equally small. If our analogies are correct, human beings must have lived in small populations for a very long time. A string of small populations covering a continental region, with natural selection taking place in different populations, and some gene flow over the borders, is just what would have impelled the evolution of races during the Pleistocene.

Let us not forget, however, that peoples who harvest fish and mammals in large numbers can have breeding units of over 1,000 persons. During the Late Pleistocene in Europe the Upper Paleolithic peoples were killing reindeer in such numbers that they could select the animals most desirable in age and sex and let the others go. One mammoth feeds many mouths, and the mammoth hunters of central Europe killed so many of these giant animals that they were able to stack the bones in piles, each kind of bone

[9] Lorna Marshall: "Marriage Among the /Kung Bushmen," *Africa*, Vol. 29, No. 4 (1959), pp. 335–65.

to its own heap. It is not unlikely that these hunters lived in communities of over 1,000 and that the same was true, later on, of the Mesolithic and Early Neolithic fish trappers who inhabited the lower banks of such rivers as the Elbe and Huang Ho.

Systems of Mating Among Food Gatherers

THE TIWI are organized in monogamous or polygynous households—mostly the latter. The same is true of most Australian tribes. Murdock has listed the matrimonial systems of 564 different peoples of the world, 88 of which qualify as food gatherers.[1] I have added one, the Kadar,[2] and changed one, the /Kung Bushmen,[3] on the basis of later information. The total is now 89. Seventy-three of them, or 82 per cent, are polygynous; 15, or 17 per cent, monogamous; and one, the Kadar, is both polygynous and polyandrous. Among Murdock's food producers, 71 per cent were classed as polygynous, 25 per cent as monogamous, and 4 per cent as polyandrous. It is clear, then, that man prefers polygyny when this form of mating is possible, although most men have only one wife. This is true of peoples of all levels of culture from the Tiwi to the Turks, living in every continent and climate, and belonging to all human subspecies. We can assume that it goes back a long way in our life as a genus. Thus, the ability to obtain more than one's share of women may have been a factor in human evolution for a long, long time.

The Longevity of Fossil Men

A REMARKABLE feature of Tiwi society is the presence of a number of old men past their muscular prime who occupy positions of prominence. Out of sixty men at Snake Bay, twenty-two

[1] G. P. Murdock: "World Ethnographic Sample," *AA*, Vol. 59 (1957), pp. 665–87.

[2] Ehrenfels: op. cit.

[3] Lorna Marshall: "The Kin Terminology System of the /Kung Bushmen," *Africa*, Vol. 27 (1957), pp. 1–25. Murdock listed the Bushmen as monogamous. Marshall, however, finds some to be polygynous.

were over fifty and five were believed to be over seventy. These figures do not indicate the proportion of such graybeards to the total number of people born in a generation; some of the younger men, we must remember, are at Bathurst and Darwin. Probably the ratio of males who lived to that advanced age is low. Still, the figure is impressive, particularly in view of the life expectancies of many peoples today. Our question is, did any men live to be old in the remote past?

The answer is yes, but not many. Of the twenty-five individuals of all ages represented by the Sinanthropus bones unearthed at Choukoutien, two were over fifty years old.[4] Of a compilation of thirty-four Neanderthals from Europe, two were "advanced in age but not senile."[5] In my opinion, the Sinanthropus remains show that as early as 360,000 years ago some peoples had attained a level of social organization in which men of fifty, who had passed their physical prime, were tolerated, if not fed, by their juniors. Later on, 70,000 to 45,000 years ago, the Neanderthals definitely fed old and crippled men. La Chapelle aux Saints, the most famous French Neanderthal, although not much past his forties, was toothless and crippled by arthritis. Shanidar 1 was born with a withered right arm, part of which was later amputated, yet he was well over forty when he was killed by a rockfall in a cave. These aging cripples were being fed; and anyone who feeds middle-aged cripples lives in a human type of social structure.

The Role of Isolating Mechanisms in Human Evolution

T w o b i o l o g i c a l problems are central to the theme of this book. (1) How did the subspecies of man become differentiated? (2) Why did they not become separate species? In other animals related species occupying the same territory (i.e., sympatric species) or adjoining territories are kept apart genetically because their members do not breed together, whether or not fertile offspring could be produced if they did. The biological mechanisms

[4] F. Weidenreich: "The Sinanthropus Population of Chou Kou Tien," *BGSC*, Vol. 14, No. 4 (1935), pp. 427–61 (also *CMJ*, Vol. 55 (1939), pp. 33–44).

[5] H. V. Vallois: "La durée de la vie chez l'homme fossile," *CRAS*, No. 204 (1937), pp. 60–3.

or procedures that prevent interbreeding are called *isolating mechanisms*. These take many forms.

Among certain invertebrates sexual relations between species A and B are prevented by the fact that the genital organs of a male of species A will not fit into those of a female of species B. Among amphibia, such as tree toads, the pitch of the mating call may be critical. Each species has its own special locus, or loci, on the sonic scale, and males and females of a given species reach each other by following these calls. Mammals also have specific calls, and in the case of the moose, the sound of a female's urine dropping in the water of a swampy lake will rouse the bull's libido to fever pitch, whereas it would leave a male deer unimpressed. On the whole, however, most isolating mechanisms in land mammals involve the sense of smell, which is also vital to them in marking out their territories.

Isolating mechanisms can arise only in isolation. Once two related subspecies have acquired different ones, they can meet without interbreeding, and have speciated.

Such mechanisms do not exist in all kinds of animals. Fish that spread their milt and eggs broadcast in the sea obviously do not have them. Others that breed in special places at special times, do. Large animals that have only one species to a genus do not ordinarily need them. In the case of man, we have modern evidence that Mongoloids, whites, Negroes, and Pygmies each finds the odor of the next one in the series unpleasant, but this olfactory barrier (based on the number of apocrine glands) has not prevented mixture between any two of these groups. What retards mixture in modern societies, as in India, South Africa, and the United States, is something else: there peoples of different races have been brought together by historic or late prehistoric invasions and kept apart by an ethnic division of labor probably unknown to simple food gatherers. The barriers which separate these racial and ethnic isolates are probably all products of the last 8,000 years of human life, that is, they are the fruit of technology, which has permitted races brought together artificially to remain apart longer than they could have done on a food-gathering level, and longer than they may be able to do once our space-age world culture becomes thoroughly homogenized.

Whether clearly differentiated subspecies or closely related and potentially interfertile species which have been artifically juxtaposed will remain genetically isolated depends to a certain extent on whether or not both sexes are present in each population. For example, at about 1907 a herd of wild mouflon that had been brought from Corsica and Sardinia was released on Lambay Island, Dublin County, Ireland. A domestic herd was also grazing there, and the island was unfenced. These two kinds of sheep are interfertile, and are either closely related species or well-differentiated subspecies—it is hard to tell when one kind is domestic. In zoos the two do not mix, nor did they on Lambay Island as long as there were both males and females in each herd. But owing to shooting and other causes, the mouflon herd declined to two rams and one ewe. The rams remained faithful to their consort until her death. Then the rams joined the domestic herd and in one season sired twenty crossbred lambs that were fertile and were absorbed into the domestic herd.[6]

Modern men behave much like the mouflons, but in reverse. Sailors and explorers, whose wives have been left at home, mate freely with native women of all races; but when the settlers follow with their wives and children, race mixture is usually forbidden. Some of the very soldiers, sailors, and marines who nearly created a new race in the Pacific Islands in World War II are opposed to the mingling of races in their native states. This is not inconsistency—it is simply biology.

But the races of man evolved long before modern technology made exploration or colonization possible. Far more pertinent to the subject of this book are the age-old systems of mating practiced by living food gatherers. In this respect food gatherers differ from other animals in that food gatherers consider their marital rights as property. A man who has many wives is a man of prestige. A stranger who visits the camp and is considered important enough to be sent home happy is loaned a woman. Many white men have been so accommodated. A temporary exchange of wives may be part of the peacemaking ceremony between tribes that have been fighting and are reconciled. If one tribe defeats the

---

[6] J. A. F. Roberts: "A Geneticist's View of Human Variability," in P. Mason, ed.: *Man, Race, and Darwin* (London: Oxford University Press; 1960), pp. 48–55.

other, the vanquished men may be slaughtered, but their women and young children will be taken as prizes. Many examples of such behavior can be cited. They are the common grist of anthropology.

But how far back does this kind of sexual behavior go? It is universal in *Homo sapiens,* including the Australians. Is it fair, then, to assume that it is at least as old as our species and nearly as old as speech? Because this mating system ensures gene flow wherever populations meet, and because isolated populations— the Australians, for example—have not been alone long enough to speciate, we can tentatively consider this system as one reason for our failure to develop watertight isolating mechanisms, and for our unity as a species.

Adaptation to Crowding: A New Theory of Evolution by Succession

ANIMAL SPECIES vary greatly in the number of individuals that can live together and tolerate one another's presence. Some kinds of insects live without friction in hives and labyrinthine hills in the hundreds and thousands. Some fish swim in schools, some birds fly in flocks, and herd mammals graze together in huge numbers. The ability to stand crowding is not confined to any one branch of the animal kingdom, and indeed it varies even among plants.

In this respect many primates are very primitive. Most if not all nocturnal species are solitary. Among the diurnal species, most of the lemurs, if not all, live in groups of from four to fifteen individuals,[7] or more. Apparently all the South American monkeys are gregarious, and the mean population of howler-monkey troops has been set at 17.3 monkeys, with a standard deviation of ±6.8 individuals.[8] The macaques and open-country baboons live in groups of about sixty and range from about ten to about two hundred. The larger groups usually include more than one dominant

---

[7] F. Bourlière: *Mammals of the World* (New York: Alfred A. Knopf; 1955).
[8] C. R. Carpenter: "Characteristics of Social Behavior in Non-Human Primates," *TNYA,* Ser. II, Vol. 4, No. 8 (1942), pp. 251–3.

male. Among the apes one species of gibbon, the hoolock, is said to live in troops; the lar gibbon is monogamous; and the three great apes live in individual harems. The primates, therefore, are for the most part gregarious but limited to bands of small numbers; and our closest kin, the great apes, live in little kingdoms of one dominant male and his family and followers.

Although we do not know how our ancestors lived in the days before speech and tools, it is unlikely, on the basis of comparisons with primates, that they constituted large bands or troops. The social unit was probably a small one consisting of one or more family units. In any case, in the evolution of the human type of society a threshold must have been crossed when individual family bands or households established peaceful relations with other such bands or households and began exchanging wives.

At this stage each individual came to recognize, know the names of, and tolerate the presence of several hundred other individuals. One adult male could then meet another adult male of a different household, a man of his own age and size, without challenging him to a fight or creeping away. As many as twenty or thirty men could get together for a ceremony without the certainty of serious physical conflict.

The peaceful widening of one's circle of acquaintances to the size of a modern, food-gathering breeding unit represented a large step forward in the process of becoming human. It could not have been accomplished without language. But even with language, it was necessary for a healthy and vigorous man to learn to suppress his emotions. Not only must he control his speech; he also had to resist the impulse to ravish an attractive woman or to attack a potential rival. Like language itself, man's ability to curb his impulses required genetic changes in the nervous system and also involved the endocrine system where these emotions are stimulated. Learning to hunt could have helped a man make this adjustment, by transferring the target of his aggression from other males of his group to animals.

Even when human beings had become able to tolerate the presence of several hundred other individuals, usually in small groups but occasionally in large ones, adaptation to what zoologists call crowding did not end. With the invention of agriculture some peoples came to live in villages and attend intervillage and tribal markets at which a visitor might see thousands of persons, many of whom he did not know. In the Bronze Age came cities and the extreme crowding characteristic of urban communities. In Asia people who grew wet rice lived in the densely built-up villages and towns that this miraculously productive cereal is able to support. The Iron Age brought empires, and the Industrial Revolution spawned slums. Today vast armies, huge corporations, and Levittowns channel the interaction patterns of millions of human beings.

Although human relations have thus been growing more and more complicated, there has usually been room for two kinds of individuals. The first and most numerous kind consists of simple villagers, peasants, petty craftsmen, laborers, and factory workers. Such people interact with each other in small, face-to-face groups, informally organized in neighborhoods, work teams, churches, and clubs. Their patterns of interaction are usually no more complex than those of primitive hunters and gatherers. As civilization has grown, they have found niches for themselves in its lower echelons.[9]

The second kind of individual is the man who has kept pace with civilization and made it grow. These men rise to high levels both in hierarchies and in social strata. They are the leaders in business, politics, religion, education, entertainment, and other activities. Their circles of acquaintances are national and international rather than local. Such a man may greet a thousand people by name in a single day. He possesses a fine sense of discrimination and of propriety, knows which words will please and which will offend, and is able to get others to do what he wants done. He is capable of choosing reliable lieutenants, delegating authority, and sleeping soundly after a strenuous day. This man is an "operator" on a scale impossible in a society like that of the Tiwi. The same qualities that enable a Tiwi to be successful in obtaining women bring him rank, wealth, and fame.

He is in many ways a bright man, but the physical equipment

[9] A. F. C. Wallace: "On Being Just Complicated Enough," *PNAS*, Vol. 47, No. 4 (1961), pp. 458–64.

responsible for his success is not limited to the quality of his brain. Other men as bright as he are failures. His vast energy and his ability to control it without breakdown depend also on his endocrine system. This we know principally by analogy, because of extensive experimental work done with other mammals.[1]

In rodents, rabbits, and hares, as well as in other animals, social pressure—an amount of interaction greater than the animal can tolerate in comfort—stimulates the part of the brain known as the hypothalamus, and this organ sends information to the anterior lobe of the pituitary, commonly called the master gland. The pituitary in turn reduces its secretion of growth hormone and of gonadotropins, the substances that stimulate the sex glands to ovulate, to secrete sperm, and to produce sex steroids, and it also deforms sperm cells. At the same time the pituitary overstimulates the adrenal cortex. The end product of this neuroendocrinological chain of events is stunting, independently of nutrition; reduced fertility; reduced lactation; an altered sex ratio at birth; increases in susceptibility to diseases; and a higher rate of mortality.

When animals die as a result of this sequence of events, it is usually through a rise in the cholesterol level accompanied by atherosclerosis. This has been shown by Ratcliffe in his autopsy studies of animals that died during the 1950's in the Philadelphia zoo despite an ideal diet high in protein and an attempt to give each animal as much privacy as possible.[2] Still, excess interaction takes its toll. Individual animals see one another but can neither attack, flee, nor drive one another away. Thousands of leering and jeering schoolchildren bait them. Like the overcrowded wild animals studied by Christian and others, they succumb to endocrine disfunction and high cholesterol level, and die young.

High cholesterol level, hypertension, and atherosclerosis are

[1] J. J. Christian: *Endocrine Adaptive Mechanisms and the Physiologic Regulation of Population Growth*, NMRI, No. 60–2, 1960.

Christian: "Phenomena Associated with Population Density," *PNAS*, Vol. 47, No. 4 (1961), pp. 428–49.

[2] H. L. Ratcliffe and M. T. I. Cronin: "Changing Frequency of Arteriosclerosis in Mammals and Birds at the Philadelphia Zoological Garden," *Circulation*, Vol. 18, No. 1 (1958), pp. 41–52.

prevalent in our own civilization. It has been shown that the amount of cholesterol in a person's bloodstream depends less on fat intake or obesity than on "other biological factors"[3] and that a tendency to the related diseases listed above is probably hereditary.[4] High blood pressure is particularly frequent in urbanized Negroes both in America and in Africa.[5] In terms of animal behavior, all this evidence—much of it quite new and not yet fully digested by the medical profession—seems to indicate that individuals vary widely in their inherited ability to resist the evil effects of large amounts of interaction, and that a higher ratio of individuals who can withstand it has arisen, by natural selection, in some populations than in others.[6] These differences are not racial *per se*, but some races have been exposed to more of this kind of pressure than others.

In our monogamous society the day has passed when a man of outstanding administrative ability, whose threshold of tolerance for crowding is high enough to keep him alive and healthy, can beget a large number of children. In our society natural selection seems to work in the other direction, by pruning off those who cannot tolerate stress. As time, television, and automation move on, the number of persons who can live as common laborers dwindles. Every plumber's son dreams of college and many get there. Stress is moving down the social scale. As Henry has shown,[7] our mental hospitals fill up faster than our maternity wards, and in mental institutions reproduction is discouraged.

[3] C. B. Thomas and S. M. Garn: "Degree of Obesity and Serum Cholesterol Level," *Science*, Vol. 131, No. 3392 (1960), p. 42.

[4] M. Kaplan: "Physician Links Hypertension to Inborn Factors, Not Stress," *NYT*, January 27, 1960. Kaplan refers to a report by Dr. G. A. Perera at the New York Heart Association's annual conference on January 26, 1960.

[5] R. K. Plumb: "Blood Pressures of Negroes Studied," *NYT*, June 3, 1960. Plumb refers to a conference sponsored by the New York Academy of Science on June 2, 1960, in which several papers were read on studies made in South Africa, Liberia, and the United States but in which no general agreement was reached. The interpretation is mine.

[6] Following a mutation in a single set of gene alleles, the number of fruitflies that can live together in the same space and with the same amount of food was trebled in three generations. See H. L. Carson: "Increase in Fitness in Experimental Populations Resulting from Heterosis," *PNAS*, Vol. 44, No. 11 (1958), pp. 1136–41.

[7] Jules Henry: "Culture, Personality, and Evolution," *AA*, Vol. 61, No. 2 (1959), pp. 221–6.

Many of the inmates of these instutitions could probably have been adequately adjusted in simpler societies.[8]

The studies of stress and crowding which have just been reviewed are of theoretical value both in general biology and in human evolution. They point to a physiological mechanism by means of which animal populations automatically keep their numerical levels constant, even without the aid of predators, which of course also help. As the selection favors individuals who have both a stress tolerance and superior intelligence (the two factors are not otherwise related), this may be a mechanism for a general increase in intelligence in competing animal species.

This non-Malthusian concept adds a new dimension—neuroendocrinological competition within a population—to Darwin's concept of natural selection. It is selection from within in addition to selection from without, and in that sense especially concerns general adaptation and evolution by succession, whereas natural selection for fitness to the environment outside the population more closely concerns evolution by branching. This seems to be a new idea and it will no doubt be challenged, repudiated, and then widely accepted (I believe) within a few years of the publication of this book.

As far as man is concerned, this theory helps us understand how *Homo erectus* evolved from whatever he was before, and how he further evolved into *Homo sapiens*. We now have an idea of what the "other factors" are, beside nutrition and disease, which cause primitive, marginal populations to drop off in numbers when faced with invaders and colonists of more elaborate cultures, and to become extinct, in some cases, through absorption.

The association between tolerance for crowding and high intelligence, which, as stated above, is apparently coincidental, must not be overworked. Neither a businessman who can tolerate the body heat and noise of a large cocktail party held in a small room nor a sergeant who can click his heels and transmit orders in a highly disciplined army is necessarily brighter than a creative

[8] The concept that selection for crowding has played a role in culture change had been thoroughly explored by Schwidetzky before the animal evidence on which this section is based had become available. See Ilse Schwidetzky: *Grundzüge der Völkerbiologie* (Stuttgart: F. Enke Verlag; 1950), and also a review of the same by Paul Leser in *AJPA*, Vol. 10, No. 1 (1952), pp. 141–4.

scientist who cannot stomach any kind of regimentation and who prefers to work alone in his laboratory or out of doors. It takes all kinds to make a world, and it took several kinds of personalities to make *Homo sapiens* and to bring him to his present position in the animal kingdom.

Dwarfing as a Solution to the Problem of Crowding

ONE OF THE most controversial subjects in human taxonomy is the classification of the Pygmies, including principally those of Africa, the Andaman Islanders, the Semang of the Malay Peninsula, and the Philippine Negritos. As yet we have no fully verified Pleistocene Negrito skeletons to tie us to facts,[9] so speculation has been untrammeled. Some authors give these little folk separate subspecific status, but others include them in a larger Negroid group among the Melanesians, Papuans, Tasmanians, and African Negroes—in other words, everyone with black skin and curly hair. To base global relationships on skin and hair alone, without paleontological support, is dangerous.

The exponents of separate status and, by the same token, a single origin as dwarfs, have to postulate early, extensive, and completely undocumented migrations from Africa to southeast Asia and Oceania, or vice versa. Those who consider them shrunken Negroes explain their distribution much more easily, as the result of independent and parallel acts of dwarfing. No one today, as far as I know, holds that the Pygmies simply retain the original human size, under 150 cm. or five feet, whereas the rest of mankind has grown larger.

As the first two explanations both involve a size reduction from larger ancestors, it behooves us to study dwarfing in other forms of life. Dwarfing is common in both plants and animals. Among wild mammals there are, or have been, dwarf deer in Cuba and Japan; dwarf elephants in the Philippines, Celebes, and Malta; a dwarf

---

[9] Two Dutch anthropologists found six or more fossil skeletons of small people in a cave in the island of Flores, Indonesia, in 1955. A report of the tentative identification of the skeletons as Negritos, and an undocumented estimate of their age as 30,000 to 40,000 years, has been published only in the press. See *Science Digest*, October 1960, pp. 62–3; also *The Interamerican*, Vol. 7, No. 8, November 1960.

Dialectic

Were the First Americans Caucasoid?

by BOB SLAUGHTER

Shuler Museum of Paleontology,
Southern Methodist University, Dallas 75222

The editor of the *Texas Journal of Science* has assured me (personal communication) that contributions to this section of the journal need not be reports of scholarly research, but may be mere reflections on recent literature and/or fodder for speculation . . . "the more controversial the better." Holding him to this I should like to pose to those better read on the subject the question, WERE THE FIRST AMERICANS CAUCASOID?

Although positive evidence is rather elusive, more and more archeologists seem to be accepting the probability of man entering the New World via the Bering Land-Briidge in excess of 18,000 B.P. (years before present). Wendorf (1966) places the event merely "in excess of 18,000 B.P. and Meuller-Beck (1966) suggests 28,000 B.P. for the initial migration. Both of these workers base their dates on the belief that the artifact industry of the earliest known Americans could not have been derived from the industry present in Siberia after 18,000 B.P. They stress that these Clovis-Folsom industries could easily have taken origin from the Asiatic industries present up until that datum.

Cro-Magnon man is often considered by the casual student as prototypic "modern" man (*Homo sapiens*). Actually, the remains studied and usually cited are from Europe and have decided causasoid charsacters. Therefore they may be considered prototypic caucasoids but probably post-date the divergence of modern races. These peoples entered Europe some 35,000 years ago, presumably from Siberia. To be sure, the divergence of the basic modern races (caucasoid, mongoloid, and negroid) had taken place prior to this time.

Early in the 20th century most of the Kuril Islands of northern Japan were inhabited by a group of people known today as the Ainu. They now have been reduced in numbers to perhaps 100 and even these are largely diluted by contact with Japanese people with mongoloid affinities. (Shin'ichiro Takakura, 1967). The Ainu are light skinned, very hairy, lack the epicanthic or mongoloid eye-fold, and often have blue eyes. When they are mentioned in the semi-popular literature they are often compared with the Australian aborigines by pointing out that both are hairy, unlike mongoloids, both lack the eye fold, etc. One gets a very poor idea of what the Ainu are like from such comparisons. Clean shaven and properly dressed, a more-or-less pure Ainu would go unnoticed on any central European street (Fig. 1). The ainu are clearly closely related to the caucasoids of Europe and the Mediterranean Basin. I find it inconceivable that a group of caucasoids could have found their way across Asia through land inhabited by mongoloids only to wind up on these obscure islands while maintaining their racial integrity. They must have been there first! The last outpost of previous peoples when being displaced by invaders is usually the farthest islands or peninsulas. Perhaps then, these early Siberians,

Fig. 1. Young Ainu Man. (Photo by, and with the permission of, Ruiko Yoshida Ante)

which are caucasoid or at least proto-caucasoid, made their way east into America at the same time or not too much later than their cousins migrated to the Middle East and Europe. It must have been after this that the mongoloids entered Siberia proper, presumably from the northeast. The 2 reasons for suggesting a northeastern point of origin for the mongoloids are (1) The only selective advantage I can imagine for the epicanthic fold would be for protection from cold or sand charged wind and these conditions were doubtless present in the proposed area (2) Even more suggestive is the distribution of the mongolian characters (broad, flat face, and the fold). These traits are most extreme in the northeastern Siberia and less prominant to the east, south, and west.

Some 40,000 years ago there were but 2 basic races in most of Asia; caucasoids to the north and people not unlike the Australian aborigines in the south. There were of course all gradients in between. Some 35,000 years ago segments of the northern group migrated west, eventually inhibiting the northern shores of the Mediterranean Sea and all of Europe. About the same time or slightly later some of the same northern Siberians came to America across the Bering Land-Bridge. Sometime later, perhaps 18,000 B.P. the mongoloids moved in on the Siberian caucasoids, probably from the Arctic. They more-or-less completely absorbed the earlier peoples in northeastern Asia but were diluted to varying degrees toward the south and even more so across the seas to the East Indies and Polynesia. Mongoloids also found their way into America in some numbers, mixing with the less numerous caucasoids to varying degrees related to distance from the mainstream of the migration. The admixing of the same 2 basic stocks, caucasoid and mongoloid could then account for the closer physical similarities of certain American Indians to peoples in other mongolian peripheral areas (*i.e.*, western and southcentral Siberia.

As this paper is designed to stimulate discussion, I shall now arrange the targets in such a way as to allow would-be participants to draw a bead on a specific thesis.

(1) The Ainu may be a relict population, essentially Cro-Magnon.

(2) Essentially Cro-Magnon stock may also have given rise to early American cultures (Llano, etc.).

(3) Mongolians are the last of the basic races to appear, at least on our screen of knowledge.

My sincere appreciation is due Mrs. Ruiko Ante for her kind permission to reproduce the photograph of the young Ainu man.

LITERATURE CITED

MULLER-BECK, H., 1966—On migrations of hunters across the Bering Land Bridge in the Upper Pleistocene. *IN*, Hopkins, D. M., Ed., *The Bering Land Bridge.* Stanford Univ. Press, Palo Alto, Calif.

TAKAKURA, S., 1966—Vanishing Ainu of North Japan. *Nat. Hist.*, 75(8): 16–25.

WENDORFF, F., 1966—Early man in the New World: Problem of migration. *Amer. Nat.*, 100(912): 253–270.

mammoth on Santa Rosa Island, California; a dwarf fox on Catalina and Santa Rosa; a dwarf hippopotamus in Liberia; a dwarf bush-baby (loris) in Africa; a dwarf marmoset in South America; and a dwarf chimpanzee in the Belgian Congo. The last three, like *Homo sapiens*, are primates. Among domestic animals there are dwarf horses in the Shetlands, Iceland, Öland Island (Sweden), the isles off Brittany, Sardinia, Corsica, Sable Island, Cape Verde Islands, Timor, Bali, Sumba, and Japan; dwarf buffalo on Mindoro and Celebes; dwarf goats on Guadalupe Island, Mexico; and a galaxy of dwarf horses, cattle, and goats on the Ryukyu Islands.[1]

Zoogeographically speaking, all these pygmy animals live either on islands or in small enclaves of tropical forest where their refuges are surrounded by zones of drier terrain. Some of the islands they inhabit are cool and all are damp; and dampness ensures an abundance of vegetation. Pygmy men are found only in tropical forests, which are islands of dense foliage in seas of grass. In such forests the dense vegetation, fallen and rotting logs, and a network of hanging lianas make travel difficult; it is easiest for a small man to move about. Furthermore, little food is available on the ground. Birds' nests, monkeys, fruits, and honeycombs are high up in trees, and a small man can climb better than a large man.

In order to continue to exist, a breeding population must remain at a greater than critical number. The mammoths of Santa Rosa Island, for example, which were confined within about 60 square miles, were more likely to maintain the required population quota as dwarfs than if they had been full sized. Human beings must attain a minimum population size within a geographical area, and in addition a minimum number of individuals is needed if they are to live together in a self-supporting band.

Other special factors, such as the availability of nutritive elements [2] and the superiority of a small body over a large one in maintaining thermal equilibrium in areas where a combination of high atmospheric humidity and lack of wind render sweating

[1] A. H. Smith: "The Culture of Kabira, Southern Ryukyu Islands," *PAPS*, Vol. 104, No. 2 (1960), pp. 134–71.

[2] J. R. de la H. Marret: *Race, Sex, and Environment* (London: Hutchinson & Co.; 1936).

nearly useless as a cooling mechanism, may add to the advantages Pygmies share with other dwarfed animals in the tropical forest. At any rate, their small size must be advantageous or they would not have become entirely dwarfed, with a 100 per cent frequency of whatever gene controls their stature.

In plants, dwarfing is caused by a single gene mutation, demonstrated in peas, beans, and maize. In peas and beans and in four of six dwarf strains of maize, the mutation simply reduced the organism's capacity to metabolize gibberellic acid. When this substance was fed to the plants in large doses, they grew to normal size. The fact that only four of six dwarf maizes responded to this treatment indicates that dwarfing may be due to any one of a number of different genes.[3]

Comparable experiments have been carried on in dwarf strains of mammals. Several teams of research biologists have shown, mostly by transplants, that dwarf mice owe their failure to grow to full adult size to the absence, from the anterior lobe of the pituitary, of either of two kinds of cells (eosinophil and acidophil) and to a deficiency of growth hormone, and that each condition is controlled by a single, non-sex-linked gene.[4]

These dwarf mice were *ateliotic;* that is, they were normal for their species and race in body proportions, with due allowance for differences of an allometric nature (see Chapter 1, p. 25). Ateliotic dwarfs occur in many species, including man, and are often infantile in some respects, including sexually. In an experiment performed on human beings, eighteen Caucasoid ateliotic dwarfs, belonging to a group of related families, grew out of the dwarf class when, like the mice, they were given pituitary growth hormone.[5]

Another class of dwarfs is called *achondroplastic.* Like bull-

---

[3] B. O. Phinney: "Growth Response of Single Dwarf Mutants in Maize to Gibberellic Acid," *PNAS*, Vol. 42 (1956), pp. 185–9.

[4] R. L. Carsner and E. G. Rennels: "Primary Site of Gene Action in Anterior Pituitary," *Science*, Vol. 131, No. 3403 (1960), p. 829.

P. E. Smith and E. C. MacDowell: "An Hereditary Anterior-Pituitary Deficiency in the Mouse," *AR*, Vol. 46, No. 3 (1930), pp. 249–57.

G. R. de Beer and H. Grüneberg: "A Note on Pituitary Dwarfism in the Mouse," *JG*, Vol. 39, No. 2 (1940), pp. 297–300.

[5] R. L. Schaefer and F. Strickroot: "Endocrine Dwarfism," Fourth Report, *Endocrinology*, Vol. 26, No. 4 (1940), pp. 599–604.

dogs, they have large heads and bodies, pushed-in faces, and short, deformed arms and legs with distorted hands and feet. Unlike the ateliotic dwarfs, they have enlarged pituitaries. The deformity of the limbs is usually inherited as a simple dominant, whereas the facial deformity is inherited in a more complex fashion.[6] Achondroplasia, as this trait is called, occurs in many species of animals and something like it is even seen in certain dwarf trees. In man, as in dogs, the achondroplastic dwarf is sexually normal.

Human Pygmies, in Africa and elsewhere, exhibit various kinds of dwarfing. Some are predominantly ateliotic, although sexually competent, and others show certain achondroplastic features. The fact that different Pygmy populations vary in these respects may be added to other kinds of evidence [7] to indicate that the Pygmies of the world have arisen from separate full-sized ancestors in several regions through parallel gene mutations. They are neither a subspecies nor a single race, and if they are mutually related it is through their separate full-sized ancestors.

The Endocrines and Temperament

AS EVERYONE who has bred or even worked with dogs knows, different breeds vary greatly in temperament. A terrier behaves differently from a bulldog, and setters and retrievers have special behavior patterns of their own. We know by experience that these specific breed temperaments are inherited, because the breeds were selected on that basis. Elaborate experiments have shown that learning has little to do with them, except insofar as capacities to learn certain aspects of behavior are inherited.[8] Furthermore, and this is particularly pertinent at this point, differences in temperament between breeds are accompanied by differences in the size, form, and histological structure of the

[6] R. R. Gates: *Human Heredity* (New York: The Macmillan Co.; 1946), pp. 1320–2.

[7] Gates: "The Melanesian Dwarf Tribe of Aiome, New Guinea," *AGMG*, Vol. 10, No. 3 (1961), pp. 277–311. Gates has shown that in both New Guinea and Africa Pygmies have blood groups similar to those of their full-sized neighbors.

[8] E. Caspari: "Genetic Basis of Behavior," in A. Roe and G. G. Simpson: *Behavior and Evolution* (New Haven: Yale University Press; 1958), pp. 103–27.

endocrines, particularly the pituitary, thyroid, parathyroids, and adrenals.[9]

Human beings also vary in temperament. It is a common observation among anthropologists who have worked in many parts of the world in intimate contact with people of different races that racial differences in temperament also exist and can be predicted. Races also differ in the size and weight of endocrine glands, and in the substances carried in the urine.[1] The study of these variations has just begun, and many readers who believe in the current dogma that all behavioral differences are due to man's unique capacity for learning will find this unpalatable, but the burden of proof is on them. If such differences are not related to the endocrine system, then man is indeed a unique animal.

Parallels Between Animal Domestication and Social Adaptation

D A R W I N was deeply interested in the biological results of domestication, and others have carried on a detailed study of this subject, particularly because of its high economic value. For present purposes, one may ask, what has domestication to do with man? Man is a self-governing animal. But whether an animal is free or captive, certain modifications take place in its anatomy

[9] C. R. Stockard: *The Physical Basis of Personality* (New York: W. W. Norton & Co.; 1931).

———: *The Genetic and Endocrinic Basis for Differences in Form and Behavior* (Philadelphia: Wistar Institute of Anatomy and Biology; 1941).

D. G. Freedman: "Constitutional and Environmental Interactions in Rearing of Four Breeds of Dog," *Science,* Vol. 127, No. 3298 (1958), pp. 585–6.

H. Oboussier: "Das Verhalten der Hyophyse bei Reciproken von Hunden gegensätzlicher Wuchsform," *ZA,* Vol. 155, No. 5/6 (1955), pp. 101–11.

[1] For differences in the size of endocrine glands, see:

E. Loth: *Anthropologie des Parties Molles* (Warsaw and Paris: Masson et Cie; 1931).

W. Freeman: "The Weight of the Endocrine Glands," etc., *HB,* Vol. 6, No. 4 (1934), pp. 489–523.

R. Pearl, M. Gooch, J. R. Miner, and W. Freeman: "Studies on Constitution, IV, Endocrine Organ Weights and Somatological Habitus Types," *HB,* Vol. 8, No. 2 (1936), pp. 92–125.

For biochemical differences, see H. E. Sutton and P. J. Clark: "A Biochemical Study of Chinese and Caucasoids," *AJPA,* Vol. 13, No. 1 (1955), pp. 53–65.

These references are only a small sample of the pertinent literature.

and physiology as a result of cultural protection. Klatt,[2] among others, has shown that animals in a state of domestication respond to crowding, and to a reduction in mobility and in sensory perception. They do not need to walk far for their food, and some of it is even brought to them; nor do they need to watch for predatory carnivores, because men and dogs protect them. They do not have to seek shelter in bad weather, because they are driven into barns or caves.

These factors bring about a reduction of bone density, an increase in adipose tissue, a reduction in the length of the snout and in some cases in tooth size, and a reduction in brain size of 10 per cent, 20 per cent, or even 30 per cent of the measurements for wild forms. This has been established in the case of dogs, ferrets, pigs, ducks, and cats. When house cats become feral, larger brains reappear.[3] Domestic animals do not ordinarily use their senses as much as their wild counterparts do. This is indicated by reductions in the *area striata* of the brain, which is concerned with vision, and by smaller eye sockets (orbits), and smaller auditory apertures on the skull. In the dog, which is a working animal (or used to be), the brain is smaller than the wolf's but shorter and higher, and the forebrain is larger. Klatt interprets the growth of the canine forebrain to a selection for the capacity to do the work hunters and shepherds require of him.

In our study of fossil skeletal material it will be interesting to watch for possible changes in man comparable to those seen in domestic animals. We shall find long skulls, protruding occiputs (*area striata*), heavy brow ridges, large orbits (eye sockets), and large auditory canals in the earliest forms, which existed when

---

[2] Berthold Klatt: *Haustier und Mensch* (Hamburg: Richard Hermes Verlag; 1948).

[3] The reversion of domestic animals to wild prototypes once they have become feral can be demonstrated by experiments on insects, particularly on body lice. The head louse, a human parasite, is so different morphologically from the body louse that they have been considered different species (*Pediculus capitis* and *P. vestimenti*). Yet, when head lice are forced to live on the body they change form drastically over several generations, and when they move back to the scalp they gradually resume their original form. The difference in environment between a covered and an uncovered part of the body may be compared to wild and domestic conditions. H. Levene and T. Dobzhansky: "Possible Genetic Difference between the Head Louse and the Body Louse (*Pediculus humanus* L.)," AN, Vol. 93, No. 873 (1959), pp. 347–53.

men were living close to nature and few could sit in the camp and be fed by others. But we cannot expect to see many of the changes which accompany domestication appear in males very early in the Pleistocene. However, as women are protected more than men, these changes could appear earlier in the female than in the male skeletons. Later on, with the advent of villages and cities and pre-cooked frozen meals, these modifications may appear in numbers. At any rate, this is another possible physical result of social adaptation in man to add to an initial increase in brain size, subsequently reduced in some populations; to an adaptation to crowding; and to dwarfing.

The Unique Adaptations of the Genus Homo

LIKE OTHER ANIMALS, *Homo* has adapted himself to living in his terrestrial environment and with other animals of his own species. Many of the forms these adaptations have taken follow common garden rules of biology, including both zoology and botany; probably all of them do. What is unique is the way man has interrelated them, or more accurately, the way the forces of nature have interrelated them for him.

He has stretched the capacity of a hairless tropical primate to its physiological limits in conquering unfavorable climates. He has learned how to make fire and shelter, carry water, and store food. He has learned to talk and to think in terms of language, and to live in larger communities than any of his fellow primates. He has found ways to tolerate crowding and a certain amount of regimentation. All these are cultural in a sense but in another and more inclusive sense they are biological because they have affected the genetic structure of the human organism. Culture and biology are parts of a single picture and both require equal treatment in the review of human racial history that follows.

4

THE ORDER OF PRIMATES

Primate Studies and the Classification
of Human Races

THE PURPOSE of this book, which must not be lost from view in the dense foliage of information—drawn from many disciplines—needed for its composition, is to trace the descent of the living races of *Homo sapiens.* To discover the genetic relationships among these living races, we shall attempt to follow them back in time to ancestral fossil races, derived in turn from one or more prototypes in the extinct species *Homo erectus,* itself descended, through the mists of the fossil record, from still earlier prehominid forms. This must be done because it is possible that the ancestors of the living races parted company very early in the history of our genus.

We must also learn certain specific facts about the other living members of our order, prosimians, monkeys, and apes, because the primates as a whole are variable in anatomy, physiology, and behavior. Some of these variations are mentioned briefly in the preceding chapter. A more detailed study of them may disclose pertinent data about the descent of our genus and also about the possibilities within the total primate gene pool for all kinds of phenomena, such as the lack of a tail, different ways of walking erect (when this is done occasionally), the capacity to live in groups, communication, different amounts of skin pigment, a prominent external nose, and so on. These variations recur in some races of man but not in others, and they may be primitive, neotenous, specialized, or adaptive. We shall be in a better position to understand these traits in man if we first examine them in other primates. Such a preliminary study will also enable us to judge between close kinship and parallelism with greater confidence.

The Classification of Primates

IF THE relationships among the units in any set of phenomena are to be studied, these units must be classified. Had chemists not classified atoms and molecules, we would have no modern industry. If zoologists and paleontologists were not able to classify the order of primates, we could not hope to formulate a valid human taxonomy. Unfortunately for present purposes, no ironclad classification has yet been made; but the problem is not as great as it seems, for most of the difficulties involve the designation of the higher categories: suborders, infraorders, superfamilies, and families, which interest us least. There is little disagreement about genera and species, which are most pertinent to our study.

The classification given in Table 1 is based on Simpson's (1945), with emendations from other sources, chiefly Fiedler (1956).[1] When Fiedler and Simpson are in disagreement, this fact is indicated by initials in parentheses: (F) and (S).

The Prosimians

ALL MODERN taxonomists group the lemurs, lorises, and tarsiers, with or without the tree shrews, in a convenient category, that of the prosimians, which distinguishes these lowly members of the primate order from New World monkeys, Old World monkeys, apes, and men. They are of particular interest because they

[1] From 1945 on, the principal sources on primate taxonomy are as follows.

G. G. Simpson: "The Principles of Classification and a Classification of Mammals," *BAMN*, Vol. 85, 1945.

W. L. Straus: "The Riddle of Man's Ancestry," *QRB*, Vol. 24, No. 3 (1949), pp. 200–23.

W. C. O. Hill: *Primates, Vol. I, Strepsirhini* (Edinburgh: University Press; 1953) and *Vol. II, Haplorhini* (Edinburgh: University Press; 1955).

W. Fiedler: "Übersicht über das System der Primates," in D. Starck and S. Karger, eds.: *Primatologia, Vol. I* (Basel: S. Karger; 1956), pp. 1–266.

My scheme will of course be superseded when Simpson's revision of his 1945 work is published.

are exceedingly primitive mammals, in many ways not far advanced beyond the marsupials, and because they have much in common with our closest mammalian kin, the insectivores. The ancestors of these prosimians formed the base from which the higher primates developed. Knowing about them will help us understand the relationships among the more advanced forms.

The Tree Shrews

STANDING NEAR the taxonomic frontier between the primates and the insectivores are the tree shrews, which have a superfamily and family of their own, divided into two subfamilies and four genera. The tree shrew proper, genus *Tupaia*, has eight species; the smooth-tailed tree shrew (*Dendrogale*) has two; and the Philippine tree shrew (*Urogale*) and the pen-tailed tree shrew (*Ptilocerus*) have one each. All are confined to the Oriental region, principally to southeast Asia and Indonesia.

Being among the smallest of mammals, they have a high metabolic rate and require much food. If two males are left together in a confined space overnight, one will eat the other. They are enormously energetic, voracious, belligerent, amorous, irascible, and omnivorous, and particularly partial to a diet of insects, which befits their size. Their excesses of courage, wrath, and libido constitute a caricature of uninhibited human behavior unparalleled by any larger and fully accredited primate.

Like the insectivores they have claws on all ten toes; other primates have at least some nails. Their tooth formula is $\frac{2:1:3:3}{3:1:3:3}$, which is zoological shorthand for: upper incisors = 2, upper canines = 1, upper premolars = 3, upper molars = 3; lower incisors = 3, lower canines = 1, lower premolars = 3, lower molars = 3. Thus, each of the four kinds of teeth commonly found in mammals is enumerated for one side of the face. To calculate the total number of teeth one would multiply by 2. The tree shrews, then, have 38 permanent teeth. We have 32. The tree shrews uniquely, among primates, have three lower incisors on each side. All the others have two or one.

TABLE 1
ORDER OF PRIMATES, LIVING GENERA
(F) Fiedler's classification   (S) Simpson's classification

SUB-ORDER	SUPER-FAMILY	FAMILY	SUBFAMILY	GENUS	ENGLISH NAME	HABITAT OR RANGE
	Tupaioidea	Tupaiidae	Tupaiinae	Tupaia	Tree Shrew (various)	Southeast Asia, Indonesia, South India
				Dendrogale	Smooth-tailed Tree Shrew	Vietnam and Borneo
				Urogale	Philippine Tree Shrew	Mindanao
			Ptilocerinae	Ptilocerus	Pen-tailed Tree Shrew	Malay Peninsula, Sumatra, Borneo
PROSIMII	Lemuroidea	Lemuridae	Lemurinae	Lemur, Hapalemur, Lepilemur	Common Lemur, Gentle Lemur, Sportive Lemur	Madagascar
			Cheirogaleinae	Cheirogaleus, Miocrocebus	Mouse Lemur, Dwarf Lemur	
		Indridae		Indri, Lichanotus, Propithecus	Indris, Avahi, Sifaka	
		Daubentoniidae		Daubentonia	Aye-aye	
	Lorisoidea	Lorisidae		Loris, Nycticebus, Arctocebus, Perodicticus	Slender Loris, Slow Loris, Angwantibo, Potto	South India and Ceylon, India to Borneo, West Africa, West Africa
		Galagidae (F)	Galaginae (S)	Galago	Bush Baby	Africa south of Sahara
	Tarsioidea	Tarsiidae		Tarsius	Tarsier	Indonesia
		Callithricidae		Callithrix (including Cebuella), Leontocebus	Plumed and Pygmy Marmosets, Maned Marmosets, Tamarins and Pinchés	Panama to Southern Brazil

			Callimiconinae	Callimico	Callimico, or Goeldi's Marmoset	
PLATYR-RHINAE	Ceboidea	Cebidae		Callimico	Callimico, or Goeldi's Marmoset	Southern Mexico to Argentina
			Aotinae (S)	Aotus	Douroucouli	
			Pitheciinae (S)	Callicebus	Titi	
				Pithecia	Saki	
				Chiropotes	Saki	
				Cacajao	Uakari	
			Alouattinae (S)	Alouatta	Howler	
			Cebinae (S)	Cebus	Capuchin	
				Saimiri	Squirrel Monkey	
			Atelinae (S)	Ateles	Spider Monkey	
				Brachyteles	Woolly Spider Monkey	
				Lagothrix	Woolly Monkey	
CATAR-RHINAE	Cercopithe-coidea	Cercopithecidae	Cercopithecinae	Macaca	Macaque	Gibraltar, Morocco, Tibet, India to Japan
				Cynopithecus	Black Ape	Celebes
				Cercocebus	Mangabey	Africa
				Papio	Baboon	Africa and Arabia
				Theropithecus	Gelada	Ethiopia
				Cercopithecus	Guenon	Africa
				Erythrocebus	Patas Monkey	Africa
			Colobinae	Presbytis	Banded Langur	India and Himalayas
				Pygathrix	Doue Langur	East Indochina
				Rhinopithecus	Snub-nosed Langur	East Tibet and Kansu
				Simias	Pagi Island Langur	Sumatra
				Nasalis	Proboscis Monkey	Borneo
				Colobus	Gueraza	Ethiopia
	Hominoidea	Hylobatidae (F)	Hylobatinae (S)	Hylobates	Gibbon	Southeast Asia and Indonesia
				Symphalangus	Siamang	Sumatra
		Pongidae		Pongo	Orangutan	Sumatra and Borneo
				Pan	Chimpanzee (including pygmy)	Congo and West Africa
				Gorilla	Gorilla	Central and West Africa
		Hominidae		Homo	Man	Global (and Spatial)

BARBARY
APE

SPIDER MONKEYS
HOWLER MONKEYS

LOWLAND
GORILLA

MAP 4

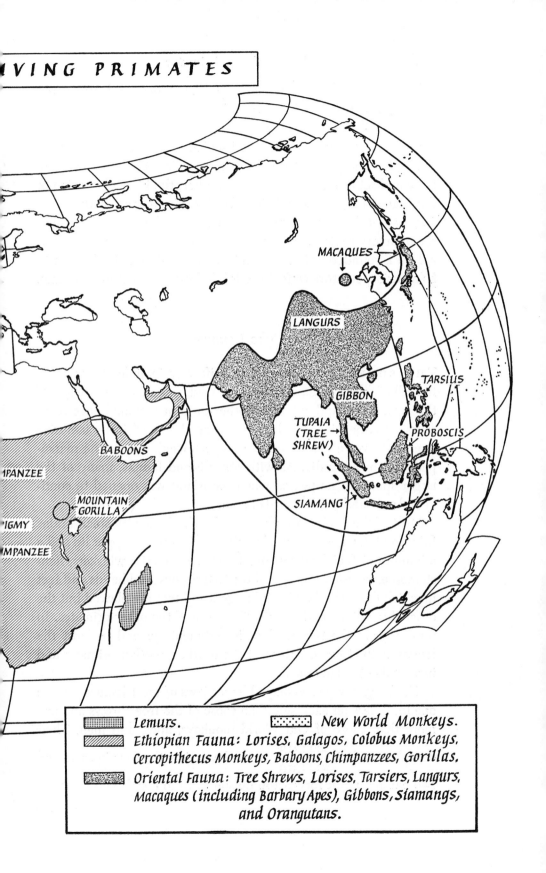

MACAQUES

LANGURS

TARSIUS

GIBBON

TUPAIA
(TREE
SHREW)

PROBOSCIS

BABOONS

CHIMPANZEE

MOUNTAIN
GORILLA

SIAMANG

PIGMY

CHIMPANZEE

Lemurs.

New World Monkeys.

Ethiopian Fauna: Lorises, Galagos, Colobus Monkeys,
Cercopithecus Monkeys, Baboons, Chimpanzees, Gorillas.

Oriental Fauna: Tree Shrews, Lorises, Tarsiers, Langurs,
Macaques (including Barbary Apes), Gibbons, Siamangs,
and Orangutans.

The male tree shrew has a large (for him) and pendulous penis, with external testicles. The female has a double-chambered uterus and each placenta has two discs. The tree shrews proper have three pairs of nipples, the smooth-tailed ones two pairs, and the Philippine and pen-tailed ones a single pair each. Their eyes are large and set at right angles to each other; the binocular vision of the higher primates is missing. Yet the visual area of the brain (*area striata*) is large compared to that of the insectivores, and the olfactory region is relatively small. In some species the external ear is rounded as in man. All in all, these little animals seem to be a curious mixture of features left behind and features to come.

The Lemurs

THE SUPERFAMILY of Lemuriformes includes three families, all of which live exclusively in Madagascar. In the shelter of this secluded island, where no other form of mammal gave them serious competition, the lemurs (using the word in its inclusive sense to cover all three families) specialized, just as the marsupials did in Australia. As with other island faunas, many of the larger species disappeared when the island was opened to continental animals by the arrival of man.

Most of the lemurs are quadrupedal climbers with small brains for primates, a good sense of smell, a tacked-down upper lip and a minimum of facial expression, a wet nose, tactile whiskers, nonstereoscopic vision like that of the tree shrews, and hands and feet in which the second and third fingers and toes are clawed but the other three digits end in nails like those of the other primates. In some species the second digit is rudimentary; and in most the longest is the fourth, instead of the third as in other primates and in most five-toed mammals.

The long, narrow, V-shaped lower jaws of most lemurs contain one tooth less on each side than those of the tree shrews and one more than those of Old World monkeys, apes, and men. Their dental formula is $\frac{2:1:3:3}{2:1:3:3}$. In the lower jaw the four incisors and two canines point forward in unison to form a stabbing or shearing device known as a dental comb, and the first lower premolar has become enlarged to assume the duties of the lower canine in other animals. These are very aberrant specializations.

However, one family, the Daubentonia, with but a single species, the aye-aye, has an even more specialized and greatly reduced rodentlike dentition, with this formula: $\frac{1:0:1:3}{1:0:0:3}$, totaling 18 permanent teeth as compared with 36 for the other lemurs and 32 for men. Its incisor teeth, which are huge, grow with wear, like those of rodents. With them these animals cut through the hard stalks of canes, especially sugar cane, to get at the sweet

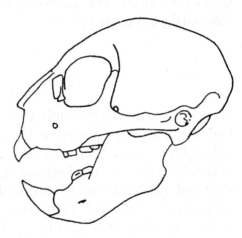

FIG. 3 THE SKULL OF AN AYE-AYE. The Aye-Aye (*Daubentonia*) is a highly specialized lemur of Madagascar which has chisel-like incisor teeth. It uses them like a rodent. (Drawing after Flower and Lydekker, 1891.)

sap. They also use the incisors in chiseling wood, like woodpeckers, to uncover grubs, which they pull out with long, slender, highly specialized middle fingers. Except for the great toe, which bears a nail, all their digits end in claws.

Unlike most primates lemurs have a breeding season, and one of them, the mouse lemur (*Cheirogaleus*), sleeps through the hot season, or more technically, it estivates. The uterus of the lemur, like that of the tree shrew, is forked. Whereas all the other primates, including the tree shrew, have disk-shaped placentas, the lemurs have bell-shaped ones. Also uniquely among primates, the lemur's placenta fails to emerge with the infant at birth. Twins are frequent, and some genera have four nipples each, others only two.

The lemurs are too specialized to have much bearing on primate origins, but they serve as classic illustrations of several principles. Ranging in size from the stature of a mouse to that of a man, they probably failed to increase much in intelligence once they had reached Madagascar. Because of lack of competition with other terrestrial mammals, intelligence was not at a premium. The lemurs achieved as complex a pattern of evolution and as great a proliferation of species as could be expected on an island the size of Madagascar. The two sets of organs most concerned with locomotion and feeding became the most specialized: the hands and feet, and the teeth. The lemurs were no match for man and the other invaders that accompanied him from the East Indies and Africa. The largest species were the most vulnerable and the first to disappear.

The Lorises

MUCH MORE widely distributed, and in a sense less specialized, than the lemurs proper are the members of the superfamily of Lorisiformes. The family of Lorisidae has four genera, and that of Galagidae but one. The Lorisidae, or lorises proper, include the slow and slender lorises of southeast Asia and India and the angwantibo and potto of West Africa. These are all small animals, squirrel- to cat-sized, heavily furred, with round heads and short ears, tails rudimentary or absent, and nails on all digits except the second toe. They breed throughout the year. They are all nocturnal and solitary, and they are all slow movers, especially the slow loris and potto. Seeing them creep along a limb is like watching a slowed-down movie.

Their slowness is due to a lowered metabolism, which is helped by the *rete mirabile*,[2] or net of blood vessels in the extremities which produce a heat exchange between outgoing arterial and incoming venous blood, as occurs, in a more simplified form, in the extremities of Australian aborigines. Like the sloth, another slow animal, the lorises need their fur, even in the tropics, to keep them warm under these circumstances.

[2] P. F. Scholander: "The Wonderful Net," *SA*, Vol. 196, No. 4 (1957), pp. 96–107.

With large thumbs pointing straight out sidewise and rudimentary index fingers, they creep about by grasping limbs, in search of leaves, buds, grubs, birds' eggs, and other immobile or slow-moving food. I once saw a potto bite clean through the thumbnail of a man who was holding it and was too busy talking to notice its snail-like movements. Uniquely among mammals this animal has four or five long, pointed vertebral spines, which stick through the skin of its neck and shoulders. By raising them when attacked, it can inflict a nasty wound on a predator.

One of the Asiatic species, the slender loris (*Loris tardigradus*), which is not quite as slow as the others, parallels man in that its body length is in the same ratio to its leg length and that it has no tail.

The galagos lack the lorises' low metabolic rate. They are quick-moving animals with large, erect, and mobile ears; they make their way through the trees by long leaps. Like several other African mammals, including man, they come in two sizes, regular and pygmy. One species, the needle-clawed euoticus (*Galago elegantulus*), has nails like the others, but each nail has a ridge running down the middle which ends in a sharp, clawlike point. They are particularly great leapers, and use these needle points for grasping branches when they land. All galagos have a secondary undertongue. That of euoticus is fringed like a comb; with it the animal cleans its fur.

The Tarsiers

THE SUPERFAMILY of Tarsiiformes is represented today by a single genus and what is probably a single species,[3] *Tarsius spectrum*. Tarsius is an extremely important animal. In its fossil form it is believed to have served as an evolutionary bridge between the Lemuriformes and all the higher primates. Also, according to the celebrated anatomist Wood Jones, man is descended directly from a tarsioid ancestor without intervening benefit of monkeys or apes.[4]

Whatever his position in the progression of primate evolution,

[3] Other species have been proposed. See Fiedler: op. cit., pp. 125–7.
[4] F. Wood Jones: *Man's Place Among the Mammals* (New York: Longmans, Green, & Co.; 1929).

Tarsius today is a pocket-sized prosimian equipped with a pair of huge, almost but not quite stereoscopic eyes; hands and feet lined with spongy pads for clinging to limbs; and a specialized lengthening of the tarsal bones, whence his name. These are bones of the ankle, heel, and the back part of the arch of the foot. In man, compared to other mammals, they are usually short; but in Tarsius they are greatly elongated to facilitate hopping, at which he is a champion. He retains claws on his second and third toes: the transition from claws to nails in his suborder is not complete.

An animal that hops in the dark needs better vision than a night crawler, which can guide itself partly by touch. Hence the huge eyes of the tarsier. To go with these, the visual cortex of his brain is correspondingly enlarged, and the back of his skull rounded, as in man. Another humanlike feature is the reduction of his jaws in relation to the size of his head. Tarsius crushes grasshoppers with his fingers, puts them in his mouth, and swallows them, just as people swallow premasticated food. His teeth are somewhat reduced in number; their formula is $\frac{2:1:3:3}{1:1:3:3}$. The upper median incisors are wider than the upper laterals, as in man, but the small jaws converge in a V-form in a very unmanlike fashion.

Clutching the shaft of a twig large enough to hold his inconsequential weight, Tarsius sits erect, looking about him for even tinier prey. He can turn his head around 180° and gaze directly behind him, thus completely covering the field. In order to rotate to this extent, his head is hafted in the center, and his foramen magnum is therefore placed forward of its location in other primates except man.

The tactile whiskers of the lemur remain, but the wet nose is gone, along with the long frenum tacking down the upper lip. Whereas in the lemur and the loris the bony ear has two pieces, the bulla and annulus, in Tarsius these are fused to make an external auditory meatus, as in man. All in all, Tarsius anticipates the higher primates in several features, some perhaps in a truly evolutionary sense, others independently developed by each, in parallel fashion, because of a special way of life.

The Living Platyrrhines: the South American Monkeys

THE PLATYRRHINES evolved in a tropical paradise much larger than Madagascar and nearly as free from competition. They produced a variety of primate forms based on a prosimian pattern, mimicking, in locomotion particularly, the monkeys and apes of the Old World tropics. Because their nostrils, like those of lemurs and many other mammals, are widely separated by a broad septum, they are called platyrrhines, in contrast to the Old World monkeys, or catarrhines, whose nostrils are pinched together, as, to a certain extent, is true in man. Their basic dental formula is also lemuroid: $\frac{2:1:3:3}{2:1:3:3}$. Their placentas, on the other hand, are single deciduous discs, as they are in Tarsius.

The most primitive members of the platyrrhine suborder are the marmosets, the three genera of the family Callithricidae. They are small monkeys with lemurlike body proportions, and a tail half as long again as head and body combined. The male, who has a scent gland at the base of his tail, raises it as a signal of sexual interest. Uniquely among primates, the female habitually gives birth to two or three young at a time and if three are born the mother kills one. Except at feeding time the father carries the babies, and when they are ready for weaning he chews food for them.[5]

The marmoset has claws on all digits but a great toe and a thumb with feeble powers of adduction. The face still has tactile whiskers, and the whole facial musculature consists of a single subcutaneous sheet, the platysma, which, as in lemurs and other primitive mammals, is not differentiated into separate muscle bundles as it is in higher primates, including man, who communicate partly by facial expression. The marmoset's dental formula is reduced, with only two molars on each side of each jaw. Like the galagos, the marmosets have a pygmy form.

The rest of the South American monkeys, the Cebidae, have

[5] W. E. Edwards: *Why the Marmoset Grew Her Tail,* paper read at Am. Assn. Phys. Anth. meeting May 13, 1960.

the standard prosimian dental formula, $\dfrac{2:1:3:3}{2:1:3:3}$, and nails on all fingers and toes. The thumb is either nonopposable or absent. The eyes of the marmosets, like those of the prosimians, point a little to one side. The eyes of the cebid monkeys, however, point forward to produce a single stereoscopic image, as in the catarrhines, including ourselves. Furthermore, in the marmoset eye the retina is largely undifferentiated.

The retina of the cebid monkeys, on the other hand, has a central depression called the fovea which is necessary for fine focusing. This is richly equipped with cones, the kind of nerve ends used in color vision. As both the platyrrhines and the catarrhines evolved separately from the prosimians, stereoscopic vision and color vision were acquired independently in the higher primates of the Old and New Worlds. Only one genus of cebid monkeys, *Aotus*, lacks color vision; this animal is nocturnal and does not need it.

The cebids also parallel the catarrhines in brain development, and in intelligence. In both groups progressive series can be laid out, from large to small brains, and from simple to complex convolution patterns. The details of brain structure differ in the two groups, regardless of size or complexity of cortical folding. This observation leads to the thought that if brains can evolve independently in size and complexity in two related suborders, then the same kind of parallel evolution could take place in equally isolated populations of smaller taxonomic magnitude, such as genera, species, and even subspecies. This concept is vital for the understanding of the origins of human races.

In their means of locomotion the cebids have diversified widely. One of their adaptations is unique; the others parallel those of the Old World monkeys and apes. The unique feature is the long prehensile tail found in the three most specialized forms, the capuchins (*Cebus*), the howler monkeys (*Alouatta*), and the spider monkeys (*Ateles*). They use the tail in locomotion as a fifth limb, and they can even hang by it. With it the spider monkey can pick up food and put it in his mouth. Such a tail is particularly useful in the rainy season, when forests are flooded. The monkeys cannot go down to the ground and if they fall they may drown.

In the use of their limbs the Cebidae fall into two categories, those that resemble the Old World monkeys and those that ape the apes. From Callimico to Callicebus to Cebus is a linear evolutionary sequence to be expected more of a fossil series than of a living assemblage.

One sideline is that of the Pithecinae, which have short tails; another is that of the Alouattinae, or howlers, which eat leaves like the Colobinae and vocalize as loudly as gibbons. Their noisemaker is a chamber in the throat enclosed by a huge hyoid bone and a pair of swollen and everted gonial corners in the mandible.

Like the apes, the Atelinae brachiate, that is, they move through the trees by swinging hand over hand between branches. This mode of locomotion is optional with Lagothrix, the woolly monkey, whose thumbs are still large and whose forelimbs are shorter than his hindlimbs, as in nonbrachiating forms. Brachyteles, the woolly spider monkey (whose nose is narrow like those of catarrhines), has somewhat longer forelimbs and brachiates more frequently. Ateles the spider monkey, the largest of all and at the end of the evolutionary line, is a full-time out-and-out brachiator except when he is swinging by his tail. He has acquired a gibbonlike body size and body build with a short trunk, long limbs, and a particularly long forearm. As his hands are used primarily as swinging hooks, Ateles, who can pick things up with his tail, has lost his thumb, and when at rest his four fingers are kept in a hooked position by short tendons that stop the fingers from straightening out except when the palm is bent forward. This apelike specialization prevents strain in his finger muscles when he hangs from his hands for long periods. On the ground he walks on his mid-phalangeal finger joints, like an ape.

The Living Cercopithecidae: Old World Monkeys

THE CATARRHINES, including the Old World monkeys, apes, and men, have in common the type of nose for which they were named. In it the nasal passages are set close together and parallel, separated only by a narrow septum; and the nostrils, of variable width, are set fairly close together and point downward.

The catarrhines have a reduced sense of smell in comparison with the other primates. They all are diurnal and have stereoscopic color vision and a fovea. They have a fused bony ear with an external auditory meatus. Another feature of the catarrhines is a dental formula, $\dfrac{2:1:2:3}{2:1:2:3}$, which they alone possess and which represents a reduction by one premolar (the first) from the lemuroid ancestral form.

Despite these common features, the Old World monkeys, apes, and men cannot be included in a single family, or even a superfamily, because of two fundamental differences. (1) The Old World monkeys have a two-disc placenta, also found in tree shrews. The apes and men have the usual one-disc form in common with the tarsiers and platyrrhines, although a two-disc placenta occurs as a rare anomaly in man. (2) The family peculiarity of the Cercopithecidae is in the form of their molar teeth.

All primate molars have cusps, or moundlike projections, on the occlusal or grinding surfaces. These cusps tend to be worn down through use during life. Although the number of cusps varies individually, racially, and otherwise, between three and six, there are characteristically four principal ones, one in each corner. The four sides of the tooth bounded by these cusps are known as the labial, on the tongue side; the buccal, on the cheek side; the mesial, or front; and the distal, or back.

Uniquely in the family of Cercopithecidae, the two mesial cusps are linked by a crossbar into a ridge, known technically as a *loph*, and the two distal cusps form a second loph. Such teeth are called *bilophodont*. Among the Old World monkeys the first and second upper and lower molars are characteristically bilophodont, and the third of either or both jaws may or may not be. The molars of apes and men lack bilophodontism. As both the two-disc placenta and bilophodontism are specializations, the absence of these features in apes and men is commonly taken to indicate that the ancestors of apes and men must have branched off the common ancestral Old World simian stock before the ancestors of the Cercopithecidae had acquired these features.

A third peculiarity of the Cercopithecidae which is almost but not quite exclusive to them is the possession of ischial callosities.

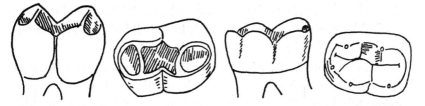

FIG. 4 THE MOLARS OF OLD WORLD MONKEYS AND APES. *Left:* A bilophodont lower molar, typical of the Old World monkeys. The molar has four cusps, in two lophs or pairs, each loph linked by a connecting ridge. *Right:* A Dryopithecus-type lower molar, typical of apes and men. Such a molar has five cusps, situated independently around the edge of the crown, with the fifth to the rear.

These are bare, rough spots on the animal's skin, which cover the projections of the ischial bones on which it sits down. As the presence of this built-in seating pad is matched by a roughened area on the underlying bone, it can be detected in fossil forms. All the Cercopithecidae have these callosities, but so do other animal forms. Small callosities are to be seen, although they are partly concealed by fur, in the gibbon, and they turn up now and then in chimpanzees. Ischial callosities have nothing but their general location in common with another and much more conspicuous primate feature, sexual skin, which is found in some genera of both monkeys and apes.

The Leaf-eating Colobinae

THE CERCOPITHECIDAE are subdivided into two subfamilies, the Cercopithecinae and the Colobinae. The latter is limited in Africa to a single genus extending from West Africa across the Congo to Ethiopia, but it has three genera in Asia, where they comprise the majority of all fully arboreal monkeys. Like the South American howlers the Colobinae specialize in eating leaves. (The langur and snub-nosed langur also eat fruit, and the latter steal food from men.) Their adaptation involves principally the digestive apparatus. The colobinian stomach is very large and, when full, contains a load of leaves equal to one third of the animal's body weight, or ten times as much food as man requires. Resembling a modern combination living room, dining room, and kitchen, this stomach is partially divided into semi-detached subchambers by a series of constrictions. The liver, crowded by the enormous food container, is lobeless, and is separated from the diaphragm, as in the human fetus.

As leaves require chewing rather than biting, the incisors and canines of these animals are relatively small, and the molars proportionately large. The chewing mechanism, which calls for sidewise grinding as well as up-and-down motion, involves a stronger development of the masseter muscles of the face than of the temporal muscles of the vault. In this whole dental and muscular complex they resemble the Hominidae, including ourselves. Furthermore, two of the three Asiatic genera of Colobinae have also acquired prominent external noses, which make them look like caricatures of people. In *Nasalis,* the common monkey of Borneo, the male starts off in childhood with a tip-tilted sensitive-looking little nose; in early maturity the nose stands out straight and strong, and it collapses grossly and pendulously to lip level when the animal is approaching the end of its life cycle. The female's nose is much smaller. *Rhinopithecus,* the snub-nosed langur of Tibet and China, retains an uptilted nose throughout life.

The stenophagic diet of the Colobinae, which provides them with an abundance of easily acquired food, thus permitting dense population growth,[6] limits them to forested regions of little seasonal change in which the foliage is nondeciduous. Although barring much of Africa, this diet permits the Colobinae to extend their range outside the tropics into the cool Himalayan and trans-Himalayan forests, which are inhabited by two kinds of langurs. Like other narrow ecological specializations, this diet is an evolutionary blind alley which primates of more than one category have entered but from which none has emerged by producing a higher form.

The Cercopithecinae

J u s t   a s the forests of the Oriental region are mainly inhabited by the Colobines, so those of Africa are typically the playground of arboreal Cercopithecines. This may be partly due to the relatively small seasonal change in rainfall in Asia and Indonesia

---

[6] In Africa hundreds of thousands have been killed for fur.

and to the availability of green leaves there throughout the year. In most of Africa, on the other hand, alternate wet and dry seasons cause many species of trees to lose their leaves once a year, so that monkeys which eat fruit, grubs, and other nonleafy foods have an advantage over leaf eaters.

Beside being omnivorous, the Cercopithecines have several peculiarities, including in most species cheek pouches in which they carry food, and in all species superorbital notches, that is, a notch in the top of the bony orbit of each eye which permits the sheltered passage of a nerve, a vein, and an artery. In man and the apes these may pass through a foramen, or small circular opening, instead. All the Cercopithecinae have well-developed, opposable thumbs, and many have relatively short tails. Their brain development is variable between genera and reaches its greatest height among primates other than apes and men. They use elaborate techniques of communication, both by voice and by facial expression.

The subfamily can be further divided into two groups according to habitat and means of locomotion, the arboreal and the terrestrial. The arboreal group, which is exclusively African, includes three genera, *Cercocebus, Cercopithecus,* and *Erythrocebus,* which are divided into many species and races. These monkeys vary greatly in hair length and thickness, coiffure styles, and color, with greens, yellows, reds, blacks, whites, and various combinations of these variations. The smallest is the talapoin of the genus *Cercocebus,* which shows many parallels to the New World *Cebus.* It has a globular brain case, a long lumbar section of spine, little protrusion of the jaws, and small teeth. From this animal a progression may be found to the patas monkey, *Erythrocebus,* a red-haired monkey of East Africa which lives in open country. It has a protruding snout and a short tail, and is as much at home on the ground as in the trees. It is thus transitional to the genera which live primarily on the ground, the macaques (*Macaca*), baboons (*Papio*), and gelada (*Theropithecus*).

These three have become specialized for a way of life not known among the primates hitherto described—life on the ground. Although they can and do climb trees without difficulty —baboons even sleep in trees when these are available—monkeys of these genera walk about on all fours, with the palms of their hands flat on the ground, seeking food in bushes, under stones, and elsewhere on the surface of the earth. Some of them even dig shallow-growing roots with their stout fingers. Thus they are able to occupy successfully lands unavailable to other subhominid primates, and to live in the forest as well. Many of them seem to prefer rocky terrain to flat country, and they are accomplished rock climbers. All of them can sit up when resting, and all have retained full mobility of their fingers despite their quadrupedal gait; they are, in fact, more dexterous than brachiating monkeys and other treetop climbers including the howler. Such is the construction of their jaws that, when sitting erect, they can open their mouths wide only by throwing back their heads. They all have muzzles and large teeth, some being more doglike in this respect than others. They are vigorous, belligerent, amorous, and formidable fighters, particularly in packs.

The least specialized anatomically and the most widely distributed is the genus *Macaca,* which is the second most widely ranging of all primate genera after *Homo. Macaca* has many regional forms. Reading from left to right on the map, the first is the Barbary ape, native to Gibraltar and parts of North Africa,[7] particularly the rocky face of Mt. Meggu, behind the city of Shehshawen in northern Morocco. At Mt. Meggu the Spanish soldiers used them for target practice during the Riffian War of the early 1920's, and these monkeys characteristically carried away their wounded, probably mostly young ones. The Barbary ape is a shaggy, yellowish-brown animal with no tail.

The second is *Macaca mulatta,* formerly called *M. rhesus,* which ranges east from Pakistan over much of India. It is the common laboratory monkey in whose honor a set of blood groups has been named, and hardly needs description. It inhabits both open country and forests; and a related form ranges high in the Himalayas along with the langurs.

A species called *Macaca arctoides,* large and hairy, lives as far

[7] The widespread notion that the Arabs brought this animal to Gibraltar, either from North Africa or from as far away as Pakistan, has no historical basis and is refuted by paleontological evidence. See N. C. Tappen: "Problems of Distribution and Adaptation of the African Monkeys," *CA,* Vol. 1., No. 2 (1960), pp. 91–120.

north as Szechuan in China, and others even get to the Amur River and Korea. The macaques of Japan dig for food under the snow in winter and swim in the sea for shellfish in summer. A Formosan macaque lives in caves along the coast and is semi-aquatic, diving for crabs and shellfish and special seaweeds. The crab-eating macaque of Indonesia and the shores of southeast Asia, *Macaca irus*, lives in mangrove swamps, and swims after sea food like the others. In Celebes lives the so-called Moor macaque (*Macaca Maura*), a black species with a stumpy tail. It goes about in packs and is said to hunt other animals.

In sum, the genus *Macaca* shows as much range of behavior as of habitat. It is one of the most versatile of mammals, not only among the primates but in any order. Mainly tree-borne in south India and Ceylon, mainly terrestrial in most other places, it is an alpinist, a swimmer, a hunter, a fisher, a mollusc gatherer, and it eats the whole menu from shellfish to nuts. No wonder, then, that medical researchers have favored it as their chief laboratory animal. If its versatility was a result of living away from the forest and on the ground, this may help explain the wide distribution of our own ancestors after they, too, had ceased to be arboreal.

The other terrestrial Cercopithecinae are the black ape, *Cynopithecus*, and the baboons. The black apes inhabit Celebes, Batchian, and some of the southern Philippines. Although related to the macaques, they have developed muzzles and cheek swellings that make them look like baboons. They, too, include sea food in their diet.

The baboons, of the genus *Papio* (*P. papio, comatus, cynocephalus, doguera, and hamadryas*), are limited to Africa and southwest Arabia. They are large animals with tails shorter than the combined length of their body and head, doglike muzzles equipped with large teeth, including long, daggerlike canines in the male. The face is bare, ribbed, and red, and the posterior adorned with a large, continuous, pillowlike crest of ischial callosities which, as Washburn has observed,[8] serves as a cushion on which the bulk of the animal's weight rests while it is sleeping in trees. The female also sports a gay patch of sexual skin that puffs

[8] S. L. Washburn: "Ischial Callosities as Sleeping Adaptations," *AJPA*, Vol. 15, No. 2 (1957), pp. 269–76.

out and becomes excessively vascular, as a signal of invitation, before ovulation.

Listed in the same genus are the drills (*Papio leucophaeus*)
—large, nearly tailless animals that roam the forest floor in West
Africa, and the mandrills (*Papio sphinx*) of Gaboon, which sally
out of the forest from time to time to raid the savannah country.
The drill has a dark green coat, a black face, and a pink posterior.
The mandrill is dark brown, with a bright red nose and a blue,
longitudinally ridged swollen area over each cheek, and a red
and blue region to the rear, a combination callosity and sexual
skin.

In a genus of its own, *Theropithecus*, is the gelada, an exceptionally large baboonlike primate, possibly of independent origin,
inhabiting southern Ethiopia. A huge mane covers its forequarters, but its chest and underside are bare. These parts are as pink
as its posterior. This is the only primate beside man, apparently,
that has both a mane top-forward and bare skin elsewhere.[9]

These terrestrial animals are all omnivorous, intelligent, aggressive, well organized in packs for concerted action, and dangerous
to man if provoked, and to carnivores. Washburn saw a pack of
baboons which were feeding in and about a herd of impala drive
off three cheetahs by simply looking threatening while the impala,
apparently confident in the protective power of their companions,
whom they served in turn as lookouts, grazed unconcerned.[1] The
inference is that life on the ground, particularly in open country,
has created a situation favorable to increased versatility, adaptability, and general intelligence in primates, as shown by the performance of the series from macaque to gelada.

The Anthropoid Apes

LESS VERSATILE, less adaptable, more specialized, and
probably even more intelligent are the anthropoid apes, including
two genera of small ones, the gibbons and siamangs, and three
genera of large ones, the orangs, chimpanzees, and gorillas. Most
authors include them all in a single family, the Pongidae, rating

[9] A comparable coat combination is seen in a terrestrial bird, the ostrich.
[1] Washburn: op. cit., pp. 273–4.

the first two as a subfamily, the Hylobatinae, and the last three as another, the Ponginae. Both Fiedler and Straus, however, categorize them as two families, Hylobatidae and Pongidae, because of the separation of the gibbons and siamangs from the other three both anatomically and in probable line of descent.

In either case, all apes have certain features in common. They all have large, interlocking canines on both jaws, so that they can chew only up and down. In the upper jaw there is a gap, or diastema, between each canine and its neighboring lateral incisor. This gap makes room for the lower canine when the jaws are closed. In the lower jaw the first premolar is long, narrow, and ridged. The outer edge of this tooth is sharpened against the upper canine, with which it acts as a pair of scissors.

The ape molars are not bilophodont, but retain separate cusps. The upper and lower molars meet in different fashion from those of the Cercopithecidae; in the monkeys the upper and lower teeth mesh alternately, with the anterior loph of each lower tooth filling the gap between its opposite number and the one in front of it, whereas in the apes the uppers and lowers meet more nearly squarely on. Furthermore, the cusps of the lower molars of all genera of apes have the Dryopithecus pattern, named for a fossil ape to be described presently. This is also called the Y-5 pattern, because a tooth of this kind has five cusps, two forward and three aft, and the grooves separating the cusps assume a pattern resembling the letter Y, with its tail to the front. Much has been made of this feature by paleontologists, who have little else but teeth to go on.

Although one of the apes, the gorilla, spends as much time on the ground as baboons do, all the anthropoid apes are anatomically adapted for arboreal life through brachiation, the mode of progression independently acquired by the spider monkeys in the Neotropical region. In all five genera the upper limbs are longer than the lower; both hands and feet are to some degree prehensile; and the tail is gone, leaving even less of a vestige than in man. The gibbon and siamang have ischial callosities, like the Old World monkeys, but the three great apes sit on enlarged *sphincter ani* muscles which look like portable doughnuts. All five have the single-disc type of placenta.

The Gibbons: Symphalangus *and* Hylobates

THE HYLOBATIDAE are long-limbed and spidery, with the longest legs in proportion to body height of any higher primate save man, and the longest arms of all, relatively speaking, with especially long forearms. They are by far the best brachiators among the anthropoids, but they vary their gait by running erect along horizontal branches with their arms extended, like high-wire artists with balancing poles. On the ground they run in exactly the same way. When crossing streams too wide for aerial jumping they swim, using the breast stroke. Compared to those of man and the other apes, their hands and feet are long and narrow, and their thumbs are short and set far back in the palm, so that the thumb tips fail to reach the first row of knuckles. This, like the thumblessness of the spider monkey, is an adaptation for fancy brachiation. Their teeth are small, but their canines are long and can inflict a nasty wound. Generally, however, they avoid direct territorial fights and instead have shouting matches, emitting liquid calls that can be heard over a mile from an inflated throat pouch. All of them have small, hard, rather than puffy, ischial callosities. There is no visible sexual dimorphism in any of the species, and as the genitals are small and shielded by hair, the only way to distinguish male from female in the field is by noticing either the nipples of a female that has borne young, or who mounts whom.

Each genus is of a different size. *Symphalangus,* the siamang, has an arm span of six feet and weighs about 24 pounds. *Hylobates,* the gibbon proper, weighs between 11 and 15 pounds, according to the species. Both genera fall well within the size range of the Old World monkeys, which all three pongid apes, as well as man, exceed. Like man, the siamang has a web between the first joints of the second and third toes and for this trivial reason he, and not man, has drawn the name *Symphalangus,* presumably to distinguish him from the gibbon. His abundant coat is a drab black to brown, and his home is the island of Sumatra, which he shares with two more colorful apes, the orang and one species of gibbon.

The latter, which occupies a wide range in the Oriental region, is divided into at least three species, a valid division because in places pairs of them are sympatric. Westernmost and northernmost is the hoolock, a small animal which is usually black but varies through a gamut of coat colors from browns to gray and cream. All, however, have a white bar across the eyebrows—their distinguishing feature. Races of the hoolock (*H. hoolockii*) range over Bhutan and Assam and up the gorges into Tibet; they cross Upper Burma and northern Siam into Indochina and the island of Hainan.

South of the hoolock, from Burma eastward, lives the white-handed, or lar, gibbon, which ranges to the tip of the Malay peninsula. The color of its coat is also variable, but all of them have a white ring around the face and white hair on the hands. The skin of the face, which is bare, and of the palms and soles, is black. To the East, in Indochina, lives the black gibbon or concolor. A fourth group comprising one or more species is called the agile gibbon in Malaya and the silvery gibbon in Java, and a related form lives alongside the siamang in Sumatra. They have no special mark, but some of the latter have bodies of one color and limbs of another. This genetic patterning in hair color, although common enough in mammals in general, including the lower primates, is absent in the three great apes and in man. He, though individually and racially variable, has a single pelage color, save for an occasional blond or red mustache with brown head hair, and the graying of age.

The Orangutan (Pongo)

THE ORANG lives in Sumatra and Borneo. Despite a separation since the flooding of the Sunda Shelf in the late Pleistocene, the two island races are still one species, *P. pygmaeus*. He is a large animal, the adult male averaging 165 pounds and reaching 200 pounds; as the females average only 81 pounds, there is a sexual dimorphism of 2 to 1 in weight. Sexual dimorphism is also evident in the excessive growth of the jaws and teeth, particularly the canines, in the adult male. The thrust of the bite is carried upward through the lateral facial bones to the forehead bones to the forehead in a single line without the need of brow ridges as braces, but so strongly are the temporal muscles developed that they meet on the top of the skull, which grows a sagittal crest to part them and give them room for attachment. A separate transverse crest at the rear supports the ends of the neck muscles needed to counterbalance the animal's deep, heavy jaw.

The orang's arms are the longest in relation to his body length of the three great apes, and he can move his legs to the side at a right angle to his trunk, because he lacks a tendon on the hip joint needed for erect posture. When he walks on the ground, he uses his arms as crutches, swinging his legs between them. Like the gibbon, he has a laryngeal sac, but instead of using it for music-making he converts it into a pneumatic shock absorber in brachiating. This specialization he shares with the other two great apes. The sac extends, in the adult animal, to the shoulders, either of which has to bear the total weight of the animal, as much as 200 pounds in his case and more in that of the gorillas, when he hangs by one arm. In man this laryngeal sac sometimes turns up in heavy vocalizers, for example, opera stars and muezzins.[2]

On his hairless cheeks the adult male orang sports a pair of coarse, fleshy flanges which look like the sidepieces of a baseball catcher's mask and which may serve as armor against biting, although this has not been proved. The orang's hair, which is reddish and very long, protects his light-brown skin from the torrential tropical rain. At night the orang, like the chimpanzee and the gorilla, sleeps in a nest of his own fabrication, and in it he likes to cover his head with leaves. He neither needs nor has ischial callosities.

The Chimpanzee (Pan)

THIS, the most familiar of primates, frequently seen on television and the stage, inhabits various parts of the tropical forests of Africa from Gambia to Uganda and south to Angola. The male

[2] Jane Enzmann: "The Structure and Function of the Laryngeal Sacs of the Chimpanzee, Gorilla, and Orang-Utan," *AJPA*, Vol. 14, No. 2 (1956), pp. 383–4.

is smaller than the male orang, with a mean weight of 110 pounds against the orang's 165 pounds, but the female chimpanzee is slightly and probably not significantly larger than the female orang, with a mean weight of 88 pounds against 81. The weight ratio between the sexes is therefore only 1.3 to 1, which still gives the chimpanzee greater sexual dimorphism in weight than is found in most races of man. The stature of this animal ranges from five feet to five feet seven inches (152–170 cm.) for the males and four feet to four feet three inches for the females (122–130 cm.). This is well within the range of human races in the male, and well below it in the female. Morphologically speaking, the sex dimorphism of the chimpanzee is not great, and little difference can be found in the skull and teeth. The male does not ordinarily have a sagittal crest.

Probably because more chimpanzees have been observed than orangs or gorillas, we know that they are extraordinarily variable in skin color, running from a grayish pink that is almost white to black, with several yellowish shades between. Their color range is essentially the same as in the races of man, and they all live within one environmental realm. The hair color, in the blacks and browns, is less variable, but the amount of hair on the body and head varies greatly. Baldness is sometimes present, and the animals gray with age. The presence or absence of ischial callosities is also variable; callosities are present in 36 per cent of the animals noted. As the chimpanzee, like the orang and gorilla, builds a nest, he has no more need of these pads than they do.

Specialists who have tested chimpanzees—and who have even reared some of them in their homes alongside human babies—find that they vary enormously in intelligence and in temperament although, compared to orangs and gorillas as a species, they may be characterized as gregarious, noisy, inquisitive, and provocative. Up to the age at which the human infant learns to talk, they are apparently our equals.

Taxonomically they are commonly divided into two species, *Pan troglodytes* and *Pan schweinfurthii*, but Schultz and others who have studied them carefully find the division unjustified. Individual variations within populations are at least as great as regional ones. Moreover, there is no evidence to support the idea that they will not interbreed, in or out of captivity.

Like the galago, the marmoset, and man, the chimpanzee has a pygmy form. It was first described in 1929 by Schwartz, who classified it as a subspecies, *Pan satyrus paniscus*. Coolidge, describing an adult specimen in 1933, called it *Pan paniscus*, giving it full species rank;[3] and in 1954 Tratz and Heck called it a genus, *Bonobo*.[4] In the opinion of other primate anatomists the subspecific designation may be the correct one, because the musculature of the two animals is the same,[5] and because the two forms are allopatric. The pygmy chimpanzee lives only south of the Congo River, where the full-sized animal is not found.

The pygmy is about half the size and weight of the full-sized chimpanzee, and it is morphologically pedomorphic, in contrast to the other races and species of great apes, which are essentially gerontomorphic. Whereas the full-sized chimpanzee has large cupped ears, its pygmy relative has small ones like those of a gorilla, and a gorillalike, relatively prominent, external nose. The pygmy has a different call from that of the full sized chimp; he calls Hi! Hi! instead of Ho! Ho! In 1923, six years before the existence of this race was known, Robert Yerkes acquired an animal which had been captured in pygmy-chimpanzee territory and which undoubtedly was a pygmy. After a little over a year, it died, probably early in its fourth year of life. In Yerkes's stated opinion, it was a simian genius and the brightest ape he had ever known, with an excess of boldness and curiosity.[6] How it would have developed as it grew older we can never know. There is one currently in the Philadelphia zoo. The taxonomic disposition of this animal is of special interest to anthropologists, because man too has pygmy races, as different from full-sized people as a pygmy chimpanzee is from his neighbors across the river. We do not consider our Pygmies a genus, however, nor even a species.

[3] H. J. Coolidge, Jr.: "*Pan paniscus*, Pigmy Chimpanzee from South of the Congo River," *AJPA*, Vol. 18, No. 1 (1933), pp. 1–57.

[4] E. Tratz and H. Heck: "Der afrikanische Anthropoide 'Bonobo,' eine neue Menschenaffengattung," *SM*, Vol. 2 (1954), pp. 97–101.

[5] R. A. Miller: "The Musculature of *Pan paniscus*," *AJA*, Vol. 91, No. 2 (1952), pp. 183–232.

[6] R. M. Yerkes: *Chimp Intelligence and Its Vocal Expressions* (Baltimore: Williams and Wilkins Co.; 1925).

The Gorilla (Gorilla)

T HE GORILLA is divided into two noncontiguous geographic populations: the lowland gorilla of the Gaboon and Cameroons, and the mountain gorilla of the eastern Congo west of Lakes Edward and Kivu, where it ranges in altitude from 7,500 feet to 12,-000 feet. The habitat of the lowland animal is ordinary tropical rain forest. The home territory of the mountain population is cool and alpine in places, with an abundance of bamboo, the shoots of which are a favorite food of the gorilla. The lowland form has traditionally been given a specific name, *Gorilla gorilla,* and the mountain form another, *Gorilla berengei,* but despite certain marked differences, as in foot form, the current tendency is to consider them geographical races of a single species and call them by the former name.

In both races the stature of adult males ranges from about five feet to about six feet (152–183 cm.), although individuals of six feet six (198 cm.) have been found. This is the human range, excluding pygmies. Probably the mean weight of adult male gorillas is about 400 pounds. Grossly heavier weights, reaching more than 600 pounds in individual zoo and circus animals, are the result of obesity caused by overfeeding and lack of exercise; human beings can reach 900 pounds under similar circumstances. The adult female is much smaller, probably weighing not more than 200 pounds. The weight ratio between the sexes, then, is about 2 to 1, as among the orangs.

Sexual dimorphism is exaggerated in the head and face. The skull of the male gorilla has enormous teeth, particularly canines, and huge brow ridges, sagittal crest, and nuchal crest, although these flying buttresses vary greatly among individuals in size and form. The considerable size of the brain case is thus overshadowed by the overdevelopment of the masticatory apparatus and its dependent braces. The female skull, however, can hardly be distinguished from that of a male chimpanzee. Gorillas almost never have ischial callosities. Their skin is usually black, their ears small, and the soft parts of the external nose stand out from the facial plane.

Most of the differences between the two races of gorillas are trivial compared to those which separate human subspecies, and concern relative trunk and limb lengths and skull form. However, the difference in foot form does suggest that they may be two species. Although the foot of the lowland gorilla is broad and short by simian standards, its great toe is pointed at an angle from the axis of the foot, whereas in the mountain gorilla the great toe, although still short, is in line with the foot, like that of a man.

Like the chimpanzee the gorilla sleeps and sometimes feeds in trees, but he moves from one tree to another by climbing down and walking from trunk to trunk on the ground; and in the bamboo forest he habitually feeds on the ground. Like the other great apes he walks on all fours, on the outer edges of his feet and on the knuckles of his hands. He can stand erect when he wishes, but when moving fast, like the others he runs on all fours.

The gorilla is less communicative than the chimpanzee and almost always silent; he is less aggressive in the wild, but sometimes more so in captivity.[7] What noise he makes he produces mostly by drumming on his chest with his fists. Which of the two apes is the more intelligent is a matter of controversy. Gorillas are the most difficult apes to rear in captivity, and the least communicative. The chimpanzee wears his intellectual heart on his sleeve, so to speak; the gorilla's is deeply concealed.

The Hominidae (Homo)

REPRESENTED, like each of the three Pongidae, by a single living genus and species, the family of Hominidae differs from its fellow giant catarrhines in a number of easily enumerated features. Man's brain is about three times as large as those of the great apes, although at birth it is smaller than the orang's. The human brain is also more specialized than those of the others. Man's teeth are generally smaller. His canines in particular are smaller. They are no longer than the incisors and premolars that

----

[7] J. T. Emlen, Jr.: "Current Field Studies of Gorillas," *CA*, Vol. 1, No. 4 (1960), p. 332.

Emlen: "In the Home of the Mountain Gorilla," *AK*, Vol. 63, No. 3 (1960), pp. 98–108.

flank them, so that they do not overlap. Consequently there is no diastema, or gap in the gum line, between the canines and the lateral incisors on the upper jaw nor one between the canines and the first premolars on the lower.

Whereas all the apes are specialized for brachiating, man is specialized for walking erect, with consequent differences in the spinal column, pelvis, upper and lower limbs, hands, skull, jaw, and vocal apparatus. As he neither sleeps in trees nor has yet become anatomically adapted to a life in chairs, man has either lost or failed to develop ischial callosities. Most men are less hairy than most apes, and in some races man is virtually hairless, except on the head, where he sports a mane, and in the axillae and pubis. In some races the male also has a beard. His skin color covers the primate range, even to the blue of the drill's nose, which is matched by the so-called Mongolian spot on the skin over the sacrum in some races, and the blue penis of some South American Indians. His hair color is less variable because it lacks greens, and his eye color is possibly more variable, with an emphasis on blues, grays, and greens as well as various browns and intermediate patterns. His hair form is more variable than that of all other primates; only man has the woolly or spiral hair of Negroes and Bushmen.

In his tolerance of extremes of climate, in the variety of terrain he is able to inhabit, in his general adaptability, aggressiveness, and ability to live in groups, man more closely resembles the monkeys who live on the ground, particularly the macaques, than he does any forest-bound ape. The human populations which live most simply differ little, if at all, from other primate populations in their relationship to other species of animals and to the landscape. Although partly carnivorous, they kill only what they need to eat, and leave nature in balance as they find it. Now and then they burn over hunting grounds, and this action favors some plant species over others and provides certain browsing and grazing animals with more food than before, but self-ignited forest fires have the same results. Still, it is possible that in various nontropical regions, particularly in the Palearctic and Nearctic, human hunters may have caused, or at least hastened, the extinction of several species of mammals, mostly oversized ones such as the mammoth in Europe and Asia, and the mastodon, giant sloth, and even the horse, in North America. Ecological disturbances caused by man may have been more substantial at the hunting level in cold climates than in warm ones, particularly the wet forests.

Nevertheless—setting aside these extinctions for the moment—it was only about 8,000 years ago that man began to enlarge his ecological niche by doing what certain invertebrates, the ants and termites, had been doing for millions of years—building elaborate houses, domesticating other species and raising vegetables, storing food in great quantities, and grouping themselves in elaborate hierarchies. As all human populations do not share modern civilization, some peoples, fast disappearing, are still in the same ecological balance as lower primates, whereas others, rapidly inceasing, have already hit the moon and are orbiting men around the earth.

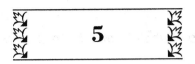

5

MAN'S PLACE AMONG
THE PRIMATES

The Bearing of Primate Studies on Racial Origins

EVER SINCE DARWIN, there has been a diversity of opinion about the position of our species among the primates. Darwin himself considered us closest to the great apes, and Huxley agreed with him. Mivart, however, argued that the Old World monkeys are our closest kin. Later on, Wood-Jones bypassed all apes and monkeys impartially and maintained that man had derived from tarsiers. Today Gregory, Schultz, and Washburn favor the apes, and Straus supports certain aspects of Mivart's earlier position.

Lacking special training or experience in primatology, I am in no position to argue on one side or the other. In fact, a question arises as to why, in a book on the origin of human races, this subject has to be discussed at all. The answer is simply that we need all the evidence we can get to solve the problem of our descent, which is inadequately documented paleontologically. If we know to which other living primates we are most closely related in anatomy, physiology, and behavior, we shall be in a better position to interpret the evidence of fossil bones than if the bones were all we had. This will help us determine the time at which our ancestors and theirs parted company. Such information will, in turn, give us some idea as to the time when the geographical races of man could have begun to differentiate. Finally, comparisons with other primates may help us decide which specializations of living human races are old and which are new.

To Brachiate or Not to Brachiate

THE MOST conspicuous difference between man and the other primates is our erect posture, with bipedal locomotion and free hands. Although not the only criterion of genetic relationship, it has become the most controversial. Most orders of mammals have one principal method of locomotion each, be it swimming, flying, running about on the ground, or climbing trees. But the single order of primates has a wide range, including climbing, hopping, tail-swinging, walking on all fours (quadrupedal), brachiating, and walking on two feet (bipedal). In an early primate stage, man's ancestors must once have been arboreal and quadrupedal. Whether or not they brachiated for a while before becoming bipedal is the moot question. Anatomists have argued it back and forth, bone by bone and muscle by muscle, largely motivated by a desire to find out, in terms of this single feature, if man is or is not descended from some kind of ape.

This concept is based on a false premise—that if man's ancestors once brachiated, he must be descended from early, brachiating apes, and conversely, that if man's ancestors did not brachiate, he is not descended from early apes. It is false because brachiation can be acquired in different primate lines independently. Spider monkeys, langurs, and apes, belonging to three different superfamilies, have all adopted this specialized means of locomotion. If man's ancestors did indeed brachiate at one time, they may have done so independently of the ancestors of the apes. This we shall explore in the following chapter when we examine the fossil record.

To my mind the essence of the argument, at this point, is not to trace the descent of man nor the history of his locomotion, but to explain the freeing of the human shoulder girdle, arms, and hands from whatever kind of locomotion man's remote ancestors practiced. The human upper extremity is unique among bipedal vertebrates in that it is neither involved in locomotion, except for guiding animals and steering vehicles, nor degenerate. Ostriches, emus, rheas, and other flightless birds have tiny degenerate wings covered with pin feathers or down. Kangaroos, jerboas, kangaroo rats, and most other nonarboreal, bipedal, jumping mammals have tiny, mostly useless, arms and hands. So did the bipedal dinosaurs. Man's arms are at least as long, in ratio to body length, as those of quadrupedal monkeys, and man's hands at least as large and as mobile as theirs. Why?

Two theoretically reasonable explanations come to mind, each involving a direct shift from one function of the forelimbs to another without time off between for degeneration.

(1)   *Descent from Brachiators.* Our remote arboreal ancestors began to brachiate and specialized to a certain extent, say, as far as the woolly monkey has done. This gave them a powerful upper extremity. Their hands did not become specialized for hanging, like those of the great apes, because our ancestors were then small animals too light to need this adaptation. When a brachiating animal is moving through the trees, and also when it is seated, the axis of its trunk is vertical to the ground. Such an animal, when it comes to live on the ground, can retain this vertical position only by walking erect. As the weight of the entire body falls on the pelvis and legs, instead of on the arms and shoulder girdle, the pelvis and legs had to become adapted for bipedal walking, particularly as the body grew heavier, whereas the arms and hands were ready-made for the use of tools and weapons, carrying infants, and other manlike and womanlike activities.

(2)   *Descent from Quadrupeds.* Let us suppose that instead of brachiating our remote ancestors left the trees while they were still quadrupeds, like the prosimians and most of the monkeys. When they got to the ground they walked about on all fours, like the macaques and baboons. Before they could acquire long snouts like baboons or bright buttocks like drills, they began, for some reason or other, to stand up and walk like men. As there are intermediate stages of standing and walking erect, our ancestors could have done this gradually, just as other primates are becoming adapted to brachiation gradually, and just as the ancestors of bats must have glided like flying squirrels before they learned to fly.

The Bearing of Hominid Teeth on the Erect Posture

WHETHER they had been brachiating or not, what caused our ancestors to find the erect posture advantageous? The answer may be related to the peculiar form of their teeth.

All primates use their hands for picking food off the stem, off the ground, out of the nest, or wherever, and for peeling, breaking, or otherwise processing it, and for putting it in their mouths. Unlike many other animals, they neither graze nor browse. Flightless birds peck their food with their beaks, and kangaroos bite off theirs with their teeth. Most of the primates, however, have long canines, with which they do a bit of food processing. Holding a tough-skinned fruit in one hand, the monkey or ape will rip off its husk with his canine teeth. With these same canines they fight, if they cannot win by scowling and bluffing. It is in order to succeed at fighting, not to process fruit, that males have longer canines than females.

Like some of the smaller monkeys, the hominids have short canines set in line with their other teeth. Because of this handicap they have to use both hands at once to peel a tough fruit. As this leaves no hands at all for support in the trees, it brings the animal down to the ground. Because of it they are also obliged to use their hands in fighting—and it is difficult to fight with your hands when on all fours. The dental eccentricity of hominids thus favors both life on the ground and life standing up. Our peculiar teeth may not explain all the whys and wherefores of the erect posture and powerful forelimbs of man, but they can easily have influenced this combination.

A Few Details of the Posture Story

THE ANATOMICAL evidence for and against the belief that our ancestors once swung hand over hand in the trees is long and involved and serves the purposes of this book only in documenting the fact that some races seem more arboreally constituted than others. This will be a very short summary of the primate evidence, and man will here be treated temporarily as a homogenous species.

Like most other four-footed animals, the nonbrachiating, subhuman primates hold their vertebral columns horizontally, slinging their internal organs downward from them by the force of gravity. Owing to the usual mechanical predominance of the hind over the forequarters, the vertebral column has a particularly long lumbar and a particularly short thoracic or rib-bearing segment. One vertebra, known as the anticlinal, which is generally the tenth thoracic, acts as the center of a spring. It is the continental divide, so to speak, between the muscles of the hind and fore-quarters; and the dorsal spines of the vertebrae in front of it point backward and those behind it point forward. This arrangement is ideal for jumping, with the bulk of the thrust coming from the rear, as is the case with most other four-footed mammals.

All four limbs are usually flexed; in many species they cannot

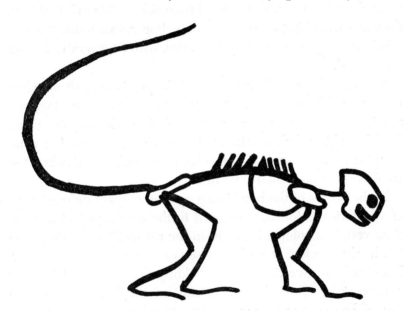

Fig. 5 THE JUMPING SKELETON. A climbing, jumping, quadrupedal primate: the marmoset *Hapale*. Note the dorsal spines of the vertebrae. The ninth thoracic vertebra acts as fulcrum, and its spine points upward. Those in front point backward, those behind point forward. (Drawing after Gregory, 1951.)

be held out perfectly straight at the elbow and knee. But seen from the front and rear each extremity seems to form a straight column, as it does in dogs, cows, and most other quadrupeds, and the two hands and two feet are a considerable distance apart when in motion. The rib cage is oval in horizontal section, with the long axis running from back to front; the thoracic vertebrae are set at or above the upper rib level; the sternum is narrow; and the scapulae are placed alongside the rib cage. The legs are longer and stronger than the arms, and the thumbs are well developed.

Fingerprint ridges of the kind made famous by the F.B.I. completely cover the skin of the palms and soles in the Old World monkeys, whereas in the New World monkeys and prosimians they cover only parts of the surfaces. New World monkeys that hang by the tail have similar ridge patterns on the business surface of that organ as well. In the Old World monkeys the ridge patterns of the palms and soles are simple. Although their hands have considerable mobility, as do the hands of all primates, in the wrist the carpal bones articulate with both radius and ulna, and this prevents them from rocking the hand from side to side as hitchhikers do when thumbing rides. When traveling on all fours, the Old World monkeys place their palms down, with fingers extended, on the ground.

As all monkeys, and even some of the prosimians, sit up when resting or sleeping, the erect posture is habitual when they are not in motion. Consequently the neck is moderately long and flexible and the skull is hafted to the cervical vertebrae in a compromise position, so that the animal can look ahead when the trunk is either horizontal or vertical.

In the bodies of the brachiating apes an entirely different type of adaptation is found. Compared to the quadrupedal monkeys, their vertebral column is longer in the rib section and shorter in the lumbar region. It no longer serves as a spring for jumping, but simply as a vertical rod for holding the body's weight. It is somewhat like a pendulum. As most of the locomotion is performed by the arms, the anticlinal position has moved down about three places, and now is in the first lumbar. The muscles of the shoulder girdle have also advanced downward, and those of the lower extremities have retreated in the same direction. Some of the shoulder muscles now reach down to the rim of the pelvis.

In the monkeys, as in many more primitive vertebrates, the muscles tend to be attached directly to the long bones, which are ridged, lumped, and pitted to receive them. But in the brachiators the same muscles join the bones indirectly through the intermediacy of tendonous sheaths, called aponeuroses, which leave the surfaces of the bones tubelike and smooth. This arrangement greatly increases the mobility of the limbs. Also, the limb muscles have relatively short, fleshy "bellies," as the main bodies of the muscle bundles are called, and relatively long, tough tendons. This combination is best suited to withstand the shock of the whole weight of the falling body as it is caught up short by the muscles of a single arm in brachiating. The shock is further cushioned in heavy adult apes by the laryngeal air sac.

In section the brachiator's rib cage is shaped like a heart without a point at the rear, and flat in front; the ribs arch behind the vertebrae, and the whole enclosure is relatively broad and flat, as is the sternum. The scapulae (shoulder blades) are set behind the rib cage, not beside it. The arms are long and mobile at shoulder and elbow, and the arm can be straightened out completely at the elbow or even bent back, as in the gorilla.

In our own bodies the legs do not form straight columns, dog-

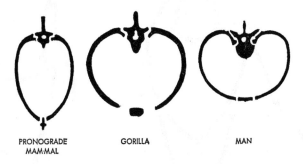

PRONOGRADE   GORILLA   MAN
MAMMAL

Fig. 6 Transverse Rib-cage Sections of Jumpers, Brachiators, and Man. (Drawings 1 and 3 after Hamilton, 1956; drawing 2 after Raven, 1950.)

and monkey-wise, when seen from the front or from behind. Our thighs converge from hip to knee, and our lower legs run parallel to each other from knee to ankle. The angle between the axes of the upper and lower leg portions is called the *carrying angle*. It keeps our trunks from swaying from side to side as we walk. It is an adaptation to the erect posture.

According to the same principle, the apes need a carrying angle at the elbow. Their upper arms converge from the shoulder and their lower arms run parallel to the wrist. When an ape is brachiating, each hand in turn passes directly over his head, and his body is thus kept from swinging back and forth sidewise.

Although they do not walk bipedally, the apes also have carrying angles in their legs. This allows them to bring their feet together in parallel fashion when grasping a straight object, such as the limb of a tree. Although we do not brachiate, we have carrying angles in our arms. This allows our arms to clear our hips, which is particularly useful to women, and it enables us to grasp a straight object with both hands, just as apes do with their feet.

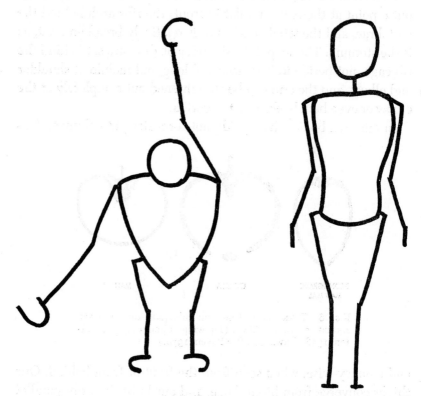

Fig. 7 The Carrying Angle in Apes and Men. The carrying angle is the angle formed at elbow and knee in brachiators and man. In an animal that moves itself with one pair of limbs at a time—arms or legs—this angle is needed to keep the body upright. It is not found in four-footed animals which walk or run with at least one limb of each side on the ground at all times, or when the body is entirely in the air, as in leaping or hopping.

The brachiator's arms are longer than his legs, and his forearm is especially long. His wrist bones articulate with the radius only, and his hand can be rocked sidewise, which is very useful in brachiating. In the three large apes the fingers cannot be straightened out when the wrist is bent forward; this is due to short, strong tendons in the fingers that make the hands into hooks and permit the animal to hang by the hands for long periods without muscle strain.

As a price of brachiation the thumbs of the apes have become short and imperfectly opposable. The great toe, in compensation, is partially opposable except in the mountain gorilla, whose feet are to a certain extent adapted to walking on the ground. In all the apes the ridge patterns of the palms and soles are relatively complicated. When walking on the ground, the three large apes walk on the backs of their fingers; the gibbons do not ordinarily touch their hands to the ground.

The ape skull is hafted more or less as in the Old World monkeys, but owing to the exaggerated weight of the teeth and jaws the neck muscles creep higher on the neck than in most monkeys. The neck itself is short and not very mobile.

The lumbar region of the vertebral column is longer and heavier in man, the bipedal primate, than in the apes. Unlike the comparable structures of either apes or monkeys, his vertebral column has an S curve when seen from the side, and the center of gravity of his body passes through this bony column vertically. His pelvis is relatively short and broad, and his ilium (hip blade) is particularly short. As among the apes, the muscles of his shoulder girdle reach far down the trunk—in some cases to the pelvis—and the muscle attachments tend to be made directly on the bone, as among monkeys.

In the ischium, the most distal and dorsal (hindmost and rearmost) of the three bones that fuse to form the *os coxae,* or pelvic bone, man differs from both monkeys and apes. Because when man walks he jolts his visceral organs downward with each step, his lower pelvic bones must converge inward as far as possible to support them, while still allowing space, in the female, for the birth canal. Between the bones stretches a firm web of ligaments and muscles. If this network fails, the result is a hernia. In the Old World monkeys the pelvic opening points backward, and in the apes the shoulder girdle takes the strain of locomotion and cushions the blows to the viscera.[1]

These differences in locomotor habit have left the Old World

[1] H. O. Elftman: "The Evolution of the Pelvic Floor of Primates," *AJAn,* Vol. 51, No. 2 (1932), pp. 307–46.

monkeys and apes with an ischium that is long and flares outward, whereas in man the ischium is short and bent inward. The
monkeys and gibbons sit on callosites covering the ends of these
bones; in the great apes the lower part of the ischium serves as an
anchor for the *gluteus maximus* muscle, which does not cover it
but extends to the side.[2] In man the *gluteus maximus* covers the
ischium, helping to hold the trunk erect and forming a buttock,
which is unique among primates.

Monkeys do not ordinarily move about bipedally. When apes
do they run to keep from falling forward; they can stand erect
without moving only a very short time, as when a male gorilla is

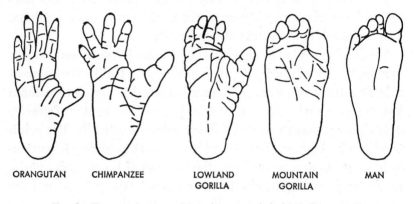

ORANGUTAN   CHIMPANZEE   LOWLAND   MOUNTAIN   MAN
                           GORILLA   GORILLA

Fig. 8   Feet of Apes and Men. (Drawings after Schultz, 1956.)

drumming on his chest. Standing erect continuously and true
walking are exclusively human attributes.

Although man's arms are shorter, relatively, than those of the
apes, they are fully as long, compared to body length, as those of
quadrupedal monkeys. They are also mobile. Like apes' arms,
they too hang at a carrying angle, and their wrist bones also
articulate with the radius alone, allowing the hand to be rocked.
However, the thumb is as long as or longer than the monkey's
thumb. Also, the hand can be extended completely, and the thumb
can be opposed to all four fingers. A baby crawling or walking on
all fours sets the palm of the hand down flat, with fingers extended, just as a monkey does. The palm- and sole-ridge prints

[2] H. C. Raven: *The Anatomy of the Gorilla* (New York: Columbia University
Press; 1950), p. 57 and figures.

are simple, like a monkey's rather than an ape's. The legs are uniquely long. Man has relatively immobile knee and ankle joints, with large, flat-faceted tarsal bones, and a long great toe, in line (when not deformed by shoes) with the other four.

The head of the bipedal primate is hafted more anteriorly than in any other primate. His neck is longer than that of apes, and the animal can look ahead without peering over the tops of his glasses, so to speak, only when he is standing or sitting in an erect position. Probably because his assumption of the erect posture has moved the female genital organ considerably forward, only he and the pygmy chimpanzee among primates copulate ventrally, like the porcupine, who does it for a different and even better reason.[3]

In evaluating these perplexing and somewhat contradictory comparisons we must remember that four closely related families of animals have become adapted to four principal means of locomotion: quadrupedal in trees, quadrupedal on the ground, brachiating, and erect bipedal. This is a wide range for so small a group. In order to achieve this degree of differentiation, the genetic capacities of these families must have been exploited to the utmost by differential growth rates. Neoteny, pedomorphism, and gerontomorphism reach their peak in man and in his close primate kin.

Large brachiating and bipedal primates have several functional requirements in common, one of which is the absence of an external tail. To both, this appendage would be useless, if not an actual hindrance. A large ape is too heavy to hang from one, and a man needs what is left of his to help close his pelvic opening. Its absence in the gibbons suggests that the monkeys which live on the ground have short tails, some mere stubs, because they need no balancing appendage. Its absence among all apes, great and small, suggests that their common ancestors spent a prebrachiating period on the ground, rather than going directly from one kind of arboreal locomotion to the other, as can be postulated in the case of the New World monkeys.

Another similarity between apes and men is the shape of the

---

[3] Other mammals said to do this are the hamster and the two-toed sloth. Bourlière: *The National History of Mammals,* p. 159.

chest. For swinging apes and walking men, a broad, flat rib cage keeps the center of gravity below or above, as the case may be, the focal point of locomotion in the anteroposterior plane, and its greater width is compensated for by the carrying angle of the propelling limbs. Four-legged animals do not have these gravity problems because, unless cantering, galloping, single-footing, or jumping, they have one foot of each side and pair on the ground at all times. Also, in apes and men alike, a broad chest extends the animal's reach and gets in the way least when the arms are busy in brachiation or work. Both apes and men need, and have, dorsally situated scapulas. As to the carrying angle, this is useful in all four limbs to both apes and men, but in opposite ways.

This brief survey does not conclusively indicate whether or not our ancestors brachiated. Even if it did, it would not settle the question of how close we are in descent to either the Old World monkeys or the apes. Other anatomical comparisons favor the apes. All the Old World monkeys have ischial callosites. The gibbons have small ones, and these are also found in roughly a third of the chimpanzees. The orang, the gorilla, and men lack them. The Old World monkeys have two-disc placentas. Men and the apes have single-disc ones. In these features the apes seem to be man's closest primate relatives.

The Evidence of Teeth

M UCH CAN BE learned from the standby of the paleontologists, teeth. Human beings have the same dental formula as both the Old World monkeys and the apes, $\dfrac{2:1:2:3}{2:1:2:3}$, which sets them all apart from the prosimians and platyrrhines. Man also differs from the Cercopithecines on three counts and from the apes in two of these. Both Old World monkeys and apes have a long upper canine, separated from the first upper premolar by a gap. In both, the first lower premolar has a shearing edge. The Old World monkeys alone have bilophodont molars. As man has none of these three dental distinctions, on this score the two groups of Old World primates are closer to each other than either is to man.

The essential feature of hominid dentition is that it enables the hominid to grind the lower against the upper teeth, from side to side and from front to back, instead of just compressing the jaws together ape-wise, up and down. Our method is highly advantageous for an omnivore with carnivorous tendencies as it gives an animal a high masticating efficiency per unit of tooth surface area in reducing coarse food, such as skin, lean raw meat, and tendons, as well as tough roots, into digestible fodder. Thus the reduction of the canines, which seemed at one point a rather infantile and disadvantageous mutation or retention, actually gave the homi-

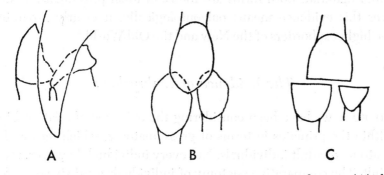

A   **B**   **C**

Fig. 9 Occulusion of Canines in Apes and Hominids. In the apes (A) the upper canine overlaps the lower first premolar and lower canine, and in biting and chewing it touches these teeth, particularly the lower first premolar, against which it grinds a shearing edge. In the hominids (Australopithecus and man) (B), the unworn canine overlaps the same two lower teeth at first, but after they have been worn down to a certain extent by a rotary motion, the points of all three are worn off and all of them have acquired smooth occlusal surfaces (C). As modern, civilized man does not chew enough to arrive at stage C, his teeth may remain at stage B until death.

nids a distinct advantage over other primates who live on the ground and seek the same kind of food, because it permits the teeth to concentrate on one task only, mastication, instead of three, fighting, mastication, and peeling coarse-skinned fruit. The change that made this transformation possible was the release of the hands from the duty of locomotion for the work of fighting off rivals, killing game, peeling and even cutting up food. The teeth of primitive men and of adult fossil hominids are worn flat from chewing, whereas those of apes retain their original cusp patterns for life.[4] Although our teeth are apelike rather than monkey-

[4] Anyone civilized enough to read this book will probably find that he cannot grind his teeth together from side to side because his upper incisors and canines overlap his lower ones. This is not the fault of his genes, but the fault of his parents, who fed him on soft food. He did not have the opportunity to develop his hominid bite.

like, they are really *sui generis* and distinctive, like the erect posture—a hominid hallmark—and we have probably had them for a long time.

In another respect, however, our teeth do resemble those of the apes and Old World monkeys, and incidentally those of the Madagascar lemurs. Seen microscopically, the enamel prisms have straight edges and are separated only by a little insterstitial material. In the platyrrhines, lorises, and tarsiers, the enamel prisms have wavy edges and are separated by larger amounts of interstitial material. Both forms are found in fossil prosimians. Whatever this evidence means paleontologically, it clearly separates the higher suborders of the New and the Old World.[5]

The Evidence of Embryology

S O F A R we have been considering the evidence of relationships within the primates in terms of gross anatomy, which means the anatomy of adult individuals. Not every individual, however, is an adult. The comparative anatomy of individuals aged six years, for example, is also of value, and we can learn a great deal from a comparative study of individuals who have not yet emerged from the womb.

These last were of particular interest to the German zoologist Ernst Haeckel, a contemporary of Darwin, although younger. Deeply moved by Darwin's work, he propounded, in 1866, the *biogenetic law,* also known as the law of *recapitulation,* the theme of which is that *ontogeny recapitulates phylogeny.* This means simply that each one of us, from fertilization to birth, passes successively through the forms of all his ancestors, being in turn amoeba, worm, fry, tadpole, and so on. This recapitulation is said to take place partly in the embryo and partly in the larva, the latter being a grub in the insect world and a tadpole in the amphibian. Among mammals the larva is called a fetus. The embryo becomes a fetus at the stage at which one species can be told from another. In man this occurs at about the beginning of the ninth week.

[5] C. T. Regan: "The Classification of the Primates," *Nature,* Vol. 125, No. 3143 (1930), pp. 125–6.

Like many other laws and rules of the nineteenth century, Haeckel's has been variously supported and attacked. In its literal sense it has been generally repudiated, but the fact remains that it is true in essence, for organisms *do* repeat ancestral forms, within certain limitations.

Each organism goes through a series of the corresponding embryonic forms of its ancestors, not of the adult forms. For reasons of economy, some stages may be skipped entirely, as in certain limbless amphibians which, although descended from four-legged ancestors, have no trace of limbs at any embryonic stage. This particular omission can be explained by neoteny, already discussed in Chapter 1. In addition, certain structures needed for survival during larval or fetal life, but of no use later, appear at that time only, without reference to general recapitulation. An example is the twig-mimicking larval form of certain caterpillars destined to grow into moths.

The sequence of developmental stages of each structure follows the evolutionary order, with or without omissions, but different structures do not necessarily keep to a single timetable. The fact that feature X reaches a more or less adult functional form at the end of fetal life whereas feature Y is still quite retarded, relatively speaking, at time of birth does not mean that X evolved earlier in the ancestral phylogeny than Y did. A fetus has immediate postnatal survival requirements of its own and only so much uterine space to develop in, and therefore prepares itself primarily for urgent needs that arise at birth. Some of the structures with lower priorities are left to complete their growth afterward, just as soldiers about to go into battle clean and load their weapons first, rather than shaving, or polishing their boots.

A fawn and a colt are born with long legs on which they can run closely behind their mothers' tails a few minutes after birth if the mother is disturbed. A newborn gibbon, which does not yet need to brachiate but needs immediately to cling tightly to its mother's fur and to stay there until after it has been weaned, is born with strong fingers and short forearms, which grow long thereafter. By the same token, a human baby, who does not need a big brain in the cradle but would have a hard time passing an oversized head through its mother's pelvic opening, is born with a head even smaller than that of an orang. Like a gibbon's forearm, the baby's brain grows prodigiously after birth and is ready for action when needed.

Schultz once compared twenty-one features in three series of fetuses of Old World monkeys, apes, and men. He considered only diameters, which he painstakingly measured, and proportions, which he calculated, at the beginning of fetal life, at what corresponds to the sixth prenatal month in man, and at full term. He found an extraordinary similarity between the three groups, and some differences.[6]

The catarrhine primates, including Old World monkeys, apes, and men, are gradually transformed in the fetal stage from a compactly packaged embryo to a more regionally differentiated organism. However, the forearm length of monkeys and apes is prenatally more nearly adult than in man because monkeys and

---

[6] A. Schultz: "Fetal Growth of Man and Other Primates," *QBB*, Vol. 1, No. 4 (1926), pp. 465–521.

Twelve features of all three develop more or less the same way and at the same rates, as follows. Chest circumference decreases relative to trunk height. Hip breadth relative to trunk height increases. Hip breadth relative to shoulder breadth increases. The position of the umbilicus moves higher on the trunk. Upper-limb length relative to trunk height increases until the sixth month and then decreases. Lower-leg length relative to thigh length increases. Hand breadth relative to hand length and foot breadth relative to foot length both decrease. Thumb length relative to hand length decreases. Average diameter of head relative to trunk height decreases. Nose breadth relative to face breadth decreases. Interocular breadth (distance between the inner eye corners) relative to face breadth decreases.

The development of four of the features takes the same direction in all three samples, but the monkey and ape fetuses change faster than man's do. These changes are as follows. Forearm length relative to upper-arm length increases. Total face height relative to head height increases. Upper-face height relative to face breadth increases. Nose breadth relative to nose height decreases.

In two features the direction is the same in all three samples, but man changes the faster, as follows. The upper-limb length relative to lower-limb length decreases. The lower-limb length relative to trunk height increases until the sixth month and then decreases.

In two features the monkeys and apes form a bloc, differing from man in the direction of change at least in part of the fetal cycle. Whereas in man the nipples migrate lower down on his chest until the sixth month and then move up again, the nipples of monkeys and apes move higher constantly. Man's head grows narrower in proportion to its length, but the heads of monkeys and apes retain a constant proportion or grow broader.

In only one feature does man split the simian bloc. In the apes and in man, the chest grows broader compared to its depth. In the monkeys it does the opposite.

apes need their forearms for locomotion. Also their face length is more nearly adult prenatally because they need to chew earlier than man does. On the other hand, man exceeds both monkeys and apes in the early growth of the lower limbs, which must be long for walking erect. The chests of both apes and men, unlike those of the monkeys, undergo a prenatal broadening and flattening which anticipates both brachiation and bipedal walking, neither of which need be derived from the other, on this evidence. In other words, the measurement of fetuses fails to tell us whether or not man's ancestors brachiated. Were we, indeed, to judge

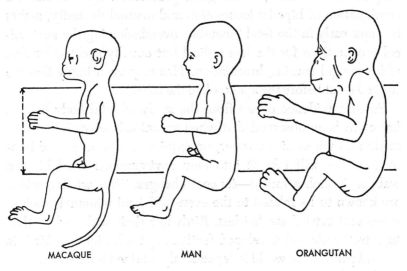

MACAQUE   MAN   ORANGUTAN

Fig. 10 Body Proportions of Newborn Primates. Note that the orangutan is born with the largest head. (Drawings after Schultz, 1926.)

from this evidence alone, we could not even be sure that apes do.

Some of Schultz's morphological observations are more helpful. The human thumb, which starts out in line with the fingers, begins very early in fetal life to rotate until it comes to rest at a 90° angle to the axis of the fingers. At the same time its place of origin, in the same knuckle line as the other digits, moves wristward. In the Old World monkeys and apes the process of rotation and migration begins later and the rotation is less complete. The human thumb remains long, whereas the thumb of the monkey and the ape does not grow as long, particularly in the apes.

In the foot of monkeys and apes a comparable rotation and migration occurs, but it does not in the human fetus. In the other primates the longest toe is usually the third, whereas in man the first or second eventually becomes the longest. In 4 to 5 per cent of human fetuses at the beginning of the third month, however, the third toe is still the longest. In both the hand and the foot, therefore, differences in the rate of growth of the digits and in the timing of the rotation of thumb and big toe separate the human fetus from those of the other two categories of Old World primates. To say that one is more fetalized than the other is an oversimplification. Rather, man's great precultural specialization, a combination of bipedal locomotion and manual dexterity, makes its mark early in the fetal timetable, overshadowing the anatomical preparations for the less radical but equally spectacular feat of his pongid cousins, brachiation. This may even imply that we walked erect before the apes took to the trees.

Further evidence comes from the study of fetal body hair. It has often been observed that when an animal moves into a new medium, such as air or water, or acquires a new means of locomotion that will take it into new environments—and bipedal walking is such a means—its coat changes. Thus whales, which are known to be related to the even-toed land mammals such as sheep and cattle,[7] are hairless. Birds lost their scales when they took to the air and developed feathers instead; flightless birds in several parts of the world independently retained fetal down.

The arboreal primates preserve the primitive mammalian hair coat that some of the monkeys living on the ground have partly lost; and man, with his new means of locomotion that takes him even farther afield than macaques, has a coat as fetal as those of ostriches, probably because, in a wide variety of climates, particularly in hot, open sun, a nearly hairless body suits our thermal requirements better than a hairy one does. Bolk indicates that in the fetal life of four selected primates the following series of coat reductions can be seen.[8] Monkeys are born completely covered with hair, as in the adult form. In the gibbon, the head and back

---

[7] P. A. Moody: *An Introduction to Evolution* (New York: Harper and Brothers; 1953), pp. 103–13.

[8] P. R. de Beer: *Embryos and Ancestors* (London: Oxford University Press; 1951), p. 58.

L. Bolk: *Das Problem der Menschenwerdung* (Jena: Fischer Verlag; 1926).

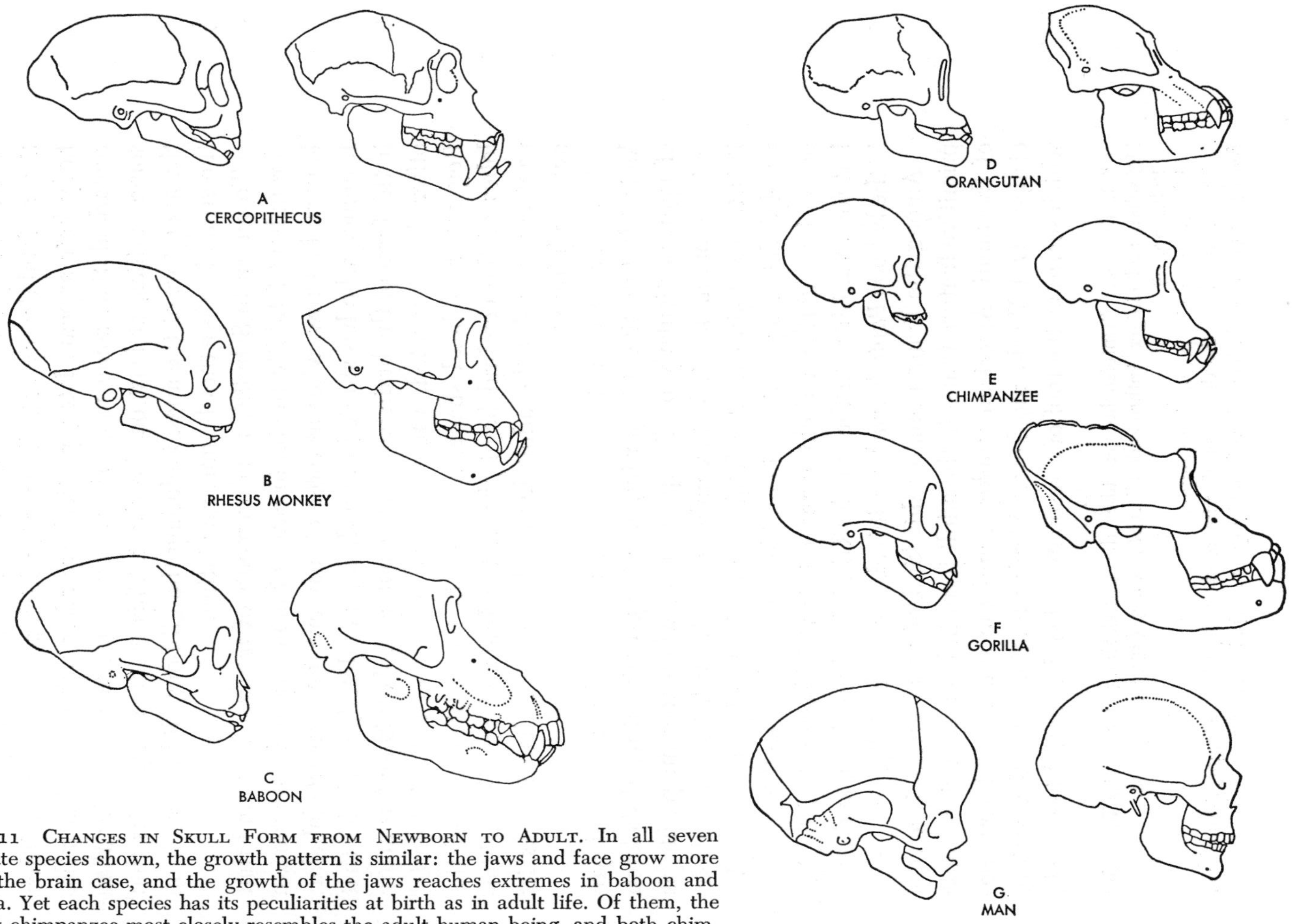

Fig. 11 Changes in Skull Form from Newborn to Adult. In all seven primate species shown, the growth pattern is similar: the jaws and face grow more than the brain case, and the growth of the jaws reaches extremes in baboon and gorilla. Yet each species has its peculiarities at birth as in adult life. Of them, the infant chimpanzee most closely resembles the adult human being, and both chimpanzee and gorilla have a humanlike nasal profile at birth, which they lose later in

A
CERCOPITHECUS

B
RHESUS MONKEY

C
BABOON

D
ORANGUTAN

E
CHIMPANZEE

F
GORILLA

G.
MAN

are covered with hair and the rest grows out after birth. In the gorilla, only the head is covered and the rest grows out later. In man also only the head is covered, although there may be a retention of fetal downy hair (lanugo), which soon disappears. Other body hair appears later, particularly after puberty. Schultz has remarked that some men of his acquaintance are hairier than some gorillas, at least on the chest. This evidence suggests that the ancestors of the apes, including the gibbons, did a stretch on the ground before they began brachiating.

To return to Schultz's measurements of fetuses: he found that throughout fetal life the brain cases of monkeys and apes remain long and narrow, whereas those of man are much more globular. Kummer, who has studied these changes in detail, concludes that in the form of the brain case man is not, as Bolk said and as many others have repeated, a fetalized ape but a creature *sui generis*.[9] Regardless of head shape, however, in the relative size of the lobes of the cerebral hemispheres the brain of the fetal chimpanzee resembles the adult human brain more than it does its own adult form.[1]

Kummer's excellent drawings bring out still another embryological fact pertinent to our inquiry: the prominent nasal skeleton of man, particularly of European man, when seen in profile, is not a gerontomorphic feature unless excessively developed. Rather, it is to a certain extent a fetal feature. In the human fetus the nasal skeleton is prominent in profile from at least the third month on. In both gorilla and chimpanzee it is visible early in fetal life but soon vanishes. In the smaller Old World monkeys, and even in the baboon *Papio hamadryas,* it is also present fetally.

Among the living primates this kind of nasal profile is a very primitive feature found in the adult form in lemurs, tarsiers, most of the South American monkeys, and the smaller and less specialized Old World monkeys.[2] Man's prominent nasal skeleton, which serves as the roof of a resonance chamber useful in speech,

[9] B. Kummer: "Untersuchungen über die Entwicklung der Schädelform des Menschen und einiger Anthropoiden," *AEB,* No. 3 (1953), pp. 1–44.

Bolk: op. cit.

[1] de Beer: op. cit., p. 58, after Coupin.

[2] See particularly the drawings of primate skulls in W. K. Gregory: *Evolution Emerging* (New York: The Macmillan Company; 1951), Vol. II.

is thus an ancient primate possession, part of the precatarrhine complex. In so far as man retains it for a new purpose, he is less catarrhine than the Old World monkeys and apes. As we shall see later, some living human races are more catarrhine than others in this respect. We cannot, therefore, call a flattish nasal skeleton pedomorphic.

Differences in Postnatal Growth

A s o u r s t u d y of fetal differences in primates has been pushing us steadily past the zero hour of parturition, let us consider postnatal growth, to round out the picture. Among the insects there is no problem. Cinderella-like, the transition from larval to adult life is an abrupt one: what was at last view a hairy, crawling grub suddenly takes wing as a beautiful butterfly, as large and perfect as it will ever be. Among the mammals no such dramatic transformation takes place. An attenuated postnatal growth period is in many ways an open-air prolongation of fetal life, lasting anywhere from a few weeks in some tiny rodents to twenty years in elephants and men. It lasts three years in the prosimians, seven in the Old World monkeys, nine in the gibbon, and eleven in the anthropoid apes.

In this postnatal growth period most of the differences between monkeys, apes, and men which in the womb were so elusive now take shape and assume proper proportions. The colobus's thumb, barely present at birth, remains a button or shrinks from sight; the gibbon's forearm grows mightily. No sooner are the great apes' milk teeth all in place than the huge permanent teeth follow, crowding them out; and the jaw early assumes its massive form. Man's teeth pursue a more leisurely sequence, waiting for the brain to reach nearly adult size before the permanent set begins to erupt, at the age of five or six.

In the monkeys and apes the sutures of the skull close not long after birth. This closing does not halt the brain's growth, but it signifies that the brain has itself ceased growing. In man the sutures do not close until much later, around the age of thirty. When, by some genetic accident, the sutures close early in man, the result can be a microcephalic idiot.

Probably the most human characteristic of man's development is not so much his posture or his brain as the fact that from birth to belated maturity it takes six times as many calories of food per kilogram of adult weight to build a man as to nurture any ordinary mammal to adulthood.[3] Man, then, is the most expensive of all animals to rear. Hence, the need of special techniques to obtain extra calories must have placed an early premium, and a survival value, on culture, which in turn depends on superior locomotion and brain power. The effects on language, the family, and technology are self-evident.

Biochemical Clues to Our Relationships with Other Primates

COMPARATIVE ANATOMY and the study of prenatal and postnatal fetal growth are not the only approaches to taxonomic relationships between primates. Scientists working with microscopes and test tubes have disclosed a set of physiological similarities and differences which are equally valuable, and usually quite technical. New information is becoming available so rapidly that only a specialist can keep up with it. I know, at the time of writing, of nine biochemical tests that relate man to other primates. The first two concern the urine, the others the blood.

(1) *Purine Metabolism.* Man resembles the apes and differs from the other primates.[4]

[3] M. Rubner: *Das Problem der Lebensdauer und seiner Beziehung zum Wachstum* (Munich and Berlin, 1908), after de Beer.

[4] Purine is a crystalline compound ($C_5H_4N_4$), the parent of other compounds of the uric acid group. All the primates in which purine metabolism has been studied, except man and the apes, carry the oxidation of purine through the uric acid stage to that of allantoin, which is excreted in the urine. In man and the apes, the process stops with the production of uric acid, only about half of which is passed in the urine, the other half circulating in the blood stream. This trait is also found in one breed of dog, the Dalmatian; there it has been traced to the recessive allele of a single gene. The circulation of uric acid in the blood stream is said to have a stimulating effect, like that of caffein, on the physiology of the brain. This explanation is flattering to humans and apes, but it is not supported by the inclusion of the Dalmatian, whose intelligence does not surpass that of other breeds.

W. L. Straus, Jr.: "Urine of Anthropoid Apes," *Science*, Vol. 124 (1956), p. 435.

W. C. O. Hill: *Man's Ancestry* (Springfield, Illinois: Charles C Thomas; 1955), p. 87.

(2) *The Rate of Excretion of Five Amino Acids in the Urine.*
Adult human beings differ from apes, but human infants resemble
them in this trait. No data is available for other primates.[5]

(3) *ABO Blood Groups.* Man resembles the apes, particularly
the chimpanzee, and differs from the macaques.[6]

S. M. Gartler, I. L. Firscheim, and T. Dobzhansky: "A Chromatographic Investigation of Urinary Amino Acids in the Great Apes," *AJPA*, Vol. 14, No. 1
(1956), pp. 41–58.

De W. Stetten, Jr.: "Gout and Metabolism," *SA*, Vol. 198, No. 6 (1958),
pp. 73–81.

[5] In the rate of excretion of five amino acids in the urine, all four apes, including the gibbon, show marked differences from man. Man excretes much more
creatinine and histidine than apes, but apes exceed man in glutamic acid, aspartic
acid, and beta-alanine. Since human infants resemble adult apes in the excretory
ratio of glutamic acids, aspartic acid, and creatinine, it is conceivable that compared to the apes man is gerontomorphic in these physiological processes. However, no reports are available to date on the excretion of these substances in other
primates, so we cannot use this test for a three-way comparison between man,
apes, and monkeys. But this study does serve to line man up in one taxonomic
camp and all four apes in another. Among ape genera, lesser differences may be
seen. Chimpanzees excrete more histidine than the others, gorillas more aspartic
and glutamic acids, and beta-alanine. In the largest nonhuman primate sample
studied, that of thirty-seven chimpanzees, individual variation was seen to be as
great as in man, which is also true of many other chimpanzee traits.

Gartler et al: op. cit.

[6] The ABO blood groups are found in the Old World monkeys and apes as
well as in man. In man and all apes except the gorilla all the substances are
carried in the blood itself. In the gorilla the anti-A substance is carried in the
blood and the anti-B in the salivary glands. Both substances are carried in the
urine. In the Old World monkeys the substances are present only in body fluids
and other tissues, but not in the blood.

The chimpanzee has both groups O and A, and the A is neither A_1 nor A_2, as
found in most human beings, but a third type called $A_{1,2}$ (Wiener & Gordon,
1960). This is also found in man, most frequently in Negroes, rarely in Caucasoids, and never in Mongoloids. The mountain gorilla has only group A; the lowland gorilla only group B, and the B substance is different from its human
counterpart. Both orangs and gibbons have A, B, and AB. Among the monkeys
the rhesus (*Macaca mulata*) has only B (Büchi, 1953), but the macaque of
Java (*Macaca irius*) has A, B, and AB.

All thirteen chimpanzees studied for the secretor trait, which is associated
with the ABO system, were found to have it.

P. B. Candela, A. S. Wiener, and L. J. Goss: "New Observations on the Blood
Group Factors in Simiidi and Cercopithecidae," *Zoologica*, Vol. 25, No. 4 (1940),
pp. 513–21.

E. C. Büchi: "A Rhesus Monkey with B Agglutinogen," *Nature*, Vol. 172
(1953), p. 873.

S. D. and L. J. Lawler: *Human Blood Groups and Inheritance* (Cambridge,
Mass.: Harvard University Press; 1957), p. 82.

A. S. Wiener and E. B. Gordon: "The Blood Groups of Chimpanzees, ABO
Groups and MN Types," *AJPA*, Vol. 18, No. 4 (1960), pp. 301–11.

(4) *MN Blood Groups.* Man resembles the chimpanzee more closely than other primates.[7]

(5) *Precipitin Test.* Man is identical with the chimpanzee, resembles Old World monkeys to a recognizable extent, and shows no kinship to the New World monkeys or the prosimians.[8]

(6) *Serum Albumin and Serum Gamma Globulin.* Tests were made on man, gibbon, macaque, mandrill, and marmoset. In these characteristics man resembles the gibbon most, the macaque and mandrill next (and equally), and the marmoset least.[9]

---

[7] Both the apes and the Old World monkeys have the M antigen of the MN series, but in the three major groups, man, apes, and Old World monkeys, this M substance varies in chemical composition. That closest to man is found in the chimpanzee, which is also the only subhuman primate known to have the N antigen.

However, when Wiener and Gordon tested thirteen chimpanzees for M and N, they found all to be MN; not one was MM or NN. Such a distribution would be impossible in man, because we inherit this trait in Mendelian fashion, and therefore only 50 per cent of any series could be MN. The chimpanzee type of MN must therefore be inherited differently. Chemically only half the chimpanzees tested had the human type of N substance. The others had a type specific for chimpanzees.

Wiener and Gordon also tested the same chimpanzees, and one dead animal, for an anti-U factor, related to the MN system. All fourteen lacked it. It is present in the blood of all Caucasoids tested but absent in some Negroes. The same authors also point out a similarity in the reaction to a certain Rhesus antigen (Rh-Hr) between the bloods of chimpanzees and Negroes. They interpret these Negro-chimpanzee similarities ($A_{1,2}$, anti-U, and Rh-Hr) as parallel mutations suited to the African environment.

Lawler and Lawler: op. cit.

Weiner and Gordon: op. cit.

[8] In the precipitin test a rabbit is immunized with small doses of human blood. The serum from this rabbit's blood is used, largely by the police, to identify human blood. If the rabbit serum is mixed with human serum, a precipitate is formed. Some cloudiness is produced if the rabbit serum is mixed with chimpanzee serum, less cloudiness if mixed with serum from the Old World monkeys, and no reaction is seen at all when it is mixed with the sera of New World monkeys or lemurs.

Hill: op. cit., p. 8.

P. Kramp: "Serologische Stammbauforschung," *Primatologia,* Vol. 1 (Basel: S. Karger: 1956), pp. 1015–34.

[9] A refinement of the precipitin test involves the comparison of rabbit and chick antisera with the serum albumin and serum gamma globulin of various mutually related species. Goodman has compared, in this fashion, the gibbon, macaque, mandrill marmoset, and man. His experiments have placed us closest, of these four animals, to the gibbon. Next come the macaque and mandrill, about equally close. Our kinship to the marmoset is traceable but most distant.

M. Goodman: "The Species Specificity of Proteins as Observed in the Wilson Comparative Analyses Plates," *AN,* Vol. 94, No. 875 (1960), pp. 184–6.

(7) *Hemoglobins, Haptoglobins, and Serum Transferrins.* Man and apes resemble each other, and the Old World monkeys are radically different from both.[1]

(8) *Whole Globulin Molecules.* Man is almost indistinguishable from chimpanzee and gorilla. Of the other primates only the orang was tested.[2]

(9) *Gamma Globulin, Gm Group.* Man is closer to the chimpanzee than to the gibbon, Old World monkeys, or New World monkeys.[3]

In these nine tests man's biochemical relationship to apes was explored. In six tests man was compared to Old World monkeys, in three to New World monkeys, and in one to prosimians. Man is shown to be closely related to the apes—more closely to the chimpanzee than to either the gorilla or the orang. The gibbon is more distant from man than the other apes are. Man's relationships to the other primates are even more distant.

Until further data is available, we may consider the order of

[1] In a paper delivered before the American Association of Physical Anthropologists on May 12, 1960, J. Buettner-Janusch reported on work in progress on *Hemoglobins, Haptoglobins, and Serum Transferrins of a Number of Old World Primates.* Apparently serum haptoglobins are the same in all primates studied, in that there are three types identical in each population, including prosimians: two homozygotes and a heterozygote. However, differences are found in the serum-transparent beta globulins, which are governed by eight or nine alleles. The beta globulins differ from species to species, and even within bands of a single species (baboons). The pattern seen in the Old World monkeys is radically different from that in apes and man. At the time of writing, Buettner-Janusch is engaged in extensive research on this and similar physiological comparisons between primates. As the beta-globulin test discloses differences among populations within a species, it should be useful for racial studies in man.

[2] In a paper delivered before the American Chemical Society on September 18, 1960, Emile Zuckerkandl stated that the patterns of whole hemoglobin molecules differ among animal species in accordance with their evolutionary relationships. "The hemoglobin patterns of man and eleven adult animals were analyzed, including the gorilla, chimpanzee, orangutan. . . . 'The . . . technique shows that man's hemoglobin is almost indistinguishable from that of the gorilla and chimpanzee,' Dr. Zuckerkandl said." (*The New York Times,* September 18, 1960.)

[3] S. H. Boyer and W. J. Young examined the gamma globulin (Gm) of 24 chimpanzees, 2 gibbons, 25 baboons, 2 rhesus monkeys, 2 spider monkeys, 1 red (?) monkey, 4 cows, and 5 mongrel dogs. Only the chimpanzee serum inhibited any of several Gm type reactions. Chimpanzee sera, like those of man, are polymorphic, and in both species the GM phenotype is not associated with gamma globulin concentration. In these three respects the chimpanzee of all animals studied is closest to man.

S. H. Boyer and W. J. Young: "Gamma Globulin (Gm Group) Heterogeneity in Chimpanzees," *Science,* Vol. 133, No. 3452 (1961), pp. 583–4.

resemblance between man and the pongids, in this characteristic, to be: chimpanzee, gorilla, orang. Man is closer to the gibbon that to the Old World monkeys, and closer to the latter than to either the New World monkeys or the prosimians. For what it is worth, these tests relate us more closely to the African pongids than to any other primates yet tested.

Parasites and Primates

S T I L L A N O T H E R test of man's kinship to his fellow primates involves mutual parasites, internal and external. Chimpanzees can serve as hosts for malaria and can be given syphilis in a mild form. This disease can also be given to baboons; it is even milder in them and soon disappears. The chimpanzee can also be given yaws. In Ruanda-Urundi the mountain gorilla can have an intestinal parasite in common with man. These comparisons are suggestive, but their validity is weakened by the versatility of disease organisms: trichinosis, for example, may pass from pigs to bears.

However, external parasites are different. Owing to an extreme biochemical specialization, a particular kind of louse, for example, can live only on its habitual host or on another genetically very close. The application of this principle to birds led to the discovery that flamingoes, despite their long legs and specialized beaks, are really ducks. Pursuing this line of evidence, we discover that body lice of the genus *Pediculus* exist on man and the chimpanzee. The Old World monkeys are infested with lice of another genus, *Pedicinus,* and the New World monkeys, lorises, and lemurs have one other genus each.[4] Aside from *Pediculus humanus* on his head and body, man supports a louse of another genus, *Phthirus pubis,* in the neighborhood of his genitals, and the gorilla has a louse of the same genus but of a different species, *P. gorillae,* around and about his private parts. No other species of *Phthirus* has been found.[5]

[4] Hill: op. cit., pp. 8–10.
[5] H. Levene and T. Dobzhansky: "Possible Genetic Difference. . . ."
R. R. Gates: *Human Genetics* (New York: The Macmillan Co.; 1946), Vol. 2, pp. 1419–21.

The Comparison of Primate Chromosomes

T H E   S T U D Y of chromosomes is a useful and relatively new tool of taxonomy. So far as we know, chromosomes are not influenced by environment except in mutations. Also, in a few species, it has been possible to equate chromosome micro-anatomy with the gross anatomy and functions of the whole organism.

Most cells are either *haploid* or *diploid*. In a haploid cell there is only one set of chromosomes. At least in primates, only sperm cells and unfertilized egg cells are haploid. Diploid cells have two sets of paired chromosomes. Fertilized egg cells and somatic cells—the ordinary cells of the body—are normally diploid. The diploid figure is commonly used to indicate the number of chromosomes in the cells of an animal.

The number of chromosomes per nucleus in each species is virtually constant. In normal human beings only about 1 per cent of the diploid cells vary from the number 46.[6] The numbers 45, 47, and 48 occur principally in hermaphrodites, persons congenitally lacking sexual parts, and others suffering from certain hereditary diseases. These deviations are principally concerned with the sex chromosomes. Similar individual variations have also been observed in other primates.[7]

With these exceptions, the number of chromosomes is constant within a species and often so within related species. Unless it is the same, animals cannot produce healthy, fertile offspring. If two or more supposed subspecies can be shown to have different normal chromosome counts, then they are separate species. For example, in the Brown lemur, *Lemur fulvus*, counts of 60, 52, and 48 chromosomes have been made on three populations classified as subspecies (see Table 2).

Within the order of primates, counts made to date range from 72 to 34. We cannot assign segments of this range to special families or subfamilies because each family or subfamily so far

[6] J. H. Tjio and T. T. Puck: "The Somatic Chromosomes of Man," *PNAS*, Vol. 44, No. 12 (1958).

[7] E. H. Y. Chu and B. A. Swomley: "Chromosomes of Lemurine Lemurs," *Science*, Vol. 137, No. 3468 (1960).

studied in which more than one or two species are represented shows a wide range of its own. As is true among other kinds of animals, within each subfamily the chromosome count is highest in the simplest, most generalized species, and lowest in those most specialized. Man, with 46 chromosomes, lies a little below the middle of the primate range. Of the 72 species studied, 35 have more chromosomes than man, 8 have the same number, and 29 have fewer. Man has the same number as certain species of lemurs, marmosets, and cebus monkeys, to which he is not particularly related; only the number 42 is as common as 46. On the basis of the chromosome count it cannot be said that man is closer to the chimpanzee, gorilla, and orang, who have 48 each, than to the macaques and baboons, who have 42.

Raw numbers of chromosomes cannot be used on a simple, linear scale to indicate taxonomic relationships because chromosomes tend to combine as the animals become increasingly specialized. The individual chromosomes in a single cell vary greatly in length. In man the autosomal chromosomes (all but the sex chromosomes X and Y) vary from 1.8 to 9.6 per cent of their combined length, or more than five to one. The total length of all the chromosomes in a cell seems to be a more useful figure than their number.

Chromosomes also vary in the position of their centromeres. A centromere is a specialized segment of a chromosome which acts both as an adhesive and as a repellent. It is the junction point of the two strands of which the chromosome is composed at certain stages. When the chromosome splits in cell division the centromeres act as the foci of separation.[8]

If the centromere is located more or less in the middle of a chromosome, that chromosome is called *metacentric*. If it comes at about the three-quarter point, so that the arms on the two ends are of unequal length, that chromosome is *subterminal*. If the centromere is set at the very end of the chromosome, the latter is *telocentric* (or *acrocentric*).[9]

---

[8] For details, see any standard textbook on elementary genetics.

[9] The thresholds between these categories seem to be arbitrary. Tjio and Puck have invented a ratio by which the categories can be standardized—the length of the long arm divided by that of the short arm. The figures range from 1.08 to 10.5.

Geneticists have devised a means of illustrating the relative sizes and shapes of the chromosomes for any species. They line up one each of the autosomal chromosomes according to size and relative arm length, and also show both sex chromosomes. Such a chart is called a *karyotype* (see plate XXI). In the human karyotype none of the autosomal chromosomes are telocentric. The male sex chromosome Y may or may not have a very short second arm. Two chromosomes, Numbers 18 and 21, have curious-looking antennae.

At any rate, two telocentric chromosomes can combine into one metacentric unit by joining end to end. By this process the number of chromosomes can be reduced in one of several closely related species. Thus, for example, the goat (*Capra sp.*) has 60 paired chromosomes, all telocentric. The sheep (*Ovis sp.*) has 54, of which 48 are telocentric and 6 metacentric. Apparently 12 telocentric chromosomes of their common ancestor became fused into 6 metacentric ones to produce the sheep.[1] Nevertheless, these two animals are so similar anatomically that a mammalian anatomist can hardly tell their bones apart, or even their teeth. Yet the two genera cannot interbreed. Most human anatomists can tell at least the skulls of human races apart; yet all human beings are members of a single species and can interbreed. If in our survey of the primate chromosome patterns we find two genera of monkeys or apes with different chromosome numbers, we must seek further data before deciding on degrees of affinity.

Bender and Mettler suggest that the original number of chromosomes for the primates was about 70 (presently the maximum is 72), all being small telocentrics, and that this number has been reduced by combination.

So far chromosomes are no more useful taxonomically, in the sense of indicating genetic affinity, than a host of other characteristics, but they may become so. Fruit-fly specialists have been able to assign special functions to individual segments of individ-

---

The authors arrange these in four categories: median = 0–1.30; submedian = 1.31–3.13; subterminal = 3.13–10.50. According to this system, man has 6 median, 22 submedian, and 16 subterminal pairs. None are terminal.

[1] S. Makino: "The Chromosome Complexes in Goat (*Capra hircus*) and Sheep (*Ovis aries*), and their Relationship," Chromosome Studies in Domestic Mammals, II, *Cytologia*, Vol. 13, No. 1 (1943), pp. 39–54.

TABLE 2

NUMBERS OF CHROMOSOMES AMONG
THE PRIMATES*

Diploid Chromosome Numbers				
Subfamily *Species*	*Source*	*Common Name*	*Number*	
Tupaiinae				
Urogale everetti	D	Philippine tree shrew	26 (?)	
Lemurinae				
Lemur mongoz	C&S	Mongoose lemur	60	
Lemur fulvus rufus	C&S	Brown lemur	60	
Lemur fulvus sp. nov.	C&S	Brown lemur	52	
Lemur fulvus fulvus	C&S	Brown lemur	48	
Lemur albifrons	C&S	Black lemur	60	
Lemur catta	C&S	Ring-tailed lemur	56	
Lemur variegatus	C&S	Ruffed lemur	48	
Lemur variegatus (subspecies)	C&S	Ruffed lemur	46	
Lemur macaca	C&B	Black lemur	44	
Hapalemur griseus olivaceus	C&S	Grey gentle lemur	58	
Hapalemur griseus griseus	C&S	Grey gentle lemur	54	
Microcebus murinus	B&C	Miller's mouse lemur	66	
Lorisinae				
Periodictius potto	C&B	Potto	62	
Nycticebus cougang	B&M	Slow loris	50	
Galaginae				
Galago crassicaudatus	C&B	Thick-tailed bush baby	62	
Galago senegalensis	Mat	Lesser bush baby	38	
Callithricinae				
Callithrix chrysoleucos	C&B	Golden marmoset	46	
Callithrix jaccus	Ch	Common marmoset	46 (?)	
Leontocebus illigeri	B&M†	Red-mantled tamarin	46	
Callimiconinae				
Callimico goeldii	C&B	Goeldi's marmoset	48	
Cebinae				
Cebus sp.	P	Ringtail monkey	54	
Aotus trivirgatus	C&B	Owl-faced monkey	54	

Symbol	*Author and Title*
YPY	C. H. Yeager, T. S. Painter and R. M. Yerkes: "The Chromosomes of the Chimpanzee," *Science*, Vol. 91, No. 2351 (1940), pp. 74–5.
C&G	Chu and N. H. Giles: "A Study of Monkey Chromosome Components," *AJPA* Proceedings, 1957, Abstract 70, pp. 452–3.
B&M	M. A. Bender and L. E. Mettler: "Chromosome Studies of Primates," *Science*, Vol. 128, No. 3317 (1958), pp. 186–90.
T&P	Tjio and Puck: op. cit., pp. 1229–37.
YMFJ	Young, T. Merz, M. A. Ferguson-Smith, and A. W. Johnston: "Chromosome Numbers of the Chimpanzee, *Pan troglodytes*," *Science*, Vol. 131, No. 3414 (1960), pp. 1672–3.
C&S	Chu and Swomley: op. cit., pp. 1925–6.
HFD	J. L. Hamerton, M. Fracatto, L. Decarli, F. Nuzzo, H. P. Klinger, L. Hulliger, A. Taylor, and E. M.

TABLE 2

NUMBERS OF CHROMOSOMES AMONG
THE PRIMATES*

Diploid Chromosome Numbers

Subfamily Species	Source	Common Name	Number
Cebus apella	B&M	Cinnamon ringtail	54
Cebus capucinus	B&M	Capuchin ringtail	54
Pithecia pithecia	B&M†	Saki	46 (?)
Cacajao rubicundus	B&M†	Uakari	46 (?)
Alouatta seniculus	B&M†	Red howler monkey	44 (?)
Callicebus cupreus	B&M	Red titi	46
Saimiri sciureus	B&M	Squirrel monkey	44
Ateles geoffroyi	B&M	Hooded spider monkey	34
Ateles paniscus chamek	B&M	Black-faced spider monkey	34
Ateles belzebuth	B&M	Golden spider monkey	34
Ateles arachnoides	Ch	Woolly spider monkey	34 (?)
Lagothrix ubericola	B&C	Brown woolly monkey	62
Cercopithecinae			
Cercopithecus l'Hoesti	C&B	l'Hoest's guenon	72
Cercopithecus mona mona	B&M	Mona guenon	66
Cercopithecus mona denti	Tap	Guenon	66 (?)
Cercopithecus mona campbelli	C&G	Campbell's guenon	66
Cercopithecus aethiops sabaeus	C&G	African green monkey	60
Cercopithecus aethiops tantalus	C&G	African white monkey	60
Cercopithecus diana	C&G	Diana monkey	60
Cercopithecus neglectus	Tap	De Brassa's guenon	60 (?)
Cercopithecus nictitans	C&G	White or spot-nosed guenon	66
Cercopithecus cephus	Ch	Mustached guenon	54 (?)
Erythrocebus patas	C&G	Patas monkey	54
Cercocebus torquatus torquatus	B&M	Sooty mangabey	42
Cercocebus torquatus lunulatus	C&G	White-crowned mangabey	42
Cercocebus albigena	Tap	Grey-cheeked mangabey	42
Cercocebus galeritus	Tap	Crested mangabey	42(?)
Macaca mulata	D&H	Rhesus macaque	42
Macaca irius	C&B	Crab-eating macaque	42

	Lang: "Somatic Chromosomes of the Gorilla," *Nature*, Vol. 192, No. 4799 (1961), pp. 225–8.
Ch	B. Chiarelli: "Chromosomes of the Orang-utan (*Pongo pygmaeus*)," *Nature*, Vol. 192, No. 4799 (1961), p. 285.
B&C	Bender and Chu, with permission.
C&B	"Chromosome Cytology and Evolution in Primates," *Science*, Vol. 133, No. 3462 (1961), pp. 1399–405.
	References Cited in C&B
P	T. S. Painter: 1924.
S	P. I. Shiwago: 1939.
Mak	S. Makino: 1943.
D&H	C. D. Darlington and A. Haque: 1955.
Mat	R. Matthey: 1955.
R&S	K. H. Rothfels and L. Siminovitch: 1958.
D	O. Dodson, in personal communication to Chu and Bender.
T	N. E. Tappan, in personal communication to Chu and Bender.
B&M†	M. A. Bender and L. E. Mettler: Unpublished.

TABLE 2

NUMBERS OF CHROMOSOMES AMONG
THE PRIMATES *

| | | *Diploid Chromosome Numbers* | | |
Subfamily	*Species*	*Source*	*Common Name*	*Number*
	Macaca nemestrina	D&H	Pig-tailed macaque	42
	Macaca cyclopis	Mak	Formosan macaque	42
	Macaca sylvana	Ch	Barbary ape	42
	Macaca assamensis	Ch	Assamese macaque	42
	Macaca fuscata	Ch	Japanese macaque	42 (?)
	Macaca sylenus	Ch	Lion-tailed macaque	42
	Papio papio	D&H	Guinea baboon	42
	Papio sphinx	B&M	Mandrill	42
	Papio doguera	C&G	Olive baboon	42
	Papio leucophaeus	B&C	Drill	42
Colobinae				
	Colobus (polycomos)	B&C	Colobus monkey	44
	Presbytis entellus	Mak	Langur	50
Hylobatinae				
	Hylobates lar	B&C	White-handed gibbon	44
	Hylobates agilis	B&C	Agile gibbon	44
	Hylobates hoolockii	C&B	Hoolock (gibbon)	44
	Symphalangus syndactylus	B&C	Siamang	50
Ponginae				
	Gorilla gorilla	HFD	Gorilla	48
	Pan troglodytes	YPY	Chimpanzee	48
	Pongo pygmaeus	Ch	Orangutan	48
Homininae				
	Homo sapiens	T&P	Man	46

ual chromosomes. All that human geneticists have accomplished in this line is to determine some of the traits that are carried on the sex chromosomes X and Y. They know that others are carried on the autosomal chromosomes, singly or in groups, but they cannot say which autosomes carry which traits. But experimental cytogenetics is advancing rapidly, thanks to the electron microscope and the use of biopsy samples from live individuals, and it may not be long before we know the function of each segment of each chromosome in the development of the human organism.[2] When that time comes, we may be able to draw karyotype charts

[2] Investigations made with the electron microscope at Cold Spring Harbor have shown that in cells of an animal's body single chromosomes excrete RNA from nucleus to cytoplasm. If we can discover which chromosomes are involved in different parts of the body, man may become as well known genetically as the fruit fly. See Helen Gay: "Nuclear Control of the Cell," *SA*, Vol. 202, No. 1 (1960), pp. 126–36.

of human subspecies, and the study of race in man will be on firm ground.

The Evidence of Behavior

THE ONE remaining category of evidence concerning man's relationship with the other primates is behavior, which taxonomists now consider as important a criterion of species as anatomy and physiology. This decision was prompted by the fact that in the course of natural selection animal populations are pruned for their individual capacities for behavior. In addition, selective behavior in mating makes species possible.

In man behavior takes two forms, technological and social. We can dismiss technology as a basis of comparison because man alone has it. (Such minor activities as temporary nest-building among the apes can be disregarded.)

Social behavior involves both nonsexual and sexual activities, both of which are concerned with family structure. In most if not all primate species, as among many other animals, the mother shows anxiety about the safety of her newborn young. Juvenile primates belonging to the same band play together as children do, exercising their muscles, learning motor habits, and establishing interpersonal relationships. Monkeys and apes groom each other's bodies and when night falls some may sleep together for mutual warmth, companionship, and protection. Human beings do all these things and in this they resemble all the other primates in general, except the prosimians, rather than any one family, genus, or species of monkey or ape.[3]

In sexual behavior, which forms another basis of group organization, man does not strictly follow the pattern of any other primate family, genus, or species. Man's closest kin, the three great apes, live in simple harems. More complex simian societies in which two or more adult males tolerate one another's presence are found among South American monkeys, Old World leaf eaters, and the terrestrial Old World monkeys such as the macaques and baboons.

Although these three groups of monkeys, which are only re-

[3] C. H. Southwick: "Letter to Editors," *SA*, Vol. 203, No. 6 (1960), p. 14.

motely related to man and to each other, have also achieved a social order in which adult males can live peacefully together, their patterns of social behavior differ from man's in other respects. The club type of sex life practiced by the howler monkeys has no counterpart in normal human society, although something similar turns up in houses of prostitution and at times of war. Among the baboons, when an adult female begins to come into heat she is first served by one or more eager, youthful males; only when in full oestrual bloom, as ripe as a persimmon, does she crawl to the old king, who then deigns to serve her. This behavior pattern has certain human counterparts that need not be over-interpreted, such as the bachelor's house in many primitive societies, patterned adultery among the Tiwi, and the noctural activity of Turkish sultans.

The primate closest to man in family life is the gibbon, to whom man is less closely related in other respects, as far as we know, than he is to the great apes. But when we consider the human trait of solicitude on the part of the male parent toward the helpless young, man's closest counterpart is the male marmoset, who carries his wife's babies about and weans them with premasticated food.

The kind of society man lives in, then, does not relate him to the kin that is closest to him anatomically and physiologically. Man has moved into new realms in locomotion and communication, and has developed a pattern of behavior of his own which finds its closest parallels in his more distant primate kin. This similarity may be due to neoteny of endocrine origin, to higher intelligence derived from competition among males for the largest harems and among females for the most desirable males, and to recombinations of genetic possibilities inherent in the primate gene structure. That we do not usually behave like apes does not mean that we are not genetically close to them.

Among living peoples vast gaps separate the behavior patterns of simple hunters and root diggers from those of sophisticated urbanites and exurbanites. Yet the hunters belong to all five geographical races and the urbanites belong to at least three. Behavior in this sense is not a matter of race.

Among the subhuman primates the species noted for highest

intelligence—and all above the prosimians are bright animals—belong to several families that also include species of lesser wit, as far as we can tell. In any colony of chimpanzees individual differences of mental aptitude are profound. The genetic basis for high intelligence has been acquired independently in different taxonomic categories of primates. There is no evidence that the most successful populations within several different human races have not also become bright independently. If we believe they did, the maze of human evolution can be straightened into a multiple-laned highway.

This is as far as the pursuit of comparisons among living primates can take us. The next step is to discard the rich evidence of flesh, fur, blood, lice, chromosomes, and conniving, and to follow the bare bones of our ancestors and their relatives backward in time to the moment when the primates first appeared.

6

THE FOSSIL RECORD FROM
LEMURS TO SWAMP APES

On the Scarcity of Primate Fossils

N o   m a t t e r how carefully we compare the anatomy, physiology, chromosomes, and behavior of the living primates, we shall not, by these means alone, completely solve the secret of their mutual relationships, or of our own descent, for each species is the end product of its own evolution. No species is standing still; not one is identical with its ancestors which lived in the early days of mammalian differentiation. By the same token, comparative embryology, although a valuable discipline, offers nothing more than a succession of fetal forms, some of which may have been omitted by neoteny. And zoogeography does not include extinct species.

To learn the details of the ancestral journey of any species or group of related species through the caverns of time there is no substitute for the study of the records of paleontology. Only through this specialized, fragmentarily documented, and all-encompassing discipline can we hope to answer the questions: Who are we? Whence do we come?

Were we sapient horses or snails, our task would be easy. Their records have been worked out from A to Z. Unfortunately, however, we are primates, kin to an untidy, grimacing lot, and members of an order whose ancestors chose the worst possible places to live and and the worst possible way of living, in terms of the preservation of skeletal material.

Plants equipped with chlorophyl turn carbon dioxide and sunlight into sugar; animals eat the plants and one another; and bacteria break down the leftover tissues into simpler substances, which repeat the cycle. Were this not so, the surface of the earth would be stacked high with logs and bodies. As scavengers abound, nearly all dead animals are transformed into the tissues of new generations and death ensures the continuity of life.

Some parts of dead animals, however, resist decay. The hardest, most durable part of a vertebrate's body (except for birds) is its teeth. Much of paleontology therefore rests on dental comparisons, just as some kinds of archaeology rely heavily on potsherds. This is fortunate, because the sizes, shapes, and structural details of teeth are hereditary, independent of environmental influence except wear, and unaffected by growth changes once erupted.

Even teeth, however, are hard to find in tropical forests where the rainfall leaches away the topsoil and where the subsoil is acid. The world's great fossil beds are located in grasslands, and particularly in swampy terrain, where animals now and then get mired, just as rhinoceros do today in muddy water holes during the dry season. Unable to get out, they sink below the surface of the mud and die, safe from predators, to be found millions of years later embedded in sedimentary rock. This happens rarely to primates. Most of them live in trees and never encounter mud. Only the genera that live on the ground, like macaques and baboons, frequent waterholes, and only their bones turn up in any abundance. Our earliest known hominid predecessors also lived in the open and quenched their thirst on the ground. Later, some of them began to live in caves, where scraps of their bones turn up in garbage heaps. Not more than seventy thousand years ago did they begin to bury their dead. Only from the latest geological period, therefore, are hominid bones at all frequent; anthropologists still have much less material to work with than do palentologists who trace the evolution of horses and rodents.

The Primate Time Scale [1]

THE primate fossil record covers the entire Cenozoic era. The duration of this period is estimated at 78 million years on the

[1] Geological time is officially divided into *eras, periods, epochs,* and *ages.* These terms are often used loosely or interchangeably. However, they are defined as follows. All geological time consists of five eras, the Archaeozoic, the Proterozoic, the Paleozoic, the Mesozoic, and the Cenozoic. Each era contains a number of

TABLE 3

THE CENOZOIC ERA IN MILLIONS OF YEARS

PERIODS	EPOCHS	Duration Each	Began X Millions of Years Ago
Quaternary	Pleistocene and Recent	1	1
T	Pliocene	11	12
e	Miocene	13.7	25.7
r	Oligocene	8.3	34
t	Eocene	21	55
i	Paleocene	23	78
ary			

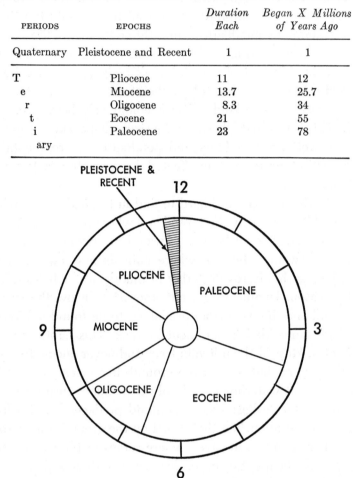

FIG. 12   THE PRIMATE TIME SCALE: THE CENOZOIC CLOCK.

basis of studies of the decay of uranium into lead, and by other methods. It is divided as shown in Table 3. No division is made

periods. Those of the Mesozoic are Triassic, Jurassic, and Cretaceous; those of the Cenozoic, Tertiary and Quaternary. Each period is divided into epochs. The epochs of the Tertiary are Paleocene, Eocene, Oligocene, Miocene, and Pliocene; those of the Quaternary are Pleistocene and Recent. The word *age* is used independently of the other terms to designate the time span of a form of life or special geological condition, thus: the Age of Fishes, the Age of Reptiles, the Age of Mammals, and the Ice Age. Archaeologists and historians use some of these words in special senses, e.g., the Stone Age, the Iron Age, the Hallstatt (Iron Age) Period, and the Christian Era. The dates giving the divisions of the Cenozoic on Table 3 are based on J. L. Kulp: "Geologic Time Scale," *Science,* Vol. 133, No. 3459 (1961), pp. 1105–14.

in this chart between the Pleistocene and the so-called post-Pleistocene, or Recent, which covers the time span elapsed since the recession of the last glacial ice sheets in Europe and North America at about 8,000 B.C. In other parts of the world it is more difficult to determine.

Primate Paleontology as a Whole

D URING the Paleocene and Eocene the earth's surface was much smoother than it has been since, and tropical forests extended much farther poleward than they do today. Consequently fossil primates are found in regions now uninhabitable for any free-living primate except man. During the Oligocene the Alpo-Himalayan and Rocky Mountain systems began to rise, and they continued to do so during the Miocene. These new highlands cooled off much of the poleward land of the Northern Hemisphere which had formerly been suitable for habitation by arboreal primates, isolating most of them in the three present-day tropical faunal regions (Ethiopian, Oriental, and Neotropical). During the Pliocene and the Pleistocene interglacials, however, parts of southern and western Europe remained frost-free and habitable by subhuman primates.

Unfortunately, the record of fossil primates is incomplete. More investigation has been carried out in some countries than in others. Moreover, in many areas whole epochs are completely unrepresented. In Africa south of the Sahara, a very accessible region where much work has been done and where hominid evolution may have gone on during the Pliocene, there are few known deposits of that period. In the Dasht-i-Lut desert of southeastern Iran, where Pliocene deposits are abundant, the ovenlike climate and general inaccessibility make paleonotological exploration virtually impossible.

Certain elements of primate history can be explained by the rise and fall of bridges between continental and off-shore land masses. Madagascar was cut off from Africa in the Jurassic epoch of the Mesozoic era, about 160 million years ago, when mammals were just beginning to evolve. More than 100 million years later, during the Eocene, the ancestors of the lemurs crossed to the island from Africa by some unknown means, possibly by a temporary land bridge. During the Miocene an incomplete bridge admitted two fresh-water aquatic mammals, a dwarf hippopotamus and a South African river pig, but no species arrived that could interfere with the arboreal life of the lemurs until man appeared, some 2,000 years ago.

Africa and Eurasia were connected intermittently, mostly at Suez as today. At one time or another these temporary bridges allowed passage to all Old World primate forms. From the Cretaceous into the mid-Eocene, the Bering Strait was a land bridge over which prosimians crossed from east to west; then it was broken until the Pleistocene, when man, along with many other land mammals, crossed it.

During the Cretaceous and early Paleocene the Isthmus of Panama connected North and South America, enabling prosimians to go south into the Neotropical forests, where they evolved into the South American monkeys and proliferated mightily. Meanwhile in North America the prosimians became extinct. Until late in the Pliocene the isthmus remained under water. Then it re-emerged, and it has been a land bridge ever since. After its rise from the deep a number of dominant mammalian species went south, extinguishing many of the hitherto sheltered local species; but this invasion did not appreciably affect the primates, as it included no competing arboreal forms. Moving in the opposite direction, some of the South American monkeys ventured north to Mexico, and men came down from the northern continent late in the Pleistocene or even during the recent period. As Australia had no Cenozoic land bridge, no primates came there until man arrived, by island hopping, at some time late in the Pleistocene when the Sunda and Sahul shelves were above water.

The Prosimian Proliferation

D u r i n g the early Cenozoic—Paleocene to mid-Oligocene— four orders of small mammals competed for a special ecological *lebensraum* by developing, in some families, gnawing or chiseling incisors like those of living beavers and squirrels. These were the multituberculates, primates, rodents, and lagomorphs (hares and rabbits). First to flourish, the multituberculates reached a peak in the Paleocene but became extinct in the Eocene, possibly because their incisors lacked dentine on the back with which to keep a sharp edge, and their roots failed to continue growing throughout life to replace wear, as the incisors of rodents do.

Next came the primates, then consisting exclusively of prosimians. They may have competed with the multituberculates and helped bring about their downfall. Some fifty-five genera of early Tertiary prosimians have been discovered—the better-known are grouped in five families. Before the mid-Oligocene, three families had become extinct. These were all chiselers and gnawers, probably forced out of action by competition with the rodents and lagomorphs. The two surviving families, the Adapidae and Anaptomorphidae, were nongnawers and owed their continued existence to a lack of specialization. The only latter-day gnawing primate is the aye-aye, who probably took up this habit later and on his own.

The third and fourth chiseling orders, the rodents and lagomorphs, were present from the Paleocene on but radiated only after the decline of the gnawing prosimians. Their advantage over the latter was physiological and behavioral rather than dental. They are very fertile animals, with short pregnancies and large litters. They are well adapted to life in deserts and cold climates because they build nests and burrows and collect and store food for lean seasons, and because some of them can live without water and others hibernate. These adaptations gave them dominance outside the tropical forests, where the nongnawing prosimians were left to evolve after their own fashion. This included long pregnancies, single births, and a long period of maturation—features disadvantageous perhaps in the Paleocene and even in the Oligocene, but essential to the eventual rise of man, who builds houses, stores food, transports water, and proliferates mightily by outwitting his competitors.

The Adapidae, found in both Europe and America, were unspecialized lemurlike primates with small brains and the dental formula $\frac{2:1:4:3}{2:1:4:3}$. They were either the ancestors of living lemurs and lorises or their close kin, but no kin of man.

The Anaptomorphidae, however, with subfamilies in the Old and New Worlds, were probably unspecialized tarsiers which had branched off even earlier from the protolemur stem. From this family all the living monkeys, apes, and man were probably derived, before the ancestors of the living tarsiers had acquired their specializations for hopping and nocturnal vision.

An important structural change that took place between the protolemur and tarsius stages was a backward and sideward shift of the line of stress on the skull which accommodates the muscular pull of the jaws. In the lemurs, as in the shrews, much of this stress is carried to the top of the head by way of the bony framework between the eyes, which are consequently set far apart and are not fully binocular. In the tarsiers this stress is shifted mostly to the side of the face and head, outside the orbital rims and behind the orbits. The eyes are then set closer together and are fully binocular. These changes, which may be related to a diminishing sense of smell and an increasingly better eyesight, were carried over into both higher primate suborders, to a more marked degree in the catarrhines than in the platyrrhines.

The Evolution of the Platyrrhines

FROM a North American anaptomorph the South American monkeys evolved into four-footed limb crawlers, brachiators, and tail-swingers; and there we leave them. Their only bearing on this story is that the same evolutionary parallelism occurs in the differentiation of the Old World primates. None of them, apparently, went down to the ground.

The Evolution of the Catarrhines

MEANWHILE, the ancestors of the Old World monkeys, apes, and men were evolving independently of the New World monkeys, apparently from one or more of the Old World anaptomorphs, but exactly when and where we do not know. There is even a slight doubt whether the Cercopithecoids and Hominoids made the transition from prosimian to catarrhine in a single evolutionary act, through a common ancestor, or whether the two superfamilies independently crossed what paleontologists call an adaptive threshold.

In Chapter 5 we discussed some considerable differences between the two superfamilies which do not concern locomotion or posture. The Old World monkeys have double-disc placentas; the apes and men, single-disc ones. Men and the apes metabolize purine only partially; the monkeys completely.

In the apes and men, ABO blood-group substances are carried in the blood; in the monkeys these substances are carried in plasma and other media. The precipitin test demarcates the two groups sharply, as do the genera of body lice with which each is infested. As far as we know, chromosome counts likewise differentiate the two groups. As long ago as 1945 Simpson divided the New World monkeys, Old World monkeys, and the apes and men into three superfamilies, the Ceboidea, Cercopithecoidea, and Hominoidea, implying the separate descent of each from a lower primate grade.[2]

Recent discoveries in paleontology have supported this position. Until a few years ago two very small and ancient fossil mandibles were believed to provide a common catarrhine link between the Old World monkeys and the Hominoids. One was *Amphipithecus,* found in an Upper Eocene deposit in Burma;[3] the other was *Parapithecus,*[4] from the Lower Oligocene beds of the Fayum in Egypt. Now both of these have been discredited.[5] Not only do we

[2] G. G. Simpson: "The Principles of Classification . . . ," p. 184.

[3] E. H. Colbert: "A New Primate from the Upper Eocene Pondaung Formation in Burma," *AMN,* No. 951 (1937).

[4] W. E. LeG. Clark: "New Paleontological Evidence Bearing on the Evolution of the Hominoidea," *QJGS,* Vol. 105, Part 2 (1949), pp. 38.

[5] J. Hürzeler: "*Oreopithecus bambolii Gervais,* A Preliminary Report," *VNGB,* Vol. 69, No. 1 (1958), pp. 1–48, especially 32–3.

C. L. Gazin: "A Review of the Middle and Upper Eocene Primates of North America," *SMC,* Vol. 136, No. 1 (1958), pp. 1–112.

Clark: *The Antecedents of Man* (Chicago: Quadrangle Books; 1960).

Hürzeler rejects both *Parapithecus* and *Amphipithecus* and also two other dubious Fayum specimens, *Apidium* and *Moeropithecus.* Gazin casts doubt on *Amphipithecus* by inference, calling it ". . . a possible primate with three molars

lack a common ancestral catarrhine, but we have no fossil Cercopithecidae older than the Lower Miocene, at which time genuine Old World monkeys appear in East Africa. A small frontal bone from the Lower Oligocene beds of the Fayum has recently been identified as that of a primate, probably a catarrhine,[6] but this does not solve the problem because we do not know what kind of a catarrhine it was. In its general configuration it resembles an ape rather than a monkey, but that is inconclusive.

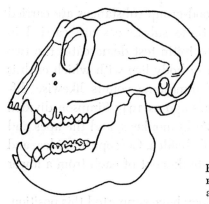

FIG. 13   *Mesopithecus,* A MIOCENE LEAF-EATING MONKEY (*Colobinae*). (Drawing after Piveteau, 1957.)

The genuine Old World monkey found in the Lower Miocene of East Africa is *Mesopithecus.*[7] Sometime later, probably no more then ten million years, the same genus is found in Greece, Czechoslovakia, and Iran in a period known as the Pontian, which the French call Late Miocene and the British and Germans Early Pliocene. The best site is at Pikermi, in Greece, where complete skeletons have been found. This animal is listed in the sub-

---

from the Eocene of Burma." Clark expresses caution about the status of *Parapithecus,* and W. L. Straus, Jr., who saw an enlarged photograph of *Parapithecus* after it had been freshly cleaned (courtesy of Hürzeler), states that the tooth originally called a canine is a premolar, making the dental formula 1:1:3:3. Straus feels that if *Parapithecus* was a primate at all it was an aberrant tarsier.

[6] E. L. Simons: "An Anthropoid Frontal Bone from the Fayum Oligocene of Egypt: the Oldest Skull Fragment of a Higher Primate," *AMN,* No. 1976 (1959).

[7] J. Piveteau: *Les Primates et l'Homme, Traité de Paléontologie Humaine,* (Paris: Masson et Cie; 1957), pp. 135–43. This reference covers the rest of this section, unless otherwise specified.

family Colobinae because its skull, jaws, and teeth resemble those of the living leaf-eating monkeys of Africa and Asia. Among other resemblances, the lower third molar has a third loph, as is true of living colobines; and the lower molars and premolars are particularly worn on their outer edges whereas the corresponding upper teeth are worn on the inner edges. This pattern of wear favors the mastication of leaves, i.e., browsing.

The rest of the skeleton, however, is less specialized than that of the living colobines and closer in form to those of macaques and baboons. The femur is longer than the humerus, as is true of the ground-living genera; the hand bones are longer than those of leaf eaters and shorter than those of macaques and baboons. The thumb is unreduced. The ischium has an enlarged, corrugated area suited for large ischial callosities like those of macaques and baboons. In Kenya, where *Mesopithecus* remains are earliest, they were part of a grassland fauna.[8]

On the whole, it looks as if this animal was close to the common ancestor of the colobines and the ground-living Cercopithecines, but had passed the taxonomic frontier into the colobine camp in terms of diet while it still had some distance to go in locomotor adaptation. It persisted in France until the Early Pleistocene, and has turned up in the Pliocene deposits of the Siwalik Hills of northern India and in the Pleistocene of Madras. Its route between Africa and India seems to have followed the Nile to the eastern Mediterranean, the Fertile Crescent, and Iran, bypassing southern Arabia.

To date, there are no true Cercopithecines available in the fossil record before the Pliocene, when macaques (*Macaca prisca* and others) appear in France, Holland, and Italy. Macaques are also found in the Pleistocene of Europe, Indochina, and China. The baboons first appear in the Late Pliocene or Early Pleistocene of East Africa.

For one reason or another, including the fact that certain fossil specimens just haven't been uncovered, the fossil record of the Old World monkeys is shorter than that of the Hominoids. More-

---

[8] B. Patterson: "The Geological History of Non-Hominid Primates in the Old World," *HB*, Vol. 26, No. 3 (1954), pp. 191–219.

over, the Old World monkeys did not acquire their present specializations any earlier than apes and men did.

The Gibbon Line

THE EARLIEST known specimens of the Hominoids are representatives of the least highly evolved of the three living families, the Hylobatidae, or gibbons. At least three excellent sets of specimens shed light on their evolution. The earliest is *Propliopithecus,* a small, nearly complete mandible unearthed, like that of *Parapithecus,* in the Oligocene beds of the Fayum. This bone is only two thirds the size of that of a living lar gibbon; if the body was in proportion to the jaws the animal weighed only 7 to 10 pounds. This places it within the weight range of a house cat.

Seen from above, the mandible is essentially V-shaped like those of prosimians. Seen from the side, its ascending rami (the paired branches behind the teeth which articulate with the skull) are higher than those of a modern gibbon, suggesting a higher face. Yet the mandible is shorter anteroposteriorly (from ear to lips) and the chin line seems to have been nearly vertical. The molars had five cusps and the premolars two. Although broken off, the canines seem to have been of normal length for a gibbon; the first premolar is not fully sectorial, that is, with a shearing edge; and the incisors are missing. As the bone of the mandible is massive in proportion to the size of its teeth, the animal must have had a powerful bite. Schlosser,[9] who described it, considered it a basal form of the gibbon family, but there is no apparent reason why it could not also have been ancestral to the other apes, although its relationship to the hominids is harder to see.

Moving on to the Lower Miocene, an animal named *Limnopithecus,*[1] undoubtedly a gibbon, has been found on Rusinga Island in Lake Victoria in Kenya. Several jaw fragments, teeth, and

[9] M. Schlosser: Oligozäne Landsäugetiere aus dem Fayum, *BPGO,* Vol. 51 (1911), pp. 51–167 (after Gregory, 1951).

[1] Clark and L. S. B. Leakey: *Fossil Hominids of East Africa, BMFM,* Series 1, 1951.

Clark and D. P. Thomas: *Associated Jaws and Limb Bones of Limnopithecus macinnesi, BMFM,* Series 3, 1951.

limb bones have been recovered. The canines are shorter than those of living gibbons and the anterior lower premolars still less specialized for shearing. The incisors are a little smaller, and the jawbones more robust. The limb skeleton, much of which is preserved, is in some ways intermediate between those of living Old World monkeys and gibbons. The arms are shorter than those of living gibbons, and the whole rotating apparatus of the shoulder girdle and elbow is only partly developed for brachiation. This gibbon had only begun his career as a trapeze artist and still lacked much of the necessary equipment. In fact, his legs were quite strongly developed, and anatomical details of his foot suggest more jumping or walking than modern gibbons indulge in.

In the Middle and Upper Miocene of Europe another ancestral gibbon turns up. *Pliopithecus* [2] may in some future taxonomic reshuffling come to be included in the same genus as *Limnopithecus*. *Limnopithecus* is represented by only a few teeth and scraps of bone, whereas almost every bone in *Pliopithecus's* body below the mandible has been recovered, as well as portions of the skull.

The dentition of *Pliopithecus* is similar to that of *Limnopithecus*, and the mandible, like that of the living siamang—an animal of the same body size—has a trace of a simian shelf, a bony strut across the inside of the jaw at chin level. This mechanical prop probably has no phylogenetic significance because it appears when needed in big-toothed and heavy-jawed primates, and disappears when no longer useful. A trace of prosimian influence is seen in the form of the jaw, which is still V-shaped in the posterior portion. The modern gibbon has lost this. Also, in what is left of the facial skeleton, the interorbital distance is greater and the nasal region wider than in modern gibbons, again a prosimian relic.

The body of this animal is gibbonlike in details of the pelvis and vertebrae. The sternum is broad and flat, as in brachiators and man, and the clavicle (collarbone) is S-shaped as in orang-

[2] H. Zapfe: "Die Pliopithecus-Funde aus der Spaltenfüllung von Neudorf an der March (Czechoslovakia)," *VGBV*, Sonderheft C. (1952). Reprinted in *Yearbook of Physical Anthropology* (New York, 1951), pp. 55–9.

Zapfe: "Results of Research on the Skeleton of Pliopithecus (*Epipliopithecus*) vindobonensis." Paper read at the Annual Meeting of the Am. Assn. of Phys. Anth., Cambridge, Mass., April 12, 1958.

utans and chimpanzees, rather than simply bowed, as in modern gibbons. The hind legs are as long as a siamang's, but the arms are only 60 per cent as long as those of the living ape. The shoulder and elbow joints are not as swivel-formed as in the modern animal, and both the radius and ulna articulate with the carpal bones in prosimian and monkey fashion.

The tarsal bones of the feet are longer and the metatarsals and toe bones shorter than in the siamang; and the same proportions are found in the hand bones. In short, *Pliopithecus* was not yet a full-time brachiator, nor was he altogether an arboreal quadruped. He was a small ape that seems to have come down from the trees, partly adapted himself to a quadrupedal life on the ground, and was only beginning to become adapted to a renewed arboreal life as a brachiator. In those anatomical details in which his limbs differed from those of modern gibbons, according to Zapfe, he resembled the prosimians as much as or more than the living Cercopithecid monkeys. The significance of this is uncertain because Miocene Cercopithecids may have also resembled prosimians in these features.

Limnopithecus and *Pliopithecus* establish the presence of ancestral gibbons in the Miocene of Europe and Africa; comparable remains of equal age have not been found in Asia. By the Miocene the gibbons had already branched off from the stock of the still-missing common ancestor of all the catarrhines, if indeed such a common ancestor ever existed. By that time they had also begun to become distinct from the ancestors of the Pongidae, or great apes, and possibly also of the Hominidae, including *Homo*.

The Ancestors of the Three Living Great Apes

DURING the Miocene, the period in which the ancestors of the gibbons appeared, the ancestors of the chimpanzees and gorillas also made their first recognizable bow, and from the same general stock. Although the ancestors of the orangutans must have existed at the same time, their bones have not yet been found or identified. Simpson, in 1945,[3] and Fiedler, in 1956,[4] classified all

[3] Simpson: op. cit.
[4] W. Fiedler: "Übersicht über das System. . . ."

the ancestral great apes in one subfamily, Dryopithecinae, and called their living descendants Ponginae. Some of the Dryopithecinae became extinct by evolving into new forms, others by simply dying out, apparently without issue. Thus the terms *Dryopithecinae* and *Ponginae* represent evolutionary grades rather than individual lines of descent, because both the chimpanzee and the gorilla, in Africa, and the orangutan in Asia, must have evolved independently from Dryopithecine ancestors.

Proconsul

T H E African Dryopithecines belong to a single genus, *Proconsul,* named after a chimpanzee called Consul who lived in the London zoo. *Proconsul* was found on the same fossil-rich island of Rusinga as *Limnopithecus.* During the Miocene this part of the island was apparently a forest, and the land below the trees was seasonally flooded. This ape has three species and sizes: *P. africanus,* little bigger than a gibbon; *P. nyanzae,* chimpanzee-sized; and *P. major,* as big as a gorilla.[5]

The three are much alike except for size and the consequent differences in proportions. As many more remains of *P. africanus* have been found than of the other two, it has received the most attention. Being the smallest and lightest, it was also, we believe, the best brachiator of the three.

Unique among primate fossils of this age is an almost complete adult female skull of *P. africanus.* As might be expected of a female of the smallest of the three species, it has a more or less globular brain case, a forehead running at an angle of about 55° to the eye-ear plane (a line drawn from the top of the ear hole to the lower border of the orbit, which places the skull in its normal operating position), no brow ridges, and an upper facial skeleton set at the same angle as the forehead. The forehead slope of a female gorilla is about 35°, and a modern human female who happens to have a vertical forehad has, of course, a slope of 90°. Many women have less of a slope than that.

[5] Clark and Leakey: *The Miocene Hominidae of East Africa,* BMFM, No. 1 (1951).

J. R. Napier and P. R. Davis: *The Fore-limb Skeleton and Associated Remains of Proconsul Africanus,* BMFM, No. 16, 1959.

Although the cranial capacity cannot be measured accurately, it probably lies somewhere between that of a gibbon (*ca.* 100 cc.) and that of a chimpanzee (*ca.* 400 cc.), which fits its body size. As far as the endocranial cast can be read, it shows a frontal area more monkeylike than apelike. In other words, the brains of these

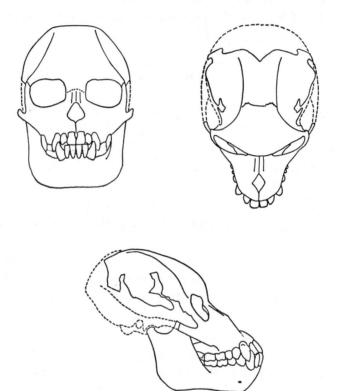

Fig. 14 *Proconsul africanus*. Note that the skull of *Proconsul africanus* retains several prosimian or platyrrhine-like features, including the relative position of the eye sockets and nasal skeleton and the V-shaped lower border of the nasal opening. The canines do not interlock very far; the bite of the unworn teeth is intermediate between those of man and apes. (Drawings after LeGros Clark and Leakey, 1951.)

fossil apes had not evolved to the modern pongid level by the Miocene.

As in some primitive men but not in living apes, the orbits are low and broad, and the distance between them is great. Seen from above, the orbits seem to face to the side more than they do in living apes or even in most living Old World monkeys; in this respect *Proconsul* resembles some of the lower primates which lack full stereoscopic vision. The lower border of the nasal opening is V-shaped, as in some Old World monkeys. In apes and men it is a horizontal line.

A more modern feature is that the plane of the occlusal border of the teeth, where uppers meet lowers when the jaws are closed, as seen from the side, is parallel to the eye-ear plane, as in most living apes (in the orangutan it actually slopes upward and foreward) and in most men. This sharply distinguishes them from the living ground-monkeys, such as the baboon, whose tooth lines slope downward and forward at a 40° angle.

The lower jaw is not massive and lacks a simian shelf. Its sides are convergent, as among some lower primates; it does not have parallel sides, as among the living apes, nor is it U-shaped as in men. That the musculature of the jaw was relatively light is shown by a wide separation of the temporal lines on the parietal bones, by a medium development of the attachment areas for the masseter muscles, and by a rather frail zygomatic arch.

The teeth, too, are not as impressive as those of modern apes. The incisors are man-sized, the canine larger but moderate for an ape, and in the maxillary bone of the face, above the root of the canine, there is a small depression known as a canine fossa, which is present in man but not in living apes. As in apes but not in men, the first lower premolar is sectorial, that is, it has a shearing edge. From numbers 1 to 3 the molars increase in size, and number 1 is quite small. In living apes the second is largest and the third smallest. The teeth of the other two species are similar but larger, and the jaw of *P. major* is gorilloid in its massiveness.

Limb bones of all three species have been found and described, but, as with the skull, the limb bones of *P. africanus* are the most nearly complete. Napier and Davis have described an almost complete left forelimb. Because of brachiation, the forelimb is critical in the identification of a pongid. In the humerus, radius, ulna, carpal bones, metacarpals, and phalanges, this animal showed some features reminiscent of the quadrupedal arboreal primates and other features unique to brachiators. No features unique to terrestrial quadrupeds like the macaques and baboons were found. On the other hand, some quadrupedal traits in the forelimb may be shared with arboreal and terrestrial forms; only the brachiators are set apart. As *P. africanus* was only a part-time or halfway brachiator, we cannot be sure that his ancestors, before beginning to brachiate, had not spent some time both in the trees and on the ground.

The hand bones of ground-living monkeys are specialized for walking and digging, as witness their long metacarpals and short phalanges. The hand bones of apes, being specialized for brachiation, have long metacarpals, long phalanges, and short thumbs. The hand bones of *P. africanus* occupy an intermediate position, one which indicates no complete form of specialization. He had long phalanges, like an ape, but he also had a fairly long thumb, like both arboreal and terrestrial monkeys, and man. The wrist bones (carpals) were like those of the arboreal quadrupeds rather than like either of the other forms, and the ulna met the carpal bones as in quadrupedal primates.

As for the lower extremity, the upper end of the femur is ape-like in general architecture, and the angle of head to shaft suggests a carrying angle, as in apes and men but not in monkeys either tree-borne or grounded. Napier and Davis have described a nearly complete foot of *P. africanus,* which they find to be largely apelike in the shortness of the tarsals, the proportions of metatarsals to phalanges, and the divergence of the great toe.

The splendid work done on the Miocene primates of East Africa by Leakey and his associates, among others, has given us a likely ancestor for the chimpanzees and gorillas, and possibly also one for man.

Dryopithecus in Europe and Asia

W H I L E the ancestors of the chimpanzee and gorilla were evolving in Africa, a much larger number of Dryopithecine genera were similarly engaged in Europe and Asia. The entire subfamily is named after a mandible found in France in 1856 by Lartet, and dated in the mid-Miocene. He called it *Dryopithecus fontani.* The genus *Dryopithecus* has since been found in other parts of Europe, where some species persisted into the Pliocene.[6] With two

[6] Piveteau: op. cit., pp. 197–206.

exceptions the specimens are limited to teeth and pieces of jaws. One humeral shaft from France has been uncertainly labelled *Dryopithecus fontani*.[7] As both ends of it are missing, this humerus tells us little. One complete femur, *Paidopithex*, found in Germany and formerly attributed to *Dryopithecus*, is listed under the gibbons in Simpson's compilation.[8] Both bones are gibbon-sized.

Recently two sets of teeth attributed to *Dryopithecus keiyuanensis* have been found in Yunnan, China[9] in Lower Pliocene lignite beds. As lignite, a brown coal intermediate between peat and bituminous coal, is an excellent preservative, we may hope for whole skulls and postcranial skeletons from this area. From illustrations, the Keiyuan teeth look nearly as hominid as they look pongid. Professor Woo, who found them, says of the lower first premolar of his new primate that its outer surface is "worn, as in other anthropoids, by the posterior inner face of the upper canine." Nevertheless, this tooth is short and broad for a pongid. Whether the type of dental articulation ascribed to it by Woo could be lost in the evolution of a hominid from a pongid is an unanswered question. In any case the Dryopithecus teeth from China seem to be more nearly hominid than those from Europe.

Ramapithecus, a Possible Ancestor of the Hominids[1]

I N 1935 G. E. Lewis and his associates found the jaws and teeth of many Dryopithecines in the rich fossil-bearing deposits of the Siwalik Hills in northwest India. They sorted these into five genera, four of which they named after Indian gods: *Sivapithecus*, *Sugrivapithecus*, *Bramapithecus*, and *Ramapithecus*. The fifth was called *Paleosimia*. Although *Ramapithecus* has been

[7] Le Gros Clark, in 1960, called it only "probably" a part of this animal. Clark: *The Antecedents of Man* (Chicago: Quadrangle Books; 1960), p. 214.

[8] Simpson: op. cit., p. 67.

[9] Ju-Kang Woo: "Dryopithecus Teeth from Keiyuan, Yunnan Province," *VP*, Vol. I, No. 1 (1957), pp. 25–32. Also "New Materials of *Dryopithecus* from Keiyuan," *VP*, Vol. 2, No. 1 (1958), pp. 38–42.

[1] W. K. Gregory, M. Hellman, and G. E. Lewis: "Fossil Anthropoids of the Yale-Cambridge India Expedition of 1935," *CIWP*, No. 495 (1938).

Elwyn Simons: "The Phyletic Position of *Ramapithecus*," *PYPM*, No. 57 (1961).

called Upper Pliocene or even Early Pleistocene, it is now assigned to the Lower Pliocene along with the other four genera, and all are roughly contemporary with the other Dryopithecines mentioned above.

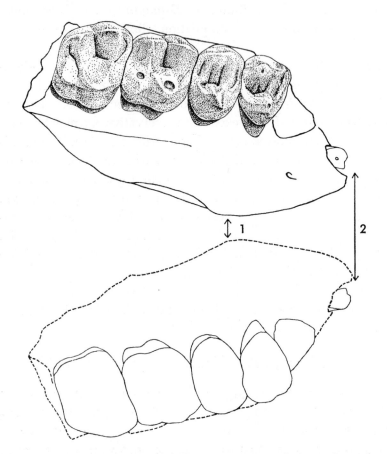

FIG. 15   *Ramapithecus brevirostis.* The type specimen of *Ramapithecus brevirostis,* a Pliocene ape from the Siwalik Hills of Northern India, whose upper molar and premolar teeth resemble those of man. In this figure Simons has projected the shape of the whole palatal arc, which appears rounded as in man. (Drawing by Simons, 1961 [PYPM, No. 57, Fig. 2] with permission.)

The most hominid-looking of these specimens is the piece of right maxilla of *Ramapithecus brevirostis,* which contains the first two molars, both premolars, and the root of the lateral incisor. The socket of the canine is also preserved, and the lateral wall of the socket of the median incisor. Simons, who has recently re-studied this specimen, has reconstructed the palate, and estimated the sizes of the missing teeth from the sizes of their sockets and the space available to each in the tooth-row.

According to this reconstruction the palate is arched, as in man; the canine was no larger than the first premolar, and was thick mesiolabially as in man, instead of spatulate, as in apes; and the ratio between the sizes of the front teeth (premolars and canines) and those of the cheek teeth (premolars and molars) is roughly the same as in man, and not as in the apes, which have relatively large front teeth. Enough of the maxilla is preserved to show that the upper jaw was more manlike than apelike in its depth and degree of prognathism. In view of these findings, Simons has committed himself to the opinion that *Ramapithecus brevirostis* was, in fact, a hominid, the first known of his subfamily. What others will say about this identification remains to be seen.

In any case, India and China may well have been the breeding places of the Hominidae, either through *Ramapithecus brevirostis* or some other species, just as Africa was the cradle of the chimpanzee and gorilla. The origin of the orangutan is still a mystery, as no bona-fide orang is known before the Pleistocene.

Kenyapithecus wickeri[3]

L A T E I N 1961 Leakey turned the putative home of the hominids back to Africa by discovering a Pontian (Early Pliocene) primate specimen in the orange grove of a white farmer, Fred Wicker, at Fort Ternan forty miles west of Kisumu in Kenya. This discovery was announced on March 22, 1962. The Argon-40 date determined at Berkeley is 14 million years, within the accepted span of the Pontian, and the fauna belongs to that period.

The specimen, like Ramapithecus, consists of a piece of the right maxilla. It contains the second and first upper molars, the second upper premolar, and the freshly broken stub of the first upper premolar. The right upper canine, found separately, has been glued into the distal cup of its socket.

The specimen is between 4 and 4.5 cm. long, and all the teeth

[2] L. S. B. Leakey: "A New Lower Pliocene Fossil Primate from Kenya," *AMNH*, Ser. 13, Vol. 14, pp. 689–96 (1961) (published May 22, 1962).

are within the human size range. Both molars have the Dryopithecus Y-5 cusp pattern, and show no special features such as a cingulum, enamel extensions, or enamel pearls (see p. 358) which characterize certain human races. The size progression from the molars to the second premolar to the first premolar to the canine is the same as that found in *Homo* but not in *Australopithecus*—the first premolar cannot have been much larger than the canine. The canine is short and does not extend downward below the occlusal level of the other teeth.

The only morphological pecularity of the teeth which I could observe was a considerable surface relief on the inner or lingual side of the canine. Like most but not all human maxillae, and no others, that of the Fort Ternan primate had a canine fossa.

It is easy to speculate on the relationship of this specimen to *Proconsul, Ramapithecus,* the living apes, *Australopithecus,* and man, but until more details are available, to do so is not only risky but also probably unprofitable.

The Pleistocene Apes of China

As CHINA is the gateway between the Oriental region and the Palearctic, we should not be surprised to find that during the Pleistocene a number of higher primate genera in addition to *Homo* had established themselves in that country. Among them is the orang and an animal with huge molar teeth known as *Gigantopithecus blacki,*[3] first described on the basis of molar teeth

[3] D. A. Hooijer: "The Geological Age of *Pithecanthropus, Meganthropus,* and *Gigantopithecus," AJPA,* Vol. 9, No. 3 (1951), pp. 265–81.

G. H. R. von Koenigswald: "*Gigantopithecus blacki* von Koenigswald, a Giant Fossil Hominid from the Pleistocene of South China," *APAM,* Vol. 43, Part 4 (1952), pp. 295–325.

W. C. Pei: "Giant Ape's Jawbone Discovered in China," *AA,* Vol. 59, No. 5 (1957), pp. 834–8.

Pei and Y. H. Li: "Discovery of a Third Mandible of *Gigantopithecus* in Lu-Cheng (Kwangsi, South China)," *VP,* Vol. 2, No. 4 (1958), pp. 190–200.

W. L. Straus, Jr.: "Jaw of *Gigantopithecus," Science,* Vol. 125, No. 3250 (1957), p. 658.

S. M. Garn and A. B. Lewis: "Tooth-Size, Body-Size, and 'Giant' Fossil Man," *AA,* Vol. 60, No. 5 (1958), pp. 874–80.

"More *Gigantopithecus,"* in *News and Activities, VP,* Vol. 2, No. 1 (1958), p. 67.

recovered from Chinese pharmacies, where they are sold as tooth-ache medicine. Between 1956 and 1958 three lower jaws of this species were removed from a cave in a high cliff in Kwangsi province. According to Pei and Li, this animal lived in the Lower Pleistocene, or Villafranchian, earlier than *Sinanthropus*. How-ever, the time gap between those two Chinese primates is too short for *Gigantopithecus* to have been an ancestor of man, as some have claimed, whatever anatomical arguments may be produced to favor such a descent, for in some ways his teeth resembled man's more than those of the living apes do. The tooth pattern was essentially pongid, but the sides of the jaw are convergent like those of prosimians, and the teeth are worn down all along the line, indicating a rotary grinding motion, as in hominids. Once again we are impressed with the capacity of the primates for parallelism. According to Remane (1960), *Gigantopithecus* was definitely a pongid, at the end of a special line. It was less human-like than a female chimpanzee and about the size of a large gorilla.

Possible Survivals of Chinese Apes

T H E P L E I S T O C E N E ended—if it ended at all—only ten thousand years ago, a mere yesterday zoologically. It would be noteworthy if all of the apes of China, the number of genera being still undetermined, could be shown to have become extinct at the close of that period. But there is evidence that they did not do so. For example, the philosopher Hsün-Tzu, who lived a hundred years after Confucius, or about 400 B.C., definitely states that an ape the size of a man and covered with hair lived in the Yellow River Valley in his day, and also that it stood erect. Furthermore, the Liang Annals, written in the time of the Warring States, 200 B.C. to A.D. 200, places apes in Sin-Kiang province, north of Tibet, near the country where the giant panda was first found as recently as 1930.

A third book, entitled *Anatomical Dictionary for Recognizing*

G. Heberer: "The Descent of Man and the Present Fossil Record," *CSHS*, Vol. 24 (1959), pp. 235–44.

A. Remane: "Die Stellung von *Gigantopithecus*," *AAnz*, Vol. 24, No. 2–3 (1960), pp. 146–59.

Various Diseases, which originated in Tibet and was published in Peking at the end of the eighteenth century [4] though it was probably written earlier, contains a systematic description of the fauna of Tibet and neighboring regions. Many species of mammals, birds, reptiles, fish, and so on, are included, and each is illustrated with a recognizable woodcut. Not one of the animals is fantastic, composite, or mythical. Among them, in a group of monkeys, a tail-less, bipedal primate is shown standing on a rock, with one arm stretched upward. Trilingual captions in Tibetan, Mongolian, and Chinese designate it as a man-animal. A different and more detailed illustration appears in an edition of the same book printed a century later, in Ulan-Bator. In this edition the text reads: "The wild man lives in the mountains, his origin [this word probably means habitat] is close to that of the bear, his body resembles that of man, and he has enormous strength. His meat may be eaten to treat mental diseases and his gall cures jaundice."

How, if at all, this wild man is related to the so-called Yeti or Abominable Snowman remains to be determined, along with its relationship to the Pleistocene fossil apes of China. If there really is, or has recently been, a large bipedal primate in central Asia, its discovery, dead or alive, would be of enormous importance, not only for primate taxonomy but for its bearing on the theoretical relationship between the erect posture, tool-making, speech, and culture.

Hominoids and Hominids [5]

F R O M *Propliopithecus* on (page 196), we have been describing Hominoids—first hylobatids, or gibbons, then pongids, or great apes—as distinguished from hominids, or man and kin of men. Two fundamental features distinguish hominids from their closest kin, the pongids: posture and teeth. Hominids, by definition, stand erect and walk with their hands free from the ground. Pon-

---

[4] E. Vlček: "Old Literary Evidence for the Existence of the 'Snow Man' in Tibet and Mongolia," *MAN,* Vol. 59, Article No. 203 (1959), pp. 132–4.

[5] The most detailed and authoritative work on this subject, including both *Oreopithecus* and *Australopithecus,* is Heberer: "Die Fossilgeschichte der Hominoidea," in H. Hofer, A. Schulz, and D. Starck: *Primatologia,* Vol. I (Basel, 1956), pp. 379–560.

gids brachiate, walk on their knuckles, or both. Hominids have small canine teeth that do not project above the line of occlusion of the other teeth; they have no gap between the upper canines and first premolars—such a gap is known as a diastema—and the two lower premolars are more or less the same in shape and function. Pongids have large, long canines, usually a diastema, and the first premolar is laterally compressed and has a shearing buccal edge for scissors contact with the upper canine. In each side of the lower jaw of pongids a hole known as the mental foramen is located near the lower border of the bone, to clear the long root of the canine. In hominids this foramen is located higher up, because the root of the canine is shorter. As we examine the fossil record in search of hominids, these points must be borne in mind.

Oreopithecus bambolii,[6] *the Swamp Ape*

A RECENT, much publicized hominid possibility is an animal found in great abundance in the so-called Pontian fossil beds of central Italy, which consist, like those of China, of layers of lignite. These beds are attributed variously to the Upper Miocene and the Lower Pliocene, and cover the period between about 10 and 16 million years ago. This is also the time of Kenyapithecus, the Fort Ternan primate.

[6] Hürzeler: "Zur Systematischen Stellung von *Oreopithecus*," *VNGB*, Vol. 65, No. 1 (1954), pp. 88–95.

Hürzeler: "*Oreopithecus bambolii Gervais*, A Preliminary Report," pp. 1–48.

Hürzeler: "The Significance of *Oreopithecus* in the Genealogy of Man," *Triangle*, Vol. 1, No. 5 (1960), pp. 164–74.

Straus: "*Oreopithecus bambolii*," *Science*, Vol. 126, No. 3269 (1957), pp. 345–6.

Straus: "A New *Oreopithecus* Skeleton," *Science*, Vol. 128, No. 3323 (1958), p. 523.

Straus: "Is *Oreopithecus bambolii* a Primitive Hominid?" *AR*, Vol. 132, No. 3 (1958), pp. 511–12.

Straus: "Cranial Capacity of *Oreopithecus bambolii*," *Science*, Vol. 132, No 3428 (1960), pp. 670–2.

Simons: "*Apidium* and *Oreopithecus*," *Nature*, Vol. 186, No. 4727 (1960), pp 824–6.

A. H. Schultz: "Einige Beobachtungen und Masse am Skelett von Oreopithecus," *ZfMuA*, Vol. 50, No. 2 (1960), pp. 136–49.

P. M. Butler and J. R. F. Mills: "A Contribution to the Odontology of Oreopithecus," *BBMN*, Vol. 4, No. 1 (1959), pp. 1–26.

E. Boné: "*Oreopithecus bambolii*, A Propos du Jalonnement Tertiare de l'Homme," *Q.S.*, April 20, 1959, pp. 215–46.

First found in the 1860's and called *Oreopithecus,* these remains were assigned to various taxonomic categories until Hürzeler reopened the question with new specimens in 1956. Early in 1958 he found a nearly complete skeleton, which at the time of writing has not been fully described. This animal had been mired in a forested swamp and covered while still whole, before

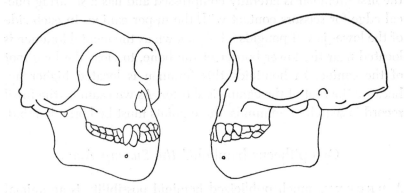

Fig. 16   The Skull of *Oreopithecus:* Hürzeler's Reconstruction. (Drawings after Hürzeler, 1960.)

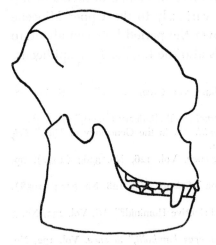

Fig. 17   The Skull of *Oreopithecus:* Drawn from a Photograph. This picture, drawn from a photograph of the skull as it lay in its matrix, differs from Hürzeler's reconstruction in two respects: the nuchal crest is higher, and the mandible is blown out in the gonial region, as among the leaf-eating langurs, and suggesting a specialized diet of soft vegetable matter. (Drawing after a photograph by Hürzeler, 1960.)

predators had had a chance to find the body. He was not a mountain ape, as his name implies, but a swamp ape.

The creature apparently stood some 120 cm. or 4 feet high, about the height of a siamang. Its skull is small, with a length of 125 mm., a breadth of 85 mm., and a capacity of between 275 cc. and 530 cc., which places it in the same brain–body-size ratio as living apes. Although there is no sagittal crest, the supra-orbital ridges are very heavy. Unlike the faces of apes and early men, its face is short. However, the zygomatic arch orginates in the malar bone forward of its position in apes but comparable to its position in man. There is a suggestion of a nasal spine and the nasal bones project beyond the surrounding level of the face; both are manlike features. The symphysis, or sagittal midline, of the lower jaw is steep but chinless, and the mental foramen highly placed.

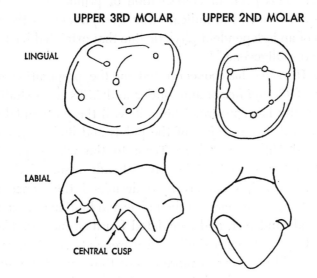

UPPER 3RD MOLAR   UPPER 2ND MOLAR

LINGUAL

LABIAL

CENTRAL CUSP

FIG. 18   THE SPECIALIZED DENTITION OF *Oreopithecus.* The tooth on the left, the upper right third molar, has a small cusp, or conulid, the center of the crown, in addition to the five cusps characteristic of the Dryopithecines, modern apes, and hominids. All of its cusps are high and pointed. The upper right second premolar has five cusps, like a molar, and the two principal cusps are high and pointed. (Drawings after Butler and Mills, 1959.)

The teeth, which have been thoroughly studied by Butler and Miles, are similar to man's in some respects and very different in others. The canines are small and short, and in eleven of twelve known jaws a diastema is lacking. Actually, a diastema appears now and then in human jaws and is sometimes absent in apes. However, the canines occlude differently from those of hominids or apes. Both lower premolars are bicuspid and of the same shape; the shearing edge of the first premolar found in apes is lacking, as one would expect because of the short canines. The molars are long and narrow. They have a high cone relief, with a very unusual central cone, and thin enamel. The enamel in human teeth is nearly twice as thick, enabling men to chew more and to live longer under primitive conditions—unless *Oreopithecus* ate soft food.

Butler and Mills find twelve features in which the *Oreopithecus* molars differ from those of men, and in most of these twelve our molars resemble those of the apes. And the *Oreopithecus* molars bear no relationship to those of Old World monkeys. The authors conclude: "This peculiar combination of primitive and specialized characters seems to indicate that *Oreopithecus* is the terminal form of an independent phyletic line that extended back probably into the Oligocene." [7]

While Hürzeler has concentrated on the preparation of the skeleton of *Oreopithecus* and Butler and Mills have studied its teeth, Schultz has concerned himself with the postcranial skeleton.[8] It was the appearance of the pelvis and limb bones which initially led Hürzeler and de Terra to the widely publicized theory that the animal might have already assumed the erect posture. Schultz has effectively undermined this concept. He took twenty measurements of the pelvic and limb bones, exclusive of the hands and feet, and calculated fourteen indices. Then he compared this data with similar measurements and indices from ten Old World monkeys of more or less the same size, a gibbon, a siamang, a male and a female orang, two male chimpanzees, a female mountain gorilla and a male lowland gorilla, a Negro, a Hawaiian, and a European.

The animal had a trunk height (supersternale to symphysion) of about 460 mm., which is in the range of the largest Old World monkeys, the orang, and the chimpanzee. Judging by its build it weighed about 40 kilograms (88 pounds), a weight equaled among the Old World monkeys only by the largest baboons, and within the orang-chimpanzee range. Its humerus was as long as those of chimpanzees and men, and longer than those of all Old World monkeys. Its femur was shorter than those of Old World monkeys and all apes but the orang. The head of the hu-

---

[7] Butler and Mills: op. cit.
[8] Schultz: "Einige Beobachtungen. . . ."

merus is much wider than that of the femur, which indicates that
the body was supported by the arms more than by the legs; and
the humerus is 122 per cent as long as the femur, a proportion
found in the siamang, orang, and lowland gorilla. Neither the
bones of the forearm nor those of the lower leg were particularly

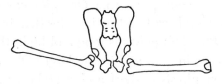

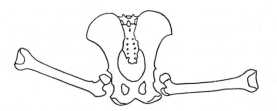

Fig. 19   The Pelvis and Femora of *Oreopithecus.* The top drawing represents
the pertinent bones of a langur, the middle one of Oreopithecus, and the
bottom one of a chimpanzee. Note the relative shortness and breadth of the
Oreopithecus pelvis, which in this respect appears hominid, and the shortness and
stoutness of the femora, which in this sense are pongid. (Drawings after Schultz,
1960.)

elongated. Although a brachiator, *Oreopithecus* was not extremely specialized in the proportions of its limb segments. That
it was arboreal is to be expected because most of the fauna of
flooded forests is either tree-borne or aquatic.

Several bones indicate that the animal had a stout body. The
femur is thick in proportion to its length, the lumbar vertebrae are
heavy, and the ribs are large. The shape of the ribs in particular
is apelike rather than monkeylike, in that the dorsal arm of the rib

lies at an obtuse angle to the main body of the bone, whereas in monkeys the angle is acute. Five lumbar vertebrae were present, compared to between six and eight in monkeys, between four and six in gibbons and men, and between three and five in the great apes.

The form of the pelvic bone (*os coxae*) is of particular interest as it led to the early conception that *Oreopithecus* stood erect. The pelvis as a whole is broad, but no broader than in apes. However, the ilium of the ape's pelvis is long and high; that of *Oreopithecus* is shorter, as in man and in the larger Old World monkeys. The pubic symphysis is short and straight, as among apes and men, but not monkeys; the ischium small and short, as among apes and men, and not long as in monkeys, gibbons, and one extinct hominid that will be discussed in the next chapter (*Australopithecus*). Apparently *Oreopithecus* had not yet developed the pelvic peculiarities of the other large brachiators.

Schultz concludes that *Oreopithecus* is a catarrhine, but that it does not belong to the Cercopithecidae because of peculiarities of both teeth and body. It belongs to the superfamily of Hominoidae, but not to the gibbons (Hylobatidae) because of its teeth and ischium, its short femur, and short lower arm bones. As for the family of Pongidae, its kinship is near but not exact: five lumbar vertebrae is a high number for this group, its ilium has not become elongated, and its teeth are aberrant. It definitely does not belong with the Hominidae; there is no evidence of upright posture superior to that of the larger apes. In its limb bones it is closest to the gorilla, which is the least efficient brachiator among living apes.

In 1916 Schwalbe called the Oreopithecidae an extinct family,[9] and it is either that or a connecting form between the Pongidae and Hominidae. This will be clearer when more evidence is available. Kälin in 1955,[1] Thenius in 1958,[2] and Butler and Mills in 1959[3] have all confirmed Schwalbe's theory. One may conclude

[9] G. Schwalbe: "Über den fossilen Affen, *Oreopithecus bambolii*," *ZfMuA*, Vol. 19 (1916), pp. 149–254.

[1] J. Kälin: "Zur Systematik und evolutiven Deutung der höheren Primaten," *Experientia*, Vol. 11 (1955), pp. 1–17.

[2] E. Thenius: "Tertiärstratigraphie und tertiäre Hominoidenfunde," *AA*, Vol. 22 (1958), pp. 66–77.

[3] Butler and Mills: op. cit.

with Schultz that *Oreopithecus* adds to the number of known forms of Hominoidea, and constitutes further evidence "of the extraordinary variability and plasticity of this group, to which man belongs." [4]

Fossil Primates and Human Evolution

A T T H E beginning of this chapter we proposed to test, on the scale of time, the conclusions of comparative anatomy, physiology, cytology, and parasitology as to the degrees of kinship between man and his fellow primates. According to these conclusions, man fell closest to the living apes; but these findings are still unconfirmed. To date we have no certain ancestor earlier than the Pleistocene, although *Ramapithecus brevirostis* and *Kenyapithecus wickeri* are distinct possibilities, and *Oreopithecus bambolii* has warm champions.

We also hoped to ferret out some evolutionary rules that might cast a few rays of light on man's evolution into geographical races. Zoologically this is a matter of relatively minor importance, but to us it is very important. Despite the meager paleontological representation of primates and despite many wide gaps in the record, we discovered a few enlightening continuities.

The primates appeared early in the history of mammals as a very generalized order of tiny animals, arboreal, virtually omnivorous but with an accent on animal proteins, and reproductively primitive. As prosimians they showed a remarkable adaptive versatility. Some became nocturnal, some acquired a slowed-down metabolism, some lost their tails, some poked the spines of their dorsal vertebrae through their skins as weapons, and some grew chiseling incisors like those of rodents. From these adaptations several superfamilies passed into a higher adaptive grade, that of monkeys (the simian), and they made this transition independently in both hemispheres. Both groups acquired stereoscopic color vision and rapid locomotion in the trees, through brachiation.

It is possible that in South America the marmosets and the cebus monkeys crossed the frontier from the prosimian to the

[4] Schultz: op. cit., p. 148; translation mine.

simian grade independently also, just as four different kinds of reptiles once became mammals. It is equally possible that the Old World monkeys and the ancestors of the apes and men made the same transition separately, although this too has not been proved. Parallel evolution, in separate but genetically similar populations, is a primate commonplace, and a zoological commonplace as well.

Another fact of outstanding significance evidenced in the paleontological record is that in the early epochs of the Cenozoic, tens of millions of years ago, all the primates were small, ranging in size from mice to squirrels and cats. In the Miocene only *Proconsul,* as far as we know, was bigger than a gibbon. In the evolution of the different primate lines the principle of allometry, or the shift of bodily proportions with growth, has been at work. In the elephants the leg and foot had to become columnar to support the animal's increasing weight. In a brachiating primate the hand needed tendinous supports once a certain weight threshold had been reached. In a bipedal primate the pelvis, legs, and feet needed special modifications for a large animal that a small animal did not need.

Several families of primates learned to brachiate independently, and it is possible by the same token—although we cannot prove this—that more than one subfamily or genus independently became bipedally erect. In different families, some genera have grown more intelligent than others. In fact, although a definitely identified early ancestor of man still eludes us, we have discovered a pattern that we might look for when we turn to the history of our own egocentric species, as well as that of other probably less articulate, and extinct, species and genera in our own family. Because changes of all magnitudes, which eventually designate species, genera, and higher taxonomic categories, begin at a subspecific level, what we have learned in this chapter provides a background for a realistic evaluation of the evolutionary parallelism that exists and has existed between various geographical races of man at successive stages of human evolution.

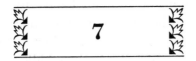

7

THE EARLIEST HOMINIDS

The Origin of the Hominids

W E HAVE TRACED in some detail the family histories of all the primates, except the Hominidae, from the Paleozoic to the present. That of the Hominidae has been postponed until now for two reasons. They include all fossil and living men, whose evolution into races constitutes the main subject of this book, as well as a subfamily of related manlike creatures, the Australopithecines. They are the only primate family lacking a known, proven ancestor who lived before the Pleistocene. Not a trace of the Hominidae has yet been found in a deposit incontestably older than the end of the first half of the Lower Pleistocene.[1] Yet between that time and the beginning of the Middle Pleistocene their bones or tools or both were deposited in several sites scattered all the way from Algeria to South Africa and Java. What happened to the Hominidae during this earliest known period of dispersal is pertinent to the study of human racial origins because the differentiation of races may have begun by or during that time.

Did the Hominidae exist before this dispersion took place, and if so, where? These questions cannot be answered conclusively on the basis of existing information: entire families and subfamilies of primates remained hidden over vast geological periods. Gaps of over 30 million years separate the tree shrews and tarsiers from their last known ancestors, and the chimpanzee and gorilla are parted from *Proconsul*, an ape whose name will appear frequently in this chapter, by 25 million years.

---

[1] Except possibly for one Australopithecine fragment from Tchad, to be described later, and unless *Ramapithecus* and the Fort Ternan primate are hominids.

Of 118 families of mammals living today,[2] 19 first appeared during the Eocene or earlier, 22 during the Miocene, 13 during the
Pliocene, 12 during the Pleistocene, and 27 in the Recent epoch.
During the Pliocene, which lies in the middle of this progression,
the several families of large land mammals evolved, including
elephants, rhinoceroses, and hippopotamuses.[3] In contrast, most
of the land mammals that first appeared as families during the
Pleistocene or Recent epoch are small creatures: rodents, insectivores, and prosimians. The Pliocene, therefore, was a reasonable
period for a family of fairly large-bodied animals with only one
living genus, the Hominidae, to have evolved in. If our family
came into being during the Upper Pliocene or during the initial
phase of the Lower Pleistocene, no paleontological precedent or
protocol was violated.

The bulk of the anatomical and physiological evidence reviewed in the last two chapters strongly suggests that our ancestors evolved from the same primate stock as the chimpanzees,
gorillas, and orangs. We differ from these three apes and from
the Early Miocene ape, *Proconsul*, in three principal respects:
locomotion, brain size, and dentition. Neither locomotion nor
brain size is significant as far as our relationship to the living
pongids is concerned. The apes might have begun to brachiate
before our ancestors quit their company, or our ancestors might
have begun to brachiate, with the apes, before walking erect.
And the brains of all evolutionary lines of primates must have
been small at the beginning. But dentition is a more serious barrier
to kinship with the living pongids, all of which have interlocking
canines and shearing lower first premolars. The shift from the
shearing and crushing type of teeth peculiar to all living and most
fossil apes to our grinding type was a dramatic one, which may or
may not have taken place more than once.

Pending more discussion about *Kenyapithecus*, the leading candidates for the title of Pliocene ancestor of the hominids
will still be the Dryopithecinae found in the Siwalik deposits of

---

[2] Calculated from G. G. Simpson's list of 1945.

[3] The hippopotamus is a land animal in the sense that it comes out of the
water at night to feed on dry land.

northern India in the 1930's by G. E. Lewis and his associates.[4] Because these consist of teeth and jaws alone we do not know whether these apes brachiated or walked, nor how large their brains were. We know only that for some reason their jaws were shorter than those of other pongids and the teeth of some of them were no larger than those of the living genus *Homo* and were, to a certain extent, manlike in form. Others had larger teeth. The body sizes of all these genera are unknown.

In the genus *Ramapithecus* an evolutionary sequence, pointing in the hominid direction, may be traced from *R. hariensis* of the Lower Pliocene to *R. brevirostis* of the Upper Pliocene and initial Pleistocene. In this sequence the molars grow wider (labiolingually) than they are long (anteroposteriorly). The premolars become bicuspid, and although the lower first premolar is still sectorial, the canines are small, and there is no diastema, or gap between the upper canines and the upper lateral incisors. The incisors rise steeply from both jaws, and the alveolar prognathism is less than in some living human beings.

Proconsul himself, who sired the gorilla and chimpanzee, was an African Dryopithecine, and the earliest member of his family yet known. He was related, either as an ancestor or as a cousin,[5] to the Dryopithecines of Europe and Asia, which lived from mid-Miocene to Early Pleistocene and which included the god-apes of India, *Gigantopithecus*, and the as yet unidentified ancestor of the orang. An ape identified in 1951 by LeGros Clark and Leakey by its teeth as *Sivapithecus africanus*, attributed to the Lower Miocene of Kenya, may have been the link between the African and Eurasiatic Dryopithecines. Therefore *Proconsul* could have

[4] G. E. Lewis: "Preliminary Notice of the New Man-like Apes from India," *AJSc*, Ser. 5, No. 27 (1934), pp. 161–79.

W. K. Gregory, M. Hellman, and G. E. Lewis: "Fossil Anthropoids of the Yale Cambridge India Expedition of 1935," *CIWP*, No. 495 (1938).

See also G. Heberer: "Die Fossilgeschichte der *Hominoidea*," *Primatologia* (Basel, 1956), pp. 379–560.

[5] In the sense of G. G. Simpson, who wrote, in 1945: "The †Dryopithecinae are probably a very heterogeneous group which represents a stage in primate evolution rather than a single phylum and its branches. Thus the different Ponginae probably arose from different Dryopithecinae so that the separation of the subfamilies is not phylogenetic classification, but the true phyla are not really distinguished at present." (p. 188)

been our ancestor, either through an African line including the Fort Ternan primate and distinct from that of the gorilla and chimpanzee, or through an Asiatic line that left Africa in the Miocene or Pliocene and returned in the Lower Pleistocene. This geographical problem cannot be decided on present evidence.

Australopithecus *and* Homo

W H E R E V E R it originates, a new family can arise when a group of animals adopts a new ecological position by a radical change of behavior, as, in the case of man, by walking erect, using tools, talking, and seeking food on the ground in groups. But it takes time for a new family to branch into a number of genera and for genera to give birth to species, either by succession, branching, or both; and our family, as we know it, has had very little time.

The known Hominidae are divided into two genera, *Australopithecus* and *Homo*. *Australopithecus* lived during the Lower Pleistocene, with a slight overlap into the Middle Pleistocene. Except in Java, *Homo* is so far definitely known only from the beginning of the Middle Pleistocene onward. The question thus arises, is *Homo* descended from *Australopithecus* by evolution through succession, i.e., by phyletic evolution, or did the two genera arise from a common ancestor through branching, after which our genus replaced its brother?

Both theories have warm champions, and the question is not likely to be decided immediately. So that we may understand the problem as clearly as possible I shall devote the rest of this chapter to the first known phase of hominid history, the Lower Pleistocene, and particularly to the Australopithecines.[6]

---

[6] The name Australopithecinae, denoting a subfamily, was coined by Gregory and Hellman in 1939. Whether these animals actually form a subfamily or just a genus is a matter of opinion. Gregory and Hellman: "The Dentition of the Extinct South-African Man-Ape *Australopithecus* (*Plesianthropus*) *transvaalensis* Broom, A Comparative and Phylogenetic Study," *ATM*, Vol. 29 (1939), pp. 339–73. To match the term Australopithecine, the word Hominine is sometimes used for man.

The Lower Pleistocene

THE Lower Pleistocene is the name given the first half of the Pleistocene epoch; it is believed to have begun about one million years ago and to have ended about one half million years ago. Lower Pleistocene deposits cannot be easily distinguished from the underlying Pliocene beds everywhere that both occur, but in some places an abrupt soil change caused by uplift and erosion marks the Plio-Pleistocene threshold and in others no Pliocene underlies the Pleistocene strata at all.

With the advent of the Pleistocene the climate cooled repeatedly in certain parts of the earth, and in others there were alternating periods of heavy rainfall and drought. New mountains rose and old ones increased their stature, volcanoes spouted lava and dust, and sea levels rose and fell, as the earth's crust buckled and waters of the oceans were first imprisoned in icecaps and then released, three such cycles occurring in a row. But the icecaps were a special feature of the second half of the Pleistocene. During the Lower Pleistocene mountain glaciers formed in stream beds several times in different places, but no ice accumulated on continental land masses. When the first icecaps appeared on continental land masses, the Middle Pleistocene had begun.[7]

In certain critical places the point in time at which the Pleistocene began is defined by the appearance of cold-adapted molluscs in previously warm waters.[8] The change in molluscan geography is matched, on land, by the appearance of modern genera and subfamilies of horses, cattle, elephants (in the form of mammoths), and camels. These animals spread rapidly and widely in the Palearctic, Nearctic, Oriental, and African regions.

The fauna to which they belonged is called Villafranchian, after a site in Italy. In the original sense the name meant a particular assemblage of mammals, but in various places these animals continued to evolve, so that many old species were replaced by new

[7] See J. K. Charlesworth: *The Quaternary Era* (London: E. Arnold & Co.; 1957).

[8] See F. C. Howell: "The Villafranchian and Human Origins," *Science*, Vol. 130, No. 3379 (1959), pp. 831–44.

ones. Some genera even replaced others. The Lower Pleistocene, with its challenging alternations of climate, was a time of rapid mammalian evolution. Many authors use the term Villafranchian as a synonym for Lower Pleistocene. This practice has caused some confusion because many local faunas of the middle and latter parts of the Lower Pleistocene are Villafranchian only in a general and derivative sense.

Lower Pleistocene sequences of the Old World, some geological, some faunal, and some both, are best known from Europe, Palestine, India, Java, China, and several parts of Africa. In western Europe a succession of mountain glaciers and associated drops in temperature produced first a cold phase, then a so-called Tiglian cool interglacial, then the two mountain glaciers known as Günz I and Günz II, and finally the Cromerian Interglacial, which was followed by the beginning of the Middle Pleistocene. In Central Europe three local mountain glaciations, called Donau I, II, and III, occupied the same general time span.[9]

In Palestine two successive earth movements, or riftings, opened the crack that created the Jordan Valley and the Dead Sea. The twisted strata and dislocated blocks so formed mark the thresholds between the Pliocene and Lower Pleistocene and between the Lower and Middle Pleistocene.

In India the Pliocene deposits of the Siwalik Hills, so rich in pongid fossils, are overlaid by two successive Lower Pleistocene levels, first the Tatrot, then the Pinjor. The Tatrot is Early Lower Pleistocene, and the Pinjor is contemporaneous with the first of a series of four Himalayan glaciations, corresponding to Günz in the Alpine series. Although much alike, the Tatrot and Pinjor faunas

---

[9] As I write, this classification is changing. B. Kurtén has proposed a new way of dividing the first half of the Pleistocene which makes excellent sense. In it the Lower Pleistocene is synonymous with the Villafranchian, which F. Clark Howell calls the Basal Pleistocene. Thus the Günz glaciations, the Cromerian Interglacial, and the Mindel-Elster glaciation (including the Cortonian Interstadial between Mindel I and Mindel II) together become the Lower Middle Pleistocene. Then the Second, Great, or Holstein Interglacial and the following Riss, Saale, or Third Glaciation become the Upper Middle Pleistocene. What is left remains Upper Pleistocene, as before. Although this scheme has much merit, it needs to be generally accepted (as it probably will be) before I can use it in a book. B. Kurtén: "The relative ages of the Australopithecines of Transvaal and the Pithecanthropines of Java," in G. Kurth: *Evolution und Hominisation* (Stuttgart: Gustav Fischer Verlag; 1962), pp. 74–80.

are differentiated by the presence or absence of certain species. For example, *Ramapithecus*, the Dryopithecine ape with the most humanlike dentition so far described, lived on into the Tatrot but is not found in the Pinjor.

Most of Java was submerged during the Pliocene, but during the Pleistocene the land rose, starting at the western end. Geological deposits in the western part of the island are clearly Lower Pleistocene, like those of the Siwaliks. In the eastern part of the island the earliest fauna is found in the Djetis beds, which have been called contemporary with either the Cromerian Interglacial or the beginning of the first Mindel glaciation of the initial Middle Pleistocene. These beds contain a so-called Sino-Malayan fauna, including the orang, gibbon, and two hominids, all of which are believed to have originated in south China and to have reached Java via the outer ring of islands.

In south China the bones of this fauna are cemented in blocks of breccia preserved in rock crevices. Because breccia can have formed at several different times, these fossils have been dated on the basis of their first appearance in stratified deposits elsewhere, in this case the well-known Siwalik Hills. There the Sino-Malayan fauna is absent from the Pinjor beds. For that reason Hooijer and others, including Howell, call the Djetis fauna Early Middle Pleistocene, whereas von Koenigswald, who did much of the original research in Java, has consistently stipulated a Late Lower Pleistocene date.[1]

At present von Koenigswald seems to be ahead in this argument. In 1961 he obtained two tektites (glassy nodules from outer

---

[1] D. A. Hooijer: "Fossil Mammals and the Plio-Pleistocene Boundary in Java," *PKAW* B, Vol. 55, No. 4 (1952), pp. 436–43.

Hooijer: "The Lower Boundary of the Pleistocene in Java and the Age of Pithecanthropus," *Quaternaria*, Vol. 3 (1956), pp. 5–10.

Hooijer: "The Correlation of Fossil Mammalian Faunas and the Plio-Pleistocene Boundary in Java," *PKAW* B, Vol. 60, No. 1 (1957), pp. 1–10.

Howell: "The Age of the Australopithecines of Southern Africa," *AJPA*, Vol. 13, No. 4 (1955), pp. 635–62.

Howell: "The Villafranchian and Human Origins," *Science*, Vol. 130, No. 3379 (1959), pp. 831–44.

Heberer: op. cit., pp. 379–560, 528.

Von Koenigswald: "Remarks on the Correlation of Mammalian Faunas of Java and India and the Plio-Pleistocene Boundary," *PKAW* B, Vol. 59 (1956), pp. 204–10.

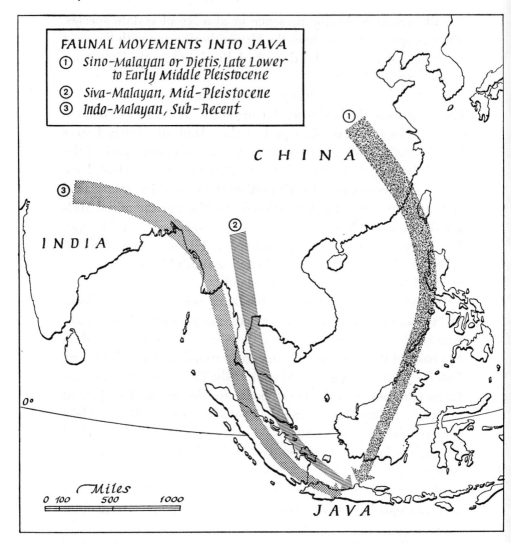

FAUNAL MOVEMENTS INTO JAVA
1. Sino-Malayan or Djetis, Late Lower to Early Middle Pleistocene
2. Siva-Malayan, Mid-Pleistocene
3. Indo-Malayan, Sub-Recent

MAP 5

space) from two different deposits in central Java, taken from beds of the Trinil fauna—the one following the Djetis, with which we are here concerned. He submitted both samples to the atomic laboratory of the Max Planck Institute in Heidelberg. There W. Gentner and H. J. Lippolt tested them by the Argon-40 method, which will be described in the following chapter. The two samples gave almost identical results. The Trinil beds were laid down about 600,000 years ago. That is before the conventional date of the beginning of the Middle Pleistocene. The Djetis beds, being older, are therefore of Late Lower Pleistocene date.[2]

In northern China, where no atom-age dating has yet been done, geological and faunal sequences have been worked out. The Pliocene was warm and mainly dry. The Pleistocene, which started with earth movements, was wetter and cooler. The Lower Pleistocene deposits consist first of basal conglomerates, then of a series of sands, marls, and clays known as the Lower Sanmenian, and finally of a bed of sands and silts containing an Asiatic version of the Villafranchian fauna. Next comes an erosion surface caused by additional earth movements, and then the Upper Sanmenian red loams, which are Middle Pleistocene.

In East Africa the giant earthquakes that cracked out the Jordan also split open the Rift valleys and lowered the lake beds. Among the flanks of the Rift faces, gullies have been eroded through 300 feet or more of Pleistocene deposits, some of which are seated on beds of basalt. There is no question about locating a Pliocene-Pleistocene border there because no Pliocene deposits have yet been identified. As they consist of alternate layers of lake-bottom accumulations and volcanic ash, some of the Lower Pleistocene beds are very thick. But these materials can accumulate rapidly; the thickness of the beds is therefore not an accurate indication of the passage of time.

Five key East African sites have yielded local Lower Pleistocene faunas: Kaiso, Omo, Kanam, Laetolil, and Olduvai. Of these Kaiso is considered to be the oldest. Omo and Kanam, roughly contemporaneous, come next and overlap those below and above them in the time scale. Laetolil is the next to youngest and Olduvai the most recent.[3] At the end of the Lower Pleistocene the East African climate, which had been moist, grew very dry, and during the drought the top of the Lower Pleistocene deposit at Olduvai

---

[2] Von Koenigswald, W. Gentner, and H. J. Lippolt: "Age of the Basalt Flow at Olduvai, East Africa," *Nature*, Vol. 192, No. 4804 (1961), pp. 720–1. "Das absolute Alter des Pithecanthropus Erectus Dubois," in Kurth: *Evolution und Hominisation* (Stuttgart: Gustav Fischer Verlag; 1962), pp. 112–19. See also H. C. Urey: "Origin of Tektites," *Science*, Vol. 137, No. 3532 (1962), pp. 746–8.

[3] In the East African faunas Ewer found the following percentages of living species: Omo, 21%; Laetolil, 29%; and Olduvai, 36%. The Kaiso fauna had only thirteen species, too few to be statistically significant. R. F. Ewer: "Faunal Evidence on the Dating of the Australopithecinae," *PTPA*, 1957, pp. 135–42.

Gorge weathered away. We do not know how much of the Olduvan faunal deposits were lost at that time.

In North Africa several sites contain Lower Pleistocene fauna, but of a relatively late date, comparable to those of the East African locations. The best known is Aïn Hanech (more properly Hanash) or Snake Spring, near St. Arnaud in the Sétif plateau, department of Constantine, Algeria.

In South Africa the picture is confused by the influence of the antarctic air masses, which make the local sequence partly independent of the glacial and pluvial systems farther north. Here the chronology of the Lower Pleistocene is based largely on fauna, some of which seems older than the East African series because it contains a larger number of extinct species. When we study the Australopithecines, this fact will assume a considerable importance.

The New Dating for the Lower Pleistocene

U N T I L A U G U S T, 1961, most geologists, paleontologists, and anthropologists were content to accept, at least provisionally, the date of about one million years ago for the beginning of the Villafranchian. Then the National Geographic Society dropped a bombshell in a press release, following it with a magazine article in October.[4]

The bombshell was a new date for the Zinjanthropus level in Bed I of Olduvai Gorge, Tanganyika, determined by the newly discovered Argon-40 method, the same one used by von Koenigswald's associates on Javanese samples. J. F. Evernden and G. H. Curtis of the University of California at Berkeley collected several samples of volcanic materials at the Gorge and measured them for Argon-40 content. The dates provided by these samples, taken from the Zinjanthropus level of Bed I, ranged from 1,570,000 to 1,890,000 years, with an average of 1,750,000 years ago.

The confusion which the publication of these dates caused was somewhat allayed five months later when von Koenigswald and Lippolt announced that the basalt underlying Bed I was only

[4] G. H. Curtis: "Clock for the Ages: Potassium Argon," *NG*, Vol. 120, No. 4 (1961), pp. 590–2.

1,300,000 years old. However, doubt was revived after a few weeks, in March 1962, when Leakey declared, on the basis of new tests at Berkeley, that the basalt was really 4 million years old.

Lippolt tested two chopping tools made of basalt which von Koenigswald had collected in Beds I and II, and a piece of the underlying basalt chipped off by Oakley. All gave a date of 1,300,000 years. Meanwhile Curtis and Evernden, according to Leakey, got dates of nearly 4 million years from the same underlying basalt, but from different samples. As Leakey himself has suggested, it seems likely that the basalt was laid down more than once and that different layers have different dates. In this sense, everyone is right.

Either the soils of Bed I were laid down by wind and water from older volcanic deposits, or else the different minerals sent to laboratories from Olduvai Gorge accumulate Argon-40 at different rates, as Straus and Hunt have suggested.[5] Otherwise the post-Villafranchian part of the Lower Pleistocene lasted much longer than had been supposed, not only in Africa but throughout the world. For the purposes of this book I shall adhere to the conventional chronology, at least in this edition.

The Evidence of Tools and Fire in the Lower Pleistocene

THE HOMINIDAE are distinguished from the other primate families by a behavioral characteristic that can be determined archaeologically—the manufacture of stone tools. Whenever hominid bones have been found in undisturbed habitation sites, tools are there also. Other tools of equal age have been found in disturbed and undisturbed sites lacking hominid remains. This does not mean that all hominids made stone tools, only that there is no proof to the contrary.

Lower Pleistocene tools whose age can be definitely certified have so far come only from North and East Africa. The principal

[5] Von Koenigswald: "Das absolute Alter des Pithecanthropus Erectus Dubois," in Kurth: *Evolution und Hominisation*, pp. 112–19. Also personal communication from L. S. B. Leakey, March 24, 1962. W. L. Straus, Jr., and C. B. Hunt: "The Age of Zinjanthropus," *Science*, Vol. 136, No. 3513 (1962), pp. 293–5.

site in North Africa is again Aïn Hanech,[6] situated in or on the edge of an old lake deposit containing a Late Lower Pleistocene fauna similar to that found at Olduvai.[7]

In East Africa tools have been found with a Kaiso fauna at Kanyatsi, Uganda; at the faunal sites of Omo and Laetolil; and at Olduvai itself. In South Africa a few tools have turned up in the more recent of the Australopithecine cave sites. They are probably no older than those from East Africa, if as old. These African sites, with the exception of the latest South African one, are older than the oldest known specimens of *Homo* in Africa, and the fossils that have been found with tools probably, if not definitely, belong to the genus *Australopithecus*.

The tools that have been found at single sites in large enough numbers to constitute complete industries follow a definite pattern. Some are simply oval, water-rounded pebbles split crosswise, lengthwise, or diagonally. Others are single-edged choppers or double-edged chopping tools, and still others are crude, simple flakes. In some of the North and East African sites stone balls have been found. These have fancifully been called bolas stones, but the most perfect ones are much more plausibly stones especially shaped for accurate throwing. Anyone who has played baseball knows that it would be easier to hit an animal with a stone shaped like a perfect sphere than with a shapeless piece of rock.

Wherever these implements have been dated, by faunal associations or otherwise, they have come from the later part of the Lower Pleistocene. As they have been found nowhere at the base of the Pleistocene, they may be considered a Middle or Late Lower Pleistocene invention, and as far as we know an African one.

In Eurasia most if not all of the tool-bearing sites or groups of sites so far found, from England to the Philippines, cannot be shown to be older than the Cromerian-Mindel threshold that marks the end of the Lower Pleistocene, with possible exceptions in France, India, and Malaya.

In 1959 two French archaeologists, R. Agache and F. Bourdier,

[6] L. Balout: *Préhistoire de l'Afrique du Nord* (Paris: Arts et Métiers Graphiques; 1955), pp. 159–73.

[7] C. Arambourg: "L'Hominien Fossile d'Oldoway," *BSPR*, Vol. 57, Nos. 3/4 (1960), pp. 223–8.

while excavating a small trench on the highest terrace of the Somme River near Amiens, uncovered a Lower Pleistocene deposit apparently of Tiglian age. In it they found a tooth of the Villafranchian horse *Equus stenonis,* several flint flakes at least one of which they identified as an implement, and what seemed to be a hearth.[8] Additional work needs be done there before this discovery can be evaluated.

In Palestine, also in 1959, a bulldozer operator accidentally uncovered what seemed to be a habitation site in a Lower Pleistocene outcrop at Tell Ubeidiya, Israel, near the southern shore of Lake Tiberias and just west of the Jordan River. In addition to very fragmentary hominid remains they found chipped balls, choppers, chopping tools, and several flakes, constituting the industry seen at Aïn Hanech and Olduvai. Although the exact age of these finds remains to be determined, they are probably no older than the two African sites, that is, post-Villafranchian.

In Northern India typologically good Lower Pleistocene implements of the so-called pre-Soan industry have been found with a fauna of Cromerian age in the gravels of the Second Himalayan Glaciation. These should be at least as old as the Lower-to-Middle Pleistocene threshold.[1]

In Malaya also, tools have recently been found in gravels of probably the same age, Cromerian or earliest Mindel, which could make them as old as the Djetis beds of Java.[2] These tools are

[8] R. Agache and F. Bourdier: "Découverte de Silex Apparemment Taillés à un Equidé Archaeique de Type Villafranchien dans la Haut Terrasse Supérieure de la Somme," *CRAS,* Vol. 248, No. 3 (1959), pp. 439–40.

[9] M. Stekelis, L. Picard, N. Schulman, and G. Haas: "Villafranchian Deposits near Ubeidiya in the Central Jordan Valley (Preliminary Report)," *BRCI,* Vol. 9-G, No. 4 (1960), pp. 175–84.

These remains are said to come from a stratum containing *Melanopsis* invertebrate fauna. The "Melanopsis stage" of the Lower Pleistocene is a very early Lower Pleistocene lake-bed formation, entirely under water, which could hardly have been a living floor at the time it was formed, although hominids could have camped on the shore. The mammalian fauna has not yet been identified in enough detail to pinpoint the exact stage of the Pleistocene to which it belongs, but the preliminary report contains no genus or species name inconsistent with a Lower Pleistocene date.

[1] R. E. M. Wheeler: *Early India and Pakistan* (New York: Frederick A. Praeger; 1959), pp. 34–62.

[2] Ann Sieveking: "The Paleolithic Industry of Kota Tampan, Perak, Northwest Malaya," *AP,* Vol. 2, No. 2 (1960), pp. 91–102.

mostly single-faced choppers. Siam and the Philippines are beginning to yield similar industries, so far undated. The earliest industries of the Far East differ in detail from those of the West. Their
principal tool is the single-faced chopper, and there are no
flaked balls.

The currently popular theory that tool-making began in Africa
in the Late Lower Pleistocene and spread to Europe and Asia only
at the beginning of the Middle Pleistocene has not yet been disproved, but it faces many challenges as more and more archaeological research is carried out in India, southeast Asia, and Indonesia (in the ethnic, not political, sense). However, it seems likely
that northern China, whose Lower Pleistocene beds have been
carefully explored, was uninhabited until the Middle Pleistocene.

Tools and fire are the unique possession of man. Except for the
unconfirmed discovery of Agache and Bourdier, however, no evidence of fire whatever has been found in any Lower Pleistocene
site, either in the form of charcoal, charred bones, or discolored
stones. And, as we shall see shortly, the teeth and jaw muscles of
most if not all known Lower Pleistocene hominids were big
enough and strong enough to masticate raw food, including meat.

Geography and Numbers of Early Hominids

A s o n e would expect, the sites containing Lower Pleistocene
tools outnumber those containing early hominid bones. An animal which makes stone implements discards thousands of chips
and tools in his lifetime, and, as stone is inedible, these artifacts
usually stay where he has left them, unless they are moved by
water or ice. He himself has only 180-odd bones in his body and
all of him except his teeth is edible. Unless he happens to drown or
sink in quicksand his remains will most likely be dragged away,
dismembered, and digested. Several of our early hominid skeletons, therefore, were found under what once was water.

Ten sites and possibly also a Chinese drugstore [3] have furnished
remains of a maximum of seventy-five hominid individuals, pre-

[3] Ralph von Koenigswald found some fossil teeth, which he considers to be
Australopithecine, in the same Chinese pharmacies in which he also found *Gigantopithecus* teeth. See page 358.

sumably Australopithecines, which will be described in this chapter. These remains have in common the fact that they were found in Lower Pleistocene deposits, or, if they are younger, that they cannot be definitely called *Homo*. Their geographical distribution is as follows.

TABLE 4

THE DISTRIBUTION OF
EARLY HOMINIDS

Region	Site	Number
South Africa	Taung	1
	Sterkfontein	21 *ca.*
	Makapansgat	5 *ca.*
	Swartkrans	35 *ca.*
	Kromdraai	3
East Africa	Olduvai Gorge	3
	Kanam	1 (?)
	Garusi	1
Sahara	Tchad	1
Palestine	Tell Ubeidiya	1
Java	Djetis Beds	2
China	drugstore	1 (?)

The order in which these sites have been arranged in Table 4 is based primarily on the amount of information available for each specimen or group of specimens. It may also reflect relative age, although this is not sure.

The South African Australopithecines: Time, Space, and Taxonomy

THE MOST numerous and most fully described of early hominids are the Australopithecines of South Africa. They seem to be divided into two successive populations of different sizes and degrees of resemblance to *Homo*. What we know about them we have learned as a result of the energy and devotion of a few dedicated South African anatomists and paleontologists, notably Dart, Broom, and Robinson. Their success is due in part to the fact that in Africa south of the Sahara limestone is scarce. With the modern building boom in Johannesburg and other cities along the Rand, whatever deposits there are have been subjected to quarrying, dynamiting, and conversion into cement. Like most limestone, the Transvaal deposits contain fissures and caves, many of which are filled with sandy breccia, useless to limeworkers. These breccias are packed with animal bones, mostly those of ungulates, but some are the bones of baboons and a few of hominids. Since 1924 when Dart first identified the infant skull of *Australopithecus africanus,* fragmentary remains of many other hominid individuals have been tediously cut out of the breccias.

So far only five such sites contain these remains. They are located in three widely separated regions (see Map 5). Taung, where the first find was made, is in Bechuanaland, six miles west of Taung Station and eighty miles north of Kimberley. Kromdraai, Sterkfontein, and Swartkrans are clustered together within a space of three miles located six to nine miles north-northwest of Krugersdorp in the Transvaal. Makapansgat is near Potgietersrust, north Transvaal, 165 miles north of Pretoria. From Taung to the three central sites is about 200 miles, and from the latter to Makapansgat about 150. Taung is in dry country, whereas the other four are well watered. These differences in relative humidity existed during the time of the Australopithecines, as they do today.

The Taung site consists of a dolomite plateau scored by deep cracks. Into these crevices animal bones had fallen or been washed, along with sand, which cemented them into two successive breccias, a gray below and a pink above. The Sterkfontein site is a cave which had a hole in its roof in Australopithecine time. As the bones inside had fallen through the roof, it could not have been a habitation site. The other three, Makapansgat, Swartkrans, and Kromdraai, were apparently ordinary caves.[4]

The remains from all these sites are as fragmentary as the bony refuse from a lamb stew, and consist largely of teeth. It is impossible, therefore, to say how many individuals are represented. However, since the initial discovery at Taung, in 1924, of an infant skull, which was promptly named *Australopithecus africanus,* the remains of several hundred similar hominids have been collected. This skull came from the pink breccia. Following hoary paleontological tradition the hominids were initially classified into four genera and six species, as follows: *A. africanus,* Taung;

[4] G. B. Barbour: "Ape or Man?" *OJS,* Vol. 49 (1949), pp. 129–45.

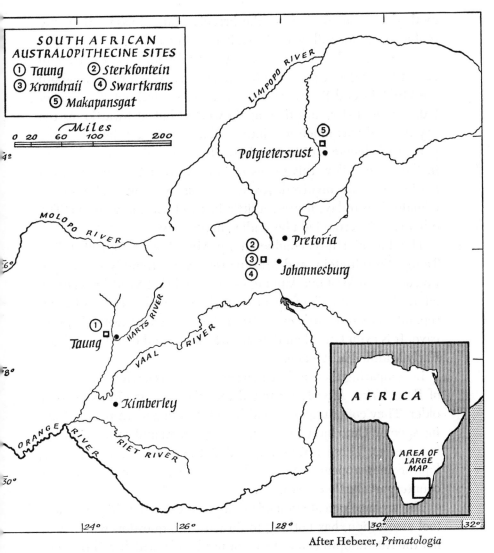

SOUTH AFRICAN
AUSTRALOPITHECINE SITES
① Taung   ② Sterkfontein
③ Kromdraii   ④ Swartkrans
⑤ Makapansgat

After Heberer, *Primatologia*

MAP 6

Plesianthropus transvaalensis, Sterkfontein; *A. prometheus,* Makapansgat; *Paranthropus crassidens,* Swartkrans; *Telanthropus capensis,* Swartkrans; and *Paranthropus robustus,* Kromdraai. Dart named the two species of *Australopithecus,* Broom and Robinson the others. The commonly known subfamily named Australopithecinae, which encompasses all of them, can be used informally in the guise of Australopithecine.

The succession of these five sites has been determined by three methods: soil analysis from the breccias, faunal association, and tool association. Soil analysis, which Brain conducted,[5] is used to determine whether a climate was wet or dry and what pattern of climatic changes occurred while each breccia was forming. In both Sterkfontein and Swartkrans the climate started out like that of today, grew drier, and then again wetter; but at Swartkrans the dry interval was much less intense than at Sterkfontein, and the pattern of change is different. As the two caves lie near each other in the same valley, this seems to indicate that two different climatic cycles are involved. Kromdraai, also nearby, had a wetter climate than today; it grew a little less wet as time went on. The other two sites could not be studied in this way.

The faunal study conducted by Miss Ewer[6] indicates that Taung, Sterkfontein, and Makapansgat were roughly contemporaneous, or at least overlapping in time, and that Swartkrans came later, after a gap. The fauna assigned to Kromdraai came from a separate site 100 yards away from the Australopithecine-bearing cave. It is even later than that of Swartkrans and could have been Early Middle Pleistocene.

In comparing the South Africa cave faunas as a whole with those of East Africa, Miss Ewer found that they are as old as Omo or older. They contain 47 per cent living genera and 12 per cent living species. Omo has 60 per cent living genera and 21 per cent living species. These results imply that the South African Australopithecines appeared on the local scene as early as did their counterparts farther north.

The archaeological evidence that constitutes the third method, tool association, has nothing to do with the question whether or not the Australopithecines made or used tools, which will be dealt with later. It is concerned only with associations outside the caves themselves. In the terraces of the nearby Vaal River Valley archaeologists, working independently of the fossil-hunters, have discovered a three-stage tool sequence, starting with Early Oldowan.

[5] C. K. Brain: "New Evidence for the Correlation of the Transvaal Ape-Man-Bearing Cave Deposits," *TCPC* (1957), pp. 143–8.

Brain: "The Transvaal Ape-Man-Bearing Cave Deposits," *TMM*, No. 11 (1958).

B. E. Sabels: review of Brain's work, *AJPA*, Vol. 17, No. 3 (1959), pp. 247–9.

[6] Ewer: op. cit.

By comparing the climates of the caves with those of the successive valley levels, Oakley [7] has found that the three early sites, Taung, Sterkfontein, and Makapansgat, were probably contemporaneous with the Early Oldowan level, whereas the other two, particularly Kromdraai, belong with the fully evolved Oldowan tool level, which is geologically separate from the first.

Although each of the three methods—soil analysis, faunal association, and tool association—has its limitations, the cumulative effect of the three is impressive. The early sites are thus associated with Omo and Kanam, Swartkrans with Olduvai Bed I, and Kromdraai could even have overlapped the beginning of the Middle Pleistocene.

This division of the five sites into two consecutive, nonoverlapping groups agrees with the anatomical evidence. The first three caves contained small hominids about the size of a living human Pygmy or even smaller, under five feet or 150 cm. tall and weighing less than 100 pounds. The Swartkrans and Kromdraai creatures were taller and heavier, within the full-sized human range in both dimensions. In fact Swartkrans may have weighed as much as 150 pounds.[8] There is some question about Telanthropus's size and status; that will be discussed later. That we are dealing with samples of two successive populations makes good sense ecologically. It is doubtful that two closely related species or subspecies of hominid could both survive competition for the same food supply while living within a mile of each other in the same valley. Whether the big species evolved out of the small one, or simply replaced it after invading from the north, this evidence does not tell us.

Despite the proliferation of taxonomic names originally given these hominids, the group as a whole was no more variable than the living chimpanzee, including its pygmy form. Washburn,[9] seconded by Dart himself,[1] has proposed that all the Australopithe-

[7] K. P. Oakley: "Dating the Australopithecines," *TPCP* (1957), pp. 155–7.

[8] These estimates, based principally on pelvis size, were made by W. L. Straus, Jr. See S. M. Garn and A. B. Lewis: "Tooth Size, Body Size, and 'Giant' Fossil Man," *AA*, Vol. 60, No. 5 (1958), pp. 874–80.

[9] S. L. Washburn, in discussion of E. Mayr: *Taxonomic Categories in Fossil Hominids* (Cold Spring Harbor Symposia, Vol. 15, 1950), p. 118.

[1] R. A. Dart: "*Australopithecus prometheus* and *Telanthropus capensis*," *AJPA*, Vol. 13, No. 1 (1955), pp. 67–96.

cines so far known constitute a single genus, and Oakley[2] has further proposed that this genus can be divided into no more than two species, *Australopithecus africanus* for the Lower Pleistocene specimens and *A. robustus* for the later ones.

We now have three sets of names for the South African Australopithecines: five site names, four of which refer to separate and single kinds of animal each, and only one of which houses two kinds; five generic names as originally proposed, two of which encompass two species each; and one new genus with two species separated by a time threshold. Of the three sets the only one which cannot be changed is the first. I shall therefore follow the current procedure employed by experts in this field and call the specimens by the names of their sites, except for Telanthropus, whose status is in doubt anyhow. The list of names is now: Taung (*A. africanus*); Sterkfontein (*Plesianthropus*); Makapansgat (*A. prometheus*); Swartkrans (*Paranthropus crassidens*); Kromdraai (*P. robustus*); and Telanthropus (*Telanthropus*).

The Australopithecine Cave Sites

U N L I K E Bed I of Olduvai, not one of the five Australopithecine sites can be called with certainty a habitation or occupation site; and since Taung and Sterkfontein are mere refuse pits, they are out of the question. The breccias of all five were broken by quarry-men into blocks, out of stratigraphic context. Even if Makapansgat, Swartkrans, and Kromdraai had contained superimposed occupation floors, we could not list them in order. Howell, in 1959, considered that the way some of the ungulate long bones were split, and their lack of tooth marks, indicated that the Australopithecines might have brought the bones into the caves. But no primate except man has been known to live in caves,[3] and even men will rarely enter them unless they have fire, or at least a light. Caves are dark, and hominids do not have night vision. Caves are dank and clammy; without fire they are uncomfortable. Caves also

---

[2] Oakley: "Dating of the Australopithecines of Africa," *AJPA*, Vol. 12, No. 1 (1954), pp. 9–23.

[3] A possible exception is the crab-eating macaque of the Philippines, which lives along the shore and has no predators to fear but man.

harbor predatory beasts, like tigers, and smaller but almost equally objectionable porcupines. We have no evidence that human beings lived in caves before they had fire. And none of the Australopithecines had it.

In the Limeworks Cave at Makapansgat a count was made of the animal bones removed from the breccia. Ninety-two per cent were the bones of antelope of different species and sizes. Baboons accounted for 1.7 per cent, and the Australopithecines for only .26 per cent. Had the Australopithecines been both residents and cannibals, like Sinanthropus, the count of their own bones would be higher. Whoever or whatever animal it was that lived almost exclusively on antelopes must have been an accomplished hunter, a far better one than the contemporary hominids of Olduvai and Tell Ubeidiya (Israel), as we shall soon see.

Howell attributes to Desmond Clark a statement that these caves contained springs and that animals entered them to drink.[4] This may well be true. But the Australopithecines would not dwell in a busy public watering place frequented by large predators as well as by their prey.

Did the Australopithecines Make Tools?

W E D O not know whether the Australopithecines made tools. We only know that someone was flaking tools in Australopithecine country when those hominids lived there, and that those tools found their way into two successive terraces of the Vaal. If the Australopithecines did not make the stone implements in question, then they could only have been made by true men, of whom no physical trace has yet been found.

Yet true men could hardly have coexisted with Australopithecines in a single valley for over a hundred thousand years (a minimal estimate) without having exterminated their close rivals for the food supply. We are left with the circumstantial evidence that the Australopithecines probably did indeed make the stone tools.

There is no reason at all for stone tools, or any other kind of implements, to be found in the breccias except by coincidence. The

⁴ Howell: "The Villafranchian. . . ."

Australopithecines almost certainly did not live in the caves, and a dead hominid who is being dragged into a cave by carnivores, in several pieces, is not likely to bring his tools with him.

At Makapansgat seventeen "pebble tools" have been found in breccia above the Australopithecine-bearing layer.[5] At Kromdraai two pieces of intrusive rock, not identified as implements, have also been found.[6] At Sterkfontein worked pebbles have been removed from an upper level of breccia which also contained an Australopithecine maxilla and several teeth.[7] Leakey calls this level Middle Pleistocene. A direct bit of evidence is Schepers's discovery of a piece of "flint-like rock" imbedded in the skull and endocranial cast of a Kromdraai specimen, who may well have died as a result,[8] but the victim could have lived late enough to have been killed by a pioneering Middle Pleistocene *Homo*. Schepers was obliged to destroy this object in cleaning the matrix.

Dart had, in 1948, a collection of fifty-eight baboon skulls from Taung, Sterkfontein, and Makapansgat, forty-two of which showed depressed fractures, some in the form of double dents as if made by blows from the distal condyles of an ungulate femur. More had been struck on the left side than on the right. He states that these baboons had been tapped on the head by such a bone weapon, held in some kind of hominid's hand, in this case, the hand of an Australopithecine.[9] In recent years he has had published widely his theory that some of the bones, horns, and teeth recovered from the breccias were used by the Australopithecines as weapons and tools.[1] I have handled some of Dart's specimens

[5] Brain, C. van R. Lowe, and Dart: "Kafuan Stone Artifacts in the Post-Australopithecine Breccia at Makapansgat," *Nature*, Vol. 175, No. 4444 (1955), p. 16–18.

[6] L. S. B. Leakey: "A New Fossil Skull from Oldoway," *Nature*, Vol. 184, No. 4685 (1959), pp. 491–3.

[7] Oakley, in comment on paper of M. Bonnardel: "La Main et L'Outil," in *Les Processus de L'Hominisation*, A Delmas, ed. (Paris, 1958), p. 131.

[8] G. W. H. Schepers, "The Endocrinal Casts . . . ," pp. 173–4. Also personal communication.

[9] Dart: "The Makapansgat Proto-Human Australopithecus Prometheus," *AJPA*, Vol. 6, No. 3 (1948), pp. 259–84.

Dart: "The Predatory Implemental Technique of Australopitheus," *AJPA*, Vol. 7, No. 1 (1949), pp. 1–16.

[1] Dart: "The Makapansgat Australopithecine Osteodontokeratic Culture," *PTPC*, 1955, pp. 161–71.

Dart and J. W. Kitching: "Bone Tools at the Kalkbank Middle Stone Age Site

and find them as unconvincing as his ingenious theory is unnecessary. Recently Pei and others have found the same kind of bone "tools" as Dart's in a Chinese mammalian fauna of Late Pleistocene date, without any evidence of man's presence.[2]

Whatever made them, the paired depressions on the baboon skulls are the likeliest evidence we have that the Australopithecines hunted at all, but they are not convincing, for two reasons. (1) Only one of the three sites, Makapansgat, was an ordinary cave into which predators dragged the remains of their kills. Most of the bones were those of adult animals. Taung and Sterkfontein were holes into which animals fell, or their bones were washed. Neither was a habitation site. Both were naturally formed refuse pits. (2) Of the twenty-two photographs of punctured baboon skulls shown in Dart's 1949 article, sixteen are adult, one is juvenile, three are infant, and two are of undetermined age. If 80 per cent of Australopithecus's primate victims were adult, then he was a mature hunter, like the unidentified killer who left the bones of his victims in Makapansgat cave. Whoever killed the antelopes of Makapansgat and the baboons of all three sites was therefore a much better hunter than the hominids who inhabited Olduvai Gorge and the Jordan Valley, where nearly all the animals killed were infants. It is hard to believe that the South African Australopithecines were better hunters than their relatives farther north.

The Postcranial Skeletons of the South African Australopithecines

A HOMINID can hunt only if his hands are free to hold weapons, and his hands are free only if he can stand, walk, and run bipedally. Whether or not an animal stood erect can be determined by studying the bones of its postcranial skeleton. In the

---

and the Makapansgat Australopithecine Locality, Central Transvaal, Part 2, The Osteodontokeratic Contribution," *AB*, Vol. 13, No. 51 (1958), pp. 94–116.
    And many other titles.
    [2] W. C. Pei, W. P. Huang, C. L. Chiu, and H. Meng: "Discovery of Quaternary Mammalian Fauna at Ch'ao-tsun, Chien-An County, Hopei Province," *VP*, Vol. 2, No. 4 (1958), pp. 226–9.

published literature on the Australopithecines [3] we have information on twelve such bones, or sets of bones, as shown on Table 5.

To this list may be added the following pieces of an adult female skeleton from Sterkfontein, which has not yet been fully described: eight thoracic vertebrae, six lumbar vertebrae, a sacrum,
two nearly complete pelvic bones, and a piece of femur, as well as
the body of a lumbar vertebra from another individual.[4]

Combining the above with the list on Table 5, we find that
Taung has no postcranial bones, Sterkfontein twenty-five, Makapansgat five, Swartkrans two, Kromdraai eight, and Telanthropus
one. As some of the bones came in groups from single individuals,
the entire set could represent as few as seven or eight creatures.

The Sterkfontein Vertebrae and Ribs

THE ADULT FEMALE found by Robinson at Sterkfontein
had eight of a putative twelve thoracic vertebrae, which have not
been described, and six lumbar vertebrae. This number is interest-

[3] The bibliography is exhaustive. Here are some of the basic references in
which new specimens are reported.

R. Broom and Schepers: "The South African Fossil Ape-Men, the Australopithecinae," *TMM*, No. 2 (1946).

Broom, J. T. Robinson, and Schepers: "Sterkfontein Ape-Man, Plesianthropus,"
TMM, No. 4 (1950).

Broom and Robinson: "Swartkrans Ape-Man," *TMM*, No. 6 (1952).

Robinson: "Telanthropus and its Phylogenetic Significance," *AJPA*, Vol. 11,
No. 4 (1953), pp. 445–501.

Robinson: "The Dentition of the Australopithecinae," *TMM*, No. 9 (1956).

Dart: "*Australopithecus africanus*, the Man-ape of South Africa," *Nature*, Vol.
115, No. 2884 (1925), pp. 195–9.

Dart: "The Makapansgat Proto-human *Australopithecus prometheus*," *AJPA*,
Vol. 6, No. 3 (1948), pp. 259–84.

Dart: "The Adolescent Mandible of *Australopithecus prometheus*," *AJPA*, Vol.
6, No. 4 (1948), pp. 391–412.

Dart: "The Cranio-facial Fragments of *Australopithecus prometheus*," *AJPA*,
Vol. 7, No. 2 (1949), pp. 187–214.

Dart: "Innominate Fragments of *Australopithecus prometheus*," *AJPA*, Vol. 7,
No. 3 (1949), pp. 301–38.

Dart: "The Second or Adult Female Mandible of *Australopithecus prometheus*," *AJPA*, Vol. 12, No. 3 (1954), pp. 313–43.

Dart: "*Australopithecus prometheus* and *Australopithecus capensis*," *AJPA*,
Vol. 13, No. 1 (1955), pp. 67–96.

Dart: "The Second Adolescent (Female) Ilium of *Australopithecus prometheus*," *AJPA*, Vol. 2, No. 1 (1957), pp. 73–82.

[4] Robinson: "The Dentition of the Australopithecinae," pp. 161, 170.

TABLE 5

AUSTRALOPITHECINE POSTCRANIAL
BONES

Bone	Common Name	Site, Animal	No. of Bones
Os Coxae	Pelvic bone	Makapansgat	2
		Sterkfontein	2
		Swartkrans	1
Femur	Thighbone	Makapansgat	1
		Sterkfontein	1
Talus	Ankle Bone	Kromdraai	1
Phalanges (Foot)	Toe Bones	Kromdraai	2
Scapula	Shoulder Blade	Sterkfontein	1
Clavicle	Collarbone	Makapansgat	1
Humerus	Upper Arm Bone	Makapansgat	1
		Sterkfontein	1
		Kromdraai	1
Radius	Outer Lower Arm Bone	Makapansgat	1
		Telanthropus	1
Ulna	Inner Lower Arm Bone	Kromdraai	1
Capitatum	A Wrist Bone	Sterkfontein	1
Metacarpals	Hand Bones	Kromdraai	1
		Swartkrans	1
Phalanges (Hand)	Finger Bones	Kromdraai	1

ing since only about 5 per cent of human skeletons have six; 92 per cent have five, and 3 per cent have four. The macaques usually have seven, the chimpanzees four, and the gorillas four or three. According to Robinson, when the lumbar vertebrae are articulated with the sacrum a distinct lumbar curve is visible, as in man. If and when Robinson's statement is substantiated, we shall have the best evidence yet that the Sterkfontein Australopithecines stood and walked erect.

None of the ribs found at this site have yet been described.

The Pelvis of Australopithecus

N O S I N G L E B O N E is more sensitive to changes of posture and locomotion than the pelvic bone, or os coxae, which is composed of three elements fused together, the ilium, ischium, and pubis. Of the four pelvic bones that have been described in publications, the two from Makapansgat [5] are immature and the ones from Sterkfontein and Swartkrans are adult.[6]

In comparing these bones to the pelves of man and other pri-

[5] Dart: "Innominate Fragments . . ."; "The Second Adolescent. . . ."
[6] Broom et al: "Sterkfontein . . ."; "Swartkrans Ape-Man."

mates we are severely limited because we have no pelvic bones for
Proconsul or other Dryopithecines, or for fossil men older than the
Neanderthals. We do have the bones of modern men, however,
and of apes and Old World monkeys. All four specimens resemble
those of living men in general form and in most details, but they
differ from the human pattern in a few features.[7]

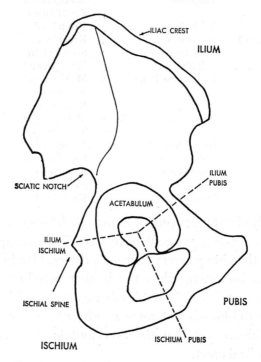

FIG. 20   THE ANATOMY OF THE HUMAN PELVIC BONE (*Os Coxae*).

For example, in man the outer surface of the ilium is ordinarily
divided into three planes, one each for the attachment of the
gluteus maximus, gluteus medius, and *gluteus minimus* muscles,
and these planes are set at different angles. In neither Australopithecines nor apes are these planes differentiated. However,
Dart (1957) has found the same condition in the pelvis of a mod-

[7] L. W. Mednick: "The Evolution of the Human Ilium," *AJPA*, Vol. 13, No. 2
(1955), pp. 203–216.

W. E. LeG. Clark: "The Os Innominatum of the Recent Ponginae, with Special Reference to That of the Australopithecinae," *AJPA*, Vol. 13, No. 1 (1955),
pp. 19–28.

Dart: "The Second Adolescent . . . ," pp. 73–82.

ern Pygmy. His discovery implies that in small and light bipedal animals, like Pygmies, Sterkfontein, and Makapansgat (if the two latter were bipedal), ridged areas of attachment for these muscles are unnecessary; but Swartkrans was as heavy as a full-sized man.

Also the ischial bone differs both among the Australopithecines and between them and man. This is the lowest and rearmost of the three fused pelvic bones. As stated in Chapters 4 and 5, in the Old World monkeys and apes the ischium extends far down and

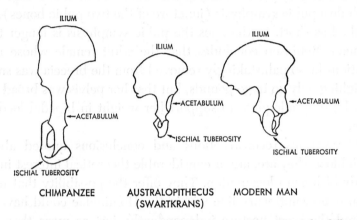

CHIMPANZEE   AUSTRALOPITHECUS   MODERN MAN
(SWARTKRANS)

FIG. 21   PELVIC BONES OF APE, *Australopithecus*, AND MAN. Note the differences between these three Hominoids in the ilium and in the ischium. Whereas the Australopithecine bone is generally short and compressed, as in man, the tuberosity of the ischium is set well below the level of the acetabulum, and in this feature it is intermediate between man and ape. (Drawings after Abbie, 1961.)

to the rear, and its tuberosity flares outward. In man it is short and bends inward. Only in man does the *gluteus maximus* muscle cover the ischial tuberosity. Makapansgat's ischium is the most manlike, Sterkfontein's slightly less so, and Swartkrans's is nearly apelike.

This evidence suggests that none of the Australopithecines sat exactly as man does, and that Sterkfontein and Makapansgat were more nearly human in posture than Swartkrans. LeGros Clark, Robinson, and some other anatomists agree that the Australopithecines stood erect, but also that their posture was less perfect than ours, and Robinson (1956) suggests that the earlier species (*Australopithecus africanus*) and the latter one (*A. robustus*) were members of separate lines which had acquired the erect posture, such as it was, independently. Washburn has recently suggested that the Australopithecines in general could not have walked erect as we do, but could only run while erect, dropping down on all fours when at rest.[8]

The undescribed sacrum mentioned by Robinson (1954) is nearly but not wholly complete. It is said to be short and broad, and to bear a close general resemblance to those of modern men. Of the pelvic bones (os coxae) found with the sacrum Robinson states that they are oriented in the human fashion and that they include a pubic symphysis (juncture of the two pubic bones), described as short. In the apes the pubic symphysis is longer than in man. Robinson concludes that the adult female whose midportions he so painstakingly removed from the breccia was small, weighing only 40 to 50 pounds, but that her pelvis was broad and sturdy, fully adequate to support her weight in bipedal locomotion.

The various reconstructions and conclusions quoted above, variable as they are, are of considerable theoretical interest in the study of human locomotion. They offer the possibility that more than one evolutionary line within the Hominidae could have acquired the erect posture independently, just as more than one reptile became a mammal, and they suggest a reason why standing and walking erect became advantageous in the first place. If primates like the earlier Australopithecines, and the forerunners of *Homo*, were able to walk erect, they could have used their hands to make and carry tools. But if they moved about on all fours except when dashing after game, they could not have carried tools, even if they made tools when sitting down. Unless they could walk, they could not have carried water and food from source to camp. Much depends on their means of locomotion, which can be further elucidated by studying other bones, particularly those of the legs and feet.

The Legs and Feet of Australopithecus

ALTHOUGH NO whole femur has been described, we have descriptions of two femoral heads, only one of which is complete

[8] Washburn: "Tools and Human Evolution," SA, Vol. 203, No. 3 (1960), pp. 63–75.

enough to be useful,[9] and of one distal, or lower, end.[1] The nearly complete head belonged to a specimen from Sterkfontein. To it is attached the crushed shaft of most of the rest of the femur, which Broom estimated to be 310 mm. long, barely within the lower border of the human range. The position of the head on the shaft fits that of the acetabulum of the pelvis described above. Although it faces outward, it does not rotate as far forward as in man, nor are its areas of muscle attachment as strongly devel-

FEMUR

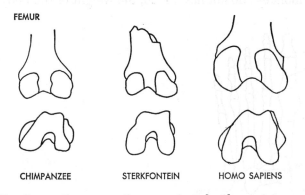

CHIMPANZEE   STERKFONTEIN   HOMO SAPIENS

FIG. 22   THE DISTAL END OF THE FEMUR IN *Australopithecus*, APE, AND MAN. In the Sterkfontein femur, the angle between the shaft and the condyles is greater than in either chimpanzee or man. In the end view (bottom row), the Sterkfontein condylar head is squarer and more deeply notched than in either chimpanzee or man. (Drawings after Broom, 1946.)

oped.[2] All that can be said of the second specimen, the one from Makapansgat (Boné, 1955) is that it is believed to come from a different individual than did the other bones from that site, and that it is larger than the Sterkfontein specimen.

[9] Broom et al.: "Sterkfontein Ape-Man, Plesianthropus."

[1] Broom: The Occurrence and General Structure of the South African Ape-Men, in Broom and Schepers: "The South American Fossil. . . ."

Broom and Robinson: Further Evidence of the Structure of the Sterkfontein Ape-Man, Plesianthropus, Part I, of Broom et al.: "Sterkfontein Ape-Man. . . ."

E. Boné: "Quatre Fragments Post-Craniens du Gisement à Australopitheques de Makapansgat (N. Transvaal)," *L'Anth.*, Vol. 59, No. 5/6 (1955), pp. 462–9.

Boné and Dart: "A Catalogue of Australopithecine Fossils Found at the Limeworks, Makapansgat," *AJPA*, Vol. 13, No. 4 (1955), pp. 621–4.

H. M. Kern, Jr., and Straus, Jr.: "The Femur of *Plesianthropus transvaalensis*," *AJPA*, Vol. 7, No. 1 (1949), pp. 53–78.

[2] The great trochanter is less sharply lipped than in a Bushman femoral head used for comparison; the trochanteric fossa is shallower, and there is no well-developed trochanteric crest.

The lower (distal) end of a femur is also credited to Sterkfontein (Broom, 1946). It is small but also within the adult human size range. In details, however, it resembles the thighbones of both men and ground-living monkeys in most recognizable features, and in no single feature does it exclusively favor the apes. It is thick enough and heavy enough to have borne the animal's entire body weight, not just momentarily but continuously. Like the femurs of apes and men, it has a carrying angle that the femurs of monkeys do not have. Also, the weight of the body passed

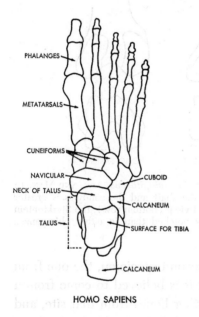

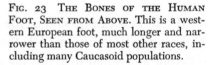

FIG. 23 THE BONES OF THE HUMAN FOOT, SEEN FROM ABOVE. This is a western European foot, much longer and narrower than those of most other races, including many Caucasoid populations.

through the outer condyle of the knee joint, as in man and land-roving monkeys but not in apes. These details suggest that as far as the femur is concerned the Australopithecus from Sterkfontein, at least, could have either walked or run erect, as he pleased, and that if his ancestors had ever brachiated in the trees, no trace of the brachiating type of adaptation remained on their femurs once they had become anatomically suited for life on the ground.

As both tibias and fibulas are missing, we must pass on to the foot, which is represented by a single major bone, a talus or ankle bone of Kromdraai (Broom, 1946). Being the bridge between the lower leg and the rest of the foot, this bone reflects, in the details of its complicated form, the degree of rigidity or mobility of the ankle joint. In the apes the advantage lies in mobility, for the foot is used more or less as a hand. In bipedal primates rigidity is advantageous, for, while the animal is walking, each talus bears in turn the entire weight of the body. In the quadrupedal monkeys, whose gait places less strain on this bone, an intermediate condition is more suitable.

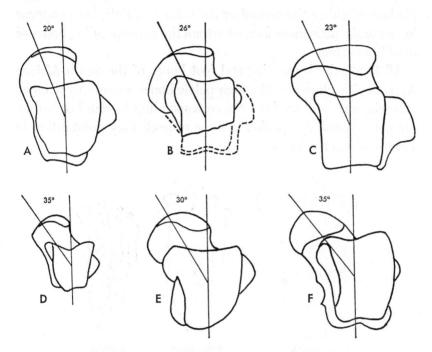

Fig. 24 The Astragulus of the Australopithecines and Other Primates. A. *Homo sapiens*, a woman; B. Kromdraai; C. Olduvai Child; D. Baboon; E. Chimpanzee; F. *Proconsul nyanzae*. In the angle of the neck of the astragulus to its main axis, the Australopithecines are intermediate between the apes and baboons on the one hand, and men on the other. (Drawings A, B, and D after Broom, 1946; C after Leakey's photograph, 1961; E and F after LeGros Clark and Leakey, 1947.)

Seen from above, the Kromdraai talus may be compared with those of several other primates, including that found with the Olduvai child, which will be discussed later. Although it is broken in the rear, enough is left so that the shape and general dimensions can be reconstructed with some accuracy. It falls within the human range in size, and probably in the length-breadth ratio, and its neck and head point inward at an angle of about 26°, a figure on the outer edge of the human range (18–25°) and below that of living apes (30–36°)[3] and of *Proconsul nyanzae* (*ca.* 35°). In the form of its facets it appears both to be of the proper size and to have the rigidity necessary for bipedal walking. It is essentially human.

The two toe bones of the same animal are an incomplete first, or proximal, phalanx of the left little toe, and a last, or distal, phalanx of either the second or the third toe. Both bones appear longer and a little more fingerlike than the corresponding bones of most human feet.

All in all, the known leg and foot bones of the South African Australopithecines are, like their pelvic bones, essentially manlike and where they differ from the corresponding human bones they are not particularly apelike. In some respects they point rather to *Proconsul* and the baboons.

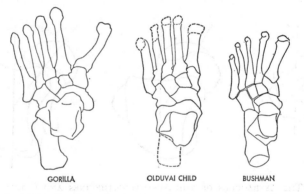

GORILLA   OLDUVAI CHILD   BUSHMAN

Fig. 25   The Foot Bones Found with the Olduvai Child (compared with those of a gorilla and a Bushman). (See page 294.) The foot bones found with the Olduvai child in Bed I are now believed to have belonged to an adult of the same species. Although twelve bones are present, the part of the calcaneus lying behind the posterior border of the talus is missing, as are the epiphyses of all five metatarsals and all of the phalanges. The fifth metatarsal overlapped the fourth, producing a pathological growth on the latter.

The Olduvai foot is essentially if not completely human, as would probably be made clear were it to be compared with the pedal skeletons of men of different races. It has the usual human pair of arches, but the tilt of the head of the talus is not completely modern and an articular facet between the first and second metatarsals suggests a certain flexibility of the big toe. (Drawing of gorilla after Raven, 1950; of the Olduvai foot after M. H. Day and J. R. Napier, "Fossil Foot Bones," *Nature,* Vol. 201, No. 4923 (March 7, 1964), pp. 969–70; Bushman after Keith and McCown, 1938).

[3] R. Martin and K. Saller: *Lehrbuch der Anthropologie,* Third Edition (Stuttgart: G. Fischer; 1958), Section 7, pp. 1117–18.

The Shoulder Girdle of Australopithecus

T H E primate shoulder girdle consists of two pairs of bones, the scapulae or shoulder blades and the clavicles or collarbones. These bones attach the arms to the trunk, not rigidly as the pelvis is fastened to the sacrum, but flexibly, through the agency of muscles and tendons, and remotely, by the articulation of the clavicles to the sternum, the sternum to the ribs, and the ribs to the vertebrae. As we have seen in comparisons between monkeys and apes, the shape and position of the scapulae and clavicles sensitively reflect each animal's mode of locomotion.

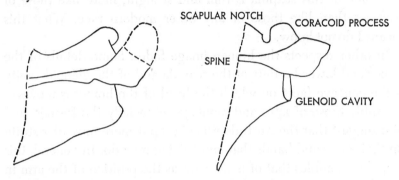

STERKFONTEIN (BROOM, 1946)   MAN (BROOM, 1946)

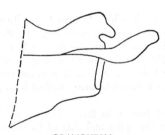

ORANGUTAN   CERCOPITHECUS (VALLOIS)
(VALLOIS, *L'OMOPLATE HUMAINE*)

FIG. 26   THE AUSTRALOPITHECINE SCAPULA.

In the Australopithecine material one scapula from Sterkfontein and one clavicle from Makapansgat [4] have so far been described. Both are fragmentary.

[4] Broom and Robinson: "Further Evidence of the Structure . . . ," pp. 55–7.
   Boné: "Une Clavicule et un Nouveau Fragment Mandibulaire *d'Australopithecus prometheus*," *PAf,* Vol. 3 (1955), pp. 87–101.

About half the Sterkfontein scapula is available, and luckily it is the more interesting half, containing the part that meets the humerus (upper arm bone) at the shoulder. Because ground monkeys, apes, and men all hold their arms in different positions, this part of the scapula is a highly diagnostic portion of the primate anatomy.

The Sterkfontein fragment has a long spine, as do apes and men but not monkeys. The head of its spine projects far out over the head of the humerus, as it does in apes and men but not in monkeys. But the head is thick, as in man alone. Oddly enough, the spine of this scapula is thin and straight, more like those of Negroes than like those of any other modern race. What this means I do not know.

In other respects the human image fades. Some details of the upper and lower borders of the scapula and of the glenoid cavity —the concave facet on which the head of the humerus moves— resemble those of apes and monkeys, especially the former, and also suggest that the Australopithecines put more muscular strain on their arms and hands than most living men do. In general, this scapula resembles that of man as far as the position of the arm in the shoulder is concerned, but where it differs from man's it is apelike rather than monkeylike.[5]

[5] The Sterkfontein specimen has no scapular notch, which in man is usually a deep, semicircular cavity at the base of the coracoid process, enclosing, with the help of a ligament, the suprascapular nerve. This notch is usually present in the Cebidae and man, and absent in prosimians, Old World monkeys, and apes, although a trace of it turns up now and then in baboons. In man it is sometimes absent altogether, as in 5 per cent of Pygmies, or it may take many variant forms, including a bridged hole.

The lower border of the scapula also is not human in form. The so-called axilospinal angle, the angle between the axis of the spine and that of its lower, outer border (next to the axilla, or armpit) is 22° in Sterkfontein. The range for apes is from 8° in the gibbon to 18° in the orang. An arboreal Old World monkey, *Cercopithecus sp.*, has an angle of 30°, and the individual human range is 24 to 58°.

Another diagnostic angle is that formed between the axis of the glenoid cavity and that of the scapular spine. Although this angle could not be measured in the conventional way because of breakage, a substitute technique, which can be applied to comparable fragments of other scapulae, gives Sterkfontein an angle of 103°, wider than those for man (about 90°) and the living apes (85° and lower).

Broom, who was able to examine the specimen closely, said that the glenoid cavity has a much larger attachment for the biceps muscle than does the corresponding part in man. This indicates further that the Australopithecus scapula

The Sterkfontein clavicle (collarbone) is even less complete than the scapula from the same site. Owing to its fragmentary condition, it is useless in our present study.

The Arms and Hands of Australopithecus

W E H A V E three pieces of humerus: one almost complete bone from Sterkfontein which is crushed flat except for the head; [6] a section of shaft about 64 mm. long from Makapansgat; [7] and a distal (elbow) portion from Kromdraai.[8] These three specimens are similar enough to be treated as a unit, if we keep in mind that the first two came from smaller animals than the third.

The first bone was originally about 30 cm. long, within the ranges for man and chimpanzee. A comparison of this figure with the length of a femur from the same deposit, but not necessarily from the same individual, gives a skeletal upper-arm–thigh index of 96. In apes the humeri are always longer than the femora, so that the individual humero-femoral indices range from 111 to 147. In the Old World monkeys the index is always below 100, and in man it is about 71 to 76. This evidence suggests that Sterkfontein's upper arms were shorter than his thighs and that he probably walked erect. At least, he did not walk on all fours the way that apes do when on the ground.

The piece of shaft from Makapansgat is heavy, thick, ridged with muscular crests, and structurally humanlike. It is more robust than either the head just described or the elbow piece about to be described.

The latter, from Kromdraai, is particularly significant. It in-

---

in question could not be mistaken for that of man, ape, or monkey, and that in general it tends rather toward the apelike than the human.

H. V. Vallois: "L'Omoplate Humaine," *BMSA* varia 1928–46 (Paris: Masson et Cie; (1946).

Martin and Saller: op cit., Vol. 1 (1957) p. 531.

[6] Broom and Robinson: "Further Evidence of the Structure . . . ," p. 57.

[7] Boné: "Quatre Fragments Postcraniens du Gisement de Makapansgat, N. Transvaal," *L'Anth*, Vol. 59, Nos. 5–6 (1955), pp. 462–9.

[8] Broom: "The Occurrence and General Structure . . . ," pp. 114–15.

Straus, Jr.: "The Humerus of Paranthropus robustus," *AJPA*, Vol. 6, No. 3 (1948), pp. 285–312.

cludes unbroken articular surfaces that permit and delimit the
movements of the forearm at the elbow, and are thus concerned
with both locomotion and the rotation of the hand when it is
free. In morphological details [9] this piece of shaft falls into the
same general category as do those of *Proconsul*, apes, and men and
is essentially different from the distal humeri of the Old World
monkeys, both arboreal and ground-living. In a few respects it is
unique. On the whole it suggests a degree of forearm mobility intermediate between those of apes and men, without settling, in
itself, the question of locomotion.

We have fragments of two real or alleged radii, the proximal
and distal ends of what is believed to be a single bone, from
Makapansgat, and an alleged distal extremity of Telanthropus.[1]
The first is doubtful. The head could be hominid or even pongid,
but the end piece is not necessarily that of a primate, for it resembles the radii of carnivores, particularly cats. The second or Telanthropus piece, according to Robinson, can be matched among
modern human radii.

At Kromdraai Broom [2] found a fragment of ulna from the same
elbow joint as the distal piece of humerus described above. It is
only 3.7 cm. long, but it contains both the diagnostic articular
surfaces and the olecranon process—the hook that locks the bone
to the humerus when the arm is fully extended. Although it seems
human in most respects, it has two anomalies. One is a thin, hol-
low-backed ridge on the inner side of the olecranon process, the
other a deep hollow near the extremity of the articular surface.

---

[9] As in *Proconsul africanus*, the apes, and man, the angle between the axis of
the shaft and that of the condyles is 100° or more; in the Old World monkeys it
is about 90°. Also, the articulation with the radius is the same as in man, but the
articular surface for contact with the ulna is oval rather than round, unlike that
in either man or ape. The inner condyle is small and more pointed than it is in
either man or ape, and the outer condyle also is "not quite human" (Broom,
1950, p. 115). The supinator ridge on the lateral condyle, for the attachment of
the supinator muscle—a muscle joining the humerus and radius and concerned
with the rotation of the lower arm—struck Broom as being more apelike than human. He also found a deep furrow and pit between the same condyle and the
radial articular surface which is present neither in apes nor in men.

[1] Boné: "Quatre Fragments. . . ."
　　Robinson: "Telanthropus and its Phylogenetic Significance."

[2] Broom: "*Paranthropus robustus* Broom," in Broom and Schepers: "The South
African . . . ," p. 115.

Broom was able to find similar characteristics in about 1 per cent of the human ulnae of various races, but he failed to find them in ape ulnae.

The only carpal bone we have is a right *os capitatum,* or capitate bone, from Sterkfontein.[3] This is a small, more or less cubical bone in the middle of the outer row of wrist bones, one which articulates, in man, with five or sometimes six other bones, thus forming the center of the wrist. Human in size and intermediate between the corresponding bones of apes and men in mobility, it is particularly human in its implication of a large and mobile index finger.[4]

The metacarpal of one thumb, that from Swartkrans, throws light on the possible manual activities of the larger Australopithecines.[5] It is 36 mm. long, which places it in the lower part of the human range, and stoutly built. As seen from the side, it appears to be more curved than the metacarpal of either men or apes (Fig. 27). On the inner side of the rear or proximal end is a sharp beak that once separated a pair of large sesamoid bones.

Sesamoids, so called because they look like sesame seeds, are small bones which form in tendons over joints that are frequently flexed in a single direction and with considerable force; they serve

---

[3] Broom: *"Plesianthropus transvaalensis* Broom," in Broom and Schepers: op. cit.

W. E. LeG. Clark: "Observations on the Anatomy of the Fossil Australopithecinae," *JANAT,* Vol. 81, No. 3 (1947). Reprinted in *Yearbook of Physical Anthropology* (New York, 1947), pp. 143–77.

[4] In man the facets by which it articulates with the other bones around it are broad and extensive, permitting considerable mobility. In the apes, particularly the gorilla and chimpanzee, these facets are small. In the apes, however, areas for the attachment of ligaments are extensive; in man they are smaller. In the apes, which have long, slender hands, the capitate is long; in man it is shorter. In the apes the bone is larger than in man.

The Sterkfontein capitate is of human rather than apelike size, being comparable to those of baboons and Bushmen. (Maximum lengths: Sterkfontein, 18.3 mm.; Bushman female, 18.3; Bushman male, 20.9; baboon male, 19.0; *Proconsul africanus,* 23.0; gorilla male, 26.5; chimpanzee male, 26.5; orang male, 31.7 mm.) It is relatively broad, like a man's. In the development of facets and ligamental attachments, it is intermediate between those of apes and those of men, but closer to the human. In particular, it has a larger articulation for the head of the second metacarpal, on the thumb side, than is found in the apes; in the gorilla there is characteristically none at all.

[5] Broom and Robinson: "Thumb of Swartkrans Ape-Man," *Nature,* Vol. 164, No. 4176 (1949), pp. 841–2.

as fulcrums. The kneecap is our largest sesamoid. Both Swartkrans and man have sesamoids of the thumb, absent in apes. But
Swartkrans seems also to have had sesamoids at the base of the
first metacarpal (rare in man), which rode high on the joint, suggesting specialization for coarse work, such as digging roots.

A metacarpal from Kromdraai, probably that of the index finger,
is 70 mm. long, as long as that of a man with long hands. In most
respects it is human-looking, but two grooves on the palmar side of

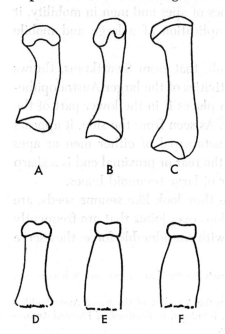

Fig. 27 The Australopithecine
Hand Bones. *The Metacarpal Thumb
Bones of Australopithecus:* A. Swart-
krans; B. Bushman; C. European.
Note that the Australopithecine bone
is curved and hooked at the base.
*Proximal Phalanges of the Third or
Fourth Finger in Man, the Olduvai
Child, and the Gorilla:* D. Man;
E. Olduvai Child; F. Gorilla. In man
the shafts of the phalanges are
rounded and narrow; in the gorilla
and other apes they are broad and
spatulate. In the shape of this bone
the Olduvai child resembles the apes.
(Drawings A and B after Broom and
Robinson, 1952.)

the distal knuckle betray the former presence of another pair of
sesamoid bones. These are rare or nonexistent in apes and normal
in baboons. In man they occur singly, but seldom in pairs.

Two proximal phalanges of the same hand belong to the second
and fifth fingers. In the apes these phalanges are flattened on the
underside, and their edges are lipped; this represents an adaptation for brachiation in a heavy animal, and reaches an extreme
form in the gorilla. It is not found in notable degree in *Proconsul
africanus,* the Old World monkeys, or man. The Kromdraai phalanges also lack it. No better indication is needed that this animal
was not a brachiator and that if his ancestors once had this adaptation they subsequently lost it.

Australopithecus, *a Primate Mermaid or a Unique Hominid?*

W E N O W have the impression that the South African Australo-pithecines from the neck down were a kind of primate mermaid, a somewhat composite animal. Either the Australopithecines were going through a transitional stage of evolution that we have not seen before, or the postcranial bones are a mixed bag of spare parts of Australopithecines, apes, big baboons, and men. In general, if not in every case, the first explanation is the more plausible.

No animal can be understood merely through comparison with others, for each species is an entity in itself, an organism adapted to its own kind of existence. From the study just made of the postcranial bones of the South African Australopithecines it may be concluded that these creatures must have followed a way of life no longer seen on the earth. The resemblances of individual bones to those of other primates living and extinct indicates principally that these creatures drew on the same primate storehouse of genetic potentialities as did monkeys, apes, and men. Moreover, it is evident that the biological forces of parallelism, differential evolutionary rates, and neoteny shaped a special organic whole to fit a new ecological requirement in a creature whose ancestors had parted company with those of the subfamily Ponginae before the latter had become fully specialized.

As far as the postcranial skeleton is concerned, *Homo* could have been descended from some kind of Australopithecine, more like *Australopithecus africanus*, perhaps, than *A. robustus*. But we can say no more until we have studied the rest of the skeletal parts of the whole animals. The skulls and teeth will shed more light on the relationships between *Homo* and his early South African relatives.

The Skulls, Jaws, and Teeth of Australopithecus

A V A I L A B L E published accounts [6] of the finds in the five caves that have yielded the known remains of the South African Australo-pithecines include descriptions of the whole and fragmentary

[6] The bibliography is essentially the same as that for the postcranial bones.

brain cases, jaws, and teeth of at least twenty-one individuals or at most about forty, three to seven times as many creatures as are accounted for by the postcranial bones. Each of the South African cave groups contains at least one skull, more or less complete. However, there is none for *Telanthropus,* whose presence from the neck up is indicated only by one nearly complete and one very fragmentary lower jaw, and a piece of palate.

TABLE 6

SKULLS, JAWS, AND TEETH
OF AUSTRALOPITHECINES

Taung	1 skull, six years old, milk teeth
Makapansgat	3 fragmentary skulls 2 maxillae 3 mandibles 1 molar tooth
Sterkfontein	2 crania (one almost complete)
Kromdraai	1 cranium, fragmentary 2 mandibles various teeth
Swartkrans	8 crania in various conditions 5 maxillae 10 mandibula 100 *ca.* loose teeth
Swartkrans, Telanthropus	2 fragmentary mandibles 1 maxillary fragment

Before going further let us familiarize ourselves with some technical terms that will appear in the descriptions of skulls and their parts. The *skull,* technically, includes the entire structure: the bones of the head, face, and both jaws. The *cranium* does not include the lower jaw. A *calvarium* is a faceless and jawless brain case; a *calva* consists of the top of the brain case only, without the base; a *maxilla,* of the upper jawbone (one on each side); and a *mandible* or *mandibula,* of the lower jawbone.

The Brain Case and Brain of Australopithecus

NEXT TO the teeth, the brain case is the most human-looking feature of this creature, as we can see (Fig. 28) from the pro-

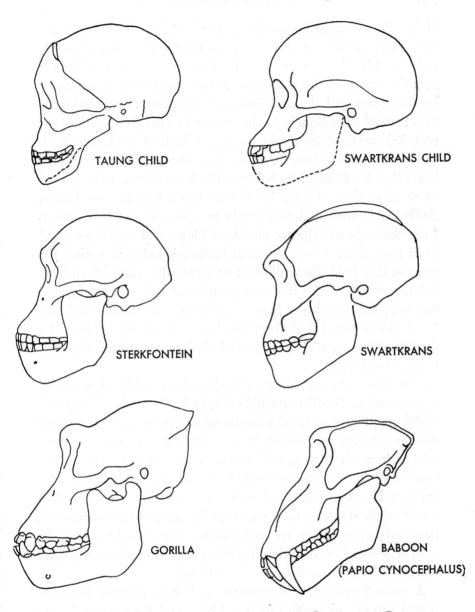

FIG. 28   SKULL PROFILES OF AUSTRALOPITHECINES, GORILLA, AND BABOON.

files of four skulls: the infant Taung, supposedly aged six years; an infant from Swartkrans, supposedly aged seven years; an adult male (?) from Sterkfontein; and an adult female (?) from Swartkrans, greatly restored. In all of them the skull is long and rather high, with a sloping forehead, and the brain case rises above the brow ridges as high, in relation to its total size, as in some early and primitive human crania. The foramen magnum is located near the center of the skull base, as far from the rear as in some human races; and the occipital condyles point downward as in man instead of obliquely to the rear as in apes. In addition, the occipital crest, which marks the upper limit of neck-muscle attachments, is even lower than in some human skulls, and much lower than in either ape or baboon. The brow ridges are heavy but no more so than in some fossil and even a few modern human skulls. As in man and only rarely in apes, the mastoid process (a protuberance of the occipital bone) is present, and it is conical as in man. Since this anatomical landmark helps to anchor the muscles that hold the skull erect on either side rather than from behind, we may infer from the position of this process that the Australopithecines had a human rather than an apelike neck. All in all, the hominid skull form had been completely achieved by Australopithecus, which suggests but does not prove that this animal stood erect.

A human brain size, however, had not been achieved, nor even approximated. The Taung child of six had a brain size of 494 cc.,[7] which could have attained a maximum of 543 cc. had the creature lived to maturity and had his brain continued to grow at the same rate as in modern man, which cannot be assumed. The Makapansgat brain case is known only from a single occipital bone. Its capacity has been estimated, very speculatively, at 600 cc.[8] Two Sterkfontein skulls complete enough for accurate measurements have capacities of 435 cc. and 480 cc. Thus, the brains of the smaller and earlier Australopithecines range from a known 435 cc. to a possible 543 cc. and a speculative 600 cc.

A quite fragmentary Kromdraai skull may possibly have attained 650 cc., although this is unlikely; and the various Swartkrans skulls, none of which is complete enough to measure properly, have been estimated at 700 cc. Washburn denies that any of these skulls can have exceeded 550 cc.: the foramen for the in-

[7] C. J. Connolly: *External Morphology of the Primate Brain* (Springfield, Ill.: Charles C Thomas; 1951). See pp. 293–5.

[8] Clark: "The Os Innominatum. . . ," p. 122.

ternal carotid artery, one of the vessels that feeds blood to the brain, is no larger than those of apes.[9]

According to the principle of allometry (see page 25), which governs the differences in proportions of similar animals of different sizes, if the large Australopithecines had the same kind of brains as the small ones, the cubic capacity figure of the large ones would be absolutely larger and proportionately smaller than those of the small group. The difference between the two groups seems to be about 100 cc., or about 20 per cent. However, the difference in body size may have been in the order of 50 to 100 per cent. These figures do not suggest any increase in intelligence between *Australopithecus africanus* and *Australopithecus robustus* such as one might expect to find if the second species were evolving from the first in the direction of man.

The variously estimated range in brain size of 435 to 700 cc. ascribed to the Australopithecines by several authors falls within the middle and upper parts of the anthropoid ape range, which is 325 to 685 cc.; and it may not exceed that of the largest known gorilla—685 cc. The brains of both putative species of Australopithecines were a little larger for their body size than the brains of the three living great apes, but not enough larger to indicate, without supplementary evidence, a substantial difference in intelligence. It is extremely unlikely that they could speak.[1]

[9] Washburn and V. Avis: "Evolution of Human Behavior," in A. Roe and G. G. Simpson: *Behavior and Evolution* (New Haven: Yale University Press; 1958), p. 430.

Although an approximately equal amount of blood also flows up through the vertebral arteries, this fact alone does not invalidate Washburn's conclusion, because the ratio of blood contributed by each pair of arteries is the same in all living primates.

[1] Schepers, who studied the internal brain casts of the Taung infant, five Sterkfontein skulls, and a fragmentary juvenile specimen from Kromdraai, after having constructed elaborate charts of the surface configurations of the cerebral hemispheres, concluded that the Australopithecines could speak. Several brain anatomists, particularly Father Connolly, have challenged his reconstructions. Moreover, Penfield and his associates have recently discovered that the speech centers of the human brain lie mostly on inner folds of the cerebral cortex, where they could not make imprints on the inside of the skull.

Schepers: "The Endocranial Casts. . . ."

Schepers: *The Brain Casts of the Recently Discovered Plesianthropus Skulls,* in Broom, Robinson, and Schepers: "Sterkfontein. . . ."

Connolly: op. cit.

W. Penfield and L. Roberts: *Speech and Brain Mechanisms* (Princeton: Princeton University Press; 1959).

The smallest cranial capacity for a fossil man is 775 cc., calculated for the Trinil Pithecanthropus skull 2.[2] This leaves, between the known ranges of *Australopithecus* and *Homo*, a gap of about 200 cc., which Vallois calls a Rubicon. At the moment this stream is still unbridged.

To summarize, the brain cases of the Australopithecines are human in form but apelike in size, and in the gross morphology of the brain, as seen dimly through the surface markings on the inner surfaces of the skulls, there is nothing to indicate that they, or other creatures like them, could not have evolved into men. The ancestors of the genus *Homo,* whoever they were, must once have had equally small brains, before they began to grow out of the Australopithecine range.

The Faces of the Australopithecines

I N 1951 Washburn stated that in the course of human evolution different parts of the body had evolved at different times and at different rates.[3] First came the erect posture; then the perfection of the upper limbs; next the brain grew larger; and finally the teeth grew smaller and the bony structures of the face and jaws which support the teeth in their work of mastication also became reduced.

In the evolution of the Australopithecines this schedule may not have been closely followed. The evidence which we have cited indicates that the erect posture may not have been fully achieved at the start, and it certainly did not become more perfect in the later and larger animals; nor did the brain grow according to this plan. The teeth, as we shall soon see, grew larger instead of smaller, and so did their supporting structures. These facts do not disprove Washburn's thesis, but they cast some doubt on the idea that the South African Australopithecines were evolving into men.

Although some fossil men may have had as massive faces as the

---

[2] F. Weidenreich: "Giant Early Man from Java and South China," *APAM*, Vol. 40, No. 1 (1945), p. 97.

[3] Washburn: "The New Physical Anthropology," *TNYA*, Ser. 2, Vol. 13, No. 7 (1951), pp. 298–304.

early Australopithecines, nevertheless a whole set of features, partly concealed by a common air of brutality, separates the Australopithecine face from that of fossil and living men. These are in what I call the *mask*, the region of the eyes and nose.

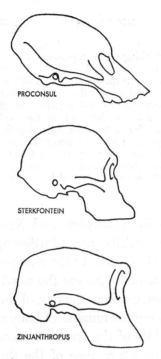

PROCONSUL

STERKFONTEIN

ZINJANTHROPUS

FIG. 29   FROM *Proconsul* TO THE SMALLER AUSTRALOPITHECINES TO THE LARGER ONES. In this comparison of facial profiles, the skull of *Proconsul africanus* is represented twice as large, proportionately, as the other two. The lower part of the occipital bone of Proconsul has been reconstructed, and the crest of Zinjanthropus has been left out. In these drawings it may be seen that the brow ridges progress from none to extremely heavy; the prognathism from extreme to great to medium; the lateral axis of the eye socket from sloping backwards to straight to sloping slightly forwards. With an elongation of the face and a reduction in prognathism, the face has moved upward in front of the brain case. Otherwise, the tooth line would be inconveniently located for an erect bipedal animal. (Drawing of Proconsul after LeGros Clark and Leakey, 1951; Sterkfontein after LeGros Clark, 1960; Zinjanthropus after Leakey, 1959.)

In man the distance between the bony orbits (eye sockets) is variable; fossil men and the more primitive living races have the greatest interorbital distances. In the Old World monkeys and apes this distance is small. Much of the pressure of their jaws is carried upward by the bony structures on either side of the orbits, leaving the eyes-nose triangle a compact island between two

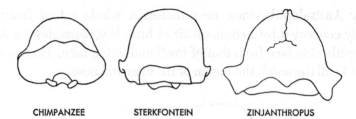

CHIMPANZEE   STERKFONTEIN   ZINJANTHROPUS

Fig. 30   Variations in the Area of Neck-Muscle Attachment in Apes and Australopithecines. The chimpanzee represents the apes; Sterkfontein, the earlier and smaller Australopithecines; and Zinjanthropus, the later and larger ones. Like the *Australopithecus robustus* specimens from South Africa, Zinjanthropus has wide-flaring temporal crests and a sagittal crest, both indicating an exaggerated development of the temporal muscles and a coarse, tough diet. But the nuchal crest, under which the muscles of the back of the neck are attached to the occipital bone, is set low on the skull in the Australopithecines and high on the chimpanzee. In Zinjanthropus it is set even lower than in Sterkfontein (*Australopithecus africanus*). This progressions suggests, but taken alone does not prove, a continuous evolutionary progression among the Australopithecines in the acquisition of the erect posture. We have no occipital bones from Proconsul with which to extend this comparison.

columns of stress. In the prosimians and New World monkeys, both the eyes and the nostrils are set farther apart and the nasal skeleton takes some of the strain. In the chimpanzee (see Fig. 31) the maxillary sinuses actually invade the nasal territory, separating the inner nasal passages from the roof of the mouth by branch air pockets, and reducing the number of bony struts passing from the palate to the middle of the forehead from three to one.[4] In man the nasal skeleton takes some of the thrust, and the nose pushes the orbits farther apart than in most catarrhine monkeys and all apes. When seen from the side, the human orbit, through variable, tends to extend to the side and rear much more than in living Old World monkeys and apes, after the fashion of prosimians, platyrrhines, and *Proconsul*. In these respects man is a relatively primitive primate.

Furthermore, the nasal skeleton stands out from the plane of the face, not only in man, but also in lemurs, fossil and living tarsiers, and most of the arboreal monkeys of both hemispheres, but not in macaques, baboons, or apes. Their nasal skeletons are flush with the bones to either side of them, or even depressed. The same is true of the South African Australopithecines. It has been said that in all these big-jawed animals the nose would be

[4] Broom: *"Plesianthropus . . . ,"* pp. 86-7.

left standing out like an island were the jaws to be reduced; but this is not true, because the nasal skeleton is flat even at eye level where the jaw protrusion makes no difference. No amount of jaw reduction could give Australopithecus a human nose. In the six-

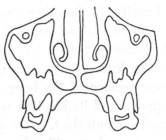

CHIMPANZEE (ADULT MALE)

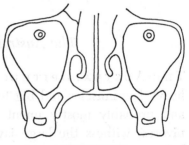

STERKFONTEIN

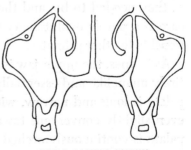

Fig. 31 Sections through the Nasal Passages of *Australopithecus*, Ape, and Man. Section through level of first upper molar. In the chimpanzee the maxillary sinuses lie between the nasal passages and the palate. In Australopithecus and man the nasal passages are directly above the palate and the maxillary sinuses lie to either side of the nasal passages only. (Drawings after Broom and Robinson, 1952.)

HOMO SAPIENS (KAFFIR)

and seven-year-old skulls of Taung and Swartkrans the nasal profile is just as flat as in the adults. Nasally the Australopithecines were more apelike, and in a sense more evolved, than we are.

In man the external nose is a useful part of the speech apparatus: it forms a resonance chamber for the amplification of sound comparable to the air sac of the gibbon and the enlarged voice box of the howler. Whether or not the Australopithecines could speak, and I have seen no conclusive evidence that they could, they seem to have lacked this special human adjunct.

Telanthropus, however, differs from the others nasally.[5] It has a distinct, though small, nasal spine situated at the front of the nasal cavity. In the other specimens the spine is located far inside and its two lateral segments are divided by the vomer, which is the lower part of the nasal septum. Telanthropus's nasal passages have a distinct floor, forming a single plane set at an angle to the outer surface of the bone. In the other specimens the floor is rounded and its junction with the outer plane of the bone guttered and indistinct. In these respects Telanthropus seems to have been more humanlike than the other Australopithecines.

The Australopithecine Jaws

THE AUSTRALOPITHECINES needed large jaws. It takes heavy jaw muscles and big teeth to chew the coarse, uncooked, and probably mostly uncut food eaten by open-country omnivores; witness the large jaws and teeth of the ground-living baboons. The Australopithecine jaws are just as large and heavy as they needed to be, and their size relative to that of the brain case is a purely evolutionary matter without implication of relationship to other primates.

As in apes, the upper jaw is long and deep, but the palate is entirely unapelike and essentially human in shape. Whereas the ape palate is long and narrow, with the cheek-tooth rows parallel or even slightly convergent toward the rear, the Australopithecine palate is continuously arched, with no apelike gaps (diastemas) between canines and lateral incisors. The key to the difference between hominid and pongid palate forms is the relative size and time of eruption of the upper canines. In juvenile apes, as in a youthful specimen of *Proconsul*, the palate is shaped much as in *Australopithecus* and *Homo*. The huge canines of the apes are cut only when the palate is big enough to accommodate them, and when the animal needs them—just before or along with the third

[5] Robinson: "Telanthropus. . . ," pp. 445–501.

molars. In the hominids the canines are small and erupt early, without altering the shape of the palate.

Apart from size, the chief difference between Australopithecine and human palates is that in the former the posterior border of the palate extends far beyond the level of the third molars, whereas in man this border is in line with the teeth. In this detail the Australopithecine palate falls halfway between those of gorilla and man. It is tempting to interpret this feature to mean that the Australopithecines could not have spoken because their pharynxes had not yet become open as in man (see page 74), but additional evidence is needed before such a conclusion can be drawn.

The mandible, which is correspondingly large and heavy, is also human in shape if compared to the chinless jaws of fossil men. As

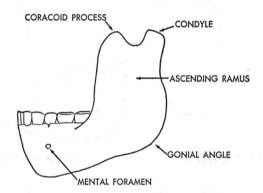

Fig. 32   The Anatomy of the Mandible: Swartkrans, female. (Drawing after Dart, 1954.)

in man, the mental foramina are high. No specimen has been found with a simian shelf to brace it, but even if one turns up, this feature will not make the creature less hominid. In general the ascending ramus is extremely long, to accommodate the great height of the upper jaw and face, and it is set at nearly a right angle to the occlusal plane in all known jaws except those from Swartkrans. In the latter the angle is wider because the temporal muscles were attached far back on the brain case. For the same reason the coracoid process, to the tip and anterior border of which the temporal tendon is attached, points backward more than in most human mandibles, particularly those of fossil men.

In all Australopithecine specimens the mandibular fossa of the temporal bone of the cranium, which is the groove in which the mandibular condyle moves in chewing, is human in form. Along with the evidence derived from the teeth, this indicates that the Australopithecines chewed their food in a rotary movement, as do primitive men, instead of up and down, like apes and most civilized men. One Swartkrans skull, called female by its discoverer, had such extensive temporal muscles that they met at the top of its head in a crest which did not, however, stretch gorilla-fashion backward to its occipital torus. As even in the gorilla such crests are confined to males, the identification of this skull as female is highly dubious. It was probably a male skull.

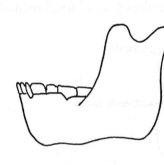
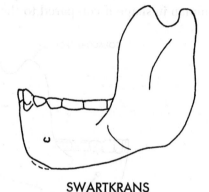

MAKAPANSGAT SWARTKRANS

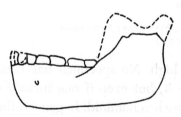
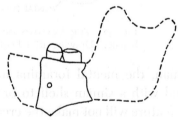

TELANTHROPUS 1 TELANTHROPUS 2

FIG. 33 THE AUSTRALOPITHECINE MANDIBLES.

The Swartkrans and Kromdraai mandibles are larger and heavier than those of the earlier and smaller Australopithecines. This difference does not necessarily imply a change in dietary habits, because it can be equally well interpreted as an application of the law of allometry, that is, that the larger an animal becomes, the larger his jaws grow both absolutely and proportionately.

The two Telanthropus mandibles, found in the Swartkrans cave in what seemed to be a separate pocket of breccia, are more slender and smaller than those of their companions in the cave, *A. robustus,* but they are not identical. The first one is virtually whole except that both ascending rami are broken off. However, the position of one condyle was indicated by the form of its stump, and when reconstructed the ramus height appears to have been moderate, as in man. Yet the ascending ramus starts to leave the body of the mandible at the level of the first lower molar, as in proper Australopithecine jaws, instead of farther back, at the level of the third molar, as in most human jaws. Also the maxilla that Robinson attributed to Telanthropus, although manlike in other respects, was long from nose to tooth line and would require a high ramus.

The second Telanthropus mandible, which in 1952 Broom and Robinson tentatively identified as human, is a piece of the right branch, about 5.5 cm. long, carrying the first and second molars. Morphologically and metrically it is indistinguishable from a human jaw fragment and in fact resembles in many ways the Mauer (Heidelberg) jaw from the Early Middle Pleistocene of Europe.

The Teeth of Australopithecus

MORE HAS BEEN written about the teeth of these creatures than about the sum of the rest of their remains, and much of the writing is highly detailed and technical, and comprehensible only to specialists. Luckily the entire subject has been exhaustively covered by Robinson in a single volume.[6]

The total number of Australopithecine teeth known in 1956 was 526. Of these 448 are permanent and 78 deciduous, or milk, teeth. The vast majority come from two sites, Sterkfontein and Swartkrans, although there are enough from the other sites to indicate what they are like. Every tooth of both upper and lower jaws, and of both milk and permanent dentitions, is represented

[6] Robinson: "The Dentition of the Australopithecinae."

by at least two specimens; and enough specimens of most kinds of tooth in the permanent dentition are available to permit detailed statistical analysis. These teeth are more abundant and more completely represented than those of any kind of fossil man except the Upper Paleolithic folk of Europe, whose teeth were modern.

TABLE 7

NUMBERS OF AUSTRA-
LOPITHECINE TEETH

		Milk	*Permanent*	*Total*			
Taung		20	4	24			
Sterkfontein		12	129	141			
Makapansgat		2	25	27			
Swartkrans		38	273	311			
Kromdraai		6	17	23			
		78	448	526			

		I-1	I-2	C	P-1	P-2	M-1	M-2	M-3
Permanent	upper	11	14	22	49	36	49	43	31
	lower	9	5	15	27	25	46	33	33
Milk	upper	4	2	2			5	8	
	lower	5	8	9			14	21	

Although some of these teeth are very large by human standards, they are essentially, if not entirely, human in form and function and quite different from those of either Old World monkeys or apes, whether fossil or living. These differences are just as marked in the milk as in the permanent dentitions. In both upper and lower jaws the incisors are practically identical with those of *Homo* both in size and in shape. The canines, too, are similar in form, but some are larger than the largest found in man. Starting with the first premolar of each jaw, the cheek teeth grow larger and larger, compared to man's, as we move down the row to the third molar, but the morphological similarity remains. No trace is found in any site of elongated, conical canines, shearing lower first premolars, or a diastema; nor are any of the molars bilophodont. There is no evidence to indicate a transition from ape to hominid nor a close relationship with the Old World monkeys. But the lower molars have the typical Dryopithecus cusp pattern in common with *Proconsul*, the other Dryopithecines, and the living

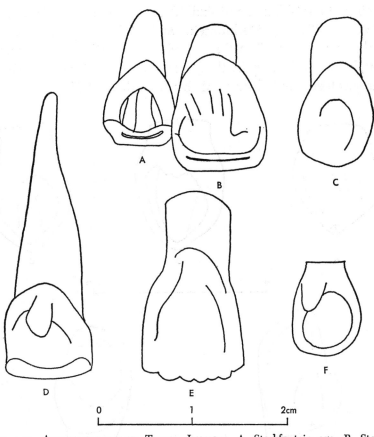

FIG. 34a AUSTRALOPITHECINE TEETH: INCISORS. A. Sterkfontein 25a; B. Sterkfontein 25a; C. Makapansgat (no number); D. Swartkrans 3; E. Swartkrans 68;
F. Swartkrans 11. The smaller and earlier Australopithecines are represented by
only two upper median incisors, a pair in a single jaw from Sterkfontein. One is
depicted here (B), along with an upper lateral incisor accompanying it, and an
upper lateral from Makapansgat (C). An upper median (E) and two upper
laterals (D and F) from Swartkrans represent the larger and later Australopithecines. In A, B, and C a certain amount of surface relief is shown on the inner
or labial side of the blade; this relief takes the form of a mild shoveling (A and C)
and ridging (A and B). These features also occur in human teeth and will be explained later. In the Swartkrans median incisor (E), the edges are slightly raised
and the lower border of the tooth is scalloped; this scalloping also occurs in human teeth when first cut. The Swartkrans laterals (D and F) show some ridging,
and each has a teatlike basal protuberance, also found in some human teeth. On
the whole, the earlier incisors seem to have more relief on the lingual side than the
later ones, but the samples are too small to be sure. (Drawings after Robinson,
1956.)

apes. In short, the Australopithecines were just as hominid dentally as we are, and in some respects even less apelike.

But they were not a single unit. In tooth size and tooth form
the Australopithecines fall naturally into three groups, just as

their postcranial bones and skulls do, as follows: *Australopithecus africanus* (Taung, Sterkfontein, and Makapansgat); *Australopithecus robustus* (Swartkrans and Kromdraai); and Telanthropus, known so far only by the lower teeth of two jaws. The Telanthropus teeth are indistinguishable from those of *Homo*.

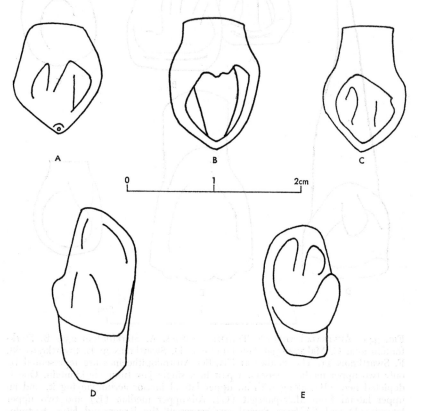

Fig. 34b Australopithecine Teeth: Canines. A. Swartkrans 93; B. Sterkfontein 52a; C. Makapansgat (uppers); D. Sterkfontein 50; E. Sterkfontein 51 (lowers). Like the incisors, the Australopithecine canines show a considerable amount of relief on the lingual side, including raised edges, ridges, basal protuberances. The ones shown here are from the smaller and earlier group except A, which is from Swartkrans. Apparently the smaller and earlier species had more elaborate relief patterns than the later and larger one. All these variations can be found in man.

Robinson, who had large enough samples of the first two groups to permit refined statistical analysis, has shown them to represent genetically different populations that probably differ as much from each other as *A. africanus* does from *Homo*. On this basis the two groups should rank at least as separate species.

The differences between them begin with the palate. The palatal index, a length-breadth ratio, falls between 90 and 96 per cent in the Australopithecines, 63 and 95 per cent in man, and 35 and 62 per cent in apes. These figures place the Australopithecines at the top of the human range. Although the two species are the same in this index, they differ in the shape of the upper dental row and consequently of the palate itself. In Sterkfontein (*A. africanus*) the tooth row consists of a smooth curve, as in most human palates, but in Swartkrans (*A. robustus*) the incisors form a flat line from canine to canine.

In both species the teeth are crowded. Some of the incisors are set crookedly in the jawbones so that their occlusal edges overlap each other. All jaws that contain worn incisors have the edge-to-edge bite typical of human populations that chew tough food, and the individual teeth are worn not only on their crowns but also fore and aft, where the teeth rub together in chewing. But in *A. africanus* the wear on the lower premolars and molars is mostly on the buccal or cheek (outer) side of the crowns, and in *A. robustus* it is on the inner or tongue side, because the palate of *A. africanus* is wider than the lower jaw; in *A. robustus* it is the opposite. In this feature *A. africanus* resembles man, and *A. robustus* the ungulates. Furthermore, only in *A. robustus* does the enamel of the crowns show extensive chipping, as if from grit encountered on uncleaned roots.

In the length and breadth dimensions of the dental crowns (see Table 8), *A. africanus* falls within the human range in fifteen of thirty-two measurements, overlaps that range in sixteen others, and falls completely outside it in only one, the breadth of the second lower premolar. *A. robustus,* however, falls outside the human range in ten measurements, all in the premolars and molars, and seven of them are breadth measurements. All the ranges of the two Australopithecine species fail to overlap, but the older species, *A. africanus,* has larger front teeth—incisors and canines—than the younger species, *A. robustus,* which has the larger premolars and molars. In this sense *A. africanus* is more nearly human than *A. robustus*. Robinson explains this as follows: "All the features of the *Paranthropus* (read *Australopithecus robustus*) dentition, as far as size and proportion are concerned, may be ex-

TABLE 8

CROWN DIMENSIONS OF AUSTRALOPITHECINE TEETH
UPPERS

		A. africanus	A. robustus	Zinjanthropus	Garusi	Homo
I-1	1.	9.3– 9.5 R	8.3–10.8 R	9.6–10.2		6.5–10.8
	b.	8.2– 8.3	7.3– 7.8	7.9		6.2– 9.0
I-2	1.	5.8– 7.3 R	6.5– 9.0 R	6.2– 7.1		5.0– 9.0
	b.	5.6– 7.0	6.3– 7.6	5.6– 7.3		5.0– 8.5
C	1.	8.8– 9.9 R	8.1–10.6 R	7.9 L	10.5 ca. S	5.8–11.0
	b.	8.7– 9.9	8.4–10.4	9.0–10.2		5.0–10.0
P-1	1.	8.5– 9.4 R	9.0–10.8 R	10.7 L	9.6 S	5.5– 9.5
	b.	10.7–13.9	13.1–15.3	14.9	12.3	5.0–12.5
P-2	1.	7.2–10.5 R	9.2–11.8 R	10.7 L	9.1 S	7.8–13.1
	b.	12.5–13.8	13.7–16.3	14.9–15.8	12.5	5.0–12.5
M-1	1.	11.9–13.2 R	13.1–14.5 R	14.7 L		7.8–13.5
	b.	13.2–14.1	13.2–16.6	17.0–18.1		9.0–14.8
M-2	1.	12.8–15.1 R	13.6–15.9 R	17.0 L		7.0–13.6
	b.	14.3–17.1	16.0–17.4	18.1–20.3		7.0–15.2
M-3	1.	11.6–15.2 R	13.9–17.0 R	12.7 L	(10.9) S	4.0–13.0
	b.	14.6–17.9	15.7–18.1	20.3–21.5	(13.0)	4.0–15.0

L = Leakey   *Nature*, Aug. 15, 1959
M = Marks   *IJNS*, Vol. 109, 1953
R = Robinson   *TMM*, No. 9, 1956
S = Şenyürek   *Belleten*, Vol. 19, No. 73, 1955
W = Weidenreich *APAM*, Vol. 40, Pt. 1, 1945

plained on the assumption that selection has retained as large a chewing area in the grinding teeth as is consistent with reducing jaw size at the expense of the less important teeth in a large vegetarian." [7]

In one particular comparison the essential difference between the two Australopithecine species is seen in sharp focus; that is, the ratio between the crown area of the canine teeth and the crown areas of the two premolars of each jaw. In *A. africanus,* as in various human populations living and extinct, the canines are nearly or just as large as any premolar of either jaw. In *A. robustus*

[7] Robinson: "Dentition of the Australopithecinae," pp. 148–9.

LOWERS

Homo	Telanthropus	Olduvai Child	A. africanus	A. robustus	Meg. jav.
3.5- 6.8 4.9- 7.7	6.5	5.9- 6.0	5.9- 6.3 R 6.1- 8.1	5.2- 5.6 R 5.5- 6.7	
4.2- 7.5 5.3- 7.6	6.9	7.0- 7.1	7.3 R 6.8	6.1- 6.7 R 6.7- 7.5	
7.0-11.8 5.8-10.4	8.2	8.7-10.0 8.0- 9.2	8.5-10.5 R 9.2-12.1	6.9- 8.5 R 7.3- 9.2	
4.5- 9.8 5.7-11.2	8.6 R 10.3	9.9-10.4 9.2	9.2-11.8 R 9.0-11.7	9.2-10.5 R 10.0-12.9	10.0 W 12.0
8.0-14.1 8.3-13.2	8.4 R	11.2 9.2- 9.3	9.8-10.1 R 11.6-11.7	10.3-12.5 R 12.0-17.0	8.5-10.5 WM 11.0
8.0-15.0 8.3-13.5	11.9-12.1 R 11.9	13.8-15.0 11.5-12.1	13.0-15.1 R 11.2-13.9	12.7-16.1 R 13.0-15.2	14.0-15.1 WM 13.0
6.3-16.0 8.0-13.7	12.1-13.6 R 12.5-13.1	15.0 11.5	14.3-16.8 R 13.2-15.3	15.0-17.4 R 13.9-16.2	14.5 M 13.0
5.8-15.0 4.0-13.0	13.9-14.1 R 12.3-12.4		13.5-16.7 R 12.7-14.8	15.4-18.5 R 12.9-16.5	15.5 M 13.0

L = Leakey	*Nature*, Aug. 15, 1959
M = Marks	*IJNS*, Vol. 109, 1953
R = Robinson	*TMM*, No. 9, 1956
S = Şenyürek	*Belleten*, Vol. 19, No. 73, 1955
W = Weidenreich	*APAM*, Vol. 40, Pt. 1, 1945

TABLE 9

A COMPARISON OF THE CROWN AREAS OF
CANINES AND PREMOLARS IN
AUSTRALOPITHECUS AND *HOMO*

	Upper Jaw		Lower Jaw	
Canine to:	First Premolar	Second PM	First Premolar	Second PM
A. robustus	1.316	1.444	1.395	1.546
A. africanus	1.077	1.107	1.050	1.109
Homo	1.021–1.065	.980–1.026	.987–1.025	1.000–1.078

the premolars are a third to a half again as large as the canines. This is a considerable difference and taxonomically of significance. Had we no other information on the Australopithecine teeth, we could divide the genus into species on this basis.

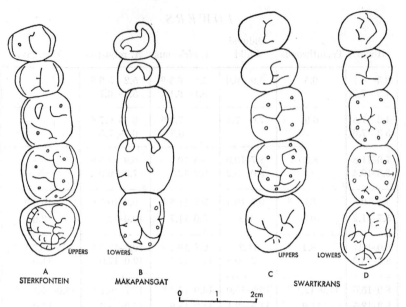

FIG. 35 AUSTRALOPITHECINE TEETH: PREMOLARS AND MOLARS. A. Sterkfontein uppers; B. Makapansgat lowers; C. Swartkrans uppers; D. Swartkrans lowers. A, C, and D are relatively new teeth; B is worn enough to obscure the cusp pattern. Although the molars are more or less the same size in both species, the premolars of *Australopithecus robustus* are larger and more molarlike than those of *Australopithecus africanus*. Also the *robustus* molars consistently have six cusps; the *africanus* molars five or six. (Drawings after Robinson, 1956.)

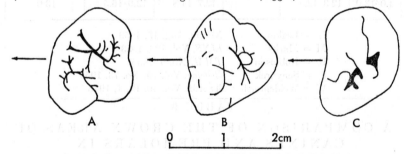

FIG. 36 IRREGULARLY SHAPED MOLARS OF *Australopithecus robustus*. A. Upper Second; B. Upper Third; C. Lower Third. All from Swartkrans. (After Broom and Robinson, and Robinson, 1956.)

In most dental measurements *A. africanus* shows more individual variation than *A. robustus,* whose teeth seem to have been selected for a rigorous, special diet; but in the breadth measurements of some of the premolars and molars the latter's teeth fall into two groups, large and larger. Robinson interprets this as evidence of sexual dimorphism, which is not noticeable in the dentition of *A. africanus.*

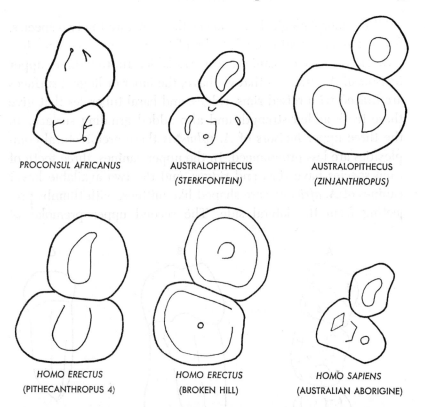

FIG. 37   THE UPPER CANINE AND FIRST PREMOLAR IN AUSTRALOPITHECINES, APES, AND MEN. In *Australopithecus* the front teeth (canines and incisors) are small in comparison with the cheek teeth (premolars and molars). In *Homo* the opposite is true, and in this respect *Homo* is intermediate between the Australopithecines and the apes. In this figure are shown the crown surfaces of six pairs of teeth, the upper left first premolar (below) and the upper left canine (above). The crown patterns reflect degrees of wear more than morphological differences. What is critical here is the relative crown sizes of the two teeth in each species. In *Proconsul africanus*, as in living apes, the crown of the upper canine is larger than that of the upper first premolar. In both the smaller and the larger Australopithecines, represented here by Sterkfontein and Zinjanthropus, the canine is less than one third as large as the first premolar. In *Homo erectus*, represented by Pithecanthropus 4 and the Broken Hill skull (the earliest and latest of the known *H. erectus* skulls), the canine and first premolar are of roughly equal size, as they are in many modern jaws, particularly among Mongoloids. The specimen of *Homo sapiens* shown here, that of an Australian aborigine, illustrates an extreme degree of size differentiation for our species—the upper canine has only about two thirds the crown area of the upper first premolar. Because these and other dental differences between *Australopithecus* and *Homo* are as old as both genera, they must have arisen longer than 700,000 years ago, the date of the earliest known specimens of either genus, except possibly that from Lake Tchad, the taxonomy of which remains to be determined. Of the two, the Australopithecine is the more specialized and the human the more conservative, at least in the feature illustrated here. (Drawing 1 from LeGros Clark and Leakey; drawings 2 and 6 from Clark; number 3 from Leakey; number 4 from Weidenreich; and number 5 from Pycraft.)

Of the morphological differences that separate the two species, few if any are great enough to be of taxonomic value. Very few unworn incisors or canines are available. In the three upper incisors of *A. africanus* that we have, the inner or lingual surfaces are braced with raised rims, ridges, and basal tubercles that give these teeth added strength and also added grinding surface. In the three upper incisors of *A. robustus* these architectural complexities are less pronounced. In the upper canines, three teeth of each species have rims and ridges, and the two available lower canines of *A. africanus* are shaped like mittens, with thumbs projecting from the lateral side. The second upper premolar of

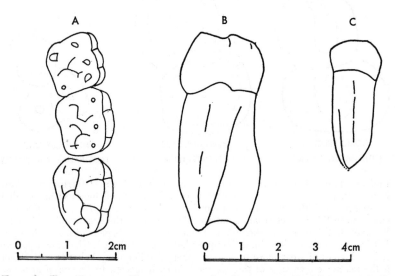

FIG. 38   THE TEETH OF TELANTHROPUS. In the cave at Swartkrans, with the Australopithecine bones, were found two pieces of mandible and a piece of maxilla of a smaller and more humanlike hominid, Telanthropus. A represents the right molars of mandible 1; C, the lower first premolar of mandible 2; and B, a lower first premolar of *Australopithecus robustus*, found in the same cave, by way of comparison. The molars are humanlike in size and shape, and so is the first lower premolar. In mandible 2 the socket that once held the lower third molar is conical and shallow, showing that it held a single-rooted tooth, as in man. As Swartkrans may be Early Middle Pleistocene in date, it is possible that Telanthropus was an early form of *Homo erectus* and not an Australopithecine, but this is not certain. (Drawings after Robinson, 1953.)

A. africanus has two roots; that of *A. robustus* three, in all cases— a total of eighteen teeth for *A. robustus* and ten for *A. africanus*. Some of the molars of *A. robustus* are not rectangular, as they usually are among primates, but have odd shapes, including parallelograms and even triangles. Those of A. *africanus* conform more closely to the usual form.

Some of the dental features peculiar to A. *africanus,* and others common to both South African species, anticipate subspecific differences found, over long periods, in the teeth of geographical races of *Homo.* In most if not all cases they are typical of either the Congoid (African Negroid) or Caucasoid branches of mankind, and differ from the corresponding features in the teeth of the Australoid and Mongoloid lines. As human racial differences in dentition will be discussed in the next chapter, they need not be

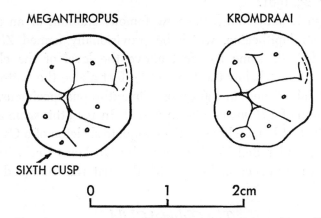

MEGANTHROPUS   KROMDRAAI

SIXTH CUSP

0   1   2cm

FIG. 39   THE AUSTRALOPITHECINE FEATURES OF THE LOWER FIRST MOLAR OF MEGANTHROPUS. On the left is a diagram of the cusp and groove pattern of the lower right first molar of the Javanese fossil mandible known as Meganthropus (see page 298); on the right, the corresponding tooth of an Australopithecine from Kromdraai, South Africa. The two specimens are virtually identical in size, shape, system of grooves, and cusp locations. Each has six cusps, a rarity among hominids except *Australopithecus robustus* (Swartkrans and Kromdraai), in which the feature is apparently invariable. Robinson uses the close similarity between these two teeth, along with other features, including the size and form of the roots, to substantiate his theory that Meganthropus was an Asiatic Australopithecine. (Drawings after Robinson, 1953.)

given in detail here. But they should be borne in mind, particularly throughout our study of the early hominid remains, including teeth, which have recently been exhumed in Tanganyika and Kenya.

The Early Hominids from East Africa

EARLY HOMINID remains have been found in three sites in East Africa: Olduvai Gorge, Garusi, and Kanam. The only finds that are completely reliable in a geological sense are those from Olduvai, and they are also the most numerous and diagnostic. In Bed I, associated with early Oldowan tools, Leakey found many hominid remains, including pieces of the skeleton of an eleven-year-old child of unknown sex, lying 27 feet below the top of the bed and 78 feet above the basalt at its bottom. This find was made late in 1960. At the time of writing the only available information comes from two short articles, with photographs.[8] I have also been given the opportunity, by Matthew Stirling and L. S. B. Leakey himself, to examine some of the specimens and fresh casts, on February 25, 1961.

In 1959 Leakey found the now famous cranium of an adult male Australopithecine, which he provisionally named *Zinjanthropus boiseii*,[9] some five feet above the level of the child's skeleton, 22 feet below the top and 83 feet above the bottom of Bed I. He also found, in 1960, more Zinjanthropus specimens, and the cranium of a *Homo erectus* in Bed II. In 1913 this same gorge yielded its first human bones—the complete skeleton of a Capsian man in or under Bed V—discovered by Dr. Hans Reck. In this chapter we are concerned only with the material from Bed I.

The Olduvai Child

THE OLDUVAI child's skeleton consists of a broken mandible, two more or less complete parietal bones, one wrist bone, and

[8] Leakey: "New Finds at Olduvai Gorge," *Nature,* Vol. 189, No. 4765 (Feb. 25, 1961), pp. 649–50.

Leakey: "New Links in the Chain of Human Evolution: Three Major New Discoveries From the Olduvai Gorge, Tanganyika," *ILN,* Vol. 238, No. 6344 (March 4, 1961), pp. 346–8.

J. R. Napier: "Fossil Hand Bones from Olduvai Gorge," *Nature,* Vol. 196, No. 4853 (1962), pp. 409–11.

[9] From *Balad al-Zanj* (or *Zinj*), Arabic for *Land of the Ethiopians.*

FIG. 40   [Facing page] A SECTION THROUGH THE PLEISTOCENE BEDS AT OLDUVAI GORGE. C. Olduvai Child; Z. Zinjanthropus; MT. Milk teeth; CH.3. Chellian-3 skull. Capsian denotes the original Oldoway man discovered by Hans Reck; all the others were discovered by Dr. and Mrs. L. S. B. Leakey. The beds are numbered I through V. Bed I is Lower Pleistocene but post-Villafranchian. Bed II is Middle Pleistocene; Beds III and IV, Upper Pleistocene. Bed V is post-Pleistocene, and some of it has slipped down the face of the gorge to the underlying basalt. In this section, five different sets of skeletal remains are placed as if they lay directly over each other. Actually some of them are several miles apart. (Drawing after Arambourg, 1961.)

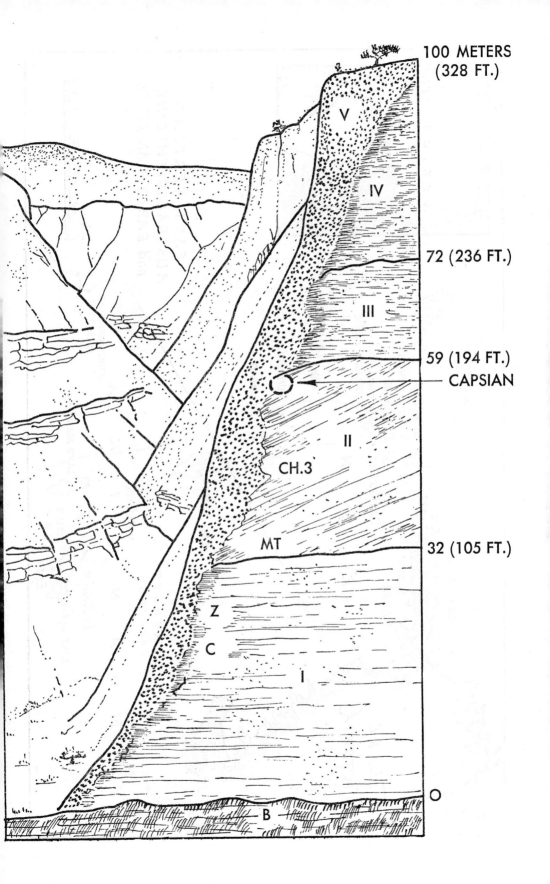

100 METERS
(328 FT.)

V

IV

72 (236 FT.)

III

59 (194 FT.)
CAPSIAN

II

CH.3

MT

32 (105 FT.)

Z

C

I

O

B

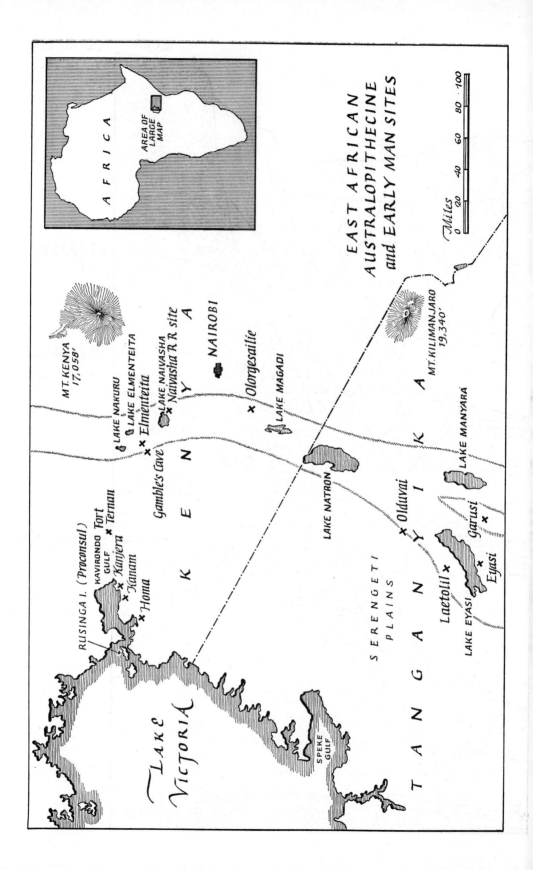

EAST AFRICAN
AUSTRALOPITHECINE
and EARLY MAN SITES

Miles
0   20   40   60   80 100

AREA OF
LARGE
MAP

A F R I C A

LAKE
VICTORIA

SPEKE
GULF

RUSINGA I. (Proconsul)
KAVIRONDO
GULF
× Fort
× Ternan
× Kanjera
× Kanam
× Homa

Gamble's Cave

K   E   N   Y   A

MT. KENYA
17,058'

LAKE NAKURU
LAKE ELMENTEITA
× Elmenteita
LAKE NAIVASHA
Naivasha R.R. site

× Olorgesailie
× LAKE MAGADI

NAIROBI

LAKE NATRON

S E R E N G E T I
P L A I N S

T   A   N   G   A   N   Y   I   K   A

× Olduvai

Laetolil ×
× Garusi
LAKE EYASI
× Eyasi

LAKE MANYARA

MT. KILIMANJARO
19,340'

seven finger bones. Also found were six finger bones, two clavicles (collarbones), twelve bones of a left foot, and "a few teeth" of what Leakey calls one or more adult individuals. Before describing these specimens I should state that the difference of five feet between the location of the child and his companions and that of Zinjanthropus may indicate a greater time span than this small vertical distance would suggest. Although the Oldowan stone tools extend to the bottom of Bed I, the fauna of the level of the child's skeleton is said to contain genera and species not seen in the 22-foot level. The future identification of this new fauna is critical.

The Child's Mandible

THE MANDIBLE was found lying bottom up, and its entire lower portion had been destroyed. On its left side the mandible extends to a point one centimeter behind the lower second molar,

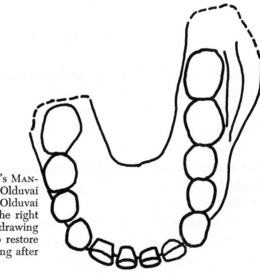

FIG. 41 THE OLDUVAI CHILD'S MAN-DIBLE. The mandible of the Olduvai child, found in Bed I of Olduvai Gorge, was crushed so that the right side was bent inward. In this drawing an attempt has been made to restore it to its original form. (Drawing after Leakey in *Nature*, 1960.)

and on the right it is broken off just in front of the rear border of the first lower molar. The profile of the chin region is moderately steep, and continuously curved downward and backward, but on the inner side the body of the bone sweeps backward almost to a line connecting the rear borders of the second premolars—farther back than in the Australopithecines or *Proconsul*. The forward flanges of the ascending rami are widely separated from the tooth row and begin to rise at the level of the forward borders of the first molars. In this feature the mandible resembles those of *Proconsul* and of all the South African Australopithecines, including Telanthropus.

Before fossilization the mandible was broken in several places, all in the canine- and incisor-bearing section. This breakage thrust the left incisors backward and drew the right side of the mandible inward. The original shape (see Fig. 41), as tentatively restored, is that of a long, narrow arch, the two halves of which diverge slightly toward the rear. In this respect it resembles the mandibles of Sterkfontein and Makapansgat, *Oreopithecus*, and the known Dryopithecines of Africa and Asia, including *Proconsul africanus*, all of which retained, in different degrees, a generalized, primitive, essentially V-shaped, primate form.

The Child's Teeth

A L L   T H E incisors, canines, and premolars, and both first molars are present, as well as the left second molar. The first molars and the incisors are well worn, but the second molar is in mint condition, having just erupted at the time of death. All the teeth are within the human range in breadth, but the crowns of the canines, the second premolars, and the second molar are longer (anteroposteriorly) than those of any specimen of *Homo* yet found (see Table 8, page 273).

The incisors are similar to human teeth in size and form, with no peculiarities foreshadowing those of any individual human race, and they also resemble the lower incisors of *Proconsul*. The canines, larger than those of the South African Australopithecines, are pointed and somewhat spatulate, as in many human beings. The premolars are longer than wide, especially the second premolars. Instead of being superhominid, like those of the Australopithecines, the premolars are, if anything, less completely bicuspid than our own, and each of the second premolars has a pit (fovea) at the rear of the crown. This pit is bordered posteriorly by a rim composed of tiny cusps, or beads, as in the corresponding teeth of *Proconsul*. The cusp pattern of the first molars is fully human, with five crowns on the left tooth and six on the right one. The left second molar has six cusps. Seen from the side, these teeth fail to form a straight row at the line of occlusion with the upper teeth: the crowns of the premolars are lower than those of either the molars or the canines and incisors.

These are clearly not proper Australopithecine teeth. Rather, they resemble those of *Homo* in form and also in relative size along the tooth row; the incisors and canines are large compared to the Australopithecine dentition, and the molars are relatively long and narrow. In fact, the molars also resemble, in this respect, those of Telanthropus, *Proconsul,* and *Oreopithecus*. Morphologically the molars look like *Proconsul's* rather than *Oreopithecus's;* the opposite is true of the premolars. Whatever the kinship and status of the Olduvai child turn out to be, his teeth seem to form a connecting link between the large apes of the Miocene and Pliocene and *Homo*. The living apes and the South African Australopithecines would then be left on either side of him. That he could have been descended from the Australopithecines so far found seems unlikely, but some of them could have been descended from him.

The Child's Parietal Bones

WITH THE mandible were found two parietal bones, the left of which is the more nearly complete. Their open sutures and thin walls confirm the eleven-year-old age ascribed to the mandible. According to the scale on the photographs, these parietals are about as long, in the sagittal chord (from bregma to lambda) as those of Sterkfontein.[1] All else being equal, this comparison suggests a capacity of 450 to 500 cc., but this is a very tentative

[1] Roughly, 70 to 75 mm. In *Homo erectus* the shortest chord known is that of Pithecanthropus 1, 87.5 mm., capacity 900 cc. Pithecanthropus 2, with a chord of 91 mm., had a capacity of 775 cc.

figure, one which does not allow for the curvature of the bones. In 1962 Leakey showed a picture of himself placing the parietals of the Olduvai child over the brain cast of Pithecanthropus 2, which had a cranial capacity of 775 cc. The bones were almost large enough to fit. The child's cranial capacity may, therefore, have been as high as 700 cc.

The cranial capacity of an eleven-year-old modern child is virtually that of an adult, and the parietals have assumed nearly adult form. These parietals are thin, and show no signs of an incipient crest seen on the larger Australopithecines. The left parietal contains a depressed fracture with radiating cracks, inflicted *pre* or *ad mortem.*

Since the original discovery more skull and jaw pieces have been found, raising the total to five individuals. Estimated cranial capacities run from 643 cc. to 724 cc. These specimens have been assigned to a new species, *Homo habilis.**

The Foot Accompanying the Child's Remains

THE BONES of the left foot found with the parietals and mandible of the first Olduvai child belonged to a second individual, an adult. The description of these bones was published in March, 1964.† In this foot, the part of the calcaneum behind the posterior border of the talus is missing. So are the epiphyses of all five metatarsals and all the phalanges. Despite these omissions, the essential parts of the skeleton of the foot are there and a conclusion can be drawn. The Olduvai foot is essentially if not completely human and bears no more resemblance to an ape's foot than do the feet of some living men (Fig. 25). This is logical, if one of the first developments in human evolution was walking erect: that kind of locomotion requires human feet.

The foot was relatively broad and the third metatarsal unusually robust. Also, the third metatarsal had a bony growth that

* L. S. B. Leakey, P. V. Tobias, and J. R. Napier: "A New Species of the Genus *Homo* from Olduvai Gorge," *Nature,* Vol. 202, No. 4927 (April 4, 1964), pp. 7–9.

† M. H. Day and J. R. Napier: "Fossil Foot Bones," in "Hominid Fossils from Bed I, Olduvai Gorge, Tanganyika," *Nature,* Vol. 201, No. 4923 (March 7, 1964), pp. 969–70.

overlapped the fourth metacarpal. As the remaining parts of the foot were about 11 cm. long, the original foot would have been about size 7, and the width at least E, about the size and shape of a Pueblo Indian's foot. It was not necessarily the foot of a person of dwarf stature, as previously suggested.

A tibia and fibula were also recovered at the same site, but higher up, on the Zinjanthropus living floor (see p. 294).[*] They too are essentially human. The tibia was originally about 277±10 cm. long. If the bones belonged to a human being of modern proportions, he or she would be only about 144.5 cm. tall, or 4 feet 8 inches. This does not necessarily have a bearing on the stature of the individual whose foot was found lower down. In the case of the unattached leg bones, also, the important fact about them is their essentially human quality, whether they belonged to a *Homo* or an *Australopithecus,* and whatever they were like from the neck up.

The Collarbone, Hand, and Fingers

L E A K E Y's preliminary notices contain pictures of one clavicle, originally attributed to the child and later called adult. That of the other adult is not shown. The clavicle shown has lost both ends, and in its present condition is 13 cm. long, but was probably at least 2 cm. longer, long enough for a full-sized modern man. Its shape is a simple, open S, as in man. In the gorilla the bone is shaped like a hockey stick, with a curve at only one end.

The finger bones are said to come from the same two individuals, and there is only one hand bone, a capitate—the most centrally located of the wrist bones. Luckily we have a comparable bone from Sterkfontein. Seen from the volar or palm side, the capitate is about 25 mm. long and 20 mm. wide, well within the human range. Although details are not easily distinguishable, it seems to lack the constrictions on both sides characteristic of this bone in *Proconsul* and the living apes. These constrictions serve as

[*] P. R. Davis: "A Tibia and Fibula," in "Homind Fossils from Bed I, Olduvai Gorge, Tanganyika," *Nature,* Vol. 201, No. 4923 (March 7, 1964), pp. 967–8.

anchors for the powerful tendons needed to keep the wrist firm for brachiation. The Sterkfontein capitate also lacks them.

The finger bones of the first individual consist of five first or second phalanges, all broken at the proximal (wristward) end, and two terminal or nail-bearing phalanges. The finger bones of the second, so-called adult individual, are two proximal or intermediate phalanges (they are not easy to tell apart when broken) and two distals (the ones that carry the fingernails). Two distals and one intermediate are intact. The phalanges of the two individuals are alike in size and shape, and as large as those of some living men.

They are not, however, fully human in form. The shafts of the proximal and intermediate bones are broad, flattened, and lipped on the palm side, as in *Proconsul* and the gorilla, and their terminal joints are narrower than their shafts, which have convex borders. In man the joints are usually wider than their shafts, the borders of which are slightly concave. In these details the Olduvai finger bones are less human than those of Kromdraai.

But in another respect the distal phalanges of both Olduvai individuals are human rather than apelike. (We have no distal phalanges from Kromdraai for comparison.) In man the end of each distal phalanx is broad and rounded, to support pressure from a broad, flattish nail, whereas in the apes the distal phalanges are tapering and pointed, to match the narrow, curved nails that cover them. In this anatomical detail both Olduvai hands were nearly if not entirely human.

Luckily one piece of thumb bone was recovered. It is the outer (distal) half of the proximal phalanx of the left hand. Its articular joint, on which the distal phalanx moves, is as wide as any corresponding joint on the fingers of the same hand, or very nearly so. This is the human condition. In apes it is narrower than the finger joints.

In brief, these Olduvai hominids had wrist bones like those of Kromdraai and man, proximal and intermediate finger phalanges like those of *Proconsul* and the gorilla, terminal finger bones like man's, and proximal thumb bones of human size compared to the sizes of the finger bones. The total picture is one of evolution in process.

The Evolutionary and Taxonomic Position of the Olduvai Child

UNTIL THE remains of the Olduvai child and his adult companions have been carefully and competently studied by specialists in primate and human anatomy, we shall not know where on the hominid family tree this child belongs, nor what we should call it. Leakey has shown admirable forbearance in declining to give it a hastily coined Latin name.

These bones and teeth may be compared to those of *Proconsul,* Kenyanthropus, the Australopithecines, the living apes, and men. In many features the child resembles *Proconsul,* so much so that, if future studies support my tentative interpretation of the pictures and hasty handling of the specimens, a case can be made for the child's probable descent from a Dryopithecine, perhaps *Proconsul* himself. The Fort Ternan primate may be even closer. The child resembles the living apes only in features which both share with *Proconsul.* As in many ways the child is like South African Australopithecines, he probably belongs to the genus *Australopithecus,* but he is at the same time both more dryopithecine and more human than any Australopithecine yet found. He resembles man enough, perhaps, to have been our ancestor—provided that Leakey does not unearth some part of him which contradicts this interpretation.

Even more important than finding the rest of the child's bones and teeth, however, is determining their geological age. Is there a soil change in the five feet that separate Zinjanthropus's lair and the child's? What, if any, is the difference in fauna between these levels? The answers to these questions will help us find out.

Zinjanthropus: His Tools, Diet, and Activities

THE SPECIMENS known collectively as Zinjanthropus (I am using the name informally, like Telanthropus) include the 1959 cranium [2] and the 1960 discoveries—a tibia, a fibula, parts of a

[2] "The Astonishing Discovery of 'Nutcracker Man'; Dr. and Mrs. Leakey at Work at Olduvai," *ILN,* Vol. 235, No. 6267 (1959), pp. 217–19.

Leakey: "The Newly Discovered Skull from Olduvai: First Photographs of the Complete Skull," *ILN,* Vol. 235, No. 6268 (1959), pp. 288–9.

Arambourg: "L'Hominien Fossile d'Oldoway," pp. 223–8.

second skull, and some loose teeth. No systematic study of any of them has yet been published, and of the 1960 discoveries only the tibia and fibula have been illustrated.[3]

The site was apparently a camping place along the shore of a lake, at the head of a small peninsula. In it animal bones are abundant, particularly those of snakes, lizards, and crocodiles. Birds too are common, including a giant ostrich that laid giant eggs. Some of the mammals are also giants: *Afrochoerus* was a pig the size of a rhinoceros; *Pelorovis* a sheep six feet at the shoulder, with a horn spread of twelve to fifteen feet; *Sivatherium* a short-necked giraffe with horns like moose antlers; and *Simopithecus* a baboon with a lower jaw the size of a gorilla's.[4]

The hominids whose bones were found in the 22-foot level of Bed I seem not to have been skilled hunters, if they were hunters at all. Zinjanthropus 1, who died just after erupting his third molars, had already worn some of his other grinding teeth down to their pulp cavities. To have achieved this degree of attrition he must have been eating gritty roots, extracted from the soil, perhaps with sticks sharpened by his stone tools, and he may have eaten them uncleaned.

Most of the reptiles and some of the small mammals fall into the category of "slow game," game usually killed by women and children among living food-gatherers. The representatives of the giant mammals were apparently sucklings or even newly born babies, which are also sometimes killed and eaten by baboons. Leakey's careful study of these bones indicates that Zinjanthropus could not have been the hunter that *Homo* was, as shown by every pre-agricultural living site attributed to the latter which has yet been found. Yet the Zinjanthropi indubitably ate more animal proteins than were consumed by any known ape. They must have already developed a taste for raw meat.

[3] Leakey: "Recent Discoveries at Olduvai Gorge," *Nature*, Vol. 188, No. 4755 (1960), pp. 1050–2.

Leakey: "New Links in the Chain of Human Evolution: Three Major New Discoveries from the Olduvai Gorge, Tanganyika," *ILN*, Vol. 238, No. 6344 (1961), pp. 346–8.

The Zinjanthropus cranium has been studied by P. V. Tobias, whose voluminous report is expected shortly.

[4] Leakey: "Finding the World's Earliest Men," *NG*, Vol. 118, No. 3 (1960), pp. 420–35.

Zinjanthropus was an Australopithecine. So were the hominids who lived in South Africa at roughly the same time. If he could not hunt full-sized, adult game, neither could they. This new evidence effectively lays the ghost of Australopithecus the Hunter conjured up by the juxtaposition, in the Transvaal breccias, of hominid and other mammalian bones, including brained baboons.

The Anatomy of Zinjanthropus: His Cranium

THE CRANIUM of Zinjanthropus 1 has been pieced together and restored enough so that we can see what it was like. Its most striking feature is an exuberant growth of bony struts to brace the movements of a pair of massive jaws. The face is enormously long, and the brow ridges rise above the level of the forehead, which slopes backward, at first, behind them. On the sagittal line of the brain case rises a crest, as in Swartkrans, to anchor the temporal muscles where they meet on top of the skull. This crest is split down the middle by the sagittal suture, which had not yet fused at the time of death. Having just cut his wisdom teeth, Zinjanthropus was barely eighteen, according to our human growth schedule, and as an Australopithecine he may have been even younger.

Other crests run backward across his temporals from the zygomatic arches, and below them is set a pair of man-sized mastoids. In the rear his neck muscles were accommodated by still another crest, which is set low down, indicating an upright hafting of the skull on the neck.

Zinjanthropus's face, although larger and more apelike in gross proportions than the faces of the other Australopithecines, is more human in three respects. His eye sockets are wide and set far apart, so that their lateral borders are cut back, as in both *Proconsul* and man. His nasal skeleton can be seen from the side along its entire length, whereas in the other crania it is recessed. The nasal spine is set forward, at the lip of the nasal floor, as it is in Telanthropus alone of the South African Australopithecines.

Leakey has published a few of the measurements of this cranium. I have tentatively added others based on all the available photographs, and I have compared them with figures similarly obtained for *Australopithecus africanus, A. robustus,* and *Proconsul africanus* (see Table 10). Let us first consider only the three Australopithecines. In twelve of fifteen measurements, a progression from smallest to greatest may be seen from *A. africanus* to *A. robustus* to Zinjanthropus. In two other measurements no figures are available for *A. robustus,* but the progression is otherwise valid. In only one measurement, head height, is the sequence reversed; Sterkfontein has the highest cranial vault and Zinjanthropus the lowest.

In these changes—assuming that we have an evolutionary sequence—the cranial vault is affected the least, and most of the growth is seen in the bony framework supporting the jaws. The greatest increase is evident in the dimensions of the face; upper face height, bizygomatic face breadth, nose height and breadth, orbital height, and palate length and breadth.

On the other hand, changes in proportions, as reflected in seven indices, are trivial or nonexistent in four, and probably significant in only three—the two height ratios of the vault and the orbital index. These simply mirror the flattening out of the vault, the great growth of the jaws, and the change from more apelike to more human facial proportions. The eyes are farther apart than in the other Australopithecines and apes, and the stress of jaw action passes more through the center of the face and less through its sides than in the South African crania. The reduction in facial flatness seen in Zinjanthropus not only harks back in a sense to *Proconsul* but also makes him look more human.

As for *Proconsul,* we can see on Table 10 that *P. africanus,*[5] the smallest ape of this genus, is much smaller in all dimensions than the Australopithecines but is similar in several cranial and facial indices. Its high length-breadth (cranial) index is due primarily to its lack of brow ridges, which stretch the cranial lengths in the Australopithecines. Its facial proportions, involving the upper face, nasal bones and apeture, orbits, and palate, are very similar. In the assessment of genetic continuity in human geographical lines these ratios seem to be more important than gross

---

[5] We are obliged to limit our comparison to that species because no skulls of the other two have been found, only jaws and teeth.

TABLE 10

TENTATIVE CRANIAL MEASUREMENTS AND INDICES OF THE AUSTRALO-PITHECINES AND OF *PROCONSUL AFRICANUS*

	Proc. af.	A. afric.	A. rob.	Zinj.	Aa to Z Directions
Maximum Length (glabello-occipital)	97??	147 H		174 L	—·↦
Maximum Breadth (supra-mastoidal)		120		138 L	—·↦
Maximum Breadth (inter-temporal)	83	99 H	116	118 L	—→
Basion-bregma Height	Aur.55+	105 H	102	99 L	←—
Bizygomatic Face Breadth	87	131	137/154 (2)	188 L	—→
Biorbital Diameter	70	88	102	122	—→
Interorbital Diameter	16	24	39	42	—→
Upper Face Height (nasion-prosthion)	45	74	86	114	—→
Nose Height	24	49	61	73	—→
Nose Breadth	14	27	32	42	—→
Maxillary Height (nasale-prosthion)		26	28/30 (2)	37	—→
Orbital Height	21	33	34	37	—→
Orbital Breath	27	33	37	46	—→
Palate Length	50	64.6 (5)	70	84	—→
Palate Breadth	50?	64.6 (5)	68	82	—→
Cranial Index	86?	67		68	○
Length-Height Index	58?	71		57	↔—
Breadth-Height Index	67	106	87	84	←—
Upper Facial Index	53	56	63/56 (2)	61	○
Nasal Index	56	55	52	58	○
Orbital Index	78	100	95	80	←—
Palatal Index	100	100	97	98	○

H = G. Heberer: *Primatologia*, Vol. I (1956), pp. 379–560.
L = L. S. B. Leakey: *Nature*, December 17, 1960.
(2) = two specimens   (5) = mean of 5 skulls: 4 Sterkfontein and 1 Makapansgat

dimensions, and the same may be true of the African primates in question.

Returning to Zinjanthropus, we note that in a preliminary estimate Leakey has set the cranial capacity of that skull at over 600 cc. If he is right, it might fall within the maximum pongid figure of 685 cc. for a male gorilla. If we postulate a generous maximum of 700 cc. and calculate a ratio between brain size and palate area,[6] the figure for Zinjanthropus appears to be between 1.1 and 1.0, compared to 1.2 for a female chimpanzee. *Homo erectus* ranges from 1.4 to 1.7, and *Homo sapiens* from 1.9 upward.

If we study the outlines of the crania of the smallest species of *Proconsul, P. africanus,* and of Sterkfontein and Zinjanthropus, as shown on Fig. 29, and consider them, at least for the moment, an evolutionary sequence, the metrical progression indicated on Table 10 takes on added meaning. The position of the skull in relation to the neck shifts from the diagonal hafting of a pronograde ape to the vertical one associated with the erect posture. The face becomes more vertical also, as it moves higher and higher up on the front of the brain case: if the face grows more rapidly than the brain it has to expand upward as well as downward, resulting in a loss of forehead. Compared to the Miocene ape *Proconsul,* the Lower Pleistocene Australopithecines have grown progressively larger-faced and more brutal-looking. Had we a sequence of the pongid line that led from *Proconsul* to gorilla, a parallel progression could presumably be seen.

This exercise does not mean that, if our premise is true, Zinjanthropus was evolving away from a common ancestor with man. It simply shows that man's face had to grow larger before it could become small again. This up-and-down sequence could reflect merely an alternation of increasing chewing needs, which began with a dietary shift from fruit to roots and raw meat, followed by a decrease brought about by the invention of cooking. We shall see a repetition of this rise and fall of the facial scaffolding in several human sequences. Here the important thing is to establish the principle that governs this kind of change.

The Teeth of Zinjanthropus

THE ONLY TEETH from the 22-foot level of Bed I of Olduvai Gorge about which anything has been published are the sixteen

[6] Sir Arthur Keith, who invented this index, compared brain size to palate area directly. I have treated brain size as a cube and palate area as a square, dividing the cube root of cranial capacity by the square root of palate area, and thus have compiled new figures for all fossil skulls found since he wrote. A. Keith: *The Antiquity of Man,* Second Edition (London: Williams and Norgate; 1925), Vol. I, pp. 213–6.

uppers in the 1959 skull. We have all sixteen. The third molars had been cut but had not yet descended to the occlusal plane and so were not worn at the time of death. These teeth are similar to those of the South African Australopithecines in size and shape, with a few exceptions (see Table 8). The incisors fall within the South African range, and the canines are even smaller; the left canine is reduced to a small, degenerate-looking cone. The premolars match those from the south, but the molars are larger, the second and third having particularly excessive breadths.

With these molar breadths we can arrange a progression from *A. africanus* to Zinjanthropus comparable to that for the cranial measurements, with the same implication. Species of a single genus grow progressively larger-toothed and heavier-jawed as they grow bulkier, and even more so as they meet increasing needs for processing coarser and tougher items of diet. A similar progression can be seen in the *Proconsul* series, among the Indian god-apes, and indeed in many other kinds of mammals. Among the pongids and hominids this increase in tooth size tends to involve a widening rather than an elongation of the cheek teeth, because in a semi-erect or erect animal there is more room in the jaw for lateral than for longitudinal expansion, and the more erect an animal stands, the more cumbersome to him a long muzzle becomes.

Morphologically the upper teeth of Zinjanthropus are Australopithecine, in the South African sense, with a few differences. Although even larger than those of *A. robustus*, the Zinjanthropus molars are generally rectangular rather than irregular in shape, recalling those of *A. africanus* in this sense. The barely erupted third molars are relatively short-crowned, and their enamel is extensively and finely wrinkled, as in the molars of the orang. Compared with the teeth of the Lower Miocene apes of Kenya, Zinjanthropus's molars recall those of *Sivapithecus africanus* rather than those of *Proconsul*, for the crown patterns of the teeth of *S. africanus* are relatively simple. Compared with the teeth of *Homo*, Zinjanthropus's exceed the human range in breadth from canines to third molars, and in the length of the first premolar and the first and second molars. In size and in most proportions Zinjanthropus's teeth are the least human of the Australopithecine teeth so far discovered.

The Leg Bones Attributed to Zinjanthropus

A TIBIA and a fibula, presumably a pair, were found in the 22-foot level of Bed I in Olduvai Gorge, where the Zinjanthropus skull lay. These bones are long, very slender, apparently straight, and broken at the lower ends. As far as one can tell from a single photograph, they appear to be essentially human, but the fibula is relatively heavier than the tibia. They must come from two individuals, or else an unusual amount of weight was carried on the outer margin of the foot.

As more than one skull has already been found in this level, there is no reason for attributing these leg bones to the first Zinjanthropus skull, and indeed they appear too slender to go with it. If these were the bones of a human being, he, or more likely she, would have had a stature of only about 136 cm., or four feet six inches, more or less. If they were the bones of a Zinjanthropus whose legs might have been short in proportion to trunk length, a stature of five feet is possible. However, until further studies are made, we can do no more than speculate about the significance of these leg bones.

The Status of Zinjanthropus

WE MAY provisionally conclude that Zinjanthropus was an Australopithecine, more manlike in some respects than the Australopithecines of South Africa and less so in others; that in the development of his teeth and of the supporting bony structures of his face and brain case he came at the peak of a divergent evolutionary line; and that his relationship to the earlier Olduvai child, who so far is represented only by bones and teeth missing in Zinjanthropus, was not so close as a stratigraphic distance of only five feet would imply. These two denizens of Olduvai seem to stand at opposite ends of the Australopithecine scale, if the child is, in fact, an Australopithecine.

The Specimen from Lake Eyasi, Tanganyika

I N 1938, when the study of the Australopithecines was in its infancy, L. Kohl-Larsen, a German paleontologist, found another specimen at Garusi, on the eastern shore of Lake Eyasi in Tanganyika, about 35 miles south of Olduvai Gorge. It lay in a Laetolil faunal bed, where it might possibly have been intrusive. It consists of a small piece of left maxilla containing two premolar teeth. A third molar picked up a few miles away and originally attributed to this specimen or one like it was probably human and less ancient.

Kohl-Larsen originally called it *Australopithecus,* with a question mark; in 1950 Weinert dubbed it *Meganthropus africanus* (the name *Meganthropus* had been previously held by a Javanese specimen that will be described shortly); and in 1955 Şenyürek labeled it *Praeanthropus africanus.* Also in 1955, Robinson showed, to the satisfaction of most primate paleontologists, not only that Garusi is an Australopithecine but that it is indistinguishable from Sterkfontein, with which it may have been contemporary.[7] In any case, subsequent discoveries have rendered the age and taxonomy of the Garusi specimen unimportant.

The Kanam Mandible

T H E S A M E may almost be said of the famed Kanam mandibular fragment discovered in 1932 by a Kikuyu assistant of Leakey. It lay in an Omo faunal deposit on the south shore of the Kavi-

---

[7] L. Kohl-Larsen: *Auf den Spuren des Vormenschen,* Vol. 2 (Stuttgart: Strecker and Schröder; 1943), pp. 379–81.

H. Weinert: "Über die Neuen Vor-und Frühmenschenfunde aus Afrika, Java, China, und Frankreich," ZFMUA, Vol. 42 (1950), p. 113–48.

A. Remane: "Die Zähne des Meganthropus africanus," ZFMUA, Vol. 42 (1951), pp. 311–29.

Robinson: "Further Remarks on the Relationship between 'Meganthropus' and Australopithecus africanus," AJPA, Vol. 13, No. 3 (1955), pp. 429–45.

M. S. Şenyürek: "A Note on the Teeth of Meganthropus africanus Weinert from Tanganyika Territory," *Belleten,* Vol. 19, No. 73 (1955), pp. 1–55.

Heberer: "Die Fossilgeschichte . . . ," pp. 379–560.

rondo Gulf of Lake Victoria Nyanza, in Kenya, about 200 miles north and a little west of Olduvai Gorge. It lay in what appeared to be basal Villafranchian soil, associated with pebble tools and a tooth of the extinct *Dinotherium*.[8] For nearly thirty years this fossil has been the center of controversy, regarding both its age and the kind of hominid it was.

Its age was questioned because the site eroded away after the specimen was removed, and could not be relocated. Later, when fluorine and uranium tests were applied to the specimen, it was found to have a high calcium carbonate content, which invalidated the comparisons made between it and other specimens of the same period and region. It is very old, but its exact date is unknown.[9]

The other source of doubt was its morphology, because it seemed to have small teeth and a chin. The fragment consists of a battered and diseased piece of lower jaw extending from the distal root of the right first molar to the region of the left second premolar. Only the two right premolars, both badly worn and broken, are *in situ*. Also, the lower margin of the mandible is missing. After an extensive study of this amorphous-looking specimen, Tobias found that it had no chin at all, that the protuberance resembling one was a bone sarcoma that had grown over an old fracture. Its greatest distinction is the massiveness of the bone, which exceeds those of all known jaws of *Homo* in at least one dimension, symphyseal height.[1]

Kanam man was either an Australopithecine contemporaneous with the other animals found with him; or he was a later Australopithecine intrusive in the deposit from which he was removed; or he was an equally intrusive *Homo* comparable in age and grade to those found in North Africa, which will be described in Chapter 12. As we now have a human cranium from the Early

[8] Leakey: *The Stone Age Races of Kenya* (Oxford: Oxford University Press; 1935).

[9] Oakley: *Physical Anthropology in the British Museum, 1958;* and personal communications.

[1] P. V. Tobias: "The Kanam Jaw," *Nature*, Vol. 185, No. 4714 (1960), pp. 946–7.

Tobias's definitive report on the Kanam mandible will be published in 1962, in the Transactions of the Fourth Panafrican Congress on Prehistory, held in Leopoldville in 1959.

Middle Pleistocene of Olduvai Gorge, it makes little difference to the history of man and the Australopithecines which of the three he was.

The Australopithecine from the Republic of Tchad

ON JUNE 3, 1961, Yves Coppen, a French paleontologist, announced his discovery of an Australopithecine skull in an unnamed Lower Villafranchian site in the Republic of Tchad, halfway between Largeau and the Nigerian frontier and about 200 miles northeast of Lake Tchad.[2] The specimen is called Lower Villafranchian because of its association with an extinct elephant, *Loxodonta africanavus*, so named by its discoverer. If this dating is substantiated after a complete study of the fauna, the Tchad Australopithecine may turn out to be the oldest of its genus.

The skull fragment consists of a frontal bone broken off a short distance in front of bregma, and parts of the bones of both sides of the face, the right of which is the better preserved. The skull has a forehead, and its cranial capacity was apparently large for its genus. The brow ridges are of moderate dimensions, and overlay large frontal sinuses. The orbits are very large, and over each of them is a supraorbital foramen, a human feature. The zygomatic bone (malar) is short and thick; the junction with the zygomatic arch is sharply curved and sloped obliquely upward and forward. The lower face is extremely prognathous, but there is a canine fossa, and the canine teeth were apparently small. Coppen provisionally considers this to be the oldest and the most nearly human of the Australopithecine specimens yet found.

The Fossil Hominid of Tell Ubeidiya, Jordan Valley

THE FOSSIL hominid found in a Lower Pleistocene outcrop at Tell Ubeidiya, Israel, near the southern shore of Lake Tiberias and on the west side of the Jordan Valley, consists of two small

[2] Y. Coppen: "Découverte d'un Australopitheciné dans le Villafranchien du Tchad," *CRAS*, Vol. 252, No. 24 (1961), pp. 3851–2.

pieces of skull and one incisor tooth. We do not yet know whether this animal was *Australopithecus* or *Homo*. Although the specimens await description, the skull fragments are said to be "of very great thickness," [3] and from other sources I have heard that the incisor is small.

As stated earlier, the tools also found are similar to those from the Zinjanthropus level at Olduvai Gorge and from Aïn Hanech in Algeria.

The animal bones are those of fish, turtles (including terrapins and tortoises), birds, and mammals. Many slow-moving and verminous animals, such as tortoises, mice, other rodents, and porcupines, were apparently eaten, but so were large mammals. Hippopotamus, rhinoceros, elephant, asses, zebras, a large cervid deer, a fallow deer, and gazelles and antelopes were all, it seems, on the menu, however their flesh was acquired. Some of the larger animal bones were split, presumably for marrow, and one of them showed scratches where flint may have been used to cut off the flesh. Still, most of the bones were those of slow game. If the fossil hominid of Tell Ubeidiya was a better hunter than Zinjanthropus, his superiority in this respect has yet to be definitely proved.

The fauna is a combination of Oriental, Palearctic, and African genera. The two kinds of deer, one of which, the fallow deer (*Dama cf. mesopotamica*), still exists in the Near East, are Palearctic whereas the zebras are African. The hippopotamus is both African and Oriental; one pig (*Sus cf. scrofa*) is Palearctic, another has not yet been identified. A fresh-water turtle (*Trionyx*) has living species in both Africa and Asia. Because Palestine stands at the crossroads of continents and faunal regions in the Old World, it could have served as a link between the Australopithecines of Africa and those of Asia, wherever they originated and to whichever regions they subsequently dispersed.

The Meganthropus Mandibles from Java

THAT THE Australopithecines dispersed widely is evident from the discovery of two mandibular fragments in the Djetis

---

[3] Stekelis et al.: "Villafranchian Deposits Near Ubeidiya . . . ," p. 182.

faunal beds of Java, known as *Meganthropus paleojavanicus*. Von Koenigswald found the first in 1941 and P. Marks, a Dutch geologist, retrieved the other in 1952. Both came from Sangiran, the site of the infant human skull that von Koenigswald calls *Pithecanthropus modjokertensis;* and at least the first one came from the same level as the human specimen.[4] More clearly than in South Africa, this evidence indicates that two kinds of hominid were sympatric, if only for a short period.

The first piece (see Fig. 56, p. 381) includes the first lower molar, both premolars, the socket of a canine, and a small section of the inner sagittal surface. The second contains the premolars and molars of the right side of the mandible; but the crowns are broken off or abraded, except that of the third molar, which is intact.

Both jawbones are large and thick, well outside the human range but within that of the larger South African Australopithecines. Morphologically the Javanese and African mandibles are similar but not identical.[5] The teeth, which have been widely discussed, fall within the South African size ranges in length and breadth, and all but the lower first premolar are closer to *Australopithecus africanus* than to *A. robustus* (see Table 8).

In seven of ten dimensions, these teeth are also within the ranges of *Homo*. The only two molars that have crowns, the first lower molar of von Koenigswald's specimen and the third of Marks's, are also closest to *A. africanus* in shape. Von Koenigswald has advanced several arguments to show that the teeth of his specimen are more nearly human than those from South Africa, but this can hardly apply to Telanthropus or to the newly dis-

[4] Weidenreich: op. cit.

P. Marks: "Preliminary Note on the Discovery of a New Jaw of Meganthropus," *IJNS*, Vol. 109, Nos. 1, 2, 3 (1953), pp. 26–33.

Robinson: "Further Remarks on the Relationship between 'Meganthropus' and Australopithecines," *AJPA*, Vol. 13, No. 3 (1955), pp. 429–46.

Von Koenigswald: *Meeting Prehistoric Man* (New York: Harper & Bros.; 1956).

[5] Von Koenigswald finds, on the inner side of the symphysis, spikelets that are also present in most human mandibles. In man they serve as hitching posts for the genio-glossal muscles. Von Koenigswald (1956, pp. 111–13) interprets their presence on the Meganthropus jaw as indicating the power of speech. This interpretation is unfounded, however. See E. L. DuBrul and C. A. Reed: "Skeletal Evidence of Speech?" *AJPA*, Vol. 18, No. 2 (1960), pp. 153–6.

covered Olduvai child. In any case, one cannot expect the jaws and teeth of related hominids located as far apart as South or East Africa and Java to be identical, any more than the jaws and teeth of the human inhabitants of those regions today are identical.

As to which, if either (and if not both), of these candidates was our ancestor, no decision can be made on present evidence. We can state, however, that Meganthropus had not deviated as far from the human form, in either bone or teeth, as had Zinjanthropus.

The Drugstore Australopithecines of China

BECAUSE the Djetis fauna is believed to have entered Java from China, there has been reason to suppose, ever since the discovery of the first Meganthropus jaw, that Australopithecine remains will also turn up in the mother country. In the search of Chinese pharmacies which turned up the first *Gigantopithecus* teeth, von Koenigswald also discovered a few other teeth, which he tentatively attributed to the Australopithecines, or to a similar creature, in the following passage. "A few additional teeth that are not definitely classifiable with either orang or *Gigantopithecus* probably indicate the presence of forms related to the Australopithecinae in our fauna. They are of large size, too large for *Sinanthropus,* with a very simple cusp pattern, and too small for *Gigantopithecus.* These teeth have not yet been studied in detail." [6]

Von Koenigswald sent casts of two canines of this collection to Broom, who found them similar to those of Sterkfontein and wrote: "We can, I think, feel fairly confident that a large Australopithecine, and probably two, inhabited China in Upper Pliocene or Lower and Middle Pleistocene times. And if this should prove to be the case it may be that they will prove to be even nearer to man's ancestor than the South African Australopithe-

[6] Von Koenigswald: "*Gigantopithecus blacki* von Koenigswald, a Giant Fossil Hominid from the Pleistocene of North China," *APAM,* Vol. 43 (1952), pp. 293–325.

cines." [7] In 1956 Robinson said that these were orangutan canines. [8] Who is right I do not know.

The above is the sum total of the data available to me concerning teeth salvaged from Chinese drugstores. Their potential significance is enormous.

The Replacement of Australopithecus *by* Homo

THE MEGANTHROPUS jaws discovered in Java, the teeth found in Chinese drugstores, and the hominid fragments unearthed in Palestine and associated with Oldowan tools suggest that the Australopithecines spread eastward from Africa across the whole range of the Old World tropics and inhabited both the Ethiopian and the Oriental faunal regions. Or they originated in Asia and spread to Africa. Except for Europe and northern China, Australopithecines already occupied, at the end of the Lower Pleistocene, the same territory *Homo* lived in a little later. In effect, at the beginning of the Middle Pleistocene *Homo* replaced *Australopithecus* in the latter's *lebensraum,* and his hominid predecessors everywhere vanished from the earth.

The arrival of *Australopithecus* was almost as sudden as his disappearance. During the last third of the Lower Pleistocene the bones or tools, or both, of these hominids appear all the way from Morocco to South Africa, Palestine, Java, and south China. This is a wide spread for a new genus of primates, which are generally restricted to single geographical regions at any one time. Just before their expansion the ancestral Australopithecines must have acquired some ecological advantage that freed them from local climatic limitations and afforded them dominance over competing species.

Tools, a more or less perfect bipedal posture, the ability to collect slow game and to carry it home, the beginnings of a human type of social structure, a rudimentary kind of hunting, and a dawning intelligence keener than that of other primates—these

[7] Broom and Schepers: "The South African Fossil Ape-Man," p. 66.
[8] Robinson: "The Dentition of the Australopithecinae."

new acquisitions may have made the Australopithecines more adaptable to all kinds of tropical environments than were the forest-bound apes. These are the only traits we know of that could have provided the needed advantage.

Yet, at the beginning of the Middle Pleistocene, this previously successful animal faded out rather rapidly and was replaced everywhere by a different but closely related hominid, man. *Homo* must have had an even greater ecological versatility than his predecessor. What gave him this added advantage? Probably not stone tools, because the earliest man-made tools are no better than those attributed to the Australopithecines. Was it fire?

Perhaps, but we have no way of knowing. Only in sheltered habitation sites, such as caves, can charcoal be expected to survive the action of wind and water over hundreds of thousands of years, and when it does we are lucky. Our earliest cave site is Choukoutien, in China. The men who lived there 360,000 years ago had fire. There is no reason to suppose that other men who camped only in the open did not have it earlier.

In most early habitation sites the broken bones of adult wild animals bear witness to true hunting. Hunting, speech, fire, and a type of social organization in which men, under competent leadership and following prearranged plans, could combine forces in hunts and raids of several days' duration, must have given *Homo* a decided advantage over his less imaginative and less communicative cousins. At the time he began to replace the Australopithecines he must have possessed such an advantage, or he would not have won.

Yet so closely similar are the bones and teeth of *Australopithecus* and *Homo* that some kind of close genetic continuity between them must be accepted. But we do not know where or when the genetic transition from one genus to the other took place. Did the known Australopithecines, having undergone an evolutionary sequence of their own, simply become men at the end of the Lower Pleistocene after they had begun to hunt, to speak, and to sit around fires; or did some early kind of Australopithecine like Sterkfontein or the Olduvai child evolve into *Homo* while Swartkrans and Zinjanthropus pursued their own genetic blind alleys to extinction? Who knows?

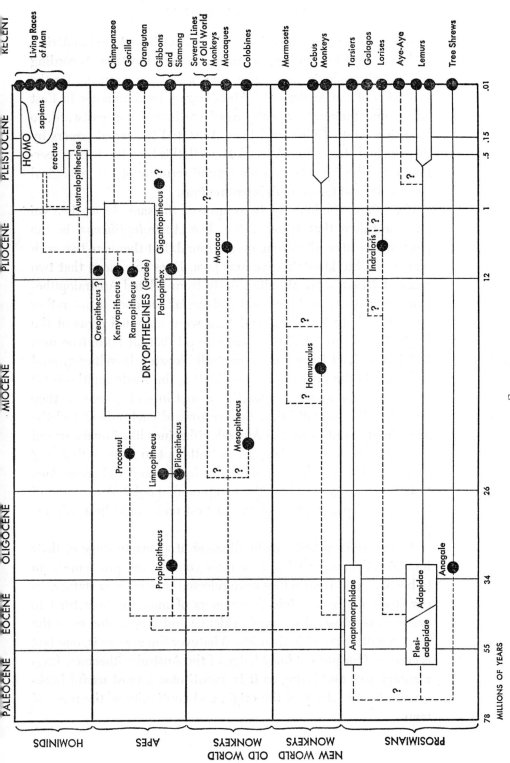

Fig. 42

The oldest known Australopithecines have been found in Africa, and the oldest known human remains come from Java. According to strict chronological sequence, then, a case can be made for the evolution of the Australopithecines from a local ancestor in East Africa and their subsequent spread northward and eastward, to Palestine, south China, and Java. As stated in several papers by its principal champion, F. Clark Howell, this hypothesis has a certain logical validity based on a careful scrutiny of the geological time scales and faunas of different regions.

If we grant the hypothesis and pursue the same logic, then we may postulate that *Homo* arose, like *Australopithecus*, in the place where his earliest remains are found. But there are two such places, the Sterkfontein cave and Java. Does this mean that two races of *Homo* arose simultaneously from related Australopithecine populations in Africa and Indonesia? Or does it not rather mean that both Transvaal and Java were marginal areas at the beginning of the Middle Pleistocene and that, at both, true men had just arrived from a more centrally located breeding ground and were in the process of exterminating the Australopithecines?

When *Homo* and *Australopithecus* met in such places, as they probably did, how did they behave toward each other? Did the men simply hunt down the Australopithecines like impala, or did they spare some of the females and attempt to mate with them? Were the two populations mutually fertile, and did some Australopithecine genes enter the conquerors' pools? If so, some of the regional peculiarities of the earliest men could be easily explained.

As research workers usually discover at a certain stage of their inquiries, the more we learn the more complex our problems seem to become, and possibilities once rejected take on new stature. In our study of the hominid forerunners of man we have tried to present every useful scrap of evidence and to examine even the most remotely possible theories. Whatever the answer is, one fact is certain. Our present knowledge of the Australopithecines, fragmentary and tantalizing as it is, constitutes a most useful background for the study of the origin and continuity of the races of man.

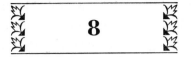

8

AN INTRODUCTION TO
FOSSIL MAN

Of Time, Space, Grades, and Lines

I N   T H E   last seven chapters I have reviewed some of the principles of evolution, particularly as they apply to man. I have described the primates as an order and have traced the descent of all of them except those that belong clearly to the genus *Homo*.

Homo can be studied with more insight after this lengthy introduction because now the nature of the scaffolding that holds up our genealogical structure is discernible. This frame extends in several dimensions. The first is *time,* the last half million years or so, covering the Middle Pleistocene, the Upper Pleistocene, and the Recent, with one or two possible dips into the tail end of the Lower Pleistocene. The second is *space,* which includes the zoogeographic regions of the world as they exist now and as they existed during the Pleistocene.

The third is *grade,* and the fourth is *line.* Within the dimensions of time and space we have seen several groups of primates evolve from simple to complex forms and also across one or more of the biological frontiers that zoologists call adaptive thresholds. The monkeys of the New and Old Worlds moved from the prosimian to the simian grade independently of each other. Each separately acquired stereoscopic color vision, and in both hemispheres some of them came to brachiate. In the Old World it is quite possible that at least the latter stages of adaptation for four-footed life on the ground were reached independently by the baboons and macaques. The gibbons and the living African apes also became arboreal separately, as probably did the orang. Thus three lines of tailless apes independently moved into the pongid grade. If the hominid grade, with erect posture, was reached by a single animal only, this border-crossing constitutes a great exception.

A *grade,* then, is a stage of physical adaptation to a special way of life, otherwise known as an ecological niche. A *line* is a lineage, a genetic continuum, a succession of animals in process of phyletic evolution (evolution by succession), from the earliest distinguishable ancestor to the present form. A line may pass through several grades and a grade may include populations of animals belonging to different lines.

Within a line, a population may become extinct in one of three ways: by dying out completely; by evolving into something else; or by hybridizing with a genetically different population, and thus being absorbed.[1] All three processes were probably involved in the evolution of *Homo sapiens* from *H. erectus.* The first way is probably the least important in human evolution because when a local population dies out, another like it will usually survive elsewhere. There is no modern evidence of complete extinction; even the Tasmanians survive in hybrid form. The second way can be demonstrated in several lines; and the third, which was probably the commonest, in many more.

This concept of grades and lines may be the most valuable we have learned in the last four chapters. In man, as in other primates, grades and lines are concerned both with ecology and with anatomy. Among colobine monkeys of Africa and Asia, leaf-eating is an ecological adaptation for which the stomachs of these animals have become anatomically suited.

In man the making of tools, the use of fire, and the manufacture of houses and clothing are all cultural adaptations that provide the basis of ecological grades, through which, or through some of which, different human lines have passed. Ecological grades in human populations involve man's relationships with the land on which he lives and with other men. The simplest grade of human

[1] E. H. Colbert: "Some Paleontological Principles Significant in Human Evolution," in W. W. Howells, ed.: *Early Man in the Far East* (Philadelphia: Am. Assn. Phys. Anth.; 1949), p. 146.

culture is collecting wild foods, such as berries, roots, grubs, and slow game. In essence this is no higher than the ecology of Australopithecines, or even of baboons. The next grade is hunting, which can be further divided technically in terms of weapons and techniques, such as clubs, simple spears, spears cast with spear throwers, the bow and arrow, elaborate traps, and the use of dogs. As previously stated (in Chapter 3), what is important here for human evolution is not so much the techniques themselves but the effects they have on human relations and the complexity of social structure.

After hunting comes agriculture, with or without animal husbandry; specialized pastoral nomadism; village life, with the rise of arts and crafts; and the births of cities, kingdoms, and empires.

Only the ecological grades preceding agriculture are useful for present purposes. By the time agriculture began, all the known subspecies of man had reached their present anatomical forms. Since then, the racial map of the world has been complicated and obscured by numerous large-scale migrations and by recent mixtures. The pertinent cultural grades may be sorted out and defined in terms of the degree of perfection and diversification of tools, by whatever conclusions about hunting, food processing, and skin processing techniques we can draw from studying animal bones as well as tools in their sites, and by a consideration of whatever works of art have survived.

In some parts of the world archaeological sequences follow clear-cut, independent lines through various grades. The most striking example known of a self-contained cultural line is that of the American Indians. From a hunting and gathering base with a technology derived from eastern Asia in the late Pleistocene, they invented fluted points, polished stone axes, agriculture, pottery, textiles, bronze metallurgy, urban architecture, writing, and the concept of zero, apparently independently of the Old World.

Although no other technological line is equally clear-cut and dramatic, we can trace independent developments, with certain overlaps, in much earlier periods in several parts of the Old World. The only line of evidence which we have from the earliest periods is that of stone tools, including those attributed to the Australopithecines. The sequence of grades that these tools follow runs in general from rough core tools to fine core tools, with or without flakes, to flakes to blades, with or without microliths, to the use of antler, ivory, and bone, and to the use of polished stone. In some areas this sequence is incomplete, in others certain stages have been skipped. In most of them refinements of tool form are the result of changes in tool-making techniques, from stone-on-stone to stick-on-stone, to the use of an elastic punch, to pecking, grinding, and polishing. By studying these technological lines we can see where contacts between cultures must have taken place; the diffusion of tool-making techniques from one area to another indicates communication between different human populations. As we know from modern examples, this in turn implies the possibility of gene flow. Where a complete technological discontinuity is evident, it generally indicates the arrival of a new population.

The final application of the concept of grades and lines comes in the analysis of the bones of the fossil men themselves. Apparently the different parts of the body have evolved to a certain extent independently of each other and at different rates. The pelvis and legs, the shoulder girdle and arms, and the skull have had separate histories. In the following four chapters I will consider the differences in the postcranial skeleton of fossil populations to the extent that I can, from the grades-and-lines point of view; but this extent will not be great because the fossil remains of these bones are few. This subject can therefore be postponed for the most part to a later volume in which the richer information on the soft parts of the living will be reviewed.

Here I shall concentrate particularly on the skull, which itself has a number of components that evolve at different rates: the front teeth (incisors and canines); the cheek teeth (premolars and molars); the jaws; the brain case; and the *mask*, meaning the region of the eyes and nose. From these components, as from the skull as a whole, it is evident that several lines of fossil men, living in different regions but within the same time spans, passed through several cultural grades at different evolutionary rates.

Of the four dimensions time is the least reliable. We do not know how old all our fossil specimens are, and moreover not all geologists and physicists agree about the time scale of the second

half of the Pleistocene, particularly in regard to the correlation of
the glacial and pluvial sequences in different regions. To allot the
remaining chapters of this book on the basis of time would be to
lean the bulk of our weight on the weakest and shakiest timber in
the scaffold.

Space, on the other hand, is the most reliable dimension. We
know exactly where each specimen came from. We also know
something about the distribution of other animals during the
Pleistocene, and in most cases we can relate fossil men to their
faunas. Geography is our strongest timber; it is bolstered, moreover, by demonstrable sequences of lines of men through various
cultural grades in several regions. In other regions these sequences
are broken, and invasions can be traced both through cultural and
anatomical discontinuities.

The Dimension of Time

I N C H A P T E R 7 the chronology of the Lower Pleistocene was
reviewed, primarily as it concerns the places where fossil hominids and tools have been found, that is, Africa, Palestine, and
Java. With the appearance of man in several continents at the
beginning of the Middle Pleistocene the whole world becomes
involved; we must therefore examine the premises on which several conflicting evolutionary chronologies are based.

The world is divided into a number of geographical regions,
in which changes in temperature, humidity, soil deposition, and
soil erosion have proceeded at different rates. Regions that lie
near the poles and at high altitudes have proved to be more sensitive to changes in temperature than those that lie near the equator and at lower altitudes. Equatorial territories, particularly in
Africa, have reflected changes in rainfall more than changes in
temperature. Geologists rely to a certain extent on fauna, which
may change more rapidly in some places than in others. Moreover, we are dealing with an exceedingly brief time span, little
more than a half million years.

The earliest glacial sequence was worked out in the Alps, with
mountain glaciers. Hence the well-known terminology, Günz,
Mindel, Riss, and Würm. However, mountain glaciers are local,

and cannot be expected to reflect global climatic changes as finely as continental icecaps. Of these latter we have three in Europe—Elster, Saale, and Weichsel—corresponding more or less to Mindel, Riss, and Würm, of the Alpine series. There was no European icecap to match Günz. In North America we have four, Nebraskan, Kansan, Illinoisan, and Wisconsian, which match, more or less, the four Alpine periods. Like the Alps, the Himalayas had four mountain glaciations.

By definition the Middle Pleistocene begins with the advance of the Elster icecap, Mindel I, and the Second Himalayan Glaciation. It does not include Günz or the First Himalayan, which have been relegated to the very end of the Lower Pleistocene, along with the Cromerian Interglacial. Before the Villafranchian was cut loose from the Pliocene and added to the bottom of the Pleistocene, the situation was much simpler; the Pleistocene was simply the Ice Age. These new complications make the problem of dating the phases of the Middle and Late Pleistocene even more difficult.

Penck and Bruckner, who worked out the Alpine sequence, set the beginning of Günz 600,000 years ago, and that of Mindel about 500,000 years ago. They allotted 60,000 years for the Günz-Mindel Interglacial, 240,000 for the Mindel-Riss, and 60,000 for the Riss-Würm. According to their scheme, Würm lasted 60,000 years and ended sometimes between 16,000 and 24,000 years ago. We know now that it ended about 10,000 years ago. As 10,000 plus 60,000 equals 70,000, their corrected date for the beginning of Würm is about 70,000 years ago. This has recently been more or less confirmed by a Carbon-14 date of 64,000 ± 1,100 years ago for a mild climatic oscillation shortly after the beginning of Würm I.[2]

This is the earliest Carbon-14 date yet determined anywhere. It sets the outer boundary of our ability to date sites by this well-known method.[3]

[2] H. Godwin: "Carbon-Dating Conference at Groningen" (September 14–19, 1959), *Nature*, Vol. 184, No. 4696 (1959), pp. 1365–6. The C-14 date number is GRO-1379.

[3] On January 10, 1961, the National Bureau of Standards announced that the half life of Carbon-14 is now 5,760 years instead of 5,568, as formerly believed. The old dates were calculated on the former basis. They must now be multiplied

Penck and Bruckner made their calculations by standard geological procedure, including measurements of rates of erosion, and estimates of the rates at which soils were deposited on land surfaces. Aside from the Würm, they did not try to date the duration of the glaciations, only that of the interglacials and of the Ice Age as a whole. As this procedure has been followed by most geologists, it is difficult to find one who will commit himself on the lengths of the periods of glaciation and thus construct a complete glacial chronology.

Zeuner, however, did suggest a complete glacial chronology, using all data available in 1951, including calculations based on the amount of solar radiation that reached various latitudes of both the Northern and the Southern Hemisphere of the earth's surface at different times. These figures, which a modern electronic computer could deliver in a few hours, were the result of twenty years' efforts by the Yugoslav M. Milankovitch and his associates. The computations are based on the correlations of three astronomical cycles: (1) changes in the angle between the equatorial plane of the earth and the plane of its orbit (40,000 years); (2) variations in the season at which either hemisphere passes closest to the sun in the course of orbit (92,000 years); and (3) the periodicity of a slight conical movement in the earth's axis (26,000 years). Unfortunately these correlations are so complicated that they may be interpreted in more than one way.

At any rate, with this and other aids, Zeuner filled in the 600,-000 year period of Penck and Bruckner as follows. Mindel began about 500,000 years ago and reached two peaks, 476,000 and 435,000 years ago. The Mindel-Riss Interglacial lasted 190,000 years; Riss reached two peaks, 230,000 and 187,000 years ago. The Riss-Würm Interglacial lasted 60,000 years; and Würm

---

by 1.0345. In most cases, the difference falls within the range of probable error of the sample, and the maximum difference is about 2,000 years. The reader may make these corrections if he wishes.

Following procedure initiated by E. S. Deevey of Yale in 1961, I have designated each Carbon-14 date by its laboratory number. For example, GRO-1379 is the date given in footnote 2. GRO means Groningen, Netherlands. Other symbols used are NZ for New Zealand, W for Washington, L for the Lamont Laboratory of Columbia University, C for Chicago, P for Philadelphia (University of Pennsylvania), BM for the British Museum (Natural History), and I (UW) for Isotopes Inc., New York.

reached three peaks, 115,000, 72,000, and 25,000 or 22,000 years ago, depending on the latitude. Since the end of Würm III, 22,000 years have elapsed.[4]

Zeuner admits the possibility of an error of 20 per cent for Würm III, and the C-14 process indicates that his dates for Würm are on the whole too early. However, he believes that the further back one goes in time the smaller the error, and he allows a deviation of 5 per cent for the earlier glaciations.

In 1946, Harold C. Urey discovered that, as water evaporates, the three isotopes of oxygen, oxygen 16, 17, and 18, go off at slightly different rates, and the lightest of the three, oxygen 16, goes off the most rapidly. He then studied the proportions of oxygen isotopes in the carbonate deposits, formed mostly of foraminifera, at the bottom of the ocean. After many refinements, he and his associates developed a method for dating long cores of carbonates drilled from the ocean's floor.

Intensive work on this material was carried out in the early 1950's, particularly by Cesare Emiliani, who finally developed a sequence that shortened Penck's and Bruckner's estimate of the Ice Age by about a half. According to Emiliani, Günz (Nebraskan) extended, in round numbers, from 300,000 to 265,000 B.P. (before present); Mindel (Kansan) from about 200,000 to 175,-000; Riss (Illinoisan) from 125,000 to about 100,000; and Würm (Wisconsin) from 70,000 to 10,000. The sea-water isotope system gives Würm only two subperiods, known as stadials, pinpointed at 71,000 to 57,000 and 28,000 to 8,000.[5]

More recently, Rhodes W. Fairbridge has worked out another timetable based on the fluctuations in sea level along the various shores of the earth. This, too, is very complex and involves a number of factors and variations in different regions. He finds that, although the interglacials were warmer, the mean sea levels were 100 meters higher than today before the glaciers began to accumulate; that at the height of the Günz-Nebraskan, despite the accumulation of ice at the poles, the shores were still 30 meters above present level; that at the peak of the Mindel-Kansan they

[4] F. Zeuner: *Dating the Past*, Third Edition (London: Methuen & Co.; 1952), pp. 144–5.

[5] C. Emiliani: "Ancient Temperatures," SA, Vol. 198, No. 2 (1958), pp. 54–6.

were virtually at present sea level; during the Riss-Illinoisan they went down to 87 meters below present sea level; and the two peaks of Würm-Wisconsin found them to be between 85 and 100 meters below the present level.

Fairbridge, by correlating his recent sea-level dates with the Carbon-14 record, has confirmed the accuracy of his method in detail for the post-Würm oscillations. Extending it backward, he finds a general agreement with Emiliani's data, but stretches the dates out a little; he would put the peaks of Günz-Nebraskan at 320,000; those of Mindel-Kansan at 230,000; of Riss at 112,000; and Würm at 62,000 and 25,000 B.P. Like Zeuner, he correlates his findings with the solar cycles of Milankovitch, but with a different result. If he is correct, the Middle Pleistocene began 250,-000, instead of 500,000, years ago. As the beginning of the Pleistocene is still placed at about one million years ago, the span of the Lower Pleistocene would then be about 660,000 years, two thirds of the Pleistocene rather than one half of it.

While these ingenious calculations were being made, teams of physicists in Germany and California experimented with a more long-ranged method, the measurement of Argon-40.[6] Argon-40 and Calcium-40 are both formed by the decay of Potassium-40. When a crystalline mineral containing Potassium-40 is heated to 500° F. or more, the Argon-40 which had previously been formed inside it, and which had been trapped, escapes. After the mineral cools, new Argon-40 atoms collect inside it.

Such a mineral is anorthoclase, one of the feldspars. Anorthoclase is ejected onto the earth's surface by volcanic eruptions, and when it emerges it is too hot to contain Argon-40. As time goes on, this gas accumulates in it at a fixed rate. The measurement of the proportion of the gas in the mineral tells, within a probable error of five to seven per cent, exactly how long ago the volcano erupted. Argon-40 is also formed in tektites, which are small glassy meteoric nodules found in many countries. As they are heated while passing through the earth's atmosphere, Argon-40 begins to

[6] R. W. Fairbridge: "The Changing Level of the Sea," SA, Vol. 202, No. 5 (1960), pp. 70–9.

G. H. Curtis: "A Clock for the Ages: Potassium Argon," NG, Vol. 120, No. 4 (1961), pp. 590–2.

form in them after they have landed and cooled, just as it does in lava.

Not only have these physicists dated deposits in Olduvai Gorge, Tanganyika, and the Trinil Beds of Java (as stated in Chapter 7), but they have also given us several critical dates for glacial events in Europe and North America.[7] The early glacial till of California, equivalent to the local Donau glaciation in Central Europe, which was pre-Günz, was dated at 850,000 B.C. This makes sense in terms of the date of one million years ago for the beginning of the Villafranchian. Günz is moved back to 500,000 years ago, and Mindel to 400,000. The latter part of the Second, or Great, Interglacial is set at 230,000 years, a date based on samples taken from the Late Acheulian site at Torre in Pietra, Italy. Hand axes from this site are similar to those found with the Swanscombe skull in England. This is as close to the present as Argon-40 had taken us early in 1962, and it leaves a gap of 160,000 years to the oldest Carbon-14 date. On the whole it ties in well with the older system of Penck and Bruckner and of Milankovitch, and fails to support those of Emiliani and Fairbridge. The last two seem to be more accurate for the latter part of the Pleistocene than for its earlier part.

Fairbridge's work sheds light on another subject—the availability of land bridges at different periods. For example, the passage across Bering Strait, where the sea-level fluctuations have been simple, was possible only during the peak of the Riss-Illinoisan, and all of the Würm. Fairbridge's view also reduces the possibility that the Djetis fauna, about which much has already been said, could have reached Java very much before the beginning of the Middle Pleistocene. This is heartening to paleontologists and archaeologists as it indicates that fewer early sites lie lost forever under the sea than we had feared.

These new dating methods and correlations unfortunately do not greatly concern Africa, where so much evidence of early

[7] J. F. Evernden, G. H. Curtis, and R. Kistler: "Potassium-Argon Dating of Pleistocene Volcanics," *Quaternaria*, Vol. 4 (1957), pp. 13–18.

W. Getner and J. Dährinder: "The Potassium-Argon Dates of Some Tektites," *ZfNF*, Vol. 14a, No. 7 (1959), pp. 686–7.

K. P. Oakley: "Dating the Stages of Hominid Evolution," *The Leech*, Vol. 28, Nos. 3, 4, 5 (1958), pp. 112–5.

hominid evolution has been found. There anthropologists work with a series of pluvials (wet periods) and interpluvials (dry periods) originally aligned as follows: Kageran Pluvial = Günz; Kamasian Pluvial =Mindel; Kanjeran Pluvial = Riss; and Gamblian Pluvial = Würm.

Unfortunately the Kanjeran Pluvial has been clearly identified only in East Africa. In other parts of the continent south of the Sahara only three pluvials are known. This discrepancy has led some geologists to believe that the Kanjeran is only a subdivision of the Kamasian Pluvial, which reached one or more peaks just as in Europe each of the four glaciations did. At any rate, the end of the Kanjeran, whatever its status, is clearly marked, for it was then that the faulting that cracked open the Rift Valley and left it in its present form is believed to have taken place.

Determining whether sub-Saharan Africa underwent three or four pluvial periods during the Pleistocene is only part of the problem, for the periods of wetness and drought varied in different parts of the subcontinent, just as today some parts are wet and others dry. In the past, zones of moist climate, with their appropirate floras and faunas, shrank and expanded gradually, so that at any one time a particular spot on the map could have been wet while another a few hundred miles away was dry, and a little later, geologically speaking, both could have been either wet or dry. The climate of South Africa has been particularly deviant because it has been affected by air masses from Antarctica which follow a pattern of their own independent of that of the Northern Hemisphere. This complicates the problem of establishing a date for the Australopithecines and for the human-looking jaw fragment, Telanthropus 2, from Sterkfontein Cave.

In North Africa and in the Near East the Pleistocene sequence is based partly on changes in fauna and partly on a complex and imperfectly understood series of local rises and falls of the sea levels along both the Atlantic and the Mediterranean coasts.

In Java,[8] which like Africa has been found to contain both Australopithecine and very early human specimens, geological research on the Pleistocene has been concentrated in the Solo River Valley in the eastern part of the island. There deep cuts through

[8] H. R. Van Heekeren: "The Stone Age of Indonesia," *VKIV*, Vol. 21 (1957).

successive layers show sequences as long as those in Olduvai Gorge, and like Olduvai's they are composed in part of volcanic materials potentially suitable for argon-potassium dating.

The Pleistocene is represented by three superimposed beds, which are, starting at the bottom, the Putjangan, Kabuh, and Notopuro. These contain, in the same order, the Djetis, Trinil, and Notopuro faunas. The first two are more or less continuous geologically and in fauna, but the Notopuro beds are distinctly marked. Just before they were formed the land rose, creating new drainage lines. At the same time Sundaland emerged from the sea during what corresponded to the Third, or Riss, Glaciation. At the end of the Notopuro period the waters again rose, and the succeeding fauna is modern.

The age of the Djetis fauna is still in dispute, but this fauna probably existed in the Late Lower Pleistocene, corresponding to the Cromerian Interglacial in Europe. The Trinil fauna is Middle Pleistocene, and it lasted until the ocean level fell again in the Third, or Riss, Glaciation. The Notopuro fauna is Upper Pleistocene. As we shall see in Chapter 10, three distinct but successive forms of man inhabited Java during these three divisions of the Pleistocene, but it is impossible for us to pinpoint their dates with greater accuracy.

In China [9] also only major divisions of the Pleistocene are readily discernible because that country was unglaciated east of the Tibetan Highlands. China is divided into two geological regions, north and south, by the ridge of the Tsinling Mountains. This range runs east and west in Shensi Province, on about the 34° latitude, just south and west of the first great bend of the Huang Ho.

In north China the Pliocene–Pleistocene threshold is marked by a series of warpings and faultings in the earth's crust, followed by the deposition of the Nihowan-Taiku, or Horse Beds, laid down in lake bottoms and river channels. They contain a local Villafranchian fauna known as the Sanmenian series, which includes horses, elephants, cattle, sheep, deer, and camels. The climate was cool.

The Lower Pleistocene of south China is harder to identify. In

[9] Cheng Te-Kun: *Archaeology in China,* Vol. 1 of *Prehistoric China,* Heffer, Cambridge, 1959.

Kwangsi, whence most of the material comes, the beds are later-ites (red soils produced by rock decay) washed from the valley slopes and deposited in terraces 12 meters above the present high-water levels. The fauna is the same as that of north China.

In north China the Middle Pleistocene deposits are called Terra Rossa, because they consist of red conglomerates and red clays. In south China a second set of terraces and river fans com-posed of water-borne laterites represents this period. At this time and in both regions many caves and fissures were opened and then filled up with air-borne earth. This earth then solidified, im-prisoning large numbers of animal bones, including those of Sinanthropus and a somewhat later human skeleton, that of the Ting-tsun man, both of which will be described in Chapter 10.

Throughout the Middle Pleistocene north China had a Pale-arctic fauna although the climate varied intermittently from cool and semi-arid to almost tropical. In south China, where the entire period was tropical, the fauna was Indo-Malayan, as described in Chapter 7. The fossil remains of this fauna come mostly from the yellow deposits of the Kwangsi caves.

As the deposition of Terra Rossa soils continued without a break, the Upper Pleistocene arrived in north China unostenta-tiously, and the only way in which geologists can tell the Early Upper Pleistocene layers from the Late Middle Pleistocene ones is by the fauna. No new species appeared, but some of the old ones had become extinct by the Upper Pleistocene.

Then in the middle of the Upper Pleistocene, the land rose again in another continental uplift, which was followed by the so-called Chingshui Erosion. After that, yellow earth was deposited in Kansu, Shensi, and Shansi by northwest winds, which also brought a cool and semi-arid climate. This was the Age of Yellow Earth, equivalent to the Würm glaciation in Europe. Its fauna was the same as before, but further impoverished by continued extinc-tions. In south China this period is unknown. At the end of the Pleistocene came the Age of Black Earth, whose soils contained a transitional fauna between the fauna of the Yellow Earth and the modern animals of China.

In the two Americas and in Australia, continents remote from the centers of human evolution, human beings arrived so late that we have little need of reviewing geological details in this book. All finds are well within the time span of the Carbon-14 clock.

More exact intercontinental correlations than those outlined here may be expected when the Chinese begin dating their sites by Carbon-14 and when the Argon-40 method shall have been more widely used. More generally, as the Space Age reaps the fruits of the Atomic Ages, these chronological problems may be solved within our lifetime. But they have not been solved yet, and several interesting fossils have been set aside by scientists because their exact age is unknown. Time is still not our most reliable yardstick.

The Dimension of Space: Glacial Geography [1]

F O R P R E S E N T purposes the dimension of space consists of the geography of the land masses of the earth during the last half million years, particularly the areas of land covered by ice, the continental shelves exposed by the drying of oceans, and the intercontinental land bridges that afforded animals and men temporary passage between zoogeographic regions.

During the glacial maxima, ice covered most of northern and eastern Europe, some of the Tibetan plateau, and parts of the diagonal mountain spine of Central Asia. It nearly sealed off Western Europe from Eastern Europe and it blocked passage between China and the West, except for those hardy animals able to negotiate chilly passes in summer. Until at least the Third Interglacial it is fairly certain that man was not one of them.

If Fairbridge is correct, both the Sunda and the Sahul shelves could have been dry land during the Riss glaciation and also during the Würm. Multiple and separate invasions of Indonesia from southeast Asia would then have been possible, and even Australia could theoretically have been invaded by man more than once. Bering Strait, which is only 200 feet deep, could have permitted the crossing of ancestral Indians from Siberia to Alaska during the Riss-Illinoisan glaciation, if any such ancestors were on hand at

[1] The most useful general source is J. K. Charlesworth: *The Quaternary Era* (London: Edward Arnold, Ltd.; 1957).

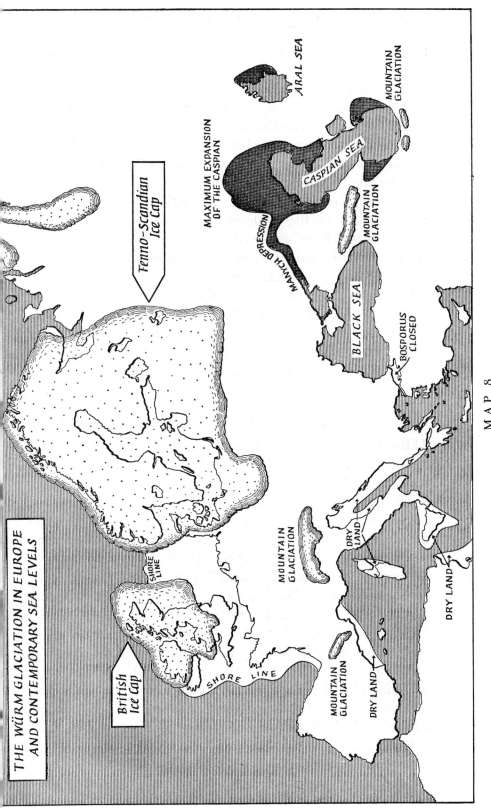

THE WÜRM GLACIATION IN EUROPE
AND CONTEMPORARY SEA LEVELS

British Ice Cap

Fenno-Scandian Ice Cap

SHORE LINE

SHORE LINE

MOUNTAIN GLACIATION

MOUNTAIN GLACIATION

DRY LAND

DRY LAND

DRY LAND

BLACK SEA

BOSPORUS CLOSED

MOUNTAIN GLACIATION

MANYCH DEPRESSION

CASPIAN SEA

MAXIMUM EXPANSION OF THE CASPIAN

MOUNTAIN GLACIATION

MOUNTAIN GLACIATION

ARAL SEA

MAP 8

that time. During the Würm-Wisconsian the passage was wide open, and before the end of that period America was inhabited by its basic aboriginal population.

During most of the time which concerns us Great Britain was part of the European continent. The Strait of Gibraltar, now 1,000 feet deep, was an open-water barrier throughout this period. Those who have crossed between Spain and Morocco in small craft know that the tides, currents, and winds can make this passage danger-ous. The sides of the cut through which the water flows are very steep. Even when the sea level was 300 feet lower, something sturdier than rafts or simple canoes would have been needed to mount an invasion mustering more than a handful of people.

Although no certain evidence exists to prove it, possibly a land bridge connected Tunisia and Italy during part of the Lower Pleistocene, allowing sabertooths and a few other African ani-mals to pass into Europe.[2] Also, momentarily during the Upper Pleistocene, narrow channels between islands in this part of the Mediterranean may have permitted human passage, but not an exchange of fauna.

During glacial maxima the Caspian Sea rose high above its pres-ent level, up to 300 feet during Riss and 250 feet during Würm. At the times of flooding the Caspian waters, fed by the Volga and by the glaciers that it drained, flowed across the strip of lowland north of the Caucasus to spill into the Black Sea. But the Black Sea had its high water when the Caspian was low, and vice versa, because only during interglacials, when the oceans were high and the Mediterranean swollen with salt water, did the Mediterranean floods break through the Bosporus to fill the Black Sea basin. Between these periods the Black Sea was a brackish lake. The Aral Sea was enlarged in rhythm with the Caspian, and south and east of the Urals stretched a vast swamp, below the edge of the ice. Europe was as difficult to approach from the northeast as from Africa. Its only gateway to the outside was the Bosporus and the Levant.

During pluvial periods similar floodings took place in Africa, in what is now the Sudan and southern Sahara. Lake Tchad, now a shrinking body of shallow water, was once a broad lake. To its

[2] Charlesworth: op. cit., pp. 1226–7.

east extended, at least intermittently during the Pleistocene, an extensive area of swamps and sometimes possibly of lakes. This barrier extended from the Sabaluka Gorge, 50 miles north of Khartum, some 450 miles southward to about 10° North Latitude.[3]

These water barriers, and the existing great lakes of East Africa, which were greatly enlarged during pluvials, must have restricted animal and human traffic in Africa, moving both north and south and east and west, to a few narrow highways, and made Black Africa nearly as inaccessible as western Europe. But after the Pleistocene the lakes and swamps shrank and the East African highlands were invaded at least twice by people from the north.

For the Lower Pleistocene the faunas of different regions serve as fair indicators of the passage of time because evolution was then working overtime. For the Middle and Upper Pleistocene the chief value of faunas lies in their record of extinctions. Time is measured by the number of species that had disappeared at each period, with a few exceptions. The spotted hyaena, *Crocuta crocuta*, first appeared early in Mindel, more or less simultaneously in Europe, Africa, and Asia, and his presence serves to correlate these continents chronologically.

There is also a geographical aspect to faunal distribution during the Pleistocene. In Europe the Middle Pleistocene is marked by the arrival of a new set of animals, the cold fauna, all of which —the mammoth, woolly rhinoceros, reindeer, and others—had become cold-adapted by means mentioned in Chapter 2. They replaced the warm or Villafranchian fauna of the Lower Pleistocene, one member of which, the hippopotamus, continued to live in his chilly rivers until the beginning of the Elster glaciation.

The cold-adapted animals of the European Middle Pleistocene were Palearctic and were more closely related to Oriental than to Ethiopian species. North African mammals were Ethiopian almost until the end of the Pleistocene, when Palearctic species appeared, including the bear, stag, and European wild boar (*Sus scrofa*), and also the European elk (moose to Americans), whose portrait has been found among the rock paintings of the Sahara. In southeast Asia three successive faunas migrated, as we have

[3] G. Andrew: "Geology of the Sudan," Chapter 6 of J. D. Tothill: *Agriculture in the Sudan* (Oxford: Oxford University Press; 1948), pp. 84–128.

already discussed, from India and China into Indonesia. These movements are important to the subject of this book, because where edible animals go, man the hunter follows.

The Temporal and Spatial Distribution of Fossil Man Sites

A T T H E T I M E of writing at least 337 sites which can be dated with some degree of accuracy have yielded skeletal remains of

TABLE 11

FOSSIL-MAN SITES IN TIME AND SPACE

Time

Region	L&M	IG3	W-1	W-2,3	P-W	Total	Per Cent of Total
Western Europe	3	6	29	78	37	153	49
Eastern Europe and U.S.S.R.	0	2	6	20	5	33	10.6
North Africa	1	4	1	2	14	22	7.1
Africa south of Sahara	1	2	3	1	15	22	7.1
Near East	0	1	10	6	4	21	6.7
India and Ceylon	0	0	0	0	2	2	.6
East Asia	5	5	0	2	2	14	4.5
Southeast Asia and Indonesia	4	1	1	1	17	24	7.7
Australia and New Guinea	0	0	0	1	3	4	1.3
America	0	0	0	4	13	17	5.4
Total Per Cent of Total	14 4.5	21 6.7	50 16.0	115 36.8	112 35.9	312 99.9%	100.0%

Time Symbols: L&M = Lower and Middle Pleistocene
IG3 = Third Interglacial
W-1 = Würm 1
W-2,3 = Würm 2 and 3
P-W = Post-Würm

fossil men that reputable scientists have recorded.[4] These bones represent a minimum of a little over one thousand individuals, ranging in completeness from a tooth to a skeleton. These 337 sites are distributed in space, and with various degrees of probability in time, as follows.

In the time scale on Table 11, the first column is labeled "Lower and Middle Pleistocene" for the benefit of the possibly human Telanthropus mandibles from Sterkfontein and of the Pithecanthropus specimens from the Djetis faunal beds of Java. There is still some doubt whether all these remains belong to the Late Lower or Early Middle Pleistocene. The rest of the sites in this column are unquestionably of Middle Pleistocene date.

In any case, this portion of the Pleistocene (85 per cent, more or less), from our standpoint the most important since it was the formative period for *H. erectus* and *H. sapiens*, is represented by only fourteen known sites, or 4 per cent of the whole. In only one of them, Choukoutien, were there more than a few fragments of one, or at the most three, individuals. The earlier half of the Upper Pleistocene, consisting of the Riss-Würm, or Third, Interglacial in Europe and the Kanjeran-Gamblian Interpluvial in much of Africa, is represented by only twenty-one sites, or 7 per cent of the whole, although some other, imperfectly dated pieces might be included. The second half of the Upper Pleistocene, that is, Würm, Wisconsian, or Gamblian, can also be divided, this time into periods of no more than 35,000 years each, covering the consecutive regimes of Neanderthal and Upper Paleolithic men in Europe and the arrival of human beings in Australia and the Americas. The first of these periods is represented by fifty sites, or 16 per cent of the whole; the second by 115 sites, or 37 per cent. Into the few thousand years between the last retreat of the Scandinavian icecap and the diffusion of agriculture must be crowded 112 sites, or 36 per cent of the total.

It is easy to read into these figures an increase in the human population in Pleistocene and early post-Würmian times similar to the increase currently taking place, but such an interpretation must be made with caution. Long after the beginning of human

[4] H. V. Vallois and H. L. Movius, Jr.: *Catalogue des Hommes Fossiles* (Algiers, 1952); and reports of other sites published since this compilation.

existence, the dead were still being abandoned, to be bitten, crunched, and dismembered like the bodies of any other creatures. Some living tribes continue this custom to this day.

Deliberate burial did not begin until the Late Pleistocene, and has never been universally practiced. Short of mummification, the best way to preserve (and unwittingly ensure the discovery of) a skeleton is to bury the body in a cave, and this was not done in many parts of the world. In any case, it was not done anywhere before the Late Pleistocene. Burial customs, or their absence, probably affect the numbers of skeletal specimens discovered in different periods much more so than population size. However, the world's population undoubtedly grew slowly as new regions were settled and new techniques of food acquisition invented.

We must also consider the geography of archaeological search. Paleolithic archaeology was born in France. The French have many archaeologists, much limestone, and many caves. More than 34 per cent of the world's known sites containing human remains are in France or in present or former French colonies or dependencies. Even outside these territories the French have been active. More than 22 per cent of the sites are in British Commonwealth territories, for the British have been almost equally enthusiastic. Three per cent are in former or present Dutch territories, which encompass only a small part of the land area of the world; and the Dutch have found five of fourteen Lower and Middle Pleistocene sites. Were the count made by the nationality of the discoverers, the French, British, Dutch, Germans, and Americans would be far in the lead, for between them they have found well over 90 per cent of all fossil-man sites and specimens.

Time, Space, and Paleolithic Tools

B E F O R E we discuss ways and means of studying the thousand-odd human fossils of the Pleistocene listed in the previous section, it may be useful for us to study the distribution of Paleolithic tools, for two reasons.

Tools are more abundant than human bones. An adult human body has only 180 or so bones, many of which contain edible substances, brain or marrow. Paleolithic stone implements are made of very hard materials, including quartz, quartzite, chert, chalcedony, and obsidian. During his lifetime a hunter makes thousands of implements that are inedible and almost as incorruptible as gold. As indicators of the presence of man, stone tools are more useful than human bones.

Moreover, stone tools constitute the principal source of information about the cultural life of Pleistocene peoples. Tool-making techniques are handed down from generation to generation, and sequences of such techniques indicate cultural lines. When two groups of people whose territories have common borders are found to have made similar tools, we may infer that one group taught the techniques to the other, with an added likelihood of gene flow between them. Conversely, when two lines of tool-making follow similar evolutionary paths, although they are widely separated in space, the possibility of independent invention and parallel cultural change must be considered.

The study of Paleolithic tools also has drawbacks. The earliest tools must have been so crude that they are indistinguishable from naturally fractured stones. Endless arguments have taken place concerning the identification of eoliths, or dawn stones, as these dubious specimens are called. In addition, we do not know whether the oldest tools were made by men or by Australopithecines. In one site, Olduvai Gorge, Australopithecine bones were found in association with stone tools on a floor on which the Australopithecines had lived. Both these problems were discussed in Chapter 7. During the Lower Pleistocene both *Australopithecus* and *Homo* may have made tools, but from the beginning of the Middle Pleistocene onward, all the tools we have were probably made by *Homo*.

Aside from choppers and chopping tools, which have already been described, these tools fall into four principal classes: bifacial hand axes, flakes, blades, and microliths. Detailed descriptions of these are readily available and need not be repeated here.[5] In general, bifacial hand axes are usually large, almond-shaped implements flaked on both sides and both bilaterally and bifacially

[5] Oakley: *Man the Toolmaker* (London: Brit. Mus. Nat. Hist.).
C. S. Coon: *The Seven Caves* (New York: Alfred A. Knopf; 1957), pp. 29–41.

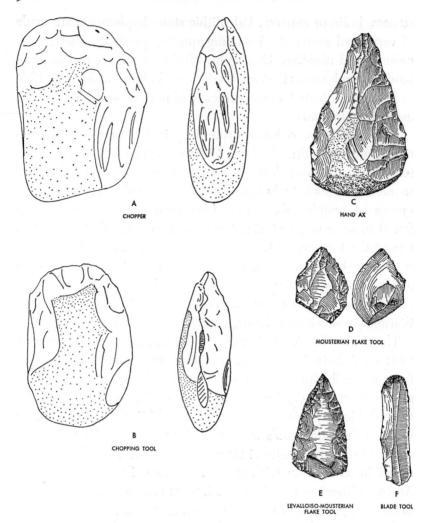

FIG. 43   BASIC TOOLS OF EARLY MEN. A. Chopper, from Melville Island, Australia (Tiwi); B. Chopping tool, from Melville Island, Australia (Tiwi); C. Hand ax, from England (Seven Caves); D. Simple flake tool, from Le Moustier, France (after Oakley, 1956); E. Levallois flake tool from Syria; F. Blade tool from Syria. The earliest tools made by man were choppers, which have a cutting edge flaked on one side only (A) and chopping tools, flaked on both sides (B). They were made from Africa to China in the Late Lower Pleistocene. In east and southeast Asia they persisted through the Pleistocene, and in parts of Australia were made in the twentieth century. Hand axes (C) were confined to Africa, Europe, and southwest Asia as far east as India. Simple flake tools were made wherever tools were used. The one shown here (D) was made by a Western Neanderthal. Flake tools made by striking prepared cores were also used by Neanderthal men, particularly in southwest Asia (E). Blade tools, characteristic of the Upper Paleolithic of Würm II, had a limited distribution from England to Afghanistan.

symmetrical. They may be shaped in either of two ways: the hand axes proper are pointed at the business end, and the cleavers have transverse, bladelike edges in place of points. The hand axe was probably an all-purpose cutting tool whereas the cleaver may have been somewhat specialized, as for skinning animals, felling small trees, or both.

Flake tools are classified by the technique used to strike the flakes off the parent core and by the treatment given the flakes after they have been detached. The crude way to make flakes consists first of trimming the chalky crust off the surface of the core by a series of glancing blows, leaving the core polyhedral rather than rounded; then searching the surface for a place where two planes form a relatively sharp angle and striking the core with a hammerstone just above that ridge, so that a more or less triangular flake will spring loose at a single blow. Unless the flake is unusually well shaped it will need trimming at the butt and along the edges before it can be used as a knife, scraper, spear point, or whatever.

Another relatively crude method consists of setting the core on an anvil stone and striking it on top with a hammerstone, so that flakes fly off both ends and all sides. Experts can distinguish these flakes, which are called bipolar, and also their cores.

But if the tool-maker knows how, he can shape the core in advance by knocking off a small chip here and another there, thereby visualizing the flake that will come off. In particular, he fashions a striking platform with an angle as close as possible to 45° so that he will get a nearly flat flake. When he strikes the critical blow, if all goes well, his flake will fall off, ready for use. This third technique produces what is known as a Levallois flake.

Once a flake has been detached, it can be used as it is, and perhaps sharpened after it has suffered a few nicks; or it can be trimmed at once into a special shape. Sharpening and trimming are called *retouching*. Its butt may be trimmed to thin it for hafting, or its edges and point retouched to make it into a side-scraper or end-scraper. A sharp blow at the tip will turn it into a narrow chisel or graver. These extra preparations suit it for special work with wood, skins, flesh, bone, antler, or ivory. In some of the most advanced flake cultures, as in the Near East and Europe, specialized flake tools are numerous.

Blades differ from flakes in that they are essentially parallel-edged instead of triangular, and usually thinner and straighter. They are elongated strips of flint or obsidian made by a special process, as follows. The tool-maker skillfully shapes his core so that it is virtually tubular, with a flat top serving as a striking platform. Near the edge of this flat surface he sets the point of a punch made of an elastic material such as fresh bone, antler, or even wood, and holds the punch at right angles to the plane of the striking platform and directly in line with the main axis of the core. Striking carefully placed blow after blow, he slivers off blade after blade. These blades are the blanks from which he can re-touch a wide variety of specialized tools.

The fourth step in tool-making is to prepare small cores in the manner just described and then strike off miniature blades that can then be retouched into microliths—fine tools such as tiny gravers, or small, individual blades set in rows inside slots carved in wooden or bone handles. Such rows of microblades are known as composite tools, which take the forms of knives, sickles, or barbed spear and arrow points.

On the basis of the five types of tools described here and in Chapter 7, the most anciently inhabited parts of the Old World—excluding Oceania and Australia—may be divided into two major provinces: a Western, situated in Europe, Africa, and West Asia, and an Eastern, in East Asia and Indonesia. During the entire Middle and most of the Upper Pleistocene, the borders of these two provinces met only in India. Thus the ancient homes of the Australoids and Mongoloids lay in the Eastern Province, and those of the Caucasoids and Africans—Capoids and Congoids—in the Western.

In the northern region of the Eastern Province the tool types were derived directly from those of the Lower Pleistocene and evolved independently throughout the Middle and Upper Pleistocene. Gradually the choppers dropped out of the sequence. At first both simple and bipolar flakes were made, but the bipolar ones also dropped out and the sequence as a whole was essentially a gradual refinement of the simple flake techniques plus an increasing use of antler and bone. During the Upper Pleistocene Western-style flakes and blades appeared at different times on the western and northern fringes of the Eastern Province, but neither of them altered the evolutionary course of tool-making in the province as a whole.

In Europe, western Asia, and most of Africa, hand axes appeared at the beginning of the Middle Pleistocene, first crudely and later finely made. The cruder ones are called Abbevillian or Chellian; the finer ones, Acheulian. The Abbevillian style lasted until the beginning of the Mindel-Riss Interglacial, and the Acheulian disappeared as an industry early in the Riss-Würm Interglacial, although special kinds of hand axes were made, as rare tools, almost until the First Würm Interstadial,[6] some 40,000 years ago. In Africa the rate of change was slower, and in the Cape Province an Acheulian industry was replaced by a flake industry as late as 30,000 years ago. The sequence in India does not mirror those of Europe and Africa exactly, and it is not certain when hand axes ceased to be made there.

From the beginning of the Middle Pleistocene flake tools coexisted with hand axes, either as elements in hand-axe cultures or as cultures of their own.[7] Only in the late Upper Pleistocene did flake tools entirely replace them. Flake tools were most elaborate and specialized in the Near East and Europe, where three partly successive and partly overlapping flake cultures filled the time span from the beginning of the Middle Pleistocene to the end of the Early Würm, some 40,000 years ago, and lasted sporadically even later than that.

These were the Clactonian, a simple flake industry that involved crude retouching; the Levalloisian, which included prepared cores and Levallois flakes; and the Mousterian, a simple flake industry that involved fine retouching. In some places the Levalloisian and Mousterian techniques were combined into a hybrid culture known as Levalloisio-Mousterian. In North Africa

---

[6] An interstadial is a mild, or cool, period between two peaks of a glacial period. It is shorter and less warm than an interglacial.

[7] The word *culture* is used here in the special archaeological sense.

a local flake culture, the Aterian, followed the Acheulian and developed into a highly specialized, technically refined way of producing knives and projectile points finely retouched on both sides. Some were tanged, barbed arrowheads strikingly similar to later American Indian specimens.

In the deep forests of Central and West Africa the tradition of the hand axe continued, in a special industry called the Sangoan, well into the Late Pleistocene and perhaps almost until its end. In East and South Africa flakes of the general Levalloisio-Mousterian type replaced Acheulian hand axes progressively, the transition working its way generally from north to south, until, as stated above, it took place in Cape Province more than 100,000 years later than it did in the Near East and Europe.

Blade-making was invented in the region of Palestine, Lebanon, and Syria, or nearby, during the Early Würm, and this new technique was apparently brought to Europe by way of the Bosporous gap in the warm Gottweig, or Würm I–II, Interstadial. By 30,000 B.C. Upper Paleolithic hunters who made both blade and flake tools reached the Atlantic, and over the next 20,000 years a bewildering (to me) sequence of Upper Paleolithic tool industries followed. Microliths were part of the European tool kit from the start. To the East blade-making extended as far as northern Afghanistan, where C-14 dates as old as those in western Europe have been determined.

From their European and central Asiatic centers blade-making techniques were carried northeastward into Siberia and over the mountains and narrow channels of icy water to Hokkaido, where a number of presumably successive blade cultures has been found.

Just before and after the end of the Pleistocene, blade cultures were brought to North Africa in two waves, the Mouillian and Capsian, and there these new techniques replaced the Aterian flake industry. Capsian tool-making was also carried to East Africa in early Recent time, and it eventually spread to South Africa in a mostly microlithic culture known as Wilton.

In southeast Asia and Indonesia the earliest tools were choppers and chopping tools, with crude flakes. These have been found in Burma, Malaya, Siam, Indochina, Luzon, Borneo, Java, and Sumatra. Only in Malaya have they been definitely dated—at the local equivalent of the Cromerian Interglacial or the beginning of Mindel I. This was the time of the Djetis fauna in Java. As in China, the flake tools in these industries gradually evolved into finer forms, followed in postglacial times by local microlithic industries.

In Australia, which was uninhabited until almost the end of the Pleistocene, all types of tools were either imported from Indonesia or invented locally. During the last century, and in some places during the twentieth, tool industries had a continent-wide distribution. Choppers as crude as any known in the early Middle Pleistocene were used until very recently (and perhaps still are), on Mornington Island in the Gulf of Carpenteria, as they were two generations ago on Melville Island. Good Levallois-like flakes were made in central Australia and blades and microliths in Victoria and neighboring parts of New South Wales. In several regions aborigines had learned to grind chopping tools to a smooth, sharp edge and to haft them as axes with sticks and gum. Archaeologically these cultures go back to a C-14 date of 6740 B.C., but undoubtedly they began several millennia earlier.

The New World industries stem from two sources, the Late Pleistocene flake culture of China, and the blade cultures of northeast Siberia, which had originally come from the West. In America these imports evolved into a number of industries some of which lasted until the arrival of Europeans. Very crude chopping tools have been collected in both North and South America, and they are as crude as the tools of Sinanthropus. We do not know how old they are, although we may soon. In South America they are found in beds underlying pottery, and were probably used by some of the Fuegian Indians until quite recently. The presence of these archaic tools cannot be taken as proof that *Homo erectus* preceded *Homo sapiens* in America.

The foregoing archaeological summary indicates that the world of the Middle and Upper Pleistocene was divided into two halves and five regions; an eastern province with a northern and a southern region, and a western province with a Eurasian, a North African, and a sub-Saharan region. These correspond, as we shall see shortly, to the distribution of the five human subspecies near the end of the Pleistocene, before the movements that relocated the

Australoids and Capoids when the two dominant northern sub-species, the Mongoloid and the Caucasoid, expanded their territories southward.

The Chronology and Distribution of the Use of Fire

M UCH HAS already been said in this book about the importance of fire to the physical and cultural evolution of man, and it need not be repeated here. But if it can be shown that some geographical races got fire before others did, the implication will be that those who had it first were also the first to receive its evolutionary benefits, and that those who obtained it last must have been correspondingly retarded.

Unfortunately, the absence of fire can be indicated only by negative evidence. We cannot expect to find charred wood and bone in disturbed sites such as gravel beds, and if we find such evidence, as found it was at Swanscombe on the Thames, we are extremely lucky. In Java we would not expect to find it for we have no undisturbed sites there. Only in Africa is there evidence that fire arrived late, as late as 59,000 years ago. In the earlier habitation sites such as Olorgesailie in Kenya, where layer after successive layer of hand axes, cleavers, and meat bones have been excavated with the most meticulous care, not a trace of charcoal or charred bone has been found.

Both Louis Leakey and Desmond Clark, who are among the most painstaking and observant excavators in the world, have stated their conviction that in East Africa the entire hand-axe period was fireless almost to the end. If future excavations confirm this erudite opinion, we shall have one explanation of the extraordinarily slow pace that human evolution followed, in the Middle and Late Pleistocene, in Africa south of the equator, and perhaps also south of the Sahara.

Grades and Species of Fossil Men

D URING the Pleistocene, hominids made tools in five traditions. As far as we know at present, tool-making began in Africa, in the

second half of the Lower Pleistocene, with split pebbles, choppers, and chopping tools. This simple technology spread as far as
southeast Asia and Indonesia. At this point the hominid world
knew but a single way of making tools.

Before the Lower Pleistocene was over, and perhaps even before the original tool-making tradition had reached southeast Asia,
the tool-makers of Africa and Palestine had added coarsely
chipped, ball-like implements to their repertoire, and these new
items were apparently not diffused to the East. Thus the split between East and West, of which Kipling sang a half million years
later, opened before the end of the Lower Pleistocene. In the
West, where hand axes were invented a little later, a further division into three parts did not occur until the end of the Middle
Pleistocene. By that time the Chinese and southeast Asian industries had also become recognizably different from each other.

If the first tools in each region were made by Australopithecines,
and we have no evidence to the contrary, we may infer that the
first split mentioned above took place between separate populations of Australopithecines belonging either to two or more species, or to two or more subspecies. But at the dawn of the Middle
Pleistocene, when *Australopithecus* and *Homo* coexisted in Java
and probably also in Africa, the same kinds of tools were apparently being made by men who, as the millennia rolled on, invented new ways of working with flint and other tool materials
and new and more efficient tool forms.

From this evidence a second inference is logical, that men
evolved from Australopithecines in either or both provinces. No
more than two such evolutionary acts are implied by existing
information. The only alternative is the theory that *Homo* and
Australopithecus lived side by side during the Lower Pleistocene,
that only *Homo* made tools, and that in both Africa and east Asia
he preyed off his hominid cousins until he had destroyed them.
This second hypothesis is not impossible but it is unsupported.

As long as we use the word *Australopithecine* in a broad sense,
including forms undiscovered as well as those known, we may
postulate without serious reservation that *Homo* was descended
from a polytypic species of *Australopithecus* inhabiting a wide
stretch of Old World tropics. By the same logic we may, as others

have done, speak of an Australopithecine grade of human evolution.

A grade is not a formal taxonomic unit, like family, subfamily, genus, species, or even waagenon (see Chapter 1, p. 17). It is an evolutionary stage or condition, as broad or as narrow as circumstances require. For example, as we saw in Chapters 4 and 6, all the New World primates and most of the Old World genera passed independently from a prosimian to a simian grade, and three lines of Old World simians passed separately to the pongid grade. Although also called a subfamily, the Dryopithecines constituted a grade through which more than one line passed. Some of these lines became independently specialized into hominids and pongids during the latter part of the Miocene or the Pliocene.

We can therefore tentatively set up, in our family tree, a succession of three grades: Dryopithecine, Australopithecine, and Hominine. The only professionals who may be expected to object to this scheme, which is not original, are the anatomists and paleontologists who believe that man is descended from *Oreopithecus,* and those others who believe that *Homo's* ancestors parted from those of *Australopithecus* by evolution through branching before the latter had evolved into their known forms. The second objection is largely one of nomenclature or semantics, and depends to a certain extent on the forthcoming study of the Kenyapithecus maxilla and teeth; on whether the Olduvai child was a true Australopithecine, a Hominine, or an unnamed ancestor of both; on a detailed study of the Tchad skull; and on the reservations we may have concerning the new finds that may await us in the ground.

Once past the Australopithecine stage, we come to the full Middle Pleistocene. *Homo* is already divided into a number of geographical populations. How many grades, from that point on, shall we recognize in fossil and living men?

Some authors prefer three, variously labelled. A compromise nomenclature is *Protoanthropic, Paleanthropic,* and *Neanthropic.*[8]

[8] This classification is derived from S. Sergi's categories *Protoàntropi, Paleàntropi,* and *Faneràntropi,* and from J. Piveteau's *Archanthropiens, Paléanthropiens,* and *Néanthropiens.* The term *Archanthropi* would make them to men what archangels are to angels; and *Faneràntropi,* from *phaneros,* Greek for *visible,* is unfamiliar.

THOUSANDS OF YEARS AGO

Years ago	RECENT / PLEISTOCENE	EUROPEAN GLACIAL SEQUENCE	AUSTRALOID	MONGOLOID	CAUCASOID	CAPOID	CONGOID
10	U P P E R	Würm II-III	Aitapé HE? / Wadjak HS / Niah HS	Upper Cave / Liu-Kiang / Ordos HS / Tze-Yang / Lai Pin / Tadoki	Upper Paleolithic-Mouillian Folk / Neanderthals Skhul Tabun StaroseI'e Qafza Egbert	Tangier HS? / Taforalt HS?	Broken Hill HE / Saldanha HE
100	P E R	Würm I	—Solo HE—	Ushikawa ?HS? Chanyang ? / Mapa HS / Ting-tsun ?	Krapina Ehringsdorf Saccopastore	Rabat HE?	
150		Last (Third) Interglacial					
200		Riss II			Fontechévade HS / Montmaurin	Sidi Abd er-Rahman HE? / Temara HE?	
250	M I D	Riss I					
300	D L E	Great (Second) Interglacial			Steinheim HS / Swanscombe HS		
350				Sinanthropus HE			Chellian 3 HE
400		Mindel II				Ternefine HE?	
450		Mindel I			Heidelberg HE?		Olduvai Milk? Teeth A?
500	L O W E R	Cromerian (First) Interglacial	Trinil Pithecanthropi HE				Kromdraai A Telanthropus A? / Swarkrans A Zinjanthropus A
550					Tell Ubeidiya HE or A?		Olduvai Child A
600		Günz					Makapansgat A
650							
700	P L E I S T O C E N E	Tiglian	Djetis Pithecanthropi HE / Meganthropus A				Sterkfontein A / Taung A
750	Villafranchian						
800							
850							
900							Tchad? A
950							
1,000							

HS = *Homo sapiens*   HE = *Homo erectus*   A = Australopithecine

The first grade includes such obviously ancient and primitive fossils as Pithecanthropus, Sinanthropus, and the new Chellian-3 skull from Olduvai Gorge. The second covers a mixed group—the European and Near Eastern Neanderthals, Solo in Java, and Broken Hill in Africa—which have little in common except long low skulls, big brow ridges, and an Upper Pleistocene date. The third includes modern man, of all races, and all fossil men that could be more or less duplicated among the living.

This threefold system is unrealistic: its grades are partly based on the time scale, and they should be entirely dependent on size, which is not considered, and form. Ignoring time, we shall see that the small-brained Solo and Broken Hill skulls belong to the first of these grades, and that other members of the second grade can be matched, in most respects, among living peoples. The second grade, then, dissolves, and the third requires subdivision.

There remain two mutually exclusive grades, the Protoanthropic and Neanthropic. The Paleanthropic does not represent a true unit; its members can be sorted and redistributed in the other two categories. These two differ sufficiently in several pertinent respects to warrant being given the status of separate, successive species, *Homo erectus* and *Homo sapiens*. For those who like to split categories more finely, each species can be divided into grades of lesser magnitude.

Between some of the fossil populations of our own species, *Homo sapiens*, anthropologists have observed what seem to be important differences in evolutionary status. But when viewed from the perspective of life as a whole, these variations are slight. Differences of equal magnitude still exist. *By definition,* every minor grade discernible in fossil specimens of *Homo sapiens* may be found in living men.

The great variability of twentieth-century human beings, in evolutionary grades as well as in racial lines, makes our lives more complicated than those of our ancestors who lived in a simpler world, when space was still a barrier to communication and travel,

---

S. Sergi: "I Tipi Umani Più Antiche," Chapter 3, pp. 69–133 of R. Biassutti: *Razze e Popoli della Terra* (Turin: Union Tipografico-Editrice; 1959), Vol. 1.

J. Piveteau: *Traité de Paléontologie,* Vol. 7 of *Primates, Paléontologie Humaine* (Paris: Masson et Cie; 1957).

and local populations kept to themselves. As we move rapidly around the world, these differences pose a challenge that we may or may not be sapient enough to meet.

The Sapiens-Erectus Threshold: the Evidence of Brain Size

IN ORDER to decide whether a given human fossil specimen belongs in the category of *Homo erectus* or that of *Homo sapiens*, we need as much evidence as we can get. Usually, however, very little evidence is available, and for practical purposes it is most often limited to the skull. Of the fossil skulls known to us only nineteen are so different from those of living peoples that they obviously belong in the *erectus* category. They are, counting adult skulls only: three Pithecanthropus specimens from Java; six Solo skulls from the same island; six Sinanthropus skulls; one newly found skull from Tze-Yang, China; and, from Africa, the newly found Chellian-3 skull from Olduvai Gorge, the Saldanha Bay skull, and Broken Hill (Rhodesian) man.

These skulls have in common small brains, low cranial vaults, heavy brow ridges, and sloping foreheads. The palates and teeth that are preserved are big; and the available lower jaws that match these skulls lack chins.

Certain other fossil skulls, like the Upper Paleolithic crania from Europe and the Upper Cave family from Choukoutien, are entirely modern. In one way or another most of the other skulls and groups of skulls are modern only in the sense that the primitive features which they possess may also be seen in the crania of surviving primitive peoples. This intermediate group is *sapiens* in the Linnean sense, that is, that all living men are *sapiens*.

With these facts in mind, just where do we draw the line? Obviously, the differences between the two species, one of which evolved by succession out of the other, are concerned with intelligence, self-control, and the abilities to provide food efficiently and to get along well in groups. The seat of intelligence is the central nervous system. The regulation of self-control is the combined task of the brain and the endocrine system, and indeed the brain and endocrines act together in many ways, and influence each other by a complex feedback system.

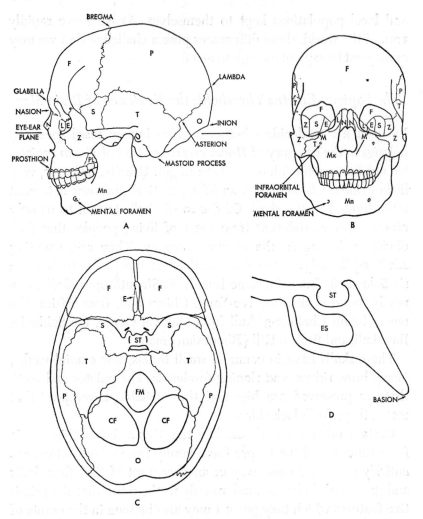

FIG. 45 ANATOMY OF THE SKULL. A. Side view; B. Front view, of a South African Bantu skull; C. Interior basal view of a laboratory skull; D. Section through the *sella turcica* region of same. *Abbreviations:* CF. Cerebella fossa; E. Ethmoid bone; ES. Ethmoidal sinus; F. Frontal bone; FM. Foramen magnum; L. Lachrymal bone; Mn. Mandible; Mx. Maxillary bone; N. Nasal bone; O. Occipital bone; P. Parietal bone; Pl. Palatal bone; S. Sphenoid bone; ST. Sella turcica; T. Temporal bone; Z. Zygomatic bones (malar). (Drawings A and B after de Quatrefages and Hamy, 1882; C and D after Hamilton, 1956.)

The size of the human brain is related to a capacity for performance in thinking, planning, communicating, and behaving in groups, as leader, follower, or both. But brain size is a sum of the masses of that organ's component parts, including the medulla, hypothalamus, cerebral hemispheres, and cerebellum. The hemispheres are divided into lobes, and their surfaces are covered with a wrinkled skin of gray matter, the cortex, which contains neurones. In living individuals and populations, differences are found in the relative sizes of the lobes and in the surface areas of the cortex; the size of the surface area varies with the complexity and depths of the folds on the inner and outer surfaces of the hemispheres. The larger a brain is, the greater the cortical surface area, both proportionately and absolutely. The cerebellum is a miniature replica of the greater part of each hemisphere, and it is covered by 75 per cent as much cortical surface, but its cortex is thinner. As the hemispheres grew larger in the course of human evolution, the cerebellum expanded proportionately.

As in the case of the Australopithecines, all that remains of the brains of fossil men are imprints left on the inside of the skull. These show gross size and form fairly accurately, and a few other details as well. The divisions between the lobes are marked in varying degree, and the seat of the cerebellum in the basal part of the occipital bone may be detected as a pair of cups. The blood supply to the covering of the brain may also be gauged to a certain extent by the imprints of the middle meningeal arteries on the parietal bones.

The inside of the skull base also contains the *sella turcica* (Turkish saddle), also known as the hypophyseal fossa. This is a depression, or cradle, in the midline of the sphenoid bone and extending to either side. In it the pituitary gland, or hypophysis, is seated. The length and depth of this depression is taken to be a rough indication of the size of the pituitary—the master gland which, among many other functions, controls growth, including that of the bony crests that brace the skull. No other endocrine gland leaves a direct mark on the skeleton.

In mammals brain size, like the face length of horses (see Chapter 1, page 25), is allometric. That is, in any closely related group of animals, such as a family or subfamily, all species of which are more or less equal in intelligence, brain weight will equal body weight times a standard fraction and carried to a given power. This formula expresses the principle that the large species will have absolutely larger but relatively smaller brains than the small species.

However, groups that differ in intelligence (more properly known as *level of cerebral evolution*) have different formulae. And as we go up the scale, from marsupials, for example, to prosimians to monkeys, apes, and finally men, these formulae grow less and less accurate. As Jerison has discovered,[9] in the most highly evolved animals brain weight acts not as a single unit but as a sum of two units, only one of which varies allometrically as expected. The other is less influenced by body size, if at all.

The first unit, which in man constitutes only 10 to 12 per cent of the total, corresponds to virtually the total brain weight of a primitive mammal, such as an opossum. The second unit, on which human intelligence primarily depends, cannot vary in a simple, allometric way: whether a man is large or small, he needs a certain number of neurones and their connecting fibers to enable him to behave like an intelligent human being.

If a fossil man of modern body weight had a cranial capacity two thirds that of the modern range (assuming brain weight and cranial capacity to be roughly equivalent), the second unit of his brain weight would have been no more than 82 per cent of the whole. Therefore the differences in intelligence between *Homo erectus* and *Homo sapiens* were presumably greater than a gross comparison of brain sizes would indicate.

Also, in comparing individuals, we need not be greatly concerned with differences in brain size due to body size. In living men the allometric (or, one might say, body-weight sensitive) proportion of brain weight varies from about 150 grams in a 100-pound person to about 225 grams in a 150-pounder. This maximum difference of 75 grams is important principally in comparing male and female skulls.

The nineteen fossil skulls which are morphologically clearly differentiated from those of living persons have cranial capacities ranging from 775 cc. to 1,280 cc. Most modern skulls range from 1,200 cc. to 1,800 cc. The only two real series of *erectus* skulls that we have, those of Sinanthropus and Solo, which have six skulls each, range from 1,035 to 1,255 cc. (the figures are identical), and both have means of 1,095 cc. The only one of the other seven skulls

[9] H. J. Jerison: "Brain to Body Ratios and the Evolution of Intelligence," *Science*, Vol. 121, No. 3144 (1955), pp. 447–9.

which exceeds this range is that of Broken Hill, Rhodesia, with 1,280 cc. Because Broken Hill man was a large male, the 25 cc. excess could easily have been due to allometry.

The smallest skull that is morphologically excluded from the *erectus* category is also the oldest one that can be called *sapiens*. It is the Steinheim specimen, a small female cranium which has not yet been thoroughly studied and which needs reconstruction because it is crushed. Its capacity is variously given as anywhere from 1,170 to 1,290 cc. If the Steinheim woman weighed as little as 90 pounds, which is possible, she can be allowed an allometric deduction of 50 cc. in brain size in comparison to the others, and this places her near the top of the *erectus* brain-size range, or even over it. In any case, she is within the modern female range.

The approximate threshold between the brain-size ranges of *Homo erectus* and *Homo sapiens* can then be set at about 1,250 to 1,300 cc., with the expectation that some of the fossil *sapiens* skulls will, like many modern ones, be smaller. The designation of a fossil skull as *erectus* or *sapiens* depends on the total configuration, and not on brain size alone.

The Evidence of Cranial Form

IN GENERAL, *Homo erectus* crania are long and broad at the base and converge toward the top, both lengthwise and sidewise. *Homo sapiens* skulls bulge more in front and back and at the sides, because a larger brain is set on a proportionately smaller base. Conventional measurements designed for the living are less useful in describing these differences than a few special measurements taken on individual bones of the skulls of both species, *erectus* and *sapiens*, particularly in the sagittal line of the frontal, parietal, and occipital bones. Two principal measurements are taken on each bone: its external sagittal arc, i.e., its length measured along the center line of the skull; and its chord, i.e., the distance, in a straight line, between its two ends.

In the nineteen skulls considered to be *erectus*, the frontal is the longest of the three bones and the parietal the shortest. In modern men the parietal is characteristically the longest and the occipital the shortest. In some of the Neanderthals, which are excluded from the *erectus* category on the basis of brain size and some other features, the frontal bone may be longer than the parietal because the lengths of the brow ridges, which are heavy, are ordinarily included in frontal length.

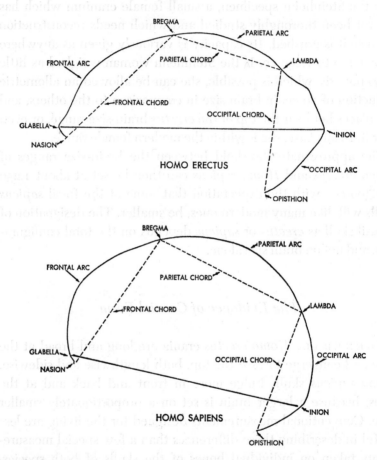

FIG. 46 SAGITTAL ARCS AND CHORDS IN *Homo erectus* AND *Homo sapiens*. One of the most reliable methods of distinguishing the two species of *Homo* is by comparing the three sets of arcs and chords of the skull in sagittal section. *Homo sapiens* is more curved in the frontal and parietal segments than *Homo erectus;* the opposite is true of the occipital segment.

For each of the three bones a sagittal curvature index may be computed by dividing the chord length times 100 by the length of the arc. The frontal bone has two curves, one extending from the root of the nose (nasion) over the crest of the brow ridges to the base of the forehead proper (glabellare) and a second from the base of the forehead to bregma—the place where the frontal and parietal bones meet at the crown of the skull. If the frontal bone is treated as a whole, these two curves tend to cancel each other out, so that no difference is seen between *H. erectus* and modern men. If, however, separate indices are calculated for the two parts of the frontal bone, the glabellar (brow ridge) part has an index of from about 75 to 85 in the *H. erectus* group, whereas in modern man this index runs from about 85 to nearly 100. In the other part of the frontal bone, the forehead section, the figures are nearly reversed, because modern men have relatively curved foreheads.

The index of curvature of the parietal bone is a better criterion, because the sagittal profile of this bone forms a simple arc. In the skulls called *erectus* in this study, the parietal chord is 93 to 97 per cent of the length of the arc; in modern skulls it runs from about 89 to 92 per cent. Little or no overlap in this ratio may be found between the successive species. In the occipital arc-chord index, the chord is 73 to 76 per cent of the arc length in the *erectus* skulls, as compared to a range of 79 to 86 per cent in *Homo sapiens*. Whereas the figures for *erectus* skulls indicate a true range, those for *sapiens* skulls indicate instead a range of means (statistical averages)—no figures for a range of individual *sapiens* skulls are obtainable. For this reason the two sets of figures are not quite comparable and the amount of overlapping between the two species in these indices is unknown.

These interspecific differences reflect principally the increase in brain height which occurred during human evolution, and the reduction of bony crests which took place as the frontal lobes grew over the eye sockets, rendering special protection above the eyes unnecessary, while the occipital crests were needed less and less as the head achieved a more perfect balance on the cervical vertebrae.

These arc-chord indices may be used along with absolute brain size as an additional set of criteria in sorting fossil skulls into the two species. Many other criteria are possible, including face breadth, forehead breadth, the dimensions of the bony eye sockets, and those of the cranial base, but because faces and bases are usually missing or defective in the oldest skulls, these constants are of less value than the three vault indices described above.[1]

The Evidence of Tooth Size

CONTRARY to what a number of textbooks say, we cannot make a blanket statement that human teeth have grown progressively smaller in the course of evolution, because this is true of some populations but not of others. Tooth reduction has moved at different rates in different lines. In certain lines, like that of the Bushmen, a rapid reduction can be traced, and in others, like that of the Australian aborigines, teeth are almost as big as ever. The size range in modern human teeth is very great but modern teeth as large as most of those of *Homo erectus* are exceptional.

We have 147 Sinanthropus teeth representing about 32 individuals, 20 Pithecanthropus teeth from at least three individuals, and 16 from the single Broken Hill cranium. Lower teeth only are also available from four mandibles found in North Africa: three at Ternefine in Algeria and one at Sidi Abd er-Rahman in Morocco. All four are old enough and morphologically suited to qualify as *Homo erectus*, if only tentatively.

With three exceptions, all the teeth listed above fall within the size ranges of the teeth of modern men, either in crown length or crown breadth, or in both dimensions. The three exceptions, which have both longer and broader crowns than any corresponding modern teeth, are the following: an upper canine in the palate of Pithecanthropus 4, from the Djetis beds of Java; a lower second premolar from the Pithecanthropus B mandibular fragment, found in the same beds; and another lower second premolar imbedded in mandible No. 2 from Ternefine. And that is all. No corresponding teeth attributed to *Homo sapiens* in this book are known to be as large as these three.

[1] R. Martin and K. Saller: *Lehrbuch der Anthropologie*, Third edition (Stuttgart: G. Fischer; 1957–1961), Vol. I, 1957, and Section 8, 1959.

F. Weidenreich: "The Skull of *Sinanthropus pekinensis*," PSNSD, No. 10 (1943), pp. 128–31.

G. Schwalbe: "Über die Beziehungen zwischen Innenform und Aussenform des Schädels," DAKM, Vol. 73 (1902), pp. 359–408 (for the frontal indices).

A Brain-Size to Tooth-Size Index

TOOTH SIZE is not the best criterion of human evolution. But teeth have, in a very general way, grown smaller while brains have been growing larger, and an index that mirrors these movements in opposite directions is more sensitive to change than either component. Two such indices can be made: a brain–palate index, already mentioned in connection with the Australopithecines,[2] and a brain–molar-size index devised for this occasion.[3]

TABLE 12

THE BRAIN-PALATE INDEX AND THE BRAIN-MOLAR INDEX

Brain-Palate Index				Brain-Molar Index		
Age-Rank	Subject	Index		Age-Rank	Subject	Index
(3)	Zinjanthropus	1.1	Australo-pithecus	(3)	Zinjanthropus	22
(2)	Swartkrans	1.2		(2)	Swartkrans	22
(1)	Sterkfontein	1.4		(1)	Sterkfontein	24
(4)	Pithecanthropus 4	1.4		(4)	Pithecanthropus 4	30
(5)	Sinanthropus	1.7	H. erectus	(5)	Sinanthropus	34
(9)	Broken Hill	1.7		(10)	Broken Hill	37
(11)	Tasmanian (mod.)	1.8		(6)	Steinheim	39
(7)	Gibraltar I	1.9		(8)	Skhul V	40
(8)	La Chapelle	1.9	H. sapiens	(9)	Combe Capelle	40
(6)	Steinheim	2.0		(7)	La Ferrassie	43
(10)	Combe Capelle	2.2		(12)	Crô-Magnon	43
(11)	Modern English	2.3		(11)	Grimaldi	43

In Table 12 the first two grades of each list are as inclusive as I could make them. However, the third grade, that of *Homo sapiens*, represents a selection, because of the enormous amount of calculations necessary to cover the entire field. In general, the columns follow the same order, from *Australopithecus* to *Homo erectus* to *Homo sapiens*. The *Homo sapiens* sections contain only

[2] This is a modified version of Sir Arthur Keith's index, explained on page 292 n.

[3] The brain-molar index is the cube root of cranial capacity divided by 100 times the square root of the sum of the crown areas (length x breadth) of the six upper (when possible) molar teeth. Or:

$$I = \sqrt[3]{cc}/\sqrt[2]{\Sigma\, l. \times b.\ (M^1, M^2, M^3)} \times 100$$

European and Near Eastern material except for the modern Tasmanians in the brain-palate index. They are listed to show that evolution proceeds at different rates in different lines, as the presence of Broken Hill man in the *erectus* category also indicates.

Had we enough patience, ingenuity, and time, it would be easy to invent dozens of other indices and ratios to finish staking out the *erectus-sapiens* frontier, but we have not. What has been presented will have to suffice. The moment has come to move on to a matter of almost equal theoretical importance, the further evolution of man once he had crossed the border into *Homo sapiens*.

Evolutionary Changes within Homo Sapiens: the Rise of the Chin

I F B Y *Homo sapiens* one thinks principally of living Europeans, and in particular of the articulated skeletons of urban paupers dangling from hooks in European and American lecture rooms, then indeed many differences may be found between some fossils that in this book have been labelled *Homo sapiens* and the mounted specimens just mentioned. But if we compare fossil men such as the Neanderthals with the peripheral, primitive populations of the world, the gap between living and fossil *sapiens* skeletons narrows, until it is closed. Brow ridges reach their peak on Melville Island, and mastoids their minimum in South Africa.

Chief among the hallmarks of the *sapiens* state in the works of many writers is the presence of a chin, despite the fact that chins have turned up in *Sugrivapithecus* (one of the Indian god-apes), Kromdraai, and gibbons. Many who sneer at phrenology believe that a prominent chin is a badge of courage, firmness, and decision. Consciously or unconsciously, those who make the chin a *sine qua non* of being *Homo sapiens* have fallen into a lexical trap. In English, French, and several other languages, the word *mental* means both "of or pertaining to the chin" (*mentum*), and "of or pertaining to the mind" (*mens*) [Webster]. We have no evidence that chins and I. Q.'s have anything in common, or that a Crô-Magnon could outwit a Neanderthal by virtue of his mental protuberance. The absence of a chin does not exclude any individual, living or dead, from the species *Homo sapiens*.

In fossil sequences modern-style chins appear toward the end of each phyletic line, starting at about 30,000 B.C. in Europe and somewhat later elsewhere. If we postulate that the chin arose through a single mutation which had to be spread by migration and mixture, or by migration and replacement, we have the Upper Paleolithic Europeans moving over the earth at nearly jet-age speed, and violate the evidence of geography and cultural history.

Chins obviously appeared in each population, if and when needed, in response to forces of a mechanical nature. Reduction in tooth size was an influential, but far from the only, factor. We know this because many modern peoples have teeth as large as those of their chinless ancestors. For example, the teeth of Heidelberg man, well preserved in the chinless Mauer mandible, are no larger than those of Upper Paleolithic Europeans.

According to E. L. DuBrul and his associates,[4] who have specialized in this subject, the chin seems to have been formed in response to a combination of separate but related changes in three organs or sets of organs: the four pairs of muscles that principally operate the lower jaw—temporals, masseters, lateral pterygoids, and medial pterygoids; the teeth; and the tongue, with its set of governing muscles. As the amount of chewing needed for survival diminished, the size of these four pairs of muscles could be reduced. A man could live out his life safely, from the nutritional point of view, with smaller teeth than his ancestors had. With smaller muscles and smaller teeth there was no further need for the mandible to remain large and massive, and, along with the palate, it eventually became smaller, and in particular, thinner and more delicate.

This general reduction in mandible and palate size produced crises for the medial pterygoid muscles and for the tongue. Each median pterygoid muscle is attached at one end to an area on the inside of the gonial angle of the mandible, and at the other end to a point on the palate just behind the third upper molar. As the rear attachments are farther apart than the forward attachments

[4] E. L. DuBrul and H. Sicher: *The Adaptive Chin* (Springfield, Ill.: Charles C Thomas; 1954).

DuBrul: *Evolution of the Speech Apparatus* (Springfield, Ill.: Charles C Thomas; 1958).

of these muscles, each time the pair of them is contracted as a unit, in order to draw the mandible back in chewing, strain is put on the center of the mandible, which must be strong; otherwise the two halves of the bone would break apart. In the process of evolution the front attachments of the medial pterygoid muscles migrated to the rear as the whole masticatory apparatus was re-

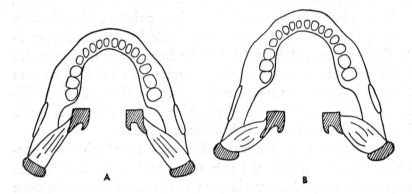

Fig. 47 THE LATERAL PTERYGOID MUSCLES AND THE CHIN. Of the five principal sets of paired muscles that move the lower jaw, the lateral (external) pterygoids have a special function which is related to the evolution of the chin. These muscles move the mandible forward in rotary chewing. They extend from the condyles of the mandible to the palatal bone, just behind the upper third molar teeth. When the jaws are at rest, these muscles are extended (A). But when the mandible is moved forward, they contract (B). Because the forward anchors of the muscles on the palatal bone lie inward from the condyles as well as forward, when the muscles are contracted (B) they pull the condyle inward as well as forward. If the jawbone were not very strong at its symphysis, it would snap like a wishbone. The shorter the mandible the stronger its symphysis, everything else being equal. When, in the evolutionary process, the jaw became shorter and the basin in which the tongue and other neighboring organs rest was lowered, a strong brace was still needed. That brace moved outward, with the formation of new bone (the mental trigonum), and became the chin. (Drawings after DuBrul and Sicher, 1954.)

duced, whereas the rear attachments remained in the same positions as before. This change widened the angle between the two muscles and increased the strain on the mid-line of the bone per unit of force exerted by the muscles themselves. As the function of these muscles is to move the jaw backward, there is no reason for it to have become reduced to the same extent as did the muscles that clamp the jaws together. Therefore the reduction in muscular effort exerted by the medial pterygoids was largely compensated for by the increase in strain on the chin area per unit of force.

In chinless primates this strain is taken by a brace on the inside of the mandible, in the form either of a general thickening or of a bar known as the simian shelf. In *Homo erectus* there is no simian shelf, but the bone is thick. Whereas the outer surface of the mandible is smoothly convex at this point, the inside is concavo-convex, and sloping strongly inward.

In a very large jaw, the presence of this brace permits space within the oral cavity for a tongue and its guiding muscles of the same size as those of living people. If the size of the mandible were to be reduced and its shape remain constant, then the tongue would be badly crowded, especially as the palate also became shorter and shallower. Therefore, in the course of the jaw reduction that took place in human evolution, the shape of the mandible had to change. Room had to be made for the tongue. The lower borders of the mandible moved outward, and the central brace migrated from the inside to the outside of the center line, producing the human chin.[5]

The tongue itself could not be reduced in size along with the teeth and jaws because we need it for talking, and we talk more than we swallow. This does not mean that the appearance of a chin made speech possible, only that it kept speech from becoming difficult as the jaws grew smaller. The absence of a chin in *Homo erectus* does not tell us whether or not he could speak, or, if he could, when he began to do so. Only through a careful study of the nervous system can these questions be answered, and in *Homo erectus* such a study is difficult if not impossible.

A reduction in the amount of chewing also affected some of the cranial bones. As the temporal muscles shrank, the zygomatic arches under which they move grew less flaring and the face became narrower. Thick skull bones and heavy braces, including the brow ridges, were no longer useful for survival as men invented more efficient ways of killing than clubbing people over the head. With (or possibly without) a change in endocrine balance, skulls

[5] It is easy to test this hypothesis. For example, I have measured the cubic capacities of shellacked casts of the Heidelberg and Crô-Magnon mandibles. Both are large. The former is chinless; the latter has a prominent chin. To the bottom and rear of each specimen I attached a cut-out floor of waxed cardboard, and then I filled each with water up to the level of the tooth line. Each contained 5.5 fluid ounces, or about 163 cc.

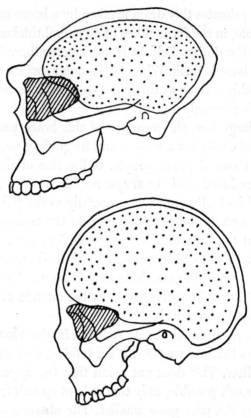

F<small>IG</small>. 48   H<small>OW</small> B<small>ROW</small> R<small>IDGES</small> P<small>ROTECT THE</small> E<small>YES AGAINST</small> B<small>LOWS</small>. In *Homo erectus*
(above), the eye sockets lie in front of the brain case, and brow ridges are needed
to protect the eyes from blows. In *Homo sapiens* (below), the eye sockets lie under
the brain case, which affords the eyes the same protection. This figure also illustrates the difference in brain shape, in the lateral view, between *Homo
erectus* (based on Pithecanthropus 4) and *Homo sapiens* (a brachycranial Aus-
trian skull). (Drawings after Moss and Young, 1960. Their drawing is based on
Weidenreich: *The Skull of Sinanthropus*, Fig. 270 B & C.)

could become thinner and brow ridges smaller by the usual
biological process that prunes organs and structures which are no
longer needed. Like tooth reduction, these changes take time, and
some living populations are closer to *Homo erectus* in these respects than are others.

Lines and Subspecies of Fossil Men: the Evidence of Teeth

I F   W E could find a few specimens of *Homo erectus* and *Homo
sapiens* frozen in the ice of the Mindel glaciation, we might learn

how ancient are the modern variations in skin color, beard and body hair development, and hair form. But as such a windfall is less than likely, we must content ourselves with the racially variable parts of the human body which are available. These parts, bones and teeth, indicate that from the very beginning the men of the Lower Pleistocene, whether called *erectus* or *sapiens*, differed from each other regionally in features and anatomical details that can still be recognized in living men. Among them are details of tooth anatomy.

In addition to variability, durability, and abundance, teeth offer still another great advantage for the student of race. They are just as firmly controlled genetically as perishable blood groups and fingerprints. No environmentalist, however biased, can demonstrate that racial peculiarities in dental details are not strictly hereditary.

Tooth size is not of primary consequence in determining evolutionary grades, but tooth form is of major importance in tracing racial lines of descent.[6] In fact, so great are the differences in tooth

[6] Following is a short bibliography on racial variations in teeth.

M. deTerra: *Beiträge zu einer Odontographie der Menschenrassen* (Berlin: Berliner Verlagsanstalt; 1905).

T. D. Campbell: "Dentition and Palate of the Australian Aboriginal," *PKSF*, No. 1 (1925).

M. Hellman: "Racial Characters in Human Dentition," *PAPS*, Vol. 67, No. 2 (1928), pp. 157–74.

M. R. Drennan: "The Dentition of a Bushman Tribe," *ASAM*, Vol. 24, Pt. 1 (1929), pp. 61–87.

A. A. Dahlberg: "The Dentition of the American Indian," in W. S. Laughlin, ed.: *Papers on the Physical Anthropology of the American Indian* (New York: Viking Fund; 1951).

I. Gleiser and E. E. Hunt: "The Permanent Mandibular First Molar, Its Calcification, Eruption, and Decay," *AJPA*, Vol. 13, No. 2 (1955), pp. 253–84.

M. Klatsky: "The Incidence of Six Anomalies of the Teeth and Jaws," *HB*, Vol. 28 (1956), pp. 420–8.

G. W. Lasker and M. M. C. Lee: "Racial Traits in the Human Teeth," *JFS*, Vol. 2, No. 4 (1956), pp. 401–19.

C. F. A. Moorrees: *The Aleut Dentition* (Cambridge, Mass.: Harvard University Press; 1957).

J. C. M. Shaw: *The Teeth, the Bony Palate, and the Mandible in Bantu Races of South Africa* (London: John Bale Sons & Danielsson; 1931).

Shaw: "Cusp Development on the Second Lower Molars in Bantu and Bushmen," *AJPA*, Vol. 11 (1927), pp. 97–100.

Shaw: "Taurodont Teeth in South African Races," *JAnat.*, Vol. 62 (1928), pp. 476–96.

morphology which first appeared in the earliest fossil specimens of each area, and which have largely persisted to this day, that the time of separation of the different lines of descent in the genus *Homo* must be set back to a period of which we have no record. I make this statement because the rates of change in tooth morphology are well known from the study of other animal genera. Some of the differences that I shall describe are both progressive, having evolved by succession, and racial, having evolved by branching, whereas others are racial only.

These variations include: (1) differences in the relative sizes of individual teeth or groups of teeth (incisors, canines, premolars, and molars) in the same tooth row of either the upper or the lower jaw; (2) differences in the length of the cheek teeth (from the first premolar through the third molar) of the upper jaw in proportion to the anterior skull length as measured from basion (the forward lip of the foramen magnum) to nasion; (3) differences in the crown patterns of the various teeth; and (4) differences in the roots and pulp cavities.

In the Australopithecines, including Zinjanthropus, the molars and premolars are very large in comparison to the canines and incisors. This disproportion is not found in any human population, either of *Homo erectus* or of *Homo sapiens*. In this respect human teeth resemble ape teeth more than the teeth of their fellow Hominids.

Among living Mongoloids the front teeth (incisors and canines) are even larger, compared to the cheek teeth (premolars and molars), than in other racial lines. The Australoids vary in the opposite direction, not because their front teeth are small, but because their cheek teeth are particularly large. Among Mongoloids the third molar is often congenitally lacking in one or more tooth rows; a fourth molar turns up now and then among Australian aborigines. Among Caucasoids the upper lateral incisor is usually much smaller than the upper medial incisor, whereas in

---

P. O. Pedersen: "The East Greenland Dentition," *MOG*, Vol. 142, No. 3 (1949), pp. 1–256.

E. K. Tratman: "A Comparison of the Teeth of People [of] Indo-European Racial Stock with [Those of] the Mongoloid Racial Stock," *DR*, Vol. 70 (1950), Nos. 2–3, pp. 63–88.

other races the difference in size between these two teeth is much less.

The second set of variations is not limited to the teeth, but compares the combined mesiodistal length of the upper cheek teeth to a sagittal dimension on the skull, the basion-nasion chord. The formula, length of the premolar-molar row × 100 ÷ BN length, is known as Flower's index, after its inventor, H. W. Flower, who was a great zoologist accustomed to classifying mammals in general and not limited to the minuscule zoological realm of man.[7] He divided the range of his index into three parts: below and including 41.9 per cent is microdont; from 42.0 through 43.9 per cent is mesodont; and 44.0 per cent and upward is megadont.

TABLE 13
FLOWER'S INDEX

	Males	Females	Males & Females	
Polynesians	40.1%	. . .	. . .	
Non-British Europeans	40.5	41.6	41.3	
Ancient Egyptians	40.8	41.2	41.0	Microdont
British	41.0	41.6	41.3	
Central & South Indians	41.4	. . .	. . .	
Bushmen, South Africa *	. . .	. . .	42.4	
Chinese	42.6	. . .	. . .	
American Indians	42.8	. . .	. . .	Mesodont
African Negroes	43.2	44.6	43.9	
Javanese & Sumatrans	43.3	. . .	. . .	
Melanesians	44.2	. . .	. . .	
Andamanese	44.4	46.5	45.5	Megadont
Australian Aborigines	44.8	46.1	45.5	
Tasmanians	47.5	48.7	48.1	

* A composite of 29 individuals from four series. Drennan: op. cit.

On the whole the Caucasoids are microdont, the Bushmen and Mongoloids mesodont, and the Australoids and their Melanesian and Negrito neighbors and kinsmen megadont. The Polynesians are classified as microdont because, although their teeth are large, their basion-nasion chord is very long. The Negroes of Africa

[7] H. W. Flower: "On the Size of Teeth as a Character of Race," *JRAI*, Vol. 14 (1885), pp. 183–6.
de Terra: op. cit., pp. 183–6.

straddle the mesodont-megadont line, with the males on one side and the females on the other.

Racial Variations in the Form and Structure of Teeth

THE MORPHOLOGICAL differences in the crowns, roots, and internal structure of human teeth constitute an enormously complex subject to which a number of specialists have devoted their lives, and which can only be summarized here, with little detail. On Table 14 are listed a few notations concerning the

TABLE 14
RACIAL VARIATIONS IN TOOTH FORM

	Caucasoid	Mongoloid	Australoid	Negro	Capoid
Shoveling	rare	extreme			probably rare*
Ridging		present		common	
Premolar Cone		present			
Cingulum (Collar)		rare			
Wrinkling		rare		rare	
Enamel Pearl	Ainu	present			present
Enamel Extensions		present			
Short Roots		present			
Extra Roots		present			
Taurodontism	rare	present		rare	rare
Cusp Formula	4–4–3 / 5–4–4	4–4–3 / 5–4–5	4–4–4 / 5–4–5	4–4–4 / 5–5–5	4–4–3 / 5–5–5
Missing Third Molars	—20%†	—70%	—13%	3% ?	10% ?
Fourth Molars			rare		
6 & 7 Cusps	3%	—20%	37%	16% ?	?
Carabelli's Cusp	common	rare	rare		

* Common among full-sized Capoid skulls, but not, apparently, among modern Bushmen, whose teeth are usually too worn to tell.
† Hellman (1928) cited a figure of 49 per cent for a series of ninth century A.D. Hungarian skulls, but we do not know how many of them were Mongoloid.

variations in fifteen items of dental morphology in the five major human subspecies postulated in Chapter 1. The term Negro is used instead of Congoid, because we are speaking of African Negroes only. For them and for the Capoids (Bushmen) less abundant and less complete data are available than for the other three groups. The Caucasoids include Europeans, Near Easterners, Hindus, and Tamils. In dental morphology these groups are all

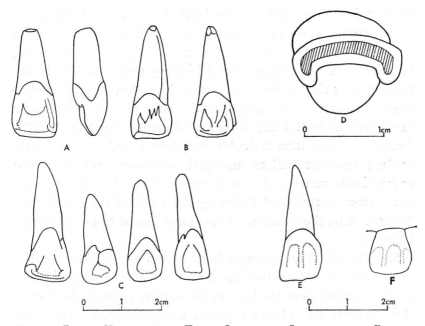

Fig. 49 Racial Variations in Tooth Structure: Shoveling and Ridging. These drawings represent only upper median incisors. A. Two views of a Sinanthropus tooth, with raised edges and a basal bulb or tubercle. (After Weidenreich, 1937.) B. Two Sinanthropus teeth with incurved edges and basal tubercles in the form of teats or swollen ridges. (After Weidenreich, 1937.) C. Four modern Aleut teeth with raised or wrap-around edges, but without basal tubercles. D. A shoveled incisor, partly worn, seen from the occlusal view and greatly enlarged. The dentine is cross-hatched. Note that in the shoveling phenomenon the thickness of the enamel remains constant; the dentine is shoveled as well as the enamel. (After Tratman, 1950.) E. A modern tooth showing a medial ridge, commonest among Negroes but also found in other races, including Europeans. (After Weidenreich, 1937.) F. An Upper Paleolithic European tooth from the so-called Negroid youth of Grimaldi, with double ridging and without raised edges. This tooth form is also seen in other European skulls, particularly among Neanderthals. Its presence does not necessarily make the Grimaldi youth Negroid.

alike. The Ainu have been included with the Caucasoids for a few features. The Mongoloids include eastern Asiatics, Malayans, Indonesians, Polynesians, Eskimo, and American Indians. As a whole they are alike, except that among the Polynesians some of the typical Mongoloid features are attenuated; among some local American Indian populations the usual Mongoloid features have beome exaggerated; and among at least two isolated Eskimo populations local tooth patterns have arisen.

Shoveling is a trait that affects the incisors and canines only, and the upper teeth, as a rule, more than the lower ones. In a mild form of shoveling the inside lateral edges of the tooth are bent backward to form a pair of rims, leaving a concavity between. In more extreme cases the edges are wrapped around to such an extent that their borders face inward, and such a tooth looks, in section, like a Gothic capital C lying prone, ⊂⊃. In the prone-C type the borders can meet at the root end and part company halfway up, like the flower of a calla lily. Or they can be fused, and the tooth is tubular or barrel-shaped (see Plate XXIV). Another extreme form is double-shoveling, found in some southwestern American Indians; among them a concavity on the front or labial side matches the usual one on the back or lingual side. For laymen accustomed to seeing the teeth of Caucasoids and Negroes only, these extreme forms have almost to be seen to be believed.

Shoveling is often accompanied by from one to three teatlike protrusions rising from the base of the crown or by vertical ridges or ribs running from the base to the cutting edge on the lingual side. As teats and ridges are part of a single complex, they have been so listed. Among Negroes one often finds them present without shoveling. In South Africa, shoveling turns up in Bantu teeth, possibly as a result of mixture of Bantu and Bushmen.

Among Asiatic Mongoloids and American Indians shoveling reaches a level of 90 to 100 per cent. Among many groups of northern Europeans and among native white Americans a simple, unspectacular form of shoveling, involving merely a raising of borders, reaches an incidence of 10 per cent or more, but this figure may be less than the frequency of the gene or genes that cause it. In children born in Japan of American fathers and Japanese mothers, the Caucasoid form, being a chisel-like nonshoveled incisor, appears in the majority.[8]

What I have called in Table 14 a *premolar cone* is a rod or cone or teatlike excrescence of enamel protruding from the center of the groove in the middle of the occlusal surface of a premolar, more often mandibular but sometimes maxillary, and usually in the second premolar. When it is present in the first premolar it is

[8] K. Hanihara: "Studies on the Deciduous Dentition of the Japanese and Japanese-American Hybrids," ZZ, Vol. 63 (1954), pp. 168–85; Vol. 64 (1955), pp. 63–82, 95–116; Vol. 65 (1956), pp. 67–87; Vol. 65 [sic] (1957), pp. 151–64. After G. W. Lasker: "Recent Advances in Physical Anthropology," BRA, 1959, pp. 1–36.

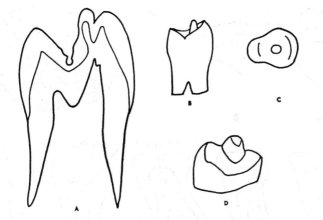

Fig. 50 Racial Variations in Tooth Structure: the Premolar Cone. A. A first premolar of an American Indian, in section and greatly enlarged. B. The same tooth, side view. C. The same tooth, occlusal view. D. An Aleut premolar with premolar cone. The premolar cone is a Mongoloid peculiarity. A cone rising from the center of an upper first premolar, it is visible in young teeth only, as it is soon broken off or worn down. As A shows, it consists of both dentine and enamel. It is disadvantageous because its destruction leads to a premature exposure of dentine. (Drawings A, B, C after Tratman, 1950; D after Moorrees, 1957.)

also to be seen in the second. Tratman (1950) called it a "dilated composite odontome," too technical a term for this book; and Pedersen (1949) labelled it an "enamel pearl," not to be recommended because the term is already in use to describe another structure. In any case, the premolar cone, owing to its position, is soon worn down, and can be detected with any conviction only in newly erupted teeth. Like several other bizarre dental details, it is confined to the Mongoloid subspecies.

A cingulum is a collarlike rim about the base of the crown of any tooth except the incisors. It may be partial or complete. It again is a Mongoloid peculiarity, although it may be expected in some very ancient teeth of other lines. Wrinkling is another Mongoloid phenomenon, commoner in ancient than in modern specimens. In some of the Mongoloid molars the surface, instead of being smooth and flat, is broken up into fine relief by a pattern of wrinkles. This is also a characteristic of both Australopithecine and orangutan teeth and may be considered an ancient feature.

An enamel pearl is a pearl-like excrescence on the labial side of a molar tooth (see Plate XXIV). It is common among Ainu, occurring with a frequency of 30 per cent, and among Eskimo. It

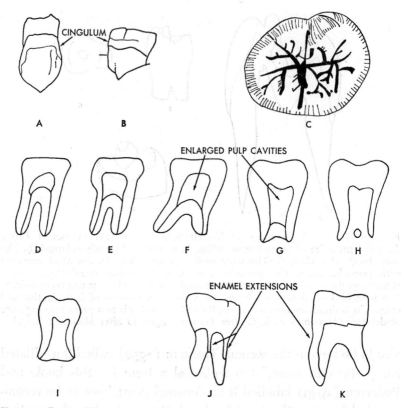

Fig. 51   Racial Variations in Tooth Structure: the Cingulum, Wrinkling, Taurodontism, and Enamel Extensions. A. Cingulum in an upper canine of Sinanthropus. B. Cingulum in a lower molar of Sinanthropus. C. Wrinkling in the crown of a third molar of Sinanthropus. D–H. Molar pulp cavities in a series of teeth from cynodont to taurodont. I. An X-ray of a taurodont tooth. J–K. Enamel extensions on the roots of molar teeth, Sinanthropus. A cingulum is an enamel collar at the base of the crown of a tooth. It may run all the way around or, more frequently in man, only part way. Wrinkling, like shoveling and the premolar cone, involves both enamel and dentine. Teeth which have this feature are wrinkled when cut, and the wrinkles soon wear down. Its function is unknown, but it is found in the molars, and sometimes other teeth, of apes, Australopithecines, and men. It is commonest among Mongoloids. Taurodontism is a neotenous condition of the molars and sometimes the premolars. The pulp cavities of taurodont teeth become enlarged because the roots fail to grow to fully adult height; the underside of the root area fails to develop completely. Thus the pulp cavity of the tooth is elongated downward from above. As the crowns wear, the dentine hardens, and the tooth can be worn down to the gums and even onto the roots. D is the molar of a European with normal pulp cavities. Such a tooth is called cynodont (dog-toothed). E is the molar of a Bushman-Bantu hybrid, with slight taurodontism (bull-toothedness). F is a tooth from the Heidelberg jaw, with medium taurodontism; and G and H are teeth from the jaw of a teen-aged Krapina youth, with extreme taurodontism. His molars had erupted at an early and incomplete stage of root development. I is the drawing of an X-ray of a taurodont tooth. Enamel extensions, found among Mongoloid teeth particularly, are extensions of the enamel of the crown onto the roots. In some cases the enamel goes under the gap between the roots like a cinch strap; in others it extends down the outside

has also been found in other Mongoloids and among Bushmen. Among Mongoloids the lower border of the enamel-covered portion of the molar crown dips down, in many cases, onto the neck of the tooth and onto its root. In other races the lower border of the enamel forms a straight line. When the border of the enamel dips down, it forms what is called an enamel extension.

The roots of Mongoloid teeth also tend to be short for the size of their crown; this is also characteristic of Lapps in Europe. Mongoloid molars also tend to have one or more extra roots in the forward part of the molars. They also lead the others in the frequency with which upper third molars are congenitally missing— up to 70 per cent in some populations—whereas this progressive trait is much rarer in all the others. The opposite tendency, to have four molars on any one side of either jaw, is rare everywhere but commonest among Australian aborigines.

In the evolution of the horse and other grazing animals teeth with long crowns, or rather high ones, which would give more years of wear than those with short or low crowns, became prevalent through the usual process of natural selection. In human beings, for whom the wear on the molars and premolars is critical, the tooth had to grow larger or its crown had to become higher. In the Australopithecines, particularly in Kromdraai and Zinjanthropus, the molars and premolars simply became huge. The genus *Homo* took the alternative solution, known as taurodontism, or bull-toothedness. Ordinary molars are cynodont (dog-toothed).

As Gleiser and Hunt (1955) discovered, taurodontism is an infantile character, a delay in the growth rhythm of the roots and inner crown structure of a tooth. In the forming molar or premolar, before it has erupted, the occlusal surface of the crown has already assumed its adult form but the pulp cavity is much larger than it will be later, under normal circumstances of growth, and the roots have failed to separate and to become defined on their inner surfaces. The roots are more or less barrel-shaped. If this infantile form is retained into later life, the large pulp cavity reach-

---

of the root to its tip. Enamel extentions give the tooth additional wear, particularly when chewed on the side. The most notable examples of these are among Sinanthropus teeth and those of the East Greenland Eskimo. (Drawings A, B, C, J–K after Weidenreich, 1937; D–H after J. M. Shaw, 1927, and Tratman, 1950; I after Tratman, 1950.)

ing well down into the combined or undifferentiated root may become an asset. As the enamel wears off, the pulp hardens to dentine, and the wear may be carried well past the point of danger in an ordinary tooth.

As one would expect, taurodont teeth are characteristic of Mongoloids, particularly of such hard-chewing Mongoloids as Eskimos. They are infrequent in living Caucasoids, but we shall encounter them in certain hard-chewing dead ones. Among Negroes they seem to occur only among southern Bantus, who are part Bushman anyway, whereas among the Capoids they are characteristic only of full-sized ancestors of the Bushmen unearthed by archaeologists.

In contrast to the dental details that we have so far summarized, the pattern taken by the cusps on the crowns of the upper and lower molars, and the numbers of these cusps on each tooth, have attracted by far the most attention from tooth experts concerned with human evolution and racial variation. The bibliography is legion, because it includes the efforts of paleontologists, zoologists, and dentists as well as of anthropologists.

As Gregory long ago demonstrated, the primordial crown pattern of human lower molars is a set of three grooves in the form of a Y lying on its side, with its tail pointing forward and its two arms pointing to the rear. In each obtuse angle are stationed two cusps, and in the acute angle a fifth cusp. This pattern, known as Y-5, is also called the *Dryopithecus pattern* because it was characteristic of that family of Hominoids from which we may all have been descended—the Dryopithecinae (see Chapter 6).

In the Australopithecines this pattern was altered by the addition of extra cusps and grooves, apparently to compensate for the added burden of chewing and grinding imposed by the coarse diet necessary for life on the ground. In the earliest specimens of *Homo* yet found, which we shall study in the next four chapters, no increase in molar crown complexity comparable to that of the Australopithecines can be observed. Some teeth show the opposite tendency, a reduction in complexity of the original Dryopithecus pattern. In all modern races, reduction has proceeded in nearly all the molar teeth, in varying degrees.

In modern teeth the molar crown patterns have been simpli-

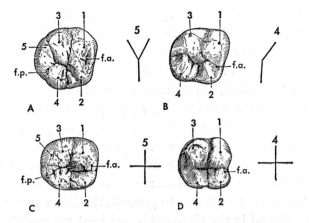

Fig. 52   Lower Molar Crown Patterns. Four stages of development of lower molar teeth, illustrating the different changes from the Dryopithecus to the most advanced pattern. (A) Dryopithecus pattern indicated by Y5, meaning primitive system of grooves and cusp formula. (B) Modified Dryopithecus pattern indicated by Y4, meaning cusp formula reduced to four and groove system primitive with the loss of the posterior limb of the Y. (C) Primitive cusp formula retained but groove system changed to cruciform, the sign being +5. (D) Cusp formula and groove system changed, sign +4. (f.a.) fovea anterior; (f.p.) fovea posterior. (Drawings and captions from Milo Hellman: "Racial Characters in Human Dentition," *PAPS*, Vol. 62, No. 2 (1928), p. 165. Courtesy of the American Philosophical Society.)

fied in two ways: (1) the groove pattern has changed from a lazy Y (to use a Western cattle-branding term) to a simple cross, +; (2) the number of cusps has dropped from five to four, or even to three or two. With five or four cusps and Y's and crosses, four combinations are possible: Y-5, Y-4, +5, and +4. Because of the symbol used, cross-5 and cross-4 are usually referred to as "plus five" and "plus four," which is confusing because *plus* implies number rather than form.

In every race for which pertinent data are available, crown-pattern reduction is greater in the upper than in the lower jaw, and only in the lower molars have both the groove patterns and the cusps numbers been systematically examined. In every race studied, the first lower molar has the original, Dryopithecus, Y-5 pattern in the majority of instances. In Caucasoids its frequency is about 75 per cent, and in all other races it is between 95 and 100 per cent. This is our most conservative molar tooth.

Y-4 is a rare pattern. In Europeans it appears in about 12 per cent of the first molars, and in African Negroes in the same percentage of the second molars. Otherwise, its appearance is sporadic. From the standpoint of reducing the mesiodistal length of a molar crown, Y-4 is less efficient than the cross pattern, and both +5 and +4 greatly outnumber it in all races.

In all races studied, +4 outnumbers +5 in the second molars. However, in the third molars the +5 pattern outnumbers the +4 pattern in all populations studied except the Europeans, Chinese, and some Eskimo groups. Considering the three lower molars as a whole, only among the Caucasoids do we find more teeth with four cusps than with five, and more groove patterns in the form of a cross than with Y patterns. In general, the lower molar crowns are most reduced in the Caucasoids and least reduced in African Negroes and Australian aborigines. Among the Bushmen, whose teeth are very small, we find the highest ratio of five-cusped lower molars. Unfortunately, we do not know the frequencies of their groove patterns.

In the upper molars all races have a majority of four-cusped crowns, nearly 100 per cent, in the first molars. In the second molars, however, racial differences in the number of cusps appear; among Caucasoids and Mongoloids three cusps are seen in 30 to 42 per cent of these teeth, whereas in Negroes the ratio decreases to 22 per cent and in Australian aborigines and Bushmen all upper second molars are apparently four-cusped. In the third molars more than half the teeth have three cusps among Caucasoids, Mongoloids, and Bushmen, whereas among Negroes and Australian aborigines more than half have four cusps.

From this statistical exercise we see that reduction in the crown pattern is most advanced among Caucasoids, least advanced among Negroes and Australian aborigines, and intermediate among Mongoloids. However, among Mongoloids and Bushmen the third molar is much more reduced in comparison to the first and second molars than in the other races, including the Caucasoid.

From the over-all cusp formula given on Table 14, it is apparent that the Caucasoid lower molar crowns are the most reduced of all, and those of the Negroes the least reduced. Among the Mongoloids and Bushmen the reduction is concentrated in the upper third molar.

In all races there is a tendency for the upper third molar to be congenitally absent, but this tendency is most marked in the Mongoloids, particularly the Eskimos. Fourth molars are rare in all races, but are found most often among Australian aborigines. They too lead in the number of teeth having six or seven cusps, which is one or two more than the standard number for the Dryopithecus pattern.

Among Caucasoids, and only sporadically in other races, a special feature known as Carabelli's cusp (described in Chapter 7; see Plate XXIV), is seen; among Europeans its frequency is as high as 40 per cent. Carabelli's cusp is an accessory cusp situated on the front part of the inside or tongue-surface of upper molars.

Carabelli's cusp is situated below the level of the surface of the crown when the tooth is freshly erupted and unworn. When the tooth has been worn down to its level, this accessory flange serves to widen the occlusal surface of the molar and thus slow down further wear. In this way it performs the same function as taurodontism in prolonging the useful life of the tooth. It is commonest on upper first molars and rarest on upper third molars. It is only found on upper second molars if it is also present on upper first molars; and when it turns up on upper third molars it is also to be seen on the other two molars of the row.

In summarizing this survey of racial tooth morphology, we are struck with several facts. The teeth of Caucasoids are plain and simple, with a single peculiarity, Carabelli's cusp. Of all races the Caucasoids show the greatest over-all reduction in tooth-pattern details, although their teeth are not the smallest in the world. Negro and Australian aboriginal teeth are also relatively simple, although less reduced than those of Caucasoids; indeed Negro teeth seem to be most like those of primitive Caucasoids.

Mongoloid teeth, however, are far from plain. They are decorated with a myriad of complicated details. They are quite different from those of the three races just mentioned, with several variations and extremes of shoveling; with premolar cones; wrinkling of molar enamel; enamel extensions onto the roots; enamel pearls; short, taurodont roots; and a tendency for the upper third molars to be greatly reduced in crown pattern as well as in size, or even to be congenitally absent. Mongoloid teeth are not so much primitive as they are deviant from those of the rest of *Homo sapiens*. Bushmen teeth, although very small, resemble those of Mongoloids morphologically more than they do the teeth of Caucasoids, Negroids, or Australoids.

Were one to classify human races on the basis of teeth alone, it would be easy to place the Mongoloids and Capoids in one category and all the other races in another. Differences in the incisors and canines alone, without reference to the cheek teeth, widely separate the Mongoloids from the Caucasoids, and as we shall presently show, these racial differences in tooth form go back as far as we can trace the ancestors of man.

Facial Flatness as a Criterion of Race

A GENERAL peculiarity of Mongoloid dentition is that the accent is on the front part of the mouth. The incisors and canines are large and elaborately braced for hard work, whereas the molars taper off rapidly from the first to the third, and the latter is often missing. Along with this forward orientation of the teeth goes a forward stance of the temporal and masseter muscles which furnish most of their motor power. In the forward part of their area of attachment on the frontal bone the temporals invade the forehead on each side, above the outer halves of the orbits, thus making the forehead look narrow, and incidentally pressing the outer portions of the orbits from behind and making them relatively shallow. As part of the same complex, the masseters are hung from forward-jutting zygomatic bones, the well-known "high cheek-bones" of the Mongoloids.

All these specialties, in combination with a low-bridged nasal skeleton, give the Mongoloids, and the Bushmen as well, an appearance of facial flatness superficially reminiscent of the apes and Australopithecines. In the case of the Australopithecines this resemblance is superficial because those hominids had very large cheek teeth and small front teeth. At the other extreme, Caucasoids have pointed, sometimes beaklike faces which remind one of some of the lower primates, particularly the South American monkeys, and of Proconsul.

Apart from the teeth, the degree of facial flatness is probably the best criterion of race which the skull offers for study because it seems to have little to do with evolutionary grades. With this in mind, T. L. Woo and G. M. Morant published, in 1934, the results of their monumental study of facial flatness in 131 series of skulls, totaling 5,788 specimens, and covering all major racial groups.[9] In order to describe this racial criterion accurately, they devised four indices, each based on the measurement of a chord between matched points on either side of the facial skeleton and the subtense drawn between the center of this chord and a given point on the sagittal line of the facial skeleton in front of that chord. The formula for each index is: subtense $\times$ 100 $\div$ chord. The four chords and their subtenses are as follows.

(1)   *The internal biorbital chord*, that is, the distance between the points on the outer edges of the orbits where the frontal and malar bones meet. The subtense used with this chord is that formed by bisecting the triangle created by joining these two points to nasion.

(2)   *The simotic chord*, that is, the minimum horizontal breadth of the paired nasal bones. The point used for the subtense is the spot on the nasal suture lying exactly between and in front of them.

(3)   *The midorbital chord*, that is, the distance between the points on the lower border of the orbit where malar and maxilla meet. The subtense is to the lower tip of the suture between the nasal bones.

(4)   *The "face breadth" of Martin*, that is, the chord between the points on the zygomatic-maxillary suture which are lowest in reference to the eye-ear plane. The subtense is to alveon, the point on the outer sagittal edge of the maxilla between the upper lateral incisors.

The indices derived from these four sets of chords and subtenses are called: (1) *frontal index of facial flatness*, (2) *simotic index*, (3) *rhinial index of facial flatness*, and (4) *premaxillary index of facial flatness*. Table 15 shows the numbers of series and ranges of means for Caucasoids, Mongoloids, Australoids and

[9] T. L. Woo and G. M. Morant: "A Biometric Study of the 'Flatness' of the Facial Skeleton in Man," *Biometrika*, Vol. 26 (1934), pp. 196–250.

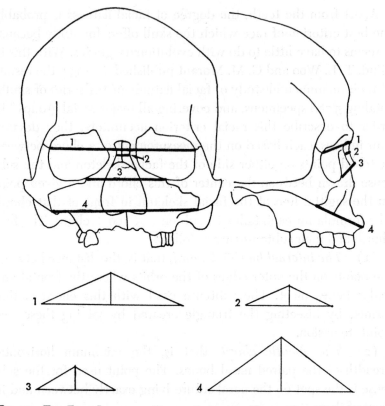

Fig. 53 The Four Indices of Facial Flatness. *Above:* The chords (left) and subtenses (right) from which the four indices of facial flatness are calculated. The order is from top to bottom: No. 1 is the frontal index, No. 2 the simotic, No. 3 the rhinial, and No. 4 the premaxillary. *Below:* The chords and subtenses laid out. Number 2, because of its small size, is scaled three times the size of the others. The skull is that of a Vedda of Ceylon. Its indices of facial flatness are: (1) 22; (2) 38; (3) 30; and (4) 34. These figures identify it as Caucasoid.

Oceanic Negroids, African Negroes and Capoids. In the Caucasoid segment the Ainu and the ancient Egyptians have been listed separately because they show a number of differences from the others. The combination of India and Ceylon (including Veddas) has also been listed separately, mainly to indicate that their inhabitants are essentially the same in these indices as the Europeans and Near Easterners. In the Mongoloid segment the Nepalese are given separate status because they are of mixed Caucasoid and Mongoloid ancestry. In the same way, an ancient Nubian series has been separated from the Negroes because the Nubians were partly Caucasoid.

TABLE 15

THE FOUR INDICES OF FACIAL FLATNESS
OF WOO AND MORANT

	No. Ser.	#1 Frontal I	#2 Simotic I	#3 Rhinial I	#4 Premax. I
Ainu	1	17.2	36.6	32.2	34.0
Ancient Egyptians	6	17.4–18.3	32.1–41.1	30.3–40.3	35.8–37.9
India and Ceylon	9	19.6–21.0	37.5–49.1	35.4–43.5	35.3–38.4
Europe and West Asia	32	17.4–20.5	40.0–53.0	37.8–48.6	33.4–37.2
Asiatic, Mongoloid and Eskimo	23	14.1–16.5	25.5–34.6	25.4–33.3	31.4–35.8
Nepalese	1	16.9	37.7	31.5	33.1
American Indians	6	16.7–17.6	29.5–49.0	32.4–39.4	34.3–36.0
Polynesians	11	16.4–18.0	36.7–43.4	31.5–39.4	34.3–37.0
Australians and Tasmanians	7	17.6–18.7	35.5–44.4	29.9–37.2	38.7–42.3
Papuans and Melanesians	9	17.2–18.4	26.1–39.8	31.1–37.4	35.7–37.9
Negritos, Philippines and Andamans	4	15.8–17.2	23.9–35.5	28.1–34.2	34.1–34.7
Nubians	2	17.7–18.3	30.2–36.3	33.6–34.6	34.5–35.3
Negroes	14	17.0–18.1	18.6–33.6	24.2–30.8	34.1–39.1
Bushmen and Hottentots	4	15.5–17.0	16.9–29.3	19.2–27.9	34.1–35.8

This table can be most easily understood in terms of the four charts on page 368. They show clearly that, in the first three indices, the Caucasoids occupy an extreme position with by far the most pointed, or least flat, faces of all. In the first three indices the Caucasoid means do not even overlap those of the Bushmen-Hottentots and Asiatic Mongoloids and Eskimos. Only in the fourth index do the Caucasoids occupy an intermediate position, because this index is influenced by prognathism and thus tends to reflect evolutionary grade more than the other three do. In this index, as in so many other criteria, the Mongoloids and Bushmen stand at one extreme; but instead of the Caucasoids it is the Australian aborigines and Tasmanians who stand at the other. The Caucasoids and Polynesians are located in the middle of the scale.

In summarizing the information yielded by these four indices of facial flatness, we find that some races are far more deviant from a standard, generalized *Homo sapiens* face form than are

WOO'S AND MORANT'S FOUR INDICES OF FACIAL FLATNESS

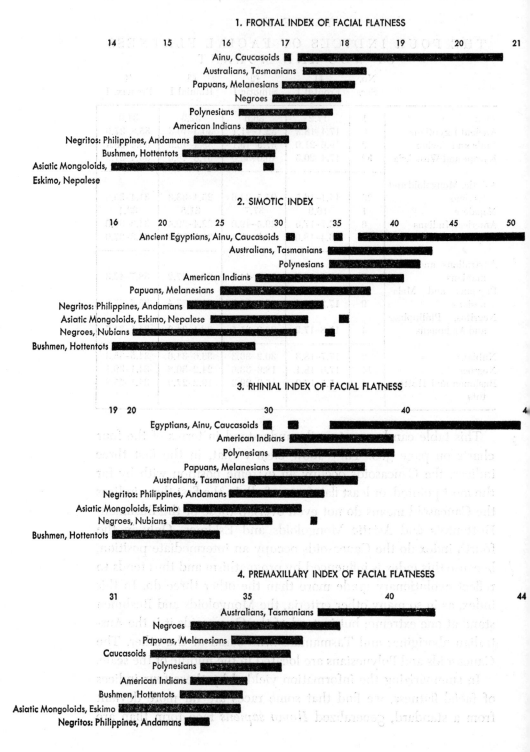

1. FRONTAL INDEX OF FACIAL FLATNESS

14 15 16 17 18 19 20 21

Ainu, Caucasoids
Australians, Tasmanians
Papuans, Melanesians
Negroes
Polynesians
American Indians
Negritos: Philippines, Andamans
Bushmen, Hottentots
Asiatic Mongoloids,
Eskimo, Nepalese

2. SIMOTIC INDEX

16 20 25 30 35 40 45 50

Ancient Egyptians, Ainu, Caucasoids
Australians, Tasmanians
Polynesians
American Indians
Papuans, Melanesians
Negritos: Philippines, Andamans
Asiatic Mongoloids, Eskimo, Nepalese
Negroes, Nubians
Bushmen, Hottentots

3. RHINIAL INDEX OF FACIAL FLATNESS

19 20 30 40 4

Egyptians, Ainu, Caucasoids
American Indians
Polynesians
Papuans, Melanesians
Australians, Tasmanians
Negritos: Philippines, Andamans
Asiatic Mongoloids, Eskimo
Negroes, Nubians
Bushmen, Hottentots

4. PREMAXILLARY INDEX OF FACIAL FLATNESS

31 35 40 44

Australians, Tasmanians
Negroes
Papuans, Melanesians
Caucasoids
Polynesians
American Indians
Bushmen, Hottentots
Asiatic Mongoloids, Eskimo
Negritos: Philippines, Andamans

others. The ranking, from most to least deviant, is: Caucasoids, Australoids, Capoids, Asiatic Mongoloids and Eskimos, Asiatic Negritos, African Negroes, American Indians, Papuo-Melanesians, and Polynesians. If we eliminate the fourth index on the ground that it confuses grade with line, the Caucasoids appear even more distinctive.

This ranking suggests that Caucasoids, Australoids, and a Mongoloid-Capoid combination are extreme or primary forms of mankind, whereas Ainu, Polynesians, Papuo-Melanesians, African Negroes, Asiatic Negritos, and even American Indians are intermediate forms. The extreme differentiation of the Caucasoids in degree of facial flatness matches that of the Mongoloids in dental anatomy, and is equally ancient.

Racial Origins and Racial Continuities

IN THIS CHAPTER a framework has been erected for the detailed study of the origins and evolutionary progress of each of the five geographical races of man, as defined in Chapter 1. We have shown that from the start of the Middle Pleistocene the Old World, in which man arose, was divided into five breeding grounds, sufficiently separated from one another by physical and climatic barriers to permit a human subspecies to evolve, almost but not quite independently of its neighbors. We have traced the archaeological sequences in each region, and shown that in them tool-making techniques followed essentially but not wholly independent paths.

Short-cutting anthropometric details, we have set the boundary between *Homo erectus* and *Homo sapiens* on the basis of brain size, the degrees of curvature of the bones composing the cranial vault, and, to a lesser extent, on tooth size, particularly as tooth size is related to brain size. We have explored and rejected the concept that *Homo sapiens* must, by definition, have had a chin, and have shown how chins came into being after the races of man had crossed the *erectus-sapiens* threshold.

From the consideration of evolutionary grades we have moved on to lines of descent, and have selected two out of many criteria of racial differentiation that are particularly easy to follow. These are tooth morphology and degrees of facial flatness. In all regions where they can be traced, both persist from the first appearance of man to the end of the Pleistocene.

With this lengthy introduction we have bridged another gap between the study of our prehuman ancestors and the details of human history. From here on we shall pursue the second subject, not by grades, for that framework has been sufficiently explored, but by racial lines.

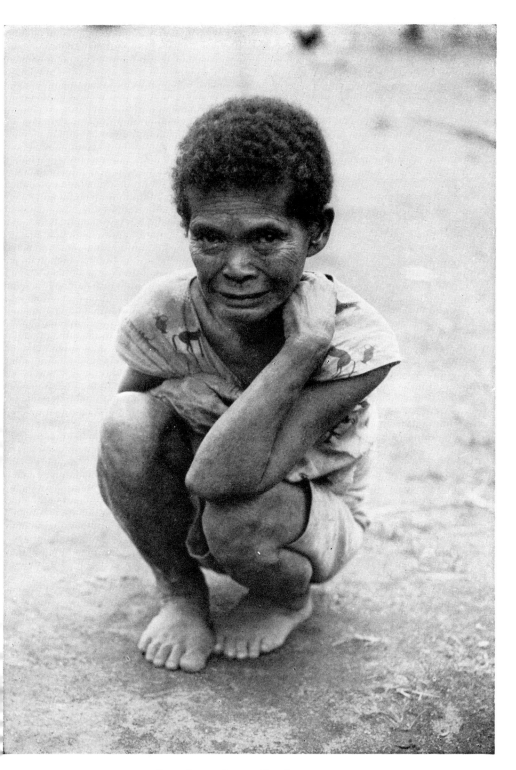

Pygmies: a Luzon Negrito woman.

Pygmies: Önges from Little Andaman Island.

Pygmies: a Kadar from the Cardamon Hills, Kerala, India.

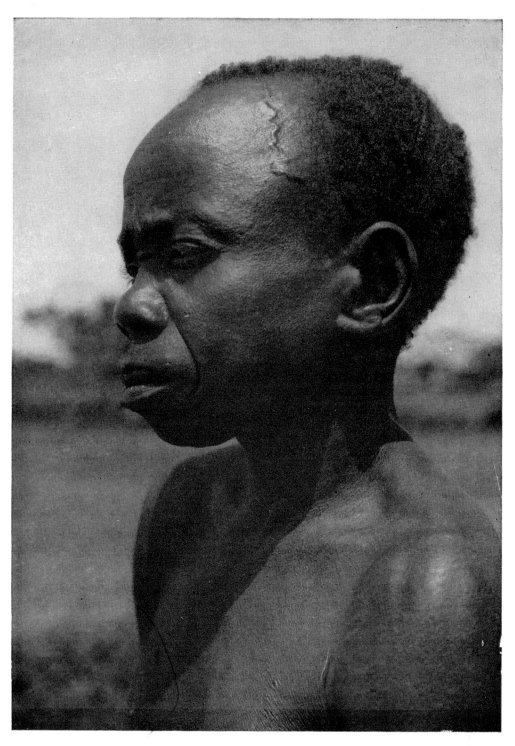

A Pygmy from the Congo.

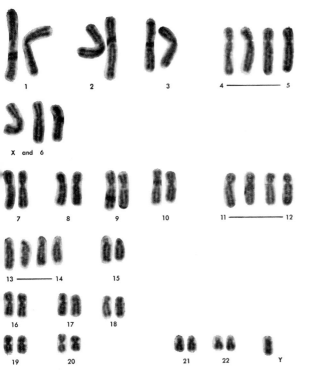

1 2 3 4 ——— 5

X and 6

7 8 9 10 11 ——— 12

13 ——— 14 15

16 17 18

19 20 21 22 Y

THE KARYOTYPE OF MAN (American Negro, Male). The forty-six chromosomes of the human cell nucleus, shown as they appear under the microscope and arranged by pairs in order of size, except for the sex chromosomes X and Y, which are of different sizes. A female would have two X chromosomes. Research in differences in details of chromosome structure in man has not yet progressed to the point at which we can identify racial differences.

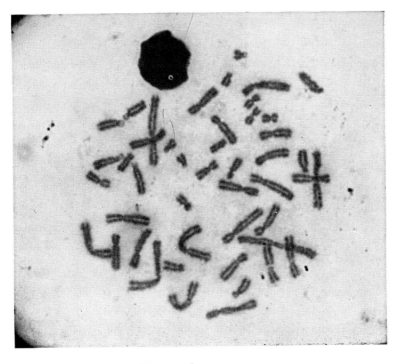

Human chromosomes.

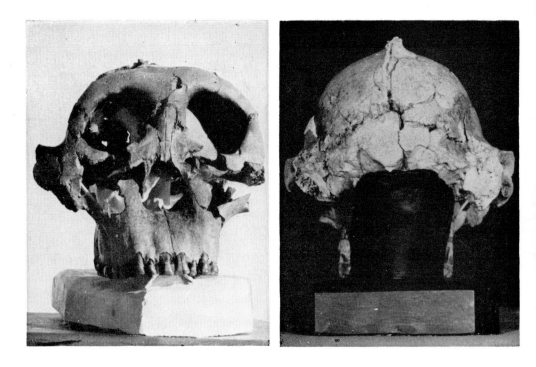

Zinjanthropus skull, three views.

Zinjanthropus palate, compared with that of an Australian aborigine.

a. Extreme shoveling of the upper incisors of a Pima Indian whose lateral incisors are barrel-shaped.

b. In the teeth of another Pima Indian shown here, the upper median incisors are double-shoveled—they are concave on both the outer and the inner surfaces.

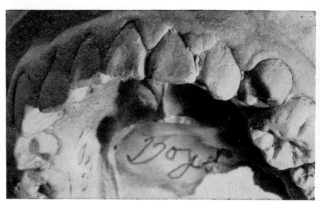

c. Carabelli's cusp, on the upper first molar of a white American.

d. e. f. The enamel pearl, a globular form of enamel extension, on the molars of East Greenland Eskimos.

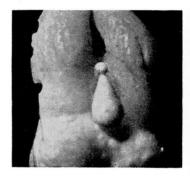

SOME RACIAL PECULIARITIES IN TOOTH STRUCTURE

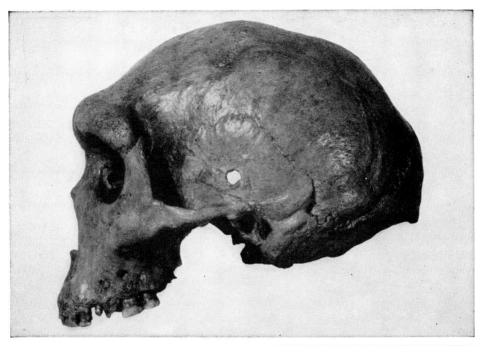

Skull from Broken Hill, front and side views.

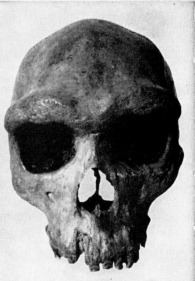

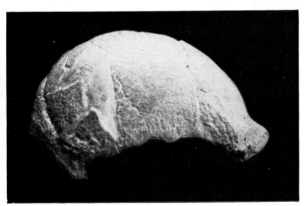

Skull from Saldanha Bay.

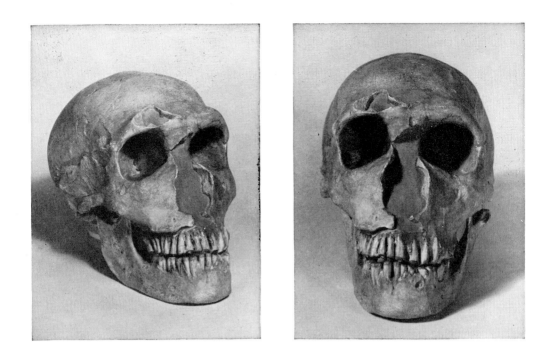

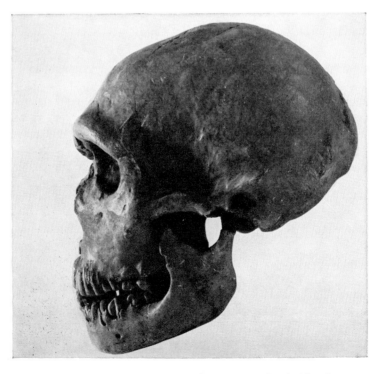

Skull of La Ferrassie 1, front, three-quarter, and side views.

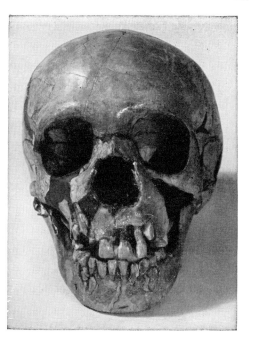

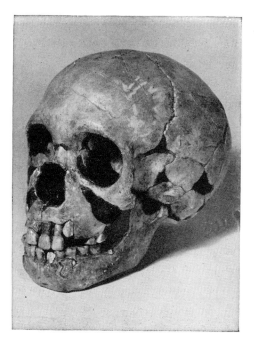

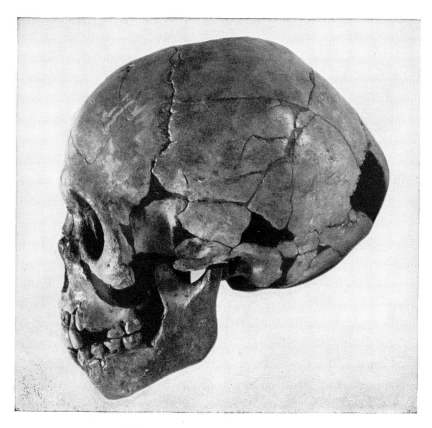

Skull from Teshik-Tash, three views.

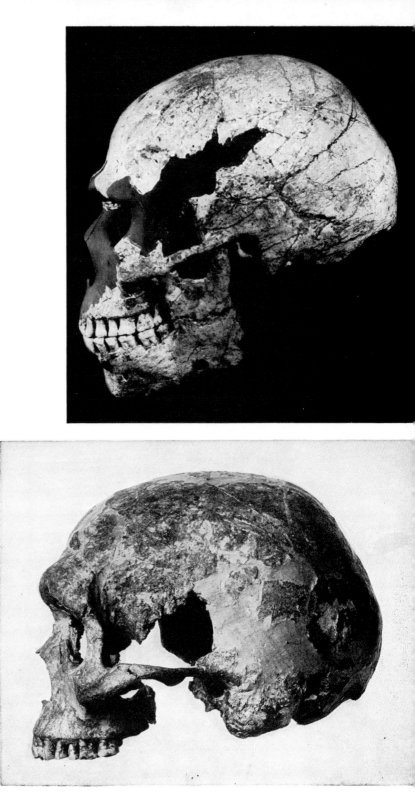

Skulls: Skhul 5 above and Jebel Qafza below.

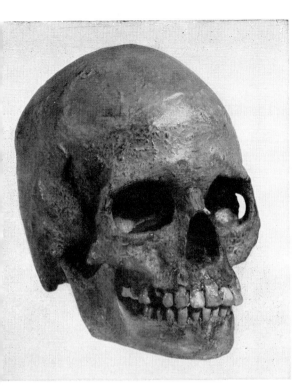

a. Grimaldi

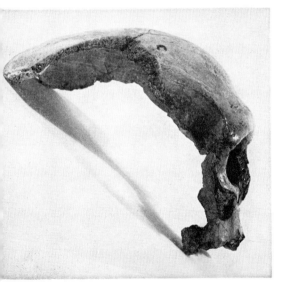

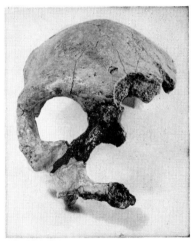

b. and *c.* Florisbad

Skulls

a. Steinheim

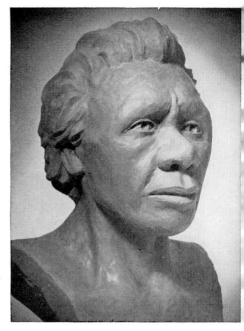

b. Wadjak 1

c. Upper Cave Male

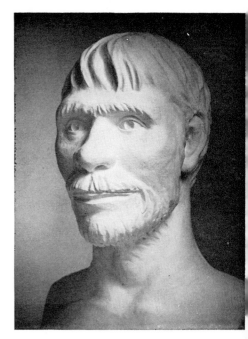

d. Skhul 5

FLESH RECONSTRUCTIONS OF FOSSIL MEN

By Maurice Putnam Coon

a. La Chapelle aux Saints

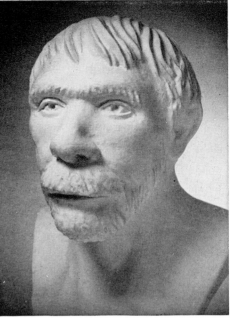

b. Circeo 1

c. Combe Capelle

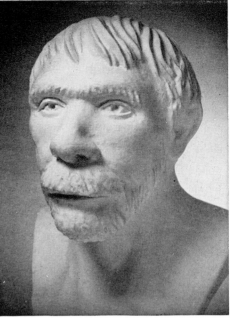

d. Crô-Magnon

FLESH RECONSTRUCTIONS OF FOSSIL MEN

By Maurice Putnam Coon

XXXI

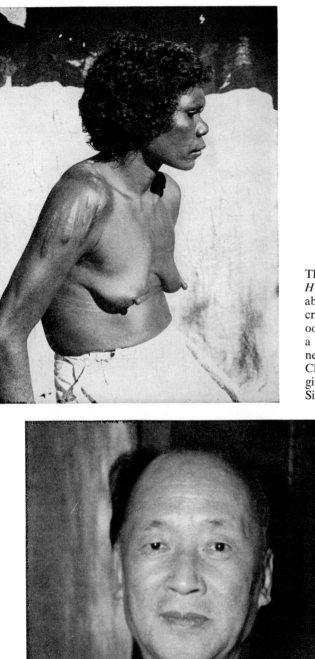

The Alpha and Omega of *Homo sapiens:* An Australian aboriginal woman with a cranial capacity of under 1,-000 cc. (Topsy, a Tiwi); and a Chinese sage with a brain nearly twice that size (Dr. Li Chi, the renowned archaeologist and director of Academia Sinica).

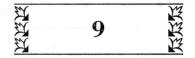

PITHECANTHROPUS
AND THE AUSTRALOIDS

The Pithecanthropus Line

O F T H E F I V E lines of human descent that we shall now
trace, the best one to begin with is the Australoid because it is the
oldest known, the simplest to follow, and the most archaic today.
The Australoid is the one human subspecies known to be native
to the Oriental faunal region, and it was the first to occupy its
present home, the Australian faunal region.

Owing to extensive post-Pleistocene migrations, the Oriental region is a racial mosaic, the most complex in the world. West of the
mountains that separate India from Burma lives a medley of peoples, mostly Caucasoids on the plains, with enclaves of Negritos,
Australoids, primitive Caucasoids, and Mongoloids in the hills.
East of the mountains the mainland population is almost solidly
Mongoloid, and so is that of the islands of Indonesia (speaking in
the geographical rather than the political sense) lying north and
west of Wallace's Line.

Like India, southeast Asia and the larger Indonesian islands
also contain relict populations tucked away in forest refuges.
These refugee groups are also racially varied, being Negrito, Australoid, and primitive Mongoloid. As one crosses Wallace's Line
and moves eastward through the Lesser Sundas toward New
Guinea, the islanders look less and less Mongoloid and more and
more Papuan or Melanesian. New Guinea, Melanesia, and Australia are (or were) inhabited by a congeries of three principal
kinds of people, Negritos, full-sized Negroids, and Australoids, all
shading into one another in such a way that the Negritos and Ne-

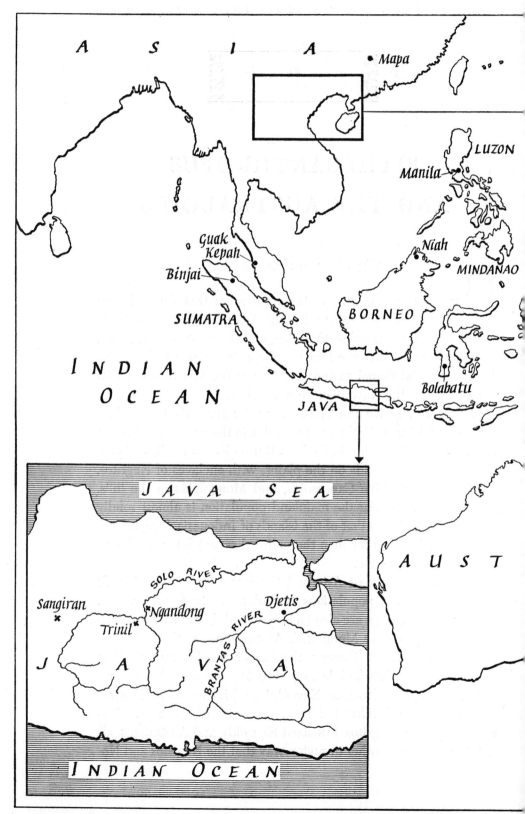

MAP 9

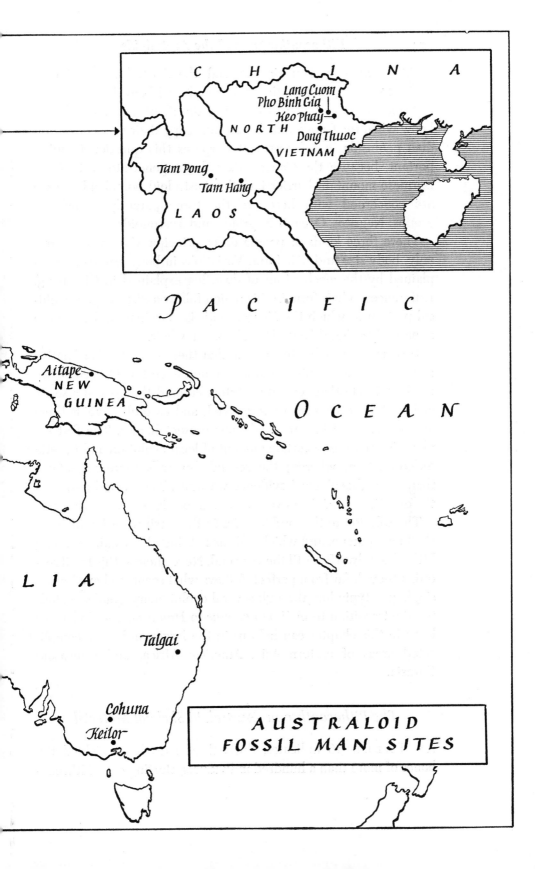

C H I N A

Lang Cuom
Pho Binh Gia
Keo Phay
Dong Thuoc

NORTH

VIETNAM

Tam Pong

Tam Hang

L A O S

P A C I F I C

Aitape
NEW
GUINEA

O C E A N

L I A

Talgai

Cohuna
Keilor

AUSTRALOID
FOSSIL MAN SITES

groids form a broken ring around the Australian aborigines.

The Mongoloids of southeast Asia and the islands began to filter in from the north toward the end of the Pleistocene. We do not know when the Caucasoids began to occupy their areas of the Indian peninsula, but for present purposes this question is unimportant, because the Caucasoids did not penetrate east of the Burmese mountain barrier into the Australoid homeland. All we are concerned with here are the three patently indigenous groups: Negritos, Oceanic Negroids, and Australoids.

These three kinds of people differ principally in two features only, body size and hair form. Variations in body size can be explained by the mechanisms of dwarfing explained in Chapter 3. Differences in hair form in this region follow a distinct geographical pattern in which the Negroid hair is marginal, and therefore apparently older, than the straight or wavy hair.

It seems reasonable to suppose that these three kinds of native peoples evolved locally from a common ancestor. Otherwise we must postulate that several ancestors entered the area in a series of invasions, each race fully evolved, and carefully avoided one another until all had reached their present homes. The first explanation requires a certain amount of local evolution and genetic differentiation, whereas the second demands more migrations than the archaeological evidence warrants. The second also begs the question of origins: every race had to originate somewhere.

The solution to this problem lies in the fossil record, which we shall now pursue, and which tells us nothing about hair form and little about dwarfs, until the very end. Nevertheless, this fossil record, although far from perfect, follows what seems to have been a single polytypic line through several evolutionary grades, including the transition from *Homo erectus* to *Homo sapiens*. What we learn in this chapter can help us in the larger and more complicated areas of eastern Asia, America, Africa, and Caucasoid Eurasia.

The Pithecanthropus-Australoid Skeletal Material

As TABLE 16 indicates, thirty-three sites have yielded the bones of more than a hundred individuals, starting with Pithecanthropus 4, a baby's skull, and two broken mandibles, and covering the entire time span from before the base of the Middle Pleistocene to almost the present. Only the sites in Australia containing patently modern burials, and two dubious sites in Indochina which contained, respectively, a tooth and a scrap of temporal bone, have been omitted.

Fossil Men from the Djetis Beds of Java

T H E O L D E S T fossil-man remains from the Oriental faunal region, and probably from the world, have been found in Java, which, among other islands of western and northern Indonesia, received invasions of Pleistocene animals from both India and China. The earliest of its hominid-bearing beds is the Djetis, which contains fossil species believed to have come from the tropical region of south China, including the pieces of mandible known as *Meganthropus paleojavanicus* described in Chapter 7. The human material found in these beds was: one specimen consisting of two parts of a cranium and two loose incisors, known, among other names, as Pithecanthropus 4 (or P-4); two fragmentary mandibles known as Pithecanthropus B and Sangiran, respectively; and the skullcap of an infant, called *Homo modjokertensis.*[1]

Pithecanthropus 4

T H E L A R G E R of the two pieces of Pithecanthropus 4 is the rear portion of a thick-walled, low-vaulted skull which had been broken shortly before its discovery, and parts of which had been lost. The occipital bone is nearly intact, as well as most of the temporals and parietals. What is missing is the frontal and the whole

---

[1] F. Weidenreich: "Giant Early Man from Java and South China," *APAM,* Vol. 40, Part 1 (1945).

G. H. R. von Koenigswald: "Neue Pithecanthropus Funde, 1936–38," *WMDM,* No. 28 (1940).

Von Koenigswald: "L'Hominization de l'Appareil Masticateur et les Modifications du Régime Alimentaire," in A. Delmas, ed.: *Les Processus de l'Hominization* (Paris: Centre Nationale de la Récherche Scientifique; 1958), pp. 60–78.

Von Koenigswald: "Fossil Hominids from the Lower Pleistocene of Java," *IGC,* No. 9 (London, 1948), pp. 51–69.

Von Koenigswald: *Meeting Prehistoric Man* (New York: Harper and Brothers; 1956).

TABLE 16

PITHECANTHROPUS—AUSTRALOID
SKELETAL MATERIAL

Country	Site	Geological Age	Material	Name
Java	Sangiran II	Late Lower Pleistocene, Djetis Fauna	1 calvarium + maxilla	Pithecanthropus 4, P. robustus
			1 mandible	Pithecanthropus B
			1 mandible	Pongo pygmaeus, Pithecanthropus dubius
	Modjokerto	Djetis Fauna	1 calvarium, infant	Homo modjokertensis
	Sangiran I	Late Lower and Early Middle Pleistocene, Trinil Fauna	1 calva	P. erectus, P-1
			2 calvas	P-2 and P-3
			6 femora	P. erectus
			3 teeth	P. erectus with P-1??
	Kedung Brubus	Trinil Fauna	1 mandible, fragmentary	P. erectus
	Sondé	Trinil Fauna (?)	1 molar	P. erectus or H. sapiens
Java	Ngandong	Late Pleistocene, Notopuro fauna	11 calvaria	H. (javanthropus) soloensis,
			2 tibiae	H. soloensis
China	Mapa, Kwangtung	Late Middle or Early Upper Pleistocene	1 calva	none
New Guinea	Aitape	Probably Late Pleistocene	1 calva	H sapiens (?)
Java	Wadjak	Late Pleistocene or Early Recent	No. 1 cranium	H. wadjakensis
			No. 2 fragments cranium, mandible	H. wadjakensis

Borneo	Niah Cave	Late Pleistocene 37,650 B.C. (C-14)	1 cranium	H. sapiens
Australia	Keilor	Probably post-Pleistocene	1 skull	H. sapiens
	Cohuna	Probably post-Pleistocene	2 frags. femur	H. sapiens
	Talgai	Probably post-Pleistocene	1 cranium	H. sapiens
Java	Wadjak	Recent, Mesolithic	1 cranium	H. sapiens
	Bodjonegoro	Recent, Mesolithic	1 skeleton	H. sapiens
	Sampoeng	Recent, Mesolithic	Scraps	H. sapiens
			Several skeletons	H. sapiens
Celebes	Bolabatu	Quite recent	7 skeletons	H. sapiens
	Lompoa	Quite recent	2 skeletons	H. sapiens
Sumatra	Bindjai Tamiang	Recent	Fragments	H. sapiens
Philippines	Manila	Unknown	1 skull	H. sapiens
Laos	Tam Pong	Recent Mesolithic	1 skull	H. sapiens
	Tam Hang	Recent, Early Neolithic	4 skeletons	H. sapiens
		Recent, Late Neolithic	22 skeletons	H. sapiens
	Lang Cuom	Recent, Late Neolithic	12 skulls	H. sapiens
	Dong Thuoc	Neolithic	1 skull	H. sapiens
	Pho Binh Gia	Neolithic	3 skulls	H. sapiens
	Keo Phay	Neolithic	1 skull	H. sapiens
Malaya	Guak Kepah, Wellesley Province, Straits Settlements	Recent, Mesolithic	1 mandible	H. sapiens
	Gunong Sennyum / Lenggong / Gunong Pondok / Bukit Chuping	Recent, Neolithic	6 skulls	H. sapiens
Ceylon	Bellan Bändi Pälässa	Recent	9 skeletons	H. sapiens

upper part of the face down to the floor of the nose. The smaller piece consists of the maxillae, including the palate, the nasal floor, and ten of the upper teeth, excluding all four incisors and the last two left molars. Several loose teeth were found in the same site and apparently fragments of the upper jaws of two other individuals.

Although there was no point of contact between the two pieces of P-4, Weidenreich restored the skull as a whole, on the model of the Sinanthropus skulls with which he had previously worked. He estimated the cranial capacity at about 900 cc., which matches the other and later skulls of the same type. The sagittal line of the

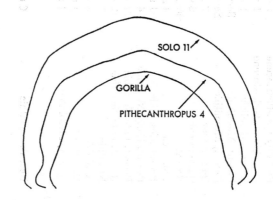

FIG. 54 TRANSVERSE SECTION OF THE SKULLS OF A FEMALE GORILLA, PITHE-CANTHROPUS 4, AND SOLO 11. The skull of a female gorilla (inner line) resembles that of Pithecanthropus 4 in general, except that the latter is more angular than the former and its sides are more nearly parallel. The largest Solo skull, No. 11 (outside line), is much the same in outline as Pithecanthropus 4, except that it is more rounded. (Drawing after Weidenreich, 1951.)

skull was keeled, but not crested as in some apes, Swartkrans, and Zinjanthropus. In fact, the temporal muscles did not extend very high on the parietals. The occipital torus was pronounced, indicating strong neck muscles, and the brow ridges must have been protuberant also. The proposed maximum length of 199 mm. and maximum breadth of 156 to 158 mm. can be matched today in large-headed Europeans, but the two sets of dimensions are not comparable. In the Europeans the figures reflect to a large extent the size of the brain, whereas in P-4 they merely bound the bony structure of its base. On the sides, the maximum diameter goes through the crest over the mastoids. The breadth of the brain case, in so far as it can be measured, is only about 125 mm. With a basion-bregma height of only 102 mm. and an auricular head-height of only 90 mm., it falls within the height range of the larger Australopithecines, whose heads, being smaller, were relatively higher vaulted than that of P-4.

The skull in general is formed of a series of planes more or less rounded at their points of juncture, so that it looks somewhat like a poorly raised loaf of bread. This is the so-called "ill-filled" look for which modern Australian aboriginal skulls are also noted. The base of the skull was relatively flat, and the positions of the fora-

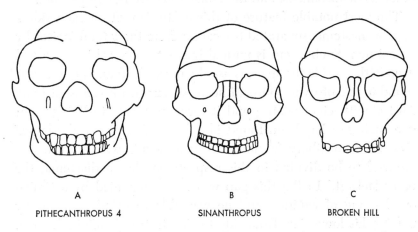

A	B	C
PITHECANTHROPUS 4	SINANTHROPUS	BROKEN HILL

Fig. 55   The Faces of *Homo erectus*. Only one *Homo erectus* specimen has a complete face—Broken Hill (C)—and it lacks a lower jaw. Weidenreich reconstructed the Pithecanthropus 4 skull, which had a maxilla and palate, with the addition of the Pithecanthropus B mandibular fragment (A). Using various fragments of face bone and the Sinanthropus 3 skull, he also reconstructed a female Sinanthropus skull (B). We have no fossil skulls for the *erectus* stage of either Caucasoids or Capoids. As shown here, the Pithecanthropus 4 skull is the most brutal and primitive of the three. The face of the Sinanthropus female is less so, but partly because of her sex. The Rhodesian skull has the largest brow ridges and the longest face of all, and its vault is about as high as that of Sinanthropus. However, it differs from the others in the flatness of the sides of its face. Its zygomatic arches are weakly developed, not because of small jaw muscles, but because of a deeply excavated postorbital constriction which gives the temporals room to contract.

men magnum and its flanking occipital condyles indicate, in so far as they can be trusted to do so, a fully erect posture, although the nuchal crest, to which the neck muscles are attached, is situated higher up than in some Australopithecines, notably Zinjanthropus. Unlike some other fossil skulls and like most modern human races, P-4 has large, downward-pointing mastoid processes.

The maxillary fragment is notable for its excessive size and massiveness, indicating that the face as a whole must have been large in all dimensions, with extreme alveolar prognathism. The floor of the nasal passages was extremely wide (36 mm.) but fully human in form. In front stands a prominent nasal spine, and the borders of the opening are guttered, as in living Australoids and Negroes. The palate is the longest on record, but not the widest. The dental arcade is parabolic, but not as smoothly rounded as in many other fossil specimens, and the molar rows are nearly parallel.

The most notable feature of this palate is that on each side a gap, or diastema, separated the canine from the lateral incisor by 5 or 6 mm. Such a gap is normal but not universal in apes, and even in the gorilla the space is usually narrower than in P-4. It was found in one of twelve Oreopithecus specimens; it is absent in all Australopithecine palates; and it turns up rarely in living men: one such gap has been found in a living Australian aborigine.[2] Two other maxillary fragments in von Koenigswald's possession are said to be divided in this respect; one has a diastema, the other lacks it.[3] In P-4 this gap was unaccompanied by a simian overlapping of canines, and he was able to grind his food by moving his lower jaw from side to side in true hominid fashion. The possession of this gap fails to make him an ape, but it also renders his descent from the kinds of Australopithecines found in South and East Africa unlikely. A second notable feature of P-4 is that the roof of the palate is smooth, as in apes, instead of ridged, as in men.

The Pithecanthropus Mandibles from the Djetis Bed

A PIECE of mandible found in the same level with P-4 is known as Pithecanthropus B. It belonged to a different individual and is just a little too small to match P-4's palate. It consists of a frag-

[2] G. Heithersay: "A Dental Survey of the Aborigines at Haast's Bluff, Central Australia," *MJA*, May 30, 1959, pp. 721–9.

[3] W. E. LeGros Clark: *The Fossil Evidence for Human Evolution* (Chicago: University of Chicago Press; 1955), p. 94.

ment of the right branch, 82 mm. long, running from a break between the two right incisors almost to the gonial angle. It contains
all three molars and the sockets of the second incisor, canine, and
first premolar. It is a very large mandible, larger in nearly all dimensions than any other unquestionably human fossil jaw, and

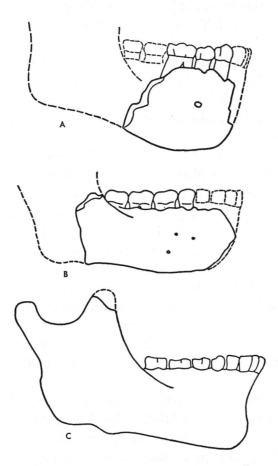

FIG. 56 MANDIBLES OF MEGANTHROPUS, PITHECANTHROPUS B, AND WADJAK 2.
A. Meganthropus (after von Koenigswald and Weidenreich); B. Pithecanthropus
B (after Weidenreich); C. Wadjak 2 (after a cast). Meganthropus is represented by
fragments of two large mandibles found in Java in the Early Pleistocene Djetis
beds. This is the first specimen, found by von Koenigswald. It is larger than any
known human jaw and as large as those of Swartkrans and Kromdraai in South
Africa. It was probably that of an Asiatic Australopithecine, although some
anatomists consider it Hominine. The Pithecanthropus B jaw was its contemporary;
Pithecanthropus B nearly matches the Pithecanthropus 4 skull. Between Pithecanthropus B and the next Australoid mandible, that of Wadjak 2, there is a gap of
over half a million years. Wadjak 2 is a large, stout, human jaw with a chin, but it
is as robust as that of Heidelberg. It also resembles that of Skhul 5 in Palestine—
the Australoid "Neanderthal"—very closely in form.

certainly the stoutest. Its circumference holds the record to date.
Nevertheless, it is only two thirds as large as the Meganthropus
fragment found in the same deposit.

Although the actual symphysis (the sagittal line at the midpoint between the two halves of the jaw) is missing, enough bone
is left in the center of the jaw to reveal the presence or absence of
a chin. It is absent. The *angle of inclination* (the angle between
the axis of the symphysis and the alveolar border) is about 58°,
the same as that of Meganthropus, and within five degrees of the
figures for the earliest Chinese and European mandibles, Sinanthropus and Heidelberg. Among living Australian aborigines this
angle runs to 75° and in many living Europeans it exceeds 90°—
a right angle.

Another fragment of jawbone from the same deposit is the so-
called Sangiran mandible, a piece 60 mm. long, again of the right
branch, and containing the first and second molars, a stub of the
second premolar, and the sockets of the first premolar and canine.
Going by the cast alone, Weidenreich described it, in 1945, as the
jaw of an orangutan. Meanwhile von Koenigswald had identified
it as a Meganthropus. In 1956 the latter wrote: "Not until later,
when I brought the original to New York and we were able to prepare (clean) it better, could I demonstrate to him that the jaw
was human, while he convinced me that it was too different from
Meganthropus to belong to the same species. Since we had both
been mistaken, I named this new form of primitive man *Pithecanthropus dubius.*" [4]

Most reviewers of the paleanthropic scene must also have considered this specimen doubtful, as they have not mentioned it. Yet
it exists. It is not, apparently, an ape, and it may be important.
(See Tables 38 and 39 for measurements of the bones and of its
two teeth.) The mandible is intermediate in size between Meganthropus and Pithecanthropus B. Its angle of inclination is 54°,
intermediate between the figure for the two jaws mentioned above
and those for living apes. How it fits into the hominid picture in
Late Lower Pleistocene Java remains to be seen.

[4] Von Koenigswald: *Meeting Prehistoric Man*, p. 114. This name also, apparently, contains a pun on the name Dubois.

The Brain Case of the Infant Modjokertensis[5]

ALSO IN the Djetis beds was found the faceless and baseless skullcap of a baby a little under two years old. The bone is thin (maximum = 3 mm.) but the tympanic plate, a part of the temporal bone near the earhole on which the condyle of the lower jaw moves, had begun to ossify prematurely, from the *sapiens*

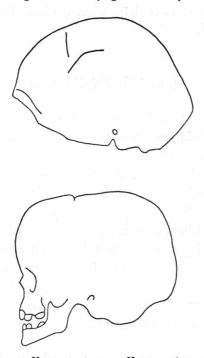

FIG. 57   THE SKULLS OF *Homo erectus* AND *Homo sapiens* AT THE AGE OF TWO (Profiles drawn to the same scale). *Above* is the skullcap of the infant from Modjokerto, Djetis beds, Java, associated with Pithecanthropus 4 and the Meganthropus jaw. Age, Late Lower Pleistocene. (After von Koenigswald.) *Below* is the skull of the infant from Starosel'e, Crimea, dated at Würm I (75,000–40,000 years ago). The race is Caucasoid. (After Roginskiĭ.) The age of the Modjokerto infant is "a little under two years"; that of the Starosel'e baby, "eighteen or nineteen months." The skull of the *erectus* baby is already elongated, its forehead is sloping, the profile of the lambda region is straight, and the occipital bone sharply curved. It already has brow ridges. The *sapiens* baby's skull has a bulbous forehead, a sharply bent parietal profile, and a more open occipital curve. This illustration shows that *erectus* and *sapiens* skulls can be told apart as early as the age of two.

[5] Von Koenigswald: *Meeting Prehistoric Man*, pp. 72–82.
Clark: op. cit., p. 92.

point of view. The forehead is more sloping than in modern babies of the same age, the occipital bone more angular. Brow ridges had just begun to sprout over the outer corners of the eye sockets, behind which there was already a postorbital constriction.

This was, without doubt, a P-4 baby, in which the critical features of *Homo erectus* had begun to show themselves at an early stage of development. We are fortunate to have an *erectus* baby of this age. When we come to diagnose the evolutionary status of other baby skulls of later date, what we have learned from this one will be useful.

Men of the Trinil Fauna [6]

FROM THE overlying beds of the Trinil fauna, also largely of south Chinese origin, and from Trinil itself and its neighborhood, three skullcaps have been taken—Pithecanthropus 1, 2, and 3— an inconsequential piece of mandible called Kedung Brubus, two whole and two broken loose teeth, and, oddly enough, six femora. P-1, the original *Pithecanthropus erectus* discovered by Dubois, is a bare skullcap without face and with an incomplete base. Its estimated capacity of 900 cc. matches that of Pithecanthropus 4, but neither skull is complete enough for accurate measurement. P-2 is a smaller skullcap similar in all respects to P-1, and it has a capacity of only 775 cc., a reasonably accurate figure because this skull is the most nearly complete of the four.[7] P-3 is a small piece

---

[6] E. Dubois: Pithecanthropus erectus, *eine Menschenähnliche Uebergangsform von Java* (Batavia, 1894).

Dubois: "Figures of the Calvarium and Endocranial Cast, a Fragment of the Mandible, and Three Teeth of *Pithecanthropus erectus*," PKAW, Vol. 27, No. 5 (1924).

Dubois: "Figures of the Femur of *Pithecanthropus erectus*," PKAW, Vol. 29, No. 9 (1926), pp. 1275–7.

Dubois: "The Sixth (Fifth New) Femur of *Pithecanthropus erectus*," PKAW, Vol. 38, No. 8 (1935), pp. 850–2.

Von Koenigswald: "Neue Pithecanthropus Funde . . ."; *Meeting Prehistoric Man.*

Weidenreich: "The Skull of *Sinanthropus pekinensis*," PSNSD, Vol. 10, ws 127 (1943).

[7] The figure of 775 cc. is Weidenreich's (1945). Von Koenigswald says 750 cc., and Boule and Vallois, 810 cc. (M. M. Boule and H. V. Vallois: *Les Hommes Fossiles* (Paris, Masson & Cie.; 1952), p. 120.

of juvenile skull consisting of a fragment of occiput, and one complete and one incomplete parietal bone.

These three skullcaps and pieces thereof are as thick as P-4, and no larger. In P-1 and P-2 the brow ridges are preserved. They are not only massive, as befits *Homo erectus,* but also they have a characteristic form. Seen in profile, they merge into the rest of the frontal bone very gradually, with little depression. This may be seen in later skulls from the same region and also among some living Australian aborigines. It is quite different from the brow-ridge profiles seen in other fossil lines, to be described presently. The frontal bone is slightly keeled along its mid-line, and this keeling continues along the sagittal suture, between the two parietal bones. The keeling has nothing to do with a crest such as we have seen in the larger Australopithecines. In fact, the temporal lines are set relatively low down on the parietal bones.

Seen from above, the brow ridges form a nearly straight bar, with no concavity in the profile line over the root of the nose, and with relatively little backward curvature at either end, indicating a relatively low figure for the frontal index of facial flatness. Behind the brow ridges at either end is a deep hollow through which heavy temporal muscles operated. This partial separation of the brain case and facial skeleton is reminiscent of, but less extreme than, the condition seen in Zinjanthropus.

The Trinil Pithecanthropus skulls (using Trinil to mean their fauna) differ from the earlier P-4 architecturally in that they are shorter and narrower at the base. They are as broad as P-4 between the parietal bones, or a little broader, and equally high in the vault or a little higher. These are changes of grade, not of line, pointing in a modern, more fully human direction. During the 200,000 years or so which separate the two faunal levels, Djetis and Trinil, evolution seems to have been at work, if not in increasing brain size, at least in giving the container of this pilot organ a less rugged and less bestial form.

The Kedung Brubus mandible is a small, triangular fragment measuring about 35 mm. on each side, and including nothing in the way of teeth except the root of a canine. As far as we can tell, it could easily have been part of a Pithecanthropus jaw.

Incidentally, the Trinil faunal beds in some of the central Javan sites contain the earliest tools known in Java. They are crude but clearly worked flakes. Because these flakes are technologically well in advance of the crudest known choppers and chopping tools, such as those found in Late Lower Pleistocene deposits in Malaya, one must assume that Pithecanthropus had been a tool-maker for some time before these flakes were made.

The Pithecanthropus Thighbones

I N 1891, a year after his discovery of P-1, Dubois also found a complete human femur in the Trinil beds at the same site as the skull. Some thirty years later he encountered five others, only one of which was whole, in a box of old animal bones in his laboratory. The first femur has a curious bony growth, or exostosis, on the inside of the shaft just below the neck. This femur—and the others were like it—was long and slender, only moderately curved, and had a pilaster (a bracing ridge running down the back of the shaft) of modern proportions. According to Loth, however, the attachment for the adductor magnus muscle on the underside of the shaft is a little higher than in modern femora.[8] Except for this detail—in view of its length of 45.5 cm.—it could have been the femur of a recently deceased Australian aborigine or Papuan standing 5 feet 6 inches (168 cm.) tall.

There is no reasonable doubt that these femora and the Trinil skulls come from the same population because their fluorine content is identical, and it matches the fauna.[9] Moreover, it is highly unlikely that two kinds of men lived in Java during the Middle Pleistocene, one race represented by four pieces from the neck up, and the other by six pieces from the waist down. Pithecanthropus, then, had the legs of an Australian aborigine and a skull that was evolving in the same direction.

[8] E. Loth: "Beiträge zur Kenntnis der Weichteilanatomie des Neanderthalers," *ZFRK*, Vol. 7 (1938), pp. 13–35.

[9] R. A. M. Bergman and P. Karsten: "The Fluorine Content of Pithecanthropus and Other Specimens from the Trinil Fauna," *MKNA*, Vol. 55, No. 2 (1952), pp. 150–2.

The Teeth of Pithecanthropus

O N L Y   T W E N T Y   teeth that have been described may be attributed to Pithecanthropus, four more than half the normal dentition of an adult human being. Ten are in their sockets in the maxillae of P-4, and two others were found loose in the same site, and were probably his also as they fit two empty sockets. Three are imbedded in mandible B; two in the *P. dubius* mandible; and the other three, two molars and a premolar, were picked up loose in the area of P-1. We will ignore the lower first molar from the Sondé site, a probably modern tooth found on the surface.

All but the three Trinil teeth are part of the Djetis Pithecanthropi. Of the three it is not certain whether the two molars are human or belonged to an orangutan,[1] and the premolar could be modern.[2] If these teeth were both human and contemporary with the Trinil skulls, they indicate no dental evolution between the Djetis and Trinil Pithecanthropus populations, and the lot can be studied as a whole, with the above caveats borne in mind.

The only incisors attributed to Pithecanthropus are a right upper median and a right upper lateral found loose in the site of P-4. They probably but not certainly had fallen out of the corresponding sockets of P-4. Both seem to be within the modern human size range, as are the corresponding Australopithecine incisors. Evidence of their shape is conflicting, and detailed descriptions have not been published. The median incisor seems to have one or more large tubercles at the base on the lingual surface, and to have had raised edges. The lateral incisor appears to have had raised edges.[3] Moderate shoveling, such as these incisors seem to

---

[1] W. K. Gregory and M. Hellman: "Further Notes on the Molars of Hesperopithecus and of Pithecanthropus," with an appendix by Gerrit S. Miller, Jr., entitled "Notes on the Casts of the Pithecanthropus Molars," *BAMN*, Vol. 48, Art. 13 (1923), pp. 509–30. Miller opted for the orang explanation; Gregory and Hellman were uncertain.

[2] Clark: op. cit., p. 51.

[3] These descriptions are based on photographs that do not show details clearly. The median incisor is depicted in von Koenigswald's *Meeting Prehistoric Man*, on page 59; the lateral in Weidenreich's "Giant Early Man from Java and South

have undergone, is found in 64 per cent of a composite series of modern Australian aborigines,[4] and the same condition has been observed in Tasmanian teeth.

The two upper canines of P-4 are a little larger than the modern maximum dimensions, and spatulate, as in man, rather than conical, as in apes. Apparently they overlapped the lower teeth a little, but not enough to have prevented rotary chewing. The upper premolars fall within the modern size range, but the upper second premolar is unusually thick (in labiolingual width). The upper first premolar also has three roots, like those of many apes and most of the *robustus* group of Australopithecines, whereas the earlier Australopithecines and most human beings have only two roots for that tooth. A lower second premolar in the Pithecanthropus B mandible again exceeds the modern range in both length and breadth. A second specimen, the loose one from the Trinil site that LeGros Clark considers of dubious age, has modern dimensions.

Not counting those of *P. dubius*, we have six upper and three lower molars. All of them, whether indubitably human or not, have wrinkled enamel surfaces comparable to those of orangs and of some Australopithecines. Their roots are long, stout, and divergent. In P-4 the second upper molar is the largest; the first next in size; and the third the smallest. In modern upper jaws the first is usually the largest, followed in descending order of magnitude by the second and third. Of the two upper molars from the Trinil site, one is a second, the other a third. The third is larger than the second, but this ranking is inconclusive because the teeth may have come from two individuals, and may not even be human.

In general these teeth fall outside the modern range—including that of the Australian aborigines—in labiolingual breadth more than they do in mesiodistal length, and this is true of the dentition as a whole. We are reminded, to a lesser degree, of the excessive width of the Zinjanthropus teeth. However, two of the molars

China," on plate 5-b. Von Koenigswald (1950, p. 59) called them both "extremely shovelled, by far surpassing the condition seen in Sinanthropus," a conclusion that may refer to the development of tubercles but not to the morphology of the dental borders.

[4] A. Riesenfeld: "Shovel-shaped Incisors and a Few Other Dental Features Among the Native People of the Pacific," *AJPA*, Vol. 14, No. 3 (1956), pp. 505–22.

are notably long and narrow; the lower third molar of Pithecanthropus B and the upper third of the Trinil trio.

As Weidenreich, following Selenka,[5] pointed out, the degree of wrinkling seen on the enamel of primate molars and the amount of surface relief seen on the unworn cusps are inversely related. Among the apes the orang has the most wrinkling and the lowest cusps; the gorilla has the reverse. The heavily wrinkled third molars of Zinjanthropus are virtually cuspless. As one would expect from this review, the Pithecanthropus molars have relatively low cusps, which are not easy to identify from available publications.

The upper molars of P-4 have at least four cusps each, and the upper second and third may have five. The three lower molars of Pithecanthropus B all have at least five, and some may have a sixth. The teeth are too worn for us to be certain. Of the questionable Trinil molars, the upper second is too worn to tell, and in the upper third, which is highly wrinkled, the cusps are marginal and hard to separate.[6]

As the first and second lower molars of the *P. dubius* mandibular fragment are close in size and form to those of Meganthropus, Pithecanthropus, and the orang, these molars have been identified, by various authors, with all three.

On the whole, those teeth which we know definitely belonged to Pithecanthropus because they were found in the sockets of unquestionably human upper and lower jaws are much closer in size to those of modern men than they are to those of the African Australopithecines (except Telanthropus), Meganthropus, or Zinjanthropus. In a few respects they are more pongid than those just mentioned, but as we have no lower first premolars, the comparison between the Pithecanthropus dentition and that of apes cannot be carried to a conclusion. It is interesting that a man of Weidenreich's stature as an anatomist should have been in doubt as to whether the Sangiran molars belonged to a man or to an orang, and that the team of W. K. Gregory and Milo Hellman, whose combined competence in primate odontology was without peer, should have had similar doubts about the Trinil molars. No one has ever confused the Australopithecine teeth of Africa with those

[5] Weidenreich: "Giant Early Man . . . ," pp. 64–8.
[6] A. Hrdlička: "Skeletal Remains of Early Man," *SMC*, Vol. 83 (1930), p. 49.

of chimpanzees or gorillas. The earliest hominids of Asia and its fringing islands were more apelike dentally than their African cousins. Moreover, the teeth of Pithecanthropus were closer to those of Meganthropus than any of the African specimens of *Homo erectus* yet found were to those of the most recent African Australopithecines. Much more, however, remains to be discovered in both the Oriental and the Ethiopian regions.

The Third Known Human Population of Java: Solo Man

I N   T H E   Solo River Valley of central Java may be seen, in various places, a high terrace above the Trinil beds from which Pithecanthropus 1, 2, and 3 were taken. This high terrace, in its Notopuro beds, contains an abundant mammalian fauna belonging to a phase of the Upper Pleistocene. Although most of the species are still alive, the specimens recovered are larger than their modern descendants. The horns of a buffalo, for instance, were extremely long and widely spread. This and other evidence suggests that the landscape was then more open and grassier than at present, for now it is dense forest in which these prehistoric beasts would have difficulty moving about. Whether this indicates the somewhat drier periods corresponding to the Third Interglacial, the major Würm Interstadial, or some other time of reduced moisture is unknown. From the standpoint of the skulls presently to be described, an earlier rather than a later Upper Pleistocene date would be more consistent with the evidence as a whole.

In this terrace, near a place called Ngandong, C. ter Haar, a Dutch paleontologist, found over 25,000 pieces of mammal bone, including eleven human calvarias and calvas, and two human tibias. These finds were made between 1931 and 1933. The skulls were all lying base upward and were in perfect condition. They had not been moved or rolled. From each the facial skeleton had been cut off, and in all but two the base had also been partially removed, apparently by prying with a stick through the foramen magnum, just as present-day Papuan head-hunters open up skulls to eat the brains. In one, Solo 6 (S-6), the base was whole, and in another, S-11, only the orbital roof had been broken out. One may surmise that these skulls had been carried to the river bank for a feast of brains. But, then, why was S-6 left unshelled, why were all the faces cut off elsewhere, why were they all lying neatly upside down, and why had the tibias been brought along? These leg bones had not been split for marrow.

Neither the dating nor the face- and brain-removing technique can be explained by the accompanying artifacts. Twenty-two stone tools, as yet undescribed, were found.[7] The discoverer picked up, with the skulls, a sting-ray barb, far from its home in the sea. Such barbs are used by modern Australian aborigines. He also found a notched bone implement, presumably a spear point, and a piece of antler that may or may not have been used.

Sex, Age, and Injuries of the Eleven Skulls

TABLE 37 gives the vital statistics of the eleven skulls, except for a small fragment of what may be a twelfth specimen adhering to S-3. Only six were whole enough for detailed measuring, as shown on Table 17. These six, S-1, 5, 6, 9, 10, and 11, are all adult. Two are called male, three female, and in one case Weidenreich, who studied them, refused to commit himself. His determination of sex, which he himself questioned at various times, was based largely on size and on the thickness of the bones of the cranial base.

In skulls S-1, 3, 5, 9, and 10, all the sutures are completely fused. This condition is rare in modern man, however aged, and few primitive men live to ripe old ages. One infers an earlier fusion of sutures in Solo than in modern man. Furthermore, the skulls are all two or three times as thick as modern crania, and just as thick as their Middle Pleistocene predecessors.

That a thick skull had a survival value in Soloese days is suggested by the roster of bone injuries in this series. Wholly aside from the post-mortem mutilations, scars left from nonfatal battles are prevalent. On S-4 a large lesion shows where a heavy, and

[7] Von Koenigswald: "Der Solo-Mensch von Java: ein Tropischer Neanderthaler," in von Koenigswald, ed.: *Hundert Jahre Neanderthaler* (Utrecht: Kemink en Zoon; 1958), pp. 21–6.

TABLE 17
THE NGANDONG SKULLS

	Sex	Age	Parts Present
S-1	probably f.	mature adult	Calvarium, base missing from nasion to mastoids, warped
S-2	?	child, 3–5 yrs.	A frontal bone
S-3	m.	mature adult	Calva: both parietals and adjacent parts of frontal and occipital
S-4	probably f.	adolescent	Calotte, frontal and both parietals
S-5	m.	mature adult	Calvarium, complete but for broken base
S-6	f.	young adult	Calvarium, complete, base whole
S-7	f.	adolescent	Fragment of right parietal
S-8	m.	adolescent	Two detached matching parietals
S-9	?	mature adult	Calvarium, most of base missing
S-10	f.	mature adult	Calvarium, most of base missing
S-11	m.	young adult	Calvarium, front of base missing

probably also sharp, implement pierced the scalp and outer bone table. The lesion then healed. S-6 bears a similar scar. S-1 and S-10 each carried to death a square injury in which the diploë had been laid bare. S-1 also showed additional minor scars. All four heavily battle-scarred victims are called females and at least two of them must have been injured while young, because they died young. Their social life seems to have been active, and S-1 may have been particularly popular.

The Racial Anatomy of the Ngandong Skullcaps

F R O M Mynheer ter Haar, who found them, the skulls passed to W. F. F. Oppenoorth,[8] who published articles about the six first discovered, then to Ralph von Koenigswald, who delivered all but S-9 to Franz Weidenreich in New York. S-9 had been presented to

[8] W. F. F. Oppenoorth: "The Place of *Homo soloensis* Among Fossil Men," in G. G. MacCurdy, ed.: *Early Man* (Philadelphia: J. B. Lippincott Company; 1937), pp. 349–60.

Emperor Hirohito during the Japanese occupation of Java and Lt. (now Dr.) Walter A. Fairservis, Jr., liberated it from an imperial collection in Kyoto and returned it to the company of its fellows. At the time of his death in 1948, Weidenreich was still writing his definitive report of them.[9]

This document was published just as he left it, ending in the middle of a sentence. It does not give the over-all dimensions of each skull, but he had earlier published a series of measurements taken on casts,[1] and more recently Ronald Singer has published some of the measurements of the originals [2] (see Table 37). These figures, combined with a family likeness evident in the photographs, indicate that the Solo skulls belonged to a single population.

The lowest cranial capacity, 1,035 cc., exceeds the highest for Pithecanthropus, 900 cc., by a considerable gap, which might be closed had we enough specimens of each to represent a population statistically. The highest, 1,255 cc., is well within the central three fourths of the modern human range. If Weidenreich's determination of sex is right, the three females have an average capacity of 1,042 cc., and the two males of 1,158 cc.; and on this basis the undesignated S-9 ought to be classed as male. The cranial capacities of the two Trinil Pithecanthropi, P-1, male, and P-2, female, differ by 125 cc., and those of modern male and female Australians by over 150 cc. These comparisons make the sex difference of 110 cc. postulated for Solo man reasonable.

Thus, we can suggest a male sequence as follows: Pithecanthropus = 900 cc.; Solo = 1,150 cc.; living Australians = 1,350 cc. The female sequence would be: P = 775 cc.; S = 1,040 cc.; Australians = 1,180 cc. This exercise in numbers places Solo almost exactly in the middle of the procession in both sexes, a grade (or a half grade, if one prefers) above Pithecanthropus and below the aborigines.

[9] Weidenreich: "Morphology of Solo Man," introduction by Von Koenigswald, *APAM*, Vol. 43, Part 3 (1951). See also Weidenreich: "Giant Early Man from China and Java," *APAM*, Vol. 40, Part 1 (1945).

[1] Weidenreich: "The Skull of *Sinanthropus pekinensis*," pp. 111–16.

[2] Ronald Singer, in von Koenigswald: "Der Solo-Mensch von Java: ein Tropischer Neanderthaler," in *Hundert Jahre Neanderthaler* (Utrecht: Kemink en Zoon N. V.; 1958), p. 22.

The cranial lengths of this series exceed both those of Pithecanthropus and those of the modern Australian aborigines, although the internal brain length is actually intermediate. Kappers, who invented an index between cranial length and the length of the endocranial cast (brain length), gives the following figures: P—1 = 83.7; S—5 = 83.97; Sinanthropus = 83.6; and among the living Australians, males = 88.5 and females = 90.19.[3] This places Solo man in the same grade as the Trinil Pithecanthropi as far as the development of bony crests is concerned.

The lateral crests were equally robust. Weidenreich gives two cranial breadths, the usual biparietal or outer brain-case width, and a so-called bicristal, which is taken lower down, across the mastoid crests. In modern men, the biparietal is almost always the greater of the two, but in Pithecanthropus and Solo it is the smaller. In Solo the lower dimension (the bicristal) remains comparable to that of Pithecanthropus, but the brain-case width increases a good ten millimeters, and both basion-bregma and auricular head heights increase about fifteen millimeters. Thus, the increase of 150 cc. in brain size from Pithecanthropus to Solo involved a parallel growth in each of the three basic cranial dimensions. The size of the brain case changed more than its shape did.

Seen from the side, the Solo profile is still Pithecanthropoid. The brow ridges still slope gradually back from glabella without the abrupt nick found in some other fossil men, notably Sinanthropus in China and Steinheim in Europe. This feature has been noted in some modern Australian crania, as well as in living aborigines. Again like Pithecanthropus, the Solo skulls have a distinct, projecting nuchal crest which forms the posterior landmark of the entire skull. The area of temporal muscle attachment is bordered not by faint lines but by raised crests. These borders follow the same contour as the skull itself, and although the enclosed area of temporal muscle attachment is adequate for a powerful jaw, they do not swing far upward as in the Australopithecines and to a lesser extent in Sinanthropus. Solo shares this feature with Pithecanthropus.

[3] C. U. Ariëns Kappers: "The Endocranial Casts of the Ehringsdorf and Homo Soloensis Skulls," *JAnat.*, Vol. 71, Part 1 (1936), pp. 61–76.

In four of the skulls, S-1, 5, 6, and 11, either a stub of the nasal bones or a scar on the frontal, indicating the place where the two join, is left. These traces show that the nasal bones came down almost straight from the frontal without the pronounced nasal notch present in many living Australian aborigines and Europeans.

Seen from front or rear, the skull looks angular and ill-filled, its profile broken into planes. This is both a Pithecanthropoid and an Australoid trait. In most living races, as in most fossil men, the profile is rounded. The base of the skull is nearly flat, both inside and out, but the back part of the occipital floor slopes gently upward from the level of the middle of the foramen magnum to the nuchal crest. Indeed, the foramen magnum itself has two levels,

TABLE 18
DIMENSIONS OF THE
HYPOPHYSEAL FOSSA*

	S-11	Modern Men (after Pruitt)
L =	22 mm.	10.7 mm. (range = 6–16)
B =	22 mm.	10.0 mm. (7–17.5)
Depth =	9 mm.	8.7 mm. (3–15)

* After Weidenreich, 1951.

horizontal to the eye-ear plane in front and inclined slightly upward behind. As in Pithecanthropus, the mastoid processes are large.

Inside the foramen magnum of S-11, Weidenreich found that the hypophyseal fossa, or *sella turcica,* which is the seat of the pituitary gland, was exceptionally large, with between three and four times the volume of the same cavity in modern crania. This discovery implies that Solo man had a very large pituitary and that therefore the endocrine balance of this population was different from that of *Homo sapiens.* From the behavioral viewpoint this is a very important observation. Washburn and Howell, however, have challenged Weidenreich's interpretation of the anatomy of S-11's cranial base, and the matter cannot be settled without further study of the skull, which is in Bandung, Indonesia.[4]

[4] S. L. Washburn and F. C. Howell: "On the Identification of the Hypophyseal Fossa of Solo Man," *AJPA,* Vol. 10, No. 1 (1952), pp. 13–22. The authors claim

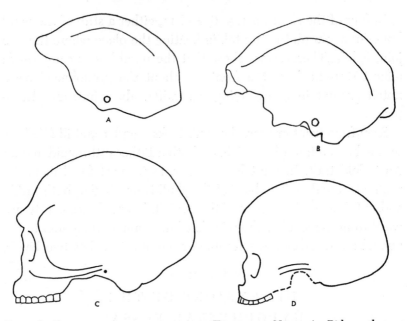

FIG. 58 PROFILES: AUSTRALOIDS FROM TRINIL TO NIAH. A. Pithecanthropus 2 from Trinil; B. Solo 11; C. Wadjak 1; D. the youth from Niah Cave, Borneo. Pithecanthropus 2 is shown here because number 1 is not available in profile view and numbers 3 and 4 are fragmentary. It is the smallest of the four, with a cranial capacity of only 775 cc., only slightly over the Australopithecine range. Its profile is characteristic of the Pithecanthropi as a group, with angular lines and brow ridges which join the forehead with little depression. The Solo skull is essentially the same but larger. The tops of the nasal bones of Solo 11 are preserved below the brow ridges. They come directly from the frontal, with little notching. Wadjak 1, the earliest *sapiens* skull from Java (with Wadjak 2), closely resembles that of an Australian aborigine. The skull from the Niah Cave in North Borneo, that of a youth of sixteen, establishes the existence of Australoid *Homo sapiens* in that island 40,000 years ago. (Drawings A and B after Weidenreich, 1951; C after Weidenreich, 1945, and a cast; D after Brothwell and Higgs, 1961.)

The Face of Solo Man

W H O E V E R removed the faces of the Solo skulls did a thorough job. All that is left is the upper borders. The brow ridges, although large, do not form a solid bar, as in the Trinil skulls, but are divided. Seen from above, they form a Cupid's bow, less projecting

---

that what Weidenreich called the hypophyseal fossa was really the sphenoid sinus, broken open from above. Yet in 1947 Weidenreich described the internal anatomy of S-11 in detail. Weidenreich: "Some Particulars of the Skull and Brain of Early Hominids . . . ," *AJPA*, Vol. 5, No. 4 (1947), pp. 387–428.

at the center than over each eye. From the front they also appear to constitute a double arch. The outer ends, which are particularly thick, bend slightly downward. The center also dips downward and the nasal bones take off from the frontal at a low level, without invading that massive bone at all. The lines marking the sutures between the frontal, lachrymal, and nasal bones lie nearly on the same level. Here there is no angularity; the region of the mask was broad and rather flat. Tentative measurements of the upper breadth of the nasal bones and of the interorbital distance in four skulls, S-1, 5, 6, and 11, show that the nose was broad at the root, and the eyes set far apart. On Solo 11 it is possible to measure the internal biorbital chord and its subtense to nasion, and to calculate, with these measurements, the frontal index of facial flatness. The figure is 15.0, matched today only by Mongoloids and approximated by Negritos and Bushmen. This particular Solo man had a very flat face, at least in the region of the eyes and the root of the nose.

When we compare the Solo skulls with the Djetis and Trinil Pithecanthropi, we find that the three sets of bones complement each other, and that they show a well-marked continuity over a period of as much as 400,000 years, in a nearly constant environment, and at a slow rate of evolution for man. This environment was the wet tropics, in its time an outer corner of the earth.

The Ngandong Leg Bones

L I K E Pithecanthropus before him, Solo man left parts of his legs for posterity, but they were different parts from those of the Trinil Pithecanthropi. Instead of six femurs we have two tibias. Tibia A is a piece of shaft 30 cm. long broken off at both ends. It was once at least 12 cm. longer. Tibia B, which is nearly complete, is 36.5 cm. long. These tibias are straight, unflattened, and, like the Pithecanthropus femurs, modern. If A was a male, as seems likely, he could have been 5 feet 10 inches tall (178 cm.) or a little shorter if his shins were disproportionately long. If B was a woman, she could have been 5 feet 4 inches tall (162 cm.).[5] These statures fall within the range of living Australoids and far exceed that of the living Javanese.

What Name, Mr. Solo?

I N Oppenoorth's initial description of the first six Ngandong skulls, he proposed the taxonomic title *Homo* (*Javanthropus*) *soloensis*. This was in 1932. Later in the same year he dropped the parenthetical *Javanthropus*, leaving only *Homo soloensis*. In 1937 he said: "In my first publication I proposed to unite *H. soloensis*, *H. rhodesiensis*, *H. wadjakensis*, all proto-australian forms, into a separate subgenus, *Javanthropus*, but—and I completely agree with Dubois that they all belong in this group—that name was not well chosen and it is better to drop it. Yet we have in *Homo soloensis* the oldest at present known representative of *Homo sapiens fossilis*." [6]

Meanwhile, in 1934, von Koenigswald had dubbed the skulls *Homo neanderthalensis soloensis*. When Weidenreich wrote his final monograph he said: "Earlier studies led me to the conviction that Ngandong man is not a true Neanderthal type but distinctly more primitive and very close to Pithecanthropus and Sinanthropus. For this reason I ranked Solo man with the same group of early hominids as the two later forms and called the whole group Archanthropines. . . . Considered from this point of view, it is entirely irrelevant whether Solo man is called *Javanthropus soloensis* or *Homo soloensis*. I decided to use simply 'Solo man.' " [7]

From the post-1960 point of view, this historical discussion seems as irrelevant to me as it did to Weidenreich in the late 1940's. Solo man was closely related to the two successive Pithecanthropus populations. He had nothing to do with Neanderthal; and as we shall see in the next chapter, he occupied the same

---

[5] The least diameters of tibia A are 28 mm. anteroposteriorly and 30 mm. bilaterally; it is also 46 mm. thick at the top where broken. The comparable figures for tibia B are: 25 mm., 25 mm., and 40 mm.
[6] Oppenoorth: "The Place of *Homo soloensis* . . . ," pp. 358–9.
[7] Weidenreich: "Morphology of Solo Man," p. 227.

evolutionary grade as Sinanthropus. Although larger-brained than his predecessors, he was still *Homo erectus.*

The Solo-like Brain Case from Aitape, New Guinea

I N A L L past and present Australoid regions, no *Homo erectus* skulls have yet been found outside of Java, with one possible exception. That is a brain case unearthed in 1925 at Aitape, in the Finsch Coast area of northeast New Guinea.[8] Its date is Pleistocene, and as the dating was carried out by oil geologists working with fossil molluscs, there is little possibility of error. What part of the Pleistocene it came from we do not know, but, on other evidence, we may suppose that it was Upper Pleistocene and late, dating from a time when New Guinea and Australia were connected by the Sahul Shelf, and Wallacea contained more dry land than it does today.

The specimen is a calva of a female aged about forty-five years, and consists of most of a frontal bone and portions of both parietals. It has very heavy brow ridges, a sloping forehead, and an angular cranial contour. The temporal lines follow the profile of the brain case. This specimen is not only clearly Australoid, but it bears a striking resemblance to the Solo calvaria. Whether it had crossed the *erectus-sapiens* line we cannot say without further study. Howells, who has seen it, thinks it had.

The Fourth Known Human Population of Java: Wadjak Man

I N 1890, before he discovered the famous Trinil skullcap, P-1, Eugene Dubois found two other fossil skulls at a place called Wadjak in central Java. They had been cemented in breccia, and were unaccompanied by implements. Because the fauna was modern in every sense, they were probably later than the Solo skulls and late Pleistocene in date, at the earliest. As the site has since been destroyed by quarrymen, the exact date may never be known. For thirty years Dubois kept the world in ignorance of

[8] F. J. Fenner: "Fossil Skull Fragments of Probably Pleistocene Age from Aitape, New Guinea," *RSAM,* Vol. 6 (1944), pp. 335–54. W. W. Howells, Jr., personal communication.

these to him relatively uninteresting skulls, and failed to describe them until 1931.[9] Luckily, we have casts of both specimens.

Wadjak 1, or W-1, is a nearly complete cranium, the base of which is largely intact, and a piece of mandible. In the cranium several considerable breaks and gaps may be seen in the right temporal and occipital regions, and both zygomatic arches are gone. Only seven upper teeth are *in situ* and unbroken: all five premolars and molars on the right side, and the second and third molars. An eighth tooth, which could be a canine, is stuck in its matrix in the roof of the palate. At the time of casting (my description is based largely on a cast), the skull had not been fully cleaned.

The piece of mandible is also still breccia-bound. It consists of 85 mm., more or less, of the right branch, running from the socket of the first molar to the gonial angle, the rear half of the first molar tooth, and the second and third molars. The ascending ramus is broken off just above tooth level. Most of the lingual surface and the bottom edge remain to be cleaned.

W-2, while more fragmentary, is in better shape, and has no adhering matrix. It consists of five pieces, which could be assembled as adequately as Weidenreich assembled those of Pithecanthropus 4. They are: (1) a piece of frontal including the brow ridges, with the upper part of the nasal bones, and with part of the left zygomatic bone extending under and defining the left eye socket; (2) the maxillae, including the palate and the floor of the nasal passages, extending 25 mm. up the side of the nasal opening (this is a little more than the corresponding piece of P-4) and containing, *in situ*, all the permanent upper teeth except the incisors and the right first molar; (3) most of the occipital bone; (4) part of the right temporal, including the mastoid and the ear hole; and (5) the mandible, the right half of which is nearly complete. The left half is broken off 10 mm. behind the level of the third molar. All the permanent lower teeth are present except the right canine, both first premolars, and the right third molar.

[9] Dubois: "The Proto-Australian Fossil Man of Wadjak, Java," *PKAW*, Vol. 23, No. 7 (1921), pp. 1013–51.

G. Pinkley: "The Significance of Wadjak Man . . . ," *PNHB.*, Vol. 10, No. 3 (1936), pp. 183–200.

Dubois, who considered Wadjak 1 a female on grounds which could be contested, gave it a cranial capacity of 1,550 cc. As the interior of the skull had not been cleaned, this figure was apparently obtained by a formula based on modern skulls. In the light of more recent knowledge, we may use the von Bonin formula for Australoid skulls. The result is a figure of 1,475 cc., which may still be too high in view of the massiveness of the bones. Wadjak 2, which Dubois classified as a male—probably correctly—may have had a brain of more or less the same size.

Despite these corrections, the Wadjak pair are large skulls; in size they fit within the upper fourth of the modern Australian range for males, and as far as brain size goes, they are fully evolved members of the species *H. sapiens.* This places them one brain-size grade above the Solo skulls, which in turn are a grade above Pithecanthropus. With this exercise, we have passed through more than 400,000 years of time, from the most primitive known human form to a man with a modern brain size, all within a small section of a single, medium-sized island having a minimum of environmental change and probably little if any advance in technology.

For the first time in the Pithecanthropus-Australoid sequence we have a population represented by the essential parts of two faces. Moreover, this is the first time since the Djetis Pithecanthropi that mandibles are available. The face, teeth, and jaws of the Wadjak specimens can be expected to reveal some progressive changes from the features of their predecessors, but not as many as brain size will indicate. It is unlikely that feeding habits, which involve the jaws and teeth, kept pace during this journey through time with advances in human relations, which are more closely linked to the growth of the brain.

The Wadjak Brain Cases

O f t h e two Wadjak brain cases, only W-1 can be described as a whole. It is a large skull in all three principal dimensions, comparing favorably with any in the world. It differs from Solo principally in height and in that the bicristal and biparietal breadths are apparently the same; this is difficult to determine because the crests are broken and the brain case is both broken and warped. The length is not from crest to crest but from a moderately prominent glabella to a rounded occipital bulge. The two heights, basion-bregma and auricular, differ by over 20 mm., whereas in the earlier Javanese skulls the differences are only from 12 to 15 mm. This reflects a change in the morphology of the brain case.

In 1947, Weidenreich observed that the truly primitive brain cases, including those of Pithecanthropus, Sinanthropus, and Solo, differed from those of modern men in two related respects.[1] In the more primitive types, the upper profile of the brain is nearly flat; in the more advanced ones it is humped. In the more primitive skulls, the floor of the brain case is virtually flat, while in the more advanced ones it is bent downward at both ends, as well as in the median sagittal line. This is caused by the growth of the parietal lobes of the brain in the center, and by the growth of the middle lobe of the cerebellum, which is concerned with voluntary movements of the muscles, particularly those of the limbs, including the fine movements of the hands in skilled work. Among other effects, this bending lowers the base of the brain relative to the position of the ear hole. It is hard to observe this phenomenon in W-1 because of breakage, warping, and poor cleaning, but in the occipital bone of W-2 the concavities that hold the base of the cerebellum and the occipital lobes of the cortex are cupped inward and downward. Wadjak man's brain was not only curved on top but it also had acquired the bending specified in Weidenreich's study. In these respects as well as in absolute size his brain was more evolved than that of Solo.

Morphologically, the Wadjak brain cases resemble those of Pithecanthropus and Solo in a familial way. There are still planes, although the contours are more nearly round, the mastoids are still large, and the temporal muscle lines still follow the contour of the skull roof. The forehead is sloping and extends upward and backward from glabella without a marked depression. Although the zygomatic arches are gone, enough is left of the zygomatic

[1] Weidenreich: "Some particulars of skull and brain of early hominids and their bearing on the problem of the relationship between man and anthropoids," *AJPA*, Vol. 5, No. 4 (1947), pp. 387–428.

process of the left malar of W-1 to indicate a bizygomatic diameter above the modern Australian maximum.

The Wadjak Faces

W-1 has a large face. It is long, broad, and flat. The brow ridges are heavy only over the nasal region, and the nasal bones take off from the frontal without much depression, but with more than we have seen previously. The nose is exceptionally flat, the interorbital distance is wide, and the orbits wide and low. Although W-1's face is too battered, bruised, and poorly cleaned to permit accurate measurements of the chords and subtenses needed for the first, third, and fourth indices of facial flatness, I have ventured to try the second, or simotic index, which expresses the degree of flatness of the saddle of the nose. It is 24.7(?),[2] which, if correct, places W-1 in the company of Negritos, Negroes, Bushmen, and Hottentots, and gives her or him a slightly flatter nose than the means for living Papuans and Melanesians. Because Wadjak 2's upper facial region is in better condition, it is possible to calculate the first index, the frontal index of facial flatness. This is 18.6, right in the middle of the range of means for recent Australian aborigines and Tasmanians and inside that of Papuans and Melanesians.

In W-1 the alveolar protrusion is tremendous, and its appearance is exaggerated by the flatness of the upper part of the facial skeleton. In both specimens the nasal aperture is very broad and its border guttered, as in Pithecanthropus 4. The palates are long, broad, and deep, within the metrical ranges of modern Australian crania in all three measurements, but definitely smaller in every way than our only previous specimen from this area, Pithecanthropus 4.

The Wadjak Mandibles

OUR first virtually complete mandible in the Pithecanthropus-Australoid sequence is that of Wadjak 2. What is missing on one side is present on the other. Because the palate of W-2 does not

[2] The question mark indicates that the figure is not certain, because of breakage.

fit it perfectly, it is apparent that the palate has been widened in the region of the right second and third upper molars in back of a break line. This distortion has been allowed for in the figure for palate breadth in Table 38.

The first thing that one notices about this mandible is that it looks modern because it has a chin, but after a little handling and matching with other mandibles a second fact becomes clear—this is a very large, heavy jawbone. It is just as large and heavily built as Pithecanthropus B. In other words, in the Pithecanthropus-Australoid line as seen in Java, the lower jaws remained equally large and strong for over a half million years. The Wadjak 2 mandible is also just as large and heavy as the famous Heidelberg jaw from Germany, which is at least 360,000 years old. But morphologically the Wadjak 2 mandible is more advanced than either Pithecanthropus B or Heidelberg in that it has a chin.

The Wadjak Dentition

I N T H E upper jaw there are two, three, or four specimens of every tooth except the incisors. In general, these upper teeth are as long as those of P-4 anteroposteriorly, but narrower labiolingually. The indices of robusticity (length times breadth) are thus lower. In particular, the second upper molars of both Wadjak specimens are smaller in every way than those of P-4. Although the Wadjak upper teeth run a little larger than the modern Australian mean, they are well within the modern range. Also, for the first time we find the modern size sequence in upper molars, in which the first molar is the largest and the third the smallest.

In the lower jaws there is at least one tooth for each place in the row. What has been said above about the sizes of the upper teeth in comparison to other specimens and series is equally true of the lowers. In the Wadjak 1 mandible the molar sequence is also the same as in the upper jaw, but in the Wadjak 2 mandible the third molar is larger than the second.

Among the Australian aborigines the cusp number for each molar tooth is usually $\frac{4\text{-}4\text{-}4}{5\text{-}5\text{-}5}$; that is, all three upper molars have four cusps, and all three lowers have five. In Wadjak 1 it is $\dfrac{4-?-3}{5-4-5}$,

and in Wadjak 2 it is $\dfrac{5-4-4}{5-4-5}$.[3] Both Wadjak 1 and Wadjak 2, then, had fewer cusps on their molars than any of the Pithecanthropus specimens; and Wadjak 1's molars were a little more reduced, that is, advanced, than those of the average modern Australian aborigine, whereas those of Wadjak 2 are identical with aboriginal teeth.

Only the teeth of Wadjak 2 are well enough reproduced in photographs or casts to permit the study of other details. Each upper canine has a teatlike ridge running up the center of the lingual side, reaching from the base of the crown to the level where the crown is worn (about 6 mm.) Comparable but narrower ridges are found on the lingual sides of the upper left canine and on all four lower incisors. On the upper left canine, the edges of the tooth are raised. These features are common in Australian teeth.

The Significance of Wadjak

THE STUDY of the two Wadjak specimens completes our series of four consecutive populations that lived in the center of one of the smaller islands of central Indonesia during the Pleistocene. This is but a tiny fraction of the total area presumably occupied by members of the Pithecanthropus-Australoid line during a period of over a half million years. It shows continuity, variability, and evolution. *Homo erectus* was still alive there less than a hundred thousand years ago, and *Homo sapiens* appeared there ten thousand years ago or earlier. Sometime between Solo and Wadjak, the transition was made.

But it was not necessarily made in Java itself. The Djetis Pithecanthropi, the Trinil Pithecanthropi, Solo, and Wadjak may represent successive invasions from a center of Australoid evolution somewhere in the north, such as Siam or Indochina, where there have been no Duboises or von Koenigswalds to seek out fossil men. If Java was a periphery of southeast Asia, Australia is a pe-

---

[3] Pinkley: "The Significance of Wadjak Man"; and also observation of casts.

riphery of Java. Bearing in mind the principle that the outer peripheries of zoogeographic regions tend to be inhabited by archaic
kinds of animals, let us see what Australia has to offer in the fossil-man line.

Fossil Man in Australia

W E D O N O T know when human beings first began to bother the
kangaroos by appearing in Australia, but it was undoubtedly later
than man's first appearance in any other continent, except Antarctica. The first people to reach North America had a broad
Pleistocene highway to walk over. The level of the earth's oceans
controlled their time of passage. The first to reach Australia and
New Guinea had no such dry road, for the islands of Wallacea
rise steeply from the sea. With or without the presence of the
Sunda and Sahul shelves, whoever made the crossing still had to
hop from island to island on rafts or small boats, and the greatest
distance that had to be traversed was about 50 miles.

When the great shelves were above water, migrants could enter
Australia by way of Timor as easily as they could get to New
Guinea via the Moluccas. When the shelves were submerged, New
Guinea was the only feasible port of entry. Which route was used
first we do not know, nor are we sure that the Timor-Sahul Shelf
route was used at all, but the present distribution of racial traits
in the entire Australian faunal area favors the latter.

The only concrete evidence favoring a late Pleistocene date of
entry is the age determination of the Aitape find, which is still an
isolated discovery and needs confirmation. The oldest Carbon-14
date yet obtained from an archaeological site is 6,740 ± 120 B.C.,
for Cape Martin, South Australia,[4] associated with an archaic culture known as the Tartangan. Because a still more primitive culture, the Kartan, has been found in several sites below the Tartangan, Tindale estimates that the Kartan must have begun at least as
early as 9,000 B.C.[5] No evidence is yet available which indicates

[4] D. J. Mulvaney: "Australian Radio-carbon Dates," *Antiquity*, Vol. 35, No.
137 (1961), pp. 37–9.
[5] N. B. Tindale: "Ecology of Primitive Aboriginal Man in Australia," in
A. Keast, R. L. Crocker, and C. S. Christian: "Biogeography and Ecology in
Australia," *MB*, Vol. 8 (1959), pp. 36–51.

that entry took place before 10,000 B.C., the very time when Mongoloid peoples had, as we shall soon see, begun pressing into southeast Asia out of China.

Linguistic evidence suggests that the dispersal of the Australoid peoples occurred less than 20,000 years ago: as explained in Chapter 1, languages lexically related to one another can be no older. All Australian languages are mutually related. The Papuan languages probably belong to the same family; so apparently does Andamanese (the languages of the Andaman Island Negritos) and even, it has been claimed, the Mon-Khmer languages of southeast Asia, which are spoken by Mongoloids, and of parts of India, where they are spoken by both Mongoloids and Australoids.

Whatever the archaeological and linguistic evidence may prove, we have a number of mineralized human remains from Australia, and more effort has beeen spent in discussing their ages than in describing them. Of the lot only three have been tentatively accepted by the profession as having any antiquity: Keilor, Talgai, and Cohuna.

The Keilor Skull

I N 1940 a fossil skull was found in a sandpit in a place called Keilor, ten miles north of Melbourne. It is heavily mineralized and a Carbon-14 date for the same terrace, but not the same site, is 6,550 ± 250 B.C. (W-169), well within the range of the Cape Martin date. The importance of this skull lies not in its age but in its close resemblance to Wadjak 1, which Weidenreich found to be within the range of twins.[6] This resemblance has been somewhat reduced by new measurements of the Wadjak-1 cast, but it is still there. If not identical twins, they could have been brothers. Keilor was an adult, and apparently a male, but this is not certain.

---

[6] Weidenreich: "The Keilor Skull: a Wadjak Type from Southeast Australia," *AJPA*, Vol. 3, No. 1 (1945), pp. 21–32.

J. Wunderley: "The Keilor Skull, Anatomical Description," *MNMM*, No. 13 (1943), pp. 57–70.

W. Adam: "The Keilor Fossil Skull, Palate and Upper Dental Arch," *MNMM*, No. 13 (1943), pp. 71–8.

The published cranial capacity, 1,593 cc., is greater than the top of the Australian range. When recalculated with the formula used for Wadjak 1, it reduced to 1,464 cm., which is a more realistic figure, close to the new figure for Wadjak 1. Keilor's face was of moderate length, his nose flat, his orbits low. He had the same Negrito-Bushman look seen in Wadjak 1. This settles the question whether people with this kind of face could have been in any way ancestral to the more pointed-faced, living aborigines.

The Talgai Skull [7]

THE TALGAI skull was found in 1884 at Darling Downs, South Queensland. It lay seven feet down in undisturbed clay under black soil, near the top of the clay. The skull eventually reached the University of Sydney, where it was described in 1918, but one upper left median incisor tooth remained in Queensland because its owner refused to sell it. The skull was heavily fossilized and badly crushed. Shortly after death, however, someone had removed the front part of the base in the usual way and presumably for the usual purpose. It was apparently a male, fourteen to sixteen years old. The skull is smaller than Keilor, with a cranial capacity of about 1,300 cc., and it is as low-vaulted as Solo. Although its brow ridges are moderate, it has a nuchal crest, and altogether it is a more primitive specimen than Keilor. The palate is as large as that of Wadjak 2, and nearly square; the molar-premolar rows are nearly parallel, and the canines and incisors form nearly a straight line across the front. In this respect it resembles the older Pithecanthropus 4, although there is no evidence of a diastema.

As neither wisdom tooth had erupted, Talgai had died young, but he had lived long enough to wear the crowns of his first molars down to the dentine. His teeth are larger than those of either of the Wadjaks or of Keilor, and approach those of Pithecanthropi 4 and B in size. In fact, his canine is a shade wider mesiodistally than P-4's, but it is not as thick labiolingually. The premolars and

[7] S. A. Smith: "The Fossil Human Skull Found at Talgai, Queensland," *TRSL* (B), Vol. 208 (1918), pp. 351–87.

first molar are nearly as large as P-4's but his second molar is considerably smaller, as in modern skulls.

Despite his big teeth, Talgai did not resemble the Javanese skulls facially. Metrically, the skull falls at about the middle of the modern Australian range in details of the nasal skeleton and orbits. Morphologically, it is not very flat-faced, but has a depressed nasion and a rather beaky profile. Its features are run-of-the-mill Australian. If it and Keilor were contemporary, the facial features of the Australian aborigines were variable at that time, as they are today.

The Cohuna Skull [8]

THE THIRD and last on our list of moderately well authenticated Australian skulls of some antiquity is Cohuna, found in 1925, two feet below the surface of the soil, in the Murray River Valley on the edge of Kow Swamp, Cohuna, Victoria. The skull was completely mineralized and filled with silt. Nearby were about fifty pieces of equally fossilized skulls and bones which have not been described, and eleven recent aboriginal skeletons.

This skull was mutilated twice. Immediately after death some fellow-aborigine broke off the base to get at the brain. Thousands of years later a modern, white Australian who owned the skull cut from it two perfect circles of bone, each 27 mm. in diameter. As one of these circles included inion, it is difficult to reconstruct the nuchal border of the occipital bone. Although the cranial capacity has not been published, the von Bonin formula for Australoid skulls places it well over 1,500 cc. This figure is probably much too high because the forehead is exceedingly low and sloping, and the auricular head height of 122(?) mm. represents a peak rather than a plane. Without doubt, the true capacity of this skull falls within the modern Australian range.

Aside from the extreme slope of the forehead, which rivals that of the Pithecanthropi except that it continues up farther, and its

[8] N. W. G. Macintosh: "The Cohuna Cranium, History and Commentary from Nov. 1925 to Nov. 1951," *Mankind*, Vol. 4, No. 8 (1952), pp. 307–29.

D. J. Mahony, W. Baragwanath, F. Wood-Jones, and A. S. Kenyon: "Fossil Man in the State of Victoria, Australia," *RIGC*, (16th) Washington, 1936, pp. 1335–42.

very heavy brow ridges, this skull is notable for its tremendous prognathism, and its wide bizygomatic diameter, which exceeds the modern Australian range. Furthermore, the palate was not horseshoe-shaped but rectangular. Unfortunately we have no measurements of the teeth. Although its face is extremely long, its features, like Talgai's, are Australian. Its nasal root is deeply sunk under the brow ridges, and its facial profile is not flat.

The Pithecanthropus-Australoid Line

T H E S E three skulls, Keilor, Talgai, and Cohuna, whatever their ages, definitely link the living Australian aborigines to the succession of four Pleistocene populations in Java, and to the Aitape brain case from New Guinea. Dubois first saw this connection and Weidenreich agreed with him. It has been more recently accepted by Boule and Vallois, and by Piveteau. Pithecanthropus of course is extinct, and so is Solo man, but neither died without progeny. Their extinction took the well-known form of evolution by succession, or, more simply, of evolving into something else.

When the ancestors of the Australian aborigines and their island-dwelling neighbors arrived at their present homes, they were already marginal people; and after they had settled there they fell into a marginal geographical pattern of their own. Among the living aborigines, for example, the curliest hair and the heaviest brow ridges are found on the peripheries of the continent and its offshore islands. Whether this implies a succession of invasions, a slow trickle of genes from the northwest during the period of Mongoloid pressure on southeast Asia and Indonesia, or local evolution radiating from a central Australian focus, we do not know, nor is the question pertinent to the thesis of this book.

Some evolution has probably been taking place, but, as one would expect in a marginal area of the Southern Hemisphere, its over-all rate cannot have been rapid. One still finds recent aboriginal female skulls with cranial capacities of 930 cc., 946 cc., and 956 cc. whose owners apparently met the demands of their culture well enough to live to maturity; [9] and I have myself measured

[9] Macintosh: op. cit.

a living married woman named Topsy (see Plate XXXII) with a head length of 184 mm., a breadth of 121 mm., and an auricular height of 109 mm., flesh included. Her cranial capacity was under 1,000 cc. and she was a normal member of Tiwi society, described in Chapter 3.

This study leads to several conclusions. One is that the Australian aborigines are still in the act of sloughing off some of the genetic traits which distinguish *Homo erectus* from *Homo sapiens*. Another is that, as rates of evolution differ in different parts of the world, populations belonging to a given evolutionary grade in different places cannot be closely related if their life spans are hundreds of thousands of years apart. Having established a base line of evolutionary tempo for the Pithecanthropus-Australoid line, we can, in subsequent chapters, see how it matches the rates of other lines.

Human Evolution North of Java in the Pleistocene

H A V I N G L E F T two areas of light, Java and Australia, we now enter a realm of virtual darkness. The skeletal history of the more northerly parts of the Eastern Oriental region is extremely fragmentary, consisting almost entirely of a few scraps of bone, a handful of teeth, preliminary notices of two or three newly discovered finds, and that is all. Only two finds can be definitely called Pleistocene, those of Mapa in south China and of the new skull from the Niah Cave of Borneo.

The Mapa Skullcap

T H E O L D E R of the two is the Mapa calva, probably that of an adult male, found in the province of Kwangtung, south China.[1] Its date is late Middle or early Upper Pleistocene, later than either the Djetis or the Trinil Pithecanthropi and probably earlier than Solo. It consists of the frontal, parietal, and nasal bones and the lower border of the right eye socket. As it bears certain resem-

---

[1] Ju-Kang Woo: "Fossil Human Skull of Early Paleanthropic Stage Found at Mapa, Shaoquan, Kwangtung Province," *VP*, Vol. 3, No. 4 (1959), pp. 176–82.

blances to both Solo and Sinanthropus, it can best be studied after we have described the latter in the following chapter. It is mentioned here merely to set the northern boundary of the area we are talking about, at the time it lived.

The Upper Pleistocene Skull from Niah Cave,
North Borneo

I N 1959 Tom Harrisson, who had been excavating the vast and famous cave at Niah, North Borneo, for several years, discovered a human skull at a depth of eight feet four inches. It was associated with chopping tools and large, coarse flakes, comparable to the Soanian of India, and it has been given a Carbon-14 date of 39,-600 ± 1,000 years ago by the Groningen Laboratory.[2] This makes it possibly as old as Solo and certainly older than Wadjak, and about as old as the first Upper Paleolithic men of Europe.

It is the skull of a youth between fifteen and seventeen years old, probably female, definitely *sapiens,* and equally definitely Australoid. Its closest resemblance is to the skulls of modern Tasmanians. It has very little brow-ridge development, a deep nasal root, and a vertical forehead. The parietal bones have high, prominent bosses; the occiput is well rounded; and the mastoids are small. The palate and teeth are smaller than those of the fossil Australian skulls but comparable in size and shape to those of living Australians and Tasmanians. The face is short, the nose broad. The tracks of the meningial arteries on the inside of the parietal bones are modern in complexity and form.

This skull indicates that, by the time of the Göttweig Interstadial in Europe, or about 38,000 B.C., the Australoid subspecies, at least in Borneo, had crossed the threshold between *Homo erectus* and *Homo sapiens,* either through local evolution alone, or as a result of gene flow from the Mongoloid region to the north.

[2] W. G. Solheim II: "The Present Status of the 'Paleolithic' in Borneo," *AP,* Vol. 2, No. 2 of 1958 (Hong Kong, 1960), pp. 83–90. The C-14 date number is GRO-1338.

D. R. Brothwell: "Upper Pleistocene Human Skull from the Niah Cave, Sarawak," *SMJ,* Vol. 9, No. 15–16 (1960), pp. 323–49.

The Mesolithic-Neolithic Transition in Indonesia

F O L L O W I N G the time of the Niah skull, we must jump at least 25,000 years until the end of the Pleistocene, and later. The main seat of the Australoids then shifted from Indonesia and southeast Asia to the Australian region, whereas in Indonesia and southeast Asia Australoids were gradually replaced, except in a few marginal refuges, by Mongoloids. We would like to know the details of this replacement. When, for example, did the ancestors of the Negritos shrink to their present size? Did they do this in one or several acts of shrinking? When did the Mongoloids come in? Did they first arrive as food gatherers, and in later waves penetrate as agriculturalists, or was the first wave already agricultural?

We cannot answer these questions satisfactorily because the existing skeletal material is scanty, and what little has been found has been inadequately described. It seemed less important to its discoverers than the older, fossilized skulls and bones, and it is mostly fragile and hard to handle. Also the archaeological sequences in this area have not yet been fully clarified and co-ordinated. The term *Neolithic* does not in itself distinguish between food-gathering and food-producing cultures but seems to include some of both. Finally, it is hard to tell which of the different "Mesolithic" and "Neolithic" tool industries evolved locally and which were derived from outside.

About the same time that he discovered the Wadjak skulls, Dubois also found a skeleton in a cave near the ancient lake of Wadjak. It was less fossilized than the Wadjak bones, and covered with red ochre. Dubois identified it as Mongoloid.[3] It was round-headed. In another cave at Bodjonegoro, also in Java, in what may have been a Mesolithic deposit, although it could be of later date, P. van Stein Callenfels[4] found some scraps and bits of human skeletal material. Of these, three molar teeth were measured. They are too big for Negritos, and a little too big for Java-

[3] Dubois: "The Proto-Australian Fossil Man of Wadjak, Java," *PKAW*, Vol. 23, No. 7 (1921).

[4] Van Heekeren: *The Stone Age of Indonesia* (The Hague: Martin Nijhoff; 1957), pp. 78–9.

nese, who for small people have large teeth. They fit easily into the Pithecanthropus-Wadjak size range.[5]

In the nearby cave of Sampoeng, in a series of "Neolithic" deposits, Callenfels and his associates found a number of burials. W. A. Mijsberg was able to restore one cranium, called Sampoeng F.[6] He measured this cranium and its teeth carefully. In every one of ten cranial dimensions, and in eight of nine cranial indices, it falls within the modern Javanese range as determined from cadaver material in Batavia. The one exception is the upper facial index, in which it exceeds the range, but this index depends to a certain extent on diet, because heavy chewing spreads the zygomatic arches and increases the face breadth. As the teeth also match those of the Batavian cadavers in size, we may well believe that this skull belonged to an early Mongoloid ancestor of the Javanese, whether agricultural or not we do not know.

To the east, in Celebes, two energetic Swiss cousins, Paul and Fritz Sarasin, discovered in 1902 a tribe of backward folk living partly in caves. They took various measurements of these people, who were called Toala, and excavated the floor of the caves they lived in, discovering some artifacts and a few human bones.[7] As a result of this research, they became convinced that the Toala were close kin of the Veddas, a hunting people still living in Ceylon, who are actually small and primitive Caucasoids. They drew this conclusion both from their study of the living and from their examination of the skeletal remains exhumed from the floor of the cave. This identification snowballed during the last half century, until the presence of Veddoids in Indonesia, and in Malaya as well, became textbook dogma. So it has remained, although

[5] Left upper first molar is 12.3 mm. in anteroposterior length and 13.1 mm. in tabiolingual breadth. The right upper first molar is 12.8 mm. by 13.4 mm.; a lower third is 13.0 mm. by 12.5 mm.

[6] W. A. Mijsberg: "Récherches sur les Restes Humains de Goewa-Lawa à Sampoeng et des Sites Préhistoriques à Bodjonegoro (Java)," in *Hommage du Service Archéologique des Indes Néerlandaises au Premier Congrès des Préhistoriens d'Extrême-Orient à Hanoi, 26–31 Jan. 1932* (Batavia: Société Royale des Arts et Sciences; 1932).

[7] Paul and Fritz Sarasin: *Reisen in Celebes* (Wiesbaden: C. W. Kreidel; 1905); *Versuch einer Anthropologie der Insel Celebes* (Wiesbaden: C. W. Kreidel; 1905).

Mijsberg refuted this identification before 1950.[8] He measured the living and found them no different from the other more or less Mongoloid inhabitants of Celebes, particularly similar to their neighbors the Buginese. He measured also some sub-Recent skeletal material from the cave of Bolabatu, Lamontjong Cave (excavated by the Sarasins), Panganrejang Cave, and Lompoa Cave.

From Bolabatu came one calvarium and a mandible. Available measurements for both are within the Buginese range, and the minimum frontal forehead breadth of 98 mm. is too great for a Vedda, and so is the mandibular height of 31 mm. One female skeleton from Lompoa Cave was four feet eight inches (142 cm.) long, which is in the Pygmy range, but many living Indonesian women are equally short. The teeth are also small, smaller than those of living Buginese, but within the Javanese range.

This material, on the whole, indicates that the people who lived in the Toalian caves in geologically Recent times were similar to the living inhabitants of the region. The deposits in the cave include Bronze Age artifacts, and also "Neolithic" implements that are called Toalian. Whether the people whose skeletons Mijsberg measured were food gatherers or slash-and-burn cultivators is not known.

Moving on to Sumatra, we come upon a report that "a few fragments of skulls, hardly sufficient for a final racial determination, were found in one of the shell heaps of north Sumatra. . . . Watsl . . . came to the conclusion that they showed Papuo-Melanoid racial characters." [9] Finding Papuo-Melanesian characters in sub-Recent but prehistoric bones was a favorite sport in southeast Asia at that time. We cannot be sure that the Sumatran cranial scraps did not belong to Negritos.

In the Philippines, a Negrito skull was found, before 1921,

[8] D. A. Hooijer: "Man and Other Mammals from Toalian Sites in S. W. Celebes," *PKAW*, Sec. 2, Vol. 46, No. 2 (1950), pp. 1–164, especially 59–74.

[9] R. Heine-Geldern: "Prehistoric Research in the Netherlands Indies," in P. Honig and F. Verdoorn, eds.: *Science and Scientists in the Netherlands Indies* (New York: Chronica Botanica Co.; 1945), pp. 129–67. After J. Watsl: "Prähistorische Menschenreste aus dem Muschelhügel von Bindjai-Tamiang in Nord Sumatra," in a Festschrift: *Otto Reche zum 60. Geburtstag* . . . (Munich-Berlin, 1939), pp. 237–43.

under ten feet of alluvial deposit below the Rio Pasig in Manila.[1] This is the first Negrito skull we have unearthed, but unfortunately it cannot be dated.

Mesolithic and Neolithic Remains from Indochina

W I T H a characteristic interest in archaeology, the French excavated widely in Indochina during the last quarter of the nineteenth century and well into the 1930's, stopping only with the advent of World War II. They found three principal post-Pleistocene cultural levels: a Mesolithic, then an early Neolithic characterized by stone axes polished on the cutting edge only, and finally a late Neolithic with axes polished all over. In all three periods, the fauna was the same as that of today, except that no bones of domestic animals have been found. Exactly when agriculture came in we do not know, but it is difficult to understand why these people needed the vast numbers of axes they made unless they were clearing garden patches, or at least ringing the bark of trees in preparation for burning.

Up to 1938, a total of thirty-five skulls intact enough for study had been found and more or less described.[2] Almost all come from Laos, although some are from Tonkin. This region is close to the Chinese border. Most of the remains were found in grassy country well over 3,000 feet high, on the main invasion route of Mongoloid peoples into Indochina. Not only was this highroad extensively used in historic times; it is even serving this purpose today. The Miao tribes of southern China advanced a full six degrees of lati-

[1] D. Sanchez y Sanchez: "Un craneo humano prehistórico de Manila (Filipinas)," *MRSE*, Vol. 11 (1921).

P. Huard and E. Saurin: "État Actuel de la Craniologie Indochinoise," *BSGI*, Vol. 25, No. 1 (1938), pp. 1–104.

[2] Huard and Saurin: op. cit.

J. Fromaget and E. Saurin: "Note Préliminaire sur les Formations Cénozoiques et Plus Récentes de la Chaîne Annamitique Septentrionale et du Haut Laos," *BSGI*, Vol. 22, No. 3 (1936), pp. 1–48.

H. Mansuy: "Contribution a l'Étude de la Préhistoire de l'Indochine: V. Nouvelles Decouvertes dans les Cavernes du Massif Calcaire de Bac-Son (Tonkin); VI. Stations Préhistoriques de Kéo-Phay, de Lai-Ta, et de Bang-Mac, dans le Massif Calcaire de Bac-Son (Tonkin); VII. Néolithique Inferieur (Bacsonien) et Néolithique Supérieure dans le Haut-Tonkin," *BSGI*, Vol. 12, Nos. 1, 2, 3 (1925).

tude southward over it in the century that ended in the 1930's. If we are to find the earliest Mongoloid skulls in southeast Asia, this is the place to look for them.

Luckily, an early Mongoloid skull has been found there, at Tam Pong.[3] It belonged to a young adult female about twenty years old, who had not yet cut her wisdom teeth. A stature of about five feet two inches (157 cm.) has been calculated from her long bones. The skull is of modern size, with a capacity of over 1,350 cc. It is delicate in structure, well rounded, has no brow ridges but does have well-developed mastoids. The orbits are not as high as in most Mongoloids, but the interorbital distance is great, and the nasal bones lie flat. Although the nasal opening is wide, the bones themselves are very narrow at the top, and constricted below nasion. The face is long and wide, and the malars (cheekbones) are salient below the lower orbital margin. There is no canine fossa. The palate is large and parabolic, the chin well developed. There is no prognathism.

The skull is certainly neither Australoid nor Negrito. It must then be either Caucasoid or Mongoloid. The shape of the orbits is Caucasoid, but the structure and protrusion of the malars, the length of the upper face, the shape and flatness of the nasal bones, as well as the guttering at the border of the nasal opening, are all Mongoloid, in a general sense. I am satisfied with the conclusion that Mongoloid food gatherers had begun to enter southeast Asia from the north fairly early in postglacial times. As Laos is a northern frontier country, this evidence does not indicate how far south these Mongoloids penetrated at what times. That they did not immediately replace the earlier peoples can be seen from a study of the Lower, or Early, Neolithic skeletons.

From the site of Tam Hang come four adult skeletons of the Lower, or Early Neolithic, the time of partially polished axes and no domestic animals. Two are males and two females. Both females were pregnant. The males are numbered S-3 and S-5, the females S-2 and S-4.

Starting with the female S-2, we note that although most of the face is missing, the mandible is present. This is a remarkably short skull, but the breadth and height dimensions make up for

[3] Fromaget and Saurin: op. cit.

its deficiency in length, giving it a cranial capacity of about
1,230 cc. The skull is thin and infantile, with a straight forehead;
the mandible modern and tiny. Without reasonable doubt, this
woman was a Negrito, resembling the modern Andamanese in
cranial structure. Her stature, four feet eleven inches, or 150 cm.,
lies on the upper border of the Negrito range.

Her companion, the male S-3, was an inch shorter, or 147 cm.
tall; and his cranial capacity, 1,430 cc., was greater. This skull is
practically complete. It is delicate, well rounded, somewhat bulbous in the forehead, with an open metopic (frontal) suture, small
malars and a feeble development of the zygomatic arches, a
sharp-bordered nasal opening, a straight chin, and no prognathism. He, too, was a Negrito.

S-5, the other male, has no cranial base, and most of the face
is gone, but the mandible is there. The cranial capacity is about
1,340 cc. The skull is narrower than S-2 or S-3, and its orbits
seem to be higher, although it is difficult to tell because they are
incomplete. Unfortunately, we do not know how tall it was. Fromaget and Saurin suspect that it is not fully Negrito, and they may
be right.

S-4, our second female, is nearly complete. The skull is broader
and higher than the others from the same site, and it has a much
more massive face. Its malars project forward, but not as much as
in the Mesolithic skull from Tam Pong, which it resembles in
many ways, including the fact that it has high orbits and alveolar
prognathism. Her stature of five feet one inch, or 155 cm., is too
great for an ordinary Negrito woman. This individual may represent a Mongoloid-Negrito mixture, if not a full Mongoloid.

In sum, this little group of Early Neolithic people interred in
the site of Tam Hang were Negritos—who had begun mixing with
Mongoloid peoples from the north—Mongoloids of the same
general type as the Mesolithic woman of Tam Pong. The Negritos
were characterized by small stature; relatively long lower legs
and lower arms; a delicate, somewhat infantile skull form that is
rounder and higher than anything we have seen before; and small
faces.

In the same site, at the base of the Upper or Late Neolithic, a
skullcap was found in a mutilated state. It had apparently been

used as a cup or bowl and is a very long, narrow calva, with a cranial index of 70, a figure we have not encountered since dealing with fully Australoid specimens. It thus represents a third element in the Indochinese population; we shall presently discuss this element more fully.

Higher up in the Late Neolithic stratum in the Tam Hang site were found a group of one adult and two juvenile skulls. Only one, that of an eleven-year-old, is complete enough to study. With a cranial index of 78, it is mesocranial; its forehead is a little bulbous, its nasal root smooth, its face rather small even for its age, but it has alveolar prognathism and shovel incisors. In general it seems to combine the elements of the Mesolithic and Early Neolithic specimens of the neighborhood.

Other sites contain the skeletons of local groups quite different from those we have just seen. We find in them a new element, already anticipated by the presence of the drinking-bowl calva at Tam Hang. Nine skulls from Lang Cuom and one from Dong Thuoc belong to this type, which the French call Melanesian, although they qualify a few as Indo-Melanesian and Australo-Melanesian. This new element is, simply, a very long and narrow-headed skull, with an index in the low seventies, which is also high-vaulted, with the height equaling or exceeding the breadth.[4]

The skull looks like an Australian aboriginal skull with some of the corners rounded off and the brow ridges and other bony struts toned down. The face also resembles a softened, less primitive-looking, Australian face. The relationship to the Australian type is clear. The reduction in primitive features could be due either to mixture with something else or to evolution.

Personally I prefer the evolutionary explanation, at least as the major cause of this change, although mixture with both Negritos and early Mongoloids cannot be ruled out. Still, neither of these two would give these modified Australoids their extreme cranial form. Moreover, it seems to me a little premature to call them Melanesian, because that implies a Negroid hair form. We know

[4] Some of the skulls from Lang Cuom and elsewhere were badly deformed by earth pressure, which reduced their breadths greatly. Cranial indices in the low sixties in this series should be discounted.

nothing of the hair form of any prehistoric skull. The Melanesians of today are believed to be Papuans modified by fairly recent Polynesian admixture. If the skulls of Lang Cuom and elsewhere resemble those of Melanesians, this simply means that a mixture which took place in the Pacific islands also occured in Indochina as an independent phenomenon. In south-central India there live several million primitive agricultural people who speak languages of an Indochinese type. These tribesmen, the Munda, Ho, and Santal, are a mixed group, with three phenotypes predominating to a certain extent in individuals. Most numerous is an evolved Australoid, next a Mongoloid, and least a Negrito or Negroid. If the ancestors of these peoples came from Indochina, it is difficult to believe that the majority had curly hair.

Six of the skulls at Lang Cuom were more or less Mongoloid, as were two from Pho Binh Gia and one from Keo Phay. Two of the Lang Cuom skulls were also credited with mixed Negrito features. Whatever the accuracy of these diagnoses, it is clear that the interesting mixture which we still see in south-central India was already in process of formation. Another conclusion is that the transformation of the countries of southeast Asia from an Australoid realm to a southern extension of the Mongoloid *lebensraum* had not been completed by the end of the Lower or Early Neolithic; and the cranial material from the Upper or Late Neolithic is too scanty to indicate whether the great rush took place then or later. One suspects that most of the replacement occurred in the full light of history, after Alexander the Great had met his end, when the Chinese empire had begun its great expansion, which has not yet ended, and after the Chinese had started to squeeze "barbarian" Mongoloid peoples like the Thai and Shan and Laos out of their cool mountains onto the steaming plains of the south. Migrating in tightly organized, Iron Age tribes, they pushed the aborigines before them.

Bypassing Siam, which has to date produced not a single prehistoric human bone, because no one has really looked, we make our next stop at a kitchen-midden near Guak Kepah, Wellesley Province, Straits Settlements, where van Stein Callenfels found a mandible in 1935. The date is Mesolithic or sub-Recent. Mijsberg, who studied it, considered it similar to the jaws of modern New Caledonians.[5] He was apparently impressed by the resemblance between certain stone discs with double perforations found at the site and similar ornaments used until recently in New Caledonia. As the New Caledonian mandibles are Australoid, this one may be called Australoid too, in a general sense.

Six skulls unearthed by I. Evans in various Malayan caves and rock shelters, notably Gunong Sennyum, Lenggong, Gunong Pondok, and Bukit Chuping, were studied by Duckworth at Oxford.[6] They are called "Neolithic," mostly late, because stone tools were used well into the Metal Age, and lack faces. All of them follow a single pattern, that of the "Melanesians" of Lang Cuom, except that at least one, from Sennyum, is more rugged, with old-fashioned heavy brow ridges, and looks more like the Australoid prototype. We can skip Burma, which is as lacking in prehistoric crania as Siam, and push on to India.

Prehistoric Populations of the Western Oriental Region

T O D A Y the eastern half of the Oriental faunal region is inhabited almost entirely by Mongoloids. Yet the evidence that we have just reviewed indicates that the ancestors of the Burmese, Thais, Indochinese, Malays, and Indonesians arrived in their present homes quite late. The movement southward out of China began in the postglacial Mesolithic, reached its peak in historic times, and is still taking place in the sense that the Chinese themselves are moving into southeast Asia.

The earlier inhabitants of southeast Asia and Indonesia are represented today by a few enclaves of Negritos and Australoids and by the food-gathering Mongoloid tribes, such as the People of the Yellow Leaves in Siam, the Kubu in Sumatra, and the Punans in

[5] Mijsberg: "On a Neolithic Palae-melanesian lower jaw found in a Kitchen-midden at Guak Kepah, Province Wellesley, Straits Settlements," PTCPFA, 1938 (Pub. 1940), pp. 100–8.

[6] W. L. H. Duckworth: "Human Remains from Rock-Shelters and Caves in Perak, Pahang, and Perlis and from Selinsing," JMBR, Vol. 12, Pt. 2 (1934), after Huard and Saurin.

Borneo. There is no evidence to indicate that these culturally primitive Mongoloids arrived in their present homes before the postglacial Mesolithic, and it is possible that some of them are feral, that is, refugees from agriculture. There are no primitive Caucasoids in the area, and no evidence exists that there ever were any.

When we cross the Burmese mountains into India, which geographically includes Pakistan and Ceylon, we encounter a comparable but different situation. Here the majority of the population, including speakers of both Indo-European and Dravidian tongues, is Caucasoid. A minority of the Dravidian speakers, composed mostly of tribal peoples outside the caste system, are Australoid, and a very few are Negroid, but both have probably taken over Dravidian speech from their culturally more advanced neighbors.

India also shelters some Mongoloids, as for example the Khasis and Garos of Assam, but none of them are food gatherers and there is no reason to suppose them to have entered India before the Neolithic. The marginal, casteless groups of food gatherers, comparable to the Negritos, Sakai, Andamanese, and so on farther east (the Andaman Islands are politically a part of India) belong to three races: Negrito or Negroid, Australoid, and Caucasoid. The Negrito or Negroid element is always found in mixture with Australoid, whereas the Caucasoid tribes are usually unmixed. In central India there also live some agricultural tribes that speak three languages, Ho, Munda, and Santal, related to the Mon-Khmer speech of Burma and Indochina. These people are Australoid with Mongoloid admixture. At least the Mongoloid element probably came in from the east in the Neolithic or later.

In southeast Asia and Indonesia the earliest population was probably Australoid in the wide sense; the Negritos and Australoids who survive there today can only be descended from this ancient polymorphic, and probably regionally variable, population pool. As India is also a part of the Oriental region, it seems logical to suppose that the same is true there also, but we cannot test this hypothesis adequately because we have little skeletal material from the subcontinent, and none of it is ancient.

The oldest we have is seven skeletons from a site called

Langhnaj near Gujarat in West Pakistan, in the Indus Valley.[7] Buried in a habitation site with mesolithic implements and without pottery, they are probably older than the Bronze Age civilization of that region. Four have been partly described; three are called males and one a female. They were moderately tall people. One male was five feet seven inches in height (170 cm.), and one female five feet four inches (162 cm.). Their lower arms and shins were moderately long compared to their upper arms and thighs, and they were of slender build. Their skulls are long and narrow, and the men had sloping foreheads, but at least one woman had a bulbous one. Owing to earth pressure, their facial bones are distorted. Nevertheless, one woman seems to have been prognathous, particularly in the upper jaw, and one man had a Caucasoid-looking lower nasal skeleton. These people were either Caucasoid or Australoid, or most likely a combination of both.

As the skeletal material from the Bronze Age civilization of the Indus Valley includes Caucasoid, Australoid, and Mongoloid skulls, all we know is that these three subspecies were represented in northwest India as early as 2400 B.C.[8]

The circumstantial evidence of geographical distribution slightly favors the greater antiquity of the Caucasoids, because of the racial situation in Ceylon. That island was settled by the ancestors of the Singhalese, who came from northern India, speaking an Indo-European tongue, about 500 B.C. Later, Tamil-speaking people from south India settled the northern part of the island. Both these peoples are primarily Caucasoid, although the Singhalese also contain a Mongoloid element.

When the Singhalese arrived, they found the island occupied by two groups of primitive hunters, which they called Yakkhas and Nagas.[9] Sometime between the arrival of the Singhalese and the period of European exploration and colonization, either one of these groups wiped out the other or they fused into a people called Veddas. The living Veddas are Caucasoid. However, they

[7] I. Karvé and G. M. Kurulkar: "Human Remains Discovered So Far," in H. D. Sankalia and Karvé: *Preliminary Report on the Third Gujarat Prehistoric Expedition* (Bombay: Times of India Press; 1945).

[8] The skulls are in Calcutta, the postcranial bones in Karachi. I have examined the skulls, which have not been completely described in publication.

[9] N. D. Wijeskera: *The People of Ceylon* (Colombo: Gunasena; 1949), p. 32.

are divided into clans, some of which are said to have light and others dark skins. Perhaps uniquely among simple food gatherers, they recognize some clans as noble and others as servile. These distinctions tend to substantiate the observations of the early Singhalese, that the aborigines consisted of more than one people.

Recently Paul Deraniyagala, the director of the museums of Ceylon, and a well-known paleontologist, found six skeletons in southern Ceylon associated with a Mesolithic stone industry.[1] These skeletons have been given a Carbon-14 date of 110 B.C. $\pm$ 200 years, which places them nearly four hundred years after the arrival of the Singhalese. No trade goods were found with the burials as might be expected were this date correct. As the graves were shallow, the charcoal samples may have been contaminated; a somewhat earlier date would make more sense.

One male skeleton had a stature of five feet six inches (167 cm.); a female skeleton was five feet one inch (154 cm.) tall. In a series of 138 living male Veddas measured in the 1930's by J. R. de la H. Marrett, the mean stature was five feet one and a half inches, or 156.78 cm., and the range was from 134 to 172 cm.[2] These two Balangodans, although taller than most modern Veddas, were within their stature range.

Although from the published measurements it is not possible to calculate cranial capacity, this capacity is probably close to that of the Veddas, whose mean is 1,260 cc. for 138 males. The teeth also are of moderate size, comparable to those of living Singhalese, who are Caucasoids. I have been unable to find a published account of Vedda teeth, but I have seen them on skulls and in the living, and am sure that they are at most only as large as those of the Singhalese. On present evidence I cannot state that the Balangodan teeth differ from those of the Veddas.

In 1957 I saw the Balangodan skulls then in Ceylon and in 1960 I inspected the one labelled T-24-B which Dr. Deraniyagala had left at the American Museum of Natural History in New York.

---

[1] P. E. P. Deraniyagala: "The Races of the Stone Age and Ferrolithic of Ceylon," *JRAS* (Ceylon Branch), Vol. 5, Pt. 1 (1956), pp. 1–23.

Deraniyagala: "An Open Air Habitation Site of Homo sapiens Balangodensis," *SZC*, Vol. 28, Pt. 2 (1958), pp. 223–60.

Deraniyagala: "The Pleistocene of Ceylon," *CNHS*, July 20, 1958.

[2] H. Stoudt: "The Physical Anthropology of Ceylon," *CMES*, No. 2 (1961).

These skulls are not, as Dr. Deraniyagala first thought (and as I did, too, when I saw them in Ceylon), Australoid. They are Caucasoid with, in a few cases, a Negroid overtone. The bones are thin, the brow ridges light, and at least on T-24-B, there is no nuchal crest. The mandible of this last skull is lightly built and delicate, and it has a sharply pointed chin. Like the upper jaw it shows a marked alveolar prognathism, which occurs in 7 per cent of living Veddas. The nose is narrow and moderately prominent, but the entrance to the nasal passages is guttered.

My present opinion, which may have to be revised after these skulls have been cleaned, repaired, and definitively studied, is that Balangoda man did not differ subspecifically from the living Veddas. If he showed some Australoid features, this should surprise no one because his island is located just south of a Caucasoid-Australoid zone of contact, and these skulls are not very old.

The Taxonomy of the Australoid Subspecies

IN THIS chapter I have demonstrated, at least to my own satisfaction, that in southeast Asia and Indonesia a pre-*sapiens* population of the genus *Homo* evolved, from the very beginning of the Middle Pleistocene onward, through three known stages into a congeries of modern races, the Australian *in sensu strictu*, the Tasmanian, the Papuo-Melanesian, and the Negrito. Even the Negritos differ among themselves. The Andamanese of the main archipelago lack the pronounced steatopygia of the Önges of Little Andaman, and both kinds of Andamanese are more infantile facially than the Philippine Negritos. The Tasmanians, though possessing Negroid hair, were morphologically close to the Australian aborigines, and perhaps even closer to the spiral-haired Melanesians of New Caledonia. We can be reasonably sure that the Negritos of the southeastern quadrant of the Old World became small independently of the African Pygmies, but we do not know whether one or several populations underwent dwarfing in the area under consideration.

Among the Australians themselves regional differentiation may be seen, and the peripheral tribes tend to be more primitive morphologically than those in the central desert. In New Guinea, the Papuans are vastly differentiated regionally. Blond hair can be seen in some of the central Australian tribes, in New Caledonia, and in Fergusson Island, one of the D'Entrecasteaux group lying off the southeastern tip of New Guinea. A strict application of the taxonomic rules stated in Chapter 1 might give the status of sub-species to some of the populations living in this geographical quadrant.

But I prefer to call them local races, particularly as they have certain features in common. All have broad noses, wide interorbital distances, dark skins; and the adult males have beards. Dentally they are also closely similar, particularly in the relationship between the size of the cheek teeth and the anterior length of the skull, as expressed by Flower's index (see Chapter 8), in which all Australoids are megadont, whether they are full-sized or pygmy-sized, curly-haired or straight-heared, or whatever.

As we have noted before, stature and hair form divide the Australoids into several groups. In Chapter 3 dwarfing was explained; the dwarfing of some of the Australoids in geologically recent times probably followed similar patterns. Because dwarfing shows on the skeleton, we have been able to trace it in at least one area, Indochina. More difficult to explain is the distribution of hair form, which is of two kinds: straight to ringlets, and negroid. The negroid type of hair is peripheral geographically to the straight, being found in Tasmania, Papuo-Melanesia, and among the mainland and Indonesian Negritos. In India it also seems to be peripheral to straight hair among the predominantly Australoid tribes. Unless we can postulate multiple mutations within our geographical quadrant, and can also explain why these mutations followed a marginal geographical pattern, we are almost obliged to consider this difference in hair form ancient. Either the straight hair of the central Australians is the result of some kind of selection, like the juvenile and female blondism of the aborigines living in the central desert; or it represents influences derived from the vanguard of the first Mongoloid invasions which reached Indonesia before the last wave of Australoids had left for Australia; or it is the result of undetected Caucasoid movements from India—these are the only explanations I can think of.

Summing up, we may divide the Australoid subspecies of mankind into three races, characterized as follows:

(1) Full-sized, with straight or wavy hair: Australoid proper

(2) Full-sized, with negroid hair: Tasmanian and Papuo-Melanesian

(3) Pygmy-sized, with negroid hair: the Negritos

Among at least the first two races, local populations differ considerably in evolutionary grade, and some of them come closest, of any living peoples, to the *erectus-sapiens* threshold.

In my own opinion, looking at this chapter in retrospect, its most important conclusion is not that the Pithecanthropus-Wadjak evolutionary line has been established, for this fact has been acknowledged before, but that we now have enough skeletal material from the period between 40,000 years ago and the present to carry that line through to modern times. No longer need we rely on hypothetical invasions from an unknown center.

It also occurs to me that the transition from *Homo erectus* to *Homo sapiens* in this quadrant was caused by gene flow from a Mongoloid source. This is suggested by, among other things, the extraordinary facial flatness of Wadjak, and by the fact that during the entire span of human history as we know it, the Australoids and Mongoloids were in contact, like the United States and Canada, over an open frontier. In the following chapter we shall try to follow the evolution of the Mongoloids from Sinanthropus to the present-day peoples of that area.

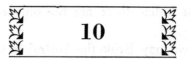

10

SINANTHROPUS
AND THE MONGOLOIDS

The Living Mongoloids and the Skeletons
of Their Ancestors

UNLIKE the three different but related races of Australoids whose common origin we tried to trace in Chapter 9, the Mongoloids of the world, from Madagascar to Tierra del Fuego, are a relatively homogenous subspecies. They have coarse, straight, black head hair which grows very long and grays only in extreme senility; and they rarely become bald. Neither sex has very much body hair, and the adult male has little beard. They have a tendency to facial flatness, protruding malars, widely separated and shallow eye sockets, nasal bones which invade the frontal bone deeply, large incisors which are usually shoveled, relatively long bodies and short lower segments of the arms and legs, along with small hands and feet.

Aside from these similarities, they are of all sizes above the Pygmy, varying according to standard zoological rules with latitude and altitude. Their skin color also tends to vary regionally, but not as much as in the Caucasoid subspecies. Some of them, like the southern Chinese, have very flat noses, whereas others, like the Nagas of Assam and the American Plains Indians, have aquiline ones. But these differences are minimal compared to those found in most other subspecies, and a common origin for all Mongoloids is clearly indicated.

Of all the living subspecies of man they are also the most differentiated, and the least like any of the others. One can see a

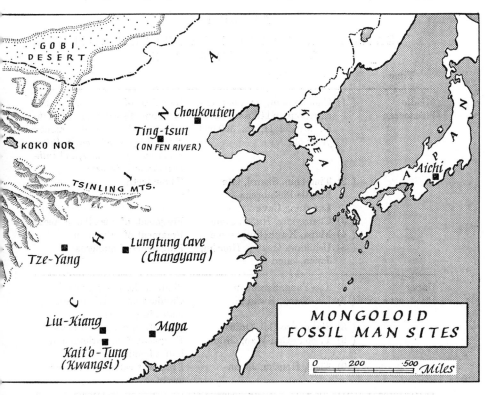

MAP 10

primitive European in an Australian aborigine and an African Negro in a Melanesian, but except for their resemblances to the African Bushmen in facial flatness and skin color, and except for the presence of a few flattish faces in north-central Europe, the Mongoloids stand alone. The questions that must be answered in this chapter are: How far back do the features that characterize the Mongoloids go in prehistory? Can they, as Weidenreich said, be derived from Sinanthropus? Let us look at available evidence.

This evidence, not including that from the Americas, is given on Table 19. It covers only fourteen sites and sixty-odd individuals, over forty of whom are Sinanthropi. Only twenty-one individuals from thirteen sites stand between Sinanthropus and the late prehistoric Chinese. However, these thirteen sites are widely scattered from the bend of the Yellow River to the Pacific, and from Kwangtung and Szechuan in China to Honshu in Japan. Also, they are well distributed on the time scale. Their temporal and

TABLE 19

EARLY SKELETAL MATERIAL FROM
CHINA AND JAPAN

Time	Place	Material
Middle Pleistocene	(1) Choukoutein, original excavations and those of 1959; all Mindel II, *ca.* 360,000 years old	Remains of 40+ individuals including 14 calvaria, 12 mandibles, and 147 teeth; named *Sinanthropus pekinensis, Pithecanthropus pekinensis,* and *Pithecanthropus sinensis*
	(2) Ting-tsun, Shansi, late Middle Pleistocene Lungtung Cave	Three teeth
	(3) Changyang, Hupei, same	Fragment of maxilla, 3 teeth
	(4) Mapa, Kwangtung, same	Fragment of calvarium
	(5) Ushikawa Quarry, Honshu, Japan, same	Fragments of humerus
Upper Pleistocene	(6) Tze-Yang, Szechuan	Skull, male, 14–15 years
	(7) Liu-Kiang, Kwangsi	Cranium and pelvic bones, male, 40 years *ca.*
	(8) Sjara-Osso-Gol, Ordos	One left upper lateral incisor
	(9) Ti-Shao-Gou-Wan, Ordos	Fragment right parietal and half a femur
	(10) Aichi, Honshu, Japan	Fragment calvarium and os coxae
Late Upper or Early Post-Pleistocene	(11) Choukoutien, Upper Cave *	Seven individuals of which 3 skulls are described
	(12) Kait'o-Tung Cave, Kwangsi	Skull base, palate, teeth
Post-Pleistocene	(13) Chalinor, Manchuria	Two skulls
	(14) Yokosuka, Honshu, Japan, Early Jomon, 6450 B.C.	One adult male skeleton

* W. C. Pei, W. P. Huang, C. L. Chiu, and H. Meng, in *VP*, Vol. 2, No. 4 (1958), pp. 226–9, call this site Final Pleistocene or the so-called Postglacial of Europe, on the basis of the fauna.

spatial distributions are thus better than what we had to work with in Chapter 9.

Sinanthropus pekinensis: *Time, Place, and People*

CHOUKOUTIEN, or Chou Gate Inn, is a limestone cliff thirty miles south of Peking. In it are breccia-filled clefts, long the haunt of dragon-bone collectors whose finds end up in Chinese pharmacies. In 1903, in a Peking drugstore, K. A. Heberer found a human tooth which was recognized as that of a fossil man. From then on for twenty-four years various paleontologists and anatomists, having traced the tooth back to Choukoutien, worked in or watched the site, which had once been a large cave. In 1927 Birger Böhlin, a Swedish paleontologist, found a molar *in situ* which Davidson Black, professor of anatomy at Peking University, named *Sinanthropus pekinensis*. From 1927 through 1937 the site was worked continuously under the direction of W. C. Pei and Père Teilhard de Chardin. Franz Weidenreich joined them before the excavations were completed and described the finds,[1] except for one skull already described in print by Black.[2] In the 1950's the Chinese Communist government resumed work at the site and a new mandible was discovered and described in 1959.[3]

Early in World War II, at the beginning of the Japanese occupation of China, all the Sinanthropus skulls were lost in an accident or military action while being transferred from Peking to the S. S. *President Harrison*. No one seems to know what happened to them. We blamed the Japanese for their disappearance and now the Communist Chinese blame us. All we have left is a set of casts made in the basement of the University Museum in Philadelphia, a lone tooth which is in Sweden, and the new mandible in China, in addition to a set of detailed monographs by Weidenreich and a few other publications.

In the course of excavation, between 1927 and 1937, Pei, Teilhard, and their associates removed from the breccia not only the celebrated fossil human remains but also many tools, some charcoal, the seeds of the hagberry, which is a kind of wild cherry,

[1] F. Weidenreich: "The Mandibles of *Sinanthropus pekinensis*," PSNSD-7, No. 3 (1936).

——: "The Dentition of *Sinanthropus pekinensis*," PSNSD, No. 1 (1937).

——: "The Ramification of the Middle Meningeal Artery in Fossil Hominids and Its Bearing upon Phylogenetic Problems," PSNSD, No. 3 (1938).

——: "The Extremity Bones of *Sinanthropus pekinensis*," PSNSD, No. 5 (1941).

——: "The Skull of *Sinanthropus pekinensis*," PSNSD, No. 10 (1943).

[2] D. Black: "On an Adolescent Skull of *Sinanthropus pekinensis* . . . ," PSD, Vol. 7, No. 1 (1927), pp. 1–28. (Black's monograph describes Skull E, or No. 3 of Weidenreich).

[3] J. K. Woo and T-K. Chao: "New Discovery of Sinanthropus Mandible from Choukoutien," VP, Vol. 3, No. 4 (1959), pp. 169–72.

and the broken and splintered bones of many animals. As the human remains had been broken in the same fashion, it was clear from the start that the Sinanthropi had been eaten by cannibals, presumably also Sinanthropi.

With a few exceptions, like that of Rhodesian man, who crawled into a narrow cave to die alone, nearly all the available skeletal material from the Middle Pleistocene, and some from the Late Pleistocene also, commemorates the ancient practice of man eat man. This does not mean that for hundreds of thousands of years every human being ended up in someone else's stomach; but if you are eaten, your bones have a better chance of being preserved for posterity than if your body is simply abandoned. Being tossed into a garbage dump is better from the archaeological point of view than being left for the wolves and hyenas on the lone prairie.

Moreover, the great cannibals of the world are farmers whose tiresome starch diets make them crave meat, as for example the Caribs, Papuans, and Azande. Hunters eat one another only when starving, not just for protein, but for calories. As the Sinanthropi were hunters, we may assume that the scraps of well-picked human bone which they threw into the cleft at Choukoutien represented moments of extreme hunger. Had the entire population been eaten over the thousands of years that this site was occupied, the excavators would have found the remains of thousands of Sinanthropi instead of a scant forty.

As the bones were both broken and scattered, it was difficult for Weidenreich to decide which pieces belonged together, and the correlation of mandibles to the correct crania, loose teeth to jaws, and long bones to skulls was nearly impossible. Nevertheless, he managed to assemble fourteen adult calvaria, which, although fragmentary, cover between them virtually the whole cranium except for the basal region around the foramen magnum. As usual, this had been broken off so that the brain could be extracted.

Table 20 lists the cranial and mandibular specimens studied by Weidenreich; calvarium 3, however, was described in 1927 by Black. Of the 147 teeth, Weidenreich was able to study all but two. Thirteen are milk or deciduous teeth; 134 are permanent.

TABLE 20

THE SINANTHROPUS SPECIMENS BY SEX AND AGE

Calvaria			Facial Bones				Mandibles		
No.	Sex	Age	No.	Bone	Sex	Age	No.	Sex	Age
1-B	M	adult	1 frag. max-				A-2	M?	adult
2-D	?	adult	illa		M	adult	B-1	F	juvenile
3-E	M	juvenile					B-2	M	juvenile
4-G	M	juv. or adol.	2 frag. zygo-				B-3	F	juvenile
5-H	M	adult	matic arch		M	adult	B-5	F	juvenile
6-I	F	adult					B-6	F	juvenile
7-I	M	adolescent	3 frag. max.				C-1	F	juvenile
8-J	F?	juv., 3 yrs.	+ 5 teeth		F	adult	F-1	M	juvenile
9-J	M	juv., 6 yrs.					G-1	M	adult
10-L	M	adult	4 ½ palate		F	adult	H-1	F	adult
11-L	F	adult					H-4	F	adult
12-L	M	adult	5 frag. max.				M-WC†	F	adult
13-O	M?	adult	+ 6 teeth		M?	adult	† WC = Woo & Chao, '59.		
14-UC*	M	adult							
* UC = upper cave			6 frag. max.						
			+ 4 teeth		M	adult			

Although only lower teeth are represented in the deciduous collection, there is at least one of each tooth, and among the permanent teeth every tooth in both jaws is accounted for. Three of the milk teeth are called male, ten female; of the permanent teeth fifty-five are called male, four male(?), and five female.

The postcranial bones, which are not listed above, consist of seven fragmentary femora designated as A-1 to A-7, of which A-2 is called adult female and the others adult male; two fragments of humerus, B-1 and B-2; one piece of clavicle; and an *os lunatum,* or wristbone. The last four bones are called adult male. None of these bones could be related to the skulls or teeth with any certainty.

As he did later with Pithecanthropus and Solo, Weidenreich sexed the Sinanthropus skulls, teeth, and long bones on the basis of size. This was possible because they varied considerably. It was an arbitrary procedure which he himself questioned in his later writings. Whether or not it was justifiable is important because the living Mongoloids do not have that much sexual dimorphism. In fact some of them have very little. If the Mongoloids are descended from Sinanthropus, then either sexual dimorphism has decreased in the Mongoloid subspecies since that time or Weidenreich's sexing is incorrect.

Another possibility is that the size difference might reflect evolutionary change, because the fissure in Choukoutien is very deep and bones were recovered over a vertical range of 150 feet. Davidson Black, who began the excavation, originally divided this range into fifteen units of 10 feet each, designated by the

TABLE 21

LOCI AND SEX OF SINANTHROPUS SPECIMENS

Specimens by Loci and Sex				Loci and Sex Correlated *			
Locus	Skulls	Mandibles	Dentitions†	Loci	Males	Females	Total
A			F,M	A-C	7	5	12
B	M	F,F,F,F,M,	F				
C		F	M,M	E-J	7	10	17
D			F,M				
E	M			K-O	5	5	10
F		M	F,M,M				
G	M	M		Total	19	20	39
H	M	F,F	F				
I	F,M						
J	M						
K			F				
L	F,M,M		M				
M		F	M				
N			F				
O			F,M				

* Only specimens designated as M or F and by level are included. Those designated as M?, F?, ?, and U.C. are excluded.

† These are sets of teeth which Weidenreich assembled.

letters A to S, and called loci. Locus A was at the top and Locus O at the bottom. We have twenty-seven definitely sexed skulls and mandibles from these loci, as indicated on Table 21 and plotted there in the form of a correlation table. There is no statistically significant difference between the loci, as combined above, and Weidenreich's sex designations,[4] and therefore no evidence that the differences in skull size and jaw size which Weidenreich interpreted as sex differences were really evolutionary in origin.

However, Weidenreich's vindication must be tempered by an-

[4] As determined by the chi-square method: $P = .33$.

other factor, the nature of the deposit itself. The fill, which later became brecciated, was only partly deposited by occupation. Some of it fell into the cave from above as debris. Although the breccia is stratified, one cannot be sure which bone entered the cave from in front and which fell in through the hole in the roof, from the land surface above. Bones and other hard objects falling 100 feet or more do not necessarily stay where they land, but can tumble and roll about. If they hit a sloping floor they can come to rest at some distance from the point of contact. So we cannot be completely sure that Weidenreich was right after all.

Recent work on the geology of the fissure indicates that the deposits were laid down over an extensive period.[5] They consist of three gravels: basal, lower, and upper. The Basal Gravels were formed, apparently during the Günz glaciation, partly as a result of gravels and red clay being washed into a large cave from outside, and partly by internal deposition. The Lower Gravels were formed by river water depositing various pebbles, gravels, sands, and clays. Their age is stated to be First, or Cromerian, Interglacial. The Upper Gravels were formed by internal deposition, in what was still a large cave, in Mindel-Elster time. Before this, the cave was not habitable. The Sinanthropus remains are, according to this new work, all of Second Glacial, or Mindel-Elster, age, but this part of the Pleistocene lasted tens of thousands of years. There was still time enough for a little evolutionary change within a single local population.

The new Chinese geological findings have been supported by Kurten's equally new paleontological determinations. He calls the date of the site Mindel-Elster II, about 360,000 years ago according to the argon-potassium dating method,[6] later than the time of the Djetis Pithecanthropi, and perhaps contemporary with Trinil. It was the time when *Crocuta crocuta*, the living spotted hyena, which had recently evolved in India, was crowding its older

[5] W. P. Huang: "Restudy of the CKT *Sinanthropus* Deposits," *VP*, Vol. 4, No. 1 (1960), pp. 45–6.

Huang: "On the Age of Basal Gravel of CKT *Sinanthropus* Site, of the 'Upper Gravel' and the 'Lower Gravel' of the CKT Region," *VP*, Vol. 4, No. 1 (1960), pp. 47–8.

[6] B. Kurtén: "New Evidence on the Age of Peking Man," *VP*, Vol. 3, No. 4 (1959), pp. 173–5.

cousin, *Hyaena brevirostis,* out of its ecological niches in Africa, Europe, and China. Commonest among the animal bones were those of deer, showing that venison was a far more popular entrée on the menu than roast Sinanthropus.

Pollen analysis conducted in Finland on a piece of Choukoutien breccia gives the following percentages for tree pollens: 33 per cent pine, 28 per cent beech, 9 per cent alder, 4 per cent spruce, 3 per cent linden, 1 per cent yew, 1 per cent willow, and 1 per cent sea buckthorn. Of the nonarboreal pollens, 11 per cent belonged to grasses, 4 per cent each to sedges and the rose family, 3 per cent to the sagebrush-wormwood tribe (*Artemesia*), and 1 per cent each to the goosefoots (*Chenopodeaciae*) and crowberry (*Empetrum*).

As the pollen-bearing breccia sample was collected by the Sino-Swedish expedition before the excavation had reached below the first few loci, it probably represents the end rather than the beginning of the Sinanthropus occupation. At that time the climate was cooler than it is today. Choukoutien then lay near the border zone which separates the northern coniferous belt, or boreal forest, from the temperate steppe. Its hills were clad with pine and spruce, their slopes bearing berries which grow today in the very north of Maine. What is left of the local vegetation at present, after thousands of years of intensive use of the land by man, is typical of steppe or parkland, and Choukoutien now lies nearer the edge of the evergreen tropical forest of southern China than that of the northern forest of Manchuria.

Sinanthropus had fire. His implements were good enough for working skins crudely. He must have been clever enough to keep from freezing during the winter months, and he was very likely physiologically adapted to cold, at least to the extent of the modern Alakalufs. One wonders how long he had lived in China before the span of the Choukoutien site. Many stone implements are turning up in China nowadays, but none is much cruder than his, except in the south. Did he make his entry with the spotted hyena, or did he evolve locally from some even more primitive kind of man? We do not know, but at the rate Pleistocene studies are moving in China, before long we may.

The Taxonomy of Sinanthropus

A s previously stated, in 1927 Davidson Black created the name *Sinanthropus pekinensis* to describe one tooth. This term was immediately applied to other remains excavated in Choukoutien as they appeared, and is still in general use. Yet Boule and Vallois renamed Sinanthropus in 1952, calling him *Pithecanthropus pekinensis*,[7] and in 1957 Piveteau dubbed him *P. sinensis*.[8] In recent years *P. pekinensis* has been widely accepted in Britain and on the continent. As I agree with Simpson, Mayr, Washburn, and others in calling all fossil men *Homo*, Sinanthropus will be called Sinanthropus without italics, and the other names given him will be mentioned again only in the index.

Still, because the new name, *Pithecanthropus pekinensis*, has been accepted by many prominent scholars, it may be worth while to trace the origin of this term. It seems to have come from a remark in 1943 by Weidenreich: "*Sinanthropus* differs from *Pithecanthropus* in characters which have not so much phylogenetic as 'racial' bearing."[9] In other words, they belong to more or less the same grade but to different lines.

Two years later G. G. Simpson, in his authoritative *opus* on mammalian taxonomy, had this to say: "All specimens of fossil hominids that differ in any discernible way from *Homo sapiens*, and some that do not, have at one time or another been placed in different genera. Almost none of these anthropological 'genera' has any zoological reason for being. All known hominids, recent and fossil, could well be placed in *Homo*. At most, †*Pithecanthropus* (with which †Sinanthropus is clearly synonomous by zoological criteria) and †*Eoanthropus* (if the apelike jaw belongs to it) may be given separate generic rank. Perhaps it would be better for the zoological taxonomist to set apart the family Hominidae

---

[7] M. M. Boule and H. V. Vallois: *Les Hommes Fossiles* (Paris: Masson et Cie; 1952), p. 145.

[8] J. Piveteau: *Traité de Paléontologie* (Paris: Masson et Cie; 1957), Vol. 7. (*P. sinensis* is used in captions of illustrations.)

[9] Weidenreich: "The Skull of *Sinanthropus pekinensis*," *PS-NS-D*, Vol. 10, ws No. 127 (1943).

and to exclude its nomenclature and classification from his studies." [1]

It is hard to see how either of these statements warrants the
definitive pooling of Pithecanthropus and Sinanthropus in a genus of their own apart from *Homo,* except as a tentative taxonomic
device which, by 1960, had lost its usefulness.

The Sinanthropus Brain Case

W E   H A V E   five Sinanthropus brain cases (see Table 37) compared to three for Pithecanthropus and six for Solo. No. 3 is a
juvenile and No. 2 has no breadth or height measurements. As all
had been opened for extraction of the brain, none has a complete
base; but No. 12 still had the posterior margin of the foramen
magnum and in No. 11 enough pieces were in contact with each
other to permit its restoration.

Omitting the juvenile No. 3, the cranial capacity of the remaining four ranges from 1,015 to 1,225 cc., almost exactly the
same as the Solo range, and a notch above that of Pithecanthropus. Sexual dimorphism in the cranial capacity of Sinanthropus
can neither be established nor disproved because only one
measurable skull out of four is called female.

In comparison with the Solo skulls, those of Sinanthropus are
both shorter and narrower, but of about equal height. How, then,
can they have the same capacities? Table 22 holds the answer. In
their internal dimensions the Sinanthropus skulls are 14 mm.
longer than the Solo average and 7 mm. narrower, and both sets
are of about equal height. In a long narrow brain, apparently, two
millimeters of length equal one of breadth ($14 = 7 \times 2$), provided
that the third dimension, brain height, remains constant.

The difference between the two groups in external skull length
is due to the more massive growth of brow ridges and nuchal
crests in Solo, particularly noticeable in No. 5. His length of 219.5
mm. is excessive in the genus *Homo* as a whole, and is a record
for fossil men anywhere, yet his internal length of 175 mm.

[1] G. G. Simpson: "The Principles of Classification and a Classification of
Mammals," *BAMN,* Vol. 85 (1945), p. 188.

TABLE 22

INTERNAL DIMENSIONS OF THE SINANTHROPUS AND SOLO SKULLS

	Sinanthropus					Solo						
Skull No.	3	10	11	12	Aver-age	1	5	6	9	10	11	Aver-age
Age	juv.	ad.	ad.	ad.		ad.	ad.	ad.	ad.	ad.	ad.	
Sex	M	M	F	M		F	M	F	?	F	M	
Length	156	184	166	175	175	161	175	153 *	164 *	159 *	157 *	161
Breadth	122	128 *	128	129	128	130	138	129	137	138	129	135
Height	105	...	102	110	106	103 *	108	109 *	105 *	100 *	109 *	107

* Qualified by (?) or *circa*.

matches that of Sinanthropus 12, whose total external length is only 195.5 mm.

Two points emerge from this comparison. (1) Although identical in size, the two sets of brains were different in shape. (2) Although he lived at least 200,000 years before Solo man, Sinanthropus was already more highly evolved than the latter in the reduction of bony superstructure about the brain case, just as he had a larger brain than his own probable contemporaries, the Pithecanthropi of Trinil. No better evidence could be found, considering the paucity of skulls at our disposal, to show that in different anthropogeographical regions evolution proceeded at different rates during the Pleistocene.

The paths followed in the evolution of the human brain can best be traced by studying the interiors of the skulls of persons of different ages, particularly the youthful and very young. In the Sinanthropus collection, No. 3, who died at the age of eight or nine, is available for study. The internal length of his brain was 20 mm. short of the figure for his elders; its breadth was within 6 mm. of theirs, and he equalled them in brain height. Judged by these figures, the gross shape of the Sinanthropus brain was modern at the age of eight, and it lengthened and flattened out later.

It would be fine if we could say that the brain of No. 3 by the age of eight or nine had not lost its infantile condition of having a bent floor, but we cannot because the appropriate bones are missing. However, much of the temporal bone is present, and the *sapiens* type of structure which includes torsion leaves its mark in this region. In the area around the internal ear, No. 3 alone

of all the Sinanthropi could pass for *H. sapiens,* which leads us
to suggest that the sapiens condition in both brain proportions
and brain floor anatomy is neotenous.[2] This evidence indicates that
the difference in brain form, as apart from brain size, which distinguishes *H. sapiens* from *H. erectus* was a product of one or
more neotenous mutations.

It is possible that *H. modjokertensis,* the ancient companion of
Pithecanthropus 4, who died while his fontanelle was still open,
also anticipated modern man in brain anatomy as it certainly did
in gross proportions.

The configuration of what is left of the basal portion of the
occipital bone after brain-picking suggests this. In any case, we
have evidence that both the Pithecanthropus-Solo and Sinanthropus populations and successions of populations bore within them
the genetic capacity for evolutionary change into *H. sapiens.*
Whether they made this change by themselves or were aided by
an injection of genes from other populations is a different question.

Another result of a close examination of the inside surfaces of
the skulls of the Pithecanthropus, Solo, and Sinanthropus adults
is that all three had a wide separation between the frontal and
temporal lobes. Each of them has a pronounced internal ridge or
Sylvian crest which is rudimentary or absent in fossil European
skulls and modern crania, as well as in ape skulls. It is an early
human trait and not a pongid heritage. Its absence in *H. sapiens*
is therefore again neotenously human rather than gerontomorphi-
cally apelike.

----

[2] So important is this point that I quote Weidenreich in full, for the benefit
of those with sufficient anatomical knowledge to understand the terminology.
In discussing the internal surface of the temporal bone, Weidenreich said: "As to
other features of the posterior surface the only noteworthy difference between
Sinanthropus and modern man concerns the apertura externa aqueductus vestibuli.
In the latter this slit opens into the impressio cerebellaris and the part covering
the slit projects more or less forming thereby the anterior boundary of the impressio. In *Sinanthropus* Skull V . . . and all the other adult specimens (right
and left side) the cover of the aperture appears as a distinct eminence and the
slit opens into a recess situated beneath the eminence. Only the juvenile Skull III
shows conditions similar to modern man. The porus acusticus internus (pai), the
fossa subarcuata, and the apetura externa canaliculi cochleae (acc) are like such
structures of modern man." Weidenreich: "The Skull of *Sinanthropus pekinensis,*"
PS-NS-D, Vol. 10 (1943), p. 68.

These skulls also have sagittal crests inside the frontal bone, separating the frontal lobes of the two cerebral hemispheres. This crest serves as an extra, unseen buttress to brace the skull. It is never found in apes and is present, but smaller, in living men. Actually, it is part of the archaic human architectural system of passing the stress of chewing up the mid-line of the face rather than to either side, as among apes and most if not all Australopithecines. The size of the crest depends on the amount of stress and on the angle between the vertical plane of the face and the slope of the forehead. When the facial profile and profile of the forehead form a straight line, as in apes and some modern people, the sagittal axis of the frontal bone is directly in the path of stress and internal bracing is unneccessary. The facial-frontal angle in Sinanthropus was close enough to 45° to make such a strut useful.

The inner surfaces of the Sinanthropus brain cases also show the paths of the middle meningeal arteries, which feed the outer sheath of the brain.[3] In fossil man and the Australopithecines these arteries split into two branches below the point at which their imprints are seen in the parietal region. Once they appear they take one of two patterns, as follows.

(A) The anterior branch crosses the Sylvian fissure and subdivides into an anterior or bregmatic branch, and a median or obelionic branch. The posterior or lower temporal branch starts out equal in size to the anterior branch and extends over the lower rear border of the parietal bone, but it forks little.

(B) The anterior branch is larger than the posterior, and both have more and finer fingers. Between them they cover the surface of the brain which they feed more closely and finely, and they are not as widely separated, so that they give the appearance of being a single system.

Type A is characteristic of the Australopithecines, Pithecanthropus, Sinanthropus, and apparently of Solo, although in the latter skulls the imprints are less easily read than in the others. It is also found in a piece of temporal bone of Early Middle Pleistocene date found at Ternefine in Algeria, and in the Late Upper

---

[3] F. C. Howell: "European and Northwest African Middle Pleistocene Hominids," *CA*, Vol. 1, No. 3 (1960), pp. 195–232.

Pleistocene skull from Broken Hill, Northern Rhodesia. Type B is characteristic of the earliest skulls from Europe, which come from the Second or Great Interglacial, and of modern men in general.

Seen from the outside, the Sinanthropus skulls are long and low, with their greatest breadths directly over the mastoids. Like the Pithecanthropus crania they suggest a poorly raised loaf. However, the frontal region is quite different. Instead of a gradual slope upward and backward from glabella, the frontal bone rises steeply to form a brow ridge, sweeps back horizontally, then bends and rises abruptly for a short distance and curves backward to bregma, the point where the frontal bone joins the parietals in the sagittal line. Bregma itself is situated directly over porion, the top of the earhole; in modern skulls it lies forward of this position. In some Sinanthropus skulls the frontal torus is solid, in others it contains a small frontal sinus. In Pithecanthopus and Solo it encloses large frontal sinuses.

Behind the brow ridges lies a deep postorbital constriction, comparable to that of the Pithecanthropi but not of Solo. In this part of the frontal bone the area of temporal muscle attachment invades the lower part of the forehead as it does in modern Mongoloids. The average distance between the temporal crests for Sinanthropus is 94.7 mm. compared to Solo's 108.7 mm. No two sets of skulls could differ from each other more, in this feature, than these.[4]

The lambdoid region is flattish, the occiput bun-shaped, and the zygomatic arches were undoubtedly flaring. Beyond their rearward anchor on the temporal bone they continue over the earhole as a supramastoid crest, but do not move on to join the nuchal crest. Although this bony framework of the skull is massive and impressive, it does not equal that of the early members of the Pithecanthopus line, as our comparison of inside and outside skull diameters indicated. As far as we can tell, the foramen magnum was set farther back in the skull base in Sinanthropus than in the Pithecanthropus-Solo skulls. The mastoid processes

---

[4] Skull 12 has two sets of temporal crests, an inner and an outer. I found the same anomaly on an Alakaluf Indian in Chile. The muscles do not extend beyond the outer crests.

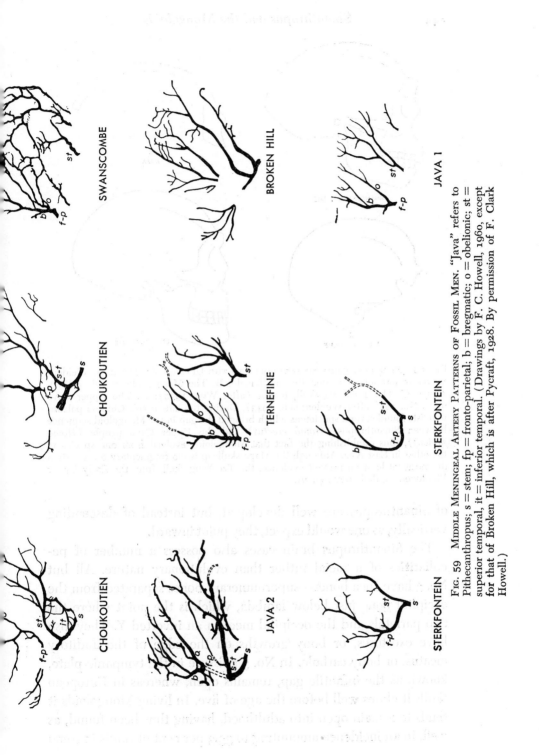

Fig. 59 Middle Meningeal Artery Patterns of Fossil Men. "Java" refers to Pithecanthropus; s = stem; fp = fronto-parietal; b = bregmatic; o = obelionic; st = superior temporal, it = inferior temporal. (Drawings by F. C. Howell, 1960, except for that of Broken Hill, which is after Pycraft, 1928. By permission of F. Clark Howell.)

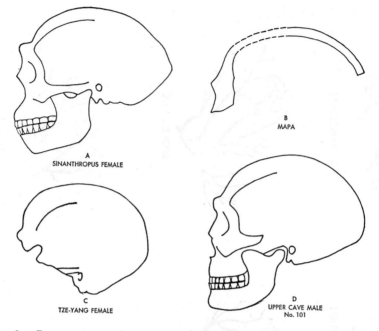

FIG. 60 PROFILES: FROM SINANTHROPUS TO THE UPPER CAVE MALE. A. Weiden-reich's restoration of a Sinanthropus female; B. The Mapa skullcap (after Woo, 1959); C. The Tze-Yang skull, female (after Woo, 1958); D. The Upper Cave male, No. 101 (after Weidenreich, 1943). During the late 1950's Chinese paleon-tologists found several specimens which bridged the gap in the Mongoloid sequence between Sinanthropus (*Homo erectus*) and the Upper Cave people (*Homo sapiens*), thus establishing the fact that Mongoloids evolved from one species to the other in East Asia. Although the Mapa skullcap is too fragmentary for a certain diagnosis, at least on present evidence, the Tze-Yang skull, from the Early Upper Pleistocene, is definitely *sapiens*.

of Sinanthropus are well developed, but instead of descending vertically, as one would expect, they point inward.

The Sinanthropus brain cases also possess a number of pe-culiarities of a racial rather than evolutionary nature. All but No. 3 have Inca bones—supernumerary bones separated from the occipital bone just below lambda, which is the point where the two parietals and the occipital meet in an inverted Y. They also have exostoses, or bony growths on the edge of the auditory meatus, or bony earhole. In No. 3 a fissure in the tympanic plate, known as the infantile gap, remains open, whereas in European skulls it closes well before the age of five. In living Mongoloids it tends to remain open into adulthood, having thus been found, as well, in an incidence amounting to 33.3 per cent of skulls in some

American Indian series, 32 per cent of prehistoric skulls from Guam, and 12 per cent of more recent North Chinese crania.

The Face of Sinanthropus

THE UPPER facial bones of Sinanthropus are represented by the six pieces listed in Table 20 and by the nasal bones and portions of orbits forming part of the brain cases. These can best be studied from Weidenreich's reconstruction of a female skull, which includes a mandible. Some of the dimensions of the reconstruction may be seen on Table 23.

TABLE 23

FACIAL DIMENSIONS OF SINANTHROPUS (FEMALE) AND WADJAK 1

	Sinanth. female †	Wadjak 1		Sinanth. female †	Wadjak 1
Minimum Frontal	84 mm.	99 mm.	Facial Index	79.7	87.1*
Bizygomatic	148	140(?)	Upper Facial Index	52.1	52.9
Biorbital	111	115	Fronto-parietal Index	64.9	66.9
Interorbital	25	29	Cranio-facial Index	105.7	94.6(?)
Bicondylar	124	140 *	Zygo-frontal Index	64.7	70.7
Bigonial	103	110 *	Zygo-gonial Index	69.6	79.6
Total Face Height	118	122 *	Nasal Index	57.2	56.0
Upper Face Height	77	74	Orbital Index	81.9	78.6
Nasal Height	52.5	50	Palatal Index	75.1	70.0(?)
Nasal Breadth	30	28			
Orbital Height	36	33			
Orbital Breadth	44	42			
Palate Length	52	60			
Palate Breadth	39	43			

* The Wadjak 1 cranium and the Wadjak 2 mandible were combined.
† The Sinanthropus female is Weidenreich's reconstruction. No Sinanthropus skull of either sex was whole enough to permit these measurements.

It is not a particularly large face. All of the dimensions given could be matched in living populations. Compared with Pithecanthropus 4, it belongs in a different order of magnitude, and it is even smaller in eight of fifteen dimensions than Wadjak I when the latter is equipped with the W-2 mandible, which may be a little big for it. The importance of this comparison is that it shows the people of northern China 360,000 years ago to have had faces, at least in the female sex, of modern size, and smaller in many dimensions than the Australoids of Java who lived at least 300,000 years later.

Both the upper face and the nose are relatively long, like those of the modern Chinese; and despite the heavy brow ridges, the Sinanthropus orbits have modern Mongoloid dimensions, although they are less rounded than in the recent skulls. From the

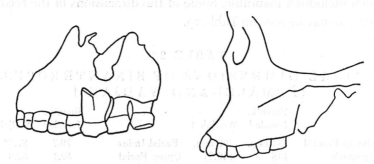

SINANTHROPUS MAXILLA No. O-1   A MODERN NORTH CHINESE SKULL

Fig. 61   Alveolar Prognathism in Sinanthropus and in Modern Chinese. (Drawings after Weidenreich, 1937.)

modern point of view the only excessive dimensions of the Sinanthropus face are the bizygomatic diameter and the palate length. These reflect evolutionary status more than racial affiliation.

The nasal bones are wide both at top and bottom, and flat, meeting the zygomatic (or malar) bones[5] in a gently rounded fashion rather than forming an angle as in the Causasoids. At the top they meet the frontal, which they invade deeply, in the form of a T, whereas in the Caucasoid face the nasofrontal suture either curves upward or looks like the head of an arrow ↑. The nasal opening is broad, as it is among all early fossil men, and the lower border is guttered as in modern Mongoloids. In profile the face is very prognathous, most of the prognathism being produced by the outward and downward curvature of the maxillae

[5] This bone is officially known as os zygomaticum, but is also popularly known by its old name, malar, which I shall continue to use.

and palate, although some of it comes from the extension of this curvature upward to the nasal region. In modern Chinese skulls an almost equal amount of alveolar prognathism is occasionally found.

Although the brow ridges make them look square, the orbits are not low. They fall within the modern Mongoloid size range; and if the brow ridges were reduced or removed, the similarity would be more apparent. The floor of each orbit opens directly and simply from the malar without lipping or sill, and the outer sides of the orbits are relatively straight, whereas in Caucasoids and Australoids this edge curves to the rear, giving the orbit a cut-away appearance and making the nasal skeleton appear more prominent. In this detail Sinanthropus resembles not only modern Mongoloids but also the orang, the gorilla, and the Australopithecines.

In Sinanthropus, as in modern Mongoloids, the temporal muscle was attached farther forward than in the Pithecanthropus-Australoid skulls, and it pushed the malar bone forward and also invaded the frontal bone over and behind the brow ridges; the temporal lines are much closer together than in Sinanthropus's grade-mate, Solo. Were one to enlarge the Sinanthropus brain by about 300 cc., reduce the brow ridges, shorten the palate, and reef in the zygomatic arches by about 15 mm., it would be hard to tell this specimen from that of a modern Mongoloid of one kind or another, at least in the upper part of the face, which is the racially critical "mask" area.

The Mandibles of Sinanthropus

F R O M   T H E lips downward the similarity still exists, but it is heavily camouflaged by the fact that the Sinanthropus mandibles are morphologically primitive and fit the evolutionary grade to which their great antiquity entitles them. The laboratory designations, sexes, and ages of the twelve which have been studied are given on Table 20.

Only three are complete enough for detailed study: the adult male G-1, the adult female H-1, and the juvenile female B-1 (see Fig. 62). H-1 was used with cranium No. 11 by Weidenreich in

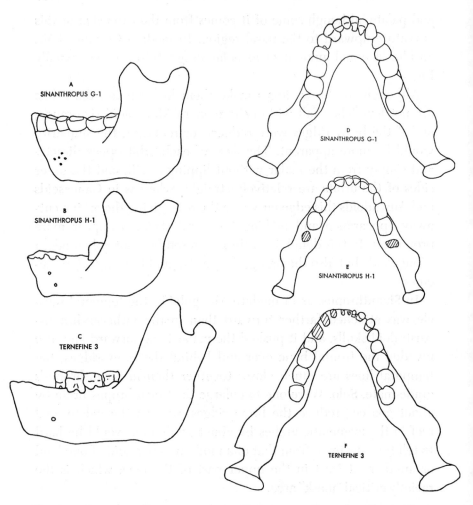

FIG. 62   MANDIBLES; SINANTHROPUS AND TERNEFINE 3. *From the side:* A. Sinanthropus G-1, male; B. Sinanthropus H-1, female; C. Ternefine 3, male. *From above:* D. Sinanthropus G-1, male; E. Sinanthropus H-1, female; F. Ternefine 3, male. Weidenreich found that the Sinanthropus mandibles were of two sizes. The larger ones he called male, and the smaller female. Both are stout, prognathous, and large-toothed. Both have multiple mental foramina. The Ternefine mandibles from Algeria are also large and robust and resemble the Sinanthropus specimens closely in many details, but Ternefine 3 has an extremely sloping ascending ramus and a very high coracoid process. The latter feature is also found in Australopithecines. Seen from above, the Sinanthropus mandibles spread far apart behind the dental arc, so that the condyles are widely separated. This is also a modern Mongoloid feature, and in it Ternefine 3 resembles Sinanthropus and the modern Mongoloids. (Drawings C and F after Arambourg, 1955; all others after Weidenreich, 1943.)

his reconstruction of a complete female skull (see Table 23). The new female mandible described by Woo and Chao closely resembles H-1 but is much less complete.

In eight measurements the female mandible H-1 attains 85.9 per cent of the size of the male G-1. In living Mongoloid populations from China, Korea, and Japan, the figure is 92.4 per cent. This difference in sexual dimorphism between ancient and living Mongoloids is of the same order of magnitude as that found in the cranial series.

The Sinanthropus mandibles as a group fall into the size range of other fossil men of the same general time span, including Javanese, European, and North African specimens. All are about equally chinless, except that in the female H-1 the chin line is angular rather than curved. The angle of inclination, which is the angle between the tooth line of the jaw and the slope of the chin line (see Fig. 62 and Table 24) comes to 63° in the Sinanthropus mandibles, including the 1959 specimen. In comparison, the angles for Pithecanthropus B, Heidelberg (Sinanthropus's European contemporary), and Wadjak 2 are 58°, 63°, and 65°. In modern Australian aborigines it averages 75° and in living Mongoloids and Europeans about 90°.

In evaluating the relative thickness of the mandible in fossil and recent jaws, anthropologists use an index of robusticity, which is thickness of the bone times 100 divided by the height of the mandibular body. The two measurements, thickness and height, are taken at the same point on the jaw when possible, but this point may differ because some jaws are fragmentary. A usual location is at the symphysis, on the mid-line of the jaw between the two lower median incisors. In Pithecanthropus B the symphysis is missing. Therefore a substitute index has been calculated at a point between the median and lateral incisors, which is present in this specimen. This index comes to 52.5, which means that the thickness is 52.5 per cent of the height. In three Sinanthropus jaws the figures are 36.6, 38.9, and 46.4, indicating a much less massive bone near the chin line. However, when the same index is taken at the conventional spot, which is the level of the mental foramen (a hole in the bone usually situated under the point where the second lower premolar and first lower molar meet), the figure for

TABLE 24

ANGLES OF INCLINATION AND INDICES OF
ROBUSTICITY OF SINANTHROPUS AND
OTHER MANDIBLES†

Angle of Inclination

Apes:		Men:	
Orang	44°	Pithecanthropus B *	58°(?)
Gorilla	47°	Sinanthropus (6)	61° (59.0–63.5)
Chimpanzee	50°	Heidelberg	63°
		Ternefine (3)	65° (62–70)
Australopithecines:		Modern Australians	75°
		Modern Whites	90° ca.
Robustus	58°	Choukoutien Upper	91°
Meganthropus	58°	Cave	

Index of Robusticity (at Mental Foramen Level)

Apes:		Men:	
Orang	50.8	Sinanthropus (4)	57.1 (48.3–62.3)
Gorilla	50.8	Ternefine (2)	55.5(?) (52?–59?)
Chimpanzee	49.5	Pithecanthropus (2)	55.4 (47.2–63.6)
		Heidelberg	48.8
Australopithecines:		Modern Australians	45.6
		Wadjak 2	42.9
Robustus *	60.0 (?)	Modern Means	
Meganthropus	58.4	(non-Australian)	38–42

* Reconstructed from drawings or photographs.
† For further details, see Table 38 in Appendix.

the four Sinanthropus mandibles comes to 55.4, against a mere 44.5 for Pithecanthropus B. Thus a racial difference is evident: the Pithecanthropus mandible is the stouter in front, and those of the Sinanthropi more robust in mid-branch.

In Sinanthropus and in other early fossil men, the gonial angle is blunted so that it becomes two angles of about 45° each. The area between the two corners is the seat of attachment of the masseter muscles on the outside of the bone, and of the internal pterygoid muscle on the inside. Because both these muscles are concerned with the rotary motion of the jaw in chewing, this similarity merely reflects the common habit of heavy chewing in unrelated lines. In Sinanthropus, as in the Eskimos and other northern Mongoloids, the gonial angles are bent outward, making the lower part of the face look very wide. This again is partly a function of chewing.

The ascending rami, which connect the tooth-bearing body of the mandible to the skull, are of moderate height in Sinanthropus, as in other early fossil men. As we saw in Chapter 7, the ascending rami of the Australopithecines are very long and high. This means only that the faces of the various lines of *Homo erectus* were diagnostically shorter than those of the Australopithecines yet discovered. Also the Sinanthropus mandibles, like those of other *Homines erecti,* have genial tubercles projecting from the insides of their symphyses, like most modern men and unlike most, if not all, Australopithecines.

While conforming to the general *Homo erectus* pattern in the details mentioned above, Sinanthropus had two special peculiarities, the *torus mandibularis* and multiple mental foramina. The

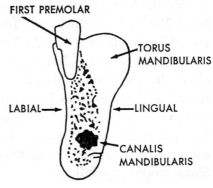

Fig. 63   TORUS MANDIBULARIS. Cross-section through the exaggerated *torus mandibularis* of the mandible of a prehistoric Chinese, in line with the first lower premolar. (Drawing after Weidenreich, 1936.)

torus mandibularis is a swelling of the jawbone on the tongue side, concentrated between the level of the canine and that of the first molar. This is solid, heavy bone, with no spongy interior. All the Sinanthropus jaws have it, and no other early fossil man had it. The *torus mandibularis* is found among some 15 per cent of the contemporary Chinese, whereas among Eskimo populations it varies in frequency between 42 and 97 per cent. It is found, as well, in 68 per cent of mediaeval Icelandic jaws. Neolithic Japanese, Lapp, Ostiak, prehistoric Chinese, Ainu, and prehistoric Scandinavian jaws all have it in ratios varying from 62 to 17 per cent; and it is just as frequent among northern Caucasoid jaws as it is among those of northern Mongoloids. If this bone is an adaptation to heavy chewing it is difficult to understand why others, particularly the Neanderthals, lacked it, unless they had some other adaptation to the same function. Oddly enough, it is also found in an extinct deer which the Sinanthropus folk ate.[6] We are reminded of other cases of convergence in special environments—for example, the case of prehensile tails in different kinds of South American mammals, including primates. As with the prehensile tail, *torus mandibularis* is hereditary.[7]

The other peculiarity, multiple mental foramina, is even more mysterious. In every jaw in which either or both sides of the bone lying immediately under the second lower premolar and first lower molar is preserved, more than one foramen may be seen. There are seven such jaws and the number of holes ranges from two to five. In other jaws, new and old, there is usually only one such perforation through which the blood vessels and nerves that service the lower part of the cheeks pass out of the body of the bone. None of the other early fossil man jaws has this anomaly, except for Heidelberg and the Ternefine mandibles from Algeria, which have two. The latter resemble the Sinanthropus jaws so closely in other respects that the two sets of jaws could have come from a single population. Later on, multiple mental foramina turn up in some of the European Neanderthals. In any case these two features, *torus mandibularis* and multiple mental foramina, indicate as well as anything could the extreme genetic isolation of the Sinanthropus population.

The Teeth of Sinanthropus

THANKS to Weidenreich, we have more information on the teeth of Sinanthropus than on those of any other fossil human population.[8] His series consists of 147 teeth, 83 of which are still in their original positions in jaws and 64 of which are loose. Of the 147 teeth, 134 are permanent, including 52 uppers and 82 lowers. Thirteen are deciduous, all lowers. The total is said to represent about 32 individuals, 20 adults and adolescents with permanent teeth, and 12 juveniles with milk teeth. This is as large a sample as we get from some living populations.

[6] H. D. Kahlke: "On the Evolution of Pachyostosis in Jaw Bones of CKT Giant Deer, *Megaceros Pachyosteous* (Young)," *VP*, Vol. 2, No. 3 (1958), pp. 117–34.

[7] M. Suzuki and T. Sakai: "A Familial Study of Torus Palatinus and Torus Mandibularis," *AJPA*, Vol. 18, No. 4 (1960), pp. 263–72.

[8] Weidenreich: "The Dentition of *Sinanthropus pekinensis*."

Like the skulls and mandibles the teeth are of two sizes, relatively large and relatively small. Large ones are found in two large mandibles and one large "male" skull, and small ones are found in two small mandibles and one small "female" skull. If we agree with Weidenreich that the large teeth are male and the small ones are female, then we have the permanent teeth of ten male adults and adolescents and of six male juveniles, and also of ten adult-adolescent and six juvenile females.

Table 39 gives the length and breadth of the Sinanthropus permanent teeth and comparable dimensions for Pithecanthropus from the two available specimens, No. 4 and mandible B, as well as the crown dimensions of the Upper Cave specimens, those of a series of modern Chinese males, and the modern length and breadth ranges for all races.

The Sinanthropus teeth are large in both mesiodistal length and labiolingual breadth diameters, but all except two of the sixteen kinds of teeth (uppers and lowers, incisors, canines, etc.) fall within the ranges of living populations. One exception is the upper canine. In five of the six specimens studied, the mesiodistal length exceeds the modern range; and one of them, with a length of 10.5 mm., is the largest such tooth in the world. The other exception is the second upper premolar. Two of twelve of these exceed the modern range in the labiolingual breadth.

In general Pithecanthropus had much larger teeth than Sinanthropus, with seven of twelve (all sixteen are not represented in Pithecanthropus) exceeding the Sinanthropus range. The two populations also differ in the ratio between the combined mesiodistal length of the three upper molars and the total length of the entire upper tooth row, from the upper median incisor to the upper third molar. In Sinanthropus the molar length is only 41.5 per cent of the total row length; in Pithecanthropus 4 it is 45.2 per cent. These differences are retained, more or less, in modern Mongoloid and Australoid peoples.

In Sinanthropus the upper first molar is the largest of the three and the upper third the smallest. This is the usual sequence in modern populations. In Pithecanthropus 4 the upper second molar is the largest and the first and third are nearly equal in size. In the lower jaw the second molar is the largest in both Sinanthropus and Pithecanthropus B, but in Sinanthropus the first molar is much larger than the third, while in Pithecanthropus B the first and third molars are nearly equal in size. These differences between the Javanese and Chinese *Homines erecti* in tooth size reflect the differences already noted in the stoutness of the lower jawbones of the two races at different locations—that in Sinan-

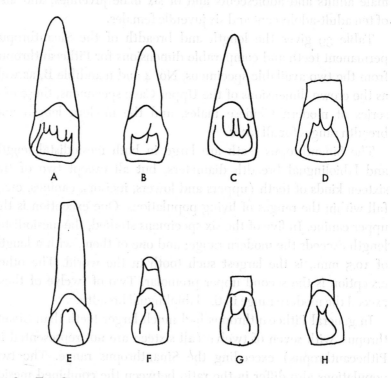

FIG. 64   THE CONTINUITY OF MONGOLOID TEETH: SHOVEL INCISORS FROM SINANTHROPUS TO THE RECENT CHINESE. *Upper Median Incisors:* A. Sinanthropus; B. Ting-tsun; C. Upper Cave; D. Recent North Chinese. *Upper Lateral Incisors:* E. Sinanthropus; F. Ting-tsun; G. Sjara-Osso-Gol; H. Recent North Chinese. This sequence of upper and lower incisors shows a continuity of tooth form in the heart of the Mongoloid realm from the Middle Pleistocene to the present. (Drawings B and F after Movius, 1956; all others after Weidenreich, 1937.)

thropus the emphasis is on the front of the mouth whereas in Pithecanthropus it is on the molars. The whole facial structure of Sinanthropus, as previously noted, is concentrated on its forward portion, which is still true of Mongoloids.

    The relationship between the teeth of Sinanthropus and those of living Mongoloids is shown more convincingly in morphological characteristics than in gross dimensions. Of these the most conspicuous is the peculiar shovel-like shape of the upper incisors, described in Chapter 8. All five of the upper median and both of the upper lateral incisors are shoveled. Not only are the edges of the teeth raised, but they are actually wrapped around on the lingual side, and they have one to three fingerlike tubercles or ridges running down the lingual surface from its upper inner rim half way to the cutting edge. Incisors comparable to those of Sinanthropus have been found in the earlier South African Australopithecines and in some of the fossil jaws from North Africa, and the element of lingual ridging occurs in the incisors of living great apes.

The upper canines of Sinanthropus are large and long-rooted, and their crowns project beyond the level of the incisors and premolars. Instead of points, as in apes and modern men, the lower canines have cutting edges. The upper canines are shoveled and fingered, braced and ornamented, in the manner of the upper incisors. Starting with the canines and moving backward, all the teeth have cingulums, or collars, sometimes completely circular, sometimes incomplete, just above the necks of the teeth, at the bases of the crowns. This feature is characteristic of apes and is slightly developed in some of the Australopithecine teeth. In Pithecanthropus it is present but not pronounced, and it is not characteristic of modern man of any race. Like Pithecanthropus, the orang, and some of the Australopithecines, Sinanthropus had fine wrinkles on the grinding surfaces of his molars. Both the cingulum and the wrinkling are more characteristic of an early grade of human dental development than of a particular line.

All the permanent molars and premolars of Sinanthropus, and all the milk molars, are taurodont; that is, each tooth has an enlarged pulp cavity extending downward into fused roots, as described in Chapter 8. A taurodont tooth can be worn down much lower than an ordinary tooth. This condition, absent in Pithecanthropus, is not unique with Sinanthropus, but is found in a number of populations, ancient and modern, particularly among the Middle Pleistocene people of North Africa, the European Neanderthals, and living Eskimos, American Indians, and Bushmen.

Taurodontism seems to have a selective advantage when the workload of the teeth is too great for their surface area, as, for instance, in a cold climate, where the teeth are used for softening skins (Neanderthals and Eskimo), or as when, after the teeth have been reduced by dwarfing, the capacity for heavy chewing is still needed (Bushmen). In Sinanthropus, skin dressing was probably the critical factor. Taurodontism is hereditary. All of the peoples who have it or had it (with the possible exception of the Neanderthals, to be studied in the next chapter) are in one way or another members of either the Mongoloid or the Capoid racial line of descent.

The Leg Bones of Sinanthropus

WEIDENREICH has described seven fragmentary femora, numbered 1 to 7. Numbers 4 and 5 are believed to be a pair. Not one has a complete head or distal end. All except No. 2, which is smaller than the others, are called male. Only No. 1 and No. 4 are complete enough to permit reconstruction of their total lengths, 400 mm. and 407 mm; these indicate a stature of about five foot one and a half inches, or 156 cm, similar to that of living Japanese, Eskimo, and Ainu, and shorter than that of Pithecanthropus.

Several peculiarities set these femora apart from those of most modern men. The walls of the shaft are extraordinarily thick and the medullary canal occupies only 35 per cent of the total diameter (33 per cent transversely and 38 per cent sagittally) as compared with about 48 per cent for other ancient men of later periods. The Pithecanthropus femora were also of normal thickness.[9] Among the apes only the orang has thick femoral walls.

In Sinanthropus the dense bone of the walls runs far up on the neck of the femur where modern femora contain mainly spongy matter. Furthermore, the trajectorial grid system of the less extensive spongy part is composed of exceptionally coarse

[9] Judging from the photographs of the broken shafts of Nos. 2 and 3 in the Leyden collection (Weidenreich, 1941, plate 29) and a photograph of No. 1 which shows a break on the inside of the lower shaft (R. Martin, 1928, p. 1153).

fibers which are laid down in a different pattern from that seen in modern femora.

The Sinanthropus femora are also extremely flat, fore-and-aft, like those of apes; this feature is also found in some other populations, including Neolithic Chinese and modern Fuegians. Uniquely, however, the Sinanthropus femora have only vestigial pilasters (bony struts along the center of the backs of the shafts); the linea aspera (a ridge superimposed on the pilaster), which is found in all human specimens, consequently lies flat on the surface on the bone. Although the shaft is bent no more than in modern specimens, the peak of the curve lies near the knee-end instead of in the middle as in other femora, including those of Pithecanthropus.

The Upper Extremity of Sinanthropus

THERE IS only one piece of humerus, and both ends of it are missing. This bone was probably about 324 mm. long, or 30 mm. longer than those of Japanese and Ainu, who have the same femur length. If Weidenreich's reconstruction of it is correct, either it belonged to a taller individual than the owners of the six femora, or else he had proportionately longer arms. Like the femora, the humerus is extremely thick-walled, although its general form is slender. Otherwise it is completely modern. It has, however, an extreme development of the tubercle for the attachment of the deltoid muscle, the function of which is to raise the arm sidewise. Similar tubercles have been found on the humeri of Neolithic Chinese and modern Fuegians. The Fuegians are great paddlers; what Sinanthropus and the Neolithic Chinese did to develop such powerful deltoids is unknown.

We have also one slightly defective clavicle in the Sinanthropus collection. As this is an extremely variable bone in modern man, it is not surprising that the specimen at hand has no special features; it is slender, highly curved, and heavily ridged for the attachment of powerful muscles, including the deltoid.

There is also one os *lunatum*, a wrist bone, which is also completely human, although it is small; but so, apparently, are those of many Mongoloids.

The Position of Sinanthropus in the Human Family Tree

EVEN THESE scanty observations make it evident that the postcranial skeleton of Sinanthropus differed from that of Pithecanthropus, and that both differed from the curiously assorted skeletons of *Australopithecus*. Among these animals the head of the femur was not rotated as far forward as in man, and the distal condyles of that bone had peculiarities of their own. In the Zinjanthropus leg bones the fibula is thicker, compared to the thickness of the tibia, than in man as a genus, and this suggests that Zinjanthropus walked on the outside of his foot. Pithecanthropus had long, slender, modern-style femora, and his successor, Solo man, a modern tibia. Sinanthropus, however, had short, heavy leg bones, with peculiar bone webbing in the head of the femur, narrow marrow cavities, a relatively short tibia, and much bowing of both bones.

Sinanthropus differed from Pithecanthropus in many other anatomical details. His brain case was larger, as large as Solo's. In some details of cranial anatomy, particularly in the configuration of the inner surface of the temporal bone, he was more apelike than Pithecanthropus. His frontal bone had a constriction behind the brow ridges, whereas Pithecanthropus's brow rose in a smoother, more gradual slope. Pithecanthropus (at least Number 4) had the largest palate, and their teeth were as different as teeth could be within a single species.

These comparisons suggest that the relationship between Pithecanthropus and Sinanthropus, which most physical anthropologists believe in, was not a close one. It also suggests that either several related hominids acquired the erect posture independently or, by the time Sinanthropus came along, different lines had been as rigorously differentiated by the evolutionary process from the neck down as from the neck up. The currently popular nostrum that except for their skins all men are alike from the neck down is nonsense.

Sinanthropus was a peculiar type of human being who had more features in common with living Mongoloids, regardless of grade, than with any other living subspecies. Among these common features are the following:

(1) A sagittal keeling of the skull vault, found among Eskimos and North Chinese. Pithecanthropus also had this, as do modern Australians and Tasmanians.

(2) Inca bones, found in three or four of five skulls. These are found in 15 per cent of the American Indians and are more frequent among Mongoloids than in other races.

(3) Broad nasal bones that show little or no difference between upper and middle breadths.

(4) A gently rounded contour of the nasal saddle.

(5) The profile angle of the roof of the nasal passages equals 89°, a little higher than in Mongoloids, who have the highest such angle among living men.

(6) The outer border of the orbit is set forward as in Australopithecines, gorillas, and orangs, and the forward part of the temporal muscle is extended anteriorly above the edge of the brow ridge, compressing the lateral half of the orbit.

(7) The infraorbital margin is rounded and even with the floor of the orbit, as in modern Mongols.

(8) Buccal exostoses (bony growths) of the mandible are found in all three upper jaws of Sinanthropus; these growths are found in from two to five per cent of the Aleuts, the Japanese, the Lapps, and the natives of Siberia.

(9) Exostoses of the internal auditory meatus (tube of the earhole).

(10) A general thickening of the tympanic plate. This and the preceding are found chiefly among Eskimos, American Indians, and Icelanders.

(11) The "infantile gap" in the tympanic bone.

(12) A special external growth on the border of the tympanic plate, found in Sinanthropus Skull X and in no other fossil hominids; it occurs in 18 to 20 per cent of the Polynesians, 12 to 30 per cent of the American Indians, and only rarely in Caucasoids.

(13) The mandibular torus.

(14) Shovel incisors.

(15) Extreme flattening of the femur, accompanied by a flat linea aspera and a distal position of the shaft curve.

(16)   A strongly developed deltoid tuberosity of the humerus.

(17)   A small wrist bone.

Weidenreich's list, given above with a few modifications,[1] implies a genetic continuity with the modern Mongoloids of Asia, Oceania, and America; but it has not been widely accepted, for two reasons. First, some of the features which appear in other populations that dwell in cold regions may have been acquired adaptively and convergently. Second, most human anatomists are reluctant to admit that more than one line of human beings could have passed the evolutionary threshold that separates Sinanthropus from the living Mongoloids. In my opinion the first objection is more valid than the second.

Still a third objection, which has held back a number of open-minded scientists who are willing to overlook the first two, is the lack of skeletal material to fill the time gap between Sinanthropus and historical races of Mongoloids. Owing to new discoveries in China and Japan, that gap is being filled.

Late Middle Pleistocene Finds in China and Japan

S I N C E 1954 four different finds of fossil man, made in the Far East, have been assigned to the later part of the Middle Pleistocene by their discoverers, three from China and one from Japan. They are listed on Table 19.

The Ting-tsun Teeth

I N 1954 fourteen paleolithic sites were excavated in the region of Ting-tsun, Shansi, northern China.[2] Although they are stated to be Middle Pleistocene by the Chinese discoverers, Movius believes that they are of Third Interglacial age. Over two thousand

---

[1] Weidenreich: "The Skull of *Sinanthropus pekinensis*," pp. 252–4.

[2] H. L. Movius, Jr.: "New Paleolithic Sites near Ting T'sun on the Fen River, Shansi Province, North China," *Quaternaria*, No. 3 (1956), pp. 13–26.

T-K. Cheng: *Archaeology in China, Vol. I, Prehistoric China* (Cambridge: W. Heffer and Sons; 1959), pp. 25–6.

G. Bushnell and C. McBurney: "New World Origins Seen from the Old World," *Antiquity*, Vol. 33, No. 130 (1959), pp. 93–101.

artifacts found here are said to indicate an evolutionary progression based on the stone-tool industry of Choukoutien, with or without influences from the Western world.[3]

The human remains from these excavations consist of three teeth, two upper incisors and a lower second molar. They are smaller than the Sinanthropus teeth and within the modern Chinese range.[4] Both incisors are shoveled in the exaggerated Sinanthropus fashion. The lower molar, which has five cusps and an incipient sixth, resembles those of Sinanthropus morphologically.

Whether these teeth belonged to the Late Middle or Early Upper Pleistocene is less important than the fact that they form a bridge between Sinanthropus and modern Mongoloids in association with a stone-tool industry derived from that of Choukoutien. This is the continuity that Weidenreich sought and died too soon to see.

The Changyang Maxilla [5]

T H R E E   Y E A R S later, a piece of fossil human maxilla, containing an upper first premolar and an upper first molar, and also an isolated lower second premolar, were found in a cave called Lungtung, at Hsiachungchiawan village, in the Ichang limestone area 28 miles southwest of the city of Changyang in Hupei Province. This is mountainous country; the cave is about 4,400 feet above sea level.

Although there were no artifacts in this site, faunal remains were abundant. They belonged to the so-called *Ailuropus-Stegodon* fauna (*Ailuropus* is the giant panda), which was also found with Sinanthropus at Choukoutien. Chia, who described it, considers the fauna of this site to be of Late Middle Pleistocene date, and to my knowledge no one has yet challenged this allocation.

---

[3] Movius states that they show no Western influence; Bushnell and McBurney that they do.

[4] Scale measurements of the illustrations give the upper median incisor a length of 9 mm., the upper lateral incisor a length of 7 mm., and the lower second molar a length of 11 mm., and a breadth of 11 mm.

[5] L-P. Chia: "Notes on the Human and Other Mammalian Remains from Changyang, Hupei," *VP*, Vol. 1, No. 3 (1957), pp. 252–7.

The maxillary fragment is part of the left side only, including the roof of the palate and the sagittal line from the nasal spine to the tooth line; in other words, half of the upper jaw. The palate is ribbed, as it should be; the anterior nasal spine is poorly developed and pointing forward; the nasal opening is wide, and its lateral wall less curved than in most modern men (this is apparently a primitive feature noted by the author of the monograph).

The relief of the bony surface of the maxilla which covers the root of the canine is high, indicating that that tooth, which is missing, had a long, thick root as in Sinanthropus. However, the three teeth that are present are intermediate in size between the teeth of Sinanthropus and the teeth of modern Chinese, although the root of the lower second premolar is longer than either of the two corresponding Sinanthropus teeth.[6] The enamel of these teeth is highly wrinkled.

Morphologically and metrically the Changyang specimens closely resemble Sinanthropus, but seem to indicate a step forward in the direction of modern Mongoloid man. Because the brain case is missing, we have too little evidence to indicate whether or not Changyang man had crossed the threshold from *Homo erectus* to *Homo sapiens;* but if he had not, he was well on the way.

The Specimen from Mapa, Kwangtung

A YEAR after the Changyang discovery, in 1958, farmers digging fertilizer in a cave in the so-called Lion Hill at Mapa, Shaoquan Municipality (formerly Chukiang District) of Kwangtung (Canton) Province, found a fragmentary human skull in the midst of many other mammalian bones, including *Stegodon,* an extinct elephant. The fauna indicates a Late Middle or Early Upper Pleistocene date.[7] The human specimen, already men-

[6] The crown dimensions of the three teeth are: upper first premolar, length = 7.4 mm., breadth = 10.6 mm.; upper first molar, 1. = 10.8 mm., br. = 12.8 mm.; lower second premolar, 1. = 8.3 mm., br. = 10.6 mm. The root length of the lower second premolar is 20.5 mm., those of the Sinanthropus specimens 17.3 mm. and 19.2 mm.

[7] Woo: Fossil Human Skull of Early Paleanthropic Stage Found at Mapa, Shaoquan, Kwangtung Province, VP, Vol. 3, No. 4 (1959), pp. 176–82.

tioned in Chapter 9, consists of the frontal bone, both parietals, the nasal bones, and the lower border of the right orbit. It is heavily fossilized; the sutures are all fused; it is certainly adult, and probably male.

With this skull two questions arise at once: Is it *erectus* or *sapiens?* Is it Mongoloid or Australoid, if either? Unfortunately, not enough of it is left to help us answer either question completely.

The frontal bone is longer than the parietals, and bregma is located farther back than in most modern skulls. These are both hallmarks of *Homo erectus*. In the indices of the arcs and chords of the frontal and parietal bones (see Chapter 8) the Mapa cranial fragment falls into the ranges of the Sinanthropus and Solo skulls, the Rhodesian and Saldanha specimens from South Africa, and also the European Neanderthals.[8] But the absolute measurements of the bones slightly exceed the Sinanthropus range, and they lie just inside the Solo range.

Woo has drawn the skull on a simulated eye-ear plane (see Fig. 60) and drawn a line from glabella, which is present, to opisthion (the rearmost point of the occiput), which is postulated. The height of the skull above this line (82 mm.) is the same as that of Sinanthropus 10, the largest of the Sinanthropi. As the Mapa skull is only 7 mm. thick at bregma, compared to 8.8 mm. for Sinanthropus, and as the skull appears to have been more rounded, its capacity probably exceeded that of Sinanthropus 10 and the largest of the Solo skulls (1,225 cc), and fell easily within the modern range.

Morphologically it is again intermediate, both in grade and in line. The brow ridges are heavy, and shaped like those of Solo rather than those of Sinanthropus. But the frontal bone behind the ridges is markedly constricted as in Sinanthropus; and the nicking of the frontal profile just above glabella is moderate, and intermediate. The nasal bones are wide and the nasofrontal suture almost straight. The frontal sinus is larger than in either Sinanthropus or Solo, and extends laterally over the eye sockets. The orbital borders are rounded, not square as in Sinanthropus; but

---

[8] The Mapa frontal arc = 134 mm., chord = 118 mm., index = 88.0. The figures for the parietal bone are 114 mm., 110 mm., and 96.5.

they are also rounded in modern Mongoloids. The orbits themselves are high, as in Mongoloids. Also the lower border of the
orbit projects forward, as in Sinanthropus and the Mongoloids.

Woo believes that the Mapa skull had evolved to the same
grade as the European Neanderthals, to what he called the Early
Paleanthropic stage. In view of the history of the Neanderthals,
which will be recounted in the next chapter, I agree with him in
this diagnosis but not in the comparison. The Mapa skull seems to
stand at the threshold between the two grades of *Homo*. If it was
not *sapiens,* it was very close to being so. In any case, it represents
a higher stage of human evolution than Sinanthropus himself,
which is the most important conclusion we can reach. As to its
race, it seems to me to be mostly if not entirely Mongoloid; and in
ways in which it differs from Sinanthropus, as in the shape of the
orbits, it is a link between Sinanthropus and the modern Mongoloid peoples.

The Humerus Shaft from Ushikawa Quarry, Japan

UNTIL AFTER the Emperor's official declaration that he was
no longer to be considered divine, the search for fossil man in
Japan was not vigorously pressed. During the 1950's, however, it
got off to a late but profitable start. In 1957, a laborer working in a
limestone quarry in the Ushikawa district, five miles from the city
of Toyohashi in Aichi Prefecture, east-central Honshu, found a
number of bones at a depth of 70 feet. Among these bones were
two broken pieces of the shaft of a human humerus. The fauna
with which they were associated is called Late Middle Pleistocene. No artifacts were found. These humeral fragments, which
are from one bone because the two sections fit together, have been
described by H. Suzuki and F. Takai.[9]

The piece is 70 cm. long, and comes from almost exactly the
middle of the shaft, which is believed to have had a total length of
230 mm. Suzuki, who thinks it female, compares it to the humeri
of nineteenth-century Japanese women, the mean of which is
265.5 mm. This suggests a stature for the Ushikawa woman of

[9] H. Suzuki and F. Takai: "Entdeckung eines Pleistozänen Hominiden Humerus in Zentral-Japan," *AAnz.*, Vol. 23, No. 2/3 (1959), pp. 224–35.

only 135 cm., or 4 feet 5 inches, which would not be very tall for a Pygmy woman.

A detailed study of the various diameters and circumferences taken at different loci on the shaft show that it differs considerably from those of the modern Japanese, being, among other things, narrower at the proximal end and thicker at the distal. Moreover, the walls of the shaft are very thick compared to the width of the marrow cavity; the walls comprise 55 per cent of the diameter, compared to 40 per cent for recent Japanese. In this respect it resembles the limb bones of Sinanthropus. This is a most unusual bone, and although it has been described exhaustively, we must, along with Suzuki and Takai, await further discoveries before it can be properly evaluated.

The Upper Pleistocene Woman from Tze-Yang, Szechuan [1]

T U R N I N G again to Table 19, we find five items from the Far East labeled as Upper Pleistocene. The first is a skull from west-central China, from the mountainous province of Szechuan, which today is inhabited not only by Chinese but also by Tibetans, Lolos, and other non-Chinese-speaking tribesmen. The skull was found in 1951 by railway workers in a bank of the Huangshanchi River, Tze-Yang District, Szechuan. Associated with it was a rather crudely made bone awl and an extensive fauna.

The animal bones, although mixed together in the deposit, could be separated into two lots on the basis of color, degree of fossilization, and fluorine content. The older fauna includes *Stegodon orientalis, Rusa unicolor,* and *Rhinoceros sinensis,* Stegodon being an extinct elephant, and Rusa simply *Cervus rusa,* the extinct deer found at Choukoutien. This fauna belongs to the Middle Pleistocene. The younger fauna includes *Muntiacus* (the muntjak deer), *Mammonteus primigenius* (*Mammuthus,* according to Simpson, a mammoth), and *Homo sapiens,* this being the Tze-Yang woman herself. This fauna is Upper Pleistocene. The sorting out of these two faunas by W. C. Pei may help clarify the dating of other sites, particularly in south China, where the faunas are also scrambled.

[1] W-C. Pei and Woo: "Tzeyang Paleolithic Man," *IVPM,* No. 1, 1957.

The skull, identified as a female over fifty years old, consists of a nearly complete vault, with both parietals intact, all of the frontal bone except for the internal part over the orbits, all of the occipital bone except for the piece immediately behind the foramen magnum, the left temporal, the left great wing of the sphenoid excepting the base, and small pieces of nasal bone adhering to the frontal. Separate and without point of contact with the vault is the palate, including parts of the maxillae and the lower part of the nasal opening. All the upper teeth are gone except for the broken-off root of the left upper second premolar. The right upper second premolar and all three left molars had been lost before death; the others had fallen out after death. There is evidence that the woman had suffered a serious dental disease.

The cranial measurements given on Table 37 indicate that the skull was quite small but well within the female range of both Metal Age prehistoric and recent North Chinese series. Compared to Sinanthropus 11, her skull is short, narrow, and high, and more voluminous by 200 cc. The minimum frontal, measured on the photograph, was probably narrower than either Sinanthropus 11, as reconstructed by Weidenreich, or the modern female mean. The nasal opening breadth, also reconstructed, was narrower than that of Sinanthropus 11 and close to the modern figures. The palate dimensions are modern, and the teeth were probably also of modern dimensions.

Although the Tze-Yang woman was essentially *sapiens,* her skull shows several archaic features. In the endocranial cast the cerebral fossae of the occipital bone are wider and deeper than the cerebellar fossae. This condition is reminiscent of Sinanthropus and the Neanderthals, and indicates that the cerebellum had neither expanded nor been pushed down by the cerebral hemispheres to the extent seen in most modern skulls. Also, on the inner surface of the parietals the impressions of the middle meningeal artery are archaic in pattern. The anterior ramus, although the larger, has fewer branches; the posterior ramus is the more intricately branched.

The outside of the skull shows heavier brow ridges than usual for Mongoloids, a relatively long frontal bone with bregma placed to the rear of its modern situation, a rounded occiput, and a swelling above the mastoids. The squamous portion of the left temporal bone is smaller than in most modern skulls of the same size. Also, according to Pei and Woo, "in modern man the zygomatic process of the temporal bone and its backward extension of the supra-mastoid crest lie nearly parallel to the eye-ear plane. In *Sinan-thropus* it forms an acute angle of 30° with the eye-ear plane, while in Tze-Yang man it forms an angle of about 20°." [2]

This excellent and detailed study, the high points of which have been given here, makes it evident that the Tze-Yang skull is an early *sapiens* form retaining some Sinanthropic features combined with, for the most part, modern proportions. The position of the temporal attachment on the frontal and its general morphology, including that of the lower nasal aperture, also indicate that it was Mongoloid, the only atypical feature being that the nasofrontal suture is slightly rounded instead of running straight across. This is not enough to upset Pei's and Woo's racial diagnosis.

The Upper Pleistocene Man of Liu-Kiang, Kwangsi

K w a n g s i is the next province to the west after Kwangtung, where the Mapa specimen was found. With Yunnan, it is the gateway through which Mongoloids crept down the fingerlike ridges that form the steep watersheds between the Irrawaddy, Salween, Mekong, and Red rivers, into the steaming jungles of southeast Asia, to replace the Australoids and Negritos who had evolved there.

In a cave called Tungtienyen, 10 miles southwest of Liuchow in central Kwangsi, workmen found, in 1958, an almost complete human skull.[3] No artifacts were with it, but it was accompanied by many animal bones of the familiar stegodon-giant panda fauna. Although it was heavily fossilized, the skull was found in red soil, whereas most of the deposit was yellow. This fact led Woo to conclude that its date is Upper Pleistocene rather than Middle Pleistocene, as would have been indicated had it been embedded in the yellow material.

The cranium is nearly complete, but there is no mandible. Also

[2] Pei and Woo: op. cit., p. 40.
[3] Woo: "Human Fossils Found in Liukiang, Kwangsi, China," *VP*, Vol. 3, No. 3 (1959), pp. 109–18.

found were four thoracic and five lumbar vertebrae; five pieces of rib; a sacrum; a right ilium-ischium combination, but no pubic bone; and two pieces of femur, one from each leg. All but the femora are said to have belonged to a male about forty years old. The leg-bones may have been his, or they may have been part of a female. They are of a different color from the other bones.

As the figures given on Table 37 indicate, it is a large and capacious skull, fully modern in the dimensions of its brain case; but its face is low, its nose short and wide, and its orbits low. Its palate is of moderate size, and its teeth the same. The incisors were shoveled—at least the lateral ones were. Although the one remaining median incisor was too worn to tell, the median incisors are always more shoveled than the lateral ones if this trait is present. Curiously enough, this man lived to be over forty without cutting his upper third molars. This, too, is a Mongoloid trait.

The brow ridges are a little heavy for modern Chinese, but not for peripheral Mongoloids like some American Indians. The position of bregma is still too far back for a modern skull, as the frontal part of the sagittal arc is more than one third of the total. The rear profile of the skull shows a moderate amount of lambdoid flattening, present in both Sinanthropus and the European Neanderthals. We have no information on the inside surface of the skull.

Is this skull, then, Mongoloid or Australoid? Woo believes that it is Mongoloid, of a primitive type, and points out that low faces and low orbits were common elsewhere in Upper Pleistocene times, particularly in Europe; this was a phase through which skulls of different lines passed independently. The form of the nose, with its guttered rim; the slight alveolar prognathism; the shape of the temporal lines on the forehead; and the teeth are all Mongoloid. The malars are prominent in the forward plane, as they should be. The skull's frontal index of facial flatness, simotic index (which indicates the degree of lateral curvature of the nasal bones), and rhinial index (which expresses the degree of flatness of the mid-face) are all within the ranges of modern Mongoloid peoples, and the first two are within the Sinanthropus range. The rhinial index of Sinanthropus cannot be calculated.[4]

[4] For the Liu-Kiang skull, F.I.F.F. = 15.7; Simotic I. = 28.3; Rhinial I. = 32.4. For Sinanthropus 12, F.I.F.F. = 16.1(?), Simotic I. = 30.0.

Woo's conclusion that Liu-Kiang man was a Mongoloid form of *Homo sapiens* still in process of evolution seems correct, except that the skull deviates somewhat from the Mongoloid line in an Australoid direction, as one would expect from an ancient skull from southeast China, the contact zone between the Mongoloid and Australoid peoples.

The Liu-Kiang Postcranial Bones

I F A L L we had from Liu-Kiang was the skull just described, our problem would be simple, but we have a number of post-cranial bones, listed on Table 19—and this raises complications. Four thoracic vertebrae, numbers 9, 10, 11, and 12, which are the bottom four, have a combined ventral body height of 84.0 mm., which is short for living peoples; and the five lumbar vertebrae have a combined height of 119.1 mm., which is even shorter. Of the living peoples occupying eastern Asia only the Sakai are known to approximate these figures, and the Sakai are aboriginal hunters, of the Malay Peninsula, of unknown origin, whose physical appearance is largely Australoid. The Sakai are not Pygmies, but they are very nearly so.

The accompanying sacrum is somewhat flattish and small, with a length of 99.2 mm., a breadth of 86.5 mm., and a length-breadth index of 93.8. It is too small for Mongoloids or for Australian aborigines, and falls into the size range of the Andamanese Negritos. It is nearly triangular, tapering toward the distal end, very much like a Sakai sacrum illustrated in Martin's *Lehrbuch der Anthropologie*.[5] The piece of pelvic bone, which is an ilium and ischium without the pubic bones, matches the sacrum, and the acetabulum is rotated somewhat forward, as in Mongoloid pelves.

The leg bones consist of two broken pieces of shaft, without condyles and of unequal length. Probably the total femur length was about 370 mm., and the stature calculated from the femur length about four feet eleven inches (150 cm.) if a male or four feet nine inches (145 cm.) if a female. These figures are on the

[5] 1928 edition, Vol. 2, p. 1085.

upper border of the Pygmy range, but they are consistent with the size of the vertebrae and pelvic bones.

Despite their shortness, the femurs are stout, with sagittal and transverse diameters close to those of Sinanthropus, and the degree of flattening of the shafts is intermediate between that of Sinanthropus and that of the modern Chinese.[6] Also, the marrow canal occupies 37.8 per cent of the shaft diameter, at its narrowest point, in the Liu-Kiang femurs; in Sinanthropus it occupies 35.7 per cent; and in the modern Chinese 45 per cent and higher.

One may place these three specimens and sets of specimens in the following order of magnitude: (1) the skull is large; (2) the femora are fairly small but rugged; (3) the trunk bones, particularly the sacrum, are very small. As there is no duplication of parts, we cannot be sure that more than one individual is represented. For a racial diagnosis each part must be taken separately. The skull is mostly but not wholly Mongoloid, with some features reminiscent of or adumbrating the Australoid or Negrito. The pelvic and vertebral skeleton suggests the modern Sakai, who are themselves an enigmatic people, and the femora suggest a small Mongoloid. Let us hope that more material will turn up from Kwangsi so that this mystery may be solved.

The Tooth of Sjara-Osso-Gol, Ordos

IN THE bed of the desert river Sjara-Osso-Gol, in the Ordos country between the Great Wall and the bend of the Yellow River, the late Père Teilhard de Chardin and E. Licent found, in 1922, one upper left lateral incisor tooth, 7.1 mm. in mesiodistal diameter, which is smaller than the smallest upper lateral incisor in the Sinanthropus series. Morphologically, however, it fits the Sinanthropus pattern, with heavy shoveling and a basal tubercle projecting downward on the lingual side. It was associated with

---

[6] Sagittal diameter = 26.2 mm.; transverse diameter = 22.0 mm. The Sinanthropus figures are 28.3 mm. and 24.4 mm. The Index of platymeria (shaft-flattening) is 67.8 for Sinanthropus, 73.7 for Liu-Kiang, and 80.2 for modern Chinese.

an Upper Pleistocene fauna and many blade implements believed to represent the Upper Paleolithic culture of that region.[7]

The Remains from Ti-Shao-Gou-Wan, Ordos

I N A N O T H E R Ordos site, near the village of Ti-Shao-Gou-Wan, two more pieces of Ordos man turned up in 1957, and they have been given the same date as the previously described tooth.[8] They are a broken parietal bone and the lower half of a femur. The parietal bone is of modern size and shape, with a sagittal arc of 125 mm., a chord of 110 mm., and a curvature index of 88. These three figures are close to the modern mean for all races. Yet the bone is a little thicker than the modern mean,[9] and the tracks of the middle meningeal artery are simple, with the posterior branch larger than the anterior.

The femur half is 203 mm. long, suggesting a stature of about five feet five inches (167 cm.) if a man, or five feet three inches (160 cm.) if a woman. Woo favors the latter sexing. The walls are thick, with the marrow canal one third the total.

These two specimens, plus the tooth from Sjara-Osso-Gol, seem to provide a continuity from Sinanthropus into the Upper Pleistocene in Inner Mongolia as well as in other parts of China.

The Upper Pleistocene Remains from Central Honshu, Japan

I N S E P T E M B E R 1958, six pieces of human skeleton were unearthed in a lens of clay in a limestone quarry in the prefecture of Aichi, town of Mikkabi, Tadaki District. Although no artifacts

[7] E. Licent, P. Teilhard de Chardin, and D. Black: "On a Presumably Pleistocene Human Tooth from the Sjara Osso Gol (South Eastern Ordos) Deposits," *BGSC*, Vol. 5, No. 4 (1927), p. 287.

Also Weidenreich: "The Dentition of *Sinanthropus pekinensis*," *PS-NS-D*, Vol. 1 (1937), p. 21 and plate 3; and Cheng: op. cit., pp. 32–4.

[8] Woo: "Fossil Human Parietal Bone and Femur from Ordos, Inner Mongolia," *VP*, Vol. 2, No. 4 (1958), pp. 208–12.

[9] The thickness of this parietal near bregma is 6.5 mm.; the modern mean 5.5 mm.; and the mean for Sinanthropus 8.8 mm., with a range of 7.0 mm. to 10.0 mm.

were found, faunal remains were abundant, including tiger, some kind of elephant, deer, boar, and badger. F. Tayaki of Tokyo University has labeled this fauna Upper Pleistocene, and H. Suzuki, who described the Ushikawa humerus shaft, is working, at the time of writing, on the human material. These consist of five pieces of skullcap and one fragmentary pelvic bone. The skull pieces are two parietal fragments, two fragments of frontal including the orbital margins, and one piece of occipital. Only the pieces of the parietals fit together. Suzuki, in a preliminary statement to the press in June 1960, said that the skull represents the same stage of development as Crô-Magnon in Europe. For further information we must await the publication of his final study.

The People of the Upper Cave of Choukoutien

AT THIS POINT we have exhausted the human skeletal material from China and Japan which most authorities agree is of Upper Pleistocene date. In eastern Asia this stretch of about 150,000 years cannot be broken down as finely into subperiods as it has been in Europe. Some of the five specimens or sets of specimens that we have studied may be older than others by as much as 100,000 or more years. Yet most if not all of them show some racial likeness to Sinanthropus, in the skull, face, and leg bones, although those in south China also reflect the proximity of Australoids. We have yet to discuss two lots of material which may be dated toward the very end of the Upper Pleistocene, corresponding to the final Würm in Europe, or even early postglacial time. The first of these consists of the famous Old Man of the Upper Cave of Choukoutien and his equally celebrated two wives, or, more properly, female fellow victims.[1]

The Upper Cave in which they were found is a dissolution cavity in the limestone, one which was not open in Sinanthropus's day. It contained an industry of an evolved type derived

[1] Pei: "A Preliminary Report on the Late Paleolithic Cave of Chou Kou Tien, *BGSC*, Vol. 13, No. 3 (1934), pp. 327–58.

Weidenreich: "On the Earliest Representatives of Modern Mankind Recovered on the Soil of East Asia," *PNHB*, Vol. 13, Part 3 (1938–9), pp. 161–74. Also referred to in his 1943 monograph.

from the old complex of earlier days of choppers and chopping-tools and flakes; there is no evidence in it of diffusion of European or other Upper Paleolithic techniques. Archaeologically, the culture of these people was a local evolutionary product. The cave soil was also crammed with fossil animal bones, including those of hares, bears, hyenas, tigers, Sika deer, roe deer, and even ostriches and cheetahs. Of these, the hyenas, bears, and ostriches represent species extinct in China. Without doubt, C-14 and pollen analysis will one day pin down the age of this deposit. Meanwhile, let us place it in the neighborhood of about 10,000 B.C., with a wide margin of error.

Parts of the skeletons of at least seven persons were found, but only three skulls have been described: a man about sixty years old, a young woman who had not yet cut her wisdom teeth, and a somewhat older woman whose dental crowns had been worn flat. They are numbered 101, 102, and 103. The man was given a stature of five feet eight and a half inches (174 cm.); female No. 102 of five feet two and a half inches (159 cm.). We have no figure for No. 103. The femora of No. 101 had the same shaft-medullary cavity ratio as those of modern north Chinese.

These people had been killed in a mass murder and left where they lay. They had apparently not been eaten. No. 101 was killed by an arrow or small-headed spear that pierced his skull at the point where the frontoparietal suture crosses the temporal lines. It was not mutilated, and was complete when found. Females Nos. 102 and 103 suffered a less unanticipated and more horrible death. Someone held their heads sidewise on a stone, while someone else dropped another stone on them, squashing them so that the bones sprang out, increasing the head height at the expense of head breadth. Furthermore, No. 102 had suffered a small degree of cranial deformation before death, because across her forehead stretches a furrow of the kind made by carrying back-loads with tump-lines. This means of transportation is still used by the Atayals of Formosa and the Ainu.

This fatal head-crushing has had an important aftereffect which the unidentified murderers could not have anticipated. The two women have gone down in history as a Melanesian (No. 102) and an Eskimo (No. 103), as stated in dozens of textbooks. This conclusion is based on a preliminary interpretation of the un-restored dimensions of the crushed skulls, as a careful reading of Weidenreich's original paper will indicate.

His suggestion that the male skull (No. 101) looked like that of an Ainu was equally hasty. He stated that he made this compari-son on the basis of some photographs and measurements sent him by S. Kodanei of Tokyo. At the time S. Kodama's monumental work on the craniology of the Ainu [2] had not yet been published.

If we compare the dimensions of No. 101 as given on Table 37 with those of four long series of Ainu skulls from Hokkaido, Sakhalin, and the Kuriles, we find many differences. The cranial length of No. 101 is 16 mm. greater than the greatest Ainu mean and 1 mm. outside all their ranges. The minimum frontal of the Upper Cave skull is 11 mm. greater than any Ainu mean, and the bigonial diameter 10 mm. greater, and both these dimensions fall just inside the maximum ranges of the Kurile and Sakhalin Ainu, who have the largest faces of all the Ainus. The biorbital diameter is 9 mm. beyond any Ainu mean, and the nose height 5 mm. beyond any Ainu mean. In both these measurements No. 101 exceeds all Ainu ranges.

The old man of the Upper Cave does not conform strictly to a Mongoloid model, but neither do all Chinese alive today. In some respects he resembled the large-faced tribes of American Indians, like those still living on the Plains. This is particularly visible in the upper part of the nasal skeleton, and the lateral borders of the orbits, but the malars and the lower part of the nasal skeleton are fully Mongoloid in the Eastern Asiatic sense.

The faces of the two female skulls resemble his in general but are fully Mongoloid in those respects in which his deviates from the Eastern Asiatic pattern. No. 103, which Weidenreich called Eskimoid, is the most exaggeratedly Mongoloid of the three. To do Weidenreich's memory justice, I will make two brief quotations.

"The Old Man of the Upper Cave appears to represent not only a very primitive form of modern man but at the same time also a type of primitive Mongolian." [3]

". . . the three individuals of the Upper Cave show certain

[2] S. Kodama: *Crania Ainoica* (Sapporo, 1940).
[3] Weidenreich: "On the Earliest Representatives . . . ," p. 168.

common features in spite of disconformities in others. The former refers especially to the configuration of the face, namely the lowness of its upper part, the quadrangular form of the orbits, the wide inter-orbital breadth, the shape of the nasal aperture and the character of its entrance, and the existence of prognathism." [4]

It may be added that although the teeth of No. 101 are not large, their smallness is largely due to extensive wear, including interproximal attrition, which reduces the mesio-distal diameters. The women, who were young when killed, had larger teeth, and the molars of all three were taurodont. In No. 101, which alone has a complete dentition, the proportion of molar tooth size to incisor size is Mongoloid, and Flower's Index, the ratio between the mesio-distal length of the cheek teeth and the basion-nasion length, is only 35.7, which is very low, reflecting in part the extensive wear and in part the exceptionally long basion-nasion diameter (112 mm). His mandible bore one of Weidenreich's criteria linking Sinanthropus with the Mongoloids, a mandibular torus.

In sum, the Upper Cave skulls from Choukoutien approach the end of the Sinanthropus-Mongoloid line, bearing the same kind of relationship to the modern Chinese that the Upper Paleolithic skulls of Europe do to modern Europeans. The sooner we forget about the Ainu-Melanesian-Eskimo label the better.

The Specimen from Kait'o-Tung Cave, Leipin, Kwangsi [5]

I N 1956, a fossil human skull base and three tools were found in a limestone cave in a hill named Chilinshan, in the Leipin District of Kwangsi. This is the same province from which the enigmatic remains of Liu-Kiang were recovered. As the fauna was all recent, there is some doubt whether this specimen is of Late Pleistocene or post-Pleistocene date. One tool was a crude pebble chopper. The other two, which were flakes, have not been described.

Found were a combination of palatal and maxillary bones, with four molars and three premolars; one each of the molar and pre-

[4] Ibid., p. 169.

[5] Chia and Woo: "Fossil Human Skull Base of Late Paleolithic Stage from Chilinshan, Leipin District, Kwangsi," *VP*, Vol. 3, No. 1 (1959), pp. 37–9.

molar teeth is represented, although all are badly worn, and the premolars have probably been broken. The palate was medium to narrow in width; the nasal aperture wide; and the molars within the size range of the Upper Cave specimens.[6] What is left of the occipital bones is modern in size and form. Otherwise this skull is too badly broken to indicate much about its racial affinities. Chia and Woo feel that the form and direction of the stub of a zygomatic process remaining on the occipital bone suggest a malar protrusion of less than Mongoloid proportions, but this seems to be reading more into the specimen than the evidence warrants.

Post-Pleistocene Skeletons

I T W O U L D seem that we have carried the northeastern peoples of the Old World through the Pleistocene in sufficient detail to show a genetic continuity from Mindel II to the end of Würm. The people who live in this area today are Mongoloid, as were the Chinese from about 3000 B.C. to modern times. The gap of 5,000 years which remains between 8000 B.C. and 3000 B.C. hardly needs filling, if, indeed, some of those finds most recently described do not fit into that period. We no longer need to scrutinize each scrap of bone nor to measure each tooth to a tenth of a millimeter. As far as northeastern Asia is concerned, our job is done, except for the problem of the Ainu, who are a white-skinned somewhat Caucasoid-looking people with as much hair as a hairy Scot or Jew.

Aside from the recent work of Suzuki, the early man finds in Japan are limited to a few skeletons from the Jomon Period, a Mesolithic-Neolithic ceramic culture which has been given an initial C-14 date of 7500 ± 400 B.P.[7] I have seen the earliest Jomon skull in Japan; this skull, like the rest of them, would look better on the neck of a modern fisherman from Osaka than on that of an Ainu. However, we do not know what the Ainu were like in

---

[6] Palate width = 37 mm.; nasal opening width = 31 mm.; upper first molar is 10 mm. long and 12 mm. wide; upper second molar = 10 mm. × 13 mm.; upper third molar = 9 mm. × 10 mm.

[7] H. Befu and C. S. Chard: "Preceramic Cultures in Japan," *AA*, Vol. 62, No. 5 (1960), pp. 815–49. (M-769)

6450 B.C. All the known Ainu skulls are recent. From Manchuria [8] there are a couple of undated, probably Mesolithic or Neolithic, skulls, which are Mongoloid, and that is all.

America: the Western Extension of the Mongoloid Realm

B O T H the American Indians and the Eskimo, which inhabit North and South America, are Mongoloid. All the skulls and bones of their ancestors which have been unearthed to date are also Mongoloid. There is not a real Australoid, Melanesian, Negroid, or Caucasoid piece of bone in the lot.

Three problems concerning the American Indians face us: How long ago did their ancestors begin to cross the broad glacial plain of what is now the Bering Strait? Was it initially crossed by people who could be called *H. erectus,* or only by *H. sapiens?* Did the incursions of Caucasoids, if there really were any, which may have produced the Ainu and the bearded tribes of the Amur River country and points north, contribute to the peopling of the Americas?

First of all, the Bering Strait "highway" to America was not always open for foot traffic. As Fairbridge's study of Pleistocene sea levels showed, it could have been open during the peak of the Riss-Illinoisan, and again during most if not all of the Würm-Wisconsin (see Chapter 8, p. 314). Theoretically, bands of hunters living on a Sinanthropus cultural level, with tools good enough to fashion weapons adequate for killing deer, with fire, and with a built-in cold adaptation as good as that of the living Alakalufs (see Chapter 2), could have made the crossing if they had adequate shelter at night, with or without clothing.

Homo erectus could have done it, but were there any populations of his grade in the north as late as the height of the Riss-Illinoisan? The only skull we have in East Asia that can have come from that period is Mapa, which is so incomplete that we are not sure whether or not it had crossed the *erectus-sapiens* threshold. If people like Mapa crossed at that time, they could

[8] A. S. Loukashin: "Some Observations on the Remains of a Pleistocene Fauna and of the Paleolithic Age in Northern Manchuria," in G. G. MacCurdy, ed.: *Early Man* (Philadelphia; J. B. Lippincott Company; 1937), pp. 327–40.

have brought genes for a very archaic skull vault, but probably also a brain of *sapiens* size.

No archaeological evidence has yet been unearthed on either the Asiatic or the American side of the Strait to indicate a Riss-Illinoisan emigration. The only facts that favor such a migration are typological. In Venezuela an industry of choppers and chopping tools has been found in association with extinct animals, including mastodon, glyptodon (a giant armadillo), megatherium (a giant mammal related to the sloths and ant-eaters), and macrauchenia (a giant three-toed ungulate). Despite the archaic nature of this fauna, the Carbon-14 date is only 16,375 ± 400 B.C. (No. O–999), but that is probably the oldest valid date yet obtained in the New World.[9] Junius Bird, who has done considerable excavating near the tip of South America, has found no evidence of human occupation older than 8,760 ± 300 B.C. (W-915). At that time the Magellanic Indians coexisted with a number of clumsy old-fashioned mammals like the megatherium, who would have been extinct in that limited area before that time had anyone been there to hunt them. If in 8,000 years Indians spread from Venezuela to the Strait of Magellan, it certainly would not have taken their ancestors 100,000 years to have gone from Bering Strait to Venezuela, and 100,000 years ago is the very last date at which a crossing could have been made over a Riss-Illinoisan land bridge.

In North America, industries of choppers and chopping tools have been found in Tennessee and Arkansas underlying modern American Indian artifacts, but these industries have not yet been dated. In Maine a similar industry has been tentatively dated at 2,019 ± 310 B.C.,[1] and in the California desert these tools were made continuously from an unknown date until recent times.

On these grounds we can probably settle safely for a Würm date of entry, but not necessarily final Würm. The Folsom site at

---

[9] I. Rouse: "The Entry of Man into the West Indies," *YPA*, No. 61 (1960), p. 8; and letter of June 13, 1962. The dating was done by the Humble Oil Company.

[1] D. S. Byers and W. S. Hadlock: "Carbon-14 Dates from Ellsworth Falls in Maine," *Science*, Vol. 121, No. 3151 (1955), pp. 735–6. The date is an average of two runs, 4150 ± 450 B.P. and 3800 ± 400 B.P. (M-89).

Lindenmeier, Colorado, now has a firm date of 8,820 ± 375 B.C. (I(UW)-141), and the Lehner mammoth site of Arizona, in which Clovis points were found, one of 9,330 ± 500 B.C. (M-811). Danger Cave, Utah, a seed-gathering site, is dated at 9,500 ± 600 B.C. (C-609). The Folsom and Clovis industries were advanced tool-making cultures, certainly not the first in America.

On July 22, 1960, *The New York Times* announced the discovery at Balsequillo, ten miles south of Puebla, Mexico, of a piece of mastodon pelvis on which someone had engraved sketches of a bison, tapir, reptile, and apparently a mastodon itself. This carving had been done when the bone was green. Whether the bone is really a mastodon pelvis and not a part of some other big animal; whether or not the drawing really represents a mastodon; and whether or not it is one of numerous archaeological fakes so commonly perpetrated in that country, remain to be determined.

Another lead regarding man's arrival in America is language. We observed that in Australia and Tasmania all aborigines speak or spoke languages of a single family, to which Papuan is probably also related. On glottochronological grounds, this unity probably sets a ceiling of 20,000 years on the first settlement of that continent and those islands. In the two Americas, no one has yet decided exactly how many linguistic stocks the Indian languages comprise, but it may well be ten or a dozen. Unless America was invaded by peoples speaking many languages over a short period of time, the ceiling of 20,000 years is unnecessary. I believe that we can postulate with safety that America was first settled some time in the second half of the Wisconsian (or Würm) glaciation, contemporaneously with the Upper Paleolithic peoples of Europe, at least in their later stages, with some of the Upper Pleistocene people of China, and possibly before the time of the Upper Cave people of Choukoutien.

One further body of evidence is the physical remains of early American Indians, none of which seem to be older than 10,000 years, if any are that old. Their enumeration and description is readily available in Wormington's latest edition of *Ancient Man in North America*[2] and need not be repeated here, because it is

[2] H. M. Wormington: *Ancient Man in North America*, Fourth edition (Denver: Denver Museum of Natural History Popular Series No. 4; 1957).

not necessary to prove that they are both *H. sapiens* and Mongoloid.

However, individuals with archaic cranial vaults turn up now and then in otherwise normal populations, in both North and South America, and particularly among some of the Fuegians, notably the Ona. These vaults have sloping foreheads and are low. Although they have been referred to as Neanderthaloids in the literature, both Stewart and Neumann[3] have rightly shown that these skulls are genetic variants in otherwise fully *sapiens,* Mongoloid populations and do not necessarily mean that whole populations of low-browed people ever entered America by themselves and were subsequently absorbed. However, that interpretation, although unlikely, is not completely ruled out as a faint possibility for which there is no evidence at present.

From the standpoint of Mongoloid history, the dating of the arrival of the American Indians is important because the Indians, by and large, are fully Mongoloid in skin texture and color range, hair form, hair texture, hair distribution, and degree of sexual dimorphism. As it is hardly likely that these characteristics of the soft parts, which distinguish the Mongoloids from all other subspecies, were acquired independently in Asia and America, the Asiatic Mongoloids must have acquired them by the time the ancestors of the American Indians had left Asia for America, in Upper Pleistocene times.

Conclusion

AS LATE as 1955 it would have been risky to endorse Weidenreich's bold speculation that the Mongoloids of the world are descended, at least in part, from Sinanthropus or similar populations of pre-*sapiens* Asiatic man, some of which became *sapiens* during or shortly after the Riss glacial period. So rapidly are new discoveries being made in China, and also in Japan, that the risk is now on the other side. The only serious doubt that remains is

[3] T. D. Stewart: "American Neanderthaloids," *QRB*, Vol. 32, No. 4 (1957), pp. 364–9.

G. Neumann: "American Indian Crania with Low Vaults," *HB*, Vol. 14, No. 2 (1942), pp. 178–91.

this: did Sinanthropus alone and unaided undergo the mutations in the central nervous system, and probably also the endocrine system, that transformed him from *H. erectus* into *H. sapiens,* or did someone else who had earlier undergone this process assist him through mixture? The same problem is involved in the transition from Solo to Wadjak and the living Australians. We may never know the answer, but we shall be in a better position to evaluate what evidence there is after studying the other two quadrants of the Old World.

11

THE CAUCASOIDS

The Caucasoid Home

IN THE NORTHWEST quadrant of the Old World we have more skeletal material to work with than in all the others put together, but still we are faced with gaps and serious problems. For example, this is the only section of the world in which no skull of *Homo erectus* has been found. The oldest ones whole enough for diagnosis are already *sapiens,* but they are not as old as the earliest *erectus* skulls from Java, China, and Africa. Yet they are older than any other sapiens skulls found elsewhere.

One reason for this unique situation may be that we have not yet located the earliest Caucasoid homeland. In Europe we have a succession of remains from the start of the Middle Pleistocene which are apparently Caucasoid. But it is hardly likely that Europe was the center of Caucasoid evolution because the succession that we find is disorderly. The changes in tool industries are in some cases too abrupt to have been the product of local technological evolution; yet the tools all emerge from a single set of traditions. By the same token, successive changes in skulls and long bones, when we have them, reflect incongruities in what seems to be a single evolutionary line.

North Africa is also a part of the Caucasoid territory, but it became so only toward the end of the Pleistocene. Western Asia is also Caucasoid country. It includes Turkey, all the Arab nations of Asia, Israel, Iran, Afghanistan, West Pakistan, Kashmir, northwest India, and parts of Soviet Central Asia west of the Tian-Shan mountain barrier. Has this broadly delimited area been, like Eu-

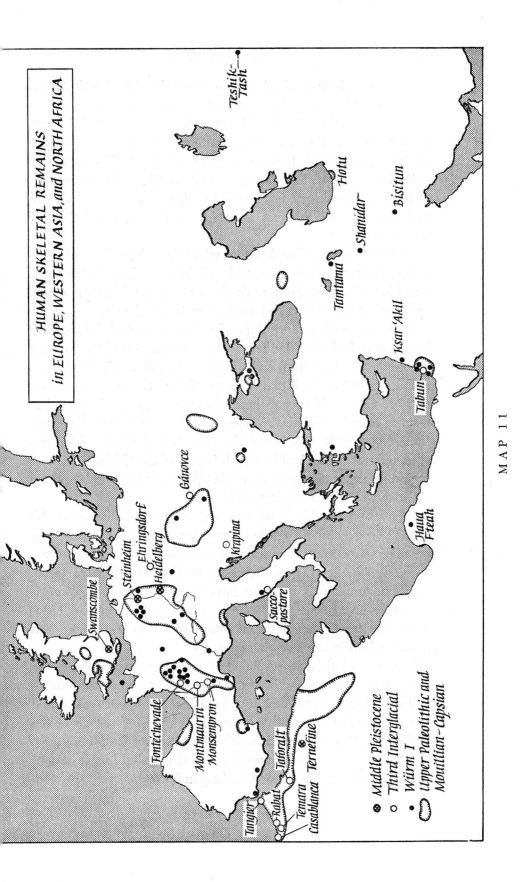

HUMAN SKELETAL REMAINS
in EUROPE, WESTERN ASIA, and NORTH AFRICA

Teshik-Tash

Hotu
Bisitun
Shanidar
Tamtama

Ksar 'Akil
Taburi
Haua Fteah

Gánovce
Steinheim
Ehringsdorf
Heidelberg
Krapina
Sacco-pastore
Swanscombe

Fontéchevade
Montmaurin
Monsempron
Tangier
Rabat
Taforalt
Temara
Casablanca
Ternefine

● Middle pleistocene
○ Third Interglacial
⊗ Würm I
● Upper Paleolithic and
   Mouillian—Capsian

MAP 11

rope, Caucasoid from the beginning; or did it, like North Africa, serve as the Pleistocene home of another subspecies?

Throughout the Middle Pleistocene the inhabitants of Europe, western Asia, and Africa were culturally unified in the sense that all three groups made hand axes, but in the Upper Pleistocene this unity broke down. The European and western Asian successors of the hand-ax people continued to follow a single tradition in tool manufacture, whereas the Africans followed traditions of their own.

Furthermore, the few skeletons which have been found in Palestine, Lebanon, Iraq, Iran, and Uzbekistan belong to the same racial line, the Caucasoid, as do those of comparable antiquity in Europe; but the African skeletons are racially different.

In the parts of western Asia where no ancient skeletons have been found, including Turkey, Syria, the countries of the Arabian peninsula, most of Iraq, and all of Afghanistan, West Pakistan, and northwest India, it may be noted that all the modern inhabitants are Caucasoid except those whose ancestry can be traced to historic invasions (Huns, Mongols, Turks, etc.) or to the slave trade (Negroes in Arabia and elsewhere). And, of all these countries, only southern Arabia, which is part of the Ethiopian faunal region, contains any trace of a relict population or similar ethnic enclaves which are not Caucasoid.

In southern Arabia hand axes and cleavers of distinctive African style are now being found, and there have long been servile populations of non-Caucasoid appearance which cannot be entirely explained away as the result of the African slave trade. Southern Arabia may therefore have been an extension of the African-Caucasoid zone of contact as early as the Middle Pleistocene, but the contact between southern Arabia and Africa was probably broken off somewhat later.

The sum of these three lines of evidence—archaeology, the study of fossil man, and the study of modern racial distribution—indicates that western Asia, as defined above, and with one stated exception, was Caucasoid territory during most if not all of the Middle and Upper Pleistocene. There we hope to find, if not now, then eventually as we do more digging, that orderly succession of culture and race which is so far lacking in Europe.

Possible Contacts Between Subspecies and
Caucasoid Evolution

IN ZOOGEOGRAPHICAL terms, western Asia is a nuclear region because it stands at the crossroads where Africa, Asia, and Europe meet and where three faunal regions, the Oriental, Ethiopian, and Palearctic, come in contact. With the cooling and moistening influence of the glacial advances and the warming and drying of the climate during interglacial periods, Western Asia has seen the comings and goings of many animal species. The climatic changes that it has undergone were great enough to be stimulating, from the evolutionary viewpoint, but not extreme enough to reduce populations quickly or to cause many extinctions. There was no better place in the Old World for men to evolve in.

The ancestors of the Caucasoids who, as we suppose, evolved there could have been in direct peripheral contact with frontier populations of three of the four other subspecies: the Australoid in India, the Capoid in North Africa, and possibly the Congoid in southern Arabia if not also in Africa. The Caucasoids did not have a common border with the Mongoloids, however, unless they met, as they do today, at the edges of the plains in Assam and Bengal. Owing to the former northward extension of Australoids in southeast Asia it is unlikely that Caucasoids and Mongoloids came into contact in India any earlier than they did in Central Asia.

It is safest to say that during most of the 500,000 years of man's known existence the Mongoloids were in a position to exchange genes with only one other subspecies, the Australoid. The Congoids were in possible contact with two (certainly Capoid and possibly Caucasoid); the Capoids with two (Congoid and Caucasoid); and the Caucasoids with three, as stated above.

This geographical situation gave the Mongoloids the isolation necessary to retain their extreme racial peculiarities while evolving from a lower to a higher grade. At the same time it placed the Caucasoids in a central position in which they could accept genes directly and simultaneously from the three other subspecies; process these new genes by exposing them to natural selection for climate and culture, in a zoologically central area; and pass the product back to the peripheral populations separately. In the same way, to a correspondingly lesser extent, the Mongoloids could deal with Australoid genes.

Peripheral gene exchanges between the five subspecies in their formative periods need not have been extensive in order to have stimulated general evolutionary change, i.e., grade-crossing, in the populations which received the new genes. Had the exchanges been much greater than they were, swampings might have occurred and some lines might have ceased to exist except in mixture.

Returning to the Caucasoids, these theoretical exercises suggest that once we have enough information we can expect to find continuity in the center of their territory and discontinuity on the peripheries, such as Europe. If a skull now and then turns up among them which looks Negroid, Australoid, Capoid, or even Mongoloid, we should not be surprised because owing to the spatial position of the Caucasoids, in the middle of the Old World land masses, they should have been the least "pure" of all human subspecies.

Continuity and Change in the Caucasoid Quadrant

B E F O R E going into details about the evolutionary history of Caucasoid peoples, let us summarize what we are going to find, because only with the help of a sweeping survey can this complicated sequence of biological and cultural events be understood.

The material can be divided into four consecutive periods: (1) from the beginning of the Middle Pleistocene to the end of the Great or Mindel-Riss Interglacial; (2) the Riss glacial period and the Last or Riss-Würm Interglacial; (3) Early Würm, a cold and wet period lasting into the Göttweig Interstadial; (4) Middle and Late Würm, beginning in the Göttweig Interstadial and ending with the last retreat of the Scandinavian ice around 8,000 B.C.

It would make our task much easier than it is if we had an adequate sample of human remains from each of the four periods in both Europe and western Asia. We could then test our thesis that western Asia was the Caucasoid cradle land and Europe a side pocket that received new populations from time to time as weather permitted. But we cannot do this. Only in Europe is the sequence of human remains adequate for comparison from period to period. In western Asia only the third period is well documented. We are lucky to have this material because it docu-

TABLE 25

PRE-WÜRM FOSSIL MAN REMAINS FROM EUROPE AND WESTERN ASIA

Country	Site	Period	Remains	Name
Germany	Mauer (Heidelberg)	Earliest Mindel	1 mandible	*H. heidelbergensis*
	Steinheim	Great Interglacial	1 cranium	*H. steinheimensis*
England	Swanscombe	Great Interglacial	1 calva	*H. cf. sapiens*
France	Fontéchevade	Last or Riss-Würm Interglacial	1 calva, 1 frontal bone	*H. sapiens*
	Montmaurin	Last or Riss-Würm Interglacial	1 mandible, 4 teeth, 1 vertebra	
	Monsempron	Last or Riss-Würm Interglacial	2 persons; #1 = cranial fragments & mandible; #2 = maxilla	
Italy	Saccopastore	Last or Riss-Würm Interglacial	1 skull, 1 calvarium	Generally credited to *H. neanderthalensis*
Germany	Taubach	Last or Riss-Würm Interglacial	2 teeth	
	Ehringsdorf	Last or Riss-Würm Interglacial	remains 4 individuals, skull & long bones	
Czechoslovakia	Gánovce	Last or Riss-Würm Interglacial	natural casts of brain, 1 radius, 1 fibula	
Yugoslavia	Krapina	Last or Riss-Würm Interglacial	remains *ca.* 13 individuals 650 ± pieces	
Palestine (Israel)	Mugharet al-Tabun	Last or Riss-Würm Interglacial	1 lower rt. molar, 1 piece of femur	

ments the interval which we need most, for the third period is a time of evolutionary discontinuity in Europe.

In Europe period 1 contains a few precious human remains which indicate that on that continent man had reached the threshold of the *Homo sapiens* grade by at least 250,000 B.C. In period 2 no substantial change is evident. As far as we can tell, the same people continued living there, until at the onset of period 3, or a little earlier, a new element was added. That new element was the famous Neanderthal man, who was more primitive morphologically than his predecessors. Either a new group of people invaded Europe, absorbing the earlier population, or the earlier population evolved backward, so to speak, into the Neanderthals. The Neanderthals continued to live in Europe until the Göttweig Interstadial, when they disappeared, being followed by the people of period 4, the Upper Paleolithic Europeans. Since then Europe has been continuously inhabited by their descendants and those of later Caucasoid invaders.

Several facets of this sequence are puzzling. The peoples of periods 1 and 2 were substantially the same, and their cultures show an uninterrupted continuity. The culture of the people of period 3 was derived from that of period 2, although with certain modifications attributable in part to a change in climate. The culture of period 4 was new in that it was focused around the production of blades, made with the elastic (horn or antler) punch, but it was old in that the types of implements used had been seen in earlier European tool kits. The burin or graver, for instance, so typical of the Upper Paleolithic, has been traced back to the Acheulean hand-ax culture of the Second Interglacial.

In the stone-tool industries of Europe there is a considerable break between periods 3 and 4, and the racial continuity of European skulls shows a minor break between periods 2 and 3, and a major one between 3 and 4. It is possible that the Neanderthals of period 3 evolved uniquely out of the population of period 2, but the Upper Paleolithic people of period 4 could not have evolved in Europe out of local Neanderthals.

In western and central Asia there seem to be no sharp cultural breaks; the succession of physical types was apparently more gradual. The peoples of period 3 included both Neanderthals of a less extreme form than those living in Europe, and other people, in Palestine, who were hardly Neanderthal at all, but transitional between the Europeans of period 2 and the Upper Paleolithic people. They apparently invented blade tools, and their implements foreshadowed those of the Upper Paleolithic. It is likely that the Upper Paleolithic people and their culture originated somewhere in western Asia at that time

The Mauer Mandible, or Heidelberg Jaw [1]

S O   F A M O U S   is the Heidelberg jaw, more correctly but less popularly known as the Mauer mandible, that it requires little description. It was found in 1907 in a sand pit in the village of Mauer, 6 miles southeast of Heidelberg. It lay 78 feet below the surface in a soil containing the bones of many animals of a Cromerian fauna, but no implements. Among the bones were those of the spotted hyena, *Crocuta crocuta,* which did not appear before an interstadial of Mindel, about 360,000 years ago, according to the chronology followed in this book. Mauer is therefore as old as Sinanthropus and the Ternefine mandibles from North Africa, which will be described in the following chapter.

Mauer is a large, massive mandible, chinless and equipped with blunted gonial angles, but it is not the largest lower jaw yet found. Both the Sinanthropus male, G-1, and Ternefine 3 are larger in most dimensions, and even more robust. In fact, Mauer's index of robusticity (see Table 38) of 48.8 per cent is lower than the figures for three of four of the Sinanthropus mandibles, four of five early North Africa mandibles, and that of Wadjak 2, whereas it is about the same as that of Pithecanthropus (Sangiran) B. Other European mandibles dated later in the Pleistocene were just as robust as Mauer, or more so. Individual mandibles from New Caledonia and the Loyalty Islands of Melanesia, whose living inhabitants are markedly Australoid, match Mauer in all measurements except the width of the ascending ramus,[2] and in this dimension Mauer exceeds all other fossil mandibles of any region or date, and probably all modern mandibles.

---

[1] O. A. Schotensack: *Der Unterkiefer des Homo Heidelbergensis* (Leipzig, 1908).

A. Hrdlička: "The Skeletal Remains of Early Man," *SMC,* Vol. 83 (1930), pp. 90–8.

F. C. Howell: "European and N.W. African Middle Pleistocene Hominids," *CA,* Vol. 1, No. 3 (1960), pp. 195–228.

[2] R. A. Dart: "*Australopithecus prometheus* and *Telanthropus capensis,*" *AJPA,* Vol. 13, No. 1 (1955), pp. 67–96.

The conventional measurement of the width of the ascending ramus is a minimum, in the case of Mauer, 53 mm. Boule and Vallois, in 1952 (*Les Hommes Fossiles*), gave a figure of 60 mm., which is a maximum.

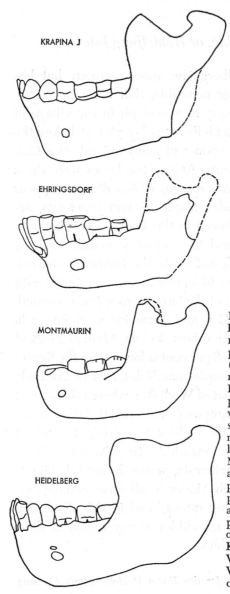

KRAPINA J

EHRINGSDORF

MONTMAURIN

HEIDELBERG

FIG. 65 MANDIBLES: KRAPINA J, EHRINGSDORF, MONTMAURIN, HEIDELBERG. The progression of European mandibles from Heidelberg (early Middle Pleistocene) to Montmaurin (Late Middle or Early Upper Pleistocene) to Ehringsdorf and Krapina J (Last Interglacial) runs from very thick and stout to slightly less so; from a wide ascending ramus to a moderate-sized one; and from chinlessness to the beginnings of a chin. Montmaurin, though small, is as stout as Heidelberg. Ehringsdorf has disproportionately large teeth, and Krapina J has condyles flattened by arthritis, a disease which sorely plagued the Neanderthals. (Drawings of Krapina J after Gorjanović-Kramberger, 1906; Ehringsdorf after Virchow, 1920; Montmaurin after Vallois, 1955; Heidelberg after a cast.)

The profile of the symphysis rises steeply in a smooth curve without any suggestion of a chin. The lower margins of the two branches of the body, underlying the molars and premolars, appear swollen in a downward and slightly outward direction, and then curve upward some 8 mm. to meet in the center line. Inside the symphyseal region, the bone retreats behind the roots of the incisors almost in the form of a shelf, and then dips steeply to the level of the genial tubercles.

The ascending ramus rises steeply from the body, and the wide coracoid process is inclined a little forward, as if to accommodate a forward attachment of the temporals. The general size and form of the whole ramus suggests a short or medium face length. Judging from the conformation of the areas of muscle attachment, Heidelberg man made extensive use of his temporal and internal (medial) pterygoid muscles, but his masseters were not as strongly developed or placed as far forward as those of Sinanthropus.

According to Howell (1960) there are three mental foramina on the left side and two on the right. But the cast shows only one small foramen on either side. There is no mandibular torus. Mauer differs from Sinanthropus in that it lacks most of the morphological features which characterize the latter, and also in the breadth of its jaw. Mauer's bicondylar diameter is only 133 mm. to 148 mm. for Sinanthropus. The Heidelberg skull base, therefore, was much narrower than Sinanthropus's, and a narrow base is a *sapiens* feature.

All the teeth were in the jaw when discovered, but the whole left row from the first premolar through the second molar was broken off in cleaning. Although the teeth are not small, they are all within the length and breadth ranges of modern man, falling closest in size to those of Australian aborigines. All the molars are within the Sinanthropus range, but most of the other teeth fall below it. In other words, the emphasis is on the cheek teeth rather than on the front teeth, as in the Australoid and Negroid dentitions and not as in the Mongoloid and Capoid. Of the molars the second is the largest, the third next in size, and the first the smallest.

Howell (1960) has furnished information concerning the molar cusp patterns. The right first is Y-5, the second and both thirds are +5. The second and probably the third had a sixth cusp. All the molars are moderately taurodont, but they lack wrinkling, cingulums, and dental pearls. The incisors and canines show no evidence of shoveling. On the whole, the Mauer lower teeth resemble those of later Europeans, are not notably different from those of living Australian aborigines or African Negroes, but differ in every pertinent detail from those of Sinanthropus and the living Mongoloids, and from these of the North African jaws of equal age.

As a single bone, the Mauer mandible belongs to the expected grade, considering its antiquity, but because there is no Mauer cranium we do not know to which species, *Homo erectus* or *Homo sapiens,* Heidelberg man belonged. Both the teeth and the narrow intercondylar width fit a higher grade than the other features of the bone itself, and both the jaw and its teeth fail to fit into the pattern of any of the other four lines of human evolution seen elsewhere in the world. Mauer therefore stands at the base of a line of its own.

The Steinheim Cranium [3]

IN JULY 1936, a female skull was found in a gravel pit at Steinheim an der Murr in Württemberg, 12 miles north of Stuttgart. It was accompanied by many animal bones, but there were no implements in the gravels. Because it was excavated under laboratory conditions by professionals there is no doubt that it belonged with its fauna. Its date is Great or Mindel-Riss Interglacial, roughly 250,000 years old, two thirds as old as the Mauer mandible and possibly 110,000 years younger than Sinanthropus. The Steinheim woman lived during a warm period.

When discovered, the skull was an almost complete cranium—the oldest yet found anywhere in the world. The basal part of the occipital bone had been broken away, as is usual in fossil skulls, but the front part of the base is present. The front part of the maxilla below the nasal aperture has been peeled, but not wholly removed, and the front teeth lost. Only the six molars and the right second premolar remain. Owing to the weight of twenty-three feet of wet earth covering it, the skull was warped and crushed; the

[3] F. Berckhemer: "Ein Urmenschenschädel aus dem Diluvialen Schotten von Steinheim an der Murr," *AAnz*, Vol. 10 (1933), pp. 318–21.

Berckhemer: "Bemerkungen zu H. Weinert's Abhandlung 'Der Urmenschenschädel von Steinheim,'" *VGPA*, Vol. 2 (1937), pp. 49–58.

H. Weinert: "Der Urmenschenschädel von Steinheim," *ZFMuA*, Vol. 35 (1936), pp. 413–518.

Howell: op. cit.

left side, forward of the earhole, had caved in, and much of the left side of the face had become detached. The skull has not yet been restored. In a detailed study Weinert tried to allow for shrinkage and distortion, but his figures must still be taken as tentative. Some of these are given in Table 37. A few of them, including the cranial capacity, have been corrected by Howell (1960), who has handled the original. All that I have had to work with are photographs and a cast.

The length, breadth, and height dimensions and the cranial

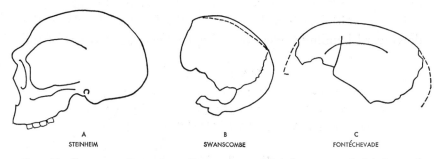

A
STEINHEIM

B
SWANSCOMBE

C
FONTÉCHEVADE

FIG. 66 PROFILES: STEINHEIM, SWANSCOMBE, FONTÉCHEVADE. Steinheim and Swanscombe are the two oldest specimens of *Homo sapiens* known. Both come from the Second or Great Interglacial. Both are designated female. Steinheim is nearly whole, but badly warped, and it has not been restored. Swanscombe consists of both parietals and the occipital bone. Fontéchevade 1 consists of a skullcap from the end of the Middle Pleistocene or Early Upper Pleistocene. The configuration of the forehead is completely modern, and it apparently had no brow ridges. Fontéchevade 2, not shown here, consists of a small piece of frontal, including the upper rim of the eye socket. It definitely has no brow ridges. (Drawing A after Weinert, 1936, and a cast; B after Morant, 1938, and casts; C after Vallois, 1949.)

capacity of 1,150 to 1,175 cc. do not differentiate Steinheim from the Javanese and Chinese *H. erectus* skulls, but morphologically it differs radically from all of them. The occiput is smoothly rounded, as in modern skulls, and the markings of the neck-muscle attachments are slight and set low. Although low, the forehead is fairly steep, and the brow ridges stand out like a thin, sharp visor over the orbits. The skull base is narrow; the mastoids small; and the side walls of the skull are parallel, as in modern crania, instead of convergent as in the Eastern *H. erecti*. The maximum breadth line is situated at a point 80 per cent of the way up from the earhole. The highest point on the profile line is located above the earholes, instead of above the mastoids. Bregma, the point where the frontal and the two parietal bones meet at the top of the skull, is located in front of a vertical line drawn over porion (the top of the earhole), as in modern skulls. In Asiatic *erectus* skulls bregma lies behind this line. Steinheim's arc-chord indices, in so far as they can be reconstructed, are also modern.

In Table 26 the internal dimensions of the Steinheim skull, tentative as they are, are compared with those of four female Asiatic *H. erectus* skulls. Steinheim's internal brain case is shorter than three, narrower than four, and lower than one, of the four. Nevertheless, its capacity is 100 cc. more than any of them, because of its shape; it is built like a cube instead of like half of a sphere.

In the sagittal section, lateral view, the frontal lobe shows the downward bending typical of *H. sapiens* and what is left of the

TABLE 26

INTERNAL DIMENSIONS AND
CAPACITIES OF STEINHEIM AND
OF FEMALE *ERECTUS* SKULLS

		Length	Breadth	Ear Height	Capacity
Steinheim		156	121(?)	103(?)	1,150–75 cc.
Sinanthropus	11	167	128	102	1015
Solo	1	161	130	103(?)	1035
Solo	6	153	129	109(?)	1035
Solo	10	159	138	100(?)	1060

occipital part of the base shows the same bending. The hypophyseal fossa, or *sella turcica,* seat of the pituitary gland, seems to be 10 mm. long and 6 mm. deep, as in modern European skulls.[4] Although we have no information on the meningeal arteries, in all known respects Steinheim's brain cast was *sapiens.*

The only skull of equal or greater age to which the facial measurements of Steinheim can be compared is Weidenreich's reconstruction of the female Sinanthropus, No. 11 (see Table 23). Steinheim's minimum frontal is 18 mm. more than S-11's; its face breadth is about 16 mm. less; and its biorbital diameter 5 mm. less. These figures indicate a fundamental difference in the relative development of the masticatory apparatus and in the position of the temporal muscle attachments on the frontal bone. Steinheim's face is a little shorter than S-11's, but still long for a modern Euro-

[4] According to Weinert's drawing, which must be considered with caution.

pean woman. Her orbits are smaller than S-11's, and they differ
from the latter's in another dimension not included in our table—
Steinheim's orbits are deep on the lateral or outer side of each cup,
whereas those of Sinanthropus are shallow on the outer side and
deeper on the inner side. The nasal dimensions of the two skulls
are the same, but the nasal bones differ greatly. In Steinheim they
are shaped like an hour glass and pointed at the top, and they
meet at an angle. In Sinanthropus they are parallel-sided and
square at the top, and they meet in a gentle curve.

Below the orbits the zygomatic and maxillary bones of Steinheim's face are recessed, as in modern Europeans, rather than
swollen, as in Mongoloids and in Sinanthropus. From the cast and
drawings I have very tentatively calculated the three first indices
of facial flatness, as follows: upper index of facial flatness = *ca.*
24; simotic index = *ca.* 55; rhinial index = *ca.* 40. In all three indices Steinheim is typically Caucasoid, so much so that even if
these figures are 10 per cent or more off, the racial diagnosis must
be the same.

The dimensions of Steinheim's seven upper teeth are given on
Table 39. These molars and one upper second premolar all fall
within the length and breadth ranges of modern men. Only the
mesiodistal lengths of the first and second upper molars are great
enough to be within the Sinanthropus range. All the teeth are
smaller than the means for living Australians, and the third molar
is even smaller than the mean for living Europeans. The first molar is the largest; the second is the next larger; and the third is
the smallest. All four first and second molars seem to have four
cusps, and the third is reduced and rounded to such an extent that
the cusps are not easy to distinguish. These teeth are also moderately taurodont. Except for this last feature, nothing notable
distinguishes them from those of a modern European woman.

The Swanscombe Cranial Bones [5]

T H E W E L L - K N O W N Swanscombe skull consists of three
separate bones, an occipital and both parietals, found at three dif-

[5] The basic report on the occipital and left parietal (the first found) is "Report
on the Swanscombe Skull," *JRAI*, Vol. 68 (1938), written by a committee of

ferent times from 1935 onward, in the 100-foot terrace of the Thames river gravels, in direct association with a Great or Mindel-Riss Interglacial fauna and a Middle Acheulean hand-ax and flake industry. The fluorine content of the skull is the same as that of the animal bones found with it. Like Steinheim's, its geological position is impeccable.

The cranial capacity, variously estimated at from 1,275 to 1,325 cc., is in the range of that of modern European women, and its breadth and height figures are modern. As one might expect of ancient bones, Swanscombe's are thick, ranging from 6.5 to 9 mm. Morphologically they are essentially modern, with a few archaic features; for example, the foramen magnum is long and narrow, and the occipital bone is broad at the base (biasterionic breadth = 123.5 mm.). On the inside, the brain cast of the occipital lobes and of the cerebellum are *sapiens* in configuration,[6] and the channels of the middle meningeal artery are full and complex, although of a pattern rare in modern peoples.

There has been a great deal of speculation about Swanscombe's face, but because Steinheim has a face, and because the threshold between *Homo erectus* and *Homo sapiens* lies in the brain, and not in the face, it is unnecessary.[7] We cannot expect Swanscombe to have had a face like that of a modern London lady, whose lineaments have been acquired over many millennia of modern living, and who would find it difficult if not impossible to survive

authors, particularly W. E. LeG. Clark ("General Features of the Swanscombe Skull Bones" and "The Endocranial Cast"); and G. M. Morant ("The Form of the Swanscombe Skull").

For the right parietal: J. Wymer: "A Further Fragment of the Swanscombe Skull," *Nature*, Vol. 176, No. 4479 (1955), pp. 426–7.

For fluorine: K. P. Oakley: "Physical Anthropology in the British Museum," in D. F. Roberts and J. S. Weiner: *The Scope of Physical Anthropology* (New York: Oxford University Press; 1958), pp. 51–3.

[6] Howell (1960, p. 221) says: "The cerebellar fossae are small in comparison with the cerebral fossae," which is true if the endocranial cast is compared with that of a typical modern European, but they are not small when compared with those of a modern Australian aborigine, or even, for example, a Bronze Age skull from Tepe Hissar, Iran, which is perfectly Caucasoid.

[7] As Howell and others have pointed out, there is a large dimplelike depression on the forward margin of the occipital bone which may be interpreted as an extension of the sphenoid sinus. As a large sphenoid sinus may be associated with a general pneumatization of the face, and hence heavy brow ridges, the conclusion is that Swanscombe had heavy brow ridges, but even if she did, my diagnosis remains unshaken.

under the cultural conditions in which both of these ancient females must have lived. The *sapiens* grade is broad and inclusive, covering many subgrades and degrees. If the modern Australian aborigines are *sapiens,* these women were *sapiens* too. And calculated according to the formula for modern Australian skulls, the cranial capacity of Steinheim is 1,145 cc., very close to Howell's figure. If these women were not *sapiens,* neither are many of the living female Australian aborigines and New Caledonians,[8] whose skulls Steinheim and Swanscombe resemble in grade, but not in line.

European Fossil Men of the Early Upper Pleistocene

N E I T H E R Steinheim, Germany, nor Swanscombe, England, were comfortable places to live in during the next to last, or Riss, glacial period. The descendants of the two women whose skulls we have just studied must have moved south as the weather grew colder. Between the two peaks of the Riss was a mild interstadial with a climate similar to that of today, and at the end of Riss came a return to warm conditions with the Riss-Würm or Last Interstadial. In Europe local populations were undoubtedly most mobile in the regions of greatest climatic change and least mobile where the climate was the most nearly constant. If the Europeans of the Last Interglacial were descended from the Europeans of

[8] In 1955 W. E. LeGros Clark accepted these skulls, at least provisionally, as primitive members of *Homo sapiens.* In 1960 Clark Howell discussed the problem at length without committing himself. He emphasized the archaic traits that foreshadowed the Neanderthals in both these skulls. Also in 1960, W. W. Howells, postulated the first appearance of *Homo sapiens* at "almost certainly . . . some 150,000 years ago." S. L. Washburn, in the same number of the *Scientific American,* wrote: ". . . the species *Homo sapiens* appeared perhaps as recently as 50,000 years ago." As no one in the Anglo-American world knows more about Steinheim and Swanscombe than these four experts, who are well aware of the date of the skulls, the disagreement is obviously a matter of how one defines *Homo sapiens.*

Clark: *The Fossil Evidence for Human Evolution* (Chicago: University of Chicago Press; 1955), pp. 63–6.

Howell: op. cit.

W. W. Howells: "The Distribution of Man," SA, Vol. 203, No. 3 (1960), pp. 113–27.

S. L. Washburn: "Tools and Human Evolution," SA, Vol. 203, No. 3 (1960), pp. 63–75.

the Great Interglacial, therefore, we may expect a certain amount of discontinuity rather than direct regional continuities; and if new populations came in from Asia we may expect to find some evidence of anatomical change.

As shown on Table 25, the Last Interglacial is represented in Europe by eight sites, and in western Asia by a single site, which contained only one tooth and a fragment of femur. Ignoring western Asia for the moment, we find that the eight European sites have yielded five skulls or sets of skulls, not one as whole as Steinheim. We have mandibles from three of these sites; teeth from five; and body bones from only two. The sites of the skulls are: Fontéchevade, Saccopastore, Ehringsdorf, Gánovce, and Krapina. The mandible sites are Montmaurin, Monsempron, and Krapina. The tooth sites are Saccopastore, Montmaurin, Monsempron, Ehringsdorf, and Krapina; and the postcranial bones come from Ehringsdorf and Krapina alone.

Except that Montmaurin may possibly belong to the Second Interglacial, that Fontéchevade probably dates from the beginning of the Last Interglacial if not from a Riss Interstadial, and that Krapina may overlap the beginning of Early Würm, we have no inkling of the chronological order of the eight sites. To describe the remains from each site one by one would only convey a false picture of an orderly succession. Instead I shall deal with skulls, mandibles, teeth, and body bones in that order. In this way Fontéchevade, where only skulls were uncovered, comes first, and Krapina, which represents the greatest store of body bones, comes last, and we shall not have to backtrack for comparisons.[9]

Fontéchevade

I N 1947 Mlle G. Henri-Martin excavated a cave at Fontéchevade in Charente. In the upper levels she found Mousterian artifacts of a kind characteristically made by Neanderthal men, but no human remains. Below this level lay a limy crust, which not only ef-

---

[9] This procedure has another advantage—it avoids anticipation of things to come. Here there will be no talk of pre-*sapiens* or pre-Neanderthals. We have already discussed *sapiens*, and we shall consider Neanderthal when we get to him.

fectively sealed off what lay below but also indicated a considerable time gap between the two layers. Under the crust there was a Tayacian flake industry with a warm fauna, including the extinct Merck's rhinoceros, fallow deer, bear, tortoise, and *Cyon*, a wild dog now found mostly in southern Asia. With these animal bones fragments of two skullcaps, Fontéchevade 1 and 2 were also discovered. Under the Tayacian level Mlle Henri-Martin found Clactonian flake tools belonging to an industry older than the Tayacian, but no human remains. Fluorine tests performed by Oakley definitely tie Fontéchevade 1 and 2 to the Tayacian fauna.[1]

Number 2, which is the more nearly complete, consists of a left parietal bone, the upper half of the right parietal, and the upper part of the frontal. A few scraps that cannot be articulated with the rest belong to the lower border of the right parietal and to the occipital. The left parietal contains a hole with depressed edges, suggesting death by violence, at an age of forty to fifty years; shortly after death the bones were charred.

If No. 2 was male, the cranial capacity was probably about 1,470 cc., and if female, about 1,460 cc. The bones are from 7 to 9 mm. thick at various places, as in Swanscombe. The skull is long, broad, and low, and it verges on brachycrany (round-skull), with an estimated cranial index of 79. Except for its greater breadth of about 12 mm. (of which we are not completely certain), Fontéchevade 2 resembles Swanscombe closely. The biasterionic breadth (lower occiput) is great—126 mm. There is, as in Swanscombe, a depression at lambda, where the two parietals and the occipital bone meet; this depression is masked, in profile, by the smoothly curved contour of the parietals. The junction of the parietal and temporal bones was low by modern standards, and the lines marking the upper limits of the temporal bones were also low; the minimum frontal diameter must have been great, close to 120 mm. Enough of the frontal bone is present to indicate that the

[1] G. Henri-Martin: "Rémarques sur la Stratigraphie de Fontéchevade," *L'Anth,* Vol. 55, Nos. 3–4 (1951), pp. 242–7.

Oakley and C. R. Hoskins: "Application du Test de la Fluorine aux Cranes de Fontéchevade," *L'Anth,* Vol. 55, Nos. 3–4 (1951), pp. 239–42.

H. V. Vallois: "The Fontéchevade Fossil Men," *AJPA,* Vol. 7, No. 3 (1949), pp. 339–60.

skull lacked massive brow ridges. The question of brow ridges in the Fontéchevade population is solved by an examination of the other and smaller specimen.

According to Vallois (1949, p. 352), Fontéchevade 1 "is represented only by a piece of the frontal 5.5 cm. high and 4 cm. wide, but it has great interest in that it comprises the region of the glabella and the left supraorbital ridge, with the internal orbital process of the same side and a small part of the overlying roof. Its general appearance and its thickness, being inferior to the skull-cap already described, shows that it derives from another individual; this one was also adult. The essential fact is the absolute absence of a supraorbital torus: the glabella and the brow ridge are less developed than in the Upper Paleolithic Europeans, or even the majority of Europeans of today. They recall, in their general configuration, skulls of female Europeans; there is no nasion depression, and the brow ridge does not extend down to the upper border of the orbit."

The fact that the two cave dwellers of Fontéchevade had smooth brows has badly shaken some of my colleagues who believe in unilinear local evolution, because the French cave dwellers of the following period, Early Würm, had heavy brow ridges. However, if we compare these skulls, and Steinheim and Swanscombe, with the skulls of modern Australian aborigines, our problem is solved. In any collection of Australian skulls, or in any living aboriginal tribe, the range of brow-ridge development is tremendous. Some have bony visors that rival Solo's, and others are as smooth-browed as Fontéchevade 1. I cannot believe that everyone living in France in Fontéchevade's lifetime lacked brow ridges, any more than all Frenchmen do today. Also, aside from brow ridges, the Fontéchevade skulls are similar to those of their predecessors of the Great Interglacial.

Saccopastore

THE TAYACIAN flake culture of Fontéchevade is believed to have been derived from the Clactonian, which it overlay in that particular cave. From the Tayacian came, presumably, the Mousterian, which in its pure form differs from the parent industry in one principal respect. Whereas the Tayacian tool-makers retouched the edges of their flakes with taps or blows from a pebble or stick, the Mousterian artificers pressed off fine flakes with a piece of bone, producing a finer, straighter edge. This second technique is called step flaking.

Not all Mousterian tool assemblages, however, follow this simple formula. In some sites Mousterian flakes are found alongside hand axes of Acheulian tradition; in others the Mousterian re-

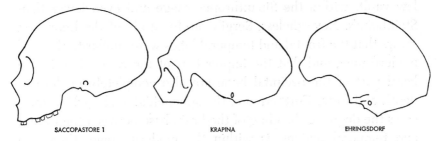

SACCOPASTORE 1   KRAPINA   EHRINGSDORF

Fɪɢ. 67 Pʀᴏғɪʟᴇs: Sᴀᴄᴄᴏᴘᴀsᴛᴏʀᴇ 1, Kʀᴀᴘɪɴᴀ, Eʜʀɪɴɢsᴅᴏʀғ. The Europeans of the Last (Third) Interglacial were a variable lot, differing regionally in skull form. The Ehringsdorf skull from Germany was the most modern-looking. Krapina in Yugoslavia yielded at least one brachycephalic skull, and the Saccopastores in Italy, with their low, barrel-shaped vaults, foreshadowed the Neanderthal skull form. (Drawings of Saccopastore 1 after Sergi, 1944; Krapina after Gorjanović-Kramberger, 1906, and Brace, 1957; Ehringsdorf after Weidenreich, 1928, and Kleinschmidt, 1931.)

touching technique was applied to Levallois flakes, which had been struck off prepared cores, from faceted striking platforms. Although the Mousterian industry, in one form or another, was characteristic of the cave sites of the Early Würm, it began in the Riss-Würm or Last Interglacial, and sites of a relatively simple and unmixed Mousterian variety from that period are particularly common in Italy.

In a gravel pit at Saccopastore, just outside the walls of Rome, in material deposited by water and containing such tools, the skull of a thirty-year-old female was found in 1929 by Sergio Sergi; and in 1936, that of a male aged about thirty-five was discovered in the same pit by A. C. Blanc and the Abbé H.

Breuil.[2] No. 1, the female, is nearly complete, although the zygomatic arches are missing, along with three teeth, and the brow ridges were cut off by a shovel at the moment of discovery, thus revealing an extensive frontal sinus. In No. 2 the skullcap is missing but the right half of the face, all the palate, the right zygomatic arch, and most of the right half of the cranial base are preserved, and the inside of the cranial base is in excellent condition.

Neither of these skulls is very large. No. 1 has a cranial capacity of 1,200 cc., close to the figure for Steinheim. The brain of No. 2, the male, probably was 100 cc. larger, but it is difficult to tell owing to the absence of the top of the vault. No. 1 had an extremely low vault, within the Sinanthropus range and even lower than Steinheim's. Nevertheless, Sergi's careful study of the brain cast shows that the frontal and temporal lobes were similar to those of modern men, and that the impressions of the cerebellum in the basal part of the occipital bone are also completely modern in depth and form. Furthermore, the sphenoidal angle, which indicates the degree of bending of the brain base between the frontal and temporal regions, is within the modern range. From the standpoint of endocranial anatomy, No. 2 was fully *sapiens*, and so, presumably, was No. 1, for the two are enough alike to have belonged to the same family.

From the standpoint of external anatomy, however, these skulls look primitive in some respects and simply strange in others. Seen from above, No. 1 looks streamlined, like a raindrop falling. The rear profile, from above, looks rounded and even swollen, whereas the walls of the brain case converge toward the front and the upper jaws appear pinched forward in the form of a muzzle. The side profile of the brain case shows a sloping forehead and rounded occiput, which curves uninterruptedly to a weak nuchal crest located below and in front of the rearmost projection of the occiput. The brow ridges were apparently not very large.

[2] S. Sergi: "Craniometria e Craniografia del Primo Paleantropo di Saccopastore," *RM*, Vol. 20–21 (1944), pp. 1–59.

Sergi: "Il Secondo Paleantropo di Saccopastore," *RA*, Vol. 36 (1948), pp. 1–95.

A. C. Blanc: "Torre in Pietra, Saccopastore, Monte Circeo—On the Position of the Mousterian in the Pleistocene Sequence of the Rome Area," *NC*, 1958, pp. 167–74.

Seen from in front and from behind, the brain case looks cylindrical, like a barrel lying on its side. The mastoids are small, and the digastric fossae lateral to them are deep, indicating large digastric muscles (the muscles that open the jaw). The foramen magnum is located in a position normal for modern European skulls, and the occipital condyles are so oriented as to indicate a fully erect posture.

At the region of lambda, this skull has no less than eleven sepa-

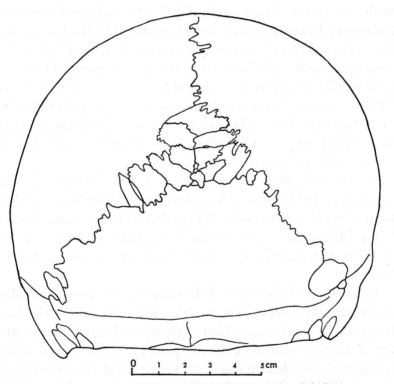

Fig. 68 SACCOPASTORE WORMIAN BONES. The Last Interglacial skull of Saccopastore 1 is notable for two things: its almost circular profile when seen from behind or in front, and its Wormian bones. A Wormian bone is an extra piece of skull vault, separated from the others by sutures, and lying in the area of lambda, the meeting place between the two parietal bones and the occipital bone. Wormian bones are so called because they are common in ancient Andean skulls. They are found principally in Mongoloid crania, in both the Old and New Worlds. The skull of Saccopastore 1, a Caucasoid Italian of the Last Interglacial, has sixteen Wormian bones, possibly a world's record; eleven major and five minor. Later on, Wormian bones were also characteristic of Neanderthal skulls. No one knows their function. (Drawing after Sergi, 1944.)

rate Wormian bones, more than Weidenreich found in any Sinanthropus skull.

The face is very long, longer than that of the reconstructed Sinanthropus female, but not exceptionally broad; and the bizygomatic diameter was probably less than the cranial breadth, as in most modern skulls. In No. 1, which retains one complete zygomatic arch, the bizygomatic diameter was only 96.6 per cent of the cranial breadth, which is a low figure for a fossil skull.

The nasal skeleton is both long and broad, to match the face; the orbits are large, and the palate is large and rounded at the tooth line. The nasal bones extend high into the frontal bone, and their upper border is curved. Seen from the side, the face is very prognathous, but only in the upper or nasal segment. Below the nasal aperture the profile is steep. The kind of prognathism seen in this skull is the opposite of that of Sinanthropus. Below the orbits the surface of the malars and maxillae is flat, rather than indented, as in Steinheim, but the two planes so produced stand at nearly a right angle to each other, instead of being nearly in line, as in Sinanthropus and the living Mongoloids.

No. 2 is larger than No. 1, and the contours of the skull are less rounded, probably because No. 2 was a male. Like No. 1 and like Fontéchevade 2, the male skull probably had a cranial index in the high seventies. No. 2 also has a less rounded tooth line than No. 1, for his canines and incisors form nearly a straight line.

As Sergi noted, these two skulls possess a curious combination of archaic and modern features. The low vault height, the long face, and the great prognathism of the upper face are characteristics of *Homo erectus,* but the morphology of the brain and the area of neck-muscle attachment are modern. Most anthropologists do not call these skulls *sapiens.* However, in terms of the criteria used in this book, they, like their predecessors of the Second Interglacial period, had crossed that threshold, yet carried many features of an earlier grade with them. As for their racial affinities, the configuration of the eye-nose triangle, the mask, is Caucasoid like that of Steinheim, but the vault form of the two Saccopastores is very different from that of the earlier cranium.

The Ehringsdorf Remains [3]

BETWEEN 1914 and 1925 a number of fragmentary human remains were found in two neighboring quarries, Kaempfe's and Fischer's, at Ehringsdorf, near Weimar, in what is now East Germany. They had been secondarily deposited in a crevice between two layers of limestone, and scraped and rolled on the way from their original resting place. This aperture had later been filled with travertine, a stalagmitic material laid down by water, which then encased them. With them were animal bones of a temperate fauna and a quantity of plant materials which indicated a climate like that of today, such as probably existed during the second half of the Last Interglacial.

The implements found with the human remains [4] were Mousterian, but not of a simple or homogenous industry, as at Fontéchevade and Saccopastore. They included scrapers of Charentian type, derived from Tayacian; small hand axes of Micoque type, derived from Acheulian; angular scrapers of a style common to Syria and the Crimea; fine and coarse drills; and crude burins or gravers. The diversity of these implements and of their geographical associations suggests that the people who lived at Ehringsdorf during late Last Interglacial time may have been the product of mixture between several related populations.

Aside from mandibles, teeth, and a few long bones that will be described later, we are concerned with a parietal from Fischer's

---

[3] H. Virchow: *Die Menschlichen Skelettreste aus dem Kämpfe'schen Bruch im Travertin von Ehringsdorf bei Weimar* (Jena: G. Fischer Verlag; 1920).

F. Wiegers, F. Weidenreich, and E. Schuster: *Der Schädelfund von Weimar-Ehringsdorf* (Jena: G. Fischer Verlag; 1928).

A. Hrdlička: op. cit.

O. Kleinschmidt: *Der Urmensch* (Leipzig, 1931)—Quoted by Behm-Blancke, 1958.

C. U. A. Kappers: "The Endocranial Casts of the Ehringsdorf and *Homo soloensis* Skulls," *JAnt,* Vol. 71, No. 1 (1936), pp. 61–76.

G. Behm-Blancke: "Umwelt, Kultur, und Morphologie des eem-interglacialen Menschen von Ehringsdorf bei Weimar," *NC,* 1958, pp. 141–50.

[4] Behm-Blancke states that there were five different strata, each containing a separate but related Mousterian industry, and that the human remains were associated with the second industry from the bottom.

quarry and a broken brain case from Kaempfe's. All we know about the former is that "it is a large, oblique fragment of the left parietal with large portions missing antero-superiorly and postero-inferiorly. It apparently proceeds from a juvenile, though hardly a child's skull, is of moderate thickness (maximum 8.5 mm.) and shows one important feature, which is a marked and nearly central parietal eminence, not dull, posterior, and low down as in the Neanderthalers, but practically like that in modern man."[5]

The specimen from Kaempfe's quarry consists of a faceless brain case. It is believed to have been that of a young adult female, twenty to thirty years old. During the process of deposition the individual bones came apart and their edges were scraped and ground, so that they do not fit together. Weidenreich made a restoration, filling the cracks with plastilene, and the measurements available in the literature are his. Others who have seen the skull recently think that the gaps were made too wide. Kleinschmidt, in 1931, published an alternative reconstruction (of the cast) which differs from Weidenreich's principally in that it makes the vault height (auricular) about 8 mm. lower—113 mm. instead of 121 mm. This controversy cannot be settled until a competent anatomist finds time to restudy the original bones.

In any case, this is a large skull, with a capacity of about 1,450 cc. according to Weidenreich and somewhat less if he was wrong. But it cannot be very much less. Even if the auricular height was only 113 mm. it is still higher than Fontéchevade 2. The brow ridges are fairly heavy, like those of Steinheim but thicker, with a depression over glabella and a fairly steep forehead. The general morphology of the brain case is modern, with a humping in the parietal region which appears in both reconstructions. The maximum breadth of the skull is high on the parietals, as in modern skulls. The endocranial cast shows a modern condition in the frontal lobes. The mastoids are modern in size.

There can be no question that the Ehringsdorf skull, although archaic in some respects, is *sapiens;* and in general morphology it shows a closer similarity to Steinheim and Swanscombe than to either Fontéchevade or Saccopastore. It seems to be on the main line of Caucasoid cranial evolution.

[5] Hrdlička: op. cit., p. 238.

The Stone Brain from Gánovce, Czechoslovakia

I N 1926 a natural endocranial cast of a human brain was found in travertine, the same marblelike material present at Ehringsdorf, in a thick deposit surrounding a thermal spring at Gánovce, near Poprad, Slovakia, at the foot of the Tatra Mountains. With it were casts of animal bones, and in 1955 casts were also found of a human radius and tibia.[6] Both fauna and geology indicate the middle of the second half of the Last Interglacial, contemporary with Ehringsdorf.

The cast itself is nearly whole, and on the left side some of the bone remained, including parts of the temporal, parietal, and occipital. Vlček's reconstruction indicates a skull with a capacity of 1,320 cc., long, narrow, and lower than any yet studied except Saccopastore 1 and possibly Steinheim. The occipital lobes are bun-shaped, with a flattening at lambda. The greatest breadth of the brain, and of the skull, lies far to the rear. The section seen from front and rear looks tubular, as in Saccopastore. The brain stem is centrally located, indicating, if such a conclusion is justified, a normal position of the head on the cervical vertebrae. The brainstem itself is long and narrow in section. The cerebellum is more or less as in Swanscombe, if not more protrusive below the occipital lobes. There is no Sylvian crest, and the pituitary fossa measures about 16 by 15 mm., within the outer part of the modern range.

This brain belonged to a member of the species *Homo sapiens*, at a fairly low subgrade; it shows no evolutionary advance over Swanscombe and it resembles most closely, of all specimens reviewed, Saccopastore 1.

---

[6] Vallois: "Un Homme de Neanderthal en Tchekoslovaquie?" *L'Anth.*, Vol. 55 (1951), pp. 166–9.

Weinert: "Zwei neue Urmenschenfunde," *ZfMuA*, Vol. 43, No. 3 (1952), pp. 265–75.

E. Vlček: "Neandertálskéno človeka na Slovensku," *SlAr*, Vol. 1 (1953), pp. 5–132.

Vlček: "The Fossil Man of Gánovce, Czechoslovakia," *JRAI*, Vol. 85 (1955), pp. 163–71.

Vlček: "Die Reste des Neanderthalmenschen aus dem Gebiete der Tschechoslowakei," *NC*, pp. 107–22 and plates.

The Round-headed People of Krapina

BETWEEN 1895 and 1906, K. Gorjanović-Kramberger and his
associates excavated some 649 shattered pieces of skull, skeleton,
and teeth in a sandstone rock shelter at Krapina in Croatia, now
Yugoslavia. One reason for the minced state of the specimens was
the fact that the excavators removed dangerous overhanging
rocks with dynamite; another that the skeletons had been broken
up at the time of death. Some of the bones were charred, and it
has been claimed but not proved that some of the deceased were
the victims of cannibalism.

The site contained nine archaeological levels, and all the human material came from the third level from the bottom. The
fauna of all but the topmost level was a warm one, consistent with
a Last Interglacial date. In the top level were the bones of cave
bear, suggesting the onset of Würm I, and those of a marmot, a
cold-weather rodent similar to a woodchuck. This last may or may
not have been intrusive. There seems little doubt that the human
bones from Krapina belonged to the latter part of the Riss-Würm
or Last Interglacial.

Over a thousand flint implements were removed from the skele-
ton-bearing level, and most of them still rest in the Natural History Museum at Zagreb, unstudied. The assembly of tools is
called Mousterian, but Škerlj [8] states that it includes both Acheulean and pre-Aurignacian elements, and Brodar [9] believes that
the commonest implements are broad blades and that there are

[7] M. de Terra: "Mitteilungen zum Krapina-Fund unter besonderer Berücksichtigung der Zähne," *SVFZ*, Vol. 13 (1903), pp. 11–31.

F. Gorjanović-Kramberger: *Der Diluviale Mensch von Krapina in Kroatien*
(Wiesbaden, 1906).

B. Škerlj: "Were Neanderthalers the Only Inhabitants of Krapina?" *BS*, Vol. 4,
No. 2 (1958), p. 44.

F. Ožegovič: "Die Bedeutung der Entdeckung des Diluvialen Menschen von
Krapina in Kroatien," *NC*, 1958, pp. 21–6.

C. L. Brace: *The Significance of the Krapina Finds* (Unpublished paper for
Seminar in Primates and Fossil Man, Harvard University, Cambridge, Mass.,
Nov. 20, 1957).

[8] Škerlj, in H. V. Vallois and H. L. Movius, Jr.: *Catalogue des Hommes Fossiles*
(Algiers, 1952), p. 250.

[9] S. Brodar: "Das Paleolithikum in Jugoslawien," *Quartär*, Vol. 1, pp. 140–72.

also some microliths in the lot. Even if the flints came from more than one level, the fact that implements of so many types came from one cave in Croatia occupied during the latter half of the Last Interglacial indicates either a gathering of different peoples or cultural evolution in process, or both. We need more information to decide.

The Krapina material includes postcranial bones from practically every part of the body, and over 270 teeth. Of the skulls, only five are intact enough even to be identified. They are labeled A

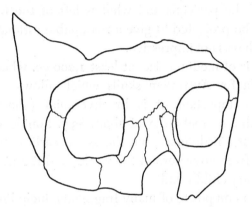

FIG. 69   THE MASK OF KRAPINA. In the Caucasoid realm, very few specimens older than the Neanderthals of Würm I have been found with intact or nearly intact faces. The best preserved is the mask of an adolescent from Krapina. It is notable for its square orbits, its lack of canine fossa, and its peculiar nasal bones. The suture between nasals and frontal has an inverted V shape, and the right nasal bone encroaches on the territory of the left. (A seven-eighth view, after Ožegovič, 1958.)

through E. Only C and D are adult, and only A, C, and D have been studied.

Skull A is the cap of a brain case belonging to a child of about three to five years of age. It consists of the frontal bone, the left parietal, and part of the right parietal. It is large, with a breadth of over 150 mm., and was undoubtedly brachycephalic. Its walls are thin, its forehead steep, and its brow ridges weak. The coronal and sagittal sutures, and also the metopic (frontal) suture, are open. For the metopic suture to remain open when the skull had acquired such size is unusual in living populations and unexpected in fossil men. Furthermore, the frontal bone shows *tubera*

frontalia, that is, bosses or projections on either side of the forehead, as in a modern child. This is the most modern European
skull we have yet considered in this survey.

Skull C belonged to a young and probably female adult. It consists mostly of a face minus the alveolar region and the lower border of the nasal opening. Although the top of the skull and most of
the base are missing, parts of the frontal, sphenoid, temporal, and
parietal bones extend around the line of greatest breadth. Gorjanović-Kramberger was therefore able to make a nearly complete
horizontal outline of the whole skull by mirror reproduction. Also,
the curve of the parietals and what is left of the frontal above
glabella can be projected to give a reasonable estimate of cranial
height, which was not impressive.

This skull is of medium size, at least 1,200 cc. when calculated
by a formula for Australian skulls which allows for the brow
ridges. More important, it is brachycranial (short or round-
skulled), with a cranial index of about 83.7. Fontéchevade 2 was
probably 79 or a little more, but this is our earliest adult brachycranial skull from anywhere in the world, and it matches skull A,
the fragmentary child's skull.

Skull D is a composite of many fragments, including an occipital bone that Loring Brace found among the unidentified pieces in
the Zagreb Museum in 1959. Its shape is the same as that of skull
C., but it is much larger, with a capacity of at least 1,450 cc. and
the extraordinary breadth of 169 mm., which is exceptional today.
Its cranial index of 85.5 is hyperbrachycranial. Skull E, a fragmentary child's headpiece consisting of parts of a frontal and both
parietals, was also brachycranial. All four skulls which are whole
enough to give an idea of head shape are those of round-headed
individuals, like the majority of living Croats.

The face of these Krapina people is best seen in skull C. The
brow ridges are heavy, but divided over nasion. The orbits are
widely separated, and squarish; the amount of facial flatness seen
in the upper orbital and nasal region is about what one would
find among round-headed central Europeans today. Nasion is
highly placed, and the union of the nasal bones with the frontals
is irregular, forming an inverted V. The upper breadth of the nasal

bones, 18 mm., is moderate; in a separate pair of nasal bones not connected to any skull, the breadth is 15 mm. In C as in spare parts of other skulls the nasal region is Caucasoid in structure. Although neither protruding nor particularly large, the zygomatic and maxillary bones are full below the orbits, and there is no canine fossa.

Six pieces of maxilla help complete the picture of the faces of these people. In all six, age can be determined by the teeth; the ages range from six to twenty years. The maxilla of the twenty-year-old individual had an alveolar height of 28 mm., which is within the modern range. The sixteen-year-old's maxillary fragment was a little prognathous, and in all of them the palate seemed broad.

Because of the large brow ridges, the low vault, the usual small mastoids, and a few other archaic features, one cannot say that the Krapina skulls are fully modern. But they are fully *sapiens* and resemble in an over-all way, particularly in that they are broad-headed, some of the living European peoples. These skulls are different from the other skulls we have studied. Within the Caucasoid framework, the pre-Würm population of Europe showed as much regional variation in cranial vault and upper facial features as the modern European population does today.

The Mandibles of the Europeans of the Last Interglacial Period

E x c e p t for the Heidelberg jaw, which may be three times as old as the skulls we have just described, pre-Würm mandibles are limited to specimens from four sites, of Last Interglacial date. These are Montmaurin (Haute-Garonne) [1] and Monsempron

---

[1] R. Baylac et al.: "Découvertes récents dans les grottes de Montmaurin, Haute-Garonne," *L'Anth.*, Vol. 54, No. 3–4, pp. 262–71.

Vallois: "La Mandibule Humaine Pré-Mousterien de Montmaurin," *CRAS*, Vol. 240 (1955), pp. 1577–99.

L. Pales: "Les Néanderthaliens en France," *NC*, 1958, pp. 32–7 and plates.

Some workers have recently stated their belief that the Montmaurin jaw is as old as Steinheim and Swanscombe. B. Kurtén: "The relative ages of the Australopithecines of Transvaal and the Pithecanthropines of Java," in G. Kurth, ed.: *Evolution und Hominization* (Stuttgart: Gustav Fischer Verlag; 1962), pp. 74–80.

(Lot-et-Garonne) [2] in France, Ehringsdorf, and Krapina. The dimensions of these mandibles are given on Table 38, alongside those of Heidelberg.

The Montmaurin specimen is a nearly complete mandible found in 1949 in a cave shaft called La Niche in the complex of caves at Montmaurin, along with implements identified as Early Mousterian. It is a small jaw, much smaller than Heidelberg, which it resembles morphologically, although its bicondylar breadth exceeds Heidelberg's slightly, indicating perhaps a somewhat broader skull base. It would be small even for a modern jaw, and it is completely chinless and very robust. Its lower border is convex so that, like certain modern Maori mandibles from New Zealand, it rocks when placed on a table. Vallois says that it has multiple mental foramina, but in Pales's picture of the left side, only one large and one very small foramen are visible.

The Monsempron mandible was one of ten scraps of human remains recovered from a site credited to the Last Interglacial, a judgment which is not completely certain as some reindeer bones were found in the site. On the other hand, the artifacts are called Early Mousterian or pre-Mousterian by Vallois.[3] The other scraps were pieces of vault too fragmentary to merit close study and a piece of maxilla which was not prognathous and which must have occluded with its missing lower jaw in a modern-style overbite, the upper incisors and canines covering the lower ones when the jaws are closed. In other fossil specimens the teeth of the two jaws meet edge-to-edge.

The mandible is a piece of the alveolar edge containing a canine and two premolars. It had a *torus mandibularis*, like the Sinanthropus mandibles and other Mongoloid jaws of various periods, and like those of some modern European peoples who live above the Arctic Circle, particularly in Scandinavia.

The Ehringsdorf collection includes one adult mandible, and one mandible of a child some ten years old. The adult jaw is nearly complete. In length and breadth it is virtually identical

[2] Vallois: "Les Restes Humaines du Gisement Mousterien de Monsempron," *APa*, Vol. 38 (1952), pp. 100–20.

J. Piveteau: *Traité de Paléontologie VII* (Paris: Masson et Cie.; 1957), pp. 482–3.

[3] Vallois and Movius: *Catalogue des Hommes Fossiles*, Section 88, p. 146.

with Heidelberg, but it is not as high at the symphysis nor as thick anywhere. Its principal morphological difference from Heidelberg lies in the chin region. Instead of a smooth curve, its lateral profile is a double curve, quite sloping in the upper or tooth-bearing segment, and steep below. It looks as if the teeth were too large for the bone, and it almost has a chin. In this respect it resembles Wadjak 2.

The child's mandible is a right half, with the left side extending around past the canine. Except for the condyle, the left ascending ramus is complete. It is steeper than the adult jaw, with a 55° angle of inclination compared to the adult's 38° angle, and lacks the forward projection of the upper portion. Despite its tender age, the body is almost as high as the adult's (28.5 as compared to 31 mm.) It looks more modern than the adult jaw, but this difference may be due to age, sex, individual variation, or a combination of these factors.

Krapina has yielded eleven mandibles or scraps thereof, nine designated by the letters A to J (there is no I) and two that were illustrated in Gorjanović-Kramberger's plates but not designated. Only F, G, H, and J are adult and complete enough to warrant inclusion in Table 38.

All eleven conform to a single general pattern and resemble in grade and line the two French mandibles and the mandibles from Ehringsdorf. They go together in the same sense as do the Sinanthropus mandibles, and those from Ternefine and other sites in North Africa. All are thick, prognathous, mostly chinless, and rounded or blunted in the region of the gonial angle. However, they vary among themselves, as might be expected in any population.

H and J are considerably larger than E, F, and G; the first two may have been masculine and the other three feminine. In F the sockets of the four incisors form a straight line between the canines, instead of the usual flattish arch. All but two of the mandibles have a single, large mental foramen on each side (if the area has been preserved); G has two foramina on the right side and one on the left, H has two on the left and one on the right. All the Krapina mandibles are thinner and more slightly built than Heidelberg, and only J approaches it in size; but J's coracoid processes are higher, narrower, and arched backward, whereas Heidelberg's incline slightly forward. Furthermore, all the Krapina mandibles are flat in frontal profile, as if in anticipation of a chin.

The Teeth of the Europeans of the Last Interglacial

W E H A V E available for study 192 permanent and 28 milk teeth from the Last Interglacial sites of Europe.[4] The permanent teeth include at least two specimens of each upper and lower tooth. From Krapina come 144; the other 48 are from Saccopastore, Montmaurin, Monsempron, Ehringsdorf, and Taubach.

These teeth (see Table 39) constitute a single population in respect to size. All are within the size range of living peoples, although some are larger than those of modern Europeans. The teeth of both Heidelberg and Swanscombe could, however, be included in this collection. We may therefore conclude that from the beginning of the Middle Pleistocene to the end of the Last Interglacial, no substantial change took place in the crown dimensions of European teeth, and not much has taken place since.[5]

However, some changes may have taken place in the relative sizes of the three lower molars. In Heidelberg the order of size is different in each side of the jaw. On the right side the second molar is the largest; the third molar is next largest; and the first is smallest. On the left side only one tooth, the third, can be measured, and it is smaller than the first molar of the other side.

Montmaurin has the very primitive order of three-two-one. In the jaw of the Ehringsdorf child, whose wisdom teeth were uncut and could not be measured, the second molar was larger than the first, whereas in the adult female from Ehringsdorf the order is two-one-three for the right side and one-two-three for the left side. In the Krapina collection the first molars are clearly the

[4] All but one of the teeth, a lower first molar from Taubach, near Weimar, are from sites already mentioned. For the Taubach tooth see A. Nehring: "Über einen menschlichen Molar aus dem Diluvium von Taubach bei Weimar," *VBGA*, Vol. 27 (1895), pp. 573-7.

[5] Some lower median incisors from Krapina seem to be larger than the modern range, but these were loose teeth and may have actually been laterals, in which case they are unexceptional.

largest, and the second and third molars are of equal size. On the whole, therefore, the teeth of central Europe are more advanced in the size-order of the lower molars than are the French ones. Or, if we compare them in time rather than by geography, the later are more progressive than the earlier ones.

Our information on the morphology of these teeth is uneven. The Saccopastore molars seem to be taurodont, judging by the appearance of a broken tooth in a photograph. The Montmaurin molars are notable in that all three are longer than they are wide. Among the Monsempron materials, an upper median incisor is moderately shoveled and has a lingual tubercle at the base. Its neighbor, an upper lateral incisor, is also moderately shoveled and has a smaller basal tubercle. The upper canine has two vertical depressions with a ridge between on the lingual side. Both the first and second upper premolars have single, moderately taurodont roots, as well as small bulbs of cement on the tips of the roots. It must be remembered that the jaw in which these teeth are still embedded has a mandibular torus. In the Ehringsdorf collection, the permanent teeth of the child's jaw are taurodont but the teeth of the adult are not. In the child's jaw, all three molars (one of which had not yet erupted) have the primitive Y-5 cusp pattern. The Taubach permanent tooth, a lower first molar, is small, narrow (width = 85 per cent of length), and five-cusped, as indeed most modern lower first molars are.

Krapina, of course, supplies the most information. The unworn upper median incisors are shoveled, like that of Monsempron, but not to the extent found in Sinanthropus or later Mongoloids. Theirs is a partial shoveling comparable to that found in certain modern European teeth, particularly among Finns. None of the Krapina teeth has the I-beam borders, the wrap-around lingual edge, the barrel-shaped form, or the double-shoveling found in Sinanthropus and modern Mongoloids, particularly some American Indians. Two of the Krapina upper median incisors have three basal tubercles on the lingual side, a feature also found in the teeth of Sinanthropus, and one upper lateral incisor has two such basal tubercles. Both an upper and a lower canine have ridges on both edges and a swollen area in between, as in the Monsempron canine.

Taurodontism, present in both Heidelberg and Steinheim, reaches an extreme development in the Krapina premolars and molars, particularly in the lower third molar. Some are tubular-rooted, with open ends. One Krapina tooth has a dental pearl—a feature found in Sinanthropus, Ainus, and Eskimos, among others. At least one upper first molar has a Carabelli's cusp, which is a European feature. The cusp number of the molars varies between four and five.

The teeth of these Europeans of the Last Interglacial period resemble those of their local predecessors in size and general proportions, but they contain morphological features that relate them in part to the Sinanthropus-Mongoloid line, unless the common possession of diagnostic Mongoloid features was a coincidence. Let us not forget that during the Last Interglacial the Caucasoids and Mongoloids may have met for the first time.

Postcranial Bones of the Last Interglacial: the Evidence from Krapina

AT SEVERAL of the European sites considered in this section, bits and scraps of long bones, ribs, and the like have been found along with the skulls and teeth, but none of them have been carefully described except those from Krapina. From what I have learned of the others from photographs and brief notes, none deviates from the Krapina models. Because the Krapina bones were measured before Rudolf Martin had standardized osteometry, in certain instances it is difficult to know how Gorjanović-Kramberger determined his dimensions. He described, or at least mentioned, some 232 bones, as given in Table 27.

In general each bone was, of necessity, treated as a separate entity. When, for instance, he discusses a series of cervical vertebrae, however, we do not know whether they came from different necks or were all part of a single neck. The same is true of all other bones that are grouped, like metacarpals and toes. Some were male, others female; some adult, others juvenile. This treatment limits the value of the study.

The neck vertebrae fall within the modern European range in

TABLE 27

POSTCRANIAL BONES FROM
KRAPINA

Vertebrae	20	Os capitatum	1	Fibula	1
Ribs	20	Metacarpals	3	Os calcis	1
Scapulae	12	Phalanges, hand	44	Talus	9
Clavicles	14	Os coxae	2	Cuboid	2
Humeri	19	Femora	2	Navicular	2
Radii	11	Patellae	15	Metatarsals	11
Ulnae	11	Tibiae	3	Foot phalanges	29

measurement and form, but they are a little small. The same is true of the thoracic and lumbar vertebrae, except that some of the individuals represented suffered from arthritis of the spinal column, which makes the vertebrae smaller. Other bones confirm the evidence of the vertebrae that, as Europeans go, these were small people.

The ribs are modern, except that although the bones are basically flat in section, the upper borders are thicker than the lower borders. The shoulder blades (scapulae) are not only modern but European in detail.

In the scapular spine, a ridge running from the coracoid process more or less diagonally toward the vertebral border of the bone, Vallois has found, among modern men, four major and several minor types, which involve differences in the attachments of the deltoid and trapezoid muscles. In the European type this spine is narrow at the junction of its outer and middle thirds. Then it swells out in the middle third and narrows at the junction of the inner third. In Negroes it is narrow throughout. In Melanesians it is thick throughout. In Japanese, and presumably other Mongoloids, it maintains a more or less constant width, but it is inclined inward and downward at a steep angle in the outer and middle thirds and then bends up again in the inner third. The other three types are less steeply inclined, and form straight lines. The Krapina scapulae resemble Vallois's first, or European, type.[6] The clavicles or collarbones of the Krapina collection are also European in size and form, but on the slender side.

[6] Vallois: "L'Omoplate Humaine," *BMSA*, in five numbers from 1928 to 1946; see Chapter 7.

The humeri also are rather small and slender, but indistinguishable from those of modern Europeans, except that in nine (we do not know out of how many, the maximum being nineteen), the olecranon fossa is perforated; that is, the lower arm could be bent backward at the elbow, as in gorillas and some contemporary women. This feature has no demonstrable racial significance but is interesting because of its high incidence. Among the living, very primitive Caucasoid Veddas of Ceylon, 50 per cent of the humeri have it. The bones of the lower arm, the radius and ulna, are also slender, and the ulna is bowed as if for heavy muscular effort. The ulna from Gánovce is similarly shaped.

A single os capitatum, a wristbone, is important here because we also have one for Sinanthropus. Krapina's is large, like those of modern Europeans; Sinanthropus's is small, like those of modern Mongoloids. The metacarpals and phalanges (finger bones) show no unusual features from a modern European point of view except that the terminal or nail-bearing phalanges—the last joint of each finger and of the thumb—were longer, in relation to the other finger bones, than is usual in living Europeans. As we do not know which bones belong together, we cannot tell whether Krapina man had attained the modern European finger-length formula in which the index finger is longer than the ring finger.

The two pieces of pelvis, one male and the other female, are completely modern and do not appear to differ in any perceptible way from those of modern Europeans. However, these pelves are fragmentary and do not include the upper branch of the pubic bone, which is peculiar in the later Neanderthals. The femur, which articulates into the pelvic bones, is distinctive. The head is set out unusually far from the shaft, and the angle between neck and shaft is 120° in two bones; this figure stands at the lower border of the modern range. Most people have a more obtuse angle. All fifteen kneecaps (patellae) are also large for the average of Europeans, but not larger than those of living individuals. Two pieces of tibia are rounder in section than they would be in modern Europeans; this indicates that these people lived out of doors and squatted while resting. Fourteen pieces of fibula are of modern design.

The foot bones are well represented, and they too are modern in form and proportions, except that the last or nail-bearing phalanges of the toes are a little long in comparison with the lengths of the other bones.

Despite the technical difficulties resulting from the scrambled state and unstandardized measurements of the Krapina skeleton, we have determined that these people were rather small; that their bones were not especially heavy; that in certain critical features, such as the wristbones and shoulder blades, they were definitely Caucasoid; and that they had achieved the modern European grade in every respect except perhaps in the articulation of the femur with the pelvis, and in the length of the last joints of their fingers and toes, which is very variable even in people alive today. In so far as we are able to interpret the data published more than a half century ago, these people were early Caucasoids, who probably resembled some of the marginal Caucasoids of Asia, like the Veddas and Dravidians, more than they did the more sturdily built living central Europeans.

The "Neanderthals" of Europe

I N 1680 a German hymn writer named Joachim Neander died in Bremen, at the age of thirty. During his short life he had had seventy-seven hymns published, and he had been honored by having a small river valley named after him, the Neanderthal, near Düsseldorf. His family name, originally Neumann, had been translated into Greek a century earlier. In 1856, in that very valley, a fossil human skullcap was unearthed and it was called Neanderthal man. Although in 1848 a similar skull had been found in Forbes's quarry in the Rock of Gibraltar, its importance was not recognized until 1864, when it was labeled a member of the Neanderthal group. Since 1856 *Neanderthal* has become a common name in many languages and been given to fossil-man remains in Asia, Africa, and even America. The Solo skulls, that of Broken Hill, and some low-vaulted American Indian crania have been so tagged from time to time and by various scientists.

In the last century the fame of Neanderthal man has increased. He is pictured as a crouching, stooping, squat and brutal creature, with huge jaws and little or no forehead, and a low grade of intelligence. Flesh reconstructions of his face make him look like an ape. In this guise he has become the prototype of innumerable cartoons, in which a slant-browed man, clad in a skin, hits a woman over the head and drags her unconscious body into a cave. This, the popular image of Neanderthal man, will probably be with us for decades to come, because it is picturesque, exciting, and flattering to ourselves. But it is wrong, and so are most of the elements in the total Neanderthal concept.

This concept stems from the method of taxonomy by which a species or subspecies is named for the first or "type" specimen collected and described. This procedure does not take into account individual and regional variations. Because the original Neanderthal specimen consisted of only a skullcap and a few long bones, there was not much to describe, and in 1911 the honor of being the type specimen was passed on to a nearly complete French skeleton, that of La Chapelle aux Saints in the Dordogne.

Nineteenth-century anatomists were struck by the heavy brow ridges and sloping brow of the original Neanderthal. They had not yet seen the skulls from Trinil, Choukoutien, Solo, and Broken Hill, nor did they realize, apparently, how heavy-browed and low-browed individual Australian aborigines can be. When other skulls with these features were found in many parts of the world, the name Neanderthal was applied to all of them, no matter where or when they lived, what kind of tools they made, or what they were like in other respects. To dub all skulls with salient brow ridges and sloping foreheads Neanderthal makes no more sense than to classify everyone with blood type B as belonging to the same race.

If the concept of a Neanderthal people is to have any validity, it must be limited in terms of time, space, and culture. Only in this way can the Neanderthals have formed a population with a gene pool of its own. Their time span is Early Würm or Würm I, from about 75,000 years ago to the beginning of the Göttweig Interstadial, about 40,000 years ago. Its *lebensraum* was Europe, western Asia, and central Asia as far east as the Altai Mountains and south to the Hindu Kush. Its culture was Mousterian, itself a complex of earlier tool-making techniques.

Neither the Neanderthal people nor the Neanderthal tool-making techniques could have sprung up out of nothing. We have a somewhat dim picture of the Europeans of the Last Interglacial; they could have been the descendants of the Europeans of the Great Interglacial who had crossed the *sapiens* threshold but had not advanced very far beyond it. The Mousterian culture had already come into being during the latter part of the Last Interglacial, as a derivative of the Acheulian, Clactonian-Tayacian, and the Levalloisian flake techniques.

The Acheulian hand-ax culture extended beyond Europe into the Arab countries, southern Iran, and India, and also far into Africa. The Clactonian-Tayacian flake culture was mostly European and Near Eastern; the Levalloisian was concentrated in western Asia. In northern Europe we do not know how far these cultures extended because the ice sheets scraped away all traces, if there were any. In Russia, which was largely unglaciated, we find a few hand axes along the northern shore of the Black Sea, and that is all. The entire central Asian realm, from the Volga to the Altai, may have been uninhabited before the Last Interglacial. The oldest implements found there are Mousterian, and Mousterian sites and surface deposits have been found on both banks of the Oxus, and east to Tashkent and the mountains. We do not yet know whether these sites and deposits date back to the Last Interglacial or merely to Early Würm, but it is more logical to suppose the former than the latter, because the Last Interglacial period was warmer than Early Würm. In one of these periods there was probably an extension to the east of the Caucasoid geographical range.

Did not some of these early Caucasoids penetrate farther, cross the passes in the mountains, and enter the homelands of Sinanthropus and the Mongoloids? We do not know the answer, but very likely they did. The flints from Ting-tsun (see Chapter 8) have been given a Last Interglacial date, and they are typologically similar to the Mousterian flints. Of them Bushnell and McBurney have said: "This industry, in which only the eye of faith can distinguish the slightest traces of Chopper-Chopping-Tool influence, is undeniably of general Middle Paleolithic character in the Western sense."[7] Let us grant, for the sake of argument, that Bushnell and McBurney are right. According to this interpretation of the flints from the Fen Valley, some Caucasoids similar to those we have seen in Europe entered central and northern China from the West, and mixed with the local population, and left their tools behind them when they died. If the Chinese population had not yet crossed the *erectus-sapiens* barrier, this injection of genes could have given them the chromosomal equipment to initiate such a transition. Chinese paleontologists and archaeologists have found no clearly *sapiens* skeletons in their country which are older than the Fen Valley flints.

In return, the invaders could have taken over some Sinanthropus-based genes, particularly those that would give them the capacity to resist the cold of the oncoming glacial winter. Passing these genes along to the peripheries of their geographical range in the west, they could have produced the Sinanthropus-like features found in some Last Interglacial specimens, such as the mandibular torus, shovel incisors, dental pearls, and a degree of facial flatness not seen in Steinheim. With the onset of the Würm cold, other such people could have infiltrated Europe from the East and reinforced in the local gene pool, by natural selection, the physical features that gave them an advantage for survival in the cold. Such a reconstruction explains the succession of peoples in Europe from the Last Interglacial period into the Early Würm, without violence to geography, cultural continuity, or genetic theory.

This hypothesis faces one serious stumbling block, the skulls from Saccopastore in Italy. They anticipate the Neanderthals morphologically; they are associated with a simple, unmixed Mousterian culture; and they were found in a country far removed from China.

But Italy lies close to Tunisia, with only Sicily and Malta in between. We know that the Palearctic fauna, including reindeer, reached Malta, but not Tunisia. A little seamanship of the kind that carried the ancestors of the Australian aborigines across Wallacea might also have served to carry a few North Africans to

[7] G. Bushnell and C. McBurney: "New World Origins Seen from the Old World," *Antiquity*, Vol. 33, No. 130 (1959), pp. 93–101.

Italy, and the North Africans of the Last Interglacial period resembled the Sinanthropus-derived peoples in a number of ways, particularly in their teeth.

We have good evidence that North Africans went to Spain during Würm II. Implements of typical Aterian form (Aterian is a local North African industry)—tanged and barbed pressure-flaked points—have been found in caves in Almeria and Valencia along with Solutrean points.[8] If some North Africans could have crossed the western Mediterranean to Europe in Würm II, others might have done so earlier.

North Africa, then, is a second potential source of genetic infiltration of Europe which could have initiated the Neanderthal racial complex, if indeed this complex did not simply arise in Europe out of local genetic materials by mutation, recombination, and natural selection.

Enough of theory. Let us examine the bones.

The Numbers and Distribution of the Neanderthals

FOR PRESENT purposes the genuine Neanderthals, or Neanderthals *in sensu stricto,* are represented by the skeletal remains of people who lived in Europe and parts of western and central Asia during Würm I, and in some places a little later; who dwelt at times in caves, made tools of a characteristic style known as Mousterian or Levalloisio-Mousterian; and who bore certain anatomical features in common, notably heavy, undivided brow ridges, small mastoids, pointed, prognathous faces, and large, projecting noses. Some also had taurodont teeth.

In the fossil-man social register of Vallois and Movius,[9] and in publications dated after 1952, some eighty-two true Neanderthals, found in forty-two sites, have been listed (see Table 28). Their geographical distribution follows a distinct climatic pattern. For the most part they favored the portions of western and southern Europe now lying south of the present-day January frost line,

---

[8] L. Pericot-Garcia: "A New Site with the Remarkable Parpalló-type Solutrean Points," *CA*, Vol. 2, No. 4 (1961), p. 387.

[9] Vallois and Movius: *Catalogue des Hommes Fossiles.*

TABLE 28

NEANDERTHAL AND OTHER REMAINS OF
WÜRM I OR LATER

Site	Country and Description
	GERMANY
Neanderthal, near Düsseldorf	Male, 40–50 years; calva and postcranial bones
Neuessing, Kelheim, Bavaria	1 milk incisor
	BELGIUM
Bay-Bonnet, Liège	1 rt. femur, lower end
Engis, Liège	No. 1, baby skull, fragmentary
La Naulette, Namur	Mandible, ulna, metacarpal, all fragmentary
Spy, Namur	No. 1, male or female, 35 years; calotte, fragments of maxilla, 14 teeth, postcranial bones No. 2, male, 25 years; fragments of maxilla and mandible, 13 teeth, postcranial bones No. 3, child; tibia and 2 teeth
	FRANCE
Bau de l'Aubesier, Monieux, Vaucluse	1 milk molar
La Chaise, Vouthon, Charente	No. 1, calva and three molars No. 2, child, 4 years; mandible, 3 teeth, parietal, 1 phalange
La Chapelle aux Saints, Corrèze	1 adult male skeleton
Combe-Grenal, Dordogne	Child, 1 fragment mandible
La Ferrassie, Dordogne	6 individuals: No. 1, adult male skeleton; No. 2, adult female skeleton, skull crushed; Nos. 3, 4, and 6, infants; No. 4, fetus
Grotte de l'Hyène, Arcy-sur-Cure, Yonne	5 individuals, mostly teeth, fragments of mandible and maxilla, fibula, and metatarsal
Grotte du Loup, same	1 molar tooth, fragments of a parietal
Malarnaud, Montseron, Ariège	Male, 21 years; mandible, 1 molar, 1 verteba
Marillac, Charente	Adult, fragment mandible with 2 teeth
Le Moustier, Peyzac, Dordogne	Male, 18 years; skeleton, complete
Pech de l'Azé, Sarlat, Dordogne	Child, 5–6 years old; cranium
Le Petit Puymoyen, Charente	4 individuals: No.1, a half mandible with teeth; No. 2, a piece of maxilla with teeth; No. 3, a piece of mandible with teeth; No. 4, two isolated teeth (originals all lost)
La Quina, Gardes-Le-Pontaroux, Charente	About 12 individuals, principally: No. 1, adult female skeleton; No. 2, 8-year-old calvarium; No. 3, 10 + pieces of skull; No. 4, fragment of a mandible; No. 5, various postcranial bones

TABLE 28 (*continued*)

Site	Country and Description
Regourdou, near Lascaux, Dordogne	Mandible, nearly complete, all teeth, various postcranial bones
Vergisson, near Solutré, Hte. Saônne	3 teeth

BRITISH ISLES

La Cotte de St. Brélade, Isle of Jersey	3 individuals: No. 1, fragmentary child's skull; No. 2, 13 teeth and a piece of tibia; No. 3, 13 teeth

SPAIN AND GIBRALTAR

Bañolas, Gerona, Catalonia	1 mandible, nearly complete, no teeth
Cova Negra de Bellus, Játiva, Valencia	1 right parietal bone
Piñar, Granada	1 adolescent skull, fragmentary
Gibraltar	3 individuals: No. 1, Forbes's quarry, adult female skull, fragmentary; No. 2, Devil's Tower, 5-year-old skull, fragmentary; No. 3, Genista Cave, 1 molar (lost) (Dating is unknown for all three)

SWITZERLAND

St. Brais	1 upper incisor

ITALY

Circeo (Rome)	3 individuals: No. 1, adult male cranium; No. 2, adult mandible; No. 3, adult mandible

CZECHOSLOVAKIA

Šipka, N. Moravia	8–10-year-old child, chin portion of mandible

HUNGARY

Subalyuk, Bükk Mts.	2 individuals: No. 1, adult female mandible, 4 vertebrae, sacrum, 7 limb bones; No. 2, 6-year-old cranium broken into over 90 pieces, various vertebrae, ribs, and metatarsals—said to be Late Mousterian

RUMANIA

Ohaba-Ponor Cave, Transylvanian Alps	1 first phalange of second right toe

U.S.S.R.

Kiik-Koba, Crimea	2 individuals: No. 1, teeth, hand, feet, tibia, fibula, patella; No. 2, a newborn infant
Starosel'e, Crimea	1½-year-old child's skull
Teshik-Tash, Uzbekistan	8–10-year-old child's skeleton

TABLE 28 (*continued*)

Site	Country and Description
	TURKEY
Karain, Adala	1 milk molar
	IRAQ
Shanidar, Kurdistan	7 individuals: No. 1, adult male skeleton; Nos. 2, 3, 4, 5, 6, adult skeletons; 1 infant skeleton
	IRAN
Bisitun, near Kermanshah	1 upper incisor, 1 fragment ulna
Tamtama, near Rezaiyeh	1 fragment femur
	PALESTINE
Mugharet al-Tabun, Mount Carmel	1 adult female skeleton, teeth of 4 individuals
Mugharet al-Skhul, Mount Carmel	Skeletons of 9 adults and 1 child
Mugharet al-Zuttiya, Galilee	1 fragmentary cranium, Galilee man
Jebel Qafza, Nazareth	Skeletons of 5 adults and 1 child
Shukba, Wadi Natuf	Skeletons of 1 adult and 6 children
Amud Cave, Lake Tiberias	1 nearly complete skeleton
	LEBANON
Ksar 'Akil, near Beirut	1 child's skeleton, "Egbert"

as well as such contemporary vacation areas as the Crimea and the coasts of Lebanon and Palestine. Very few remains of these men, or their implements, have been found in colder places. Most of central and eastern Europe was apparently too cold for them during Würm I, although some of them lived on the western slopes of the Zagros Mountains in Iraq and Iran, and just north of the Elburz and Hindu Kush Mountains in Iran, Soviet Central Asia, and Afghanistan.

The western European Neanderthals, living in parts of Germany and in Belgium, France, Spain, and Italy seem to have formed an essentially isolated population, with little if any gene flow elsewhere.[1] Possibly a thin line of communication led from Germany across Czechoslovakia and Hungary to the Black Sea coast, but this was probably genetically inconsequential.

Owing to the glaciated barriers of the Alps and Pyrenees, the western Neanderthal domain can be subdivided into three partially isolated regional groups, one living in France, Belgium, and western Germany, a second in Spain and Portugal, and a third in Italy. Of these the Italian subregion may have been the oldest. A. C. Blanc has traced the Mousterian in Italy back to the Riss glacial period,[2] where it seems to have evolved locally. Also the Saccopastore skulls are the most Neanderthaloid of any of the Last Interglacial specimens reviewed earlier in this chapter.

Because the skulls from Spain and Italy, few as they are, resemble those from France, Belgium, and Germany in most respects, we can consider the western Neanderthals as a population and study them as a unit, with regional variability borne in mind.

The Western Neanderthals

O U R S A M P L E includes the remains of about fifty-five individuals, but many of them are too fragmentary for detailed description. Some consist of items like one femur, one milk molar, and one crushed baby's skull. Although they have been found over the span of a century, some are still in private hands, others have been lost, and few have been competently described. To bring them all together, to measure or to remeasure them where necessary, and to treat them statistically would be a monumental task beyond the scope of this book. The nearest published approach to such a treatment is Morant's work.[3]

Along with Krapina C and Galilee, which belong elsewhere, Morant measured the following seven skulls of western Neander-

---

[1] Howell: "Pleistocene Glacial Ecology and the Evolution of 'Classic Neanderthal' Man," *SWJA*, Vol. 8, No. 4 (1952), pp. 377–410.

[2] Blanc: "Torre in Pietra, Saccopastore, Monte Circeo . . . ," pp. 167–74.

[3] Morant: "Studies of Paleolithic Man. II. A Biometric Study of Neanderthaloid Skulls and of their Relationships to Modern Types," *Biometrika*, Vol. 2 (1927), pp. 310–80.

thals, and a cast of an eighth: Neanderthal, Spy 1, Spy 2, La Chapelle aux Saints, Le Moustier (adolescent), La Quina 1, La Quina 2 (a child, and a cast), and Gibraltar 1. To these I have added La Ferrassie 1, which is the most complete skull we have, Circeo 1,[4] and the child's skull of Pech de l'Azé,[5] making a total of eleven. These, along with a small, basic bibliography,[6] will form the basis of the following description.

---

[4] I measured a cast of La Ferrassie 1 bought from the Musée de l'Homme, Paris, and of Circeo 1 in the Philadelphia collection.

[5] E. Patte: *L'Enfant Néanderthalien du Pech de l'Azé* (Paris: Masson et Cie; 1957).

[6] The literature on this subject is extensive, but most of it is secondary. The following works are either original or comprehensive.

S. Alcobé: "Die Neanderthaler Spaniens," *NC*, 1958, pp. 1–62.

R. Bay: "Das Gebiss des Neanderthalers," *NC*, 1958, pp. 123–40.

M. Boule: "L'Homme Fossile de la Chapelle aux Saints," *APa*, Vols. 6 & 7, pp. 1911–12.

Boule and Vallois: *Les Hommes Fossiles* (Paris: Masson et Cie; 1952).

M. Fusté: "Morfología cerebral de un ejemplar neanderthalense procedente de la cueva de la Carigüelu, en Piñar (Granada)," *TIBS*, Vol. 15 (1956).

M. García Sánchez: "Restos humanos del paleolítico medio y superior y del neo-eneolitico de Piñar (Granada)," *TIBS*, Vol. 15, No. 2 (1960), pp. 17–72.

F. C. Howell: "Pleistocene Glacial . . ."

Howell: "The Evolutionary Significance of Variation and Varieties of 'Neanderthal' Man," *QRB*, Vol. 32, No. 4 (1957), pp. 330–47.

Howell: "Upper Pleistocene Stratigraphy and Early Man in the Levant," *PAPS*, Vol. 103, No. 1 (1959), pp. 1–65.

Hrdlička: "The Skeletal Remains of Early Man."

A. Leroi-Gourhan: "Étude des Restes Humains Fossiles Provenants des Grottes d'Arcy-sur-Cure," *APa*, Vol. 44 (1958), pp. 1–62.

E. Loth: "Beiträge zur Kenntnis der Weichteilanatomie des Neanderthalers," *ZfRK*, Vol. 7 (1938), pp. 13–35.

Morant: "Studies of Paleolithic Man. . . ."

Pales: "Les Néanderthaliens en France."

Patte: *Les Néanderthaliens* (Paris: Masson et Cie; 1955).

Patte: *L'Enfant Néanderthalien du Pech de l'Azé.*

Patte: "L'Enfant du Pech de l'Azé," *NC*, 1958, pp. 265–6.

Piveteau: *Traité de Paléontologie, VII.*

Sergi: "La Mandibola Neandertaliana Circeo II," *RA*, Vol. 41 (1954), pp. 305–44.

Sergi: "La Mandibola Neandertaliana Circeo III," *RA*, Vol. 42 (1955), pp. 337–404.

Sergi: "Die Neanderthalischen Paleanthropen in Italien," *NC*, 1958, pp. 38–51.

W. L. Straus, Jr., and A. J. E. Cave: "Pathology and Posture of Neanderthal Man," *QRB*, Vol. 32, No. 4 (1957), pp. 348–63.

F. Twiesselmann: "Les Néanderthaliens découverts en Belgique," *NC*, 1958 pp. 63–71.

The Western Neanderthal Crania

A s S e r g i (1958) has remarked, whereas the Europeans of the Last Interglacial varied considerably in skull form, the Neanderthals of Würm I are much alike. They are in fact so homogenous that a strong selective agency must have been pruning off deviant individuals. Data to document this will be found in Table 37.

All had large brains, with capacities ranging from 1,525 to 1,640 cc. in six male skulls and from 1,300 to 1,425 cc. in three female

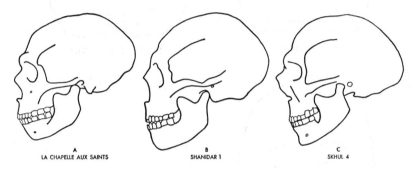

A	B	C
LA CHAPELLE AUX SAINTS	SHANIDAR 1	SKHUL 4

FIG. 70 FROM NEANDERTHAL TO NORDIC IN WÜRM I. Profiles of the skulls of La Chapelle aux Saints (A), Shanidar 1 (B), and Skhul 4 (C). Although these three men were possibly contemporary, their skulls form an evolutionary sequence from the low-headed, prognathous La Chapelle aux Saints to the high-headed, orthognathous Skhul 4. The difference is geographical. One interpretation is that La Chapelle aux Saints lived on the periphery of the Caucasoid racial area during Würm I; Shanidar 1 closer to the center; and Skhul 4 nearest the probable center of Caucasoid evolution. A second interpretation is that La Chapelle aux Saints shows the most extreme form of cold adaptation and Skhul 4 the least. A third is that Skhul 4 was the product of mixture with local Caucasoids who had never become Neanderthaloid. All three interpretations have merit. (Drawings after Boule and Vallois, 1952; Stewart, 1958; and Keith and McCown, 1939.)

ones. The sex difference of 200 cc. is great, and reminiscent of Sinanthropus. By and large these are more capacious skulls than the earlier European ones, and Circeo 1 is notably larger than the Saccopastores, which anticipated the Neanderthal cranial form in Italy.

Like that of Saccopastore 1, which was a more primitive skull in many ways, the Neanderthal crania are globular in the rear; broad, low, widely curved outward over the earholes; and overhanging the area of neck-muscle attachment behind. Their foreheads are sloping and the arc-chord indices of the frontal and parietal bones are close to the figures for *Homo erectus* (see Chapter 8, and Table 36), but not the occipital arc-chord index, because the Neanderthal occiputs are well rounded.

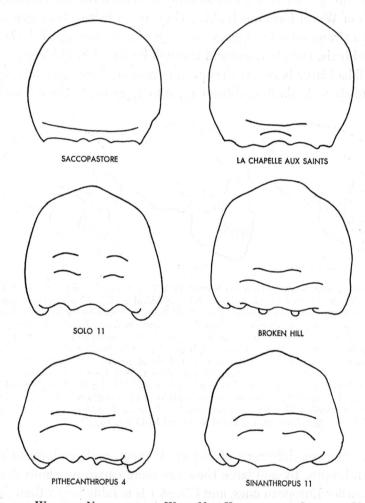

FIG. 71   WHY THE NEANDERTHALS WERE NOT *Homo erectus*: OCCIPITAL VIEWS OF SIX SKULLS. Seen from the rear, the skulls of *Homo erectus* (A to D) are pentagonal in form. This is true of all of them, from the earliest (Pithecanthropus 4) to the youngest (Broken Hill). The skull of Saccopastore 1, the first European skull to show the Neanderthal form (E), and La Chapelle aux Saints (F), generally taken as the type specimen of the European Neanderthals, are not pentagonal but circular, flattened at the bases. A circular occipital profile is a purely *sapiens* skull form. This, as well as their high cranial capacities, separate the Neanderthals from *Homo erectus*. (Drawings of Saccopastore after Sergi, 1955; La Chapelle aux Saints after a cast; Broken Hill after Pycraft, 1928; Solo 11, Pithecanthropus 4, and Sinanthropus 11 after Weidenreich, 1943.)

It is commonly stated that Neanderthal man could not have stood or walked erect because his foramen magnum, the hole in the base of the skull through which the spinal cord passes into the cervical vertebrae, was slanted backward. But this anatomical observation is not true; and even if it were true, the position of the foramen magnum would not have affected his posture.[7]

The bases of these skulls are very large, as witness La Chapelle aux Saints, La Ferrassie 1, and Circeo 1, the most nearly intact of which is La Ferrassie 1.

In Table 29 an unconventional measurement, inion-prosthion, expresses the maximum length and a conventional one, bimastoid, expresses the breadth of the bases of these three Neanderthals. For comparison, the dimensions of the earliest Upper Paleolithic

TABLE 29

SIMPLE DIMENSIONS OF THE
NEANDERTHAL CRANIAL BASE

	Inion-Prosthion	Bimastoid
La Chapelle	226	142
La Ferrassie 1	220 (?)	147
Circeo I	222	144
Combe Capelle	191	124

skull, Combe Capelle, are also given. The difference of 30 mm. in length and 20 mm. in breadth show how much larger-based the Neanderthal crania were than the cranium of Combe Capelle, which may have been contemporaneous with the last of the Neanderthals in the Würm I–II Interstadial.

The combination of a large base and flattened brain case suggests the possibility of artificial deformation, like the cradling of some modern peoples of the Balkans and of the mountains of the Near East. But this is unlikely, for two reasons. No single technique of cranial deformation, intentional or incidental to some other practice, is likely to have been employed all over western

[7] C. Arambourg: "Sur l'Attitude, en Station Verticale, des Néanderthaliens," *CRAS*, Vol. 240 (1955), pp. 804–6.

Patte: *Les Néanderthaliens;* and Straus and Cave: "Pathology and Posture. . . ," loc. cit.

The misconception arose when Boule faultily reconstructed the cranial base of La Chapelle aux Saints. In La Ferrassie 1 the foramen magnum slants forward.

Europe for 40,000 years. And in modern, artificially deformed skulls, the infant and adolescent specimens are more flattened than the adult ones. In the Neanderthal infant of Pech de l'Azé, and in the adolescents of Le Moustier and Piñar, there is less flattening than in the adult skulls. It was not the hand of man, but natural forces, that flattened the brows of Neanderthal man.

This flattening is combined with another special feature: a remarkable forward projection of the face, or beakiness, dependent on the excessive size of the nose. The Neanderthal nose projects like a prow, influencing everything around and below it. The oft-cited fact that the brow ridges, particularly those of La Chapelle aux Saints, form a continuous torus over the nose is due to the prominence of the nose. What prognathism these skulls possess is confined to the nasal region. There is little or none of the sub-nasal prognathism—projection of the alveolar borders of the palate—seen in Pithecanthropus and Sinanthropus and in many modern Australoids and Mongoloids. Although grotesquely so, the nasal and alveolar region of the Neanderthal skulls is Caucasoid.

The Neanderthal face protrudes because of the nose only. The jaws, which were carried forward by the nasal skeleton, could have functioned more efficiently for chewing had they been set two or three centimeters farther back. Inside the Neanderthal skulls the nasal passages dip downward below the level of their openings, thus producing an enlarged nasal chamber. In consequence, the maxillae are long, stretched out on the side, and puffy on the surface. There is no canine fossa. These peculiarities, which have led some authors to consider the Neanderthals a species apart, are a structural unit caused by this nasal domination.

The importance of the nose as the prime architect of the Neanderthal face has been generally overlooked because in both La Chapelle, which is too well known, and in La Ferrassie 1, which is still virtually undescribed, the nasal bones were missing at the time of discovery. Both skulls bear scars suggesting post-mortem surgery. In both it looks as if the brain had been teased out through the resulting aperture, anticipating, in a clumsy way, the handiwork of ancient Egyptian embalmers. Such an operation may have been substituted for the older and more conventional one of cutting open the skull base to remove the brain, as was done in Circeo 1. Because La Chapelle aux Saints and La Ferrassie 1 were both to be buried whole, the brain was removed through the nose.

Despite this mutilation, the nasal margins of the maxillae in both skulls are preserved, as is the location of nasion. From these loci we can see that far from being flat-nosed, as in the widely copied MacGregor restoration of La Chapelle aux Saints, these noses could have had straight or even convex profiles, as in the skull of the eight-year-old child from La Quina, and as in Shanidar 1 from Iraq. In both those skulls the nasal bones are intact and the nasal profile was prominent. In Cicero 1 and Gibraltar 1, the nasal bones were also intact. These "Mediterranean" Neanderthals, who lived in a milder climate than that of western France, were less beaky than La Chapelle aux Saints or La Ferrassie 1, and their upper jaws, from nasion to prosthion, were shorter.

The western Neanderthals, and particularly the French ones, must have needed big noses for some reason. The nose serves the purpose, among others, of warming and moistening the inhaled air on its way to the lungs.[8] In most modern populations living in cold or dry, or both cold and dry climates the nasal opening is narrow, but narrowness was impossible for Neanderthal because of the size of his front teeth. A correlation between nasal-opening breadth and intercanine breadth was established by Schwalbe seventy-five years ago.[9]

Recent military research has shown that in very cold climates it is not so much the lungs but the brain that is in danger of chilling by inhaled air. The lungs are a long way from the nose. In arctic populations necks are generally short, skulls broad and low, and the distance from nose to lungs less than in many long-necked tropical peoples. In ordinary human heads and necks the nasal passages are quite close to the arteries that feed blood to the brain. In a flat-headed, short-necked individual exposed to intense cold the proximity of nasal passages to these blood vessels could be critical, for the brain must be kept at a constant

---

[8] A. W. Proetz: *Essays on the Applied Physiology of the Nose* (St. Louis: Annals Publishing Company; 1953), 2nd. ed.

[9] G. Schwalbe: *Lehrbuch der Anatomie der Sinnesorgane* (Erlangen: Besold; 1887).

temperature. It cannot tolerate variations as can the arms and legs (see Chapter 2). The size of the nose in the western Neanderthals, the expansion of the maxillary sinuses, and the forward position of the nose in reference to that of the brain case may have had a survival value under conditions of extreme cold without adequate headgear or protection for the neck.

As the climate grew colder, Neanderthal men may have increasingly needed a large, projecting nasal "radiator," particularly as there is no archaeological evidence of cultural improvement that would help mitigate the severity of the climate. Their adaptation was probably anatomical and physiological, that is, requiring a large caloric intake, like the adaptation of the Alakalufs, who are exposed to much milder conditions.

In Chapter 2 we saw that the Greenland Eskimo, who live in the shadow of an ice sheet, keep their faces from freezing in part by a relatively great blood flow, as indicated by the large bore of the infraorbital foramina of their malar bones. In the Neanderthals these foramina are also very large. In the left malar of La Ferrassie 1, the foramen measures 10 mm. by 16 mm. La Chapelle has two foramina on each side. The largest, on the left, is 8 mm. by 7 mm. Modern European foramina, which are single, are about 3 mm. in diameter. Thus, the Neanderthal foramina were capable of supplying six or seven times as much blood to the face as those of modern Europeans, whereas the Neanderthal faces were no more than twice as large. This evidence strengthens the concept that the peculiarities of the Neanderthal face were adaptive, and not simply archaic survivals.

Despite these adaptive features, the Neanderthal faces are essentially Caucasoid. The brow ridges, which form a bar over nasion, sweep in a double arc over the eye sockets and trail out far to the rear on either side. All indices of facial flatness which can be calculated (see Chapter 8) indicate that the Neanderthals were the least flat-faced of ancient mankind. The orbits are large, as in most early men, and they are round. Although the Neanderthal faces are absolutely broad, they could not have appeared so in the flesh, for the zygomatic arches are flat rather than bowed. The facial breadth was, in fact, smaller than the breadth of the skull, as in modern Europeans. In all other fossil skulls yet studied, the faces are wider than the brain cases. This last peculiarity was largely concerned with a disparity in the relative development of the various muscles which operated the jaw.

The Western Neanderthal Mandibles

TEN ADULT or nearly adult mandibles are available for study. They are La Chapelle aux Saints, La Ferrassie 1, Spy 1, La Naulette, Le Moustier, La Quina 9, Regourdou, Arcy 2, Circeo 2, and Circeo 3. Five others, Spy 2, Malarnaud, Marillac, Petit Puymoyen, and Bañolas are either very fragmentary or undescribed (see Table 38).

Morphologically they are all more or less alike, but they vary in size. Arcy 2 is large and massive, as much so as the Heidelberg jaw, but the others are slenderer. La Ferrassie 1 is less massive than many modern jaws, being almost paper-thin in the gonial region. Not one of them has Heidelberg's peculiar conformation at the chin region; indeed, it is not found in any of the Last Interglacial mandibles. La Ferrassie, La Naulette, Arcy 2, and Circeo 3 have rudimentary chins. The most nearly chinless is La Chapelle aux Saints, the one usually taken as the type specimen.

At least five of these mandibles have multiple mental foramina. La Chapelle aux Saints, La Ferrassie 1, and La Naulette have two each on the right side; La Quina 9 has five. Only Malarnaud has more than one on the left; it has two on each side. When the foramina are single, they are very large. Because La Chapelle and La Ferrassie 1 were both apparently right-handed (as will appear shortly), it seems legitimate to wonder whether there might not be some connection between handedness and the multiple foramina phenomenon.

The most unusual feature of these jaws is that the coracoid process rises from the horizontal ramus well to the rear of the third molar. In this region the jaw looks stretched out, to match the protrusion of the upper face, which in turn accommodates the forward thrust of the nose. In La Ferrassie 1 the distance between the back edge of the third molar and the front edge of the mandibular foramen (a perforation of the table of the inner face of the ascending ramus) is 37 mm. on the left side and 38 mm. on the right. In Combe Capelle, the oldest Upper Paleolithic skeleton, the figure is 23 mm. for each side. This measurement could not be taken on the other mandibles, but in all of them the forward edge of the ascending ramus clears the third molar by about

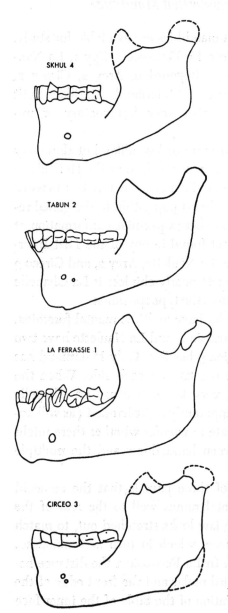

FIG. 72 CAUCASOID NEANDERTHAL MANDIBLES: SKHUL 4, TABUN 3, LA FERRASSIE 1, CIRCEO 3. The Neanderthal mandible usually illustrated is that of La Chapelle aux Saints. It is omitted here because it is nearly toothless and altered by senile degeneration. Also, it is probably the only completely chinless Neanderthal mandible. Circeo 3 is large and stout, recalling Heidelberg in some respects. La Ferrassie 1 is long and slender, almost paper-thin in parts of the gonial region and ascending ramus. Tabun 2 is shorter, deeper, and more prognathous; and its Palestinian successor, Skhul 4, is virtually modern. The extreme forward growth of the European Neanderthal mandibles is shown in La Ferrassie 1, in which the third molar clears the ascending ramus by a full centimer. (Drawings of Skhul 4 and Tabun 3 after Keith and McCown, 1939; La Ferrassie 1 after Pales, 1958, and a cast; Circeo 3 after Sergi, 1955.)

the same distance. In most other human jaws, ancient or modern, Caucasoid or otherwise, the rear edge of the third molar and the front of the coracoid process more or less coincide. In the Australopithecines the coracoid process overlaps the third molar and part if not all of the second.

On the inner sides of the Neanderthal jaws the muscular relief is excessive. Loth, who had only La Chapelle aux Saints and Le Moustier to study, found that both had powerfully developed attachments for the internal and external pterygoids, that neither had had very strong temporal muscles, and that the areas of temporal muscle attachment on the skulls extended far to the rear but not high on the vault. Loth's observations apply to the other specimens now available; indeed, to the group as a whole. With such an elongated jaw, the temporal muscles were at a mechanical disadvantage when compared with such types as Heidelberg and Sinanthropus.

In all the jaws the insertions for the digastric muscles are wide and deep, matching the digastric fossae on the bases of the skulls; these fossae are situated between the mastoid and paramastoid prominences.

Compared with the older mandibles one notes that the basin-shaped interior configuration is gone, particularly in La Ferrassie 1. The muscles that control the movements of the tongue are given as much room to work in as in any ordinary modern jaw.

Finally, the mandibular torus, that ridge of dense bone running on the tongue side from molars to canine, just below the tooth line, turns up in Marillac, La Quina 9, and Arcy 2. We have seen it in Sinanthropus and noted that it occurs among arctic peoples of both the Mongoloid and the Caucasoid subspecies. Like multiple mental foramina, it is associated with life in cold regions. Whether or not its presence among the Neanderthals is due to a genetic association, parallelism, or both is an open question.

In conclusion, the western Neanderthal mandibles may be assessed from three points of view: grade, line, and special adaptation. Arcy 2 is quite primitive, reminiscent in some respects of Heidelberg, and this jaw is probably the oldest of the lot, dating from the base of Würm I. La Ferrassie 1, which may be among the latest, is the most nearly modern. The group as a whole falls close

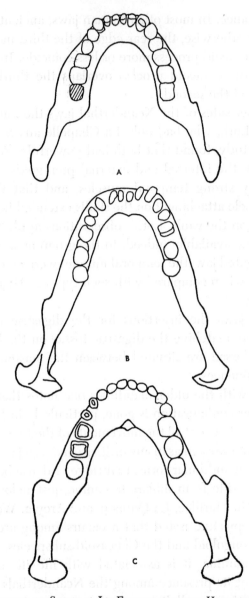

FIG. 73   MANDIBLES OF SKHUL 4, LA FERRASSIE 1, AND HEIDELBERG, SEEN FROM
ABOVE. A. Skhul 4; B. La Ferrassie 1; C. Heidelberg (after a cast). This sequence
illustrates more clearly than the profiles the progression in Caucasoid mandibles
shown in the preceding figures. The Heidelberg jaw is thick; its ascending rami
moderately flaring; and its symphysial region wide fore and aft, receding, and
braced from inside. The jaw of La Ferrassie 1 is extremely long, and its ascending
rami more nearly parallel. The Skhul 4 jaw is virtually modern. Note the marked
racial difference between these jaws and the flaring Mongoloid and North African
mandibles shown in Fig. 62.

to the mandibles of the Last Interglacial as a whole, but in general is a little more modern. The grade of these jaws therefore fits their chronological position. The line is patently Caucasoid, unless one considers multiple foramina and the mandibular torus to be peculiarly Mongoloid characteristics. All the jaws complete enough to judge show special adaptation, not only in the above-mentioned features but also in the separation of the tooth row from the ascending ramus. This last feature is merely a part of the whole complex of the skull in which the nasal apparatus is projected forward. The special adaptation of both jaw and cranium are toward the bitter cold of western Europe in which the Neanderthals lived.

The Teeth of the Western Neanderthals

THE CUSTOM of burying the dead, which the Neanderthals seem to have invented, insured the preservation of skulls and bones, but it did little to increase the number of teeth in any fossil man collection, because, even if unburied bones decay, their teeth tend to remain intact. Only 138 western Neanderthal teeth are available for study. I could find published measurements of only forty-five of these,[1] and had to measure casts and photographs to obtain figures for the others. Thirty-two from a cast of La Ferrassie 1 are reduced by wear, and the two teeth of La Chapelle aux Saints (a pair of left second premolars) are stumps. As the western Neanderthals overworked their teeth, only those of the very young can validly be compared with other series.

Table 39 presents the figures on these teeth. Their minimum sizes are mostly dictated by degree of wear; their maxima are true values. They fall in the same general range as those of Heidelberg, the teeth of Third Interglacial Europeans, and modern people. There has been little change in tooth size in Europe from Heidelberg to the present, except for a few of the Krapina teeth. The proportions between molars, premolars, canines, and incisors

---

[1] Spy 1 and 2, La Quina H-5, and La Cotte de St. Brélade, Jersey (Hrdlička, 1930); Peche de l'Azé (Patte, 1957); Arcy (Leroi-Gourhan, 1958); and Circeo 2 and 3 (Sergi, 1954, 1955).

are normal for Caucasoids. There is no common pattern in the molar rows reflecting consistent size gradation.[2]

It is an anthropological stereotype that Neanderthal man's teeth were taurodont, but this is an unwarranted generalization,

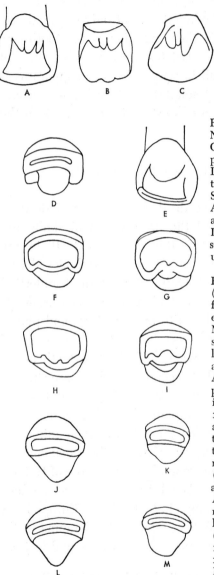

Fig. 74 The Upper Incisors of Neanderthals and Other Early Caucasoids. A. Ehringsdorf; B. Krapina; C. Le Moustier (Neanderthal); D and E. Arcy-sur-Cure (Neanderthal); F and G. Tabun 1; H and I. Skhul 7; J and K. Skhul 5; L and M. Australian Aborigine. A through E are upper median incisors, labial view; D through L are upper median incisors, occlusal view; G through M are upper lateral incisors, occlusal view.

The upper median incisors of the Europeans of the Last Interglacial (A and B) and of the Neanderthal from Le Moustier (C) are only moderately shoveled, in European, not Mongoloid, fashion. Each has only slightly raised borders and three teat-like projections at the base. The Neanderthal incisor (D and E) from Arcy-sur-Cure has a ball-like basal projection. The median and lateral incisors from Palestine, those of Tabun 1 (F and G) and Skhul 7 (H and I), although considerably worn, still show the effect of moderate shoveling of the European type. But the less worn median and lateral incisors of Skhul 5 (J and K) show no sign of shoveling and closely resemble those of an Australian aborigine (L and M). This resemblace corresponds to the Australoid character of Skhul 5's face. (Drawings A, B, C after Weidenreich, 1937; D and E after Leroi Gourhan, 1958; F through M after Keith and McCown, 1939.)

[2] The pattern 1–2–3, in which the first molar is largest, the second molar is next largest, and the third smallest, occurs once; 2–1–3 occurs twice; 2–3–1 four times; 3–1–2 twice; and 3–2–1 three times.

true of less than half the molars and premolars. And not one of these is as taurodont as those from Krapina. La Ferrassie 1, La Quina, Regourdou, and Arcy had no taurodontism at all.

The crowns are also variable. The Dryopithecus pattern, Y-5, is the commonest, but sixth cusps occur, and the plus-4 pattern is frequent in upper molars. A cingulum and wrinkling are seen in one molar from Arcy, and another cingulum is present at the base of the only unworn Le Moustier canine. Upper incisors from Le Moustier, St. Brais, and Arcy are moderately shoveled in that they have raised lateral ridges. A lateral incisor from Le Moustier has short, fingerlike mesial ridges on the tongue side; the St. Brais and Arcy specimens have, instead, well-developed basal eminences that make them very thick at the gum level. The Le Moustier canine with the cingulum also has a spatulate cutting edge, like that of an incisor, whereas one of the Arcy canines has a median vertical ridge.

All these special features are reminiscent of Sinanthropus and the modern Mongoloids in an attenuated way. The cingulum and wrinkling are also generally archaic, whereas the moderate shoveling is frequent among northern Europeans. We seem to have in the western Neanderthal series a watering down of the partially Mongoloid, or pseudo-Mongoloid, dental features of Krapina.

The condition of these teeth gives some idea of the cultural activities of these cold-weather people. All but the teeth of the very young are heavily worn, and some are worn in such a fashion that activities other than chewing food must have been responsible. In La Ferrassie 1 the outer surfaces of the upper incisors and left upper canine are polished down, as if by some object like the corner of a skin or a thong held in the teeth, and in the mandible there is a gap between the left second incisor and the canine. These two teeth were twisted away from each other and there is a pit, as of an abscess, in the outer surface of the mandible, exposing the root of the left lower canine. There are also similar gaps between the first and second molar on either side of the mandible.

These dental peculiarities, when added to the evidence for a special development of the pterygoid and digastric muscles, suggest that the western Neanderthals softened skins with their teeth. The abundance of flint tools identifiable as fleshers supports this inference. The bitter cold of Würm I must have placed a premium on warm clothing, particularly on serviceable footgear, as a necessity for survival.

Having good teeth was important to the western Neanderthals; yet a man did not necessarily die when his teeth were gone. La Ferrassie 1 had such severe arthritic erosion of the condyles of his jaw that he could not have chewed his food. La Chapelle aux Saints had only two teeth; he also was arthritic, and for many years before his death could not possibly have hunted, nor could he have chewed roasted meat. Someone must have brought him his food, and softened it for him. Despite his economic uselessness, he was important enough to warrant being buried in a cave. This could not have happened to everyone who died in a cave in winter, or the caves would be full of skeletons. During the lifetime of La Chapelle aux Saints the French Neanderthals were not poor providers on the verge of death from exposure or starvation. They were competent hunters with some kind of division of labor based on age and with solicitude for the old and incapacitated.

The Postcranial Skeletons of the Western Neanderthals

EXCEPT for an odd bone here and there, all we know about western Neanderthal anatomy from the neck down is derived from seven skeletons: Neanderthal, Spy 1, Spy 2, La Chapelle aux Saints, La Ferrassie 1, La Ferrassie 2, and La Quina H-5. The first five are masculine, the last two feminine. Not one is complete. The most fully described is that of La Chapelle aux Saints, who suffered from disease when alive and whose bones were, as we shall see, inaccurately reconstructed after exhumation.

Earlier European comparative material consists almost entirely of the bones from Krapina, which, although more numerous, were scattered and broken because they had not been buried. In general, the Neanderthal bones resemble those from Krapina morphologically but are heavier, as the western Neanderthals were powerfully built people.

The only vertebral column thoroughly studied is that of La

Chapelle aux Saints, which had been shrunken and distorted by arthritis and senility. The neck vertebrae are short-bodied, and he undoubtedly had a short neck, even in his prime.[3] So did the female, La Quina H-5. The thoracic and lumbar vertebrae of La Chapelle aux Saints are also small, but according to Hrdlička (1930) the lumbar vertebrae have unusually large articular facets on their transverse processes and large neural canals. In both La Chapelle aux Saints and Spy 2, the top third or fourth of the sacrum is preserved. In both, the upper margin is narrower than the modern European mean, but within its range. At least in La Chapelle aux Saints, the wings of the sacrum rise to a higher level than the central body. This condition is super-Caucasoid; it is found in 21.5 per cent of living Europeans and is rare or absent in other races.

The Neanderthal ribs are known from five fragments from La Chapelle aux Saints, and the nearly complete rib cages of both La Ferrassies. These ribs are variable in section. Those of La Chapelle aux Saints were round or triangular, like Krapina's, but those of both La Ferrassies were ribbon-shaped, as in modern Europeans. As in Krapina, these ribs all curve so as to produce a deep chest.

The clavicles of five specimens, Neanderthal, Spy 1, La Chapelle aux Saints, La Ferrassie 1, and La Quina H-5, are longer, slenderer, and straighter than those of most living Europeans, and their shape indicates a deep chest. In four fragmentary scapulas (from the skeletons cited above, excepting La Quina H-5) the same configuration is seen as in Krapina; but in the Neanderthal fragment and in La Ferrassie 1 the glenoid cavity, in which the head of the humerus rotates, is inclined a little more to the rear than usual in modern specimens, and the ridge for the insertion of the *teres minor* muscle is strongly developed. This is the muscle that rotates the humerus sidewise when the upper arm is held close to the body. These features are absent in Spy 2, a female,

---

[3] Boule (1911–13) made much of the fact that the dorsal spines of this specimen's cervical vertebrae pointed backward instead of downward and backward, and that the dorsal spine of the sixth cervical vertebra was not bifurcated. As Arambourg (1955), Patte (1955), and Straus and Cave (1957) have shown, these features are common in living Europeans.

who probably did not do the same kinds of work with her arms that men did.

In six skeletons (all but La Quina H-5) pieces of both right and left humeri are present, but only the right humerus of Neanderthal is complete. His left humerus had been injured early in life and was underdeveloped. Judging by the relative development of his two humeri, La Chapelle aux Saints was strongly right-handed. Neanderthal's right humerus is 31.4 cm. long, exactly the modern European mean. It is a stout bone, but no stouter than those of many living Europeans.[4]

In all the western Neanderthal humeri the olecranon fossa, a pit on the dorsal side of the lower end of the bone which receives the olecranon process of the ulna when the arm is extended, is large and deep. It is also perforated in La Quina H-5, both La Ferrassies, and Spy 2, making a ratio of perforation of 44 per cent in nine bones. Virtually the same ratio occurs at Krapina.

We have radii (the paired lower arm bone on the outer or thumb side of the wrist) for all but La Ferrassie 2. Like the humeri, they are as long as the European mean (22.7 cm. for both sexes). They are strongly built, and characteristically curved outward, more so than in any known modern population. Such a curvature provides a great deal of room between radius and ulna (the companion lower arm bone) for the development of powerful forearm muscles. The western Neanderthals must have had, and probably needed, very strong hands.

The ulnae of these skeletons match the radii in length and stoutness, but vary in curvature. That of La Chapelle aux Saints is nearly straight; La Ferrassie 1's is slightly curved and La Ferrassie 2's is very curved. In all of them the olecranon process, which is the peak of the elbow (the "funny bone") and fits into the olecranon fossa of the humerus when the arm is extended, is exceptionally long. This gives the triceps muscle a great mechanical advantage in extending the forearm.

Nearly complete hand skeletons were found with both La Fer-

---

[4] Boule calculated an index of robusticity by dividing the minimum shaft circumference by the maximum length of the humerus. The result was a figure of 23 per cent for Neanderthal. The mean for modern white American males is 21.5 per cent, and the upper range far exceeds 23 per cent.

rassie specimens.[5] Spy 1 has two metacarpals, Spy 2 six each of metacarpals and phalanges; and La Chapelle aux Saints has one fragmentary scaphoid (the wrist bone articulating with the thumb side of the radius), one capitate (the central wrist bone of the outer row articulating with the third and fourth metacarpals), three metacarpals, and two phalanges, all from his little used, probably defective, left hand.

Only the two wrist bones of La Chapelle aux Saints have been described. The scaphoid is said to be small and flattened, but this description does not apply to the half of a scaphoid present in La Ferrassie 2's right hand.[6] The capitate of La Chapelle aux Saints is as long as Krapina's (24 mm.) but narrower (14 mm. as compared to 18 mm.); La Ferrassie 2's capitate is of normal size and proportions for a European woman (22 mm. by 16 mm.), as are the rest of her surviving wrist bones.[7]

La Chapelle aux Saints's left first metacarpal (that of the thumb) is a little short by European standards—much has been made of this point [8]—but the corresponding bone of La Ferrassie 2 is longer than the mean for European women. Her metacarpals and phalanges also fall close to modern female European means, except that the terminal phalanx of her right little finger is short and conical, apparently a congenital defect. A single fourth left metacarpal from Arcy is also perfectly modern.[9] On the whole, no evidence yet produced indicates that the western Neanderthal hands were notably different from those of hard-working modern Europeans.

Scanty but generally adequate specimens are available for most of the bones of the lower extremity. Among the least satisfactory are those of the *os coxae*, or pelvic bone. These consist of one piece of left ilium from Neanderthal, and two similar pieces, one

[5] F. Sarasin: "Die Variationen im Bau des Handskeletts verschiedener Menschenformen," *ZfMuA*, Vol. 30 (1931), pp. 252–316.

[6] Piveteau: *Traité de Paléontologie*, Vol. VII, photograph on p. 458.

[7] The lunate and triquetral are missing.

[8] Boule also stressed the fact that the proximal articular surface of this bone is convex rather than saddle-shaped, as in modern metacarpals; but in this respect both La Ferrassies are normal.

[9] Leroi-Gourhan: op. cit., p. 54.

Length is 55 mm. (?); knuckle breadth = 14 mm.; minimum shaft diameter = 6 mm. The last measurement is actually small.

left and one right, from La Chapelle aux Saints. All observers since Boule [1] agree that they are similar to those of modern men.

Femora are available for Neanderthal, Spy 2, La Chapelle aux Saints, both La Ferrassies, and La Quina H-5. They are of medium length (44 cm. for four males), about as long as those of modern Bavarians. They are also relatively thick and heavy, like those of the most solidly built modern populations, for example, the Japanese. The diameter of the femoral head (54.7 mm. for four males) is great compared to the same diameter in most people, but not compared to modern Europeans, whose femoral heads are large. But the western Neanderthal femora differ from the modern European norm in three respects. They have weakly developed pilasters on the backs of their shafts; these shafts are strongly bowed, like those of modern peoples who squat on their heels; and the angle between the neck of the femur and its shaft is low, about 118° for males. Most modern femora of all races have mean angles of from 121 to 133°. However, the femoral angle of the female La Ferrassie 2 was 123°, or quite modern. What this angle signifies is not clear.

We also have four tibias, one each for Spy 2, La Chapelle aux Saints, and the two La Ferrassies. Only that of Spy 2 is complete. It is 33.7 cm. long, or 78.7 per cent of the length of its femur. This tibiofemoral ratio is among the lowest known, the same as that for modern Lapps. Relatively short tibias are characteristic of circumpolar peoples. Like the femora, the western Neanderthal tibias are bowed. Their heads are bent back at angles of as much as 20°, like the heads of other notable squatters, the Fuegians and the California Indians.

Also available are patellas, or kneecaps, for Spy 2, La Chapelle aux Saints, and one of the odd La Quina skeletons. They are all perfectly human, and large. Fibulae were found with Spy 1 and both La Ferrassies, but none has been described.

The feet of the western Neanderthals were almost as distinctive as their skulls, as we can see from a set of footprints found in an Italian cave by A. C. Blanc (see Fig. 75). They look somewhat

[1] Straus and Cave: op. cit.
Piveteau: op. cit.

like the prints of a modern Alakaluf Indian foot used to walking in icy water and snow, and very unlike the slender, tapering marks left by an Upper Paleolithic man in another cave in Italy. The Neanderthal prints are very wide, in heel, ball, and toe, and the toes are very short, except for the great toe. Despite the extreme proportions, there is nothing about these prints that is not, as some have stated, completely human.

The available fossil foot bones tell the same story.[2] We have a right calcaneum and a left astragulus for Spy 2; a calcaneum, an astragulus, and five metatarsals—all seven bones broken and incomplete—for La Chapelle aux Saints; and three nearly complete, articulated feet for the two La Ferrassies, one of which, the right foot of La Ferrassie 2, is depicted in a scale photograph,[3] which I measured.

The calcanea are large and thick, with long heel portions, as in European (and not, as supposed, in Negro) heels. On the underside of every calcaneum is a facet called the *sustentaculum tali*, the outermost of the three which hold up the astragulus, or ankle bone. In the western Neanderthal calcanea this facet is unusually large, indicating that a great deal of weight fell on the outer half of the foot. The astragali are short in proportion to height, and the other metatarsal bones, as seen in the foot of La Ferrassie 2, are wide and square. La Ferrassie 2's metatarsals are about 2 mm. longer than those of European women of today. Also the metatarsals of the Neanderthal woman differ less in length than those of modern European women; in La Ferrassie 2 the second metatarsal is only 6 mm. longer than the fifth, whereas in European women the difference averages 10 mm. The proximal phalanges (the toe joints nearest the body of the foot) are a little shorter than the modern means, except for that of the great toe, which is just as long. La Ferrassie 2, therefore, had a foot of normal length for a European woman, but her toes were shorter and her feet were wider and squarer. They looked like Russian rather than English feet.

[2] D. J. Morton: "Significant Characteristics of the Neanderthal Foot," *NH*, Vol. 26, No. 3 (1926), pp. 310–4.
[3] Piveteau, op. cit., p. 462.

The Height and Build of the Western Neanderthals

ACCORDING to the Neanderthal legend, he was a squat, stunted fellow, about five feet one inch tall, or 155 cm. As indicated by careful calculations from his long bones, La Chapelle aux Saints stood five feet four and a half inches tall, or 164 cm., about half an inch taller than the Frenchmen who lived in the region of his cave at the time his remains were excavated. Neanderthal, Spy 2, and La Ferrassie 1 were of about the same height, five feet four, five feet four, and five feet six (163 cm., 163 cm., and 165.7 cm.), whereas the female La Ferrassie 2 was four feet ten inches, or 148 cm. tall, as might be expected from the relatively small size of her head.

With large heads, deep chests, heavy bones, and large feet, the western Neanderthals must have been heavy for their stature, probably a good 160 pounds or more. They were prime examples of what students of human constitutional types call mesomorphs. They were indubitably muscular, but some of their muscles were more developed than others. The muscles of the upper back and neck had to be strong to support the weight of the head and particularly of the prowlike face. The muscles that roll the humerus outward from the trunk were powerfully developed, but the biceps and triceps of the arm need not have bulged greatly because of special leverage. The forearm, however, must have been very impressive. The calf muscles also were probably as filled out as those of Alpine mountaineers. People built more or less like these Neanderthals may be seen today in the Abruzzi Mountains, in the Alps, and in Bavaria. Whether the resemblance is due to the infiltration and absorption of Neanderthal genes into later populations, or merely to parallelism, we do not know.

The Fate of the Western Neanderthals

WITHOUT much doubt the Neanderthal population of western Europe was greatly reduced by the end of the Würm I glaciation, but it did not die out completely until after the Upper

Paleolithic people arrived during the Göttweig Interstadial. In France the Mousterian culture lasted into the beginning of that same warm period in at least one site, the Grotte du Loup at Arcy-sur-Cure. Late Mousterian sites also exist in Italy and Spain. In a Spanish site, Piñar, near Granada, in a level above that which contained the Neanderthal frontal bone already mentioned, J-C. Spahni found a basically Mousterian industry that contained traces of Upper Paleolithic techniques of tool-making, implying contact between Neanderthal and Upper Paleolithic peoples.[4] The date of the level is Würm I–II, the Göttweig Interstadial. In it Spahni also found a mandible of Upper Paleolithic type.

The implication of this and other contemporaneous sites is that the two peoples met, and mixed. There is no valid anthropological or biological reason for some of the western Neanderthals not to have been absorbed into the immigrant populations. At least in these southern regions some Neanderthal genes must have been taken into the Upper Paleolithic pool. The Neanderthals became extinct; of that there is no question. But their extinction was probably of the usual human form, extinction by absorption. Some of the physiological peculiarities of the Neanderthals probably became useful in the mixed population that followed, particularly with the advance of the second Würm ice sheet.

The Central European Neanderthals

CENTRAL EUROPE is as poor in Neanderthal remains as western Europe is rich. The difference is not due to a lag in search and excavations, for archaeologists in Central Europe have been nearly as busy in the last century as their western colleagues. Mousterian sites are rare in the middle of the continent. They are concentrated in a few favored spots, like the Bükk Mountains of north central Hungary. These are not really mountains but promontories on a small, detached highland no more than a thousand feet in elevation. It was colder in central than in western Europe

---

[4] It is also possible, but less likely, that Upper Paleolithic invaders found Mousterian artifacts and reworked them into their own kinds of tools, which they then left in the cave.

during Würm I, just as it is today, and the difference in winter temperatures between the Upper Danube and the Dordogne could have been critical for the survival of any kind of people living at that time, including Neanderthals.

The skeletal material which we have for that period is extremely scanty. It consists primarily of three lower jaws and a total of thirty-five teeth. In addition, we have some of the postcranial bones of an undersized adult female, a child's skull as thoroughly smashed as Humpty-Dumpty, and one toe bone. That is all. They are listed in Table 28.

The Three Mandibles

THE MANDIBLE first found came from the Šipka Cave near Štramberk, North Moravia, in 1880.[5] Not until 1955 did Czechoslovakian archaeologists decide that it belonged to a Mousterian culture, probably in Würm I. Destroyed in a fire in 1945, it was the front part of the jaw of a child who had not yet cut his permanent canines; his premolars were not only uncut but still rootless. It was a large and stout jaw for a child of nine.[6] The sagittal profile, below the bulge of the dental area, ran straight up and down, and the center of the lower border projected downward, as in La Ferrassie 1.

The Ochoz mandible was discovered in a cave in Central Moravia in 1905. At the time no implements were found with it. Later, in 1954–1955, archaeologists discovered two successive industries, a Mousterian from Würm I and an Upper Paleolithic from Würm II or III. It was impossible to tell which industry the Ochoz jaw belonged to, but it has been assigned to the earlier one on morphological grounds.[7] The fauna fits both dates.

Although both ascending rami are missing, about 1 cm. of the

[5] R. Virchow: "Der Kiefer aus der Šipkahöhle und der Kiefer von La Naulette," *ZFE,* Vol. 14 (1882), pp. 277–310.

K. J. Maška: *Der diluviale Mensch in Mähren* (Neutitschein, 1886).

E. Vlček: "Die Reste des Neanderthalmenschen aus dem Gebiete der Tschechoslowakei," *NC,* 1958, pp. 107–20.

[6] Sagittal height = 30 mm.; thickness = 14. mm.

[7] It is listed in the *Catalogue des Hommes Fossiles,* edited by Vallois and Movius and published in 1952, as Würm II or III. The archaeological work was done later. See Vlček: op. cit.

body is left to the rear of the left third molar and in this portion there is no trace of the beginning of the left ascending ramus that would be there if it were an Upper Paleolithic type of jaw. This is a specific Neanderthal condition. Also, the molars are taurodont. For these reasons I consider the Würm I date correct.

The whole lower portion of the jaw is missing, which makes it impossible to tell whether it had a chin, but the profile of the symphyseal region is an open double curve. The jaw was slightly prognathous, and probably had a slight chin, like some of the Krapina mandibles.

The Subalyuk mandible was found, along with other human remains, in a cave located near the edge of the Bükk Mountains in Hungary. The cave was named after Michael Suba, a legendary bandit who used to hide in it. After human remains had been unearthed there, the Hungarian government renamed it the Mussolini cave, and this name persists in the literature.[8] It is the only site in Hungary containing stratified Mousterian artifacts. There were two cultural levels, a "high" Mousterian of fine quality, and a later, decadent Mousterian. The human remains are said to have come from the latter level.

The mandible is that of an adult woman. It consists of two disconnected pieces: the chin portion, extending from the left lateral incisor to the right first premolar; and the left side of the body from the second premolar to the third molar and beyond, including a large part of the left ascending ramus. Morphologically it fits the western Neanderthal pattern except that it, like the Ochoz jaw, is prognathous. As in La Ferrassie 1, the bone is very thin.[9] The ascending ramus slopes back widely, and the distance from the rear edge of the third molar is as great as in La Ferrassie. Also, the inside of the chin portion has the same exaggerated relief for the insertion of the digastric muscles as does the French jaw.

In general, these three mandibles are closely similar to those

---

[8] L. Bartucz, J. Dancza, F. Hollendonner, O. Kadić, M. Mottl, V. Pataki, E. Pálosi, J. Szabó, and A. Vendl: "Die Mussolini Höhle (Subalyuk) bei Cserépfalu," *GHSP*, Vol. 8, No. 14 (1939), pp. 1–320.

[9] The symphysial height is 14 mm.; the height at the canine level, 33.7 mm.; and its thickness, 13 mm., compared to a thickness of 16 mm. for La Ferrassie 1, a male.

of the western Neanderthals except for one feature—a considerable prognathism. In this they favor their central European predecessors, the men of Ehringsdorf and Krapina.

The teeth imbedded in these jaws are also Neanderthaloid. Although all of them are within the modern size range, they are not entirely modern in form. As far as I can tell, all three jaws, and certainly Subalyuk, have taurodont molars. The unworn incisors of Šipka are moderately shoveled.

The Postcranial Bones from Subalyuk

WITH THE Subalyuk mandible were found other parts of the woman's skeleton: a fragmentary atlas (first cervical vertebra), three dorsal vertebrae, one lumbar vertebra, one fragmentary sacrum, one manubrium sterni (the lower section of the breast bone), one metacarpal, one patella, three metatarsals, and two toe phalanges. Together, these pieces indicate a small, poorly muscled woman of the usual Neanderthal type. However, two, the sacrum and the manubrium, are notable.

The sacrum consists of two pieces broken during excavation, including the top. It is tiny and would fit an Andamanese Pygmy, or a European child. Whether it really belongs with the rest of the skeleton is an open question.[1] The manubrium of the sternum is a bone rarely found in fossil deposits, because it is soft and spongy and decays rapidly. This is the only Neanderthal manubrium we have. It is small, like the rest of the skeleton, but it is also distinctive in form. On its inner side it is deeply concave, with a depth of 7.5 mm. Most manubria are flat or slightly concave. This can only mean that the woman had a deep chest, a standard Neanderthal feature.

The Subalyuk Child's Skeleton

WITH THE woman was found the skeleton of a child; it was badly smashed, mostly in excavation. Only the skull has been

---

[1] Published photographs of this excavation show men swinging heavy pickaxes over their heads.

studied. Bartucz painstakingly reconstructed the brain case from about sixty pieces and the face from about twenty. The child was about six or seven years old, judging from the eruption of the teeth, which have not been studied. It has been compared with the eight-year-old La Quina skull from France, and is similar in all pertinent respects. There is no canine fossa, the nasal opening is great for a child of that age, and the left nasal bone is concave at the top and convex below, as befits a Neanderthal nose.

The Rumanian Neanderthal Toe Bone [2]

R U M A N I A's contribution to the Neanderthal problem is so far negligible. It consists of the discovery of one phalange from a second toe, found in a rare Mousterian site in the Transylvanian Alps, a region that ethnically and geographically belongs to Hungary. Because no one whom I know can tell a single toe phalange of a Neanderthal from that of an ordinary European, this discovery only adds an osteological item to the archaeological evidence that people of Mousterian culture lived in those mountains in Würm I.

The Significance of the Neanderthal Remains from Central Europe

T H E   E X T R E M E L Y limited roster of Neanderthal remains from central Europe leads us to the following conclusions. Compared to France, Italy, and Spain, central Europe was very sparsely inhabited in Würm I times, probably because the climate was too cold. The people who lived there were Neanderthals, but they differed from their western relatives in having a considerable alveolar prognathism, a trait also seen in their predecessors of the Last Interglacial. It is doubtful that they were numerous enough, or in sufficient contact with their neighbors, to have served as a genetic bridge between the western Neander-

[2] M. N. Morosan: "Les Restes de l'Homme Fossile en Roumanie," *IGC*, 1936, pp. 1239–47.

thals and the contemporary inhabitants of the Soviet Union and western Asia.

Yet they seem to have survived into the Göttweig Interstadial, long enough to have made contact with the first wave of Upper Paleolithic invaders. In a cave called Veternica, near the village of Gorni Stenjevic in the neighborhood of Zagreb, Yugoslavia, three skulls were found under a stone cover in a cultural level attributed to the threshold between the Mousterian and the Aurignacian.[3] According to Malez, who found them, they are youthful and modern in type. One level below, another skull turned up in soil containing Mousterian implements. C. Loring Brace, an American anthropologist who saw this skull in 1959, says that it is an ordinary modern *sapiens* skull, associated with an ordinary Mousterian industry, dated at the first interstadial of the last glaciation.[4] Croatia, then, vies with Spain as the place where the two then existing kinds of Caucasoids, Neanderthal and modern European, may have met.

Neanderthal Remains from the Soviet Union

FROM THE Alps to the Himalayas, the northern zone of the Palearctic region, west of the Tian-Shan Mountains, is separated from its smaller and more southern portion by an east-west mountain barrier, which was glaciated locally in several centers during the Würm period. Even unglaciated, these mountains have always been difficult to cross, and human traffic has usually been routed to either side of them. That is why the Carpathians, Caucasus, and Hindu Kush are refuge areas still inhabited by culturally archaic peoples.

From the mouth of the Rhone to India there is only one major gap in this mountain wall. It is the Bosporus gateway. Because of this open passage, which was dry land during much of the Pleistocene, the shores of the Black Sea were accessible to peoples moving to and from the warmer lands of western Asia, notably

[3] M. Malez: "Die Höhle Veternica, eine neue paläolitische Fundstelle in Kroatien, *BSY*, Vol. 3, No. 1 (1956), pp. 11–12.
[4] Letter dated October 23, 1959.

Palestine and Lebanon. The Acheulian hand axes found in southern Russia owe their presence to penetration from the Levant rather than from western Europe. In the days of the Neanderthals the sea-level route between the Levant and the Black Sea must have been easier to travel than the chill mountains and forests of central Europe. The Crimea, a vacation spot today, was a particular favorite of the Neanderthals. It contains many Mousterian sites, two of which, Kiik-Koba and Starosel'e, have yielded human remains.

The Kiik-Koba Tooth and Limb Bones [5]

K I I K - K O B A is a cave lying at an altitude of about 1,400 feet in the Zuya River Valley, about 15 miles east of Simferopol. It was excavated in 1924 by Bonch-Osmolovskii, who found two cultural levels: a relatively crude flake industry with a temperate fauna, and above it an evolved Mousterian with a cooler fauna. In the middle of the limestone floor of the cave the remains of a human body were buried in a shallow trench. Like the French Neanderthal burials, the trench ran east and west. At some point but still within glacial times, the burial had been disturbed and all the bones removed excepting the feet and left lower leg, which were left in their original position. From the disturbed area parts of the right hand and one incisor tooth were recovered. Although this is not certain, the skeleton was probably associated with the later culture, and belonged to Würm I. It might be older, but it is not younger.

The incisor tooth was worn down to the neck. In size and form it could fit in the western Neanderthal series.

The right hand is represented by the trapezoid and trapezium (the wrist bones nearest the thumb), by the first and fourth metacarpals, and by three proximal, four middle, and three terminal phalanges. As indicated in Fig. 75, not one of the five

[5] G. A Bonch-Osmolovskii: "Paleolit Krima, No. II, 1941, Kist iskopaemogo Cheloveka iz Grota Kiik-Koba" (Moscow-Leningrad: Izdat. Akad. Nauk SSSR; 1941).

Bonch-Osmolovskii: "No. III, 1954, Skelet stori i goleni iskopaemogo Cheloveka iz Grota Kiik-Koba" (Moscow-Leningrad: Izdat. Akad. Naut. SSSR; 1954).

H. Ullrich: "Neanderthalfunde aus der Sowjetunion," *NC*, 1958, pp. 72–106.

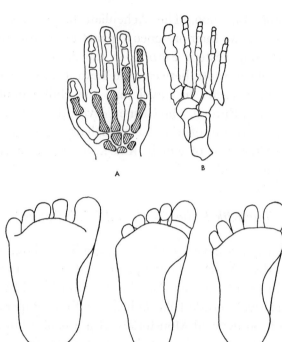

FIG. 75   NEANDERTHAL HANDS AND FEET. A. Hand skeleton from Kiik-Koba (after Bonch-Osmolovskii, 1958); B. Foot skeleton from Kiik-Koba (after Bonch Osmolovskii, 1958); C. Footprint in the cave of Basua, Toirano, Liguria, Italy (after Leonardi, 1958); D. Sole of the right foot of an Alakaluf Indian woman, Wellington Island, Chile (after a photograph by the author); E. Another footprint from the cave of Basua (after Leonardi, 1958). The Neanderthal hand skeleton (A) is short and broad, like those of many modern Russians; but no single finger is complete. The foot skeleton (B) is of the same general build. Of the two Neanderthal footprints, E is the longer (*ca.* 20 cm.). Both show a gross similarity to that of the Alakaluf woman, who walks barefoot every day in briny water. The resemblance is not racial, but convergent and adaptive. Both Neanderthals and Fuegian Indians are, or were, cold-adapted.

finger skeletons, including the metacarpal and all phalanges, is complete; it is therefore impossible to reconstruct the whole hand in its original proportions. The bones were nearly identical in size with those of La Chapelle aux Saints and larger than those of La Ferrassie 2, which suggests that Kiik-Koba was a male. The metacarpals and phalanges are very broad at the articulating ends, and the hand itself must have been correspondingly wide. The proximal end of the first metacarpal (thumb) is rounded as in La Chapelle.

The right foot, which is nearly complete, closely resembles that of the woman from La Ferrassie, except that it is larger. The total length of the foot skeleton is about 226 mm., or nine inches. It was undoubtedly masculine. The foot is long in the tarsal portion, and short in the toe. The great toe is shorter than the second one. All bones are broad, particularly in their articulating surfaces. The measurements of the individual bones closely match those of La Chapelle aux Saints. This foot could have made the prints found by Baron Blanc in an Italian cave.

Its left tibia is almost exactly the same length as the left tibia of La Chapelle aux Saints, and it is equally robust, but straighter. The fibula that matches it is also a stout bone, and has a large distal end where it articulates with the astragulus. It, too, is straight. Kiik-Koba man was probably about as tall as his French counterpart, and similarly built.

The Infant Skeleton of Starosel'e [6]

I N 1952 a Russian archaeologist, A. A. Formosov, discovered the skeleton of an infant in a cave in the Crimean village of Starosel'e, overlooking the Tschuruk-su River. Associated with it were Late Mousterian implements. The date was probably late Würm I.

Like most skeletons of infants that have been unearthed, this one was badly squashed. But M. M. Gerasimov, a Russian sculptor who is also an anthropologist, painstakingly restored the skull (see Fig. 57). The result is a startlingly modern skull; in fact it looks like a caricature of Mr. Molotov, with his bulbous forehead and square chin. The resemblance is superficial, however, because Mr. Molotov is an adult and the Starosel'e infant was only eighteen or nineteen months old.

To the unpracticed eye, the skull looks completely modern and completely Caucasoid. But babies' skulls are deceptive, and we have no Neanderthal skulls of equal age to compare it with. The forehead is high and steep, and somewhat bulbous. It is even more strongly rounded and bowed forward than most modern

---

[6] I. I. Roginskii: "Morfologischeskie Osobennosti Cherepa Rebenka i Pozdne-must'erskogo Sloia Pschery Starosel'e," *SE*, Vol. 1 (1954), pp. 27–39.
Ullrich: op. cit., pp. 72–106.

baby skulls of the same age. The face is shorter than most comparable baby faces; the mandible has a firm chin and the lower borders of the mandible spread outward. It has a distinct canine fossa. The back of the head is high and rounded. All these essential features are completely modern.

On the other hand, the vault is thick for an eighteen-months-old baby, especially the lower part of the forehead. The mastoids are weakly developed, and the milk incisors, although wide, lack the thickness of Neanderthal milk incisors. The milk molars, however, are large. In Roginskii's opinion, it would have developed heavy brow ridges had it lived, but it had none of the prowlike features of the Neanderthal nasal region.

It is either an early example of modern Caucasoid *Homo sapiens*, a product of mixture with local Neanderthals, or the end result of an evolutionary progression from Neanderthal to modern European man. Which alternative is correct cannot be decided at this point, but we shall come back to the question after describing the Würm I populations of the Levant.

The Youthful Neanderthal of Teshik-Tash [7]

IN 1938 a Russian archaeologist, A. P. Okladnikov, excavated a Mousterian deposit in a cave located in the flank of a gorge in the Baisun-Tau Mountains of southwestern Uzbekistan, about 78 miles south of Samarkand and 60 miles north of the Afghan border. The cave was Teshik-Tash. In it Okladnikov found five successive layers of habitation deposits, with hearths, Mousterian implements, and animal bones, 84 per cent of which were of one

[7] A. P. Okladnikov: "Issledovani Musterskoi Stoianki Pogrebenia Neadertal'tsa v Grote Teshik-Tash, Iuzhnyi Uzbekistan," *Sbornik Teshik-Tash* (Moscow, 1949), pp. 7–85.

N. A. Sinelnikov and M. A. Gremiatskii: "Kosti Skeleta Rebenka-Neandertal'tsa iz Grota Teshik-Tash Iuzhnyi Uzbekistan," ibid., pp. 123–36.

Gremiatskii: "Cherep Rebenka-Neandertal'tsa iz Grota Teshik-Tash Iuzhnyi Uzbekistan," ibid., pp. 137–82.

Weidenreich: "The Paleolithic Child from the Teshik-Tash Cave in Southern Uzbekistan (Central Asia)," *AJPA*, Vol. 3, No. 2 (1945), pp. 151–62.

Movius: "The Mousterian Cave of Teshik-Tash, Southeastern Uzbekistan, Central Asia," *ASPR*, Vol. 17 (1953), pp. 11–71.

Ullrich: op. cit.

species, *Capra sibirica*, a local wild goat. The other animal bones were from the modern horse, leopard, bear, hyena, and small rodents. All except the hyena, which was of the cave-dwelling variety, exist in Uzbekistan today.

In a shallow grave under the top layer Okladnikov found the remains of a nine-year-old boy surrounded by five pairs of wild goat horns. He considered it a burial, although few of the post-cranial bones were present and the skull was badly broken. Since 1938, some authors have expressed the belief that the burial had been disturbed by a hyena, others that the bones had been stripped of their flesh before being placed in the cave.[8]

Whichever may have been the case, of far greater importance for our purposes is the determination of the age of the find. The Russian scientists consider it to have been deposited in the Riss-Würm Interglacial; and although Movius believes that its date is most probably the Würm I–II Interstadial, he does not exclude the possibility of a late Third Interglacial age. In favor of a Würm I–II Interstadial dating are three facts: the climate was the same as it is today; the fauna is modern; and the industry is an evolved Mousterian. If this date is correct, the Teshik-Tash child was roughly contemporaneous with an Upper Paleolithic blade culture 150 miles to the south, in Afghanistan.[9]

Gerasimov skillfully reconstructed the child's skull from more than a hundred pieces, most of which are very small. However, about forty are large enough to permit identification and the final product is a nearly complete cranium. The mandible was intact.

The cranial capacity is 1,490 cc., and had the child lived to maturity, this capacity probably would have reached a figure of 1,600 cc. Its basic dimensions, length, breadth, and basion-bregma height (185 mm., 144 mm., and 132 mm.), can easily be matched among skulls of modern children of both European and Mongoloid populations, and its height is greater than that of the skull of any

---

[8] The argument of the anti-hyena school is that when a hyena eats a femur, he starts at the head of the bone and works down to the marrow cavity. In the Teshik-Tash specimen the femur head was intact, except for the epiphysis, and only the shaft was broken. See Ullrich: op. cit.

[9] In the cave of Kara Kamar, near Haibak. See my *The Seven Caves* (New York: Alfred A. Knopf; 1957). However, between the Upper Paleolithic blade culture and a Mesolithic level was a layer containing a still undiagnosed flake culture.

adult western European Neanderthal. The forehead is high and well rounded, the occiput somewhat bun-shaped, and the lambdoid region somewhat flattened. The brow ridges are heavy for a nine-year-old child, and continuous across the mid-line of the skull. The orbits are high and the nasion depression slight. In all pertinent details it closely resembles the frontal fragment and nasal bones of the Piñar child from Spain, said to be about eight years old.

The nasal opening is broad. There probably was no canine fossa, although this is not certain because the parts of the maxillae in which this feature is seen are missing on both sides. The maxillae are not, apparently, very much inflated by sinuses, in the western Neanderthal manner, and there is little prognathism either nasal or alveolar. The upper index of facial flatness is 22, a Caucasoid figure, and the upper edge of the orbit clearly overhangs the lower.

The mandible has a definite if weakly developed chin, and looks square in front because the lower permanent canines are fully formed but unerupted and imbedded in the bone. The teeth are larger than those of most western Neanderthals, but within the modern size range. The upper incisors are slightly shoveled, and thick at the base of the crown, with basal shelves typical of the Neanderthals.

In sum, this skull is difficult to evaluate because we lack material of a comparable age with which to contrast it. Except for the fragmentary Piñar specimen, all other youthful Neanderthal crania are either younger or older. Although the Teshik-Tash skull bears many of the hallmarks of the western Neanderthal, it is more modern-looking than most if not all of the western Neanderthal skulls, because the vault of its brain case is higher and less baggy-looking than theirs, and its face seems less muzzlelike and less puffy in the maxillae.

It is the kind of skull one would expect to find in a Neanderthal population which had not undergone the specializations of the western Neanderthals, or which had lost them, either through progressive evolution, mixture with a more modern Caucasoid people, or both. Weidenreich, in 1945, saw in it certain features characteristic of Sinanthropus, but to my mind these are less marked in the Teshik-Tash child than in Krapina or the western Neanderthals.

The postcranial bones include the atlas; twelve ribs; two clavicles, one of which is broken; the left humerus, which lacks both ends; the upper part of the right femur; the left tibia, which lacks both ends, and the shafts of both fibulae. These have been described by Sinelnikov and Gremiatskii.

The atlas is large, slenderly built, and of only medium height; its opening for the medulla is large. The clavicles are of normal size for a nine-year-old boy, and they are curved more than modern clavicles. The western Neanderthal clavicles are the opposite—they are less curved than modern ones. The ribs are more curved than those of the western Neanderthals, but some of them are triangular in section, like one of the ribs of La Chapelle aux Saints. The humerus shaft is straight and without torsion. The femur is modern in size and proportions, with none of the extreme bowing seen in western Neanderthal femora. Its neck goes off the shaft at a wider angle (130°) than that of the western Neanderthal ones. The tibia is thick, triangular in section, and straight, and the fibulas are straight and of the proper length for a modern Caucasoid.

From the neck down, therefore, the nine-year-old boy of Teshik-Tash was a modern Caucasoid in all essential respects; his body was even less Neanderthaloid than his skull. He was not, however, unique. We shall see others like him in Western Asia; in Iraq, Palestine, and Lebanon.

The Eastern Neanderthals of Shanidar

IN 1949 a Turkish archaeologist, I. K. Kökten, found two teeth in a Mousterian deposit in a cave near Adalia, on the southern shore of Anatolia. These teeth have been identified as Neanderthaloid.[1] In 1954 M. S. Şenyürek, a specialist on fossil teeth, and E. Bostanci, a physical anthropologist, discovered three more such teeth in a lake-shore cave at the foot of Musa Dagh, some 700

[1] M. S. Şenyürek: "A Short Preliminary Report on the Two Fossil Teeth from the Cave of Karain . . . ," *Belleten,* Vol. 13, No. 52 (1949), pp. 833–6.

miles to the east-northeast.[2] These widely separated sites indicate the presence of Neanderthal man, and his Mousterian culture, in Turkey.

In 1949 I found a piece of strongly bowed ulna and a lower incisor tooth in Bisitun Cave in the western flank of the Zagros Mountains of Iran, along with an evolved Mousterian industry, and also what seems to be a small piece of human femur shaft in Tamtama Cave, on the east side of the Zagros, in Iranian Azerbaijan.[3] I am not certain that these three specimens belonged to Neanderthals, although the ulna fragment looks as if it did; all I know is that some kind of man lived in or near the Zagros Mountains during Würm I or the Würm I–II Interstadial. The Turkish teeth and these Iranian finds half encircle the site of Shanidar, in which Ralph Solecki found seven Neanderthal skeletons between 1953 and 1960.

Shanidar is a huge, majestic cave in the western Zagros of northern Iraq, inhabited from early Mousterian times to the present; several Kurdish families still live in it. Now and then, owing to an earthquake or to the formation of ice in cracks in the roof, slabs of limestone crash to the floor, killing everyone below. In 1953 Solecki found a baby's skeleton; in 1957, three adult skeletons, numbered 1, 2, and 3; and in 1960 three more.

All lay in Mousterian deposits. Shanidar 1 has been given a Carbon-14 date of 46,000 ± 1,500 years;[4] Shanidar 3 was perhaps a few hundred years older. Shanidar 2 and the baby were probably about 60,000 years old, and the 1960 skeletons probably 60,000 years old or older. Shanidar 1 was found at the very top of the Mousterian deposit, indicating that the cave may have been abandoned during the height of the Würm I cold, after which, judging by the overlying deposits, it was reoccupied by Upper Paleolithic people about 35,000 years ago, during the Würm I–II Interstadial.

[2] Şenyürek and E. Bostanci: "The Excavation of a Cave Near the Village of Mağracik in the Vilayet of the Hatay, Preliminary Notice," *Anatolia*, Vol. 1 (1956), pp. 81–3.

[3] C. S. Coon: "Cave Explorations in Iran, 1949," *UMM*, 1951.

[4] R. S. Solecki: "Three Adult Neanderthal Skeletons from Shanidar Cave, Northern Iraq," *SRP*, No. 4414 (1959–60), pp. 603–35. The C-14 date number is GRO-2527.

To date, the baby's teeth have been studied,[5] and called Neanderthal, and preliminary reports on Shanidar 1 have been published by T. D. Stewart.[6] Other reports should appear shortly.

Shanidar 1 and 2 were males, and Şenyürek believes that the baby was a girl. The others have not yet been sexed. Shanidar 3 was not killed by rockfall but was buried against the cave wall. A projectile point, found in his rib cage, may have been the cause of death.

Shanidar 1 died at about age forty. He was approximately five feet seven or eight inches tall (170–173 cm.), four or five inches taller than the French Neanderthals whose statures have been computed.[7] Judging from published photographs, his limb proportions were normal for Caucasoids and unlike those of La Chapelle aux Saints and his western European companions.

Because Shanidar 1 had been born with a damaged brachial plexus, his right scapula and clavicle were atrophied and his right arm hung limply until some time before death, when a Neanderthal surgeon amputated it above the elbow, presumably with a flint knife. Either before or after this successful operation, Shanidar 1 had been severely wounded by blows with a sharp instrument around and particularly above the left eye, which may then have been blinded. He also had a bone lesion from a blow on the right parietal. Despite these injuries and adventures he died at home, standing in his own cave, crushed by a slab of limestone.

When the complete measurements are available,[8] Shanidar 1's skull may prove to be the largest fossil-man skull of its date or earlier yet found. The cranial capacity is probably well over

[5] Şenyürek: "The Skeleton of the Fossil Infant Found in Shanidar Cave, Northern Iraq, Preliminary Report," *Anatolia*, Vol. 2 (1957), pp. 49–55.
Şenyürek: "A Further Note on the Paleolithic Shanidar Infant," *Anatolia*, Vol. 2 (1957), pp. 111–21.

[6] T. D. Stewart: "First Views of the Restored Shanidar I Skull," *Sumer*, Vol. 14, Nos. 1–2 (1958), pp. 90–6.
Stewart: "Restoration and Study of the Shanidar I Neanderthal Skeleton in Baghdad, Iraq," *YAPS*, 1958, pp. 274–8.
Stewart: "The Restored Shanidar I Skull," *SRP*, No. 4369 (1958), pp. 473–8.
Stewart: "Form of the Pubic Bone in Neanderthal Man," *Science*, Vol. 131, No. 3411 (1960), pp. 1437–8.

[7] This figure was calculated by Stewart from the length of the ulna; a more accurate estimate will be made when the leg bones are described.

[8] Any figures given here are tentative, made from scale drawings and photographs.

1,700 cc. The forehead is sloping, but the parietal arc is greater than the frontal, as in modern men, and both the parietal and occipital profiles are well rounded. Seen from the front and rear, the brain case lacks the bagging or "soft watch" appearance of the western Neanderthals; in this respect it resembles Teshik-Tash.

The face is as long as those of La Chapelle aux Saints and La Ferrassie 1; and characteristically of Neanderthals, the bizygomatic face breadth is less than the breadth of the brain case. The brow ridges are heavy and overlie extensive sinuses; but unlike those of the western Neanderthals, they do not form a continuous bar over the nose but are divided, as in most other early skulls. The nasal bones, which are intact, rise high under the frontal, and the nasal profile is projecting. The orbits, which are large and rounded, fall away to either side, giving the skull an index of upper facial flatness of about 27, which is almost super-Caucasoid.

Yet morphologically the face closely resembles those of the French Neanderthals. The maxillary bone is puffy both under the orbits and over the canines and does not have a canine fossa. The face is prognathous only in the upper or nasal portion. Inside the nasal aperture the floor of the cavity falls away steeply, giving the nasal passages more depth than one would expect from the size of the opening. La Chapelle aux Saints and La Ferrassie 1 apparently also possessed this feature, but one cannot be completely sure because of the damage to their nasal bones after death.

The mandible is deep, and it is shaped essentially like those of the French Neanderthals, except that it has more chin than all but La Ferrassie 1, and its lower border is square in front. All the teeth but the two lower median incisors are present, and all are heavily worn. In size and form they resemble those of other Neanderthals. The canines and incisors are worn not only on the crowns but on their anterior surfaces, as if Shanidar 1 had held objects in his teeth to compensate for the loss of his right hand. The teeth of La Ferrassie 1 are similarly worn, and he also had a damaged arm.

Other details of the postcranial skeleton remain to be described. However, Stewart has studied the pubic bones of Shanidar 1 and

3. In each of them the upper ramus of the bone is thin and plate-like, flattened from above and below. In modern Caucasoid pelves, if not in all others, the ascending ramus of the pubis is much thicker. No pubic bones of the western Neanderthals are available for comparison, but, as we shall see presently, the pubic bone of a Neanderthal woman from Palestine, Tabun 1, is similar to those of Shanidar 1 and 3. Stewart sees in this feature as great a difference between the Neanderthals and modern men as in the form of their head and face.

He has also stated that because Shanidar 1 and 3 lived late in Würm I in what has always been a marginal, refuge area, they lived too long to have sired modern Caucasoid man. But evolution was moving at a faster pace on the eastern shore of the Mediterranean, in Palestine particularly, as we have known since the excavation of the Mount Carmel caves some thirty years ago.

The Inhabitants of Palestine During Würm I

ALTHOUGH human remains from the Last Interglacial are virtually nonexistent in Palestine, remains from Würm I are fairly abundant. They come from six caves: Zuttiya, near the Sea of Galilee;[9] Tabun and Skhul at Mount Carmel;[1] Jebel Qafza, near Nazareth;[2] Shukba in the Wadi Natuf, seventeen and half miles northwest of Jerusalem; and Amud, near Lake Tiberias.[3]

[9] F. Turville-Petre: *Researches in Prehistoric Galilee, 1925–6* (London: British School of Archaeology in Jerusalem; 1927).

Hrdlička: op. cit.

[1] A. Keith and T. D. McCown: *The Stone Age of Mt. Carmel* (Oxford: Clarendon Press; 1939), Vol. 2.

C. E. Snow: "The Ancient Palestinian: Skhul V Reconstruction," *BASP*, Vol. 17 (1955), pp. 5–10.

[2] R. Neuville: "Le Paléolithique du Désert de Judée," *AIPH*, Mem. 24 (1951), pp. 179–84.

[3] Keith: *New Discoveries Relating to the Antiquity of Man* (London: Williams & Norgate; 1931), Chap. 13–14, for Shukba.

H. Suzuki, personal communication, Nov. 16, 1961, concerning the Amud Cave skeleton.

For the entire group, see Howell: "Upper Pleistocene Men of the Southwest Asian Mousterian," *NC*, 1958, pp. 185–98.

The names of these sites are rendered here in a close approximation of correct Arabic transliteration. Elsewhere the reader will see some of them spelled in French transliteration, e.g., Djebel Kafzeh, which is incorrect. I have omitted the words *Mugharet al* (Cave of the) wherever they occur.

Some of these remains may be older than the Shanidar skeletons, others of the same age or younger. It is difficult to tell because all but the new skeleton from Lake Tiberias, which has not
yet been studied, were excavated before the Carbon-14 dating
technique had been invented. It is not correct to call these skeletons, as a group, Neanderthals. Only one deserves that name in
the strict sense. Others are modern Caucasoids, and still others
intermediate between both extremes. One of them does not seem
to be either Neanderthal or modern Caucasoid, but looks Australoid. This is a varied and complex group of skeletons which we
must use every means at our disposal to study, for in it may be the
key to the problem of modern European and western Asiatic Caucasoid origins.

The Galilee skull, from Zuttiya, consists of a frontal bone and
parts of the right zygomatic, the nasal bones, and the sphenoid.
Galilee man died at about twenty-five years of age. Keith first
called it a female, then a male; Hrdlička identified it as an "effemi-
nate" male. From Tabun come a previously mentioned molar and
piece of femur shaft of Third Interglacial date, a complete female
skeleton known as Tabun 1, and a mandible, Tabun 2. Breccias
at Skhul have yielded parts of ten skeletons, consisting of five
adult males, Nos. 3, 4, 5, 6, and 9; two adult females, Nos.
2 and 7; one male child, No. 8; and two infants, Nos. 1 and 10;
and assorted postcranial bones of at least two other individuals.
Jebel Qafza's contribution is five adults and one infant, all still
unstudied, and Shukba's is seven children and one adult, also undescribed.[4] So is the Lake Tiberias skeleton, discovered by H. Suzuki in 1961.

The date of the Galilee skull is uncertain. It is either the end
of the Last Interglacial or early Würm I. Tabun 1 and 2 are early
Würm I, and the rest are later Würm I. Recent investigations by
D. Brothwell and E. S. Higgs at Cambridge[5] have shown that
Tabun 1 and 2 are about 10,000 years older than the Skhul group.
According to Brothwell, we can divide all these Palestinian

---

[4] The Jebel Qafza remains were found in 1933; those of Shukba in 1928.

[5] E. S. Higgs and D. R. Brothwell: "North Africa and Mount Carmel: Recent
Developments," *Man*, Vol. 61, No. 166 (1961), pp. 138–9.

Brothwell: "The People of Mt. Carmel," *PPS*, October–December 1961, pp.
155–9.

skeletons into two lots, an older one, including Galilee and the Tabuns, and a younger one, including those from Skhul, Jebel Qafza, and Shukba.

Tabun and Galilee

T H E Tabun material from the Acheulian deposit of Last Inter-glacial age consists of a femur shaft with both ends missing, and a lower first molar tooth. The femur shaft is flattened from front to back and has a weak linea aspera and no pilaster. The bone is not strongly bowed. The tooth, which is badly worn, is indistinguish-able from those of Tabun 1 and 2. Both femur and tooth can be called Neanderthaloid, to the same extent that the specimens from Ehringsdorf and Krapina can be so called.

The same may be said of the Galilee skull fragment. It has heavy brow ridges divided in the middle by a depression, and a well-rounded forehead of moderate breadth. The zygomatic (malar) bone is not massive and is so shaped that the face may have had a canine fossa. The orbits are of moderate size and rectangular; the interorbital distance is great; and the nasal bones are arched from side to side. The Galilee skull could have evolved from a Last Interglacial pre-Neanderthal population like that of central Europe.

Tabun 1 was a short woman, about five feet tall (154 cm.). Her cranial capacity was 1,270 cc., the same as that of the female Gibraltar 1, and the skull as a whole is small. The brow ridges are heavy and continuous, the forehead retreating but curved, and the parietal and occipital bones well rounded. There is no lamb-doid flattening, nor an occipital bun. Although the vault is low, with its greatest breadth well to the rear of the earholes, it lacks the baggy configuration of the western Neanderthals. The orbits are rounded; the face is long but in no sense prognathous; the nose was apparently prominent and the chin retreating. The tooth line forms an angle to the eye-ear plane, so that the mouth opened somewhat downward; and the chinless profile of the lower jaw is retreating to a large degree. The teeth are of moderate size for a Neanderthal, but the incisors are characteristically thick, with a distinct heel or shelf at the base on the tongue side.

The male mandible, Tabun 2, is large, deep, and squarish in front. Its ascending ramuses are spread far apart to accommodate a broad cranial base. In sagittal profile it is concave below the tooth line and convex toward the chin, like the mandibles of Ehringsdorf and Shanidar 1.

In general morphology the Tabun 1 skull and the Tabun 2 jaw fall between the central Europeans of the Last Interglacial and the western Neanderthals, and possess some special features that are also present in the Skhul series. They also resemble Shanidar 1 in those features in which they deviate from the western Neanderthals.

Tabun 1's postcranial skeleton confirms this diagnosis. Her vertebrae, few of which were preserved, are short-bodied; her ribs rounded in section and deeply curved; her sternum long. Her scapulae resemble those of La Chapelle aux Saints, and her clavicle is long for her stature. Her humerus is not stout, but its head is directed somewhat upward as in the western Neanderthals and its distal end is large, with a large olecranon fossa. Her lower arm bones, radius and ulna, are widely separated as a result of bowing; the head of the ulna is long, and the distal end of the radius is wide. The hand is slenderer than that of La Ferrassie 1; her thumb is short and her terminal phalanges long and slender.

Her pubic bone is flattened like those of Shanidar 1 and 3. Her femur is flattened, but not very curved, and its neck is long. The tibia is short and thick; the fibula rounded in section, like that of La Chapelle aux Saints. Her foot is as long as that of a modern western European woman of the same stature, but broader, with the emphasis on the outer side of the foot; and her big toe was short. In general, her feet resemble those of La Ferrassie 2 and are less spatulate than Kiik-Koba's.

Tabun 1 looks on the whole like a Third Interglacial European woman who had acquired some but not all of the western Neanderthal specializations, or she might be a Neanderthal who had lost some of these specializations through mixture. She fits into the Asiatic Neanderthal population as we are beginning to know it from Shanidar and Teshik-Tash; and her upper face and frontal bone were a little more Neanderthaloid than the Galilee fragment. Whether or not she was an ancestress of the tall men who, some ten thousand years later, were buried in a neighboring cave, we shall do our best to discover.

The Skhul Skulls: No. 4 and His Group

T H E   S K U L L S   from the Skhul cave fall naturally into two groups. Number 4 is the best preserved of the first group, and Numbers 2, 7, and 9, although more fragmentary, are whole enough to show a family resemblance to it. These four skulls show both Neanderthal and modern Caucasoid features. The second group consists of Skhul 5, the best known and most completely restored of all, and probably also of Number 6, which is too fragmentary to be aligned with certainty in either camp. These skulls are neither Neanderthaloid nor Caucasoid but belong to a different racial line. The other four are either the skulls of babies, or adult specimens too fragmentary for racial identification. As Skhul 5 is generally considered the type specimen of the entire cave population, the difference between the two groups may come as a surprise to those who have not studied the other skulls with equal care.

Skhul 4 was a male, about forty-five years old and five feet eight and a half inches tall (174 cm.). Most of his skull is preserved, but the region around glabella and nasion is missing. It is a large skull, with a cranial capacity of 1,554 cc., long and low-vaulted, but no lower than many modern European crania. It has a thick, wide brow ridge, as big as that of La Chapelle aux Saints; a wide mandible; a long face; and a deep palate.

In sagittal profile it looks much like La Chapelle aux Saints, with two principal exceptions. Its occiput is rounded and not bun-shaped. Its nose projected in a beak, but the facial skeleton between the lower border of the nasal opening and the tooth line is drawn backward and flat. There is no prognathism, either nasal or alveolar. There is no canine fossa. The face is as long as those of the western Neanderthals, and the palate as deep; but the mandible has a firm chin. The parietals do not project sidewise as in the western Neanderthals, and the zygomatic arches flare widely, as in modern men who chew heavily, making heavy use of their temporal muscles.

If we shift our comparison from the western Neanderthals to Shanidar 1, we see that to make Shanidar I into Skhul 4 one need only deflate the facial sinuses and pull back the palate. Skhul 4 looks like an evolutionary product from an earlier eastern Neanderthal base through Tabun toward a rugged, long-headed modern Caucasoid. Skulls which are called Nordic and which resemble it in general form but with smaller brow ridges appear in northern Europe from the Neolithic onward, and particularly in the Iron Age.

Skhul 9, another male, had a cranial capacity of 1,587 cc., the same type of brain case as Skhul 4, and the same hyperorthognathous (the opposite of prognathous) facial structure, and probably the same kind of nose.

Skhul 2, a female five feet four inches tall (162.5 cm.), with a cranial capacity of 1,300 cc., is a feminine version of Skhul 4. So, as far as we can tell, for the skull is very crushed, was Skhul 7, a female five feet two inches tall (158 cm.), with heavy brow ridges and a long face.

The skulls of this group show an orderly progression from a Neanderthal to a modern European form.

The Skull of Skhul 5

EXCEPT possibly for Skhul 6, a thirty-five-year-old male who was five feet seven and a half inches tall (171 cm.) and of whose skull we have only an occiput, Number 5 is unique. He bears little resemblance to the Neanderthals before or the Nordics after him; rather, he looks in many ways non-Caucasoid.

He was about thirty-five years old, five feet eleven inches tall (180.6 cm.), and had a cranial capacity of 1,518 cc. The sagittal profile of his skull starts with the usual heavy brow ridge, then rises steeply and is well rounded the rest of the way, except for a short interval of flattening at lambda. The skull has an ill-filled look, like those of Australian aborigines, with prominent parietal bosses. Seen from above, the brow ridge is nearly a straight bar, instead of a bow curved backward at each end as it is in the Neanderthals and Skhul 4. Deep under glabella the stubs of his nasal bones remain, fused into a single flat plate. His orbits are low and square, and their sides form only shallow curves. This feature, combined with his deeply set nasal root and flat nasal bones, give him a flat upper face, with an index of upper facial flatness of only 13.5, below any living racial mean and closest to some of the ancient Australoid skulls, notably Wadjak 1, and to some of the Bushmen. His upper jaw is very prognathous subnasally, and the teeth in his lower jaw project well beyond his chin, as in Wadjak 2.

To my mind, Skhul 5 was not fully Caucasoid, and the features in which he deviated from the Caucasoid line cannot be brushed away as evolutionary grades. They are essentially Australoid. These comparisons are not surprising in view of the geographical position of Palestine at the crossroads of the Old World and the fact that its fauna during Würm I was a mixture of Oriental, Ethiopian, and Palearctic species.

Skhul 4 and his group seem to represent a station on an evolutionary line from something like Swanscombe and Steinheim via a local equivalent of the European Third Interglacial group to Tabun 1 and an ancestor of Shanidar 1. Skhul 5 patently represents the product of a contact between the line just mentioned and members of another subspecies.

The Mount Carmel Teeth

THE PICTURE that is beginning to emerge is supported by a study of the teeth. Keith and McCown published descriptions of sixty-five permanent and three milk teeth from Tabun and seventy-one permanent and twelve milk teeth from Skhul. None is markedly taurodont, nor do any possess unusual enamel patterns like those seen at Krapina.

In the unworn Tabun incisors and canines may be seen a moderate shoveling with a labial heel, which takes the form of a cingulum in one canine. One of the Tabun upper median incisors has three tubercles and others have vertical ridging. The premolars are relatively small, and the molars show no distinctive features.

The Skhul teeth resemble those of Tabun but have less shovel-

ing and ridging. Keith and McCown saw in this series a sequence from Krapina to Tabun to Skhul. Yet between Skhul 4 and
Skhul 5 certain differences may be detected. Skhul 5's palate is
enormous, big enough to fit Heidelberg or Wadjak 2. Its upper
incisors and canines show none of the Krapina-Neanderthal characters; and in Flower's index, the ratio between cheek teeth (the
premolar-molar row) and the basion-nasion diameter, it reaches
the high figure of 49.2 (see Chapter 8, page 353). This is extremely macrodont, beyond even the Tasmanian mean, whereas
Skhul 4's Flower's index is only 41.5, which is microdont and
Caucasoid. Although these contrasting ratios do not involve tooth
size as such, they involve the relationship between tooth size and
the proportions of the skull base and face. The combination is
racially diagnostic, and in this comparison its meaning is clear.

The Postcranial Skeletons of the Skhul Population

THE POSTCRANIAL skeletons of the Mount Carmel population are not divided into the same three categories as the skulls,
but possess a separate dichotomy of their own. Essentially, Tabun 1 and Skhul 7 form one distinct category, and all the others
form a second category. Skhul 4 and Skhul 5, which differ crani-
ally, are alike in the sense that both were tall men with slender
limb bones and relatively long forearms and lower legs. But
Skhul 7, a female whose skull belongs to the group exemplified
by Skhul 4, differs from the others found in the same cave in that
her long bones resemble, in certain respects, those of Tabun 1
and of the Neanderthals from western Europe and Shanidar.

We have vertebrae from Skhul 4 and 5 only. Skhul 5's neck
was short, and its vertebrae small. Skhul 4's dorsal vertebrae
were large enough to match his limb bones, but narrow from front
to back and perforated by large neural canals. His ribs were also
modern, except that the lower part of the rib cage was unusually
large. In both specimens the scapulae are small, indicating narrow shoulders, and they have a lipped groove along the axillary
margin which Boule had found earlier in La Chapelle aux Saints.
The clavicles are modern, the humeri long and slender, with small
olecranon fossae. The radii and ulnae are long in proportion to

their humeri, as in living Australoids and Negroids, but not long enough to exceed the modern European range. The forearm bones are curved, in the usual Neanderthal fashion, in only one skeleton, the female Skhul 7. The olecranon process, long in Neanderthals, is of normal European proportions in the Skhul males.

Skhul 4 had large, long hands, and Skhul 5 had similarly shaped hands, which were small for his stature. The pelves are modern, without the pubic specialization of Tabun 1 and Shanidar; and like the pelves of Krapina, they are narrow-hipped. The femurs are long and straight except for that of the female Skhul 9, which is very bowed. In the angle between the axis of the neck and head of the femur to the axis of its shaft, Skhul 4 and 5 again part company. Skhul 4 has an angle of 122°, a Neanderthaloid feature; Skhul 5's angle is 132°, a modern one. In this angle the faceless Skhul 6 resembles Skhul 5 (its angle is 135°), as it does in other respects.

The Skhul tibiae are long, so long in the males as to give the two segments of the leg—the thigh and lower leg—Negroid or Australoid proportions. All but that of Skhul 7 are sharp on the leading edge, like modern European shins, but the tibiae of Skhul 7 are rounded, in Neanderthal fashion. We have only two whole feet, from Skhul 4 and Skhul 7. Number 4's foot is long, slender, and modern; Number 7's is similar to that of Tabun 1.

In sum, Skhul 4 and Skhul 5 are alike from the neck down, but of the two, Skhul 4 was the stockier and had two Neanderthaloid features, a large lower rib cage and a low femoral neck-to-shaft angle. Skhul 5 lacked at least the second of these, and was more Negroid or Australoid in build than Skhul 4. The female Skhul 7 shows a number of Neanderthaloid features in her extremities: widely bowed forearm bones, a round-sectioned tibia, and a Tabun-like foot. Skhul 9, for whom few bones are available, also had a Neanderthaloid femur.

The Meaning of the Mount Carmel Skeletons

E V E R   S I N C E the discovery of the Mount Carmel skeletons, anthropologists and anatomists, myself included, have been discussing their significance. In 1939 I expressed the opinion, later shared by others,[6] that the Mount Carmel population was the product of a mixture between a local Neanderthal group comparable to those known from western Europe, and a more modern stock. At the time I wrote, no eastern Neanderthals had been described (although Teshik-Tash had already been discovered) and Keith's and McCown's monumental work was not yet available. All we had to work with was essentially a preliminary description of Tabun 1, Skhul 5, and the western Neanderthal material.

My present position is that, except for Skhul 5, the Mount Carmel population shows an orderly descent from a local, Last Interglacial population similar to that of Ehringsdorf and Krapina, in a modern, Caucasoid direction. Like the Ehringsdorf-Krapina group, this local population had become partially specialized in a Neanderthal direction and this specialization had reached a peak in Tabun 1. In the Skhul skeletons this specialization was, apparently, being progressively lost. Whether as a statistical accident, for the series is small, or by some mechanism such as sex-linkage, it was, apparently, being lost more rapidly in the males than in the females.

Had Skhul 5 never been found, there would have been little reason to talk of hybridization. But Skhul 5 was not only found; it was publicized as the type specimen of the Mount Carmel population. Its differences from the others buried in the same cave at presumably the same period are not differences of grade but of line. Its face is Australoid, and it resembles the skulls from Wadjak more than any others that I have been able to find. Strongly implied is a contact between Caucasoids and Australoids in some part of southern Asia.

When other Palestinian skeletons of Würm I, from Jebel Qafza, Shukba, and other sites yet to be excavated, have been described, we shall be in a better position to interpret the racial variations

[6] C. S. Coon: *The Races of Europe* (New York: The Macmillan Company; 1939), p. 38.

M. F. Ashley-Montagu's review of A. Keith and T. D. McCown: *The Stone Age of Mt. Carmel*, in *AA*, Vol. 42 (1940), pp. 518–22.

T. Dobzhansky: "On Species and Races in Fossil Man," *AJPA*, Vol. 2 (1944), pp. 251–65.

A. Thoma: "Métissage ou Transformation? Essai sur les Hommes Fossiles de Palestine, *L'Anth.*, Vol. 62, No. 1–2 (1958), pp. 30–52.

seen at Skhul. One Jebel Qafza skull, No. 6,[7] looks more modern than any of the Skhul specimens. Essentially it is the same as the Upper Paleolithic skulls from western Europe, which we shall presently describe.

Egbert, the Boy from Ksar 'Akil

I N 1938 two American Jesuit priests, Fathers J. G. Doherty and J. Franklin Ewing, who were excavating the cave site of Ksar 'Akil, about seven miles northeast of Beirut, in Lebanon, discovered the skeleton of a male child who had died in his seventh year. Later Father Ewing restored the skull, and a plaster cast of it is available, but full details have not been published.[8] Father Ewing named it Egbert, and this name has had wide circulation.

The date is Würm I, the same as that of the Palestinian specimens just described. Although the skull was broken in many pieces and there are gaps in the reconstruction, there can be no doubt about Egbert's evolutionary and racial status. The brain case is perfectly modern; there are no brow ridges; the forehead is steep, the face orthognathous, and the chin firm. Egbert was a modern Caucasoid, and probably would have grown into a man resembling Jebel Qafza 6 had he lived. Moreover, the Starosel'e infant might have grown to look like Egbert had his life been spared for another six years.

Between the Würm I Palestinians and Egbert and Starosel'e, there is a perfectly valid transition from earlier Caucasoid people to Upper Paleolithic Europeans.

More About Neanderthal Origins

I N T H E light of what we have learned about the eastern Neanderthals, including in a wide sense the Palestinian and Lebanese skeletons of Würm I, we may return to the discussion of Neanderthal origins left open on page 558.

[7] Judging from its photograph (see Plate XXVIII). Its dimensions have not yet been published.

[8] J. F. Ewing: "Human Types and Prehistoric Cultures at Ksar 'Akil, Lebanon," *FICA*, 1960, pp. 535–9.

D. A. Hooijer: "The Fossil Vertebrates of Ksar 'Akil, a Paleolithic Rock Shelter in the Lebanon," *ZV*, No. 49 (1961).

It is clear that the Neanderthals, eastern and western, were derived, at least in large part, from the preceding Caucasoids of the Last Interglacial, but it is not certain whether the distinctive Neanderthal traits, both cranial and postcranial, arose through mutation and selection alone, or were introduced into Europe and western Asia by mixture with a non-Caucasoid population.

The finds from Teshik-Tash and Shanidar do not support, nor do they completely disprove, the theory of mixture with Sinanthropus-descended Mongoloids across the mountain spine of north-central Asia. However, the theory that the Saccopastore people, whose skulls were the first to bear a Neanderthaloid stamp, could have been the product of mixture between local Caucasoids and North Africans is enhanced, purely fortuitously, by Keith's and McCown's painstaking work on the Mount Carmel skeletons.

In studying the postcranial bones of this series, Keith and McCown compared them with the skeleton of a South African Bushman and expressed their surprise at finding in the latter many striking resemblances to the skeleton of Tabun 1, and also to that of the western Neanderthal, La Chapelle aux Saints. These resemblances may be seen in the vertebrae, the ischial part of the pelvis, the sciatic notch, and the limb bones, including the hands and feet, and particularly the wrists and ankles.

These resemblances are too numerous and too striking to be dismissed as concidental on the grounds that it is a long way from South Africa to Sicily. As I shall indicate in the next chapter, the ancestors of the Bushmen, who were then full-sized people, probably lived in North Africa at the time of the Saccopastores, and what remains we have of these pre-Würm North Africans resemble Sinanthropus in details of the face, jaws, and teeth.

It is therefore easier to suppose that, if the Sinanthropus-like features of the Saccopastores were due to race mixture, the alien element came overseas from Cape Bon to Sicily, a distance of only 90 miles (60 if the immigrants stopped on the way at Pantellaria), rather than that they walked overland all the way from China. Once they were in western Europe, and once the cold of Würm I had set in, natural selection may have placed a premium on these features, and the Neanderthal race came into being.

Of the three theories of Neanderthal origins—(1) mutation

and natural selection within a western European population during the Last Interglacial and Würm I, (2) an infusion of favorable genes from the descendants of Sinanthropus in China, and (3) a penetration of Sinanthropus-like genes from North Africa— the third seems the most likely at the time of writing, but the other two should not be forgotten. Ten years from now all three theories may have been proven wrong.

The Upper Paleolithic People and Their Culture

I N   E U R O P E   the Würm I–II or Göttweig Interstadial, lasting from about 40,000 to about 29,000 B.C., was a period of mild, but not hot, climate, like that of the present, and of favored spots like Palestine during Würm I. It was a time of important racial and cultural change. During it, the Neanderthals were replaced by Upper Paleolithic people similar to modern Europeans, and the Mousterian flake culture was succeeded by a blade culture that endured, in many forms and under many names, to the end of the Pleistocene, around 8,000 B.C. Similar but not indentical blade cultures have been found in Siberia, in northern Afghanistan, in the Zagros Mountains of Iraq and Iran, in Turkey, and in Lebanon, Syria, and Palestine.

A favorite cliché of anthropology, as widespread as the image of the brutal Neanderthals, is that Upper Paleolithic Europeans belonged to three races: the Crô-Magnon, which was Caucasoid; the Negroid Grimaldis; and the Eskimoid race of Chancelade. This concept is a product of the type-specimen procedure. There was, in fact, only one Upper Paleolithic European race. It was Caucasoid and it inhabits Europe today. We know this not only from skeletons but also from the representations of the human body in Upper Paleolithic art.

There was, as well, in the broad sense only one culture, although archaeological splitters, after the fashion of their zoological brethren, as defined in Chapter 1, are constantly dividing, subdividing, and recombining it, treating the divisions as separate cultures. Where sites are abundant, as in France, subdivisions of cultures appear, vanish, and reappear in a manner perplexing even to specialists. We are led to wonder whether these sequences indicate invasions, diffusions of new techniques of making tools, or a combination of both. I feel that the local populations remained fairly constant but that genes flowed freely enough from one region to another to prevent the rise of genetically different races inside the Caucasoid subspecies. My concept of racial and cultural homogeneity seems to be supported by the fact that Upper Paleolithic art styles show a remarkable continuity over a span of 20,000 years.

In my opinion, the origins of the Upper Paleolithic culture have been determined in a general way, but not all professional archaeologists agree with me. I believe that this culture and its accompanying racial type were imported into Europe and could have come only from the East. Claims have been made that the culture arose from a Mousterian prototype in Hungary, but the only part of the Old World in which a blade culture is known to have arisen from a flake culture in Würm I is the Near East—Palestine, Syria, Lebanon, and possibly western Iran.[9]

Also, the makers of the blade tools were modern men, similar enough anatomically to the Upper Paleolithic Europeans to have been their ancestors. Palestine, Lebanon, and Syria are on the Mediterranean coast, and anyone who walked west and then north along the shores of Anatolia would soon find himself either in Greece or on the shores of the Black Sea. This is the water-level route that makers of hand axes followed in the Second Interglacial; and makers of blade tools could just as well have traveled it in the Göttweig Interstadial.

This is a logical and attractive theory, but it is too soon for us to adopt it without reservation. In Turkey, Iran, and Afghanistan many caves remain to be excavated, and who knows what will turn up in them? It is not too soon, though, for us to feel that in turning to the East we are on the right track.

[9] For a detailed review of the extensive literature on this subject, including the pioneer work of Dorothy Garrod, see:

Howell: "Upper Pleistocene Stratigraphy and Early Man in the Levant," *PAPS*, Vol. 103, No. 1 (1959), pp. 1–65.

E. Anati: *Palestine Before the Hebrews* (New York: Alfred A. Knopf; 1962).

For the Iranian evidence, see also R. J. Braidwood, B. Howe, and C. A. Reed: "The Iranian Prehistoric Project," *Science*, Vol. 133, No. 3469 (1961), pp. 2008–10.

According to Movius's interpretation of about 120 Carbon-14 dates,[1] the Göttweig Interstadial began about 40,000 B.C. and ended about 29,000 B.C. At its end intense cold set in. This marked the beginning of Würm II, or, as Movius calls it, the Early Phase of the Main Würm. It lasted about 2,000 years. Then came a long interval of generally cold conditions, known as Würm III or the Late Phase of the Main Würm. This lasted some 17,200 years and was followed by two short cycles, each of which consisted of a mild and a cold episode, totaling about two thousand years and ending with the close of the Pleistocene, about 8,000 B.C.

According to Movius's reconstruction, there were four main Upper Paleolithic industries in the Dordogne region, which is the key area for Europe, because it contains the most complex sequence and because more Upper Paleolithic digging has been done there than anywhere else. First came the Perigordian, then the Aurignacian, then a foretaste of the Magdalenian, then the final Aurignacian, followed by the Solutrean, and then the rest of the Magdalenian.

The Perigordian was a local industry, the oldest in that region. The Aurignacian was a widespread industry, ranging from Spain to Russia, and in central Europe it was probably as old as the Perigordian was in France. The Solutrean was also widespread but sporadic, with centers in Spain and Hungary, and the Magdalenian, which was probably derived from the Aurignacian, was also widespread. In England there was only one industry, the Creswellian, a local equivalent of the Aurignacian, and it lasted until the end of the Pleistocene.

Upper Paleolithic Sites in Space and Time

T A B L E 30[2] lists the Upper Paleolithic sites that have yielded human skeletal material. I have not stated which bones were

[1] Movius: "Radiocarbon Dates and Upper Paleolithic Archaeology," *CA*, Vol. 1, No. 5–6 (1960), pp. 355–91.

[2] All but four sites in this list may be found in the *Catalogue des Hommes Fossiles* of Vallois and Movius. The four exceptions may be found in:

(1) Movius and Vallois: "Crane Proto-Magdalénien et Vénus du Perigordien Final Trouvés dans l'Abri Pataud, Les Eyzies (Dordogne)," *L'Anth*, Vol. 63, No. 3–4 (1959), pp. 213–32. A complete female skull, proto-Magdalenian.

(2) D. Ferembach: "Note sur une Mandibule Presumée du Magdalénien III,"

TABLE 30
UPPER PALEOLITHIC FOSSIL MAN SITES

COUNTRY	CULTURE	COUNTRY	CULTURE
Germany—12		Limeuil, Dordogne	M
Andernach am Rhein	M	Lussac-le-Château, Vienne	M
Fühlingen, near Köln	A	*La Madaleine, Dordogne	M
Honert, nr. Dortmund	A	Le Ruth, Dordogne	M
Kleine Scheuer, nr. Stuttgart	M	Massat, Ariège	M
Neuessing, nr. Regensburg	S?	Montconfort, Haute-Garonne	M
*Oberkassel, nr. Bonn	M	Montesquieu-Avantés, Ariège	M
Petersfels, nr. Nordlingen	M	Pair-non-Pair, Gironde	S
Ranis, nr. Weimar	M	*Le Roc, Charente	S
Rothekopf, nr. Freiburg i. B.	M	La Rochette, Dordogne	A
Sirgenstein, nr. Ulm	A	Les Rois, Vienne	A
*Stettin, nr. Ulm	A	Roset, Tarn	S
Ursprung, nr. Ulm	M	St.-Germaine-la Rivière, Gironde	M
		St.-Vincent-Arlay, Rhone	M
Benelux—6		*Solutré, Saône-et-Loire	A or S
Hengelo, Netherlands	?	Téoule, Haute-Garonne	M
Chaleux, Belgium	M	Terrasson, Dordogne	M
Goyet, Belgium	M	*Veyrier, Haute-Savoie	M
Magrite, Belgium	A		
Reviaux, Belgium	M	*Britain—7*	
Oetrange, Luxemburg	A or M	*Aveline's Hole, Somerset	C
		Barcombe Mills, Sussex	C
France—43		Flint Jack's Cave, Somerset	C
*Abri Pataud, Dordogne	M	*Gough's Cave, Somerset	C
Aurenson, Hautes-Pyrénées	M	*Kent's Cavern, Devon	C
Badegoule, Dordogne	S or M	Paviland, Glamorgan	C
Blanchard, Dordogne	A	Whaley, Derby	C
Bourdeilles, Dordogne	S		
Brassempouy, Landes	M	*Spain—7*	
*Bruniquel, Tarn-et-Garonne	M	Barranc Blanc, Valencia	S
*Cap Blanc, Dordogne	M	Carmago, Santander	A
*Chancelade, Dordogne	M	Castillo, Santander	A
La Combe, Dordogne	A	Cobalejos, Santander	M
*Combe Capelle	A	Morin, Santander	M
Les Cottés, Vienne	A	*Parpallo, Valencia	S
*Crô-Magnon, Dordogne	A	Serinya, Gerona	M
Duruthy, Landes	M		
Entzheim, Haut-Rhin	?	*Switzerland—1*	
Espalungue, Basses-Pyrénées	M	*Bichon, Neufchatel	M
L'Éspelungue, Landes	M		
Les Eyzies, Dordogne	M	*Italy—2*	
Farincourt, Haute-Marne	M	* Arena Candide, Savona	A
Grotte des Fées, Gironde	M	* Báoussi Ráoussi, Liguria	A
*Gourdan, Haute-Garonne	M	Grotte des Enfants, Grimaldi	
*Les Hoteaux, Ain	M		
Isturitz, Basses Pyrénées	A or M	*Austria—1*	
La Cave, Lot	S	Miesslingtal, Lower Austria	A
Laugerie-Basse, Dordogne	M		

TABLE 30 (*continued*)

COUNTRY	CULTURE	COUNTRY	CULTURE
Czechoslovakia—8		*Iran—1*	
* Brno, Moravia	A	* Hotu Cave, Mazandaran	O
* Dolni Věstonice, S. Moravia	A		
Dzerava Skála, W. Slovakia	S	*Palestine—5*	
* Mladeč, N. Moravia	A	Erg al-Ahmar	O
Podbaba, Prag, Bohemia	A	Jebel Qafza	O
* Předmostí, N.E. Moravia	A	Skhul	O
Sv. Prokop, Prag, Bohemia	A	Mugharet al-Wad	O
Zlatý Kůň, Central Bohemia	A	Mugharet al-Kebara	O

COUNTRY	CULTURE
Hungary—4	
Barla-Barlang, Borsod, N. Hungary	M
Czakvari-Barland, Fejer, W. Hungary	M
* Nagy-Sap, Esztergom, N.W. Hungary	M
Pilisszantou-Köfülke, near Budapest	M

Code to Cultural Symbols:
A = Aurignacian, incl. Perigordian
S = Solutrian
M = Magdalenian
C = Creswellian
O = Others

COUNTRY	CULTURE
Rumania—1	
Cioclovina, Transylvanian Alps	A

Complete Skulls or Skeletons Described Numbers of Sites

by Countries		by Cultures	
Germany	2	A =	9
France	11	S =	3
Britain	3	M =	10
Spain	1	C =	3
Switzerland	1	O =	1
Italy	2		26
Czechoslovakia	4		
Hungary	1		
Iran	1		
	26		

COUNTRY	CULTURE
U.S.S.R.—6	
Puškari, Ukraine	O
Tsulatovo, Ukraine	O
Korman, N. Bessarabia	A
Siuren'i, Crimea	A
Devis-Khreli, Georgia	A
Mal'ta, Siberia	O

* Published studies of complete skulls or skeletons are available.

found in each site because I do not intend to go over all the material in detail. The sites for which published studies of complete skulls or skeletons are available have been starred.

The geographical distribution of these sites resembles that of

BSA, Vol. 5 (1954), pp. 25–34. A mandible from St.-Vincent at Arlay, Lyon; Late Magdalenian.

(3) M-R. Sauter: "Étude des Vestiges Osseux Humains des Grottes Préhistoriques de Farincourt (Haute-Marne, France)," *ASAG*, Vol. 22, No. 1 (1957), pp. 6–37. A late Magdalenian mandible and maxilla from Farincourt.

(4) Sauter: "La Squelette Préhistorique de la Grotte du Bichon (Côtes-du-Doubs, La Chaux-de-Fonds, Neuchatel)," *AS*, Vol. 9, No. 3 (1956), pp. 330–5 A Magdalenian skeleton from the cave of Bichon, Neufchatel, Switzerland.

the Neanderthals. Places too cold for comfort in Würm I were also difficult to live in during Würm II, III, and later. Southern France was again the favored spot. In Germany only the Rhineland and western Bavaria were popular, and most of the Czechoslovakian skulls are from the Interstadial.

Of 161 listed sites, only the remains of 25 have been adequately described in publication. Eleven are from France, and, by coincidence, eleven of these skulls or skeletons are Magdalenian. Not one was found east of Moravia and northwestern Hungary. Many of the publications are so old that the measurements were not based on standard techniques; and old calculations of stature are usually much too high. Two physical anthropologists, G. W. Morant and G. von Bonin, have remeasured and reworked as many skulls and long bones as possible; their monographs principally document the following survey.[3]

The Racial Characteristics of the Upper Paleolithic Europeans

T H E Upper Paleolithic Europeans, who lived from about 30,000 to about 10,000 years ago, were modern Caucasoids. Were they barbered and dressed in the current styles, they could sit in any western European restaurant without arousing particular comment except for their table manners. A few very observant fellow customers might notice that they closed their deeply worn teeth with an edge-to-edge bite, and that their well-developed temporal and masseter muscles bulged as they chewed.

As von Bonin has shown, the men were not notably tall. The mean stature for twelve adult male skeletons is only five feet eight inches (173 cm.), shorter than modern Americans. The famous Old Man of Crô-Magnon, depicted in textbooks as a giant, was only five feet six (168.4 cm.). The two tallest men of the series, Grotte des Enfants and Barma Grande 2, were five feet eleven and a half inches (181.8 cm). The shortest Upper Paleolithic man was

[3] Morant: "Studies of Palaeolithic Man, IV, A Biometric Study of the Upper Palaeolithic Skulls of Europe," *AE*, Vol. 4 (1930), pp. 109–214.

G. von Bonin: "European Races of the Upper Paleolithic," *HB*, Vol. 7, No. 2 (1935), pp. 196–221.

Chancelade. He was only five feet three (160 cm.),[4] and he lived during a brief spell of intense cold. As we know, intense cold tends to reduce stature.

The five female skeletons have a mean stature of five feet one inch (155 cm.), and the range is only from 154 to 157.5 cm. Females were, then, much shorter than the men. The sex difference was probably real, and not merely an accident of sampling in a small series, because the women's skulls are also much smaller than the men's.

The long bones of these skeletons are on the whole slender, like those of Krapina and Mount Carmel, and a lean body build is indicated. In two respects the long bones of these skeletons are variable—in the proportion of the length of the forearm to the length of the humerus, and in the ratio of the thigh to the lower leg. The Aurignacian Grimaldi woman, found in a double burial with her so-called Negroid son, had a long radius and a short humerus. Elongated shin bones were found in the skeleton of Combe Capelle, who lived in the mild Göttweig Interstadial, and in two Aurignacian skeletons from the Riviera, one from Grotte du Cavillon and the other (not to be confused with the Grimaldi pair) from Báoussi Ráoussi.[5] None of these men, nor the Grimaldi mother and child, was exposed to great cold. Both Skhul 4 and Skhul 5 had similar limb proportions.

The hands and feet of the Upper Paleolithic Europeans are better known to us from archaeological than from osteological evidence. Many negative silhouettes of hands, made by spraying pigment out of a bone tube over a hand held against a wall, have been found on the walls of French caves; bare footprints have been found on cavern floors in France and Italy. Both the hands and the feet were normal for slenderly built Europeans.

Morant's series of twenty male skulls and von Bonin's series of thirteen female skulls represent nearly all countries from France

---

[4] Vallois: "Nouvelles Réchérches sur la Squelette de Chancelade," *L'Anth*, Vol. 50, No. 1–2 (1941–6), pp. 11–202. Vallois calculated stature from the humerus, femur, and tibia; von Bonin, who got a lower figure, used the humerus only.

[5] Von Bonin also found high humeroradial and femorotibial indices for the Magdalenian skeleton of Obercassel, but he doubted the accuracy of the original measurements.

to Czechoslovakia, and all archaeological cultures. The male skulls are large, with a mean cranial capacity of 1,580 cc.; the female skulls are much smaller, with a capacity of 1,370 cc., about the size of Swanscombe. The detailed measurements of these skulls reveal a very long, moderately broad and high brain case of fully modern proportions; a face of moderate to great length, and a considerable breadth. In fact, the bizygomatic diameter exceeds the cranial breadth. This was not the case among the Neanderthals, nor is it among most modern Europeans. Heavy chewing, combined with a relatively narrow brain case, is responsible for this archaic feature, found also among the Eskimo. It has no racial significance.

Most of the skulls are not prognathous, an exception being the recently discovered female skull from the Proto-Magdalenian of Abri Pataud. Brow ridges are of moderate size or they are missing in most of the skulls, except in the Czechoslovakian ones of the early Aurignacian, which come closest to Skhul 5 and Jebel Qafza 6. They, however, show no trace of Skhul 5's alveolar prognathism. The series of male skulls also resembles a later, Neolithic series from France, Iron Age skulls from Norway, and Anglo-Saxon ones from the east coast of England.

Although most of the teeth are too worn to permit accurate observation, those of the so-called Negroid boy of Grimaldi are in perfect condition. His upper jaw shows irregular tooth eruption, gaps, and malocclusion. The upper median incisors have vertical ridges on the lingual side, and a basal protuberance. These are dental characteristics of the Negro, but not exclusively. They are also seen on a number of teeth from Krapina and on those of Neanderthals, and are also present, as we have just mentioned, in the Mount Carmel population. An upper canine from the Magdalenian maxilla of Farincourt [6] has the same features. The Grimaldi child was no more Negroid than the Palestinians of Skhul and many living Europeans of the Mediterranean region.

The other alleged intruder in the European population, Chancelade, had wide zygomatic arches and flaring gonial angles, as befitted a heavy chewer living in extreme arctic conditions. But he

[6] Sauter: "Études des Vestiges. . . ."

had high-rooted, aquiline nasal bones; a face that was far from flat; and a completely Caucasoid configuration of the malars.[7] He was as European as the rest of the Upper Paleolithic people.[8]

The Upper Paleolithic Europeans were great artists: they worked in bone, ivory, antler, and limestone and carved in the round and in relief, and engraved and painted. But they were interested more in depicting animals than in depicting people. Very few human faces and figures appear in any of the media. Of these, some are exaggerated, others are humorous, and a few are realistic.[9] The statues in the round and the bas-reliefs, known as "Venuses," invariably represent grossly obese women, whose fat is deposited on the same parts of the body and in the same fashion as in living fat women of European origin, many of whom also have slender bones.

A unique wall engraving in La Magdaleine cave shows a long-breasted woman with tapering extremities, her hips and waistline only a little fuller than is currently fashionable. Another notable wall engraving, found in Sicily, depicts some kind of ceremony; the men taking part have normally proportioned Caucasoid bodies.

Wall paintings, wall engravings, and ivory carvings contain a number of portraits of human faces. Some are bearded, some bald. Most of the men shown have prominent noses. One woman has

[7] Morant: "Studies of Palaeolithic Man, I, The Chancelade Skull and its Relation to the Modern Eskimo Skull," *AE*, Vol. 1 (1926), pp. 257–76.

Vallois: "Nouvelles Réchérches. . . ."

[8] There is, however, a possibility that a few North Africans may have visited Europe during Würm II or III. This is indicated not only by the discovery of Aterian arrowheads in Solutrean deposits in Spanish caves, mentioned on page 523, but also by the discovery of a skullcap, cut in the form of a bowl, which was found lying on the floor of a cave containing Upper Paleolithic implements and paintings. It has very heavy brow ridges and a receding forehead, and could hardly have belonged to an Upper Paleolithic Caucasoid. In the only available photograph it looks, in profile, like the Florisbad skull from South Africa, an ancestral Bushman specimen of a group which probably originated in North Africa. Until this skullcap has been studied, no definite statement about it can be made. A. H. Brodrick: "A Newly Discovered and as yet Unexplored Treasure-House of Spanish Cave Art: The Fantastic and Beautiful Caves of Nerja—a Preliminary Note." *ILN*, Vol. 239, No. 6366 (1961), pp. 216–9.

[9] Paolo Grazioso: *Palaeolithic Art* (New York: McGraw-Hill Book Co.; 1960).

J. A. Mauduit: *40,000 Ans d'Art Moderne* (Paris: Librairie Plon; 1954).

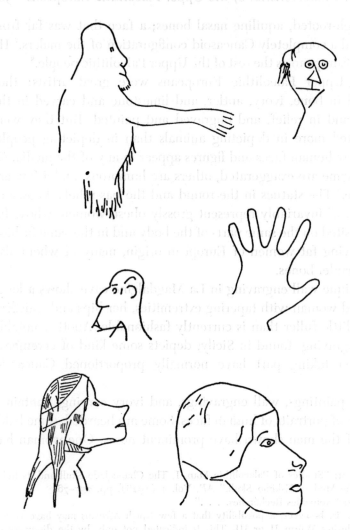

Fig. 76   The Human Face and Hand in Upper Paleolithic Art. These engravings made on the walls of French caves are probably all of Magdalenian, or Late Upper Paleolithic, origin. They have been selected from a large number of copies, some of which are of doubtful authenticity. They show both that Upper Paleolithic Europeans were Caucasoid and that they had a sense of humor. (Drawings after P. Graziosi, 1960.)

nasal prognathism to a marked degree, and another is chinless. Some of these drawings reflect to a certain degree the imagination of modern archaeologists who copied them by lamplight in the depths of the caves; but most are accurate. The total effect is that of a set of caricatures of modern Europeans.

The Fate of the Upper Paleolithic Europeans [9]

T H E Upper Paleolithic Europeans did not vanish with the mammoths on whose succulent flesh they feasted, nor with the Neanderthals. They survived the Pleistocene, and their descendants became Mesolithic salmon-seiners, Neolithic villagers, Bronze Age warriors, and Iron Age Vikings. They followed the reindeer to the edge of the ice, and when it melted, there they remained. But they were a restless people, and their descendants still are. After they had learned agriculture and cattle breeding from others like them who had come from the East, they expanded, migrating southward and eastward in many waves, one of which even reached India; and their descendants are to be seen in America, Australia, New Zealand, and South Africa.

Their Asiatic Relatives

V E R Y L I T T L E skeletal material is available from the Upper Paleolithic sites in western Asia, largely because it has not been looked for. However, from the cave of Hotu, on the Caspian shore of Iran in west-central Asia, we do have three skeletons that date from the penultimate millennium of the Pleistocene.[1] In brief, this man and two women from Hotu were indistinguishable from their western European contemporaries.

What little we have from Palestine, mostly scraps of bone and a few teeth, is also Caucasoid. For example, the Mesolithic Natufian skulls and long bones from that country are those of ancestral Mediterraneans.[2] As we shall see in the next chapter, some of the Near Eastern Caucasoids invaded North Africa before the Pleistocene was over. Others, remaining in western Asia, were the first people to grow crops and to tame the ancestors of our domestic animals. The Neolithic culture that they had invented spread in many directions, and became the basis of our modern civilization.

[9] If I may do so without immodesty, I recommend my *Races of Europe* for a review of this subject.

[1] J. L. Angel: "The Human Skeletal Remains from Hotu Cave, Iran," *PAPS*, Vol. 96, No. 3 (1952), pp. 258–69.

[2] McCown: *Natufian Crania from Mt. Carmel* (Berkeley, California: University of California Library; 1940).

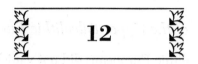

12

AFRICA

The Darkest Continent

SEVERAL YEARS AGO a number of old friends and neighbors sat in my house talking. Among them was Sarah Jones, a Negress born shortly after emancipation. Two of the group, being New Englanders, were, as might be expected, discussing ancestors. Mrs. Jones listened intently. Then she turned to me and asked: "Professor, who were *my* ancestors?"

I had to reply that I did not know. Thanks to Louis Leakey and his recent discoveries, I know a little more now than I did then, but not enough to be certain. The origin of the African Negroes, and of the Pygmies, is the greatest unsolved mystery in the field of racial study. In this chapter I shall present all the evidence I can find and offer a tentative solution.

To begin with, Africa is not the home of one subspecies but of two. The Bushmen evolved there as well as the Congoids—Negroes and Pygmies. The Caucasoids of North Africa, Berbers and Arabs, are late arrivals. When the southern Mongoloids were invading southeast Asia and Indonesia, the ancestors of the Berbers invaded North Africa, pushing the earlier inhabitants southward, just as the Australoids were crowded eastward and southward over Wallace's Line into their present home.

In Asia and Indonesia the question of who crowded whom is easy to answer because there was only one invader and only one displaced group. In Europe the same was also true of the Neanderthals and of the Upper Paleolithic peoples who replaced them. But in Africa two subspecies were displaced by the Caucasoid invaders. Our first problem is to discover where each of the native races lived before the invasions, and where each went afterwards.

In recent centuries Negroes have inhabited most of Africa between the Sahara and the Limpopo River, whereas Bushmen and their cattle-breeding kin, the Hottentots, have occupied South Africa and parts of southern Rhodesia. The boundary between Negroes and Bushmen is not an impenetrable geographical barrier but a clinal region, and the two subspecies could not have evolved each on its own side of it because the isolation needed for subspecific evolution did not exist. By simple zoogeographical logic we must therefore assume that at least one of the two subspecies initially moved into its present territory after each had evolved, during the Pleistocene, in a state of comparative isolation. And it is easier to believe that one moved first than that both moved simultaneously. Obviously, the subspecies that felt the Caucasoid pressure first moved first and farthest.

The Pygmies hold the key to the problem because North Africa is not the kind of country in which Pygmies could have evolved. It is not, and never has been, a tropical forest region. The present home of the Pygmies is, quite appropriately, the rain forest of the Congo and of sections of West Africa, and it is the logical place for them to have evolved in. During parts of the Pleistocene the Congo Basin was under water, and the ancestors of the Pygmies must then have lived in the edges of the forest, and have entered the more elevated parts of that refuge in times of drought. Once in the forest, they became dwarfs, according to the rules governing dwarfing as discussed in Chapter 3.

Pygmies are obviously related to Negroes, and a full-sized Pygmy ancestor and a Negro ancestor of the same period may have been indistinguishable. The Negro homeland must therefore have been the savannahs at the edge of the forest, an environment to which Negroes are physiologically adapted. They could not have acquired their ability to withstand heat, particularly damp heat, during the 12,000 years since the Caucasoids pushed their predecessors out of North Africa. The South American Indians of the Amazon basin have failed to become heat-adapted in an equal length of time. The African forest and its peripheries are therefore the Congoid home.

The Bushmen, who are not heat-adapted, do not fit this picture.

But, as we shall presently see, there is fair evidence that the ancestors of the Bushmen were full-sized people and that they evolved in North Africa, north of the Saharan barrier which gave them the isolation they needed to become a separate subspecies. When the present Palearctic fauna invaded North Africa near the end of the Pleistocene, the Caucasoids who came with it drove out the Capoids, who crossed the Sahara via the central Saharan Tibesti highlands, and then followed the cool East African highlands southward to their present home.

There they entered an underpopulated area inhabited by human beings of a lower evolutionary grade, who were related to the ancestors of the Negroes and Pygmies living farther north and west. These aborigines gave the ancestors of the Bushmen little trouble, and were absorbed by the invaders. Much later, in full historical times, some of the Negroes of West Africa who had acquired agriculture and iron metallurgy moved eastward and southward and in turn absorbed many of the Bushman tribes. They arrived in South Africa simultaneously with the Dutch. Bantu and Boer then formed the jaws of a giant pincers that drove the Bushmen into the Kalahari and led to the racial conflicts that beset that troubled land today.

This is the most plausible outline of African racial history that it seems to me can be drawn from available evidence. In the rest of this chapter I shall try to document this outline.

Fossil Man in North Africa: the Ternefine-Tangier Line

As STATED in Chapter 7, Lower Pleistocene archaeological sites are as old in North as in East Africa. Moreover, what may be the oldest Australopithecine yet found comes from the heart of the Sahara, in the Republic of Tchad, halfway between these two most ancient archaeological regions. Thus, North Africa has as good a claim to the title of Cradle of Mankind as Tanganyika.

It is therefore disappointing that we have no North African Australopithecine or human remains older than the Early Middle Pleistocene and that for the vast period between then and the arrival of the Mouillians, shortly before the end of the Pleistocene,

TABLE 31

PRE-MOUILLIAN SKELETAL MATERIAL FROM NORTH AFRICA

Country	Site	Age	Material	Name
Algeria	Ternefine, Oran	Early Middle Pleistocene	1 piece parietal 3 mandibles	*Atlanthropus mauritanicus*
Morocco	Sidi Abd er-Rahman Casablanca (Litorina Cave)	Riss or Third Pluvial	1 piece mandible	none
	Temara (Smugglers' Cave)	Early Last Interglacial	1 piece mandible	none
	Rabat	Late Last Interglacial	1 piece mandible 1 piece maxilla, fragments cranial vault	none
	Mugharet al-'Aliya Tangier (High Cave)	End Last Interglacial to Würm I	1 fragment child's maxilla	none
	Taforalt	Prob. Würm I	1 piece calva	none
Libya	Haua Fteah	34,000 BP (Göttweig Interstadial)	1 fragment mandible	*H. neanderthalensis*

all we have is seven mandibles, some quite fragmentary, a piece of an adult maxilla, another from a child, and several small pieces of cranial vault (see Table 31).

The Ternefine Discoveries [1]

IN 1954 and 1955 Camille Arambourg, a renowned French paleontologist, discovered human remains in a rich deposit of fos-

[1] C. Arambourg: "L'Hominien Fossile de Ternefine (Algerie)," *CRAS*, Vol. 139 (1954), pp. 893, 895.

Arambourg: "A Recent Discovery in Human Paleontology, Atlanthropus of Ternefine (Algeria)," *AJPA*, Vol. 13, No. 2 (1955), pp. 191–6.

Arambourg: "Une Nouvelle Mandibule 'd'Antlanthropus' du Gisement de Ternefine," *CRAS*, Vol. 241 (1955), pp. 431–3.

Arambourg: "Le Pariétal de l'Atlanthropus Mauritanicus," *CRAS*, Vol. 241 (1955), pp. 980–2.

Arambourg: "Une IIIme Mandibule 'd'Atlanthropus' Découverte à Ternefine," *Quaternaria*, Vol. 3 (1956), pp. 1–4.

Arambourg: "Récentes découvertes de paléontologie humaine en Afrique du Nord française," *PTPA*, 1957, pp. 186–94.

F. C. Howell: "European and N. W. African Middle Pleistocene Hominids," *CA*, Vol. 1, No. 3 (1960), pp. 195–232.

sil animal bones in a flooded sandpit at Ternefine near Palikao, eleven miles (17 km.) southeast of Mascara in the Department of Oran, Algeria. The Early Middle Pleistocene date was determined by examination of the fauna, which was typically African and indicated a savannah type of landscape. The associated industry was early Acheulian mixed with many choppers, chopping tools, and flakes reminiscent of the Far East. It seems to have been a generalized early industry into which the making of hand axes

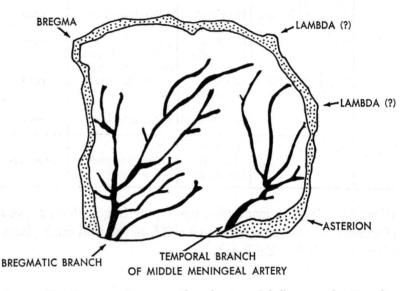

Fig. 77　The Ternefine Parietal. The only piece of skull recovered at Ternefine was this parietal, shown from the inside. No scale was given, but this drawing is exactly the same size as that published. The middle meningeal artery pattern suggests that it belonged to a member of *Homo erectus*. (Drawing after Arambourg, 1955.)

had been introduced, or in which hand-axe manufacture had been invented. The human remains consisted of a right parietal bone and three mandibles.

The right parietal bone belonged to an immature individual. We know this because all the sutures are open, and the bone is no thicker than that of a modern adult. Its curvature suggests a low vault, with the maximum cranial breadth lying below its juncture with the temporal. Although the dimensions of this bone have not been published and the drawing[2] has no scale, I have been

[2] Arambourg: "Le Pariétal. . . ."

told by two professionals who have handled it that it lies some-where between Sinanthropus and Neanderthal in size, and that it approximates the size of Swanscombe's right parietal.

The size as stated does not tell us whether the bone belonged to a large *Homo erectus* skull or a small *Homo sapiens* one, but the morphology and the endocranial surface configuration suggest the former. Like the Pithecanthropi and Sinanthropi, it has a prominent Sylvian crest and a simple meningeal artery pattern.

Mandible 1 is nearly complete, with all its molars and pre-molars and its right lateral incisor. Number 2 consists of an en-tire left side and enough of the right side to allow room for the two right incisors, but its only teeth are its left molars and pre-molars. Number 3 is complete except for the post-mortem loss of seven teeth; those present are the right lateral incisor, right ca-nine, left first premolar, both second premolars, and all six molars.

Mandible 3, which Arambourg classifies as masculine, is the largest lower jaw yet found which all investigators agree is hu-man. Its bicondylar breadth is very great, for example, so great that the cranium which it fitted must have had a very wide base—an *erectus* feature.

In many respects Number 3 is almost Australopithecine. In fact, it resembles the Swartkrans mandibles in its dimensions and also in one particular morphological detail. Its ascending ramus is very high and inclined far backward, with a 70° angle of inclina-tion; and the coracoid process of its ascending ramus is higher than its condyle. Ternefine 3 shares this overall configuration of the ascending ramus, to a lesser degree, with its contemporary, Sinanthropus, and the Neanderthals, who lived much later. The low broad ascending ramus of the Heidelberg jaw is so different that it must represent an entirely separate evolutionary line.

The other two Ternefine mandibles are similar to Number 3 in shape but they are much smaller, so much so that a sexual dimor-phism is suggested for the North African population, as among the Sinanthropi. Mandible 1 has two mental foramina; Number 3 has two on the right and three on the left; and the one-sided Number 2 has a single foramen. In these respects the Ternefine jaws resemble both Sinanthropus and the Neanderthals.

Despite its size, Ternefine 3 does not have the largest teeth;

these are found in the jaw of Number 2, supposedly a female. Her molars and premolars are larger than those of Sinanthropus, and the first and second molars are larger than those of Pithecanthropus B, who lived more than 100,000 years earlier. The molars and premolars of Ternefine 1 and 3 fit comfortably within the Sinanthropus range and are a little smaller than the Pithecanthropus B teeth. However, in the Pithecanthropus B mandible the third molar is the largest, followed in order by the second and then the first molars, whereas in all three Ternefine jaws the second molar is the largest and the third the smallest, as in Sinanthropus.

In all three Ternefine jaws the incisors and canines seem small in relation to the premolars and molars, but this is difficult to establish because these teeth are either badly worn or absent altogether and represented only by sockets.

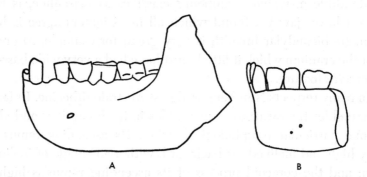

A   B

FIG. 78 MANDIBLES: TERNEFINE 1 AND RABAT. The Ternefine mandibles are not all alike. No. 1 (A) has a steep, rounded sagittal profile. The Rabat fragment (B), probably 200,000 years younger, is still steep, but has the beginnings of a chin.

The premolars and molars are heavily wrinkled, as in Sinanthropus and some of the Australopithecines, and they are taurodont. Nearly all have basal cingulums, and all the molars have the Y-5 or +5 cusp pattern. The canine of Number 3 has a long, thick root. The form of the incisors cannot be determined. All in all, these teeth resemble those of the Australopithecines, Pithecanthropus, and Sinanthropus, but the closest resemblance is to Sinanthropus. Except for taurodontism, they have little in common with the Heidelberg teeth.

The Ternefine specimens are important and tantalizing. The

skull was apparently *erectus* in general form, but large enough to have been either *erectus* or *sapiens;* the face, judging by the length of the ascending rami of the mandibles, was very long, and the jaws themselves formed a bridge between those of the larger Australopithecines and the *Homines erecti* of China and Indonesia.

The Litorina Cave Mandible

I N 1953 a French archaeologist, P. Biberson, found human remains in a former cave in the quarry of Sidi Abd er-Rahman (named for a saint's tomb perched atop it) in the Anfa section of Casablanca, Morocco. The culture was an evolved Acheulian industry, and the deposit that of the so-called Tyrrhenian I period, identified by means of associated sea-levels, which fluctuated on the Moroccan coast during the Pleistocene. It probably coincided with the Riss glaciation in Europe.

The specimens consist of two small pieces of mandible containing three right molars and a left first premolar.[3] Morphologically these fragments resemble those of Ternefine, but they are a little smaller. Had we three Litorina Cave jaws to match the three of Ternefine, we might find no difference at all.

The first premolar has a cingulum, and the molars are wrinkled. The first two molars have five cusps each, and the third one six. The size gradation of the three molars is second, first, and then third, as in Ternefine and Sinanthropus.

Despite the time gap of about 200,000 years, the genetic continuity between Ternefine man and that of the Litorina Cave seems just as clear as their cultural continuity.

The Mandible from Smugglers' Cave, Temara, Morocco [4]

D U R I N G or before 1958, Father Jean Roche excavated a cave called Grotte des Contrabandiers on the Moroccan coast at Te-

[3] Arambourg: "Récentes découvertes. . . ."
Howell: "European and N. W. African Pleistocene Hominids."
[4] H. V. Vallois and J. Roche: "La Mandibule Acheuléene de Temara, Maroc," *CRAS,* Vol. 246 (1958), pp. 3113–6.

mara, 48 miles (78 km.) northeast of Casablanca. Among other undescribed human remains, he found a mandible, nearly complete except that parts of both ascending rami had been broken off. The artifacts belonged to the final Acheulian industry or to the threshold between the Acheulian and the succeeding flake culture, the Aterian, and were roughly contemporaneous with the Litorina Cave mandible.

The Smugglers' Cave mandible resembles those of Ternefine and the Litorina Cave fragments in most respects, but it is the smallest yet found of the North African group. Unlike the others, it had a nearly straight profile and as much chin as some of the Neanderthals. The teeth are as large as those of the Litorina Cave jaw. The first molar is the largest of the three, followed in turn by the second and third.

The canine, which is very large, is ribbed on the lingual side into a three-chambered surface, and its cutting edge is horizontal rather than pointed. As among the Australopithecines, the second premolar is molarlike in structure. All the molars are moderately taurodont, and all of them have a Y-5 cusp pattern, except for the right first molar, the pattern of which is +4.

The Rabat Remains [5]

I N 1933 quarrymen blasted what was probably a complete skull from a sandy marine consolidation on the outskirts of Rabat. All that was recovered, however, were portions of the lower and upper jaws and brain case, as follows: (1) the front half of a mandible containing three incisors, one canine, three premolars, and a row of three molars; (2) the lower part of the right maxilla with a small piece of palate, to which is attached a natural cast of most

---

[5] Vallois: "L'Homme Fossile de Rabat," *CRAS*, Vol. 221 (1945), pp. 669–71.

M. Boule and Vallois: *Les Hommes Fossiles* (Paris: Masson et Cie; 1952), pp. 443–4.

Vallois and Roche: "Le Mandibule Acheuléene. . . ."

Vallois: "L'Homme de Rabat," *BAM*, Vol. 3 (1960), pp. 87–91.

L. C. Briggs: "The Stone Age Races of Northwest Africa," *BASP*, Vol. 18 (1955), pp. 17–19.

Howell: "European and N.W. African Pleistocene Hominids."

Bruce Howe, personal communication regarding date.

of the rest of the palate, and two incisors, one canine, two premolars, and two molars; and (3) twenty-one small fragments of
the cranial vault, not one of which is larger than a twenty-five-
cent piece. The date of this find is a period called Tyrrhenian I–II,
in shore-line chronology probably equivalent to the end of the
Last Interglacial in Europe and almost certainly no older than the
onset of Würm I.

The cranial fragments have not been, and probably could not
be, reassembled. But they are not much thicker than the mean for
modern skulls. On the basis of the sutures and of the teeth, the
skull is attributed to a seventeen-year-old male.

The maxilla lacks a canine fossa, and indicates pronounced
alveolar prognathism; the palate was large. The mandible, about
the size of the Temara specimen, is smaller than any of the three
Ternefine jaws, and morphologically is similar to the other North
African jaws in this series. It has two mental foramina on the right
side, and a large one on the left. Its symphyseal profile resembles
those of Ternefine, and its angle of inclination, 65°, is the same as
that of Ternefine 2.

The lower molars also fit the Ternefine range. The first is the
largest, followed by the second and the third. In size and shape
the molars resemble those from the other early North African sites,
except that the third molar has six cusps.

The upper incisors (the first we have seen from North Africa)
are shovel-shaped, although not to the degree found in Sinanthropus, and the lower incisors form a nearly straight line from canine
to canine. The upper canines, like those of Sinanthropus, have
heavy cingulums on the outer sides of the base of each crown, and
the lingual surface is divided vertically by a double ridge. These
teeth are pointed and extend a little beyond the level of the incisors. The lower canines, however, are incisorlike, as in the Neanderthals.

The upper premolars have a complicated cusp pattern, as in
Sinanthropus; the first has two roots, the second a single long
root. The lower premolars are asymmetrical, like those of Swartkrans, with diamond-shaped crowns. The first lower premolar has
a high lingual cusp, the second lower premolar has two roots and
a large distal portion; it is thus "molarized" as in the Australo-

pithecines and Sinanthropus. Some of the Neanderthals share these special dental features with Rabat man and Sinanthropus, but to a lesser degree.

Tangier Man

O u r last find in this series, dated at Würm I or even Würm II, comes from the northern end of the Moroccan coast and is much younger than the Rabat specimen. I found it in 1939 while excavating the High Cave (Mugharet al-'Aliya), one of the Caves of Hercules facing the Atlantic on Ras Ashagar, a few miles south of Cape Spartel, to the southwest of Tangier. It lay on an excavated floor in an early Aterian level where it had apparently fallen from some late Aterian soil cemented to a tip of the cave roof immediately above. The late Aterian material included refined bifacial points equipped with tangs suitable for hafting as arrowheads.[6]

It was a piece of a child's maxilla, with erupted and unerupted teeth. Of these, a permanent canine and first premolar have been measured. The child had died at about the age of nine. In sifting the earth from the same layer, I also found a badly worn upper first molar of an adult.

The piece of maxilla extends from the socket of the left first permanent upper incisor to that of the unerupted second molar, and includes the floor of the nasal aperture, the base of the nasal wall, and a small piece of the zygomatic process. The bone is massive, indicating a face already large and long at an early age; the canine fossa is absent, and the lower border of the nasal margin is smoothly rounded, as in Negroes and Australoids. It resembles in essential details the maxilla of the seventeen-year-old from Rabat.

The upper canine and first premolar are large, large enough to match those of Ternefine and the other early North Africans. Whereas the canine is particularly thick labiolingually, the first

[6] B. Howe and H. L. Movius, Jr.: "A Stone Age Cave Site in Tangier," *PMP*, Vol. 28, No. 1 (1947). The late Aterian dating is by K. P. Oakley on the basis of the uranium content of the specimen determined in 1962.

H. Hencken: "The Prehistoric Archaeology of the Tangier Zone, Morocco," *PAPS*, Vol. 92, No. 4 (1948), pp. 282–8.

M. S. Şenyürek: "Fossil Man in Tangier," *PMP*, Vol. 16, No. 3 (1940).

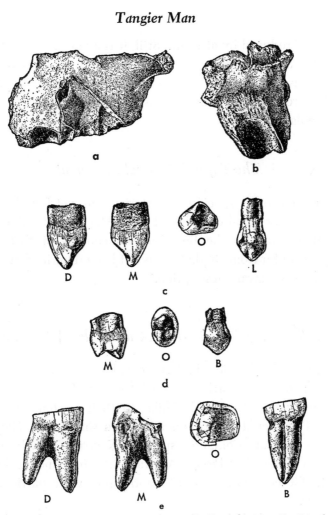

FIG. 79 THE TANGIER MAXILLA AND TEETH. B. Buccal view; D. Distal view; L. Lingual view; M. Mesial view; O. Occlusal view. a. Lateral view of the Tangier maxilla after the extraction of the teeth; b. Anterior view of the Tangier maxilla after the extraction of the teeth; c. Left permanent upper canine of Tangier man; d. Left permanent upper first premolar of Tangier man; e. Left upper second molar of the Tangier man. Approximately natural size. Note that the maxilla is puffy, as in Mongoloids and Neanderthals, and that there is no canine notch. The teeth, with low crowns and stout roots, resemble those of Sinanthropus. (Drawings from Şenyürek, 1940.)

premolar is relatively narrow in that dimension. The canine, like that of the Rabat specimen, has a cingulum. It lacks the fingering ridges of the labial side, which is smooth, but it has a marked triangular eminence, or heel, found also in some Neanderthals.

The first upper molar of the second individual is so badly worn that its cusp pattern cannot be detected, and its dimensions may have been reduced by attrition. Still, it is a very large tooth, well above the Sinanthropus mean and it probably was above the Sinanthropus maximum before wearing down. Indeed, it may well have approached the dimensions of Pithecanthropus 4's first upper molar.

The Taforalt Cranial Fragment

T H E   O N L Y other specimen of Aterian man yet found is a very small piece of cranial vault found in an Aterian cultural level in a cave at Taforalt, in the Beni Znassen country of northeastern Morocco not far from Oujda.[7] It has not been described, and probably does not warrant description.[8]

The Ternefine-Tangier Line, Cannibals, and Bushmen

A L L in all, the Tangier child and his older companion were true successors of other North Africans from Ternefine, Litorina Cave, and Smugglers' Cave, and similar to their contemporary from Rabat. Together these specimens form a single line. They were certainly not Caucasoid, nor especially Negroid. They bear a similarity on the one hand to the Australopithecines and on the other to both Pithecanthropus and Sinanthropus, more particularly to the latter.

They probably belonged to the *erectus* grade when they first appeared, but whether they had achieved the *sapiens* grade by the time the Caucasoid Mouillians invaded shortly before the end of the Pleistocene is unknown. However, the implements from later phases of the Aterian culture were sophisticated flake tools, pressure-flaked on both sides, and some of them had tangs for hafting. They were as good as the recent work of Bushmen, and this circumstantial evidence suggests that the men who made these tools were *Homines sapientes*.

The relationship of the Tangier child and his companion to

[7] J. Roche: "La Grotte de Taforalt," *L'Anth*, Vol. 57, No. 3–4 (1953), pp. 375–80.
[8] Briggs: "The Stone Age Races. . . ."

Pithecanthropus and Sinanthropus can be explained only on a theoretical basis, since we do not know the antecendents of the three populations. Either the Ternefine-Tangier people were descended from immigrants from east Asia; or the ancestors of Pithecanthropus and Sinanthropus came from North Africa; or, as a third possibility, the ancestors of all three fossil subspecies came from some point geographically in between.

In view of what we know of Lower Pleistocene archaeology, the most likely possibility is that all three originated in North Africa and at an earlier evolutionary level than any yet seen in the skulls of the genus *Homo,* but this theory cannot be proved or disproved until more, and earlier, skeletal material is unearthed both in North Africa and in Asia.

On the other hand, it now seems fairly likely that the Ternefine-Tangier people had something to do with the origin of the Neanderthals, as was suggested in Chapter 11.

Several of the peculiarities that we first saw in Saccopastore and later in the Würm I Neanderthals are present in the ancient North Africans as well as in Sinanthropus, and North Africa is nearer to the Neanderthal home than China is.

But a principal question remains: did these North Africans simply die out, or did they evolve further into one of the five living human subspecies? Certain archaeological, anatomical, and geographical facts support the concept that they were the ancestors of the Bushmen. One of these is a persistent folk memory in the oral literature of the Riffians of northern Morocco, descendants of the Mouillians.

The Riffians have a vivid image of their predecessors, food gatherers who would have survived longer in the inaccessible Riffian mountains than on the plains below. They were, according to legend, a people called *amziw* (male) and *thamza* (female), and dwelt in huts built on the sides of mountains. The women were exceedingly ugly, and their breasts dragged on the ground, squirting milk as they walked. Their lips were long and slobbering; their hair long, tangled, and curly. The men had similar lips and hair. These people were cannibals and took delight in crunching and gnawing human bones. They had the ability to transform themselves: a *thamza* could turn into a bewitchingly beautiful

Berber damsel, and an *amziw* into a Negro. Obviously, then, they were, in their natural forms, neither Caucasoid nor Negro.[9]

Aside from these powers of transformation, there was nothing supernatural about these cannibals, admittedly long extinct. They were not concerned with jinns, shaitans, angels, gnomes, ghosts, or other categories of spooks, haunts, and *genii loci* familiar throughout most of the Islamic world. As nothing is said about their size, it was probably normal, like that of the ancestors of the Bushmen whose bones have been exhumed in other parts of Africa.

If the Ternefine-Tangier folk were not the ancestors of the Bushmen, they were a sixth subspecies that uniquely died without modern descendants, and the Bushmen would have had no discernible ancestors.

The Mandible from Haua Fteah, Cyrenaica [1]

S O F A R, we have described the pre-Caucasoid fossil remains from only the western part of North Africa, Morocco and Algeria. Egypt has yielded no known early human remains, nor, until 1952, had Libya. In that year Charles McBurney excavated a huge limestone solution cavity called Haua Fteah (the open cistern) in Cyrenaica. He had reached the bottom of a Lower Levalloisio-Mousterian level and was unearthing a jumble of animal bones, four feet lower down, when he found a fragment of human mandible.

Although the industry resembled that of Tabun in Palestine, the Carbon-14 date of the bottom of the level in Haua Fteah was only 32,000 B.C. (No. W-85, 34,000 ± 2,800 years). McBurney interpolated the date of the manible at about 38,000 B.C. Both dates fall within the time span of the Göttweig Interstadial of Europe, much later than the supposed date of Tabun.

The fragment consists of a left side, including nearly all of the ascending ramus, from the location of the second premolar to the gonial angle and up to the condyle. Only the second and third

---

[9] C. S. Coon: "Tribes of the Rif," *HAS*, Vol. 9 (1931), p. 155.

[1] C. B. M. McBurney, J. C. Trevor, and L. H. Wells: "The Hauah Fteah Fossil Jaw," *JRAI*, Vol. 83 (1953), pp. 71–85.

molars are present, and the third molar is freshly erupted, indicating an age of eighteen to twenty-five years. Trevor and Wells consider the specimen female.

This mandible is much smaller than any of the northwest African ones in all dimensions and falls within the size range of the Mount Carmel series, being closest to Tabun 1; but the wide angle of its ascending ramus (113°) is closer to that of Tabun 2 (118° compared to 104° for Tabun 1). Morphologically, it is difficult to compare this mandible with others because it is badly battered. However, the leading edge of the ascending ramus is flush with the rear border of the third molar, and this is a non-Neanderthal feature.

The second molar is much smaller than any of the Ternefine-Tangier line, and the third is smaller than any but Ternefine 3, which is abnormally short anteroposteriorly. Both Haua Fteah teeth fit within the Mount Carmel range. The second molar is larger than the third and neither is taurodont; the cusp pattern of the third molar is +5.

Eastern Barbary, then, was during the Göttweig Interstadial a refuge for a Levalloisio-Mousterian industry of an earlier Palestinian type—unless the whole Mount Carmel dating is wrong. In the latter case, the Haua Fteah industry was a contemporaneous extension of the Tabun industry into Africa. In either case, this evidence suggests that by the time of the Göttweig Interstadial a presumably *sapiens* Caucasoid people, like the Mount Carmel population, may have penetrated northeast Africa. These people must have been in contact with the northwest Africans of that period, and may perhaps have occupied the Nile Valley. If the northwest Africans had not already become *sapiens* by local evolution, here was their opportunity to rise to the *sapiens* grade through gene flow, and to acquire a measure of Caucasoid characteristics some 25,000 years before the arrival of the Mouillians.

The Earliest Caucasoid Invaders of North Africa: the Mouillians

BEFORE the Pleistocene was over, northwest Africa was invaded by Caucasoids, contemporaries of the late Magdalenian peoples of Europe. They brought with them a blade and microlith culture called Mouillian after its type site, La Mouillah, 35 miles west of Tlemcen in western Algeria.[2]

We know that Mouillians came in with a Palearctic fauna, because bones of the brown bear (*Ursus arctos*), the Barbary sheep, or aoudad (*Ammotragus lervius*), and the Barbary ape (*Macaca inuus*), were found in the Mouillian site of Afalou-bou-Rhummel in Algeria. We also know roughly the date of their arrival—not long before 10,000 B.C.—because of a Carbon-14 dating in the next to earliest Mouillian level in the Moroccan cave of Taforalt (No. L-399E, 11,900 ± 240 B.P.). Because McBurney could find no exact counterpart of the Mouillian flint industry or of their physical type in the Near East, and because of their westerly geographical distribution, he believes that they came from Spain.[3] Briggs, on other grounds, derives them from the Near East,[4] and I am inclined to agree with Briggs, for three reasons: we do not yet know everything about the Upper Paleolithic industries of the Near East; the earliest Mouillian skull we have is Near Eastern Caucasoid in type, and the others could have been affected by local mixture; and bears, aoudads, and Barbary apes could hardly have swum across the Strait of Gibraltar, but they could easily have walked from Palestine during a climatically suitable period, such as the last advance of the Würm.

The Mouillian culture lasted well into the post-Pleistocene period, and its most characteristic physical type—stocky, broadfaced, and snub-nosed—may still be seen among individual Berbers living in relatively inaccessible regions along the Mediterranean coast, particularly in Kabylia and the Moroccan Rif. As late as the time of the Spanish conquest of the Canary Islands, during the fifteenth century A.D., some of the native Canarians, called Guanches, especially those living on Tenerife and Gran

---

[2] This culture was originally named Ibero-Maurusian because of its resemblance to a Mesolithic industry in Spain. Its name was later changed to Oranian because of its concentration in the Department of Oran, and finally to Mouillian, after the site in which it was first found.

[3] McBurney: *The Stone Age of Northern Africa* (London: Penguin Books; 1960), p. 225.

[4] Briggs: op. cit., p. 58.

Canaria, were Mouillians physically, as are some of their mixed descendants today.

The roster of Mouillian skeletons and parts of skeletons listed on Table 32 indicates a total of more than 252 individuals. Many of these cannot be used here, however, because they were ex-

TABLE 32

MOUILLIAN SKELETAL MATERIAL

Site	Material
ALGERIA	
Afalou-Bou-Rhummel, south shore of Gulf of Bougie, Constantine	32 skeletons and 5 mandibles in upper level; 1 adult male skeleton and 1 infant's skull in lower level
Ali Bacha, near Bougie, Constantine	Remains of 9 individuals
Gambetta, 10 mi. SSE of Souk Ahras, Constantine	Remains of 2 individuals
Kef-oum-Touiza, 45 SE of Bône, Constantine	1 skeleton
La Mouillah, 35 mi. W of Tlemcen, Oran	Remains of over 15 individuals
MOROCCO	
Dar es-Soltan, 4 mi. SW of Rabat	Remains of 4 individuals
Taforalt, 33 mi. NW of Oujda, in Beni Znassen country	Skeletons of 96 babies, 6 adolescents, and 80 adults

humed long ago and are lost, or else details have not been published. The most useful are twenty-eight skeletons from Afalou-bou-Rhummel which have been thoroughly described, and the Taforalt series, twenty-three skulls and twenty-six mandibles of which have recently been studied by Mlle Denise Ferembach.[5]

[5] Briggs: op. cit.

Boule, Vallois, and R. Verneau: "Les Grottes Paléolithiques de Beni Seghoual," *AIPH*, Mem. 13 (1934), Part 2.

Vallois: "Diagrammes Sagittaux et Mensurations Individuels des Hommes Fossiles d'Afalou-Bou-Rhummel," *TLAB*, No. 5 (1952).

Vallois: "Les Restes Humains de la Grotte de Dar es-Soltan," *CH*, No. 11 (1952), pp. 179–202.

D. Ferembach: "Les Restes Humains Epipaléolithiques de la Grotte de Taforalt (Maroc oriental)," *CRAS*, Vol. 248 (1959), pp. 3465–7.

Ferembach: "Les Hommes du Mésolithique d'Afrique du Nord et le Problème des Isolats," *BSPC*, Vol. 8 (1960), pp. 1–16.

The Capsians

A SECOND Mesolithic blade and microlith culture has been identified in northwest Africa. This is the so-called Capsian, named after its type site of Gafsa, about 50 miles south of Kasserine, of World War II fame. Its affinities are broadly Palestinian and there is little question but that it came from the Near East early in post-Pleistocene time.

Capsian sites fringe the Mouillian area on the east and south, and in some sites Capsian levels overlie Mouillian deposits. But in the northwest, particularly along the coast, the Mouillian lasted into the Neolithic, with which both these cultures gradually merged.

The oldest Capsian Carbon-14 date is 6,450 B.C. (8,400 ± 450 B.P., L-134), from el-Mekta, a site 10 miles northwest of Gafsa in Tunisia. As this is an Upper Capsian site, the Lower Capsian industry of the entire region must have been an earlier date, but not as early as the Early or even Middle Mouillian.

Although the Mouillians and Capsians were both Caucasoids, the broad-faced, heavily-muscled Mouillian type is less common among the Capsians, who tend to be more like the original Near

TABLE 33

CAPSIAN SKELETAL MATERIAL

Site	Material
TUNISIA	
Ain Meterchem, 40 mi. SE of Tebessa	1 skeleton
ALGERIA	
Aioun Beriche, 8 mi. N of Aïn Beidha, Constantine	More than 8 skeletons
Mechta al-Arbi, 35 mi. SW by W of Constantine	32 skeletons, 8 skulls of which have been described
Grotte du Cuartel ⎫ in the Grotte du Polygone ⎬ city of Grotte des Trogdolytes ⎭ Oran	Many skeletons; 3 skulls survive
MOROCCO	
Sidi Ahmed el-Habib, 12 mi. W of Berkane near the Algerian frontier	1 skeleton

Eastern prototype. As we shall see later, the Capsian culture was carried across the Sahara into East Africa, as far south as Olduvai and beyond, and the Capsian skeletons of East Africa bear a family likeness to those north of the Sahara.

On Table 33 are listed more than fifty-eight Capsian skeletons, mostly from Tunisia but represented by one site each from Algeria and eastern Morocco. Briggs, our chief source for this material, was able to locate and measure only eleven of the skulls, four of which are male and seven female. He published them not in a separate series, but in a composite North African Mesolithic series that also included thirty-three Mouillian skulls from Afalou-bou-Rhummel and elsewhere. In his analysis of this series by morphological types, Briggs distinguishes between the skulls of the two cultures, which differ as previously indicated.

The Racial Anatomy of the Mesolithic North Africans

IN ADDITION to Briggs's series, we have Vallois's of twenty-eight Afalou-bou-Rhummel skulls, and Ferembach's of twenty-three skulls and twenty-six mandibles from Taforalt. The Mouillians are far better known than the Capsians, therefore, and the following description applies principally to the former.

The mean cranial capacity of the males is 1,614 cc. for a pooled series of thirty-nine male skulls (Briggs and Ferenbach) and 1,519 cc. for seventeen female skulls. These skulls are very large, and show considerable sexual dimorphism in their dimensions. In metrical details the two series (Briggs's includes the skulls published in Vallois's series) generally resemble the European Upper Paleolithic crania. They have high-vaulted brain cases of variable shape, a few of which, from Afalou-bou-Rhummel, are brachycranial. Most of them have short, broad faces with low orbits and deep, broad mandibles with everted gonial angles.

In many of the male skulls the brow ridges are heavy, but concentrated over the centers of the orbits with little lateral extension. Most of the chins are projecting. Mid-facial prognathism is usually slight or absent, whereas alveolar prognathism is medium or pronounced in about 70 per cent of the specimens in Briggs's series. The malars are large in 60 per cent of them, and the sub-nasal fossa slight or absent in 60 per cent also. Some of the skulls show a forward projection of the malars below the orbits, a condition similar to that seen in Mongoloids and Bushmen; and one male skull (Afalou 40) apparently has an index of upper facial flatness of about 8, which is very low and within the Bushman range.

We know very little about the teeth of these people. Their upper median incisors had been removed in childhood, as had also, in some cases, the upper lateral and lower median incisors. All the adult and most of adolescent teeth were extremely worn, and only the teeth of the Dar es-Soltan skull (C-1) have been measured. These are not remarkably large. In the mandible of this specimen the first molar is the largest of the three; the third is the smallest.

In general, these skulls, disproportionately drawn from two cultures, fluctuate metrically and morphologically between two poles. At one extreme is a long-headed Caucasoid which resembles not only Combe Capelle but also several skulls of its own geological age in western Asia, such as my Mesolithic material from Hotu, and the Early Bronze Age skulls from Tepe Hissar in northern Iran. At the other is a local type characterized by a number of features not seen before in combination—a broad, short vault; a broad, short face; low orbits; a combination of a flattish upper face with alveolar prognathism; a prominent chin; and flaring gonial angles. Later on we shall see a more extreme version of the same combination in Africa south of the Sahara, where it was apparently ancestral to the living Bushmen.

The oldest known skull of whose age we can be sure, Afalou 28, belongs to the first type, and so does the Dar es-Soltan specimen (C-1), which presumably is as old. Five of eleven Upper Capsian skulls fall into a generalized modern Mediterranean category, whereas only three of twenty-eight Mouillian skulls do. This evidence suggests that the modern Mediterranean element common to North Africa today was largely if not wholly a Capsian introduction.

Information on the long bones comes entirely from Vallois.[6] He

[6] Vallois: "Les Restes Humains . . ."

measured eleven male and eight female skeletons from Afalou-bou-Rhummel. The male mean stature was five feet eight inches (173 cm., range = 162–180 cm.), and the female mean was five feet five inches (165 cm., range = 155–180 cm.). Unless these figures are capricious because of sampling, the sexual dimorphism of these people in terms of stature was less than that among the Upper Paleolithic Europeans.

Like the Upper Paleolithic Europeans, the Afalou people had relatively long forearms and lower legs. Their hands and feet were large. Nothing is known of the body bones of the Capsians except for the male skeleton from Sidi Ahmed el-Habib in eastern Morocco. It is five feet four inches tall (162 cm.) and the bones are lightly built, lacking the strong muscle markings of the Mouillians from Afalou-bou-Rhummel and Taforalt.

In sum, the racial history of northwest Africa from about 12,000 B.C. to the beginning of the Neolithic was roughly as follows. First came a robust Near Eastern Caucasoid, along with the Palearctic fauna. These immigrants mixed with the local Aterian folk, producing a population with short, broad faces, flattish upper faces, alveolar prognathism, and square jaws. While this mixture was taking place, many of the Aterian people were being pushed southward beyond the Sahara. Finally a Near Eastern Mediterranean of modern type, like that of the Natufians, came in from the East with the Capsian culture, and the result is, essentially, the present-day North African Berber population.

Human Evolution in Africa South of the Sahara

A L T H O U G H the evidence for human evolution in North Africa before the arrival of the Mouillians is scanty, at least it is internally consistent with the concept of the local development of a separate human subspecies linked at the base with Sinanthropus and at the top with the Bushmen. In the rest of Africa evidence is just as scarce and in addition it is confusing. The confusion stems from three facts. South Africa is a vast refuge area which drew more than one kind of people from the East African highlands. Several of the key skulls found in sub-Saharan Africa are dubiously dated. Some of them are misleading because they were hastily reconstructed at the time of discovery and have never been dismantled and redone, as, for example, Skhul 5 was refashioned by Charles Snow. Any skull that is important enough to serve as a document of human evolutionary history merits this treatment.

The skeletal material available, after the elimination of several particularly dubious pieces, is listed in Table 34. It comes from twenty-two sites, eight of which may be generally labelled Early Man, five Capoid, four Caucasoid, and only three definitely Negro.

The "Milk" Teeth from Olduvai

A Y E A R before the discovery of Zinjanthropus at Olduvai Gorge, Tanganyika, Louis Leakey found two hominid milk teeth in the deposit just above the Zinjanthropus level.[7] As they were associated with early hand axes and the appropriate fauna, they were attributed to the base of the Middle Pleistocene, in Bed II.

One is a mint-fresh, completely unworn molar. Leakey called it a lower second milk molar. Howell suggested that it might be an upper second milk molar, and von Koenigswald called it an upper left permanent second molar. According to Leakey, the second tooth, which is badly worn, is a left lower milk canine. Von Koenigswald called it an upper milk canine. If both were milk teeth they could have come from the same individual, but if the molar was a permanent and the canine a milk tooth, they probably did not, because the milk canines are shed before the permanent second molars erupt.

The Olduvai molar is larger than any known tooth of *Homo*, milk or permanent, in both the length and breadth of its crown. Its dimensions fall close to those of the Australopithecines from Swartkrans, but are smaller than those of Zinjanthropus. The tooth is longer than it is wide, as in four of the Swartkrans teeth. In Zinjanthropus and *Homo* the breadth exceeds the length. The

[7] L. S. B. Leakey: "A Giant Child among the Giant Animals of Olduvai," *LIN,* Vol. 232, No. 6212 (1958), pp. 1104–5.

Howell: "European and N.W. African Middle Pleistocene Hominids."

G. H. R. von Koenigswald: "Remarks on a Fossil Human Tooth from Olduvai, East Africa," *PKNAW,* Vol. 63, No. 1 (1960), pp. 20–5.

crown pattern of the Olduvai tooth, with six cusps, a slight beading on the forward edge, and a fovea at each end, can be matched in Swartkrans.

The milk canine is not distinctive morphologically. Its crown dimensions place it within the human range if it is an upper, and a little outside it if it is a lower. Its size dimensions are also like those of the South African Australopithecines. This tooth, therefore, has little diagnostic value.

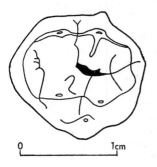

FIG. 80 THE MOLAR FROM OLDUVAI BED II. At the bottom of Bed II in Olduvai Gorge, Lewis Leakey found a molar and a canine. The canine is a milk tooth. The molar is probably a left upper first permanent molar. In its size, shape, and cusp pattern it closely resembles the corresponding teeth of *Australopithecus robustus* from South Africa. (Drawing after von Koenigswald, 1960.)

0   1cm

In all likelihood the two teeth did not belong to the same individual. Nothing more can be said about the canine, but the molar is probably Australopithecine. It resembles those of the South African *robustus* group closely, and differs in size and shape from those of Zinjanthropus, whose remains were found lower down in the same site.

Either Australopithecines coexisted with men when the bottom of Bed II was formed; or the teeth, particularly the molar, were eroded out of the top of Bed I and found their way into the bottom of Bed II; or else the earliest men of Olduvai had bigger teeth than those seen in the genus *Homo* elsewhere in the world. In my opinion the third alternative is virtually impossible. These teeth probably tell us nothing about early man in East Africa.

A Possible Negro Evolutionary Line

A S I D E from the milk teeth just described, the remaining nine specimens or sets of specimens listed at the top of Table 34 seem to form a sequence, although no one else to my knowledge has in-

TABLE 34

SKELETAL MATERIAL FROM AFRICA SOUTH OF AND INCLUDING THE SAHARA

Country	Site	Date	Material	Name or Race
Tanganyika	Olduvai	Early Middle Pleistocene	2 milk teeth	Australopithecine(?)
Tanganyika	Olduvai	Early Middle Pleistocene	1 calvaria	Chellian-3 Man
Kenya	Kanjera	Uncertain	4 calvaria, long bones	*H. kanamensis*
Cape Province	Saldanha Bay	Upper Pleistocene	1 calvaria, 1 piece mandible	None given
N. Rhodesia	Broken Hill	Upper Pleistocene	2 individuals: 1 cranium, 1 maxilla, long bones	*H. Rhodesiensis*
Tanganyika	Lake Eyasi	Upper Pleistocene	Fragments 1 skull	*Africanthropus njarensis*
Ethiopia	Diré Dawa	Upper Pleistocene	Fragment mandible	None given
Transvaal	Cave of Hearths	Upper Pleistocene	Fragment mandible	None given
Cape Province	Cape Flats	Late Upper or post-Pleistocene	3 individuals: 2 crania, long bones	"Australoid"
Natal	Border Cave	Post-Pleistocene	1 adult skeleton, 1 infant	"Australoid"
Sudan	Singa	10,000–5,000 B.P.	1 calvaria	*H. sapiens* Capoid
Kenya	Homa Shell Mound	Post-Pleistocene	7 skeletons	*H. sapiens* Capoid
Transvaal	Boskop	Post-Pleistocene	1 calvaria, fragment mandible	*H. sapiens* Capoid
Orange Free State	Florisbad	Late Upper or Early post-Pleistocene	fragment cranium, tooth	*H. (africanthropus) Helmei*
Cape Province	Fish Hoek	Post-Pleistocene	1 skeleton	Capoid
Cape Province	Matjies River	Post-Pleistocene	Remains 27 *ca.* individuals	Capoid
Kenya	Elmenteita	Post-Pleistocene	30 skeletons	*H. sapiens* Caucasoid
Kenya	Gamble's Cave	Post-Pleistocene	5 skeletons	*H. sapiens* Caucasoid
Tanganyika	Olduvai	Post-Pleistocene	1 skeleton	*H. sapiens* Caucasoid

TABLE 34 (*continued*)

Country	Site	Date	Material	Name or Race
Tanganyika	Naivasha RR	Post-Pleisto-cene	1 skeleton	*H. sapiens* Caucasoid
Sudan	Khartoum	Post-Pleisto-cene	5 individuals	*H. sapiens* "Negroid"
Sahara	Asselar	Post-Pleisto-cene	1 skeleton	*H. sapiens* "Negroid"
Mali	Kourounko-rokalé	Post-Pleisto-cene	11 skeletons, 2 fossil mand-ibles	*H. sapiens* "Negroid"

TABLE 35

THE TEETH FROM BED II OF OLDUVAI

	The Molar Compared to Lower Second Milk Molars				The Molar Compared to Upper Second Permanent Molars		
	Length	Breadth	Robustic-ity		Length	Breadth	Robustic-ity
Olduvai	15.0	14.0	210 mm.²	Taungs	12.8	14.0	179 mm.²
Taungs	11.0	9.0	99	Sterkfon-tein 89	14.6	15.0	219
Makapans-gat	12.5	10.5	131	Sterkfon-tein 20	14.0	13.2	185
Swartkrans	13.2	12.1	159	*Olduvai*	15.0	14.0	210
Kromdraai	12.0	9.7	116	Zinjan-thropus	17.0	18.1/20.3	308/345
Sinanthro-pus 127	12.2	10.1	123	Pithecan-thropus 4	12.0	14.0	168
				Sinanthro-pus 33	12.1	13.4	162

The Canine Compared to Upper and
Lower Milk Canines

		Length	Breadth	Robusticity
	Olduvai	6.7	5.7	38 mm.²
Upper	Taungs	6.8	5.8	39
Lower	Taungs	6.5	5.3	34
	Sterkfontein (largest)	6.4	5.6	36
	Swartkrans (largest)	6.4	4.7	30
	Kromdraai	5.2	4.9	26

terpreted them in this fashion. They begin with what is clearly a *Homo erectus* brain case and end with skeletons that are primitively *sapiens*.

In my opinion this is a Negro line, located in East and South Africa, a line which is separated in space, and probably also in time, from the three specimens at the bottom of the table, which are indubitably Negro. In studying each specimen in turn, we must remember that East Africa was closer to the sources of more rapid evolutionary change in the north than South Africa was, and that the farther south one goes, the slower the pace of human evolution and the greater the time lag in the procession of Paleolithic industries. What happened in the Sudan and West Africa, the homelands of the modern Negroes, is still a complete mystery.

The Chellian-3 Skull from Olduvai

D U R I N G his 1960 excavations at Olduvai Louis Leakey found a human skull in Bed II, 43 feet above the dividing line between Bed I and Bed II, and in association with hand axes and cleavers of the African Chellian industry. Because the tools at that level belong to the third of several recognized stages, the specimen is called, temporarily, the Chellian-3 skull of Olduvai. Like the remains below it, this skull was associated with animal bones, in this case the bones of full-sized game, which had been broken for marrow. Chellian-3 man was apparently a full-scale hunter.

The skull consists of a faceless calvaria, broken open at the top as well as in the base. It has very large brow ridges, a sloping forehead, a nuchal crest, and small mastoids: the hallmarks of the *Homo erectus* grade. Its length of 209 mm. is excessive, and its breadth of about 133 mm. is narrow, for an otherwise large *erectus* skull. In fact, this breadth dimension would fit the intercondylar breadth of the Heidelberg jaw. Its probable auricular vault height of about 109 mm. is low. Its walls are apparently thick. Probably its cranial capacity was between 1,100 and 1,200 cc., nearly equivalent to the capacities of the largest Solo and Sinanthropus skulls.[8]

However, it differed from both morphologically. The brow ridges form a double arch when seen from in front and sweep far to the rear on either side. Although very much larger and longer, these brow ridges resemble those of Steinheim in details of form.

---

[8] Only the length and breadth measurements have been published. The other figures are my own, derived from a scale photograph and calculations.

FOSSIL MAN SITES IN AFRICA
South of and in the Sahara

Asselar

Kourounkorokalé

Tchad
Australopithecine

Khartum

Singa

Diré Dawa

Kanjera
Homa

Olorgesailie
(ARCHAEOLOGY ONLY)

Nakuru
(Nairobi)
Naivasha
Elmenteita
Gamble's Cave

Lake Eyasi

Olduvai

Kalambo Falls
(FIRST FIRE IN AFRICA)

Broken
Hill

Cave of
Hearths
Boskop

Florisbad

Border Cave

Saldanha Bay
Fish Hoek
Cape Flats

Matjies River

MAP 12

The index of upper facial flatness, impossible to calculate accurately from present evidence, probably fell within the Caucasoid and Negro ranges. This contemporary of Heidelberg and Sinan-

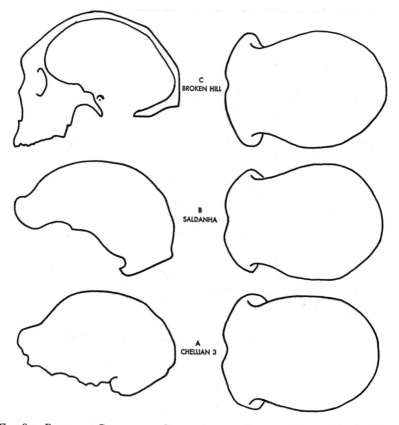

FIG. 81 PROFILES: CHELLIAN 3, SALDANHA, AND BROKEN HILL. Of the five lines of human descent, the two African ones are the most poorly represented by fossil specimens. The oldest of what seems to be the Congoid line is the Chellian 3 skull from Olduvai, shown here in a restored form. The top of the skull is missing but enough is left of the parietals to make a fair reconstruction. Although its brow ridges are heavy, its nuchal area is nearly modern in form. The Saldanha skullcap, presumably over 300,000 years younger, is essentially the same; and the Broken Hill skull, younger still, shows little advance over its predecessors. Unless the dating of the last two skulls is wrong, human evolution proceeded at a snail's pace during the Middle and Upper Pleistocene in Africa south of the Sahara. (Drawing A after Leakey; B after a photograph by the author; C after Pycraft.)

thropus (Leakey, Evernden, and Curtis set the date at 360,000 years by Argon-40 analysis) [9] could have been close to an even earlier common ancestor of both Caucasoids and Congoids.

[9] Leakey, J. F. Evernden, and G. H. Curtis: "Age of Bed I, Olduvai Gorge, Tanganyika," *Nature*, Vol. 191, No. 4787 (1961), pp. 478–9.

It is tempting also to relate Chellian-3 man to its local predecessor, Zinjanthropus. But in at least two respects Chellian-3 is
more primitively hominid, or even pongid, than Zinjanthropus, or
indeed any other known Australopithecine. Its nuchal crest, like
that of Pithecanthropus 4, sits higher on its occipital bone, and its
foramen magnum lies farther to the rear in the base of the skull.
To derive Chellian-3 man from Zinjanthropus would be biologically impossible.

We must not let ourselves be misled into interpreting the continuity of stone implements in Beds I and II of Olduvai Gorge to
indicate a continuity of tool makers—from Zinjanthropus to Chel-
lian-3 man. The crude tools that both beds have in common were
of a type made all the way from Morocco to South Africa and from
Palestine to Indonesia by several kinds of hominids, including,
no doubt, both Australopithecines and men. But in Bed II, for the
first time in the Gorge, hand axes appear, and they are the hallmark of Western man. These hand axes are few in number, compared to the cruder tools, and less skillfully fashioned than those
made in Europe at the same time. What evidence there is suggests
that Chellian-3's ancestors had come from farther north in Africa
and had not evolved from local, East African Australopithecines.

The Kanjera Specimens [1]

I N 1932, the same year in which Louis Leakey found the Kanam
mandible (see Chapter 7), he also found human remains at Kanjera, a neighboring site on the south shore of the Gulf of Kavirondo, Lake Victoria Nyanza. Kanjera is the type site of the Kanjeran Pluvial period, the third in the East African sequence, believed to correspond roughly to the Riss glaciation in Europe.

Three of the four specimens had weathered out and were lying
on the surface, but one of them, Kanjera 3, was still partly imbedded in the ground. All were covered with a crust of the grayish, calcified sand in which Number 3 had lain. All four were
equally mineralized, and had the same fluorine content as the

[1] Leakey: *The Stone Age Races of Kenya* (Oxford: Oxford University Press;
1935).

animal bones that accompanied them.[2] They were also apparently, but not positively, associated with late Acheulian hand axes. We do not know the exact age of the Kanjeran fauna, nor do we know when hand axes ceased to be made in Kenya. If, as now seems likely, the human specimens belong to the geological setting to which they have been attributed, they are probably of Upper Pleistocene date. But they could be only 40,000 to 30,000 years old. Or they could be of an earlier date, or possibly intrusive. No one really knows, which is unfortunate because they are anatomically unique.

Number 1, consisting of seven fragments, covers most of the sagittal profile of the brain case, except for its base, and also includes pieces of a zygomatic bone and maxilla. Number 2 is represented by three small pieces of parietal. Number 3, like Number 1, consists of seven pieces of vault, although they are less complete and the bones do not all articulate. Number 4 is a piece of frontal bone with nasion intact, and a smaller piece of vault.

The first three specimens are thick-walled, the fourth thin. Numbers 1 and 3 are long, narrow, and low-vaulted,[3] with deeply curved frontal and occipital bones and a flat profile on top. Numbers 1 and 3 lack brow ridges and have a general infantile appearance whereas Number 4, the thin bone, has moderately strong brow ridges. Inside the frontal of Number 1 an extensive sagittal crest served as an internal brace. The left frontal bone of Number 3 has a high temporal crest, indicating a heavy jaw musculature. In Numbers 1 and 4 nasion is placed high and the nasal bones could not have been excessively broad, at least at the root of the nose. The zygomatic and maxillary fragments of Number 1 are small and slight, with a canine fossa. The endocranial cast shows an enlarged *area striata* (the visual region of the occipital lobes) and an ill-filled parietal region, as in the *Homo erectus* specimens from Java and China and in some modern Australian aboriginal skulls.

The capacities of Numbers 1 and 3 have been estimated at 1,350 to 1,400 cc., and these figures, along with the morphology

[2] K. F. Oakley: *Physical Anthropology in the British Museum* (London, 1958).
[3] The reconstructed length and breadth dimensions of Number 1 are 207 mm. and 137 mm.; the cranial index is only 66. The comparable figures for Number 3 are 208 mm., 140 mm., and 67 mm.

of the skulls, mark them as *sapiens*. Without more of the faces and with no teeth available for study, it is difficult to give them a racial designation, but they fit the category of Negro more than any other. A perfectly modern toe phalanx associated with Number 3, three pieces of rib belonging apparently to Number 2, and a femur shaft found near Number 3 are all modern, although racially undiagnostic.

Whatever their date, these specimens are a primitive grade of *Homo sapiens*, and are probably Negro. As the femur was full-sized, they were presumably not Pygmies.

The Saldanha Bay Skullcap [4]

T H E Saldanha Bay skullcap was discovered in 1953 by Ronald Singer and Keith Jolly in a huge bed of fossil animal bones at Elandsfontein Farm, 15 miles east of Saldanha Bay and about 90 miles north of Capetown. Along with it were found many stone implements, including both hand axes and flake tools. A piece of mandible was later found in the same site and attributed to the same individual.

The date of the skull has not yet been firmly established. On the

[4] M. R. Drennan: "A Preliminary Note on the Saldanha Skull," *SAJS*, Vol. 50, No. 1 (1953), pp. 7–11.

Drennan: "The Saldanha Skull and its Associations," *Nature*, Vol. 172, No. 4383 (1953), pp. 791–3.

Drennan: "Saldanha Man and his Associations," *AA*, Vol. 56, No. 5 (1954), pp. 879–84.

R. Singer: "The Saldanha Skull from Hopefield, South Africa," *AJPA*, Vol. 12, No. 3 (1954), pp. 345–62.

Drennan and Singer: "A Mandibular Fragment, Probably of the Saldanha Skull," *Nature*, Vol. 175, No. 4452 (1955), pp. 364–5.

A. Mabutt: "Geomorphology, Archaeology, and Anthropology from Bok Baii, Darling District, Cape Province I, Physiography and Surface Deposits," *SAAB*, Vol. 10, No. 39 (1955), pp. 85–6.

Singer: "Man and Mammals in South Africa," *JPSI*, Vol. 1 (1956), pp. 122–30.

Singer: "Investigations at the Hopefield Site," *PTPA*, 1957, pp. 175–82.

Singer: "The Rhodesian, Florisbad, and Saldanha Skulls," *NC*, 1958, pp. 52–62.

Singer: "The New Fossil Sites at Langebaanweg (South Africa)," *CA*, Vol. 2, No. 4 (1961), pp. 385–7.

Singer and J. R. Crawford: "Archaeological Discoveries at Hopefield," *JRAI*, Vol. 88, Part I (1958), pp. 11–19.

Oakley: "Dating the Stages of Hominid Evolution," *The Leech*, Vol. 28, Nos. 3, 4, 5 (1958), pp. 112–15.

basis of faunal associations, confirmed by fluorine tests, it could be 100,000 years old, but on the basis of associated artifacts it could be no more than 40,000 years old.[5] For present purposes it makes little difference which of these dates is correct, because Saldanha man lived, in either case, between the dates of Chellian-3 man and Rhodesian man, and forms a close anatomical link with them.

The Saldanha Bay specimen is a skullcap reconstructed from twenty-seven pieces and completely lacking a base except for two triangular fragments of the occipital squama, situated on either side of the center line. Although the cranial capacity cannot be measured exactly, Singer places it between 1,200 and 1,250 cc., a little over the estimated figure for the Chellian-3 skullcap, which it closely resembles morphologically. In grade it is also equivalent to the larger skullcaps from Solo and Choukoutien, and is a classic example of *Homo erectus*.

Its sagittal profile is very much like that of Chellian-3, except that its brow ridges and occipital region are a little less protuberant. It is somewhat shorter (200 mm. as compared to 209 mm.) and probably broader (144(?) mm. as compared to 134(?) mm.), but the vault height above the glabella-opisthion line is apparently the same in both specimens (84 mm.). Like those of Chellian-3, its brow ridges sweep back laterally, and its index of upper facial flatness, about 20, is somewhat high for modern Negroes but normal for Caucasoids.

The piece of mandible consists of the upper forward half of the ascending ramus, including the coracoid process and the nutrient foramen. As reconstructed by Singer, it extends onto the body of the right condyle and down to within 10 mm. of the lower margin

---

[5] Singer (1961) has equated the fauna at Hopefield and that of the upper of two levels at a very rich nearby site, Langebaansweg, which is Late Middle to Early Upper Pleistocene. On the other hand, the accompanying Fauresmith artifacts, which include both very late hand axes and Middle Stone Age flakes, seem to indicate a later date. According to Oakley (1958), the implements represent a transition from one industry to another rather than a sequence of two distinct cultures. This particular local form of the Fauresmith culture has been assigned the same general date as a forest-culture called Sangoan, which was given a Carbon-14 date of about 40,000 years ago. The Lamont Laboratory has produced one date of 41,000 ± 3,300 B.C. (L-399 C), which, it advises, should be used with caution.

of the jawbone. The ascending ramus was therefore about 57 mm. high and 47 mm. wide. It was not high, and it rose at nearly a right angle from the body of the mandible. The coracoid process slopes forward, as in Heidelberg, rather than backward, as in Ternefine and Sinanthropus. In general, it closely resembled the corresponding portion of the Heidelberg jaw, but it is thinner by 1 mm. to 4 mm. at all points that can be measured.

The Saldanha Bay skullcap and mandible patently come from the same line as Chellian-3, although the Saldanha Bay specimen is several hundreds of thousands of years younger. This line resembles the Caucasoid much more closely than it does the Australoid, Mongoloid, or Capoid. The degree of its resemblance to the Congoids will be seen once we have examined other specimens that still have facial bones, particularly that of the Broken Hill skull, otherwise known as Rhodesian man.

The Broken Hill or Rhodesian Specimens [6]

T H E Broken Hill skull, also known as *Homo rhodesiensis*, or Rhodesian man, was discovered in 1921 in the course of mining opera-

[6] F. A. Bather, W. P. Pycraft, et al: *Rhodesian Man and Associated Remains* (London: British Museum [Natural History]; 1958), including:

W. P. Pycraft: "Description of the Human Remains," pp. 1–51.

G. Eliot Smith: "Endocranial Cast," pp. 55–8.

M. Yearsley: "Pathology of the Left Temporal Bone," pp. 59–63.

J. T. Carter: "Teeth of Rhodesian Man," pp. 64–5.

R. A. Smith: "Associated Stone Implements," pp. 66–9.

A. T. Hopwood: "Mammalia," pp. 70–3.

D. M. A. Bate: "Aves," p. 74.

W. E. Swinton: "Reptilia," p. 75.

A. Hrdlička: "The Skeletal Remains of Early Man," *SMC*, Vol. 83 (1930), pp. 98–144.

F. Weidenreich: "The Skull of *Sinanthropus pekinensis*"; "Some Particulars of Skull . . ."

J. D. Clark, et al: "New Studies on Rhodesian Man," *JRAI*, Vol. 77, Pt. 1 (1947), pp. 7–32.

Clark: "Further Excavations at Broken Hill, N. Rhodesia," *JRAI*, Vol. 89, Pt. 2 (1960), pp. 201–32.

Oakley: *New Evidence Regarding Rhodesian (Broken Hill) Man* (New York: Paper read at Viking Foundation Conference; June 20, 1950).

Oakley: "The Dating of the Broken Hill, Florisbad, and Saldanha Skulls," *PTPA*, 1955, pp. 76–9.

Oakley: "Physical Anthropology in the British Museum."

Singer: "The Rhodesian, Florisbad, and Saldanha Skulls."

tions at the Broken Hill Mine, Northern Rhodesia. The mine then consisted of two kopjes or hills composed of lead and zinc ores. The mining procedure was simply to break up the rock and carry it to the smelters. In 1907 the miners cut a hole through Kopje 1 and found inside it a pocket full of animal bones. As these were highly mineralized, they were smelted. Only in 1921 did the miners notice human bones among them, and some of these were saved.

The principal specimen is a virtually complete cranium that came from the very bottom of the deep pit at the end of the cave. In the same general area one tibia and one clavicle were also found, but the clavicle was later lost. Higher up in the main shaft and some distance away were found one broken *os coxae* or pelvic bone, one sacrum, pieces of two femora, the distal end of a tibia, and the distal half of a humerus, as well as a piece of a second maxilla with the right second and third molars in place. There is no assurance that any of these bones go together, even in the case of the tibia found with the skull, but they are all of roughly the same age.[7]

The associated artifacts are flake tools of an industry known as Proto-Stillbay to Stillbay, one of a series of African flake cultures of the so-called Middle Stone Age. Similar tools were found by Desmond Clark and his associates in a trench dug in the front of the kopje. They come from the end of the Lower Gamblian Pluvial period, about 23,000 B.C.[8]

The associated fauna contains only species still in existence, with two exceptions; a rhinoceros (*Diceros whitei* Chubb), and a serval cat (*Leptailurus hintoni*), both of which could have become extinct only recently.

The late Aleš Hrdlička, who was given neither to overstatement

[7] At first it was believed that the skull and the other bones were of different ages because the skull was found in lead ore and the bones in zinc ore. Subsequent analysis showed that both skull and bones were impregnated with zinc, and therefore the mineral in which each lay simply reflected its eventual position in the cave (Oakley, 1950). Still further analysis indicated that the nitrogen content of the skull and that of the bones are the same, and so is the age of both (Oakley, 1955).

[8] J. D. Clark (1947, 1960) determined this date by comparing the finds in the trench with the previously established sequence at another Rhodesian site, Mumbwa Cave.

nor to displays of unbridled emotion, called the Broken Hill skull "a comet of man's prehistory." [9] In 1930, when he made this pronouncement, Solo, Saldanha, Zinjanthropus, and Chellian-3 had not yet been discovered and Sinanthropus was being chiseled from its breccia. Thirty years later, the Broken Hill skull is still unusual in appearance, probably because it is the only complete skull of its evolutionary grade that we have. Also, it shows an incongruous combination of archaic and modern, brutal and delicate features, which label it a tired-looking peripheral survivor of an ancient and vigorous race of very primitive men.

In general morphology, Broken Hill closely resembles both Chellian-3 and Saldanha. It is as long as Chellian-3 and as broad as Saldanha. Its auricular height was less than Chellian-3's (105 as compared with *ca.* 109 mm.), but its projected height above the glabello-opisthion line was greater (85 as compared with 79 *ca.* mm.) The reason for these contradictions in the two height measurements is that in the Broken Hill skull, as in Saldanha, the nuchal crest is set lower on the occipital bone than in Chellian-3.

The cranial capacity of the Rhodesian skull is 1,280 cc., a little more than that of any other *Homo erectus* specimen we have yet seen, if the reconstructed figures for fragmentary skulls are correct. Its internal dimensions [1] match Solo's; the Rhodesian skull, however, is internally higher, but by only about 4 mm.

As the skull had been protected in the cave, it was not weathered or battered internally or externally. Because nearly all the right side of the base had been broken off at the time of discovery, Mr. Barlow of the British Museum, a peerless technician, was able to make a perfect endocranial cast, which was studied by the distinguished brain specialist Sir Eliot Smith.

Sir Eliot found that the track of the middle meningeal artery was simple, as in Sinanthropus, Solo, and Ternefine, but that its anterior branch was large. There is a large Sylvian crest, and the prefrontal, upper parietal, and lower temporal areas of the cortex were poorly developed in comparison with those of living men and of the Neanderthals. The imprint of the basal surface of the

[9] Hrdlička: "The Skeletal Remains . . . ," p. 130.
[1] Length is 173 mm.; breadth is 136.5 mm.; and height is 114 mm.

cerebellum shows that its lobes were more rounded and bent farther downward than in Solo.

The imprint of the pituitary fossa indicates a *sella turcica* of about the same size as that of Solo 11 (20 by 20 mm.). As the basal portion of the sphenoid bone was in perfect condition and the *sella turcica* easily visible, neither the shape nor the size of the seat of the pituitary is open to question.

The bones of the cranial vault are thinner than Saldanha's, the thickness of the right parietal ranging only from 6 to 10 mm. Next to Chellian-3, the Rhodesian specimen has the broadest, most

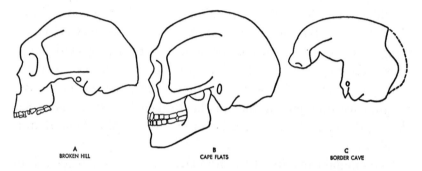

A
BROKEN HILL

B
CAPE FLATS

C
BORDER CAVE

Fig. 82 Profiles: a Possible Negro Line—Broken Hill, Cape Flats, and Border Cave. The modern Negroes seem to have evolved in West Africa and the Sudan, where we have no Negro skulls of Pleistocene age. In East and South Africa a number of skulls have been found which are apparently of early post-Pleistocene date. Of these the most authentic seem to be the Cape Flats and Border Cave skulls. These two are apparently earlier than the first Bushman remains in those regions, and they may provide a continuity between the Broken Hill skull, which was morphologically Congoid, and a primitive Negro population which preceded the ancestors of the Bushmen in South Africa. (Drawing A after Pycraft, 1928; B after A. Keith, 1931; C after Cooke, Malan, and Wells, 1945 and 1950.)

massive brow ridges of any human skull yet found; they match those of Zinjanthropus.[2] In form the Rhodesian brow ridges closely resemble those of Chellian-3 and Saldanha, sweeping far backward to either side.

Before we study the most remarkable part of the Rhodesian skull, its face, let us consider the teeth. The right lateral incisor had been lost during the individual's lifetime; both right premolars, the left second premolar, the left first molar, and the third

[2] The width and thickness of the brow ridges of Chellian-3 are, tentatively, 147 by 25 mm.; of Saldanha, 122 by 21 mm.; of Rhodesian man, 140 by 21 mm.; and of Zinjanthropus *ca.* 140 by *ca.* 20 mm.

right molar had been reduced by a combination of caries and attrition to mere shells, and the right canine had been worn or broken to a stub. (For the dimensions of the other nine teeth, see Table 39.)

The measurable teeth are as large as those of Sinanthropus, and one of them, the right upper second molar, is larger than the corresponding tooth of Pithecanthropus 4. The Rhodesian teeth are also larger than the three upper teeth from Tangier. The Rhodesian front teeth, from the upper lateral incisors to the first upper premolars, are as large as those of Zinjanthropus or larger; the remaining teeth, from the second upper premolar to the third molar, are smaller. The length of the outer dental arc, from third molar to third molar, is 175 mm. in the Rhodesian skull and 195 mm. in Zinjanthropus. The dental equipment of Rhodesian man was as massive as that of any other *Homo erectus.*

As in Sinanthropus and most modern individuals, the first molars were the largest and the third molars the smallest. The Rhodesian molars were taurodont. There is no evidence of a cingulum, Carabelli's cusp, or other unusual excrescences, and as far as we can tell the incisors were not markedly shoveled, if they were shoveled at all. A Flower's index of 44.2 makes Rhodesian man megadont. In general, these teeth resemble those of modern Negroes more than those of any other race.

As in Zinjanthropus and the Neanderthals, the palate of the Rhodesian skull is perched far forward of the middle portion of the skull base. Although this position indicates a considerable total facial prognathism, the face itself is so long that the principal inclination of the upper jaw is downward. The upper face height, 93 mm., is the greatest recorded for any fossil skull, except for the Neanderthal La Ferrassie male, whose face may have been 3 mm. longer. Weidenreich's reconstruction of Pithecanthropus 4 has an upper face height of only 89 mm.

On the other hand, Rhodesian man's bizygomatic diameter of 148 mm. is not remarkable. The same figure is found for the Crô-Magnon skull. Rhodesian man did not need flaring zygomatic arches because the forward position of his face left enough room behind his eye sockets to accommodate his temporal muscle bundles, despite heavy chewing. This does not mean that his orbits were shallow like those of Sinanthropus. They were high, wide, and deep—as far as I know the largest orbits yet found in *Homo*.

Like the Neanderthals he had a puffy facial surface, without canine fossae. In the frontal index of facial flatness and in the simotic index (reflecting the arching of the nasal bones at their root), the Rhodesian skull falls within the Caucasoid range, and in the third or rhinial index of facial flatness it resembles the ancient Egyptians and approaches the means of published series of living Negroes. In the fourth or premaxillar index of facial flatness it leaves all modern populations far behind it. In other words, this face is Caucasoid in its upper portion, Congoid in the middle, and virtually pongid below. On the whole this face is mostly Negro.

The tibia, which was found in the bottom of the cave with the skull, resembles that of a modern Negro in all essential details, and indicates a stature of about five feet seven inches (169.5 cm.).

The palate of a second individual, recovered from the front of the cave, consists of the lower half of the right maxillary bone, with the posterior half of the right second molar and the entire right third molar still embedded in it. The outer surface of this piece of bone has been scraped off except for that portion immediately over the third molar. The maxillary height, from the base of the nasal cavity to prosthion, was 24 mm., compared to 35 mm. for the skull. This difference indicates either that the Rhodesian male population was variable in upper jaw height, that this palatal fragment belonged to a female, or that this palate may not have been that of a member of the Rhodesian population. Its third molar is even larger than that of the corresponding tooth in the Rhodesian skull, which it resembles in form.[3]

In the debris from the front of the cave were also found two fragments of pelvic bone, a right and a left, which belonged to two individuals. The right one is modern in type whereas the left one has a number of peculiarities, including a high ilium and a shallow acetabulum, which led Pycraft[4] to assign not only this bone but also Rhodesian man as a whole to a new genus, *Cyphanthropus rhodesiensis* Woodward (Stooping Man). This designa-

---

[3] Length is 10 mm.; breadth, 12 mm.

[4] Pycraft: *Description of the Human Remains*.

tion has been ignored by subsequent authors. Also available are a small sacrum, the lower portion of a large humerus, and parts of two femora from different individuals. None of these bones deviate conspicuously from those of modern Negroes.

The Cranial Fragments from Lake Eyasi, Tanganyika [5]

A N O T H E R specimen from East Africa probably belongs to the same category as Rhodesian man, if it can be given any taxonomic position. It is the so-called *Africanthropus njarensis* discovered by Ludwig Kohl-Larsen on the shore of Lake Tanganyika, in 1935 and 1938.[6]

Eyasi man, as this specimen may be called, consisted of over two hundred scraps of skull, probably belonging to as many as three individuals, which Weinert painstakingly fitted together, finally producing a complete brain case. It was lost when Kiel was bombed during World War II, and we have only Weidenreich's estimate [7] that it was probably a member of the Rhodesian population and a female. Animal bones and stone tools were found on the surface with the skull fragments. But as chemical tests of the human bones cannot be made, the specimen cannot be dated.

The Mandibular Fragment from Diré Dawa, Ethiopia [8]

I N 1923 the dean of French prehistorians, the late Abbé Henri Breuil, found a piece of human mandible in the so-called Porcupine Cave in the hill of Balla, two kilometers from the Ethiopian city of Diré Dawa. Although the floor of the cave contained a number of industries, the mandible, which was fossilized, was

---

[5] H. Weinert, W. Bauermeister, and A. Remane: "Africanthropus njarensis, Beschreibung und phyletische Einordnung des ersten Affenmenschen aus Ostafrika," *ZfMuA*, Vol. 38 (1940), pp. 252–308.

[6] The generic name *Africanthropus* was subsequently dropped because it had already been assigned, equally without justification, to the Florisbad cranial fragment.

[7] Weidenreich: "The Skull of *Sinanthropus pekinensis*," p. 221.

[8] H. Breuil, P. Teilhard de Chardin, and P. Wernert: "Le Paléolithique du Harrar," *L'Anth*, Vol. 55, No. 3–4 (1951), pp. 219–30.

Vallois: "La Mandibule Humaine Fossile de la Grotte du Port-Épic près Diré-Dauoa (Abyssinie)," *L'Anth*, Vol. 55, No. 3–4 (1951), pp. 231–8.

probably of the same age as the Stillbay implements; these are similar to those found at Broken Hill.

The mandible consists of a piece of the right branch extending from the first premolar past the third molar, and lacking both symphysis and ascending ramus. Enough is left, however, for us to see that it was a large jaw, in the size range of Heidelberg, the North African mandibles of the Ternefine-Tangier line, the larger Sinanthropus mandibles, and those of some of the Neanderthals.[9]

The teeth are in poor shape, with most of the enamel and dentine gone from the crowns. Their measurements, published by Vallois,[1] are individually within the modern range and smaller than those of the Broken Hill skull.[2] Yet Vallois finds a total length of the premolar-molar row, from the front of the first premolar to the back of the third molar, of 52 mm., the same as for Heidelberg, and more than the figure for Broken Hill.

Although this mandible is classified in the literature as that of a Neanderthal, I see no justification for this label, nor can I find any clue to its actual relationship. It is included here in the Chellian-3 to Rhodesian group solely because of its geographical and cultural position.

The Mandible from the Cave of Hearths [3]

I N the Cave of Hearths at Makapansgat, Transvaal, the scene of Australopithecine discoveries, Raymond Dart found, in 1947, a human mandible cemented in red breccia and associated with the

[9] At the level of the mental foramen its height is 34.0 mm., its thickness 16.3 mm., and its robusticity index 47.9.

[1] Vallois: "La Mandibule . . . de Dire Dawa."

[2] The Dire Dawa tooth measurements are:

	First Premolar	Second Premolar	First Molar	Second Molar	Third Molar
Mesiodistal	5	5.5	9.9	10.5	10 (?) mm.
Labiolingual	7	6.5	9	10	9 mm.
Robusticity	35	36	89	105	90 (?) mm.[2]

[3] R. A. Dart: "The First Human Mandible from the Cave of Hearths, Makapansgat," *SAAB*, Vol. 3, No. 12 (1948), pp. 96–8.

P. V. Tobias: "The Kanam Jaw," *Nature*, Vol. 185, No. 4714 (1960), pp. 946–7.

Tobias: "Early Members of the Genus Homo in Africa," in G. Kurth, ed.: *Evolution und Hominisation*, Festschrift zum 60. Geburtstag von D. G. Heberer (Stuttgart: G. Fischer Verlag; 1962).

final type of hand axes known in South Africa. It probably dates to about 40,000 years ago, plus or minus 10,000 years,[4] and it was certainly no more recent than the Broken Hill skull.

It consists of a piece of the symphysis and right body of a mandible, running from the socket of the lower left median incisor to the place where the right lower third molar would have been had it erupted. Only the first premolar, first molar, and second molar are preserved, the other teeth being represented by broken roots, or having been lost. As the first molar was worn and the second molar mint-fresh and crisp-cusped, Dart gives the specimen's age as twelve.

It is a stout little mandible, probably chinless, with an angle of inclination of about 62°, which places it in the same class as Ternefine 1, Sinanthropus G, and Heidelberg.[5] Morphologically it shows no distinctive features. It has only one foramen on its remaining side, and no torus mandibularis.

The three teeth are too small to match the upper teeth of Broken Hill man, and smaller than those of the Ternefine-Tangier folk of North Africa; their closest counterparts are in the Heidelberg jaw.[6] The first lower premolar is pointed and looks like a canine, with a very low buccal cusp. The molars are plain, without wrinkles or cingulums, and the second molar has a standard Y-5 cusp pattern.

This mandible and its teeth probably belong to the Chellian-3 to Rhodesian group. However, if I were to see it without knowing where it came from, I would probably guess that it was of European origin, and set the time at the Third Interglacial.

[4] I arrive at this general date by comparison with the known dates of other sites in East and South Africa. In the Cave of Hearths itself a Middle Stone Age level was given a Carbon-14 date of 15,111 ± 730 B.P. (C-925). Libby gives Middle Stone Age III a date of 9,650 ± 700 (C-924).

[5] At the level of the first molar the height is 25.5 mm., the thickness 16.0 mm.; the index of robusticity 47.9. The indices of robusticity are 54.5 for the symphyseal region and 46.4 for the region of the mental foramen. The bone constituting the chin region had been scraped off.

[6]

	First Premolar	First Molar	Second Molar	
Length	8.0	12.0	11.5	mm.
Breadth	8.0	11.8	10.7	mm.
Robusticity	64	142	123	mm.²

The Cape Flats Skull

THE LINE that we have tried to trace, from Kenya to Cape-town and from the Early Middle Pleistocene to almost the end of the Upper Pleistocene, must have survived into the Recent period. Very likely it evolved eventually from a subspecies of *Homo erectus* into a subspecies of *Homo sapiens*, either by a purely local evolutionary process or by gene flow from outside. It may even have been wholly absorbed into another line. I think that we can rule out independent mutation as the cause of change, because the territory inhabited by this ancient line is fully exposed to contacts from the north.

Because South Africa is the most remote and isolated part of the continent—next to the rain forest, from which no pertinent information is available—it is there that we may expect to find survivors of the Chellian-3 to Rhodesian line in post-Pleistocene time. During the last half century a number of local archaeologists, both amateur and professional, have found hundreds of buried skeletons, mostly in rock shelters, which date from shortly after the end of the Pleistocene to the time when Dutch gin bottles appear amid the cultural debris, and after. Most of these finds are difficult to date, and some are actually post-Dutch, but among them it may be possible to locate what we are looking for.

This search is not helped by the fact that, except for Ronald Singer, apparently everyone who has worked with this material assumes that all skeletons found in South Africa, whatever their antiquity, must in some way be ancestral to the living Bushmen, Hottentots, and Korana (a kind of Hottentot), all of whom, in their opinion, were autochthonous.[7] However, there is an alternative theory of the origin of the Capoids: that they came from the north in postglacial times. With this in mind, we can examine each of the postglacial South African skulls critically to see if some of them are not only early in date but also racially non-Capoid. A number of non-Capoid skulls are indeed available. They have

[7] Singer: "The Boskop 'Race' Problem," *MAN*, Vol. 58, Art. No. 232 (1958), pp. 1-5.

been set aside by the South African anthropologists and classified as "Australoid" or "gerontomorphic." Two of them seem to be of moderate antiquity; these are the skulls from Cape Flats and the Border Cave.

In 1929 M. L. Drennan discovered an open-air site at Cape Flats, near Capetown, which contained, at a depth of three feet, the remains of three individuals, one skull of which has been partly described.[8] It was found without fauna in a deposit containing Stillbay flake tools, but there were also Wilton implements in the neighborhood. Stillbay tools are the kind associated with Broken Hill, and Wilton is a local Capsian derivative made by Bushmen. In South Africa the Middle Stone Age continued as late as 5,000 years ago,[9] and the Cape Flats site could have been, but was not necessarily, of that late.

The Cape Flats skull is long and narrow, with a cranial capacity of 1,230 cc., the same as Saldanha's and slightly less than Broken Hill's, and its vault is but two millimeters higher than the latter's. According to Drennan, the endocranial cast reveals the same primitive features seen in the Broken Hill skull. So far it indicates little or no advance in the shape of the brain of the line to which it seems to belong. But the external morphology of the brain case is more modern.

The brow ridges, although heavy and sweeping backward, are smaller than those of the earlier skulls. The brain case is angular, but in contour it is modern. Indeed, it generally resembles some Australian skulls, but it also looks somewhat like Steinheim. The face is long but not in the same class as the Broken Hill face, and in the degree of facial flatness, which cannot be measured without access to the original specimen, it follows the Rhodesian pattern of combining Caucasoid and Negro. The lower jaw has a chin.

Unfortunately no incisor teeth were preserved in either jaw. There are five upper teeth, from canine to first molar, and six low ers, from canine to third molar. The upper teeth are smaller than

[8] Drennan: "An Australoid Skull from Cape Flats," *JRAI*, Vol. 59 (1929), p. 417.

A. Keith: *New Discoveries Relating to the Antiquity of Man* (London: Williams & Norgate; 1931), pp. 140–2.

[9] A Middle Stone Age date from the Holley II site is 4,490 ± 150 B.P. (BM-34).

those in the Broken Hill skull, and the lowers match those from the mandible of the Cave of Hearths. All fall within the modern Negro range.

As Drennan pointed out, this skull does not resemble that of a modern South African Bantu, but there is no reason for it to do so. The Bantu are as recent as the Boers in South Africa, and this skull may well be old enough to have antedated the arrival of the ancestors of the Bushmen. If that is the case, then this skull may represent a descendant of the Chellian-3 to Broken Hill line which had crossed the *sapiens* threshold but had not evolved very much further and had lingered on in South Africa, to be eventually absorbed by the oncoming ancestors of the living Bushmen.

The Border Cave Skull [1]

I n 1934 Raymond Dart dug a trench in a cave on the border between Swaziland and Zululand (because it is on the border it is called the Border Cave), and in 1940 W. E. Horton of Nsoko, Swaziland, while continuing the excavation, found a human frontal bone in a late Stillbay cultural context. Further excavations and screening in 1941 yielded additional pieces of the skull, which is still fragmentary, consisting mostly of a frontal bone and parts of a left parietal, temporal, and occipital. Its basic measurements are given in Table 37.

The Border Cave skull is 200 cc. larger than the Cape Flats skull and has a vault 8 mm. higher. Its brow ridges are still large, and its general morphology is as expected if the Chellian-3 to Rhodesian line continued to evolve past the Cape Flats grade. It looks no more like a Bushman than did the late Mrs. Jones, with whose remark we began this chapter.

Writing before the discovery of the Chellian-3 skull, Briggs saw in the Border Cave cranial vault a resemblance to the Mouillians

[1] H. B. Cooke, B. D. Malan, and L. H. Wells: "Fossil Man in the Lembobo Mountains, South Africa; the Border Cave, Ingwavuma District, Zululand," *Man*, Vol. 45, Art. No. 3 (1945), pp. 6–12.

Wells: "Photographs with Note: The Border Cave Skull," *AJPA*, Vol. 8, No. 2 (1950), pp. 241–3.

of Afalou-bou-Rhummel.[2] His interpretation does not conflict with mine, however, because in the part of the skull represented by the Border Cave specimen Caucasoids (including the Mouillians) and Congoids have much in common. Ronald Singer, the discoverer of the Saldanha Bay skull, permits me to say that he is not convinced that either the Cape Flats or the Border Cave skull belongs to any group ancestral to the Bushman.[3]

There can be little doubt that the Cape Flats and Border Cave skulls were those of Negroes, and the Cape Flats skull had not evolved far beyond the *erectus-sapiens* threshold. We can interpret the presence of these skulls in South Africa in post-Pleistocene time in two ways. Either they represent an invasion or infiltration of Negroes from the north, along with the complex of cattle-breeding and metal-using which gave rise to the culture of the Hottentots; or else they were the remnants of a local population that had evolved from the Chellian 3–Saldanha–Broken Hill line into a local race of Negroes, one which became extinct by absorption into the ranks of the invaders.[4]

Whether or not a local race of Negroes evolved in South Africa before the ancestors of the Bushmen arrived has little to do with the origin of the Congoids as a subspecies. South Africa was not the principal center of the evolution of that or any other subspecies. The Negro home has traditionally been West Africa, a part of the Dark Continent from which we have not a single scrap of evidence.

---

[2] Briggs: "The Stone Age Races of North Africa," p. 65.

[3] Personal communication, January 18, 1962.

[4] To this second interpretation may be added a piece of evidence worthy only of a footnote. In or about 1941 a local naturalist named W. E. Jones excavated a nearly complete skeleton in a gorge of the Tugela River in Natal. It was buried in warm moist acid soil of a type inimical to the preservation of bone for more than a few centuries. Furthermore, the burial was accompanied by ostrich eggshell beads of Bushman type, which would not have lasted long in that soil. According to Jones, the skull was very similar to the Broken Hill specimen, particularly in the size of its brow ridges and the slope of its forehead. Realizing the importance of his discovery, Jones gave the skull to a Dr. Warren, director of the Natal Provincial Museum, who apparently took it to London during the latter part of World War II. Dr. Warren died in London and the skull has disappeared. O. Davies: "A Missing Skull of Early Type from Zululand," *Man*, Vol. 57, Article 54 (1957), p. 48.

The Capsian Settlers of the White Highlands [5]

I N T H E highlands of Kenya, Tanganyika, and Ruanda-Urundi, where the altitude is from 5,000 to 7,000 feet, the weather is cool the year around. Early in the present century a number of Europeans set up farms in the coolest parts of this region, and built Nairobi. Thousands of years earlier this same climate seems to have attracted other Caucasoid immigrants, a tall, long-faced, narrow-nosed people who buried their dead in a contracted posture and made blade tools in the Capsian style. We have seen these people and their tools before, in North Africa.

The first of these burials was discovered by Hans Reck of Berlin in Olduvai Gorge, in soil that Leakey has since identified as Bed V (see Fig. 40), a Capsian level. The second site was a series of burials along the face of a cliff on a farm in the Elmenteita district of Kenya. They were discovered in 1918. After the bodies had been buried, the waters of Lake Nakuru had risen, disturbing and redepositing the skeletons, and then later had subsided. At least thirty individuals were interred in this ancient cemetery.

In Kenya Leakey found the third site, Gamble's Cave, after which the Gamblian Pluvial period was named. He excavated five skeletons from this cave. Mrs. Leakey and A. J. Poppy discovered the fourth site, which contained a skeleton of the same type as the others, lying in the edge of an ancient lake at Naivasha Railroad Station, Kenya. Except for Olduvai, these sites are close to each other (see Map 12).

Only Gamble's Cave is completely stratified, and it alone contained adequate samples of implements and fauna. The implements are Capsian throughout, but between the second and fourth occupation levels from the top, an intrusive stratum of African Middle Stone Age tools was found, with Capsian artifacts below and above it. The fauna was modern.

[5] W. Giesler and T. Mollison: "Untersuchungen über den Oldowayfund," *VGPA*, Vol. 3 (1929), pp. 50–67.

Leakey: *The Stone Age Races of Kenya.*

Leakey: "The Naivasha Fossil Skull and Skeleton," *JEAN*, Vol. 16, No. 4–5 (1942), pp. 169–77.

S. Cole: *The Prehistory of East Africa* (London: Pelican Books; 1954).

Briggs: "The Stone Age Races of Northwest Africa."

McBurney: *The Stone Age of Northern Africa.*

The key to the age of this site lies in three facts. Potsherds were found in two of the three Capsian layers. Pottery was not made in the Near East or anywhere else, except Japan, before 5,400 B.C. As the Capsians were a culturally peripheral folk, it is unlikely that they were the first to invent pottery. Also, in an upper layer was found a bone harpoon identical with others from an upper layer in a Congo site dated at 6,000–4,500 B.C.[6] All the other Capsian sites in Kenya are postglacial. Therefore, the Gamble's Cave site fits into the local time scale where it belongs, well after the arrival of the Capsians in North Africa.

How the Capsians got to East Africa from North Africa we do not know, but we do not really need to. There is a direct overland route across the Sahara, following a diagonal path across the Tibesti Highlands. There is also the Nile Valley. At the time of their migration, during the early millennia of the post-Pleistocene, the Sahara had more surface water than it has today and it supported herds of game and was more densely populated than it has been in recent times.

Eleven skulls from the four sites are all essentially Caucasoid (see Table 37). They belonged to a rugged form of the Mediterranean race (a division of the Caucasoids), with long brain cases, narrow faces, and long noses. They all have modern-style chins, and in the males the mandibles are deep and the gonial angles everted. Most of them could pass unnoticed in a collection of Capsian skulls from North Africa. Between the males and females, considerable differences are evident. This is best indicated in their respective cranial capacities, which average 1,497 cc. for seven males and 1,223 cc. for three females.

Although their teeth have not been systematically studied, we know that no incisors were shoveled and that one milk molar in the Elmenteita series has a Carabelli's cusp. A lower first molar of an Elmenteita male has the extraordinarily large crown dimensions of 13 by 13 mm., well above the Caucasoid range. Also, the Elmenteita skulls, which Leakey considers younger than those from Gamble's Cave, are more prognathous than the others. To

[6] J. de Heinzelin: "Les Fouilles de Ishango," *Exploration du Parc National Albert* (Brussels: Institut des Parcs Nationaux du Congo Belge; 1957), pp. 64–1.

K. P. Oakley: "Bone Harpoons from Gamble's Cave, Kenya," *The Antiquaries Journal*, Vol. 41, Nos. 1–2 (1961), pp. 86–7.

my eye it looks as if they were the product of a mixture between the invading Capsians and an earlier element, either ancestral Bushmen who had preceded them across the Sahara or people like those whose skulls we have already seen in Cape Flats and the Border Cave.

These people were taller than the North African Capsians. The Olduvai V skeleton was that of a man five feet eleven inches tall (180 cm.); No. 4 from Gamble's Cave was the same or a trifle taller; and the Naivasha Railroad Station man, according to Leakey, was six feet eight inches tall (203 cm.)—a giant. These statures compare well with those of the living Watusi and other tall Hamitic peoples of the present-day white highlands.

Leakey and his associates also excavated a number of Neolithic sites in the same region. At least some of them were agricultural, and all antedate the main push of the Bantu expansion. These sites include the Nakuru burial ground, with nine skeletons, one of which was measured, and Willey's Kopje, near Elmenteita, with three skeletons, all measured. All twelve indicate that the Caucasoid racial type of the earlier Capsian invaders persisted in the highlands until the Iron Age, or until the Bantu arrived. Whatever mixture took place was probably with the old, indigenous East and South African line and with ancestral Bushmen rather than with modern Negroes. Despite the predominance of Bantu speech and culture in the highlands today, many of the native tribesmen who have black or brown skins and Negroid hair still retain Caucasoid facial features.

The Origin of the Capoids [7]

THE CAPOIDS, named by Broom after the Cape of Good Hope, constitute one of the five subspecies of modern man as

[7] Dart: "Three Strandloopers from the Kaokoveld Coast," *SAJS*, Vol. 51, No. 6 (1955), pp. 175–9.

Drennan: "The Dentition of a Bushman Tribe," *ASAM*, Vol. 24 (1929), pp. 61–87.

H. S. Gear: "A Further Report on the Boskopoid Remains from *Zitzikama*," *SAJS*, Vol. 23 (1926), pp. 923–34.

Gear: "Cranial Form in the Native Races of South Africa," *SAJS*, Vol. 26 (1929), pp. 684–97.

stipulated in Chapter 1. They include the living Bushmen, the living Hottentots and that branch of the Hottentots known as the Korana, a few beachcombing remnants of an earlier coastal Bushman population known as Strandloopers, and certain relict populations in Tanganyika and possibly farther north.

Capoid skeletal material is abundant in South Africa. Among it may be found specimens similar to contemporary Bushmen, with their reduced stature, small brain bent at the base to produce a bulging forehead, and small, neotenously infantile, very flat face. In addition there are specimens of a larger and less infantile variety commonly known as the Boskop race. To these two types may be added individual skulls and groups of skulls which show mixture with some other element, Hamitic (like the highland skulls we have just studied) or Negro or "Australoid." The result is a considerable confusion.

Two principal theories have been advanced to explain the origin of the Capoids. The first is that their ancestors came from North Africa or the Sahara, mostly if not entirely in postglacial

A. J. H. Goodwin: "A Comparison Between the Capsian and South African Stone Cultures," *ASAM*, Vol. 24, Part 1 (1929), pp. 17–32.

Keith: *New Discoveries Relating to the Antiquity of Man.*

Keith: "A Descriptive Account of the Human Skulls from the Matjes River Cave, Cape Province," *TRSS*, Vol. 21 (1933), pp. 151–85.

Leakey: *The Stone Age Races of Kenya*, 1935.

J. F. Schofield: "The Age of the Rock Paintings of South Africa," *SAAB*, Vol. 3, No. 12 (1948), pp. 79–88.

G. W. Grabham: "Note on the Geology of the Singa District of the Blue Nile," *Antiquity*, Vol. 12, No. 46 (1938), pp. 193–5.

Singer: "The Boskop 'Race' Problem," *Man*, Vol. 58 (1958), pp. 1–5.

D. Slombe: "The Osteology of a Bushman Tribe," *ASAM*, Vol. 24 (1929), pp. 33–60.

G. Eliot Smith: "The Influence of Racial Admixture in Ancient Egypt," *ER*, Vol. 7, No. 3 (1915), pp. 163–83.

P. V. Tobias: "Bushmen of the Kalahari," *MAN*, Vol. 57 (1957), pp. 33–40.

L. H. Wells: "The Status of the Bushman as Revealed by a Study of Endocranial Casts," *SAJS*, Vol. 34 (1932), pp. 47–58.

Wells: "The Fossil Human Skull from Singa," *FMA*, No. 2 (1951), pp. 29–42.

A. S. Woodward: "A Fossil Skull of an Ancestral Bushman from the Anglo-Egyptian Sudan," *Antiquity*, Vol. 12, No. 46 (1938), pp. 190–3.

R. Biassutti: "Crania Aegyptica," *AAE*, Vol. 36, Fasc. 2 (1906), pp. 165–73.

V. Giuffrida-Ruggeri: "I Crani Egiziani del Museo Civico di Milano," *AAE*, Vol. 37 (1907), pp. 399–410.

F. C. Shrubsall: "Notes on Some Bushman Crania and Bones from the S. African Museum, Capetown," *ASAM*, Vol. 5, Part 5, No. 6 (1906–10), pp. 227–70.

times, pushed south by the expanding Capsians. The second is that they evolved from local ancestors, including not only Saldanha Bay man and Broken Hill man, but also Florisbad, a fossil skull which will be described presently. This evolution consisted of two steps. First they acquired large, very modern brain cases, and then they shrank, through infantilism partly accompanied by dwarfing. At the same time, according to this second theory, these indigenous ancestors mixed sporadically with Hamites, "Australoids," and possibly others who wandered into the marginal territory that some of the Bushmen still occupy.

The proponents of both theories admit that the Bushmen are descended from full-sized ancestors, and that they began to grow small and infantile only a few thousand years ago, and that they did so in South Africa. No one has yet offered a satisfactory explanation of why they shrank. This subject, discussed in Chapter 3 (see pp. 112–15) and later in this chapter, does not concern us here. Our present task is to trace the history of the skeletons of Bushmen, large and small, in time and space.

The first theory, that of a northern origin, is based on data concerning chronology, archaeology, and the geographical distribution of Capoids, dead and alive. First, in all of South Africa there is not a single Bushman-like skull or skeleton of geological antiquity, although a few, such as Boskop, cannot be dated one way or the other. Second, as Goodwin has shown, all the Bushman-like specimens that are associated with a stone-tool industry are accompanied by artifacts known to South African archaeologists as Wilton, and Wilton is nothing but a derivative of the Capsian of North and East Africa. Third, the famous Bushman rock paintings, which extend northward into Rhodesia, cannot be much more than a few centuries old because they do not extend below the soil level in the caves and rock shelters in which they are found; because they have not been smoke-blackened by herdsmen's fires; because the granite on which they were painted had not exfoliated (peeled off) very much from weathering; and because the fauna depicted is all recent.[8]

The theory that the ancestral Capoids migrated southward from North Africa goes back to the discovery, during the last cen-

[8] Schofield: "The Age of the Rock Paintings. . . ."

tury, of Bushman-like rock paintings in the Sahara. In 1905 Bias-sutti first noticed Bushman-like traits in some of the oldest ancient Egyptian skulls, and since then the theory has been proposed and rejected several times. This is the first time, I believe, that the evidence favoring it has been presented as a unit.

The Singa Skull from the Sudan

I N 1924 the theory of a northern origin was re-enforced by the discovery, made by W. R. G. Bond, of a Bushman-like skull at Singa, 200 miles south of Khartoum, on a bank of the Blue Nile. Grabham, who had studied the site geologically from the standpoint of rates of soil deposition caused by the overflow of the Nile, stated, in 1938, that it could not be less than 5,000 nor more than 10,000 years old. The skull, however, was completely mineralized, despite the fact that it is thought to be of fairly recent date.

In 1951 Miss Dorothea Bate,[9] who studied the animal bones, found that two and possibly three supposedly extinct species of mammals were contemporaneous with the skull. They are *Homoioceras singae* Bate, an extinct antelopine; *Hystrix atasobae* Bate, an extinct porcupine; and *Sivatherium*, an extinct member of the giraffe family. Because no other specimens of the first two species had ever been found, we cannot be sure when they became extinct, and she herself was not altogether certain that she had correctly identified *Sivatherium*, which did not survive the Pleistocene.

In any event, the Singa skullcap is clearly as old as, if not older than, any known and competently dated Capoid skull found yet in South Africa. The skullcap is nearly complete, but the face is missing. The bone is thick (13 mm. on the parietals) and the brow ridges moderately heavy, with a distinct notch above glabella, like Sinanthropus and like the least infantile of the Bushman skulls. The forehead is narrow, but bulging; the parietals also bulge, giving the brain case a pentagonoid appearance. The orbits were apparently rectangular. Morphologically the skull could have been that of a full-sized progenitor of a Bushman. It is

[9] Wells: "The Fossil Human Skull. . . ."

brachycranial (length = 188; breadth = 154; cranial index = 82) but it may have been distorted. Even if the index of 82 is correct, this does not invalidate the racial identification of the Singa skull, because there are some living brachycephalic Bushmen. Indeed, some of the Mouillian skulls from Algeria and Morocco are also voluminous, brachycranial and rugged, presumably from mixture with the local Aterian population which they partly absorbed and partly displaced.

The Homa Shell-Mound Skulls

FOLLOWING the hypothetical migration route of the ancestors of the Bushmen to the south, we come to the Homa shell mound, a Mesolithic midden of fresh-water mollusk shells situated on the shore of Lake Victoria in Kenya. This midden contained Wilton A (Early Wilton) tools, typical of Bushmen, and six skeletons in various states of preservation. Two of the skulls, Numbers 1 and 4, have been measured and illustrations of them have been published [1] (see Table 37).

Number 1 belonged to a middle-aged male who had a large brain case, weak brow ridges, and a strongly arched forehead. Although his mandible was large, his teeth were small, especially his canines and incisors. His largest lower molar was the first one, and the third was greatly reduced. Number 2, which consists of postcranial bones and a mandible, belonged to a tall, massive man with a big mandible and five cusps on all his lower molars. Number 3 is said to be a virtually complete skeleton of a short, thickset adult male with a large head.

Number 4's face is nearly complete, and we have a profile drawing of the whole skull. The cranial capacity is very great, and the skull long and high. The forehead is bulbous, the top of the head comparatively flat. The face has much alveolar prognathism, the nasal skeleton is flat, and the lower rim of the orbits project. Despite its great size, this skull is morphologically that of a Bushman. Number 4's body was correspondingly large and heavy.

These Homa Shell Mound skeletons are significant not only because they place the Bushmen's ancestors well north of the mod-

[1] Leaky: *The Stone Age Races of Kenya.*

ern range of the Capoids, but also because, along with Singa, they are still large, unreduced, and not infantile. Had the Bushmen spread north to Kenya after they had completed their peculiar pattern of evolution in South Africa, as Tobias (1957) has suggested, Leakey would have found small Bushmen in the Homa mounds instead of big ones.

The Boskop Brain Case and the "Boskop Race"

I N 1913, when the study of human paleontology was in its infancy, F. W. Fitzsimmons of the Port Elizabeth Museum found part of a brain case, a loose temporal bone, a piece of mandible, and several bits and pieces of long bones in a layer of laterite four feet from the surface on the east bank of the Mooi River, in the Potchefstroom District, southwest Transvaal. These remnants of an ancient burial were to become famous as the Boskop man, which has gone into the literature as the type specimen of the so-called Boskop race.

The bones were mineralized as one might expect after they had lain for some time in laterite. No fauna was found with them, nor any implements, although later a single blade tool was picked up nearby.[2] The only blade industry in that region was Wilton. Although the find cannot be dated, it probably belonged to the early Capoid group which arrived in South Africa several thousand years B.C.

As Table 37 shows, the Boskop calvarium would fit in the Homa shell-mound population without difficulty; as it was a little broader than Homa 1 or 2, it deviated from them in the direction of Singa. Morphologically it possessed the earmarks of the Bushman in vault form and forehead shape, small mastoids, and other details; and, like the Homa skulls, its mandible has a chin. It has no face, but neither does the type specimen of the Neanderthals. Anyone who wishes to call the unreduced ancestors of the Bushman the "Boskop race" is, of course, free to do so. But I consider the continued use of this name unnecessary.

[2] C. van R. Lowe: "An Artifact Recovered with the Boskop Calvaria," *SAAB*, Vol. 9, No. 36 (1954), pp. 135–7.

The Florisbad Cranial Fragment [3]

T o those familiar with the conventional classifications of geologically ancient skulls it may come as a surprise to see the Florisbad
cranial fragment treated separately from the Saldanha and
Broken Hill skulls, with which it is generally grouped in a fossil
triumvirate. Actually, Florisbad has little in common with the
other two skulls except birth in Africa and membership in the genus *Homo*. Two factors have created this confusion: inconclusive
dating and faulty reconstruction.

In 1932 T. F. Dreyer was excavating the complex deposits of
the site of a mineral spring named Florisbad, 25 miles north of
Bloemfontein in the Transvaal. At a depth of 20 feet he found a
fragmentary cranium consisting of most of the frontal bone, parts
of the parietal and occipital, various pieces of the facial bones,
mostly from the right side, and a loose right third upper molar.

The position of the skull in the site was unusual (see Fig. 83)
because of the nature of the spring. The spring consists of a row
of eyes or fountains that have taken turns flowing to the surface at
different times. Periodically the active eye stops flowing and a
layer of peat forms over it. At the eye where the skull was found
there were four layers of peat, numbered I to IV, starting at the
bottom. Layers II, III, and IV had been deposited after the eye
had died, but layer I was older than the eye, which had broken

[3] T. F. Dreyer: "A Human Skull from Florisbad," *PASA*, Vol. 38 (1935), pp.
119–28.

Dreyer: "Endocranial Cast of the Florisbad Skull," *SNNM*, Vol. 1 (1936),
pp. 21–3.

Dreyer: "The Fissuration of the Frontal Endocranial Cast of the Florisbad
Skull Compared with that of the Rhodesian Skull," *ZfRK*, Vol. 8 (1938), pp.
129–98.

Drennan: "The Florisbad Skull and Brain Cast," *TRSS*, Vol. 25 (1937), pp.
103–14.

A. Galloway: "Man in Africa in the Light of Recent Discoveries," *SAJS*, Vol.
34 (1937), pp. 89–120.

Galloway: "Nature and Status of the Florisbad Skull as Revealed by its Non-
metrical Features," *AJPA*, Vol. 23, No. 1 (1937), pp. 1–16.

Oakley: "New Evidence Regarding Rhodesian (Broken Hill) Man."

Oakley: "The Dating of the Broken Hill, Florisbad, and Saldanha Skulls."

Oakley: "Dating the Stages of Hominid Evolution."

Singer: "Man and Mammals in South Africa."

Singer: "The Rhodesian, Florisbad, and Saldanha Skulls."

through it from below, bringing with it sand, animal bones, and probably also artifacts. The skull lay in a depression in the top of the first layer, next to the edge of the eye hole. Resting on the top of the peat of layer I was a perfectly modern-looking grindstone and muller (metate and mano to American archaeologists).

The most logical interpretation of this unusual situation is that the cranial fragment, which judging by toothmarks had been part

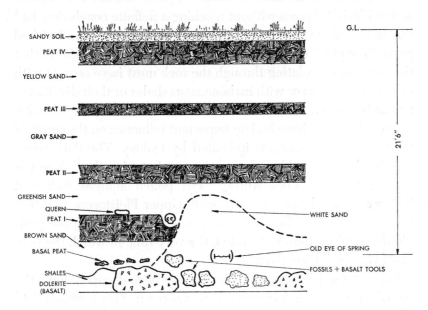

F.G. 83 THE FLORISBAD SITE. The Florisbad skull site is a thermal spring with many eyes, most of which ceased to bubble thousands of years ago. The Florisbad skull fell into one of these eyes while it was still active. Later the flow of mineral water ceased, and three sets of alternate layers of sand and peat were laid down above it. Because the skull is younger than Peat I, which is under it, and older than the overlying undisturbed Peat II, its age depends on the dates given the two layers of peat. (Drawing after Oakley, 1954.)

of a carnivore's meal, had been dropped into the spring after the water had burst through layer I and before the formation of layer II. It thus is not necessarily associated with any of the animal bones or artifacts, except for the grindstone and muller, which could hardly have been cast up by the spring. The dates of these peat layers are therefore critical.

In 1954 Libby published the following Carbon-14 dates: Layer III = 6,700 ± 500 years (C-852); Layer II = 9,104 ± 420 years (C-851); Layer I = older than 41,000 years (C-850). In 1956 the Lamont Laboratory of Columbia University published the following: Layer III = 19,530 ± 650 years (L-271D); Layer II = 28,450 ± 200 years (L-271C); Layer I = 35,000 years (L-271B). Libby tested solid carbon; the Lamont Laboratory used carbon dioxide. Which one, if either, of these sets of figures is right?

In 1955, E. M. van Zindern Bakker, a paleobotanist who worked on the Florisbad peats without reaching a definite conclusion, had this to say about using the Carbon-14 method on the Florisbad peat: "The production of much methane by the spring shows that the water in percolating through the rock must have contact with Ecca coal deposits or with carbonaceous shales or their distillation products formed under the influence of the intruding dolerite. This contact may have had an important influence on the result of the age determination, as indicated by Oakley. The dark layers may be dated too old as they may contain 'old carbon' from the above-mentioned Ecca strata." [4] His pollen analysis indicated that the peat of layer I was probably Upper Pleistocene and that much time elapsed before layer II was formed, during the post-Pleistocene Makalian wet period, the very time in which the people of Gamble's Cave lived.

In short, the Florisbad skull could have been dropped down the eye of the spring as late as 7,000 to 5,000 B.C. This terminal date would be consistent with the anatomical identification of Florisbad as an ancestral Bushman, which it seems to have been.

Dreyer reconstructed the fragment by adding plaster to the original bone, of which no cast had been made. Probably with a Neanderthal image in mind, he tilted the bone backward and stretched out the maxilla, adding to the actual tooth sockets to produce an elongated, prognathous upper face. The result was an unnatural composite that has plagued textbook writers for three decades.

After Dreyer's death, A. C. Hoffman, director of the National Museum of Bloemfontein, had the plaster removed and six casts were made of the original bone, one of which he presented

[4] E. M. van Zinderen Bakker: "A Pollen Analytical Investigation of the Florisbad Deposits (South Africa)," *PTPA* (1957), pp. 56–67.

to me (see Plate XXXI).[5] The work was done in the Department of Anatomy of the University of Capetown. Seen in its original form, the Florisbad fragment is part of a large *sapiens* skull, with a sharply curved frontal bone; a very broad forehead; a short, orthognathous face; square orbits; and teeth of modern size, judging by the sockets and by the remaining upper third molar. It would fit in the Homa series; it resembles Boskop; and it patently belonged to an ancestral Bushman. Further details may be expected from Hoffman. If the fragment is older than I think it is, I shall be surprised, and my reconstruction of the origin of the Capoids will be dealt a serious blow.

The Formation of the Modern Capoid Peoples

THE REMAINDER of the skeletal material from South Africa does not present serious problems. Owing to the diligence and enthusiasm of local archaeologists, many prehistoric Capoid skeletons have been discovered. The best known are Fish Hoek, a complete skeleton; the collection from Zitzikama, consisting of five imperfect specimens; and the Matjes River group, consisting of eighteen skeletons in various states of preservation. Some of these may be as old as Florisbad or older, but all are without much doubt post-Pleistocene.

This material indicates that the process variously known as shrinking, fetalization, or general size reduction, which affected the Capoids, took place in large part, if not completely, after their arrival in South Africa. Fish Hoek has a large brain case, but his face is small. One Zitzikama specimen, possibly hydrocephalic, has a very bulging forehead and a tiny face. In the Matjes River group there are full-sized and shrunken individuals in the same population. Singer (1958) has pointed out that even among living Bushmen and Hottentots individuals who fit the ancestral racial dimensions may be found.

The size reduction began no more than eight or nine thousand years ago and has not yet affected the entire Capoid population to

[5] Hoffman has invited five physical anthropologists, including myself, to make our own reconstructions while he makes a sixth. He plans to compare the results.

the same degree. The coastal Bushmen, or Strandloopers, a few of whom survive in southwest Africa and Angola, were taller and had larger brains than the Bushmen of the Cape and Kalahari. Moreover, as one moves northward in South Africa and Bechuanaland, the Bushmen grow taller. In South Africa itself the Hottentots are less infantile and a little larger than the Bushmen. Why this is so, I am not prepared to say, but two possibilities suggest themselves. The Hamitic racial element which the Hottentots are believed to have acquired along with their cattle may have

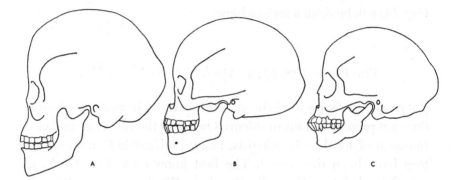

FIG. 84 THE CAPOID LINE: PROFILES OF HOMA, FISH HOEK, AND A MODERN BUSHMAN. A. Skull 4 from the Homa Shell Mounds in Kenya (after Leakey, 1935); B. Fish Hoek (after Drennan, 1929, and a cast); C. A Bushman, the so-called "Hottentot Venus" (after de Quatrefages and Hamy, 1882). According to the theory presented in this book, the Capoids originated in North Africa as the Ternefine-Tangier line, and moved to East and finally South Africa when pushed out by the invading Mouillians and Capsians, who were Caucasoid. Capoid skulls have been found all the way from the Sudan (Singa) to the Cape of Good Hope. At first large and rugged, they gradually become small and infantile. Yet they preserved one special facial feature—facial flatness, which may be observed in the three specimens shown here.

slowed down the process, or the pastoral life may in some way favor small size and infantilism less than hunting does.

Frankly, I am unable to explain the pedomorphism and partial dwarfing of the Bushmen. They do not live in tropical forests and apparently never did. It can have nothing to do with food economy because before they were disturbed in South Africa they had all the game they could eat. A parallel might be drawn between them and the Lapps, who are also stunted and tend to have small faces and small teeth. The Lapps occupy the most poleward part of their racial realm; the Bushmen the most poleward of theirs. Under certain circumstances there must be some selective advantage in pedomorphy, or it would not have become general in either of these unrelated populations.[6]

Pedomorphy did not spread among the Capoid peoples who lived north of its South African center of origin, as we know from excavations at two modern, Metal Age sites in northern Transvaal near the Limpopo River. These sites are Mapungubwe and Bambandyanolo, two neighboring hilltop forts or shrines excavated between 1933 and 1940.[7] These sites were occupied between A.D. 1,000 and 1,400, as established by Carbon-14 tests.[8] Their inhabitants were Metal Age people, undoubtedly food-producing, who wore gold ornaments. By A.D. 1,400 the younger of the two sites, Mapungubwe, is known to have been inhabited by Bantus, and the local Bantus still hold these hills in reverence.

Galloway has studied seventy-four skeletons from Bambandyanolo and eleven from Mapungubwe. Not one was that of a Negro. All were full-sized Capoids, some of whom had taurodont teeth. Clay figurines found with the skeletons show the elongated labia minora and steatopygia characteristic of Bushmen and Hottentots. Galloway's careful work on these skeletons also illustrates the differences between Capoids and Negroes in many details of anatomy, particularly in respect to the vertebrae and the bones of the feet. These show that the two subspecies are no more alike in the postcranial skeleton than in the skull, or in the anatomy of the soft parts.

The skeletons which Galloway described indicate that an unreduced Capoid population lived on the banks of the Limpopo

[6] A fantastic idea that I give only in a footnote stems from the fact that the Bushmen use poison. Every man normally has enough of it on his person to kill a rival in a few minutes during the victim's sleep. This knowledge, according to Mrs. Lorna Marshall, who has lived among them, is a powerful deterrent to adultery. Whether or not the self-control needed to refrain from adultery, and therefore avoid being killed, has an endocrine basis which favors pedomorphy I do not know, but I do know that adultery is said to be rare among Andamanese and other Pygmies.

[7] Galloway: "The Skeletal Remains of Mapungubwe," in L. Fouché, ed: *Mapungubwe* (Cambridge: Cambridge University Press; 1937), pp. 127–74.

Galloway: "The Skeletal Remains of Bambandyanalo" (Johannesburg: Witwatersrand University Press; 1960).

[8] Mapungubwe = A.D. 1430 ± 60 (Y-135–9) and A.D. 1390 ± 60 (Y-135–14); Bambandyanolo = A.D. 1060 ± 65 (Y-135–17).

only two hundred years before the Dutch settled Capetown, and if these skeletons were those of Bantu-speakers, then the early waves of Bantus across the Limpopo must have been thin indeed, like the first waves of Mongoloids into southeast Asia.

It should be noted also that several populations between Libya and the Rhodesias still show traces of Capoid origin or at least Capoid mixture. The first of these is a small group of desert dwellers called Duwwud, or Worm-People in Arabic, who live on the banks of three salt lakes in the Fezzan, Libya.[9] The Duwwuds, black-skinned, curly-haired people, specialize in netting *Artemia*, the brine shrimp, in vast numbers in September, when these animals reach their seasonal peak of abundance. The women pound the catch into a shrimp paste which they pat into cakes and let dry. These cakes are sold to Arab caravan men. During the rest of the year the Duwwuds run about the dunes hunting jerboas and other small game, which they kill with thrown sticks. In Cipriani's photographs, some of these people resemble the classic description of a Boskop type, with a flat face and a big jaw. Others show traces of Arab, or Negro, admixture. Although this is not concrete evidence of the former presence of an unreduced Capoid population in Libya, it is at least a lead that would warrant further investigation. According to Briggs, the Sahara contains more than one such population.[1]

Better evidence is afforded by the presence in central Tanganyika of a tribe that still speaks a Bushman-Hottentot language. They are the Sandawe, some of whom were measured in 1944 by J. C. Trevor of Cambridge University.[2] Although somewhat mixed with Bantu, the Sandawe still resemble the Capoid peoples, and particularly the Hottentots, anthropometrically. From the zoogeographical standpoint it is much easier to interpret the Sandawe living today in central Tanganyika as a relict population left behind during a southward movement than as the result of a northward push against the main current of migrations in East Africa,

[9] L. Cipriani: "Un Interesante Pueblo del Sahara: los Dauada," *RGA*, Vol. 2, No. 2 (1934), pp. 141–52.

[1] Briggs: *Tribes of the Sahara* (Cambridge, Mass.: Harvard University Press; 1960).

[2] J. C. Trevor: "The Physical Characters of the Sandawe," *JRAI*, Vol. 77, Pt. 1 (1947), pp. 61–80.

particularly since Bushman rock paintings, perforated stones, and so on, are not found that far north.

All the evidence that we have reviewed, then, including that of archaeology, of skeletons, and of relict populations, would indicate that the Bushmen, Hottentots, and their larger ancestors are descended from the Ternefine-Tangier line of North Africa; that their ancestors were driven out of that region by an invasion of Caucasoids toward the end of the Pleistocene and during the early post-Pleistocene period; and that they did not begin to undergo a reduction in size until after arriving in their historic homeland, South Africa, Southwest Africa, Bechuanaland, and the Rhodesias.

The Earliest Skeletons of Modern Negroes

N O W T H A T the racial history of the Capoids has been traced more or less satisfactorily, only one subspecies remains to be accounted for, and that is the Congoid. It is the weakest warp in our racial fabric. The ancient line running from Chellian-3 man to to Cape Flats and the Border Cave is Negro more than anything else, but it is not fully Negro in the modern sense. The Negroes as we know them are a distinctive people, anatomically and physiologically, and must have arisen in another part of Africa, probably north and west of the Congo basin. There evidence is scarce and of late date.

The oldest skeleton that all writers agree was that of a Negro is the so-called Asselar man, found in 1927 by M. V. Besnard and T. Monod in the dry bed of a once wide and perennially flowing river near the Tilemsi depression in the Sahara, 400 kilometers north of Timbuktu at 19° N. latitude and a little east of the Greenwich Meridian, latitude 0° [3]

No implements were associated with this skeleton. With it, however, were found the remains of fresh-water molluscs, fish, crocodiles, and various gazelles and antelopes, all of which still exist, but not in the Sahara. It obviously dates back to a time when this part of the Sahara was well watered, and is probably

[3] Boule and Vallois: "L'Homme Fossile d'Asselar, Sahara," *AIPH*, Mem. No. 9, 1932.

post-Pleistocene. It was that of an adult male at least five feet seven inches tall (170 cm.), whose long bones were slender, whose forearms were long in relation to his upper arms, and whose lower legs were long in relation to his thighs. His pelvis, vertebrae, and hand and foot bones were all Negroid. In fact, from the neck down he was altogether a Negro.

His skull is not so easily categorized. Its capacity of 1,520 cc. lies on the high side of the Negro range, and its vault proportions can be matched today in Negro skulls from the Sudan, particularly in a series of Wolof skulls with which Boule and Vallois compared the skull of Asselar. As for the face, it deviates from that of the Wolofs only in its shortness, but short faces are common in West Africa. Its two upper median incisors had been removed soon after eruption, presumably in some initiation rite. This loss caused considerable bone damage and may have reduced the upper face height (nasion-alveon).

The teeth of Asselar man are typically Negro in dimensions and, as far as we can tell, in form. In the upper jaw the second is the largest molar, followed in size by the first and then the third. In the lower jaw the ranking is second, third, and first, which is both primitive and unusual. In the upper jaw only the third is preserved well enough to permit the counting of cusps. It has four. In the lower jaw all three molars have five cusps each.

In this skeleton Boule and Vallois saw a type of Negro closer to the South African Bantu of today than to the living Negroes of the Sahara and western Sudan. They attributed this postulated relationship to mixture between a true Negro and an ancestral Bushman before the latter had journeyed southward. They may be right; but to me Asselar is simply a Negro, the first true Negro that we have found in Africa who can meet all the specifications of his race.

Remains of at least ten other individuals associated with Neolithic cultural materials, and possibly Mesolithic materials as well, have been found in a rock shelter at Kourounkorokalé in Mali, in a part of what used to be the French Sudan, 37 kilometers southwest of Bamako in the Mandingo Hills.[4] Although these speci-

---

[4] G. Szumowski: "Fouilles de l'Abri Sous Roche de Kourounkorokalé (Soudan Français), *BIAF*, Vol. 18, Ser. B., No. 2–3 (1956), pp. 462–508.

mens have not yet been studied, preliminary observations indicate that they are Congoid and that some are of very small stature.

A specimen stated to have been that of a Negro was found in 1948 in Khartum, near the railroad station. Several skeletons had been buried in a mound along with Mesolithic stone tools and with pottery. According to McBurney, the Khartum Neolithic began about 3,253 ± 295 B.C.,[5] and the Mesolithic material, including the pottery, could hardly be much more than 500 years older.[6] One skull has been partly described.[7] It is Negroid, but to me it looks like the skull of a modern, local Sudanese, a mixture of Hamite and Negro, rather than like the skull of a full Negro. As these burials may not have been much more than a thousand years older than the earliest Egyptian mural representations of Negroes, the presence of a Negro or Negroid in the Sudan at 3,700 to 4,000 B.C. is not surprising.

Do the Pygmies Hold the Answer?

U N T I L N O W we have neglected one of the four principal racial assemblages in Black Africa, that of the Pygmies. They are estimated to number about 168,500 persons [8] living in several isolated portions of the tropical forests of Central Africa from Gabon and the Cameroons to Uganda and Ruanda-Urundi, nearly all north of the Congo River. The western, central, and northeastern Pygmies live in the lowland forests, the southeastern in the upland forest around and on the slopes of Mount Ruwenzori. There is some historical evidence to indicate that the western Pygmies once extended along the entire west coast of Africa as far as Liberia, and that as late as the sixteenth century the Pyg-

---

[5] This date is apparently a combination of two dates: C-753 = 5,060 ± 450 B.P. for charcoal from Shaheinab; and C-754 = 5,446 ± 380 B.P. for shell from the same site. The average of the two is 5,253 ± 415 B.P., or 3,253 ± 295 B.C., if 2,000 years are subtracted in conversion from B.P. to B.C.

[6] McBurney: *The Stone Age of Northern Africa* (New York: Pelican Books; 1960), p. 244.

[7] D. E. Derry: "Report of Human Remains," in A. J. Arkell: *Early Khartoum* (London: Oxford University Press; 1949), pp. 31–3.

[8] M. Gusinde: "Pygmies and Pygmoids," *AQ*, Vol. 28 (NS Vol. 3), No. 1 (1955), pp. 3–61.

mies were the principal if not the only inhabitants of the forest between Lakes Albert and Edward.

Because we have no Pygmy skeletal material other than the remains of the recently deceased, and no archaeological industries that can be attributed, with confidence, to the Pygmies, we know nothing about these little people except that they have lived in the equatorial forests of Africa for as long a time as is covered by the records of history. Nor is there any evidence that Negroes lived in the forests with them before the Negroes had acquired iron and agriculture.

Since entering the forests Negro men have taken Pygmy wives and there are whole tribes of Negroes that are part Pygmy in origin and appearance; but the Pygmy men have not married Negro women, and even if a Negress should bear a child to a Pygmy the child would remain in the village and be considered a Negro. There are no hybrids in the Pygmy camps in the deep forests. To live like a Pygmy you have to be one. Gene flow between Pygmies and Negroes is thus a one-way stream which may have made the Negroes biologically more adaptable to forest living than were their ancestors out on the savannahs and grasslands.

The sickle-cell trait, an inherited malformation of the red corpuscles that limits their ability to carry oxygen and renders men immune to malignant malaria, is found among 26 per cent of the Pygmies living in malarial regions. Although not the highest frequency in Africa, this figure suggests that the trait may have originated among the Pygmies: owing to the unique direction of gene flow between Pygmies and Negroes, the Pygmies could not have got it from the Negroes.

In the Stanleyville region, including the Ituri forest, the home of the eastern Pygmies, the Pygmy birth rate is constant or increasing whereas that of the Negroes is declining. The survival of Negroes in this area seems to depend essentially on a steady rate of absorption of Pygmy genes. To the extent that forest Negroes exchange genes with savannah and grassland Negroes, Pygmy genes can be carried outside the forest to Negro populations that have never lived in it.

It appears possible, therefore, that the modern Negro is, in general, part Pygmy, but he has only become so to a considerable extent since Negro cultivators first entered the forest to plant their gardens, between two and three thousand years ago. Before that, the gene flow between Pygmies and Negroes was probably limited to peripheral contacts on the edges of the forests.

The Bantu tribes of East and South Africa may have been particularly affected because the Bantus originated in erstwhile Pygmy country in West Africa and passed through the forests on their migrations eastward and southward. The difference between the old Negro skeletons that we have reviewed and the skeletons of modern Negroes may reflect the presence and absence of Pygmy genes.

If this exercise in historical reconstruction is true, then what are the Pygmies? As they are a living people without prehistoric or even historic skeletal antecedents, their description belongs in another book, a book devoted to the living peoples of the world; but a few facts about the Pygmies must be given here if we are ever to unravel the racial history of Africa.[9]

The Pygmies are small, Negroid people. The mean stature of the men is below 150 cm. in most groups, although those that live in the chilly forests of Mount Ruwenzori have a mean stature of 153 cm., as one would expect in view of Bergmann's rule (see Chapter 2). There is considerable sexual dimorphism, the women being as a rule much smaller than the men.

They are not miniature dwarfs, like some of those in the Australoid quadrant of the Old World, nor are they as neotenous as the Bushmen; the Pygmy men have genitals as large as those of Negroes. Their manner of dwarfing verges on the achondroplastic but does not reach the extremes of achondroplasia[1] seen in indi-

[9] The literature is voluminous. A bibliography of 132 titles will be found in R. R. Gates: "The African Pygmies," *AGMG*, Vol. 7 (1958), pp. 159–218.
In the preparation of this section I have also directly consulted:
Gusinde: "Pygmies and Pygmoids."
Gusinde: *Die Twiden. Pygmäen und Pygmoide um Tropischen Afrika* (Vienna: Wilhelm Braumüller; 1956).
Twiesselmann: "Les Pygmées de l'Afrique Centrale," *RM*, No. 4 (1952), pp. 1–20.
Vallois: "New Research on the Western Negrillos," *AJPA*, Vol. 26 (March 1940), pp. 449–71.
[1] A type of dwarfing characterized by short, deformed extremities, as in bulldogs.

vidual mutations in European or Negro populations. Their arms are long in proportion to their legs, and their lower legs are particularly short. Their heads are not small—Twiesselmann has given cranial-capacity figures of 1,428 cc. for males and 1,268 cc. for females in a series of eight skulls. Although this is not statistically impressive, eight is as many skulls as we have had to work with in most fossil lines, and more extensive measurements on the heads of living Pygmies confirm these figures.

Their faces are very short; their noses are short and wide, with a nasal index, on the living, of 100 and more. In many cases their eyes protrude, as if from exophthalmic goiter. Their hair is spiral, as Negro hair is, but rarely peppercorn as among Bushmen. The men have abundant beards, and many of them have hairy bodies, with a particular abundance of chest hair. This is not fetal lanugo, as some authors have claimed, but ordinary body hair. Many Pygmy children have red hair, but this is caused by a nutritional disease, kwashiorkor.

Although variable in skin color, the Pygmies are not black; neither are they yellow like Bushmen. Their usual skin color is dark reddish brown, which Gates calls mahogany. Their eyes are dark brown, but the sclera is white, not flecked with melanin patches as it is among many Negroes and Australian aborigines.

Little has been written about Pygmy teeth, except that they are frequently carious and fall out early in life. Aside from this, we know only that they are not small, like those of Bushmen.

I have studied several hundred photographs of Pygmies, but in these I have seen only one man, Ilombé, chief of the Bambenga in the northwestern Belgian Congo, who looks in the least Caucasoid, or Hamitic.[2] Very few if any Pygmies resemble Bushmen or Hottentots. This evidence suggests that the Pygmies began to shrink before the ancestors of the Hamites and Capoids moved southward; otherwise we would see more evidence among the living Pygmies of the passage of these migrants.

I agree with Gusinde and with Gates that the Pygmies are descended from the old pre-Hamitic, pre-Capoid population of the parklands and grasslands of Africa which was driven into the forest by drought affecting both their water supply and their

[2] Twisselmann: op. cit.

hunting. Once they were in the forest, one or more mutations for dwarfing, which had already occurred among them outside the forest, now acquired a survival value, and natural selection soon spread this new trait through the forest populations. For our purpose it does not matter whether all the Pygmies are descended from one group of full-sized refugees or from several groups.

If we want to know what the full-sized ancestors of the Pygmies looked like, all we need do is select a group of Pygmy children, feed or inject them with the hormones the lack of which makes them small, and see what they grow into. This is a perfectly feasible experiment and the Pygmies would probably co-operate.

In the meantime, we can reconstruct the image of a full-sized man with a big body, a full-sized head, a broad face and broad nose, eyes set wide apart, and probably heavy brow ridges, for the Pygmies do not lack brow ridges. His skin was either mahogany-colored or black (the Pygmies may have become slightly depigmented in the forest), and his body was hairy. He may have had convex, uneverted lips like the Pygmy instead of roll-out lips like the Negroes. Such a man could well have been a descendant of the Saldanha-Rhodesian-Cape Flats group and the ancestor of both Pygmies and Negroes, the Pygmies, despite a reduction in size, retaining the more archaic form.

Let us suppose that a population of these archaic, proto-Negro and proto-Pygmy people comparable to those we have seen in East and South Africa continued to live in West Africa well into post-Pleistocene time, away from the path of Capsian and Capoid migrations. Let us next suppose that such a population mixed with Pygmies. By this mixture they would have acquired the bulbous forehead, protruding eyes, and other infantile features characteristic of living Negroes, features which distinguish them from the Caucasoids whom their ancestors more closely resembled.

To me this theory—that the modern Negroes resulted from a backcross between an original proto-Negro stock and Pygmies, which had evolved from the same ancestors by dwarfing—makes sense. It explains the physical characteristics of the modern Negroes, and it conforms with the evidence we have of their age, as a race. In fact, their transformation need only have occurred a few millennia before the historic expansion of Negroes over much of Africa. And had modern Negroes existed very much earlier, some would have wandered into East Africa and we might have seen their remains.

This theory of the origin of Negroes does not exclude the possibility of mixture between proto-Negroes and Hamites or Capoids. Such mixtures probably took place, and without doubt they would explain some of the regional variations among Negroes. But in this theory such mixtures are not a primary cause of the rise of the Negroes. Because hybrids tend to return to one of their parental stocks, no valid subspecies can arise through mixture. Like the other four subspecies, the Congoids had an ancient, if still little known, history.

Was Africa the Cradle of Mankind?

D A R W I N considered Africa to be the cradle of mankind. Later, under the influence of Matthews, Osborn, and Andrews, the pendulum of popular opinion swung to central Asia, where, we now know, human beings were marginal and late. With the discovery of Pithecanthropus, the cradle was thought to be southeast Asia, and now Dart, Leakey, Arambourg, and others have again located it in Africa.

It now seems likely that the Australopithecines evolved in Africa, whence they spread to the east through the tropics of the Old World. It is also possible, although it cannot be proved, that the primary evolutionary step from *Australopithecus* to *Homo* was taken, not on African soil, but in the Meganthropus-Pithecanthropus sequence. Java, and by extension all of southeast Asia, is a serious rival.

Wherever *Homo* arose, and Africa is at present the likeliest continent, he soon dispersed, in a very primitive form, throughout the warm regions of the Old World. Three of the five human subspecies crossed the *sapiens* line elsewhere. If Africa was the cradle of mankind, it was only an indifferent kindergarten. Europe and Asia were our principal schools.

Postscript

I N T H E summer of 1961 a workman found a fossilized skull in a barium mine at Jebel Ighoud, halfway between Safi and Marrakesh, in Morocco. Émile Ennouchi, of Rabat, made a preliminary study of it,[3] and H. V. Vallois is preparing a detailed report. In grade it appears to be incipiently *sapiens*, with a cranial capacity of 1,480 cc., heavy continuous brow ridges, a low vault, a long upper-face height, large orbits, and a large palate. Racially it seems, as expected, to have been an ancestral Bushman, with a flat upper facial region (index of upper facial flatness = 13) and great alveolar prognathism.

On December 23, 1962, in loose yellow earth in front of the same site, I found the left half of the calvarium of a younger and similar individual. Although it had no face except for the nasal bones, it has a base, which was lacking in the first specimen. Vallois will study this one also.

The fauna, studied by Ennouchi, could be that of the Third Interglacial or perhaps early Würm. So far, only trimming flakes of a Levalloisio-Mousterian type have been found there, and they could be from either a Levalloisian or an Aterian industry.

[3] Emile Ennouchi: "Un crâne d'homme ancien au Jebel Irhoud (Maroc)," *CRAS*, t. 254, pp. 4330–2. Séance du 18 Juin, 1962.
—— "Un Néanderthalien: L'Homme du Jebel Irhoud (Maroc)," *L'Anth,* Vol. 66, No. 3–4 (1962), pp. 279–99.

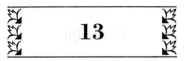

13

THE DEAD AND THE LIVING

T HE LAST four chapters are a unit. They constitute the documentation for the racial history of man. The procession of skull after skull with accompanying teeth and long bones may seem a lengthy catalogue, but in reality it is not an overburdening mass of evidence. A total of a little over three hundred bone-bearing sites is not a large number: these sites encompass all our knowledge about the ancestry of a species that now numbers over two billions. All the pertinent information available in the literature on the subject and elsewhere had to be brought forth and considered. Only by examining every scrap of data could I hope to discover when and where each of the five lines of human descent began, and where each led.

But before I could start on this documentation, I had to establish some degree of credibility for my thesis, which I state in Chapter 1. My thesis is, in essence, that at the beginning of our record, over half a million years ago, man was a single species, *Homo erectus,* perhaps already divided into five geographic races or subspecies. *Homo erectus* then gradually evolved into *Homo sapiens* at different times, as each subspecies, living in its own territory, passed a critical threshold from a more brutal to a more *sapient* state, by one genetic process or another.

This point of view is not wholly original—I know, for instance, of two younger men who have thought it out independently of myself and of each other [1]—nor is it generally accepted. As I was working alone, with only Weidenreich's interpretation of the Si-

[1] Frank Livingstone of the University of Michigan and Loring Brace of the University of California at Santa Barbara.

nanthropus material to guide me, I decided, before writing this book, to marshal many kinds of cognate evidence.

I studied genetic theory, zoogeography, and human physiology (with special reference to adaptations to climate and culture); the history of the primates, with its marvelous record of parallelism, by which such similar creatures as the Old and the New World monkeys could evolve from different prosimians; and the record of our hominid predecessors, the Australopithecines. I also made a survey of world archaeology covering the Pleistocene. In addition, I had to explain the differences among fossil men between evolutionary characteristics and those that are racial. These efforts filled eight chapters, numerically two thirds of the book, but without them, Chapters 9 through 12 would not have been solidly grounded.

Now that the task is over, I feel that the three Eurasiatic lines—the Australoid, Mongoloid, and Caucasoid—have been traced fully enough so that future discoveries will entail no major surprises. The African material, however, is less well documented and new conclusions may be reached as new evidence becomes available.

As far as we know now, the Congoid line started on the same evolutionary level as the Eurasiatic ones in the Early Middle Pleistocene and then stood still for a half million years, after which Negroes and Pygmies appeared as if out of nowhere. The Ternefine-Tangier line has left us enough jaws and teeth to work with, only one very early but still unmeasured parietal from Ternefine, and two new pre-Mouillian skulls from Jebel Ighoud, Morocco. These skulls seem to support my hypothesis that the ancestors of the Bushmen and Hottentots originated north of the Sahara and only reached South Africa postglacially. After these skulls have been properly studied, they may also help explain why in the Middle Pleistocene North Africans resembled the earliest Mongoloids, whereas the East Africans were closest to the Caucasoids, and what role they may have played in the still enigmatic genesis of the Congoids.

We also urgently need new evidence concerning the details of the transition from the australopithecine to the human grade. The search for more early hominid fossils should be accelerated in the few suitable areas of the Old World which contain Lower Pleistocene deposits. Only when the key fossils have been found will we know where and when the major lines of human descent embarked on the separate paths that they have followed to this day.

Toward the end of the Pleistocene, after all five geographical races of man had become *sapiens* but before the two northern-most, the Mongoloid and Caucasoid, had completed their south-ward invasions and expansions, each race may have contained nearly equal numbers of individuals. However, by the time agri-culture and animal husbandry had been invented, by Caucasoids and Mongoloids, these two had begun to outnumber the others. With the wide spread of food production, the numerical dis-proportion between the races increased; and today Mongoloids and Caucasoids together constitute the vast majority of the earth's inhabitants.

The Australoids are on the decline, except among the aboriginal tribes of India; and the Bushmen and Hottentots number only tens of thousands. The Pygmies are few, but hold their own. The African Negroes, on the other hand, have shown extraordinary vitality. They have been particularly versatile in adopting new cultures wherever they have been taken, as laborers, by Cauca-soids and Mongoloids, and they have become the dominant racial element in many of the tropical lowland regions of the New World, as well as of Madagascar and parts of the Arabian coast.

Once a race has become established as the principal population of a region, it has a tendency to stay there and to resist the genetic influences swept in by later invasions. Less than a thousand years

FACING PAGE: This schematic map shows the distribution of the five subspecies of *Homo* during most of the Pleistocene, from 500,000 to 10,000 years ago. This distribution matches that on the diagram in Chapter 1. Of the five subspecies, the Congoid was the most isolated; it was in contact with only one other, the Capoid, then resident in North Africa. The second map shows what happened at the end of the Pleistocene, when the Mongoloids and Caucasoids expanded and burst out of their territories. The Mongoloids entered and inhabited America, and extended their domain southward into Southeast Asia and Indonesia, while the Australoids crossed Wallace's Line and occupied Australia and New Guinea. The Caucasoids thrust northward. More significantly, they drove the Capoids out of North Africa and occupied the White Highlands of Kenya and Tanganyika. The Congoids were reduced to a small part of their earlier domain, including the Congo forests and the lands to the north, where they later evolved rapidly and spread, as Negroes, over much of Africa.

Shifts of Human Subspecies
from PLEISTOCENE to POST-PLEISTOCENE

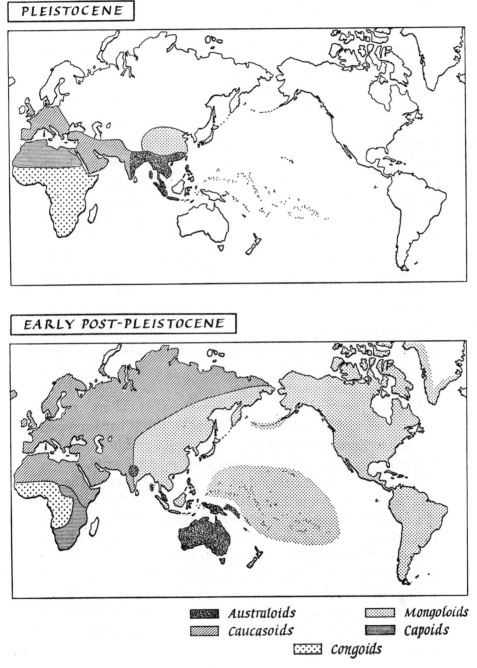

PLEISTOCENE

EARLY POST-PLEISTOCENE

Australoids   Mongoloids
Caucasoids   Capoids
Congoids

MAP 13

ago the Arabs had a city near Amoy on the China coast, complete with minarets and bazaars. Thousands of Arab men must have impregnated Chinese women; yet today there is little if anything about the Fukienese to show it. Kashmiri traders live, marry local women, and die in the cities of Tibet, and Spaniards by the thousands have settled in the Andean *altiplano,* but today Tibetans and Andean Indians are as mongoloid as ever.

When two races come into contact and mixture occurs, one race tends to dominate the other. The local advantage that the genetically superior group (superior for its time and place) possesses may be primarily cultural or primarily physiological, or a combination of both. For example, the dominance of the Europeans over the native peoples of North America, Australia, and New Zealand is primarily cultural; that of the Negroes in the tropical lowlands of the New World and of the Indians in the Andes is primarily physiological.

There is, however, a third kind of dominance, expressed by the resistance of a population to the intrusion of large numbers of outsiders into its social and genetic structures. Call it xenophobia, prejudice, or whatever, people do not ordinarily welcome masses of strangers in their midst, particularly if the strangers come with women and children and settle down to stay. Social mechanisms arise automatically to isolate the newcomers as much as possible and to keep them genetically separate. This has happened historically to Jews (who wanted to preserve their culture) nearly everywhere, and to Negroes in the New World. It has happened recently to Europeans in India and Indonesia, and in Africa it is happening very dramatically to Europeans, even as I write.

The above is the behavioral aspect of race relations. The genetic aspect operates in a comparable way. Genes that form part of a cell nucleus possess an internal equilibrium as a group, just as do the members of social institutions. Genes in a population are in equilibrium if the population is living a healthy life as a corporate entity. Racial intermixture can upset the genetic as well as the social equilibrium of a group, and so, newly introduced genes tend to disappear or be reduced to a minimum percentage unless they possess a selective advantage over their local counterparts.

I am making these statements not for any political or social purpose but merely to show that, were it not for the mechanisms cited above, men would not be black, white, yellow, or brown. We would all be light khaki, for there has been enough gene flow over the clinal regions of the world during the last half million years to have homogenized us all had that been the evolutionary scheme of things, and had it not been advantageous to each of the geographical races for it to retain, for the most part, the adaptive elements in its genetic *status quo.*

This *status quo* entails not only the variations in bones and teeth that are evident in fossil man, and those of the surface features of living men, like skin, hair, lips, and ears, by which we can distinguish races almost at a glance, but also subtler differences seen only on the dissecting table or through the eyepieces of microscopes. Races differ in the extent and manner in which the fine subcutaneous muscles of the lips and cheeks have become differentiated from the parent mammalian muscle body; in the chemical composition of hair and of bodily secretions, including milk; in the ways in which different muscles are attached to bones; in the sizes and probable secretion rates of different endocrines; in certain details of the nervous system, as, for example, how far down in the lumbar vertebrae the neural canal extends; and in the capacity of individuals to tolerate crowding and stress. These and other details of racial difference I hope to describe and document in a later volume.

In studying racial differences in living men, physical anthropologists are now relying less and less on anthropometry and more and more on research in blood groups, hemoglobins, and other biochemical features. This is all to the good because the inheritance of these newly discovered characteristics can be accurately determined. In them, racial differences have been found, differences just as great as the better known and much more conspicuous anatomical variations. Being invisible to the naked eye, they are much less controversial than the latter in an increasingly race-conscious world. To me, at least, it is encouraging to know that biochemistry divides us into the same subspecies that we have long recognized on the basis of other criteria.

To readers who find these simple biological facts disconcerting, let me repeat something I said in Chapter 1. Until the present century, and in some countries until the present day, all five subspecies of man whose racial histories I have traced include populations of food gatherers and hunters living in the same regions that their ancestors occupied at least as early as early postglacial times. Some of the most backward in a cultural sense belong to the Mongoloid and Caucasoid subspecies, other populations of which have achieved the highest levels of civilization yet known in the world. But these backward populations do not live in their ancestral homelands; they hunt in distant regions that their ancestors invaded.

Caucasoids and Mongoloids who live in their homelands and in recently colonized regions, such as North America, did not rise to their present population levels and positions of cultural dominance by accident. They achieved all this because their ancestors occupied the most favorable of the earth's zoological regions, in which other kinds of animals also attained dominance during the Pleistocene. These regions had challenging climates and ample breeding grounds and were centrally located within continental land masses. There general adaptation was more important than special adaptation. Any other subspecies that had evolved in these regions would probably have been just as successful. Now the success of these groups is being challenged in many parts of the world as other groups who evolved later learn to use their inventions, especially modern means of communication. And evolution is still taking place, particularly natural selection resulting from crowding and stress, as described in Chapter 3.

In any case, neither the future of man nor the detailed description of the bodies, biochemical peculiarities, or behavior patterns of the living races of man is the subject of this book. I have, I hope, shown as accurately as the evidence warrants whence each of them came, and what steps guided it to its present position. Further details may be found in my new book, *The Living Races of Man.* (New York: Alfred A. Knopf; 1965).

STATISTICAL APPENDIX

BIBLIOGRAPHY

GLOSSARY

ADDENDA

INDEX

TABLE 36

ARCS AND CHORDS OF THE FRONTAL, PARIETAL, AND OCCIPITAL BONES IN THE SAGITTAL PLANE

Skull	Frontal			Parietal			Occipital		
	Arc	Chord	Index	Arc	Chord	Index	Arc	Chord	Index
Pithecanthropus 1	(100)	98	(98.0)	91	87.5	96.0	(103)	78	(75.7)
Pithecanthropus 2	90?	88	97.7?	9?	91	95.8	101?	75	74.2
Sinanthropus 2	123	113	91.8	112	104	93.1			
Sinanthropus 3	115	102	90.5	100	94	94.0	106?	80?	74.2?
Sinanthropus 10	129	115	89.2	113	106	94.0			
Sinanthropus 11	122	106	86.9	92	86	93.5	118	86	72.9
Sinanthropus 12	124	113	91.2	102.5	91	95.7	118	86	72.9
Solo 1	139	120.5	86.5	106	101	95.5	11?	81.5	74.1
Solo 5	136	120	88.3	117	111	95.2	128?	94?	73.3
Solo 6	122	112	91.7	107	102	95.6	109	82	75.2
Solo 9				103?	99?	96.3	115?	88	76.4
Solo 10	135	120	89.0	105	102	97.3	114	78	68.4
Solo 11	122	112	91.8	102	97	94.2	122	90	73.4
Mapa	134	115.6	86.3	114	107	87.2	(109.0)	(87.2)	(79.9)
Liu-Kiang	136.5	117.2	85.9	117.2	119.2	91.5	105.5	91.5	86.7
Tze-Yang	103?	92?	89.0	116	104	90	98?	84	86
Wadjak 1	136	119	87.5	130	113	86.9			
Rhodesian	137.5	121	88.0	117	112	96.0	118	?9	74.1
Steinheim	118	110	84.7	103	96	93.2	(117)	(90)	(76.9)
Swanscombe				118	109	92.3	118	95	80.5
Ehringsdorf	135	115	85.4	128	119	93.2	117	87	74.3
La Chapelle	121	107	88.5	121	112	92.5	115	91	79.1
La Ferrassie 1	125?	114?	91.2	114?	106?	93.0?	124	99	79.8
Neanderthal	133	116	87.3	110	104	94.7			
Spy 1 M	100.0?	102.8?	93.4?	126.0?	114.9?	91.2			
Le Moustier (adolescent)	120.2?	108.2	90.0?	121.8	109.2	96.3?			
Gibraltar 1 F	124.0?	107	86.3?				106.0	81.1	76.5
La Quina 1 F	116.3	106.4	91.5	106.9	102.9?	96.3?			
Spy 2 F				115.0	109.0	94.8			
Combe Capelle	138	123	89.1?	132?	123?	93.2?	128?	100?	78.1?
Crô-Magnon	144	119	82.6	138	123	89.1	128	109	85.1
Grimaldi	135	115?	85.2?	145?	131	90.3	130?	97?	74.6?

TABLE 37

CRANIAL DIMENSIONS AND INDICES
A. HOMINES ERECTI

	Pithecanthropus			Solo						Sinanthropus					Saldanha	Broken Hill
	4	1	2	1	5	6	9	10	11	2	3	10	11	12		
Sex (± Age)	M	M	F	F	M	Fy*	?	F	M	?y	My	M	F	M	M	M
Cranial Capacity	900?	935	775	1035	1225	1035	1135	1055	1060	1030	915	1225	1015	1030	1225	1280
Maximum Length	199?	183?	176.5?	196	220.3	192.5	201	202.6	200	194?	188	199	192	185.5	200	208
Maximum Breadth	158	130	135	148c	147c	144c	150c	155c	144c		137.2	143	139.8	141	144?	144.5
Biparietal Breadth	125?	126?	131	142	144	140	145	152	143		133	138?	135	139?		137
Basion-Bregma Height	102	105	105?	118?	131?	124	123?	118	124				115R†			130
Auricular Height	90	92	89							100		95	105	93.5		105
Minimum Frontal	78?	85	79	105c	106c	106c	109	112.5	106	84?	81.5	89	84	91	102	97.5
Bizygomatic													148R			148
Upper Face Height													77R			93
Nose Height													52.5R			58
Nose Breadth	36												30R			31
Alveolar Height	31.5															35
Orbital Height													36R			39.5
Orbital Breadth													44R			45.5
Interorbital				29c	28c								25R			28
Biorbital													111R			124
Palate Length	72?												52R			65
Palate Breadth	49?												39R			50
Palate Height	26															18
Cranial Index	62.8?	68.8?	74.2?	75.5c	66.7c	74.8c	74.6c	76.5c	72.0c		72.3	71.4	72.4	72.6	72.6	65.9
L. H. I. (BB Ht.)	51.2?	57.4	59.4	60.2?	59.4?	61.2	58.2	62.0					59.6R			62.5
L. H. I. (Aur. Ht.)	45.2?	50.3	50.4							51.5	50.5	52.8	48.7			50.5
B. H. I. (BB Ht.)	81.6?	83.3	80.1	83.1?	91.0?	88.6	84.8?	77.6	86.7				75.6R	51.2		90.0
B. H. I. (Aur. Ht.)	72.0	73.0	67.9	73.9	73.6	75.7	75.2	72.6	74.1				67.2			72.7
Fronto-parietal 1	62.4?	67.4	60.3								69.6	74.0	60.4	70.3		67.5
Cranio-facial 1											59.7	62.6	64.9R	64.1		108.2?
Upper Facial 1													52.1R			62.8
Nasal 1													57.2R			53.4
Orbital 1													81.9R			86.8
Palatal 1	68.1?												75.1R			76.9

* y = Young, subadult; all others are adult

† R = Reconstruction

TABLE 37 (continued)

B. HOMINES SAPIENTES, AUSTRALOID

Sex (± Age)	Wadjak 1	Wadjak 2	Keilor	Talgai	Cohuna	Mesolithic Tam Pong	Living Australians (M)	Living Australians (F)
	F	M	M	M	M	F	M	F
Cranial Capacity	1475		1464	1300	1450c	1270	1347	1181
Maximum Length	202		197	192?	203c	175	183	175
Maximum Breadth	148		143	141	142c	136	132	127
Basion-Bregma Height	136		143		122c	138	131	125
Auricular Height	115		120	105?				
Minimum Frontal	99	103	101	99	86	102	98	91
Bizygomatic	140?		136	128	145?	137	131.7	117
Upper Face Height	65		74	65	78c	74	65.9	61
Nose Height	50		52	45	50c	52	48.0	45
Nose Breadth	28	30	27	25		36	27.1	26
Alveolar Height	17c	27	13.5c		22c		17.9	16
Orbital Height	33	29	30	32.5		32	33.6	31
Orbital Breadth	42	39	39.5	40	44	49	41.4	38
Interorbital	29	32	32.5	29	27		25.0	25
Palate Length	52c	58c	56.5	62			57.8	57.8
Palate Breadth	42	53	47.2	42			39.0	39.0
Cranial Index	73.3		73.0	73.4	70.0	77.2	72.1	72.6
L. H. I. (BB Ht.)	67.3		73.0		60.2	78.9	71.6	71.4
L. H. I. (Aur. Ht.)	56.9		60.1	54.7?				
B. H. I. (BB Ht.)	91.9		100.0		85.9	101.4	99.2	98.4
B. H. I. (Aur. Ht.)	77.7		83.9	74.5				
Fronto-parietal 1	70.7?		70.6	70.2	60.6	75.0	74.2	71.6
Cranio-facial 1	94.6		95.1	90.8	102.1	100.4	99.8	92.1
Upper Facial 1	46.4		54.4	50.8	53.8	54.0	50.0	52.1
Nasal 1	56.0		51.9	55.6		60.1	66.0	57.8
Orbital 1	78.6	74.4	75.9	81.2		65.0	81.2	81.6
Palatal 1	80.8	91.4	83.5	67.7			67.5	67.5

TABLE 37 (continued)

C. MONGOLOID CRANIA

Sex (± Age)	No. 11 Sin. Rest. F	Tze-Yang F	Liu-Kiang M	Upper Cave 101 M	Upper Cave 102 F	Upper Cave 103 F	"Pooled Prehistoric" 42 M	"Pooled Prehistoric" 14 F	Recent North China 86 M	Recent North China 14 F
Cranial Capacity	1015	1210	1480	1500	1380	1300	1417	1288	1400	1273
Length	192	169.3	189	204	196	184	180.3	175.4	178.5	172.4
Breadth	135	131.1	142	143	140R	133R	138.6	134.8	138.2	133.6
Basion-Bregma Height			135	136	138R	138R	137.0	130.1	137.2	132.4
Auricular Height	94	110	114.5	113	110R	113R	116.0	111.7	115.5	112.8
Minimum Frontal	84	80R	95	107	104R	105R	91.1	87.6	89.4	87.2
Bizygomatic	148		136	143	138R	140R	132.2	125.8	132.7	124.8
Biorbital	111		98.8	110	103	106	95.7	92.5	94.4	91.4
Interorbital	25		21	24	21	21	21.4	21.1	20.2	20.7
Upper Face Height	77		66	77	69	70	75.2	70.2	75.3	69.6
Nose Height	52.5		46	58	46.5	48R	54.7	51.6	55.3	50.4
Nose Breadth	30	26? R	27	32	26	25.5	25.8	25.9	25.0	23.4
Orbital Height	36		29	31.5	32R	32.0R	33.8	33.9	35.5	33.5
Orbital Breadth	44		43	48.5	40.5R	43.5R	44.4	43.5	44.0	40.8
Palate Length	52	42.6	45?	52.0	47.0	48.0	46.1	44.5	45.2	44.3
Palate Breadth	39	39.0	36	43.0	40.0	38.0	43.6	42.8	40.5	41.0
Cranial Index	72.4	77.4	75.1	70.2	71.4R	72.3R	76.8	77.8	77.6	77.6
L. H. I. (BB)	48.7		71.2	66.7	70.4R	75.0R	76.0	75.4	77.0	76.4
L. H. I. (Aur.)		65	60.5	55.4	56.1R	61.4R	64.1	64.4	64.9	65.6
B. H. I. (BB)	67.2		94.8	95.0	98.6R	103.8R	99.2	96.9	99.5	98.2
B. H. I. (Aur.)	79.7	84	80.5	80.3	79.7R	85.0R	83.7	83.7	83.6	84.4
Facial 1				86.0	79.0R	79.6	90.7	90.4	93.6	92.2
U. F. I.	52.1		48.5	53.8	50.0R	50.0R	56.1	54.5	56.8	56.0
Fronto-parietal 1	64.9	61	66.9	74.8	74.3R	79.0R	65.7	65.0	64.7	65.3
Cranio-facial 1	105.7		95.6	100.0	98.6R	105.3	95.1	94.8	96.1	93.4
Zygomatic Frontal 1	64.7		70.0	74.8	75.4	75.0	68.3	69.7	67.5	66.9
Nasal 1	57.2		58.5	55.2	56.3	53.1	47.6	51.5	45.3	46.4
Orbital 1	81.9		68.3	64.9	79.0R	74.4	76.2	77.9	80.7	82.0
Palatal 1	75.1	91.3	80.0?	82.8	85.2	79.2	85.0	97.0	89.3	92.0

TABLE 37 (continued)

D. EUROPEAN PRE-WÜRM CRANIA

Sex (± Age)	Stein-heim	Swans-combe	Fonté-chevade 2	Saccopastore		Gánovce	Ehrings-dorf	Krapina	
				1	2			C	D
	F	F	F	F	M	?	F	F	M
Cranial Capacity	1170	1275	1460	1200	1300?	1320	1450	1200?	1450
Length	185		194	182		200	196	178	197.5
Breadth	132.5	142?	154	142	150?	145	145	149	169
Basion-Bregma Height	111?	125?		109		115			
Auricular Height	98		109	101			121	105	110
Minimum Frontal	102		120?	101			113	99	
Bizygomatic	132?				145				
Upper Face Height	74.5			86?	87			107	
Biorbital	106			112	118				
Interorbital	30			22	25.5		30	26	
Orbital Height	30			39	38.5			38	
Orbital Breadth	41			46.5	47			39?	
Nose Height	52			59	60				
Nose Breadth	30			31	34				
Palate Length				53	57				
Palate Breadth				40	41				
Cranial Index	71.6		79	78		72.5	74	83.7	85.5
L. H. I. (BB)	60.5			59.9		57.5			
B. H. I. (BB)	83.5	88		76.8		79.3			
L. H. I. (Aur.)	53.5		56				83.4	59	
B. H. I. (Aur.)	74.9		71				96.7	70.5	
Cranio-facial 1	99.6				96.6				
Fronto-parietal 1	76.9		78?	71.1	60		77.9	66.4	65.1
Upper Facial 1	56.4			90.2	81.9				
Orbital 1	73.2				56.7			97.4?	
Nasal 1	57.2			75.5	71.9				
Palatal 1									

TABLE 37 (*continued*)

E. NEANDERTHALS AND SKHUL CRANIA

Sex (± Age)	La Chapelle	La Ferrassie 1	Neanderthal	Spy 1	Circeo 1	Le Moustier Y	Gibraltar	La Quina	Spy 2	Tabun 1	Skhul 4	Skhul 5	Skhul 9
	M	M	M	M	M	M	F	F	F	F	M	M	M
Cranial Capacity	1550–1600	1641	1450	1525	1550	1564	1300	1350	1425	1271	1554	1518	1587
Length	208	209	199	201	204	196	192?	204	200?	183	206	192	213
Breadth	156	159	147	144?	156	150	149?	138?	153	141	148	144	145
Basion-Bregma Height	130	136			123?	128?	122			115	128	126	130
Auricular Height	110	114		113	103?	107				105	114	115	116
Minimum Frontal	109	109	105?	101?	113?		102?	101	108	98	106	100	96
Bizygomatic	152?	150			153	148?		126?		130	160	146	140
Upper Face Height	87.8?	96?					78.5?			79	79	79	74
Biorbital	114	109	111	109	108?	106	106	101		102	117	111	108
Interorbital	23?	23			23		25?			32	33	28	35
Orbital Height	36	36			36		38?			33	34	30	37
Orbital Breadth	46	46			43		45			42	44	46	44
Nose Height	63	65			64?		58			58	55	53	55
Nose Breadth	34	34			36		34			34	30	28	30
Palate Length	56?	54?				56.8?							
Palate Breadth	49	49				50.0	45.0?	43.8?					
Cranial Index	75.2	76.1	73.6	71.6?	76.4	76.6	77.4?	67.7?	76.6?	77.0?	71.8	74.5	68.0
L. H. I. (BB)	62.5	65.1			60.3	65.6?	63.5?			62.8	62.1	65.6	61.0
B. H. I. (BB)	83.3	85.5			78.8	85.3?	81.9?			81.6	86.5	87.5	90.0
L. H. I. (Aur.)	52.8	54.5		56.2	50.5?					57.4	55.3	59.9	54.5
B. H. I. (Aur.)	70.5	71.7		78.5?	66.0?					74.5	77.0	79.9	80.0
Cranio-facial 1	97.4	94.3	71.6	70.1	98.1	98.7		91.3?	70.4	92.9	108.1	101.4	96.6
Fronto-parietal 1	69.9	68.5			66.0	71.6	68.8?	73.2?		69.5	71.6	69.4	66.2
Upper Facial 1	57.8?	64.0?								60.8	49.4	54.1	52.9
Orbital 1	78.2	78.2			83.7		84.4?			78.5	77.3	65.2	84.1
Nasal 1	53.9	52.3			56.2?					58.6	54.5	52.8	54.5
Palatal 1	87.5?	90.7?				88							

TABLE 37 (continued)

F. MOUILLIANS AND CAPSIANS; NORTH AND EAST AFRICA

	Taforalt		Gamble's Cave 5		Naiva-sha R.R.	Olduvai Bed 5	Elmenteita					
	(14)	(13)	4	5			A	B	C	D		F-1
Sex (± Age)	M	F	M	M	M	M	M	M	M^y	F	F	F
Cranial Capacity	1647	1376	1470	1530	1453	1540	1290	1585	1610	1273?	1255	1140?
Maximum Length	194.6	182.7	191.5	193.5	197	203	190	197	192	183	177	174
Maximum Breadth	146.1	139.7	136.0?	143.0	125.5	133	128.5	144	147	132	138.5	140
Basion-Bregma Height	144.0	132.7	139.5?	132.0?	135		131.5	141.5	141.5	138		124
Auricular Height	118.3	111.0	112.0	112.0?	116	115	109.5	119	117	113.5	107	108
Minimum Frontal	94.0	92.9	107.0?	107.0?	103		102	102?	103	106?		89
Bizygomatic	147.4	131.5	137.0?		126		134	137.5?	120?	127?	116.5?	123?
Upper Face Height	68.6	62.6	74.5?	74.5?	60	75?	80	81?	73?	72.5	71	59
Nose Height	54.0	49.4	57.0	60?	46.5	51	58.7	57.5?	50.2	50.2	49	43.5
Nose Breadth	28.5	26.7	26.4	24.0?	26	26	20	23?	22	22.5	20.5	18.5
Orbital Height	32.4	29.8	39.4?	40.0?	32.5		34	37	33.7	35	37.5	30
Orbital Breadth	43.7	41.5	43.1?	46.5	38.5		43.5	41.7	40.5	42.5		37.5?
Biorbital	104.8	98.3										
Palate Length	48.8	46.0					57?					
Palate Breadth	47.5	43.4		42.7?			43	42	39	40	27.5	
Cranial Index	74.5	77.0	71.0	73.7	65.4	65.5	67.4	72.7	76.4	71.7	78.2	80.4
L.H.I. (BB Ht.)	74.0	72.6	72.1	68.3	68.5		69.2	71.8	73.7	75.4		71.3
L.H.I. (Aur. Ht.)	61.8	60.9	58.5	57.9	56.6	56.6						
B.H.I. (BB Ht.)	98.6	95.0	102.6	92.3	107.6							
B.H.I. (Aur. Ht.)	81.4	79.1	82.4	78.3		86.5						
Fronto-parietal 1	64.9	66.3										
Cranio-facial 1	102.3	95.3										
Upper Facial 1	46.4	47.8	54.4	40.0	47.6		59.7	58.9	60.8	57.1	60.9	48.0
Nasal 1	52.1	54.2	45.8		55.9	51.0	49.6	40.4	43.6	44.6	41.8	43.0
Orbital 1	74.4	73.1					78.2	83.4	83.4	82.4		80.6
Palatal 1	98.7	90.2					75.4					

TABLE 37 (continued)

G. CAPOIDS AND CONGOIDS

	Florisbad	Boskop	Homa 1	Mound 4	Fish Hoek	Matjies River Range (4)	Bushmen (Slombe) Range (26)	Cape Flats	Border Cave	Asselar
Sex (± Age)	M	M	M	M	M	M F	M	M	M	F
Cranial Capacity		1650	1514?	1683	1550	1230–1660	995–1370	1230	1450?	1520
Maximum Length		205	203	205	198	178–203	165–185	191	197?	193
Maximum Breadth		150	135?	140	149	135–149	120–134	132	141?	137
Basion-Bregma Height					128					136
Auricular Height	120	115	120	132	115	114–124	98–110	107	115	
Minimum Frontal		102	106	107	105	90–102	87–120		108	
Bizygomatic					136		110–120			135
Upper Face Height	76			73	58		47–69	67		68
Nose Height	58			42	42		38–50			
Nose Breadth	31				25		21–30			
Orbital Height	35				32		28–38			
Orbital Breadth	47			36	40		35–41			
Interorbital	27				28		19–28			
Biorbital	124				101					
Cranial Index		73.1	66.5	68.3	75.2	67–73	70–80.5		71.6	71.0
L.H.I. (BB Ht.)					64.6					70.5
L.H.I. (Aur. Ht.)		56.1	59.1	64.4	58.1	59–67	54–65.5		58.4	
B.H.I. (BB Ht.)					85.9					99.3
B.H.I. (Aur. Ht.)		76.1	88.9	94.3	77.2	83–98	73–83	81.8	81.6	
Frontal-parietal 1			78.5	76.4	70.5				76.6	
Cranio-facial 1					91.3					98.5
Upper Facial 1					42.6		44–55			50.3
Nasal 1	53.4				59.5		50–70			54.9
Orbital 1	74.5				80.0		76–99			80.9

TABLE 38

DIMENSIONS AND INDICES OF MANDIBLES

	Pithecanthropus B	Sangiran 2	Wadjak 2	Sinanthropus G-1	Sinanthropus H-1	Upper Cave 101	Heidelberg	Montmaurin	Ehringsdorf
Sex (± Age)	M?	?	M	M	F	M	M	F?	M
Mandibular Length				103.0	94.0	90	120	96	
Bicondylar Breadth				146.4	101.8	137	150	137	
Bigonial Breadth			113	108.6	97.8	115	110	94	
Symphysial Height	42.2	38.2	41	40.0	31.5	37	34	29	31
Ht. at Mental Foramen	35	38.5	41	34.0	26.0	36	34	27	
Ht. at M_2–M_3	31	30?	38.5	33	26	33	32	31	30
Ascending Ramus Ht.			62	75	63	58	71	70	
Ascending Ramus Br.			46	42	40	41	52	45	
Thickness at Symphysis	16.4	19.0	14	13	14	16	16	14	16?
Thickness at Mental Foramen	16.5	19.3	16.5	16.4	15.4	12	17	15	
Thickness at M_2–M_3	17.8	20.3	22	19	16	15	22	16	16?
Index of Robusticity at Symphysis	38.9	49.7	34.1	32.5	44.4	43.2	47.1	48.3	51.6
I. of R. at Mental Foramen	47.1	50.1	40.2	48.2	59.2	33.3	50.0	55.6	
I. of R. at M_2–M_3	57.4	67.6	57.1	57.6	61.5	45.4	68.8	51.6	53.3
Angle of Inclination (Symphysial)	58°?		73.5°	59°	60.5°	91°	63°	62°	38°?
Mandibular (Gonial) Angle			111°	97°	108°	117°	105°	110°	

TABLE 38 (continued)

Sex (± Age)	Krapina F	Krapina G	Krapina H	Krapina J	La Chapelle	La Ferrassie 1	Spy 1	La Naulette	Le Moustier	La Quina H-5	Regourdou	Circeo 2	Circeo 3
	F	F	M	M	M	M	?	?	M	M	M	M	M?
Mandibular Length				114	112	110			104				
Bicondylar Breadth				155	147.3	134			133		128?		129?
Bigonial Breadth				111?	99.2	104							
Symphysial Height	31	31.5	40	42	39?	38	38	31	30		40	36	38
Ht. at Mental Foramen						32		26					
Ht. at M$_2$–M$_3$		28	34		32?	31	33	22	28	34	33	36	38
Ascending Ramus Ht.				73	70	64	61			75	66		
Ascending Ramus Br.				38	49	44	44		36	47	37?		48
Thickness at Symphysis	14.5	15	15		16	16.3	15	14				16?	16?
Thickness at Mental Foramen						14		12.7					
Thickness at M$_2$–M$_3$		14.5			18	14.5		16				16.4?	14?
Index of Robusticity at Symphysis	46.7	47.6	37.5	35.7	41.0	42.9	45.4	45.2					
I. of R. at Mental Foramen			51.8			43.8		48.8					
I. of R. at M$_2$–M$_3$					56.2	46.8		72.7					
Angle of Inclination (Symphysial)	70°	62.5°	63.5°		63°	73°	74°	65°					
Mandibular (Gonial) Angle				118°	110°	109°							

TABLE 38 (continued)

Sex (± Age)	Tabun		Skhul		Ternefine			Sidi Abd er-Rahman	Temara	Rabat	Fish Hoek	Asselar
	1	2	4	5	1	2	3					
	F	M	M	M	F	F	M	F?	F?	M	M	F
Mandibular Length	95	119	118	109	110	129					86	
Bicondylar Breadth	133	130	132	132	130?		158				121	123
Bigonial Breadth	93	88	110	98							99	97
Symphysial Height	30.3	42	42.5	36.5	39	35	39		26	30	38	34
Ht. at Mental Foramen	27.5	42.5	40.5	36.0							34	
Ht. at M₂–M₃	26.2	38.5	35.5	34.5	35 *	34 *	38 *	34.5 *	26 *	30 *	24	
Ascending Ramus Ht.	65.5	79.0	67.0	78.5		72	93				53	
Ascending Ramus Br.	38.0	40.0	42.5?	36.2		45	48				39	
Thickness at Symphysis	13.2	17.0	15.0	15.5							15	
Thickness at Mental Foramen	15.0	16.4	15.0	13.2							14	
Thickness at M₂–M₃	15.2	18.0	19	13	19 *	16 *	20 *	17 *	14 *	17 *	18	
Index of Robusticity at Symphysis	43.6	40.5	35.3	42.5							44.1	
I. of R. at Mental Foramen	54.5	38.6	37.0	35.9							41.2	
I. of R. at M₂–M₃	58.0	46.8	53.5	37.7	54.3 *	47.1 *	52.6 *	49.4 *	55.5 *	53.7 *	75.0	
Angle of Inclination (Symphysial)	61°	72°	75°	69°	62°	64°	70°		65°	76°	74°	74°
Mandibular (Gonial) Angle	98°	107°	96°	97°	98°	98°	111°				107°	

* Measured to scale from a photograph.

TABLE 39

DIMENSIONS AND INDICES OF TEETH
UPPERS

		Pithecanthropus 4	Trinil	Wadjak 1	Wadjak 2	Keilor	Talgai	Modern Australian Aborigines Max.	Modern Australian Aborigines Mean	Sinanthropus No.	Sinanthropus Range	Sinanthropus Mean
I¹	L	10.0				7.5	10.9	10.6	9.3	4	7.5– 8.1	7.7
	B					7.5	8.6	9.0	7.9	5	7.5– 8.1	7.6
	R					56	94		74			60
I²	L	8.0				6.0		9.0	7.6	2	8.2– 8.3	8.2
	B					6.0		8.5	6.9	3	8.0– 8.2	8.1
	R					36			53			66*
C¹	L	9.5			10.0	9.0	9.6	9.3	8.4	6	9.1–10.5	9.4
	B	11.8			9.6	10.5	10.9	11.0	9.0	6	9.8–10.6	9.2
	R	112			93	94	105		76			86
P¹	L	8.4		9.0	8.4	6.0	8.6	9.5	7.8	4	7.4– 9.2	8.3
	B	12.4		9.4	10.6	10.5	12.3	12.5	10.3	4	10.5–12.8	11.9
	R	104		85	88	63	106		80			99
P²	L	8.4		8.8	8.0	7.1	8.0	8.8	7.2	9	10.3–12.5	11.4
	B	12.2		10.0	10.4	10.6	11.0	12.0	10.1	9	10.3–12.5	11.4
	R	102		88	80	75	88		73			90
M¹	L	12.2	11.3	11.0	12.1	11.2	12.6	13.0	11.4	7	10.0–13.1	11.2
	B	13.6	15.3	13.2	12.7	13.2	13.1	14.8	10.1	6	11.7–13.7	12.5
	R	154	173	145	161	148	165		145			140
M²	L	13.6		10.7	11.9	9.9	11.3	12.5	10.9	7	10.2–12.2	10.9
	B	15.2		13.0	13.8	13.0	13.5	16.0	12.8	7	12.2–13.4	12.7
	R	207		137	152	129	150		142			
M³	L	10.8	12.0	10.3	10.9	9.7		13.0	10.0	9	9.1–10.4	9.6
	B	14.8	13.8	12.4	13.2	12.0		15.0	12.3	9	10.5–12.5	11.6
	R	160	166	125	125	116			123			111

* I² is larger than I¹ because teeth are from different individuals.   L = length, B = breadth, R = robusticity.

TABLE 39 (continued)

		Upper Cave 101†	Recent Chinese Mean	Stein-heim	Sacco-pastore 2	Mon-sempron	Krapina No.	Krapina Range	Neanderthals No.	Neanderthals Range	Neanderthals Mean	Tabun No. 1
I¹	L	8.0	8.7			9.0	14	9.9-10.4	8	8.0-10.0	8.8	9.0
	B	7.6	7.5			8.5		8.0- 8.9		7.5- 9.0	8.3	8.2
	R	61	65			76				64-90	74	74
I²	L	6.9	7.0			8.0	2	9.0-10.5	2	5.8- 7.3	6.6	7.3
	B	7.6	6.4			9.0		6.0- 9.0		7.0- 7.2	7.1	7.7
	R	52	45			72				61-65	63	56
C¹	L	7.7	8.1		8.0	9.0	13	9.0-10.5	2	7.0	7.0	7.9
	B	8.8	8.3		9.2	9.5		9.6-11.3		9.0-10.0	9.5	8.8
	R	66	67		74	86				63-70	66	70
P¹	L	6.7	7.2		7.0	8.0	22	7.8- 8.5	2	6.5- 7.5	7.0	7.5
	B	10.0	9.4		10.0	11.0		9.0-11.5		9.0	9.0	9.8
	R	66	68		70	88				58-68	63	74
P²	L	6.4	6.9	7.1	6.5	8.0			3	6.1- 7.0	6.7	6.5
	B	10.0	9.2	9.3	9.0	10.5				9.0-11.3	9.9	9.6
	R	64	63	66	58	84				57-69	63	62
M¹	L	10.0	10.0	12.3	11.0	11.0	16	10.0-13.3	3	7.0- 9.6	8.5	10.8
	B	10.8	11.2	11.5	11.5	12.0		11.5-13.0		11.7-12.6	12.1	11.5
	R	118	112	141	126	132				88-123	106	124
M²	L	10.5	9.4	11.3	10.0	11.0	9	10.2-12.1	3	10.0-11.1	10.6	10.5
	B	12.8	11.0	11.7	11.5	14.5		10.2-14.0		11.7-12.7	12.1	11.7
	R	134	103	152	115	160				120-141	129	123
M³	L	8.4	8.6	9.0	11.2		4	10.0-12.2	3	9.0-10.7	9.2	8.3
	B	11.3	10.3	10.0	10.9			12.0-12.5		11.5-11.0	12.4	10.2
	R	94	89	88	101					104-124	114	85

† Worn by mesiodistal attrition as well as crown reduction.

TABLE 39 (continued)

		Skhul No.	Range	Mean	Modern European Mean	Tangier	Broken Hill	Cape Flats	Asselar	Fish Hoek	Modern Human Range
I¹	L	4	8.5–10.9	9.6	9		8			8	6.5–10.6
	B	4	7.5–8.7	8.2	7		8.5			6	6.2– 9.0
	R	4	64–95	79	63		68			48	
I²	L	4	6.2– 8.8	7.2	6.4		7			7	5.0– 9.0
	B	4	6.2– 8.0	7.2	6		8			6	5.0– 8.5
	R	4	45–55	52	38		56			42	
C¹	L	5	7.5– 8.9	8.4	7.6	8.2	10	7.5	7.5	6	5.8– 9.3
	B	5	8.0– 9.5	8.9	8	10.5	11	9.5	8.5	6.8	7.0–11.0
	R	5	68–83	75	61	89	110	71	64	41	
P¹	L	3	7.4– 8.7	8.1	7.2	7.7	7.5	7.5	7	6.2	5.5– 9.5
	B	3	10.0–10.8	10.4	9.2	10.3	11	10.5	9	6.8	5.0–12.5
	R	3	74–91	84	66	79	82	79	63	42	
P²	L	3	7.0– 7.5	7.2	6.8			7.0	6.5	6.2	5.0– 8.8
	B	3	8.4–11.7	10.3	8.8			10.5	9	7	5.0–12.0
	R	3	63–77	74	60			74	58.5	43	
M¹	L	7	9.9–12.4	11.2	10.7	11.7	14	10.0	10.5	9	7.8–13.0
	B	7	11.2–12.5	12.0	11.8	13.7	13.5	12.5	13	10.5	9.0–14.8
	R	7	116–150	134	126	160	189	125	136.5	94	
M²	L	5	8.6–12.2	10.2	9.2		13		11	10	7.0–12.5
	B	5	11.5–12.2	12.0	11.5		14		13	11	6.3–16.0
	R	5	110–146	122	106		182		143	110	
M³	L	3	8.6– 9.4	9.0	8.6		19		10.5	8	4.0–13.0
	B	3	11.0–11.8	11.3	10.6		12		12.5	9	5.8–15.0
	R	3	95–111	102	91		108		131	72	

TABLE 39 (continued)

LOWERS

		Pithecanthropus B	Wadjak 2	Modern Australians Max.	Modern Australians Mean	Sinanthropus No.	Sinanthropus Range	Sinanthropus Mean	Upper Cave 101	Modern Chinese	Heidelberg	Montmaurin
I₁	L		6.1	6.7	6.0	7	6.0– 6.8	6.4	4.0	5.6	6.0	
	B		7.0	7.7	6.3	7	5.8– 6.8	6.9	5.6	6.2	6.2	
	R		43		38			44	22	34	33	
I₂	L		7.0	7.7	6.7	9	6.3– 7.2	8.1	4.0	6.2	6.2	
	B		7.0	7.6	6.6	10	6.7– 7.3	7.0	6.0	6.2	7.2	
	R		49					57	24	38	45	
C₁	L		8.1	9.0	7.6	7	8.1– 9.0	9.2	6.4	7.3	7.7	
	B		8.2	10.0	8.3	7	8.2–10.4	9.2	8.6	7.9	8.5	
	R		66		63			85	54	58	65	
P₁	L		8.0	9.0	7.6	14	7.9– 9.8	8.6	6.5	7.2	8.1	
	B		8.2	10.0	8.8	13	8.9–10.8	9.9	8.1	8.1	9.0	
	R		66		67			85	51	58	73	
P₂	L	10.0	8.2	9.0	7.7	6	8.5– 9.2	8.8	6.6	7.3	7.5	
	B	11.0	8.3	10.0	8.9	7	8.0–11.1	9.8	8.6	8.1	9.2	
	R	110	68		69			86	56	59	69	
M₁	L	13.8	13.0	14.0	12.3	13	9.9–14.1	12.6	10.6	11.3	11.6	12.5
	B	13.2	12.0	13.5	11.9	13	10.9–12.8	11.8	10.8	10.7	11.2	10.7
	R	182	156		146			149	114	107	130	134
M₂	L	13.8	11.2	14.2	12.5	8	11.3–12.9	12.6	12.0	10.7	12.7	12.5
	B	13.5	11.0	13.5	11.7	8	11.4–12.9	12.0	11.0	10.4	12.0	11.0
	R	186	122		146			151	132	111	152	138
M₃	L	14.5	11.0	15.0	11.9	10	10.0–12.9	11.7	10.8	10.6	12.2	13.0
	B	12.5	10.1	13.0	11.1	9	10.0–12.4	11.2	10.4	10.4	11.5	11.0
	R	181	111		132			131	111	110	140	143

TABLE 39 (continued)

		Mon-sempron	Ehringsdorf Child	F	Krapina No.	Krapina Range	Neanderthals No.	Neanderthals Range	M	Tabun 1	Tabun 2
I₁	L			4.5	12	7.6– 8.9	9	4.0– 5.5	5.0	5.7	5.9
	B			8.0		8.4– 9.5	6	7.4– 8.0	7.6	7.0	8.0
	R			36			6	30–41	38	40	47
I₂	L			5.8	1	7.5	12	5.8– 7.0	6.3	6.7	6.1
	B			8.2		8.2	7	5.0– 8.1	6.7	7.6	8.2
	R			47		62	6	41–60	52	51	50
C₁	L	8.0	8.5	8.5	9	7.6– 8.4	12	6.2– 9.0	7.6	8.0	8.0
	B	9.0	8.2	9.0		8.2–11.1	10	8.5–10.0	9.5	8.3	9.0
	R	72	70	76			9	62–81	75	66	72
P₁	L	7.5	8.3	7.8	14	7.8– 8.3	9	5.0– 8.0	6.3	7.0	7.8
	B	9.5	8.5	8.7		8.8–10.0	9	6.1– 9.8	7.5	8.5	9.0
	R	79	71	68			9	40–76	59	60	70
P₂	L	8.0		7.3	1	8.5	9	5.0– 7.0	5.8	5.9	7.9
	B	10.0		10.0		9.9	9	5.8–11.3	7.7	8.7	9.5
	R	80		73			9	42–69	53	51	75
M₁	L		12.0	11.8	11	11.2–13.8	12	9.6–12.5	11.2	10.0	11.0
	B		10.5	11.0		10.5–12.4	12	8.7–11.8	10.6	10.5	11.0
	R		12.6	130			12	99–138	119	105	121
M₂	L		12.9	12.3	9	10.7–12.5	14	10.6–12.0	11.5	11.2	10.8
	B		10.8	13.0		10.2–11.4	14	10.2–12.4	11.4	10.6	11.0
	R		139	160			14	107–148	132	119	119
M₃	L			10.2	7	11.1–13.6	10	10.6–12.0	11.2	10.9	11.5
	B			9.7		10.0–11.0	10	10.4–12.0	11.0	9.8	10.8
	R			99			10	113–139	124	107	124

TABLE 39 (continued)

		No.	Skhul Range	Mean	Haua Fteah	Modern European Mean	Ternefine 1	Ternefine 2	Ternefine 3	Sidi Abd er-Rahman	Rabat	Cave of Hearths
I_1	L	4	4.5– 6.5	5.2		5.4	5.6		5.5			
	B	4	6.4– 7.7	6.9		6.0						
	R	4	26–50	35		32						
I_2	L	3	6.0– 7.2	6.5		5.9						
	B	3	7.0– 8.0	7.4		6.4						
	R	3	43–58	48		38						
C_1	L	5	6.4– 9.1	7.5		6.9	7.5	7.0	8.0			
	B	5	7.0– 9.0	8.1		7.9	9.0	10.0	11.0			
	R	5	52–72	61		55	68	70	88			
P_1	L	3	5.8– 8.2	7.1		6.9	8.0	9.0	8.0	9.0	9.0	8.0
	B	3	7.7– 9.2	8.3		7.9	9.0	11.2	10.0	9.6	10.0	8.0
	R	3	45–75	59		55	76	101	80	86	90	64
P_2	L	3	7.2– 7.7	7.5		7.1	8.0	9.5	8.2			
	B	3	8.3– 9.1	8.7		8.0	10.0	10.5	10.0			
	R	3	62–70	65		57	80	100	82			
M_1	L	6	10.5–13.0	11.7		11.2	12.8	14.0	12.0	13.0	13.0	12.0
	B	5	10.5–11.5	11.1		10.3	12.0	13.0	11.8	11.6	11.0	11.8
	R	5	121–146	132		115	154	182	142	151	143	142
M_2	L	4	9.5–11.6	10.4	11.7	10.7	13.0	14.2	12.0	14.4	12.5	11.5
	B	4	10.5–11.4	10.9	11.4	10.1	13.7	13.7	12.1	11.4	11.3	10.7
	R	4	100–132	114	133	108	178	195	145	164	141	132
M_3	L	5	10.3–12.2	11.0	10.6	10.7	12.0	13.2	8.0	12.2	12.0	
	B	5	9.9–10.5	10.2	10.8	9.8	12.5	12.5	11.5	11.2	10.6	
	R	5	104–127	113	114	105	150	165	92	137	127	

TABLE 39 (continued)

		Cape Flats	Asselar	Fish Hoek	Modern Men Range
I_1	L		6.5	4.5	3.5- 6.7
	B	R		4.2	4.9- 7.7
	R			22	
I_2	L		6.5	5.2	4.2- 7.5
	B			4.3	5.3- 7.6
	R			22	
C_1	L	7.0	6.5	6.8	5.0- 9.0
	B	9.0	8	6.0	5.8-10.0
	R	63	52		
P_1	L	8.0	7	6.0	4.5- 9.0
	B	9.0	9	6.0	5.7-10.0
	R	72	63	36	
P_2	L	7.5	7.5	6.1	5.0- 9.0
	B	9.0	8	6.5	5.0-10.0
	R	70	60		
M_1	L	11.8	10	11.3	8.0-14.0
	B	11.8	11	9.5	8.3-13.5
	R	139	110		
M_2	L	11.5	11	10.0	7.0-14.2
	B	12.0	11	9.0	8.0-13.5
	R	138	121	90	
M_3	L	11.3	11	10.0	4.0-15.0
	B	11.5	10.5	8.0	4.0-13.0
	R	13.0	115.5	80	

BIBLIOGRAPHY

Abbie, A. A.: "The Quest for Man's Birthplace." *AuS*, Vol. 1, No. 4 (1961), pp. 201–7.

Adam, W.: "The Keilor Fossil Skull, Palate, and Upper Dental Arch." *MNMM*, No. 13 (1943), pp. 71–8.

Adams, T., and Covino, B. G.: "Racial Variations to a Standardized, Cold Stress." *JAP*, Vol. 12, No. 1 (1957), pp. 9–12.

Agache, R., and Bourdier, F.: "Découverte de Silex Apparemment Taillés à un Equidé Archaeique de Type Villafranchien dans la Haute Terrasse Supérieure de la Somme." *CRAS*, Vol. 248, No. 3 (1959), pp. 439–40.

Alcobé, S.: "Die Neanderthaler Spaniens." *NC*, 1958, pp. 9–62.

Alexander, P.: "Radiation-Imitating Chemicals." *SA*, Vol. 202, No. 1 (1960), pp. 99–108.

Allen, J. A.: "The Influence of Physical Conditions in the Genesis of Species." *RR*, Vol. 1 (1877), pp. 108–40. (Reprinted in *ARSI*, 1905 [1906], pp. 375–402.)

Anati, E.: *Palestine Before the Hebrews.* New York: Alfred A. Knopf; 1963.

Andersen, K. L., Løyning, Y., Nelms, J. D., Wilson, D., Fox, R. H., and Bolstad, A.: "A Metabolic and Thermal Response to a Moderate Cold Exposure in Nomadic Lapps." *JAP*, Vol. 15, No. 4 (1960), pp. 649–53.

Andrew, G.: "Geology of the Sudan," in Chapter 6 of *Agriculture in the Sudan*, pp. 84–128. Oxford: Oxford University Press; 1948.

Angel, J. L.: "The Human Skeletal Remains from Hotu Cave, Iran." *PAPS*, Vol. 96, No. 3 (1952), pp. 258–69.

Anonymous: "The Astonishing Discovery of 'Nutcracker Man'; Dr. and Mrs. Leakey at work at Olduvai." *ILN*, Vol. 235, No. 6267 (Sept. 12, 1959), pp. 217–19.

——: "More *Gigantopithecus*." *VP*, Vol. 2, No. 1 (1958), p. 67.

Arambourg, C.: "L'Hominien Fossile de Ternefine (Algerie)." *CRAS*, Vol. 239 (1954), pp. 893–5.

——: "A Recent Discovery in Human Paleontology, Atlanthropus of Ternefine (Algeria)." *AJPA*, Vol. 13, No. 2 (1955), pp. 191–6.

——: "Sur l'Attitude, en Station Verticale, des Néanderthaliens." *CRAS*, Vol. 240 (1955), pp. 804–6.

——: "Une Nouvelle Mandibule d' 'Atlanthropus' du Gisement de Ternefine." *CRAS*, Vol. 241 (1955), pp. 895–7.

——: "Le Parietal de *l'Anthropus mauritanicus*." *CRAS*, Vol. 241 (1955), pp. 980–2.

——: "Une IIIme Mandibule d' 'Atlanthropus' Découverte à Ternefine." *Quaternaria*, Vol. 3 (1956), pp. 1–4.

——: "Récentes Découvertes de Paléontologie Humaine en Afrique du Nord Française." *PTPA* (1957), pp. 186–94.

Arambourg, C.: "L'Hominien Fossile d'Oldoway." *BSPF*, Vol. 57, No. 3–4 (1960), pp. 223–8.

Ashley-Montagu, M. F.: Review of *The Stone Age of Mount Carmel* by A. Keith and T. D. McCown (Oxford: Clarendon Press; 1939), in *AA*, Vol. 42 (1940), pp. 518–22.

Baker, P. T.: "Racial Differences in Heat Tolerance." *AJPA*, Vol. 16, No. 3 (1958), pp. 287–305.

——: "American Negro-White Differences in Thermal-Insulative Aspects of Body Fat." *HB*, Vol. 31, No. 4 (1959), pp. 316–24.

——: "Climate, Culture, and Evolution." *HB*, Vol. 32, No. 1 (1960), pp. 3–16.

Bakker, E. M. Van Zinderen: "A Pollen Analytical Investigation of the Florisbad Deposits (South Africa)." *PTPA*, 1957, pp. 56–67.

Balout, L.: *Préhistoire de l'Afrique du Nord.* Paris: Arts et Métiers Graphiques; 1955.

Barbour, G. B.: "Ape or Man?" *OJS*, Vol. 49 (1949), pp. 129–45.

Barnicot, N. A.: "Climatic Factors in the Evolution of Human Populations." *CSHS*, Vol. 24 (1959), pp. 115–29.

Bartucz, L., Dancza, J., Hollendouner, F., Kadič, O., Mottl, M., Pataki, V., Pálosi, E., Szabó, J., and Vendl, A.: "Die Mussolini Höhle (Subalyuk) bei Cserépfalu." *GHSP*, Vol. 8, fasc. 14 (1939), pp. 1–320.

Bate, D. M. A.: "Aves," in W. P. Pycraft, ed.: *Rhodesian Man and Associated Remains*, p. 74. London: British Museum (Natural History); 1928.

Bay, R.: "Das Gebiss des Neanderthalers." *NC*, 1958, pp. 123–40.

Baylac, R., Cammas, R., Delaplace, E., Lacombe, P., Laplace-Jauretche, G., Méroc, L., Mothe, L., Simonnet, G. and R., Trouette, L.: "Découvertes Récentes dans les Grottes de Montmaurin, Haute-Garonne." *L'Anth*, Vol. 54, No. 3–4 (1950), pp. 262–71.

Befu, H., and Chard, C. S.: "Preceramic Cultures in Japan." *AA*, Vol. 5 (1960), pp. 815–49.

Behm-Blancke, G.: "Umwelt, Kultur und Morfologie des Eem-Interglacialen Menschen von Ehringsdorf bei Weimar." *NC*, 1958, pp. 141–50.

Bender, M. A., and Mettler, L. E.: "Chromosome Studies of Primates." *Science*, Vol. 128, No. 3317 (1958), pp. 186–90.

Berckhemer, F.: "Ein Urmenschenschädel aus dem Diluvialen Schotten von Steinheim an der Murr." *AAnz*, Vol. 10 (1933), pp. 318–21.

——: "Bemerkungen zu H. Weinert's Abhandlung 'Der Urmenschenschädel von Steinheim.'" *VGPA*, Vol. 2 (1937), pp. 49–58.

Bergman, R. A. M., and Karsten, P.: "The Flourine Content of Pithecanthropus and of Other Specimens from the Trinil Fauna." *MKNA* B, Vol. 55, No. 2 (1952), pp. 150–2.

Bergmann, C.: "Über die Verhältnisse der Wärmeökonomie der Thiere zu ihrer Grösse." *GS*, Vol. 3, No. 8 (1847), pp. 595–708.

Biasutti, R.: "Crania Aegyptica." *AAE*, Vol. 35 (1905), pp. 322–62.

——, ed.: *Razze e Popoli della Terra*, Vol. I. Torino: Unione Tipografico-Editrice; 1959.

Birdsell, J. B.: "Some Environmental and Cultural Factors Influencing the Structuring of Australian Aboriginal Populations." *AN*, Vol. 87, No. 834 (1953), pp. 171–207.

Black, D.: "On an Adolescent Skull of *Sinanthropus pekinensis* in Comparison with an Adult Skull of the Same Species and with Other Hominid Skulls, Recent and Fossil." *PS-D*, Vol. 7, ns No. 1 (1931), pp. 1–144.

Blanc, A. C.: "Torre in Pietra, Saccopastore, Monte Circeo. On the Position of the Mousterian in the Pleistocene Sequence of the Rome Area." *NC*, 1958, pp. 167–74.

Bolk, L.: *Das Problem der Menschenwerdung.* Jena: G. Fischer; 1926.

Bonch-Osmolovskii, G. A.: *Paleolit Krima, No. II, 1941, Kist iskopaemogo Cheloveka iz Grota Kiik-Koba.* Moscow-Leningrad: Izdat. Akad. Nank. SSSR; 1941.

——: *Paleolit Krima, No. III, Skelet Stori i Goleni Iskopaemogo Cheloveka iz Grota Kiik-Koba.* Moscow-Leningrad: Izdat. Akad. Nank. SSSR; 1954.

Boné, E.: "Quatre Fragments Post-Craniens du Gisement à Australopitheques de Makapansgat (N. Transvaal)." *L'Anth*, Vol. 59, No. 5–6 (1955), pp. 462–9.

——: "Une Clavicule et un Nouveau Fragment Mandibulaire *d'Austropithecus prometheus.*" *PAf*, Vol. 3 (1955), pp. 87–101.

——: "Oreopithecus bambolii, A Propos du Jalonnement Tertiare de l'Homme." *RQS*, April 20, 1959, pp. 215–46.

—— and Dart, R. A.: "A Catalogue of the Australopithecine Fossils Found at the Limeworks, Makapansgat." *AJPA*, Vol. 13, No. 4 (1955), pp. 621–4.

Bonin, G. von: "European Races of the Upper Paleolithic." *HB*, Vol. 7, No. 2 (1935), pp. 196–221.

Boule, M.: *L'Homme Fossile de la Chapelle aux Saints* (Extracts from *APa*, 1911–12). Paris: Masson et Cie; 1912–13.

—— and Vallois, H. V.: "L'Homme Fossile d'Asselar." *AIPH*, Mem. No. 9 (1932).

——: *Les Hommes Fossiles.* Paris: Masson et Cie; 1952.

—— and Verneau, R.: "Les Grottes Paléolithiques de Beni Seghoual." *AIPH*, Mem. No. 13, Pt. 2 (1934).

Bourlière, F.: *Mammals of the World.* New York: Alfred A. Knopf; 1955.

——: *The Natural History of Mammals.* New York: Alfred A. Knopf; 1956.

Boyd, W. C.: "Blood Groups." *TB*, Vol. 17, Pt. 2 (1939), pp. 113–204.

Boyer, S. H., and Young, W. J.: "Gamma Globulin (GM Group) Heterogeneity in Chimpanzees." *Science*, Vol. 133, No. 3452 (1961), pp. 583–4.

Brace, C. L.: "The Significance of the Krapina Finds." Unpublished paper for Seminar in Primates and Fossil Man, Harvard University, Cambridge, Mass., November 20, 1957.

Braidwood, R. J., Howe, B., and Reed, C. A.: "The Iranian Prehistoric Project." *Science*, Vol. 133, No. 3469 (1961), pp. 2008–10.

Brain, C. K.: "New Evidence for the Correlation of the Transvaal Ape-Man-Bearing Cave Deposits." *PTPA*, 1957, pp. 143–8.

——: "The Transvaal Ape-Man-Bearing Cave Deposits." *TMM*, No. 11 (1958).

——, Lowe, C. van R., and Dart, R. A.: "Kafuan Stone Artefacts in the Post-Australopithecine Breccia at Makapansgat." *Nature*, Vol. 175, No. 4444 (1955), pp. 16–18.

Breuil, H., Teilhard de Chardin, P., and Wernert, P.: "Le Paléolithique du Harrar." *L'Anth*, Vol. 55, No. 3–4 (1951), pp. 219–30.

Briggs, L. C.: "The Stone Age Races of Northwest Africa." *BASP*, No. 18 (1955).

——: *Tribes of the Sahara.* Cambridge, Mass.: Harvard University Press; 1960.

Brodar, S.: "Das Paleolithikum in Jugoslawien." *Quartär*, Vol. 1 (1938), pp. 140–72.

Brodrick, A. H.: "A Newly Discovered and as yet Unexplored Treasure-House of Spanish Cave Art: The Fantastic and Beautiful Caves of Nerja—a Preliminary Note." *ILN*, Vol. 239, No. 6366 (1961), pp. 216–9.

Brody, S., Ragsdale, A. C., Yeck, R. G., and Worstell, D.: "Milk Productions, Feed and Water Consumption, and Body Weight of Jersey and Holstein Cows in

688 *Bibliography*

Relation to Several Diurnal Temperature Rhythms." *RBMO*, Vol. 578 (1955), pp. 1–26.

Broom, R., and Robinson, J. T.: "Thumb of Swartkrans Ape-Man." *Nature*, Vol. 164, No. 4176 (1949), pp. 841–2.

———: "Swartkrans Ape-Man." *TMM*, No. 6 (1952).

——— and Schepers, G. H. W.: "Sterkfontein Ape-Man, Plesianthropus." *TMM*, No. 4 (1950).

Broom, R., and Schepers, G. H. W.: "The South African Fossil Ape-Man, The Australopithecine." *TMM*, No. 2 (1946).

Brothwell, D. R.: "Upper Pleistocene Human Skull from the Niah Cave." *SMJ*, Vol. 9, No. 15–16 (1960), pp. 323–49.

———: "The People of Mt. Carmel," *PPS*, Oct.–Dec. 1961, pp. 155–9.

——— and Higgs, Z. S., eds.: *Science in Archeology*. London: Thames and Hudson, 1962.

Brown, A. R.: *The Andaman Islanders*. Cambridge: Cambridge University Press; 1922.

Brown, G. M., and Page, J.: "The Effect of Chronic Exposure to Cold on Temperature and Blood Flow of the Hand." *JAP*, Vol. 5, No. 5 (1953), pp. 221–7.

Büchi, E. C.: "A Rhesus Monkey with B Agglutinogen." *Nature*, Vol. 172, No. 4384 (1953), p. 873.

Bushnell, G., and McBurney, C.: "New World Origins Seen from the Old World." *Antiquity*, Vol. 33, No. 130 (1959), pp. 93–101.

Butler, P. M., and Mills, J. R. E.: "A Contribution to the Odontology of *Oreopithecus*." *BBMNH*, Vol. 4, No. 1 (1959), pp. 1–26.

Byers, D. S., and Hadlock, W. S.: "Carbon-14 Dates from Ellsworth Falls in Maine." *Science*, Vol. 121, No. 3151 (1955), pp. 735–6.

Campbell, T. D.: "Dentition and Palate of the Australian Aboriginal." *PKSF*, No. 1 (1925).

Candela, P. B., Wiener, A. S., and Goss, L. J.: "New Observations on the Blood Group Factors in Simiidae and Cercopithecidae." *Zoologica*, Vol. 25, No. 4 (1940), pp. 513–21.

Carpenter, C. R.: "Characteristics of Social Behavior in Non-Human Primates." *TNYA*, Ser. II, Vol. 4, No. 8 (1942), pp. 251–3.

Carsner, R. L., and Rennels, E. G.: "Primary Site of Gene Action in the Anterior Pituitary." *Science*, Vol. 131, No. 3403 (1960), p. 829.

Carson, H. L.: "Increase in Fitness in Experimental Populations Resulting from Heterosis." *PNAS*, Vol. 44, No. 11 (1958), pp. 1136–41.

Carter, J. T.: "Teeth of Rhodesian Man," in W. P. Pycraft, ed.: *Rhodesian Man and Associated Remains*, pp. 64–5. London: British Museum (Natural History); 1928.

Caspari, E.: "Genetic Basis of Behavior," in A. Roe and G. G. Simpson, eds.: *Behavior and Evolution*, pp. 103–27. New Haven: Yale University Press; 1958.

Charlesworth, J. K.: *The Quaternary Era*, 2 vols. London: E. Arnold; 1957.

Cheng, T-K.: *Archaeology in China*, Vol. I, *Prehistoric China*. Cambridge: W. Heffer & Sons; 1959.

Chia, L-P.: "Notes on the Human and Other Mammalian Remains from Changyang, Hupei." *VP*, Vol. 1, No. 3 (1957), pp. 252–7.

Chiarelli, B.: "Chromosomes of the Orang-Utan (*Pongo pygmeus*)." *Nature*, Vol. 192, No. 4799 (1961), p. 285.

Christian, J. J.: "Endocrinic Adaptive Mechanisms and the Physiologic Regulation of Population Growth." *NMRI*, No. 60–2 (1960).

——: "Phenomena Associated with Population Density." *PNAS*, Vol. 47, No. 4 (1961), pp. 428–49.

Chu, E. H. Y., and Bender, M. A.: "Chromosome Cytology and Evolution in Primates." *Science*, Vol. 133, No. 3642 (1961), pp. 1399–405.

Chu, E. H. Y., and Giles, N. H.: "A Study of Monkey Chromosome Components." *AJPA* Proceedings, Abstract No. 70 (1957), pp. 452–3.

Chu, E. H. Y., and Swomley, B. A.: "Chromosomes of Lemurine Lemurs." *Science*, Vol. 137, No. 3468 (1960), pp. 1925–6.

Cipriani, L.: "Un Interesante Pueblo del Sahara: Los Dauada." *RGA*, Vol. 2, No. 2 (1934), pp. 141–52.

Clark, J. D.: "Further Excavations at Broken Hill, N. Rhodesia." *JRAI*, Vol. 89, Pt. 2 (1960), pp. 201–32.

——, Oakley, K. P., Wells, L. H., and McClelland, J. A. C.: "New Studies on Rhodesian Man." *JRAI*, Vol. 77, Pt. 1 (1947), pp. 7–32.

Clark, W. E. LeG.: "General Features of the Swanscombe Skull Bones and the Endocranial Cast." *JRAI*, Vol. 68 (1938), pp. 58–67.

——: "Observations on the Anatomy of the Fossil Australopithecinae." *JAnat*, Vol. 81, No. 3 (1947). Reprinted in *Yearbook of Physical Anthropology, 1947*, pp. 143–77. New York: Viking Fund; 1948.

——: "New Paleontological Evidence Bearing on the Evolution of the Hominoidea." *QJGS*, Vol. 105, Pt. 2 (1950), pp. 225–64.

——: *History of the Primates*. London: British Museum (Natural History); 1950.

——: *The Fossil Evidence for Human Evolution*. Chicago: University of Chicago Press; 1955.

——: "The Os Innominatum of the Recent Ponginae, with Special Reference to That of the Australopithecinae." *AJPA*, Vol. 13, No. 1 (1955), pp. 19–28.

——: *The Antecedents of Man*. Chicago: Triangle Books; 1960.

—— and Leakey, L. S. B.: "The Miocene Hominidae of East Africa." *BMFM*, No. 1 (1951).

Clark, W. E. LeG., and Thomas, D. P.: "Associated Jaws and Limb Bones of *Limnopithecus macinnesi*." *BMFM*, No. 3 (1951).

Colbert, E. H.: "A New Primate from the Upper Eocene Pondaungia Formation in Burma." *AMN*, No. 951 (1937), pp. 1–18.

——: "Some Paleolontological Principles Significant in Human Evolution," in W. W. Howells, Jr., ed.: *Early Man in the Far East*, pp. 103–47. Philadelphia: American Association of Physical Anthropologists; 1949.

Cole, S.: *The Prehistory of East Africa*. London: Pelican Books; 1954.

Connolly, C. J.: *External Morphology of the Primate Brain*. Springfield, Ill.: Charles C Thomas; 1951.

Cooke, H. B. S., Malan, B. D., and Wells, L. H.: "Fossil Man in the Lemombo Mountains, S. Africa: The Border Cave, Ingwavuma District, Zululand." *Man*, Vol. 45, Art. No. 3 (1945), pp. 6–13.

Coolidge, H. J., Jr.: "*Pan paniscus*, Pigmy Chimpanzee from South of the Congo River." *AJPA*, Vol. 18, No. 1 (1933), pp. 1–57.

Coon, C. S.: "Tribes of the Rif." *HAS*, Vol. 9 (1931), p. 155.

——: *The Races of Europe*. New York: The Macmillan Co.; 1939.

——: "Cave Explorations in Iran, 1949." *UMM*, 1951.

——: *The Story of Man*. New York: Alfred A. Knopf; 1954 and 1961.

——: *The Seven Caves*. New York: Alfred A. Knopf; 1957.

——: Review of *Mankind in the Making* by W. W. Howells, Jr. (New York:

Doubleday & Company; 1959), in *Science*, Vol. 130, No. 3386 (1959), pp. 1399–400.

Coppen, Y.: "Découverte d'un Australopitheciné dans le Villafranchien du Tchad." *CRAS*, Vol. 252, No. 24 (1961), pp. 3851–2.

Curtis, G. H.: "Clock for the Ages: Potassium Argon." *NG*, Vol. 120, No. 4 (1961), pp. 590–2.

Dahlberg, A. A.: "The Dentition of the American Indian," in Laughlin, W. S., ed.: *Papers on the Physical Anthropology of the American Indian.* New York: Viking Fund; 1951.

Darlington, P. J.: *Zoogeography.* New York: John Wiley & Sons; 1957.

Dart, R. A.: "*Australopithecus africanus,* the Man-Ape of South Africa." *Nature,* Vol. 115, No. 2884 (1925), pp. 195–9.

——: "The Makapansgat Proto-human, *Australopithecus prometheus.*" *AJPA*, Vol. 6, No. 3 (1948), pp. 259–84.

——: "The Adolescent Mandible of *Australopithecus prometheus.*" *AJPA*, Vol. 6, No. 4 (1948), pp. 391–412.

——: "The First Human Mandible from the Cave of the Hearths, Makapansgat." *SAAB*, Vol. 3, No. 12 (1948), pp. 96–8.

——: "The Predatory Implemental Technique of *Australopithecus.*" *AJPA*, Vol. 7, No. 1 (1949), pp. 1–16.

——: "The Cranio-facial Fragments of *Australopithecus prometheus.*" *AJPA*, Vol. 7, No. 2 (1949), pp. 187–214.

——: "Innominate Fragments of *Australopithecus prometheus.*" *AJPA*, Vol. 7, No. 3 (1949), pp. 301–38.

——: "The Second or Adult Female Mandible of *Australopithecus promethus.*" *AJPA*, Vol. 12, No. 3 (1954), pp. 313–43.

——: "*Australopithecus prometheus* and *Telanthropus capensis.*" *AJPA*, Vol. 13, No. 1 (1955), pp. 67–96.

——: "Three Strandloopers from the Kaokoveld Coast." *SAJS*, Vol. 51, No. 6 (1955), pp. 175–9.

——: "The Second Adolescent (Female) Ilium of *Australopithecus prometheus.*" *AJPA*, Vol. 2, No. 1 (1957), pp. 73–82.

——: "The Makapansgat Australopithecine Osteodontokeratic Culture." *PTPA*, 1957, pp. 161–71.

—— and Kitching, J. W.: "Bone Tools at the Kalkbank Middle Stone Age Site and the Makapansgat Australopithecine Locality, Central Transvaal, Part 2, The Osteodontokeratic Contribution." *AB*, Vol. 13, No. 51 (1958), pp. 94–116.

Davies, O.: "A Missing Skull of Early Type from Zululand." *Man*, Vol. 57, Art. No. 54 (1957), p. 48.

de Beer, G. R.: *Embryos and Ancestors,* Second edition. New York: Oxford University Press; 1951.

—— and Grüneberg, H.: "A Note on Pituitary Dwarfism in the Mouse." *JGen*, Vol. 39, No. 2 (1940), pp. 297–300.

Delmas, A., ed.: *Les Processus de l'Hominisation.* Paris: Centre National de la Recherche Scientifique; 1958.

Demarec, M.: "The Nature of the Gene." *AJHG*, Vol. 13, No. 1 (1961), pp. 122–7.

Deraniyagala, P. E. P.: "The Races of the Stone Age and Ferrolithic of Ceylon." *JRAS*, Vol. 5, Pt. 1 (1956), pp. 1–23.

——: "The Pleistocene of Ceylon." *CNHS*, July 20, 1958.

———: "An Open Air Habitation Site of *Homo sapiens* Balangodensis." *SZC*, Vol. 28, Pt. 2 (1958), pp. 223–60.

Derry, D. E.: "Report of Human Remains," in Arkell, A. J.: *Early Khartoum*, pp. 31–33. London: Oxford University Press; 1949.

de Terra, M.: "Mitteilungen zum Krapina-Fund unter besonderer Berücksichtigung der Zähne." *SVfZ*, Vol. 13 (1903), pp. 11–13.

———: *Beiträge zu einer Odontographie der Menschenrassen.* Berlin: Berliner Verlagsanstalt; 1905.

Diamond, A. S.: *The History and Origin of Language.* New York: Philosophical Library; 1959.

Dobzhansky, T.: "On Species and Races in Fossil and Living Man." *AJPA*, Vol. 2, No. 3 (1944), pp. 251–66.

Drennan, M. R.: "An Australoid Skull from Cape Flats." *JRAI*, Vol. 59 (1929), p. 417.

———: "The Dentition of a Bushman Tribe." *ASAM*, Vol. 24, Pt. 1 (1929), pp. 61–87.

———: "The Florisbad Skull and Brain Cast." *TRSS*, Vol. 25 (1937), pp. 103–14.

———: "The Saldanha Skull and Its Associations." *Nature*, Vol. 172, No. 4383 (1953), pp. 791–3.

———: "A Preliminary Note on the Saldanha Skull." *SAJS*, Vol. 50, No. 1 (1953), pp. 7–11.

———: "Saldanha Man and His Associations." *AA*, Vol. 56, No. 5 (1954), pp. 879–84.

——— and Singer, R. R.: "A Mandibular Fragment, Probably of the Saldanha Skull." *Nature*, Vol. 175, No. 4452 (1955), pp. 364–5.

Dreyer, T. F.: "A Human Skull from Florisbad." *PASA*, Vol. 37 (1935), pp. 119–28.

———: "Endocranial Cast of the Florisbad Skull." *SNNM*, Vol. 1 (1936), pp. 21–3.

———: "The Fissuration of the Frontal Endocranial Cast of the Florisbad Skull Compared with That of the Rhodesian Skull." *ZfRK*, Vol. 8 (1938), pp. 129–98.

Dubois, E.: Pithecanthropus erectus, *eine Menschenähnliche Übergangsform von Java.* Batavia: Landes Druckerei; 1894.

———: "The Proto-Australian Fossil Man of Wadjak, Java." *PKAW*, Vol. 23, No. 7 (1921), pp. 1013–51.

———: "Figures of the Calvarium and Endocranial Cast, a Fragment of the Mandible and Three Teeth of *Pithecanthropus erectus.*" *PKAW*, Vol. 27, No. 5 (1924).

———: "Figures of the Femur of *Pithecanthropus erectus.*" *PKAW*, Vol. 29, No. 9 (1926), pp. 1275–7.

———: "The Sixth (Fifth New) Femur of *Pithecanthropus erectus.*" *PKAW*, Vol. 38, No. 8 (1935), pp. 850–2.

DuBrul, E. L.: *Evolution of the Speech Apparatus.* Springfield, Ill.: Charles C Thomas; 1958.

———: "Structural Evidence in the Brain for a Theory of the Evolution of Behavior." *PBM*, Vol. 1, No. 4 (1960), pp. 40–57.

——— and Reed, C. A.: "Skeletal Evidence of Speech." *AJPA*, Vol. 18, No. 2 (1960), pp. 153–6.

DuBrul, E. L., and Sicher, H.: *The Adaptive Chin.* Springfield, Ill.: Charles C Thomas; 1954.

Duckworth, W. L. H.: "Human Remains from Rock-Shelters and Caves in Perak, Rahang, and Perlis and from Selinsing." *JMBR*, Vol. 12, Pt. 2 (1934), after Huard and Saurin.

Ehrenfels, U. R.: *Kadar of Cochin.* Madras: University of Madras; 1952.

Elftman, H. O.: "The Evolution of the Pelvic Floor of Primates." *AJAn,* Vol. 51, No. 2 (1932), pp. 307–46.

Elsner, R. W., Andersen, K. L., and Hermanssen, L.: "Thermal and Metabolic Responses of Arctic Indians to Moderate Cold Exposure at the End of the Winter." *JAP,* Vol. 15, No. 4 (1960), pp. 659–61.

Elsner, R. W., Nelms, J. D., and Irving, L.: "Circulation of Heat to the Hands of Arctic Indians." *JAP,* Vol. 15, No. 4 (1960), pp. 662–6.

Emiliani, C.: "Ancient Temperatures." *SA,* Vol. 198, No. 2 (1958), pp. 54–6.

Emlen, J. T. E., Jr.: "In the Home of the Mountain Gorilla." *AK,* Vol. 63, No. 3 (1960), pp. 98–108.

——: "Current Field Studies of Gorillas." *CA,* Vol. 1, No. 4 (1960), p. 332.

Emperaire, J., and Laming, A.: "The Last Fuegians." *Diogenes,* No. 8 (1954), pp. 37–68.

Ennouchi, E.: "Un crâne d'homme ancien au Jebel Irhoud (Maroc)." *CRAS,* Vol. 254, pp. 4330–2 (Séance du 18 Juin, 1962).

——: "Un Néanderthalien: L'Homme du Jebel Irhoud (Maroc)." *L'Anth,* Vol. 66, No. 3–4 (1962), pp. 279–99.

Enzmann, J.: "The Structure and Function of the Laryngeal Sacs of the Chimpanzee, Gorilla and Orang-Utan." *AJPA,* Vol. 14, No. 2 (1956), pp. 383–4.

Evernden, J. F., Curtis, G. H., and Kistler, R.: "Potassium-Argon Dating of Pleistocene Volcanics." *Quaternaria,* Vol. 4 (1957), pp. 13–18.

Ewer, R. F.: "Faunal Evidence on the Dating of the Australopithecinae." *PTPA,* 1957, pp. 135–42.

Ewing, J. F.: "Human Types and Prehistoric Cultures at Ksar 'Akil, Lebanon." *FICA,* 1960, pp. 535–9.

Fairbridge, R. W.: "The Changing Level of the Sea." *SA,* Vol. 202, No. 5 (1960), pp. 70–9.

Fenner, F. J.: "Fossil Skull Fragments of Probably Pleistocene Age from Aitape, New Guinea." *RSAM,* Vol. 6 (1944), pp. 335–54.

Ferembach, D.: "Note sur une Mandibule Presumée du Magdalénien III." *BSA,* Vol. 5 (1954), pp. 25–34.

——: "Les Restes Humains Epipaléolithiques de la Grotte de Taforalt (Maroc oriental)." *CRAS,* Vol. 248 (1959), pp. 3465–7.

——: "Les Hommes du Mesolithique d'Afrique du Nord et le Problème des Isolats." *BSPC,* Vol. 8 (1960), pp. 1–16.

——: "Squelettes du Natoufien d'Israël, Étude Anthropologique." *L'Anth,* Vol. 65, No. 1–2 (1961), pp. 46–66.

Fiedler, W.: "Übersicht über das System der Primates," in Hofer, H., Schultz, A. H., and Starck, D., eds.: *Primatologia,* Vol. I, pp. 1–266. Basel: S. Karger; 1956.

Flower, W. H.: "On the Size of Teeth as a Character of Race." *JRAI,* Vol. 14 (1885), pp. 183–6.

—— and Lydekker, R.: *Mammals, Living and Extinct.* London: Adam and Charles Black; 1891.

Fouché, L., ed.: *Mapungubwe.* Cambridge: Cambridge University Press; 1937.

Freedman, D. G.: "Constitutional and Environmental Interactions in Rearing of Four Breeds of Dogs." *Science,* Vol. 127, No. 3298 (1958), pp. 585–6.

Freeman, W.: "The Weight of the Endocrinic Glands." *HB,* Vol. 6, No. 4 (1934), pp. 489–523.

Fromaget, J., and Saurin, E.: "Note Préliminaire sur les Formations Cénozoiques et Plus Récentes de la Chaîne Annamitique Septentrionale et du Haut Laos." *BSGI,* Vol. 22, No. 3 (1936), pp. 1–46.

Fusté, M.: "Morfología Cerebral de un Ejemplar Neandertalense Procedente de la Cueva de la Carigüelu en Piñar (Granada)." *TIBS*, Vol. 15 (1956).

Galloway, A.: "Man in Africa in the Light of Recent Discoveries." *SAJS*, Vol. 34 (1937), pp. 89–120.

——: "Nature and Status of the Florisbad Skull as Revealed by its Non-Metrical Features." *AJPA*, Vol. 23, No. 1 (1937), pp. 1–16.

——: "The Skeletal Remains of Mapungubwe," Pt. 8 in Fouché, L., ed.: *Mapungubwe*, pp. 127–74. Cambridge: Cambridge University Press; 1937.

——: *The Skeletal Remains of Bambandyanalo.* Johannesburg: Witwatersrand University Press; 1960.

García Sánchez, M.: "Restos Humanos del Paleolítico Medio y Superior y del Neo-eneolítico de Piñar (Granada)." *TIBS*, Vol. 15, No. 2 (1960), pp. 17–72,

Garn, S. M., and Lewis, A. B.: "Tooth-Size, Body-Size, and 'Giant' Fossil Men." *AA*, Vol. 60, No. 5 (1958), pp. 874–80.

Gartler, S. M., Firscheim, I. L., and Dobzhansky, T.: "A Chromatographic Investigation of Urinary Amino-Acids in the Great Apes." *AJPA*, Vol. 14, No. 1 (1956), pp. 41–58.

Gates, R. R.: *Human Heredity*, 2 vols. New York: The Macmillan Company; 1946.

——: "The African Pygmies." *AGMG*, Vol. 7 (1958), pp. 159–218.

——: "The Melanesian Dwarf, Aiome, New Guinea." *AGMG*, Vol. 10, No. 3 (1961), pp. 277–311.

Gay, H.: "Nuclear Control of the Cell." *SA*, Vol. 202, No. 1 (1960), pp. 126–36.

Gazin, C. L.: "A Review of the Middle and Upper Eocene Primates of North America." *SMC*, Vol. 136, No. 1 (1958), pp. 1–112.

Gear, H. S.: "Cranial Form in the Native Races of South America." *SAJS*, Vol. 26 (1926), pp. 684–97.

——: "A Further Report on the Boskopoid Remains from Zitzikama." *SAJS*, Vol. 23 (1926), pp. 923–34.

Getner, W., and Dährinder, J.: "The Potassium-Argon Dates of Some Tektites." *ZfNF*, Vol. 14a, No. 7 (1959), pp. 686–7.

Giesler, W., and Mollison, T.: "Untersuchungen über den Oldowayfund." *VGPA*, Vol. 3 (1929), pp. 50–67.

Giuffrida-Ruggeri, V.: "I Crani Egiziani del Museo Civico di Milano." *AAE*, Vol. 37 (1907), pp. 399–410.

Gleiser, I., and Hunt, E. E.: "The Permanent Mandibular First Molar, its Calcification, Eruption, and Decay." *AJPA*, Vol. 13, No. 2 (1955), pp. 253–84.

Godwin, H.: "Carbon-Dating Conference at Groningen, September 14–19, 1959." *Nature*, Vol. 184, No. 4696 (1959), pp. 1365–6.

Goodale, J. C.: "Alonga Bush, a Tiwi Hunt." *BUM*, Vol. 21, No. 3 (1957), pp. 3–36.

——: "The Tiwi Women of Melville, North Australia." Ph.D. Dissertation, University of Pennsylvania, 1959.

——: "The Tiwi Dance for the Dead." *Expedition*, Vol. 2, No. 1 (1959), pp. 3–13.

Goodman, M.: "The Species Specificity of Proteins as Observed in the Wilson Comparative Analyses Plates." *AN*, Vol. 94, No. 875 (1960), pp. 184–6.

Goodwin, A. J. H.: "A Comparison Between the Capsian and South African Stone Cultures." *ASAM*, Vol. 24, Part 1 (1929), pp. 17–32.

Gorjanović-Kramberger, F.: *Der diluviale Mensch von Krapina in Kroatien.* Wiesbaden, 1906.

Grabham, G. W.: "Note on the Geology of the Singa District of the Blue Nile." *Antiquity*, Vol. 12, No. 46 (1938), pp. 193–5.

Graziosi, P.: *Paleolithic Art.* New York: McGraw-Hill Book Company; 1960.

Gregory, W. K.: *Evolution Emerging*, Vol. 2. New York: The Macmillan Company; 1951.

—— and Hellman, M.: "Further Notes on the Molars of Hesperopithecus and of Pithecanthropus," with an appendix by G. S. Miller, Jr., Notes on the Casts of the Pithecanthropus Molars." *BAMN*, Vol. 48, Art. No. 13 (1923), pp. 509–30.

——: "The Dentition of the Extinct South-African Man-Ape, *Australopithecus* (*Plesianthropus*) *transvaalensis* Broom, A Comparative and Phylogenetic Study." *ATM*, Vol. 19, Pt. 4 (1939), pp. 339–73.

—— and Lewis, G. E.: "Fossil Anthropoids of the Yale-Cambridge India Expedition of 1935." *CIWP*, No. 495 (1938).

Gremiatskii, M. A.: "Cherep Rebenka-Neandertal 'tsa iz Grota Teshik-Tash Iuzhnyi Uzbekistan," in Okladnikov, A. P., Sinelnikov, N. A., and Gremiatskii, M. A.: *Sbornik Teshik-Tash;* pp. 137–82. Moscow, 1949.

Gusinde, M.: "Pygmies and Pygmoids." *AQ*, Vol. 28 (ns Vol. 3), No. 1 (1955), pp. 3–61.

——: *Die Twiden. Pygmäen und Pygmoide im Tropischen Afrika.* Vienna: Wilhelm Braumüller; 1956.

Hallowell, A. I.: "Self, Society, and Culture," in Tax.S.: *Evolution After Darwin*, pp. 309–71. Chicago: University of Chicago Press; 1960.

Hamerton, J. L., Fraccaro, M., Decarli, L., Nuzzo, F., Klinger, H. P., Hulliger, L., Taylor, A., and Lang, E. M.: "Somatic Chromosomes of the Gorilla." *Nature*, Vol. 192, No. 4794 (1961), pp. 225–8.

Hamilton, W. J., ed.: *Textbook of Human Anatomy*. London: Macmillan and Co. Ltd.; 1956.

Hammel, H. T.: "Thermal and Metabolic Responses of the Alacaluf Indians to Moderate Cold Exposure." *WADC*, No. 60–633 (Dec. 1960).

——, Elsner, R. W., LeMessurier, D. H., Andersen, K. L., and Milan, F. A.: "Thermal and Metabolic Responses of the Australian Aborigine Exposed to Moderate Cold in Summer." *JAP*, Vol. 14, No. 4 (1959), pp. 605–15.

Hanihara, K.: "Studies on the Deciduous Dentition of the Japanese and Japanese-American Hybrids." *ZZ*, Vol. 63 (1954), pp. 168–85; Vol. 64 (1955), pp. 63–82, 95–116; Vol. 65 (1956), pp. 67–87; Vol. 65 [sic] (1957), pp. 151–64. After G. W. Lasker: "Recent Advances in Physical Anthropology." *BRA*, 1959, pp. 1–36.

Hart, C. W. M., and Pilling, A. R.: *The Tiwi of North Australia*. New York: Henry Holt and Company; 1960.

Heberer, G.: "Die Fossilgeschichte der Hominiodea," in Hofer, H., Schultz, A. H., and Starck, D., eds.: *Primatologia*, Vol. I, pp. 379–560. Basel: S. Karger; 1956.

——: "The Descent of Man and the Present Fossil Record." *CSHS*, Vol. 24 (1959), pp. 235–44.

Heine-Geldern, R.: "Prehistoric Research in the Netherlands Indies," in Honig, P., and Verdoorn, F., eds.: *Science and Scientists in the Netherlands Indies*, pp. 129–67. New York: Chronica Botanica Co.; 1945. After Watsl, J.: "Prähistorische Menschenreste aus dem Muschelhügel von Bindjai-Tamiang in Nord Sumatra," in a Festschrift: *Otto Reche zum 60 Geburtstag*, pp. 237–43. Munich-Berlin, 1939.

Heinzelin, J. de: "Les Fouilles de Ishango," *Exploration du Parc National Albert*. Brussels: Institut des Parcs Nationaux du Congo Belge; 1957.

Heithersay, G.: "A Dental Survey of the Aborigines at Haast's Bluff, Central Australia." *MJA*, May 30, 1959, pp. 721–9.

Hellman, M.: "Racial Characters in Human Dentition." *PAPS*, Vol. 67, No. 2 (1928), pp. 157–74.

Hellström, B., and Andersen, K. L.: "Heat Output in the Cold from Hands of Arctic Fishermen." *JAP*, Vol. 15, No. 5 (1960), pp. 771–5.

Hencken, H.: "The Prehistoric Archaeology of the Tangier Zone, Morocco." *PAPS*, Vol. 92, No. 4 (1948), pp. 282–8.

Henri-Martin, G.: "Rémarques sur la Stratigraphie de Fontéchevade." *L'Anth*, Vol. 55, No. 3–4 (1951), pp. 242–7.

Henry, J.: "Culture, Personality, and Evolution." *AA*, Vol. 61, No. 2 (1959), pp. 221–6.

Higgs, E. S., and Brothwell, D. R.: "North Africa and Mount Carmel: Recent Developments." *MAN*, Vol. 61, Art. No. 166 (1961), pp. 138–9.

Hill, W. C. O.: *Primates*, Vol. I, *Strepsirhini*. Vol. II, *Haplorhini*. Edinburgh: University of Edinburgh Press; 1953 and 1955.

——: *Man's Ancestry*. Springfield, Ill.: Charles C Thomas; 1955.

Hockett, C. F.: "The Origin of Speech." *SA*, Vol. 203, No. 3 (1960), pp. 88–96.

Hofer, H., Schultz, A. H., and Starck, D., eds.: *Primatologia I*. Basel: S. Karger; 1956.

Hooijer, D. A.: "Man and Other Mammals from Toalian Sites in S. W. Celebes." *MKNA*, Sec. 2, Vol. 46, No. 2 (1950), pp. 1–164.

——: "The Geological Age of *Pithecanthropus, Meganthropus,* and *Gigantopithecus.*" *AJPA*, Vol. 9, No. 3 (1951), pp. 265–81.

——: "Fossil Mammals and the Plio-Pliocene Boundary in Java." *PKAW* B, Vol. 55, No. 4 (1952), pp. 430–43.

——: "The Lower Boundary of the Pleistocene in Java and the Age of *Pithecanthropus.*" *Quaternaria*, Vol. 3, No. 1 (1956), pp. 5–10.

——: "The Correlation of Fossil Mammalian Faunas and Plio-Pleistocene Boundary in Java." *PKAW* B, Vol. 60, No. 1 (1957), pp. 1–10.

——: "The Fossil Vertebrates of Ksar 'Akil, A Paleolithic Rock Shelter in the Lebanon." *ZV*, No. 49 (1961).

Hopwood, A. T.: "Mammalia," in Pycraft, W. P., ed.: *Rhodesian Man and Associated Remains*, pp. 70–73. London: British Museum (Natural History); 1928.

Howe, B., and Movius, H. L., Jr.: "A Stone Age Cave Site in Tangier." *PMP*, Vol. 28, No. 1 (1947).

Howell, F. C.: "Pleistocene Glacial Ecology and the Evolution of 'Classic Neanderthal' Man." *SWJA*, Vol. 8, No. 4 (1952), pp. 377–410.

——: "The Age of the Australopithecines of Southern Africa." *AJPA*, Vol. 13, No. 4 (1955), pp. 635–62.

——: "The Evolutionary Significance of Variation and Varieties of 'Neanderthal Man.'" *QRB*, Vol. 32, No. 4 (1957), pp. 330–47.

——: "Upper Pleistocene Men of the Southwest Asian Mousterian." *NC*, 1958, pp. 185–98.

——: "Upper Pleistocene Stratigraphy and Early Man in the Levant." *PAPS*, Vol. 103, No. 1 (1959), pp. 1–65.

——: "The Villafranchian and Human Origins." *Science*, Vol. 130, No. 3379 (1959), pp. 831–44.

——: "European and Northwest African Middle Pleistocene Hominids." *CA*, Vol. 1, No. 3 (1960), pp. 195–232.

Howells, W. W., Jr.: *Mankind in the Making*. New York: Doubleday & Company; 1959.

——: "The Distribution of Man." *SA*, Vol. 203, No. 3 (1960), pp. 113–27.

Hrdlička, A.: "The Skeletal Remains of Early Man." *SMC*, Vol. 83 (1930).

Huang, W. P.: "Restudy of the CKT *Sinanthropus* Deposits." *VP*, Vol. 4, No. 1 (1960), pp. 45–6.

——: "On the Age of Basal Gravel of CKT *Sinanthropus* Site and of the 'Upper Gravel' and 'Lower Gravel' of the CKT Region." *VP*, Vol. 4, No. 1 (1960), pp. 47–8.

Huard, P., and Saurin, E.: "Etat Actuel de la Craniologie Indochinoise." *BSGI*, Vol. 25, No. 1 (1938), pp. 1–104.

Hürzeler, J.: "Zur systematischen Stellung von *Oreopithecus*." *VNGB*, Vol. 65, No. 1 (1954), pp. 88–95.

——: "*Oreopithecus bambolii* Gervais, A Preliminary Report." *VNGB*, Vol. 69, No. 1 (1958), pp. 1–48.

——: "The Significance of *Oreopithecus* in the Genealogy of Man." *Triangle*, Vol. 4, No. 5 (1960), pp. 164–74.

Hutchinson, G. E., and MacArthur, R. H.: "A Theoretical Ecological Model of Size Distributions among Species of Mammals." *AN*, Vol. 93, No. 869 (1959), pp. 117–25.

Huxley, J. S.: "Clines: An Auxiliary Taxonomic Principle." *Nature*, Vol. 142, No. 3587 (1938), p. 219.

——, Hardy, A. C., and Ford, E. B., eds.: *Evolution as a Process*. London: Allen and Unwin; 1954.

Hymes, D. H.: "Lexicostatistics So Far." *CA*, Vol. 1, No. 1 (1960), pp. 3–44.

Irving, L., Andersen, K. L., Bolstad, A., Elsner, R. W., Hildes, J. A. Løyning, Y., Nelms, J. D., Peyton, L. J., and Whaley, R. D.: "Metabolism and Temperature of Arctic Indian Men During a Cold Night." *JAP*, Vol. 15, No. 4 (1960), pp. 635–44.

James, P.: *Outline of Geography*. Boston: Ginn and Co.; 1935.

Jerison, H. J.: "Brain to Body Ratios and the Evolution of Intelligence." *Science*, Vol. 121, No. 3144 (1955), pp. 447–9.

Jones, F. W.: *Man's Place Among the Mammals*. New York: Longmans, Green & Company; 1929.

Kahlke, H. D.: "On the Evolution of Pachyostosis in Jaw Bones of CKT Giant Deer, *Megaceros Pachyosreous* (Young)." *VP*. Vol. 2, No. 3 (1958), pp. 117–34.

Kälin, J.: "Zur Systematik und evolutiven Deutung der höheren Primaten." *Experientia*, Vol. 11, No. 1 (1955), pp. 1–17.

Kaplan, M.: "Physician Links Hypertension to Inborn Factors, not Stress." *NYT*, January 27, 1960.

Kappers, C.U.A.: "The Endocranial Casts of Ehringsdorf and *Homo solensis* Skulls." *JAnat*, Vol. 71, Pt. 1 (1936), pp. 61–76.

Karvé, I. and Kurulkar, G. M.: "Human Remains Discovered So Far," in Sankalia, H. D. and Karvé: *Preliminary Report on the Third Gujarat Prehistoric Expedition*. Bombay: Times of India Press; 1961.

Keast, A., Crocker, R. L., and Christian, C. S.: "Biogeography and Ecology in Australia." *MB*, Vol. 8 (1959).

Keith, A.: *The Antiquity of Man*, Vol. I. London: Williams and Norgate; 1925.

——: *New Discoveries Relating to the Antiquity of Man*. London: Williams and Norgate; 1931.

——. "A Descriptive Account of the Human Skulls from the Matjes River Cave, Cape Province." *TRSS*, Vol. 21 (1933), pp. 151–85.

—— and McCown, T. D.: *The Stone Age of Mt. Carmel,* Vol. 2. Oxford: Clarendon Press; 1939.

Kern, H. M., Jr., and Straus, W. L., Jr.: "The Femur of *Plesianthropus transvaalensis.*" *AJPA,* Vol. 7, No. 1 (1949), pp. 53–78.

Kinsey, A. C., Pomeroy, W. B., Martin, C. E. and Gebhard, P. H.: *Sexual Behavior in the American Female.* Philadelphia: W. B. Saunders Company; 1953.

Klatsky, M.: "The Incidence of Six Anamolies of the Teeth and Jaws." *HB,* Vol. 28 (1956), pp. 420–8.

Klatt, B.: *Haustier und Mensch.* Hamburg: Richard Hermes Verlag; 1948.

Kleinschmidt, O.: *Der Urmensch.* Leipzig; 1931. (Quoted by Behm-Blancke, 1958).

Kodama, S.: *Crania Ainoica.* Sapporo, Japan, 1940.

Kohl-Larsen, L.: *Auf den Spuren des Vormenschen,* Vol. 2. Stuttgart: Strecker und Schröder; 1943.

Kramp, P.: "Serologische Stammbauforschung in Primatologia," in Hofer, H., Schultz, A. H., and Starck, D., eds.: *Primatologia,* Vol. I, pp. 1015–34. Basel: S. Karger; 1956.

Krog, J., Folkow, B., Fox, R. H., and Andersen, K. L.: "Hand Circulation in the Cold of Lapps and North Norwegian Fisherman." *JAP,* Vol. 15, No. 4 (1960), pp. 654–8.

Krzywicki, L.: *Primitive Society and its Vital Statistics.* London: The Macmillan Company; 1934.

Kulp, J. L.: "Geological Time Scale." *Science,* Vol. 133, No. 3459 (1961), pp. 1105–14.

Kummer, B.: "Undersuchungen über die Entwicklung der Schädelform des Menschen und einiger Anthropoiden." *AEB,* Vol. 3 (1953), pp. 1–44.

Kurtén, B.: "New Evidence on the Age of Peking Man." *VP,* Vol. 3, No. 4 (1959), pp. 173–5.

——: "Rates of Evolution in Fossil Mammals." *CSHS,* Vol. 24 (1959), pp. 205–15.

——: "Chronology and Faunal Evolution of the Earlier European Glaciations." *SSF-CB,* Vol. 31, No. 5 (1960), pp. 1–62.

——: "The relative ages of the Australopithecines of Transvaal and the Pithecanthropines of Java," in Kurth, G.: *Evolution und Hominisation,* pp. 74–80.

Kurth, G.: *Evolution und Hominisation.* Stuttgart: Gustav Fischer Verlag; 1962.

Lasker, G. W.: "Recent Advances in Physical Anthropology." *BRA,* 1959, pp. 1–36.

—— and Lee, M. M. C.: "Racial Traits in the Human Teeth." *JFS,* Vol. 2, No. 4 (1956), pp. 401–19.

Laughlin, W. S., ed.: *Papers on the Physical Anthropology of the American Indian.* New York: Viking Fund; 1951.

—— and Jørgensen, J. B.: "Isolate Variation in Greenlandic Eskimo Crania." *ActG,* Vol. 6 (1956), pp. 3–12.

Lawler, S. D. and L. J.: *Human Blood Groups and Inheritance.* Cambridge, Mass.: Harvard University Press; 1957.

Leakey, L. S. B.: *The Stone Age Races of Kenya.* Oxford: Oxford University Press; 1935.

——: "The Naivasha Fossil Skull and Skeleton." *JEAN,* Vol. 16, No. 4–5 (1942), pp. 169–77.

——: "A Giant Child Among the Giant Animals of Olduvai." *ILN,* Vol. 232, No. 6212 (1958), pp. 1104–5.

Leakey, L. S. B.: "A New Fossil Skull from Olduvai." *Nature,* Vol. 184, No. 4685 (1959), pp. 491–3.

——: "The Newly Discovered Skull from Olduvai: First Photographs of the Complete Skull." *ILN,* Vol. 235, No. 6268 (1959), pp. 288–9.

——: "Recent Discoveries at Olduvai Gorge." *Nature,* Vol. 188, No. 4755 (1960), pp. 1050–2.

——: "Finding the World's Earliest Men." *NG,* Vol. 118, No. 3 (1960), pp. 420–35.

——: "New Finds at Olduvai Gorge." *Nature,* Vol. 189, No. 4765 (1961), pp. 649–50.

——: "New Links in the Chain of Human Evolution: Three Major Discoveries from the Olduvai Gorge, Tanganyika." *ILN,* Vol. 238, No. 6344 (1961), pp. 346–8.

——: "A New Lower Pliocene Fossil Primate from Kenya," *AMNH,* Ser. 13, Vol. 14 (1961), pp. 689–96 (pub. 1962).

——, Evernden, J. I. C., and Curtis, G. H.: "Age of Bed I, Olduvai Gorge, Tanganyika." *Nature,* Vol. 191, No. 4787 (1961), pp. 478–9.

Lerner, A. B.: "Hormones and Skin Color." *SA,* Vol. 205, No. 1 (1961), pp. 98–108.

Leroi-Gourhan, A.: "Étude des Restes Humains Fossiles Provenants des Grottes d'Arcy-sur-Cure." *APa,* Vol. 44 (1958), pp. 1–62.

Leser, P.: Review of *Grundzüge der Völkerbiologie,* by I. Schwidetzsky (Stuttgart: F. Enke Verlag; 1950), in *AJPA,* Vol. 10, No. 1 (1957), pp. 141–4.

Levene, H., and Dobzhansky, T.: "Possible Genetic Difference Between the Head Louse and the Body Louse (Pediculus humanus L)." *AN,* Vol. 93, No. 873 (1959), pp. 347–53.

Lewis, G. E.: "Preliminary Notice of the New Man-like Apes from India." *AJSc,* Ser. 5, No. 27 (1934), pp. 161–79.

Licent, E., Teilhard de Chardin, P., and Black, D.: "On a Presumably Pleistocene Human Tooth from the Sjara Osso Gol (South Eastern Ordos) Deposits." *BGSC,* Vol. 5, No. 4 (1927).

Loth, E.: *L'Anthropologie des Parties Molles.* Warsaw and Paris: Masson et Cie; 1931.

——: "Beiträge zur Kenntnis der Weichteilanatomie des Neanderthalers." *ZfRK,* Vol. 7 (1938), pp. 13–35.

Loukashin, A. S.: "Some Observations on the Remains of a Pleistocene Fauna and of the Paleolithic Age in Northern Manchuria," in MacCurdy, G. G., ed.: *Early Man,* pp. 327–340. Philadelphia: J. B. Lippincott Company; 1937.

Lowe, C. van R.: "An Artefact Recovered with the Boskop Calvaria." *SAAB,* Vol. 9, No. 36 (1954), pp. 135–7.

Mabutt, A.: "Geomorphology, Archaeology, and Anthropology from Bok Baii, Darling District, Cape Province, I, Physiography and Surface Deposits." *SAAB,* Vol. 10, No. 39 (1955), pp. 85–6.

MacCurdy, G. G., ed.: *Early Man.* Philadelphia: J. B. Lippincott Company; 1937.

Macfarlane, W. V., Pennycuik, P. R., and Thrift, E.: "Resorption and Loss of Fetuses in Rats Living at 35° C." *JPH,* Vol. 135, No. 3 (1957), pp. 451–9.

Macintosh, N. W. G.: "The Cohuna Cranium, History and Commentary from November 1925 to November 1951." *Mankind,* Vol. 4, No. 8 (1952), pp. 307–29.

Mahony, D. J., Baragwanath, W., Wood-Jones, F., and Kenyon, A. S.: "Fossil Man in the State of Victoria, Australia." *IGC,* 1936, pp. 1335–42.

Makino, S.: "Chromosome Studies in Domestic Mammals, II, The Chromosome

Complexes in Goat (*Capra hircus*) and Sheep (*Ovis aries*) and Their Relationship." *Cytologia*, Vol. 13, No. 1 (1943), pp. 39–54.

Malez, M.: "Die Höhle Veternica, eine neue Paläolitische Fundstelle in Kroatien." *BS*, Vol. 3, No. 1 (1956), pp. 11–12.

Mansuy, H., and Colani, M.: "Contribution a l'Etude de la Préhistoire de l'Indochine, V, Nouvelles Découvertes dans les Cavernes du Massif Calcaire de Bac-Son (Tonkin). VI, Stations Préhistoriques de Keo-Phay, de Lai-Ta, et de Bang-Mac, dans le Massif Calcaire de Bac-Son (Tonkin). VII, Néolithique Superieure dans le Haut-Tonkin." *BSGI*, Vol. 12, Nos. 1, 2, 3 (1925).

Marks, P.: "Preliminary Note on the Discovery of a New Jaw of Meganthropus." *IJNS*, Vol. 109, Nos, 1, 2, 3 (1953), pp. 26–33.

Marret, J. R. de la H.: *Race, Sex and Environment*. London: Hutchinson & Co.; 1936.

Marshall, L.: "The Kin Terminology System of the /Kung Bushman." *Africa*, Vol. 27, No. 1 (1957), pp. 1–25.

——: "Marriage Among /Kung Bushmen." *Africa*, Vol. 29, No. 4 (1959), pp. 335–65.

Martin, R., and Saller, K.: *Lehrbuch der Anthropologie*, Third edition. Stuttgart: G. Fischer; 1958.

Maska, K. J.: *Der diluviale Mensch in Mähren*. Neutitschein: Landes-Oberschule; 1886.

Mason, P., ed.: *Man, Race, and Darwin*. London: Oxford University Press; 1960.

Matthew, W. D.: "Climate and Evolution." *ANYA*, Vol. 24 (1915–39), pp. 171–318.

Maudit, J. A.: *40,000 Ans d'Art Modern*. Paris: Librairie Plon; 1954.

Mayr, E.: "Taxonomic Categories in Fossil Hominids." *CSHS*, Vol. 15 (1950), pp. 109–18.

——: "Change of Genetic Environment and Evolution," in Huxley, J. S., Hardy, A. C., and Ford, E. B., eds.: *Evolution as a Process*, pp. 157–80. London: Allen and Unwin; 1954.

——: "Geographical Character Gradients and Climatic Adaptation." *Evolution*, Vol. 10, No. 1 (1956), pp. 105–8.

——, Linsley, E. G., and Usinger, R. C.: *Methods and Principles of Systematic Zoology*. New York: McGraw-Hill Book Company; 1953.

McBride, A. F.: "Meet Mr. Porpoise." *NH*, Vol. 45, No. 1 (1940), pp. 16–29.

—— and Hebb, D. O.: "Behavior of the Captive Bottle-nose Dolphin, *Tursiops truncatus*." *JCPP*, Vol. 41, No. 2 (1948), pp. 111–23.

McBurney, C. B. M.: *The Stone Age of Northern Africa*. London: Penguin Books; 1960.

——, Trevor, J. C., and Wells, L. H.: "The Hauah Fteah Fossil Jaw." *JRAI*, Vol. 83 (1953), pp. 71–85.

McCown, T. D.: *Natufian Crania from Mt. Carmel*. Berkeley: University of California Library; 1940.

Mednick, C. W.: "The Evolution of the Human Ilium." *AJPA*, Vol. 13, No. 2 (1955), pp. 203–16.

Mijsberg, W. A.: "Recherches sur les Restes Humains de Goewa-Lawa à Sampoeng et des Sites Préhistoriques à Bodjonegoro (Java)," in *Hommage du Service Archéologique des Indes Néerlandaises au Premier Congrès des Préhistoriens d'Extrême-Orient à Hanoi, 26–31 Jan. 1932*. Batavia: Société Royale des Arts et Sciences; 1932.

——: "On a Neolithic Palae-Melanesian Lower Jaw Found in a Kitchen-midden at Quak Kepah Province, Wellesley Straits Settlements." *PTCPFA* (1938), pub. 1940, pp. 100–8.

Miller, R. A.: "The Musculature of *Pan paniscus*." *AJA*, Vol. 91, No. 2 (1952), pp. 183–232.

Moody, P. A.: *An Introduction to Evolution*. New York: Harper and Brothers; 1953.

Moorrees, C. F. A.: *The Aleut Dentition*. Cambridge, Mass.: Harvard University Press; 1957.

Morant, G. M.: "Studies of Palaeolithic Man, I, The Chancelade Skull and Its Relation to the Modern Eskimo Skull." *AE*, Vol. 1 (1926), pp. 257–76.

——: "Studies of Paleolithic Man, II, A Biometric Study of Neanderthaloid Skulls and of Their Relationships to Modern Racial Types." *Biometrika*, Vol. 2 (1927), pp. 310–80.

——: "Studies of Palaeolithic Man, IV, A Biometric Study of the Upper Palaeolithic Skulls of Europe." *AE*, Vol. 4 (1930), pp. 109–214.

——: "The Form of the Swanscombe Skull." *JRAI*, Vol. 68 (1938), pp. 67–97.

Morosan, M. N.: "Les Restes de l'Homme Fossile en Roumaine." *IGC*, 1936, pp. 1239–47.

Morton, D. J.: "Significant Characteristics of the Neanderthal Foot." *NH*, Vol. 26, No. 3 (1926), pp. 310–14.

Mountfort, C. P.: *The Tiwi, Their Art, Myth, and Ceremony*. London: Phoenix House; 1958.

Movius, H. L., Jr.: "The Mousterian Cave of Teshik Tash, Southeastern Uzbekistan, Central Asia." *ASPR*, Vol. 17 (1953), pp. 11–71.

——: "New Paleolithic Sites near Tiny T'sun on the Fen River, Shansi Province, North China." *Quaternaria*, Vol. 3 (1956), pp. 13–26.

——: "Radiocarbon Dates and Upper Paleolithic Archaeology." *CA*, Vol. 1, No. 5–6 (1960), pp. 355–91.

—— and Vallois, H. V.: "Crânes Proto-Magdalenien et Venus du Périgordien Final Trouvés dans l'Abri Pataud, Les Eyzies (Dordogne)." *L'Anth*, Vol. 63, No. 3–4 (1959), pp. 213–32.

Mulvaney, D. J.: "Australian Radiocarbon Dates." *Antiquity*, Vol. 35, No. 137 (1961), pp. 37–9.

Murdock, G. P.: "World Ethnographic Sample." *AA*, Vol. 59, No. 4 (1957), pp. 665–87.

Napier, J. R.: "Fossil Handbones from Olduvai Gorge." *Nature*, Vol. 196, No. 4853 (1962), pp. 409–11.

Napier, J. R., and Davis, P. R.: "The Fore-limb Skeleton and Associated Remains of *Proconsul africanus*." *BMFM*, No. 16 (1959).

Nehring, A.: "Über einen Menschlichen Molar aus dem Diluvium von Taubach bei Weimar." *VBGA*, Vol. 27 (1895), pp. 573–7.

Neumann, G.: "American Indian Crania with Low Vaults." *HB*, Vol. 14, No. 2 (1942), pp. 178–91.

Neuville, R.: "Le Paléolithique du Desert de Judée." *AIPH*, Mem. 24 (1951), pp. 179–84.

Newman, M. T.: "The Application of Ecological Rules to the Racial Anthropology of the Aboriginal New World." *AA*, Vol. 55, No. 3 (1953), pp. 311–27.

——: "Adaptation of Man to Cold Climates." *Evolution*, Vol. 10, No. 1 (1956), pp. 101–5.

——: "Man and the Heights." *NH*, Vol. 67, No 1 (1958), pp. 9–19.

Oakley K. P.: "New Evidence Regarding Rhodesian (Broken Hill) Man." Paper read at Viking Foundation Conference, New York, June 20, 1950.

——: "Dating of the Australopithecines of Africa." *AJPA*, Vol. 12 (1954), pp. 9–23.

———: *Man the Tool-Maker*. London: British Museum (Natural History); 1956.

———: "The Dating of the Broken Hill, Florisbad, and Saldanha Skulls." *PTPA*, 1957, pp. 155–7.

———: "Dating the Stages of Hominid Evolution." *The Leech*, Vol. 28, Nos. 3, 4, 5 (1958), pp. 112–15.

———: Comment on paper of M. Bonnardel, "La Main et l'Outil," in Delmas, A., ed.: *Les Processus de l'Hominisation*, p. 131. Paris: Centre National de la Researche Scientifique; 1958.

———: "Physical Anthropology in the British Museum," in Roberts, D. F., and Weiner, J. S., eds.: *The Scope of Physical Anthropology and Its Place in Academic Studies*, pp. 51–4. Published for the Society for the Study of Human Biology, and the Wenner-Gren Foundation, London, 1958.

———: "The New Fossil Sites at Langebaaweg (South Africa)." *CA*, Vol. 2, No. 4 (1961), pp. 385–7.

———: and Hoskins, C. R.: "L'Application du Test de la Flourine aux Crânes de Fontéchevade." *L'Anth*, Vol. 55, No. 3–4 (1951), pp. 239–42.

Oboussier, H.: "Das Verhalten der Hyophyse bei Reciproken von Hunden Gegensätzlicher Wuchsform." *ZA*, Vol. 155, No. 5–6 (1955), pp. 101–11.

Okladnikov, A. P.: "Issledovani Musterskoi Stoianki Pogrebenia Neandertal'tsa v Grote Teshik-Tash Iuzhnyi Uzbekistan." *Sbornik Teshik-Tash*, pp. 7–86. Moscow, 1949.

———, Sinelnikov, N. H., and Gremiatiskii, M. A.: *Sbornik Teshik-Tash*. Moscow, 1949.

Oppenoorth, W. F. F.: "The Place of *Homo solensis* Among Fossil Men," in Mac-Curdy, G. G., ed.: *Early Man*, pp. 349–60. Philadelphia: J. B. Lippincott Company; 1927.

Ozegovic, F.: "Die Bedeutung der Entdeckung des diluvialen Menschen von Krapina." *NC*, 1958, pp. 27–31.

Pales, L.: "Les Néanderthaliens en France." *NC*, 1958, pp. 32–7.

Patte, E.: *Les Néanderthaliens*. Paris: Masson et Cie; 1955.

———: *L'Enfant Néanderthalien du Pech de l'Aze*. Paris: Masson et Cie; 1957.

———: "L'Enfant du Pech de l'Aze." *NC*, 1958, pp. 265–6.

Patterson, B.: "The Geological History of Non-Hominid Primates in the Old World." *HB*, Vol. 26, No. 3 (1954), pp. 191–219.

Pearl, R., Gooch, M., Miner, J. R., and Freeman, W.: "Studies on Constitution, IV, Endocrine Organ Weights and Somatological Habitus Types." *HB*, Vol. 8, No. 2 (1936), pp. 92–125.

Pederson, P. O.: "The East Greenland Dentition." *MOG*, Vol. 142, No. 3 (1949).

Pei, W. C.: "A Preliminary Report on the Late Paleolithic Cave of Chou Kou Tien." *BGSC*, Vol. 13, No. 3 (1934), pp. 327–58.

———: "Giant Ape's Jawbone Discovered in China." *AA*, Vol. 59, No. 5 (1957), pp. 834–8.

———, Huang, W. P., Chiu, C. L., and Meng, H.: "Discovery of Quaternary Mammalian Fauna at Ch'ao-Tsun Chien-An County, Hopei Province." *VP*, Vol. 2, No. 4 (1958), pp. 226–9.

Pei, W. C., and Li, Y. H.: "Discovery of a Third Mandible of Gigantopithecus in Lu Cheng, Kwangsi, South China." *VP*, Vol. 2, No. 4 (1958), pp. 190–200.

Pei, W. C., and Woo, J. K.: "Tzeyang Paleolithic Man." *IVPM*, No. 1 (1957).

Penfield, W., and Roberts, L.: *Speech and Brain Mechanisms*. Princeton: Princeton University Press; 1959.

Pericot-Garcia, L.: "A New Site with the Remarkable Parpalló-type Solutrean Points." *CA*, Vol. 2, No. 4 (1961), p. 387.

Phinney, B. O.: "Growth Response of Single Dwarf Mutants in Maize to Gibberellic Acid." *PNAS*, Vol. 42, No. 2 (1956), pp. 185–9.

Pinkley, G.: "The Significance of Wadjak Man, and a Homo sapiens from Java." *PNHB*, Vol. 10, No. 3 (1936), pp. 183–200.

Piveteau, J.: *Traité de Paléontologie, VII, Traité de Paléontologie Humaine, Les Primates et l'Homme.* Paris: Masson et Cie; 1957.

Plumb, R. K.: "Blood Pressure of Negroes Studied." *NYT*, June 3, 1960.

Proetz, A. W.: *Essays on the Applied Physiology of the Nose,* Second edition. Saint Louis: Annals Publishing Company; 1953.

Pycraft, W. P., ed.: *Rhodesian Man and Associated Remains,* pp. 1–51. London: British Museum (Natural History); 1928.

Ratcliffe, H. L., and Cronin, M. T. I.: "Changing Frequency of Arteriosclerosis in Mammals and Birds at the Philadelphia Zoological Garden." *Circulation,* Vol. 18, No. 1 (1958), pp. 41–52.

Raven, H. C.: *The Anatomy of the Gorilla.* New York: Columbia University Press; 1950.

Regan, C. T.: "The Classification of the Primates." *Nature,* Vol. 125, No. 3143 (1930), pp. 125–6.

Remane, A.: "Die Zähne des Meganthropus afrikanus." *ZfMuA,* Vol. 42 (1951), pp. 311–29.

Rensch, B.: "Some Problems of Geographical Variation and Species Formation." *PLSL,* 149th session (1936–1937), pp. 275–85.

——: "The Relation Between the Evolution of Central Nervous Functions and the Body Size Animals," in Huxley, J. S., Hardy, A. C., and Ford, E. B., eds.: *Evolution as a Process,* pp. 181–200. London: Allen and Unwin; 1954.

——: *Homo sapiens. Vom Tier zum Halbgott.* Göttingen: Vandenhoeck & Ruprecht; 1959.

——: "Trends Toward Progress of Brains and Sense Organs." *CSHS,* Vol. 24 (1959), pp. 291–303.

——: *Evolution above the Species Level* (New York: Columbia University Press; 1960).

Riesenfeld, A.: "Shovel-shaped Incisors and a Few Other Dental Features Among the Native Peoples of the Pacific." *AJPA,* Vol. 14, No. 3 (1956), pp. 505–22.

Roberts, D. F.: "Body Weight, Race and Climate." *AJPA,* Vol. 11, No. 4 (1953), pp. 553–8.

——, Weiner, J. S., eds.: *The Scope of Physical Anthropology and Its Place in Academic Studies.* Published for the Society for the Study of Human Biology, and the Wenner-Gren Foundation, London, 1958.

Roberts, J. A. F.: "A Genetic View of Human Variability," in Mason, P., ed.: *Man, Race, and Darwin,* pp. 48–55. London: Oxford University Press; 1960.

Robinson, J. T.: "Telanthropus and Its Phylogenetic Significance." *AJPA,* Vol. 11, No. 4 (1953), pp. 445–501.

——: "Further Remarks on the Relationship between 'Meganthropus' and *Australopithecus africanus." AJPA,* Vol. 13, No. 3 (1955), pp. 429–45.

——: "The Dentition of the Australopithecinae." *TMM,* No. 9 (1956).

Roche, J.: "La Grotte de Taforalt." *L'Anth,* Vol. 57, No. 3–4 (1953), pp. 375–80.

Roe, A., and Simpson, G. G., eds.: *Behavior and Evolution.* New Haven: Yale University Press; 1958.

Roginskii, I. I.: "Morfologicheskii Osobennosti Cherepa Rebenka i Pozdnemust'erskogo Sloia Peschery Starosel'e." *SE,* Vol. 1 (1954), pp. 27–39.

Rouse, I.: "The Entry of Man into the West Indies." *Yearbook of Physical An-*

thropology for 1961, p. 8. New York: The Viking Fund; 1961.

Rubner, M.: *Das Problem der Lebensdauer und seiner Beziehung zum Wachstum*. Munich-Berlin, 1908. After de Beer.

Sabels, B. E.: Review of C. K. Brain's "The Transvaal Ape-Man-Bearing Cave Deposits" (*TMM*, No. 11, 1958) and "New Evidence for the Correlation of the Transvaal Ape-Man-Bearing Cave Deposits" (*PTPA*, 1957), in *AJPA*, Vol. 17, No. 3 (1959), pp. 247–9.

Sánchez y Sánchez, D.: "Un Craneo Humano Prehistórico de Manila (Filipinas)." *MRSE*, Vol. 11 (1921).

Sankalia, H. D. and Karvé, I.: *Preliminary Report on the Third Gujarat Prehistoric Expedition*. Bombay: Times of India Press; 1945.

Sarasin, F.: "Die Variationen im Bau des Handskeletts verschiedener Menschenformen." *ZfMuA*, Vol. 30 (1932), pp. 252–316.

Sarasin, P. and F.: *Reisen in Celebes*. Wiesbaden: C. W. Kreidel; 1905.

——: *Versuch einer Anthropologie der Insel Celebes. Die Toala Höhlen von Lamontjong*. Wiesbaden: C. W. Kreidel; 1905.

Sauter, M-R: "La Squelette Préhistorique de la Grotte du Bichon (Côte-du-Doubs, La Chaux-de-Fonds, Neuchâtel)." *AS*, Vol. 9, No. 3 (1956), pp. 330–5.

——: "Étude des Vestiges Osseux Humains des Grottes Préhistoriques de Farincourt (Haute-Marne, France)." *ASAG*, Vol. 22, No. 1 (1957), pp. 6–37.

Schaefer, R. L., and Strickroot, F.: "Endocrine Dwarfism." *Endocrinology*, Vol. 26, No. 4 (1940), pp. 599–604.

Schepers, G. W. H.: "The Endocranial Casts of the South African Ape-Men," in Broom, R., and Schepers, G. H. W.: "The South African Fossil Ape-Man, the Australopithecine." *TMM*, No. 2 (1946).

Schlosser, M.: "Oligozäne Landsäugetiere aus dem Fayum." *BPGO*, Vol. 51 (1911). After Gregory, 1951.

Schmidt, C. F.: *The Cerebral Circulation in Health and Disease*. Springfield, Ill.: Charles C Thomas; 1950.

Schoetensack, O. A.: *Der Unterkiefer des Homo heidelbergensis aus den Sanden von Maner bei Heidelberg*. Leipzig, 1908.

Schofield, J. F.: "The Age of the Rock Paintings of South Africa." *SAAB*, Vol. 3, No. 12 (1948), pp. 79–88.

Scholander, P. F.: "Evolution of Climatic Adaption in Homeotherms." *Evolution*, Vol. 9, No. 1 (1955), pp. 15–26.

——: "Climatic Rules." *Evolution*, Vol. 10, No. 3 (1956), pp. 339–40.

——: "The Wonderful Net." *SA*, Vol. 196, No. 4 (1957), pp. 96–107.

——, Hammel, H. T., Hart, J. S., LeMessurier, D. H., and Steen, J.: "Cold Adaptation in Australian Aborigines." *JAP*, Vol. 13, No. 2 (1958), pp. 211–18.

Schultz, A. H.: "Fetal Growth of Man and Other Primates." *QRB*, Vol. 1, No. 4 (1926), pp. 465–521.

——: "Einige Beobachtungen und Masse am Skelett von *Oreopithecus*." *ZfMuA*, Vol. 50, No. 2 (1960), pp. 136–49.

Schwalbe, G.: *Lehrbuch der Anatomie der Sinnesorgane*. Erlangen: Besold; 1887.

——: "Über die Beziehungen zwischen Innenform und Aussenform des Schädels." *DAKM*, Vol. 73, (1902), pp. 359–408.

——: "Über den fossilen Affen *Oreopithecus bambolii*." *ZfMuA*, Vol. 19 (1915), pp. 149–254.

Schwidetzky, I.: *Grundzüge der Völkerbiologie*. Stuttgart: F. Enke Verlag; 1950.

Sclater, P. L.: "On the General Distribution of the Class Aves." *JPLS-Zool.*, Vol. 2 (1857), pp. 130–45.

Scott, J. H.: "The Growth of the Human Face." *PRSM*, Vol. 47, No. 2 (1954), pp. 91–100.

Şenyürek, M. S.: "Fossil Men in Tangier." *PMP*, Vol. 16, No. 3 (1940).

——: "A Short Preliminary Report for the Two Fossil Teeth from the Cave of Karain." *Belleten*, Vol. 13, No. 52 (1949), pp. 833–6.

——: "A Note on the Teeth of Meganthropus africanus Weinert from Tanganyika Territory." *Belleten*, Vol. 19, No. 73 (1955), pp. 1–55.

——: "The Skeleton of the Fossil Infant Found in Shanidar Cave, Northern Iraq, Preliminary Report." *Anatolia*, Vol. 2 (1957), pp. 49–55.

——: "A Further Note on the Paleolithic Shanidar Infant." *Anatolia*, Vol. 2 (1957), pp. 111–21.

—— and Bostanci, E.: "The Excavation of a Cave Near the Village of Magracik in the Vilayet of the Hatav. Preliminary Notice." *Anatolia*, Vol. 1 (1956), pp. 81–3.

Sergi, S.: "Craniometrici e Craniografia del Primo Paleantropo di Saccopastore." *RM*, Vol. 20–21 (1944), pp. 1–59.

——: "Il Secondo Paleantropo di Saccopastore." *RA*, Vol. 36 (1948), pp. 1–95.

——: "La Mandibola neandertaliana Circeo II." *RA*, Vol. 41 (1954), pp. 305–44.

——: "La Mandibola neandertaliana Circeo III." *RA*, Vol. 42 (1955), pp. 337–404.

——: "Die Neanderthalischen Paleanthropen in Italien." *NC*, 1958, pp. 38–51.

——: "I Tipi Umani Piu Antichi," in Biasutti, R., ed.: *Razze e Popoli della Terra*, Vol. I, Chap. 3, pp. 69–133. Torino: Unione Tipografico-Editrice; 1959.

Shaw, J. C. M.: "Cusp Development on the Second Lower Molars in Bantu and Bushmen." *AJPA*, Vol. 11 (1927), pp. 97–100.

——: "Taurodont Teeth in South African Races." *JAnat*, Vol. 62 (1928), pp. 476–96.

——: *The Teeth, the Bony Palate, and the Mandible in Bantu Races of South Africa*. London: John Bale Sons and Danielsson; 1931.

Shrubsall, F. C.: "Notes on Some Bushman Crania and Bone from the South African Museum, Capetown." *ASAM*, Vol. 5, Pt. 5, No. 6 (1906–10), pp. 227–70.

Sieveking, A.: "The Paleolithic Industry of Kota Tampan, Perak, Northwest Malaya." *AP*, Vol. 2, No. 2 of 1958 (1960), pp. 91–102.

Simons, E. L.: "An Anthropoid Frontal Bone from the Fayum Oligocene of Egypt: the Oldest Skull Fragment of a Higher Primate." *AMN*, No. 1976 (1959).

——: "*Apidium* and *Oreopithecus*." Nature, Vol. 186, No. 4727 (1960), pp. 824–6.

——: "The Phyletic Position of *Ramapithecus*." *PYMP*, No. 57 (1961).

Simpson, G. G.: "The Principles of Classification and a Classification of Mammals." *BAMN*, Vol. 85, 1945.

——: *The Meaning of Evolution*. New Haven: Yale University Press; 1949.

——: *Tempo and Mode in Evolution*. New York: Columbia University Press; 1949.

——: *The Major Features of Evolution*. New York: Columbia University Press; 1953.

——: "The Nature and Origin of Supraspecial Taxa." *CSHS*, Vol. 24 (1959), pp. 225–71.

——: *Principles of Animal Taxonomy*. New York: Columbia University Press; 1961.

Sinelnikov, N. A., and Gremiatskii, M. A.: "Kosti Skeleta Rebenka-Neandertal'tsa iz Grota Teshik-Tash Iuzhnyi Uzbekistan," *Sbornik Teshik-Tash*. Moscow, 1949.

Singer, R.: "The Saldanha Skull from Hopefield, South Africa." *AJPA*, Vol. 12, No. 3 (1954), pp. 345–62.

——: "Man and Mammals in South Africa." *JPSI*, Vol. 1 (1956), pp. 122–30.

——: "Investigations at the Hopefield Site." *PTPA*, 1957, pp. 175–82.

——: "The Boskop 'Race' Problem." *Man*, Vol. 58, Art. No. 232 (1958), pp. 1–5.

——: "The Rhodesian, Florisbad and Saldanha Skulls." *NC*, 1958, pp. 52–62.

—— and Crawford, J. R.: "Archaeological Discoveries at Hopefield." *JRAI*, Vol. 88, No. 1 (1958), pp. 11–19.

Škerlj, B.: "Were Neanderthalers the Only Inhabitants of Krapina?" *BS*, Vol. 4, No. 2 (1958), p. 44.

Slombe, D.: "The Osteology of a Bushman Tribe." *ASAM*, Vol. 24 (1922) pp. 33–60.

Smith, A. H.: "The Culture of Kabira, Southern Ryukyu Islands." *PAPS*, Vol. 104, No. 2 (1960), pp. 134–71.

Smith, G. E.: "The Influence of Racial Admixture in Ancient Egypt." *ER*, Vol. 7, No. 3 (1915), pp. 163–83.

——: "Endocranial Cast," in Pycraft, W. P., ed.: *Rhodesian Man and Associated Remains*, pp. 52–8. London: British Museum (Natural History); 1928.

Smith, P. E., and MacDowell, E. C.: "An Hereditary Anterior-Pituitary Deficiency in the Mouse." *AR*, Vol. 46, No. 3 (1930), pp. 249–57.

Smith, R. A.: "Associated Stone Implements," in Pycraft, W. P., ed.: *Rhodesian Man and Associated Remains*, pp. 66–9.

Smith, S. A.: "The Fossil Human Skull Found at Talgai, Queensland." *TRSL B*, Vol. 208 (1918), pp. 351–87.

Snow, C. E.: "The Ancient Palestinian: Skhul V. Reconstruction." *BASP*, No. 17 (1955), pp. 5–10.

Solecki, R. S.: "Three Adult Neanderthal Skeletons from Shanidar Cave in Northern Iraq." *SRP* for 1959 (1960), No. 4414, pp. 603–35.

Solheim II, W. G.: "The Present Status of the 'Paleolithic' in Borneo." *AP*, Vol. 2, No. 2 of 1958 (1960), pp. 83–90.

Southwick, C. H.: "Letters to Editors." *SA*, Vol. 203, No. 6 (1960), p. 14.

Sprague, J. M.: "The Innervation of the Pharynx in the Rhesus Monkey and the Formation of the Pharyngeal Plexus in Primates." *AR*, Vol. 90, No. 3 (1944), pp. 197–208.

Stekelis, M., Picard, L., Schulman, N., and Haas, G.: "Villafranchian Deposits Near Ubeidiya in the Central Jordan Valley. Preliminary Report." *BRCI*, Vol. 9-G, No. 4 (1960), pp. 175–84.

Stern, C.: *Principles of Human Genetics.* San Francisco and London: W. H. Freeman & Co.; 1960, 2nd ed.

Stetten, De W., Jr.: "Gout and Metabolism." *SA*, Vol. 198, No. 6 (1958), pp. 73–81.

Stewart, T. D.: "American Neanderthaloids." *QRB*, Vol. 32, No. 4 (1957), pp. 364–9.

——: "First Views of the Restored Shanidar I Skull." *Sumer*, Vol. 14, No. 1–2 (1958), pp. 90–6.

——: "Restoration and Study of the Shanidar I Neanderthal Skeleton in Baghdad, Iraq." *YAPS*, 1958, pp. 274–8.

——: "The Restored Shanidar I Skull." *SRP*, No. 4369 (1958), pp. 473–8.

———: "Form of the Pubic Bone in Neanderthal Man." *Science*, Vol. 131, No. 3411 (1960), pp. 1437–8.

Stockard, C. R.: *Physical Basis for Personality.* New York: W. W. Norton and Company; 1931.

——: *The Genetic and Endocrinic Basis for Differences in Form and Behavior.* Philadelphia: Wistar Institute of Anatomy and Biology; 1941.

Stoudt, H.: "The Physical Anthropology of Ceylon." *CMES*, No. 2 (1961).

Straus, W. L., Jr.: "The Humerus of *Paranthropus robustus.*" *AJPA,* Vol. 6, No. 3 (1948), pp. 285–312.
——: "The Riddle of Man's Ancestry." *QRB,* Vol. 24, No. 3 (1949), pp. 200–23.
——: "Urine of Anthropoid Apes." *Science,* Vol. 124, No. 3219 (1956), p. 435.
——: "Jaw of *Gigantropithecus.*" *Science,* Vol. 125, No. 3250 (1957), p. 658.
——: "*Oreopithecus bambolii.*" *Science,* Vol. 126, No. 3269 (1957), pp. 345–6.
—— and Hunt, C. B.: "The Age of Zinjanthropus," *Science,* Vol. 136, No. 3325 (1962), pp. 293–5.
Sutton, H. E., and Clark, P. J.: "A Biochemical Study of Chinese and Caucasoids." *AJPA,* Vol. 13, No. 1 (1955), pp. 53–65.
Suzuki, H.: *Recent Discoveries of Pleistocene Man in Japan.* Read at VIth International Congress of Anthropology and Ethnology at Paris, 1960.
—— and Takai, F.: "Entdeckung eines pleistozänen hominiden Humerus in Zentral-Japan." *AAnz,* Vol. 23, No. 2–3 (1959), pp. 224–35.
Sukuki, M., and Sakai, T.: "A Familial Study of Torus palatinus and Torus mandibularis." *AJPA,* Vol. 18, No. 4 (1960), pp. 263–72.
Swinton, W. E.: "Reptilia," in Pycraft, W. P., ed.: *Rhodesian Man and Associated Remains,* p. 75. London: British Museum (Natural History); 1928.
Szumowski, G.: "Fouilles de l'Abri Sous Roche de Kourounkorokale (Soudan Français)." *BIAF,* Vol. 18, Ser. B, No. 2–3 (1956), pp. 462–508.

Tappan, N. C.: "Problems of Distribution and Adaptation of the African Monkeys." *CA,* Vol. 1, No. 2 (1960), pp. 91–120.
Tax, S.: *Evolution After Darwin.* Chicago: University of Chicago Press; 1960.
Thenius, E.: "Tertiärstratigraphie und Tertiäre Hominoidenfunde." *AAnz,* Vol. 22 (1958), pp. 66–77.
Thieme, F. P., and Otten, C. M.: "The Unreliability of Blood Typing Ancient Bone." *AJPA,* Vol. 15, No. 3 (1957), pp. 387–97.
Thoma, A.: "Metissage ou Transformation? Essai sur les Hommes Fossiles de Palestine." *L'Anth,* Vol. 62, No. 1–2 (1958), pp. 30–52.
Thomas, C. B., and Garn, S. M.: "Degree of Obesity and Serum Cholesterol Level." *Science,* Vol. 131, No. 3392 (1960), p. 42.
Thompson, D'A. W.: *Growth and Form.* New York: The Macmillan Company; 1945.
Thompson, W. R.: "Social Behavior," in Roe, A., and Simpson, G. G., eds.: *Behavior and Evolution,* pp. 291–310. New Haven: Yale University Press; 1958.
Thomson, A., and Buxton, D.: "Man's Nasal Index in Relation to Certain Climatic Conditions." *JRAI,* Vol. 53 (1923), pp. 53–92.
Tindale, N. B.: "Ecology of Primitive Aboriginal Man in Australia," in Keast, A., Crocker, R. L., and Christian, C. S.: "Biogeography and Ecology in Australia." *MB,* Vol. 8 (1959), pp. 36–51.
Tjio, J. H., and Puck, T. T.: "The Somatic Chromosomes of Man." *PNAS,* Vol. 44, No. 12 (1958), pp. 1229–37.
Tobias, P. V.: "Bushmen of the Kalahari." *Man,* Vol. 57, Art. No. 36 (1957), pp. 33–40.
——: "The Kanam Jaw." *Nature,* Vol. 185, No. 4714 (1960), pp. 946–7.
——: "Early Members of the Genus Homo in Africa," in G. Kurth, ed.: *Evolution und Hominisation,* Festschrift zum 60 Geburtstag von Dr. Heberer. Stuttgart: G. Fischer Verlag; 1962.
Tothill, J. D.: *Agriculture in the Sudan,* pp. 84–128. Oxford: Oxford University Press, 1948.

Tratman, E. K.: "A Comparison of the Teeth of People of Indo-European Racial Stock with Those of the Mongoloid Racial Stock." *DR*, Vol. 70, No. 2–3 (1950), pp. 63–88.

Tratz, E., and Heck, H.: "Der afrikanische Anthropoide 'Bonobo,' eine neue Menschenaffengattung." *SM*, Vol. 2 (1954), pp. 97–101.

Trevor, J. C.: "The Physical Characters of the Sandawe." *JRAI*, Vol. 77, Pt. 1 (1947), pp. 61–80.

Turville-Petre, F.: *Researches in Prehistoric Galilee 1925–1926*. London: British School of Archaeology in Jerusalem; 1927.

Twieselmann, F.: "Les Pygmées de l'Afrique Centrale." *RM*, No. 4 (1952), pp. 1–20.

——: "Les Néanderthaliens découverts en Belgique." *NC*, 1958, pp. 63–71.

Ullrich, H.: "Neanderthalfunde aus de Sowjetunion." *NC*, 1958, pp. 72–106.

Urey, H. C.: "Origin of Tektites." *Science*, Vol. 137, No. 3532 (1962), pp. 746–8

Vallois, H. V.: "La durée de la vie chez l'homme fossile." *CRAS*, No. 204 (1937), pp. 60–3.

——: "New Research on the Western Negrillos." *AJPA*, Vol. 26 (March 1940), pp. 449–71.

——: "L'Homme Fossile de Rabat." *CRAS*, No. 221 (1945), pp. 669–71.

——: *L'Omoplate Humaine*. Paris: Masson et Cie; 1946. (Extracts from *BMSM*, 1928, 1929, 1932, 1946.)

——: "Nouvelles Recherches sur la Squelette de Chancelade." *L'Anth*, Vol. 50, No. 1–2 (1941–6), pp. 11–202.

——: "The Fontéchevade Fossil Men." *AJPA*, Vol. 7, No. 3 (1949), pp. 339–60.

——: "Un Homme de Néanderthal en Tshekoslovaquie?" *L'Anth*, Vol. 55, No. 1–2 (1951), pp. 167–9.

——: "La Mandibule Humaine Fossile de la Grotte du Port-Épic près Diré-Dauoa (Abyssinie)." *L'Anth*, Vol. 55, No. 3–4 (1951), pp. 231–8.

——: "Les Restes Humains du Gisement Mousterien de Monsempron." *APa*, Vol. 83 (1952), pp. 100–20.

——: "Les Restes Humains de la Grotte de Dar es-Soltan." *CH*, No. 11 (1952), pp. 179–202.

——: "Diagrammes Sagittaux et Mensurations Individuels des Hommes Fossiles d'Afalou-Bou-Rhummel." *TLAB*, No. 5 (1952).

——: "La Mandibule Humaine pre-Mousterien de Montmaurin." *CRAS*, No. 240 (1955), pp. 1577–99.

——: "L'Homme de Rabat." *BAM*, Vol. 3 (1960), pp. 87–91.

—— and Movius, H. L., Jr., eds.: *Catalogue des Hommes Fossiles*. Algiers: XIX Congrès Géologique International; 1952.

Vallois, H. V., and Roche, J.: "La Mandibule Achenéene de Témara (Maroc)." *CRAS*, No. 246 (1958), pp. 3113–16.

Van Heekeren, H. F.: *The Stone Age of Indonesia*. The Hague: Martin Hijhoff; 1957.

Virchow, R.: "Der Kiefer aus der Šipkahöhle und der Kiefer von la Naulette." *ZfE*, Vol. 14 (1882), pp. 277–310.

Virchow, H.: *Die menschilichen Skelettreste aus dem Kampfe'schen Bruch im Travertin von Ehringsdorf bei Weimar*. Jena: G. Fischer, Verlag; 1920.

Vlček, E.: "Neandertálskéno Človek na Slovensku." *SlAr I*, 1953, pp. 5–132.

——: "The Fossil Man of Gánovce, Czechoslovakia." *JRAI*, Vol. 85 (1955), pp 163–71.

Vlček, E.: "Die Reste des Neanderthalmenschen aus dem Gebiete der Tschechoslowakei." *NC*, 1958, pp. 107–22.

——: "Old Literary Evidence for the Existence of the 'Snow Man' in Tibet and
Mongolia." *Man*, Vol. 59, Art. No. 203 (1959), pp. 132–4.

Von Koenigswald, G. H. R.: "Neue Pithecanthropus Funde 1936–1938." *WMDM*,
No. 28 (1940), pp. 1–232.

——: "Fossil Hominids from the Lower Pleistocene of Java." *IGC*, No. 9 (1948),
pp. 51–69.

——: "*Gigantopithecus blacki* Von Koenigswald, a Giant Fossil Hominid from the
Pleistocene of South China." *APAM*, Vol. 43, Pt. 4 (1952), pp. 295–325.

——: *Meeting Prehistoric Man*. New York: Harper and Brothers; 1956.

——: "Remarks on the Correlation of Mammalian Faunas of Java and India and
the Plio-Pleistocene Boundary." *PKAW* B, Vol. 59, No. 2 (1956), pp. 204–10.

——: "L'Hominisation de l'Appareil Masticateur et les Modifications du Régime
Alimentaire," in Delmas, A., ed.: *Les Processus de l'Hominisation*, pp. 60–78.
Paris: Centre National de la Recherche Scientifique; 1958.

——, ed: *Hundert Jahre Neanderthaler* (Neanderthal Centenary). Utrecht: Kemink en Zoon; 1958.

——: "Der Solo-Mensch von Java: ein tropischer Neanderthaler," in Von Koenigswald, G. H. R., ed.: *Hundert Jahre Neanderthaler*.

——: "Remarks on a Fossil Human Tooth from Olduwai, East Africa." *PKAW*,
Vol. 63, No. 1 (1960), pp. 20–5.

——, Gentner, W., and Lippott, H. J.: "Age of the Basalt Flow at Olduwai, East
Africa." *Nature*, Vol. 192, No. 4804 (1961), pp. 720–1.

——: "Das absolute Alter des Pithecanthropus Erectus Dubois," in Kurth, G.;
Evolution und Hominisation, pp. 112–19.

Wallace, A. F. C.: "On Being Just Complicated Enough." *PNAS*, Vol. 47, No. 4
(1961), pp. 456–64.

Wallace, A. R.: *The Geographical Distribution of Animals*, 2 Vols. London: The
Macmillan Company; 1876.

Ward, J. S., Bredell, G. A. C., and Wenzl, H. G.: "Responses of Bushmen and
Europeans on Exposure to Winter Night Temperatures in the Kalahari."
JAP, Vol. 15, No. 4 (1960), pp. 667–70.

Washburn, S. L.: Comment "Taxonomic Categories in Fossil Mammals" by E.
Mayr. *CSHS*, Vol. 15, pp. 109–18.

——: "The New Physical Anthropology." *TNYA*. Ser. 2, Vol. 13, No. 7 (1951),
pp. 298–304.

——: "Ischial Callosities as Sleeping Adaptations." *AJPA*, Vol. 5, No. 2 (1957),
pp. 269–76.

——: "Tools and Human Evolution." *SA*, Vol. 203, No. 3 (1960), pp. 63–75.

—— and Avis, V.: "Evolution and Behavior," in Roe, A., and Simpson, G. G.,
eds.: *Behavior and Evolution*, p. 430. New Haven: Yale University Press;
1958.

Washburn, S. L., and Howell, F. C.: "On the Identification of the Hypophyseal
Fossa of Solo Man." *AJPA*, Vol. 10, No. 1 (1952), pp. 13–22.

Weidenreich, F.: "The Sinanthropus Population of Chou Kou Tien." *BGSC*, Vol.
14, No. 4 (1935), pp. 427–61. (Reprinted in *CMJ*, Vol. 55 [1939], pp.
33–44.)

——: "The Mandibles of *Sinanthropus pekinensis*." *PS-NS-D*, Vol. 7, ws No. 3
(1936).

——: "The Dentition of *Sinanthropus pekinensis*." *PS-NS-D*, Vol. 1, ws No. 101
(1937).

———: "The Ramification of the Middle Meningeal Artery in Fossil Hominids and Its Bearing upon Phylogenetic Problems." *PS-NS-D*, Vol. 3, ws No. 110 (1938).

———: "On the Earliest Representatives of Modern Mankind Recovered on the Soil of East Asia." *PNHB*, Vol. 13, Pt. 3 (1938–9), pp. 161–74.

———: "The Extremity Bones of *Sinanthropus pekinensis*." *PS-NS-D*, Vol. 5, ws No. 116 (1941).

———: "The Skull of *Sinanthropus pekinensis*." *PS-NS-D*, Vol. 10, ws No. 127 (1943).

———: "Giant Early Man from Java and South China." *APAM*, Vol. 40, Pt. 1 (1945).

———: "The Keilor Skull: a Wadjak Type from Southeast Australia." *AJPA*, Vol. 3, No. 1 (1945), pp. 21–32.

———: "The Paleolithic Child from the Teshik-Tash Cave in Southern Uzbekistan (Central Asia)." *AJPA*, Vol. 3, No. 2 (1945), pp. 151–62.

———: "Some Particulars of Skull and Hair of Early Hominids and Their Bearing on the Problem of the Relationship between Man and Anthropoids." *AJPA*, Vol. 5, No. 4 (1947), pp. 387–428.

———: "Morphology of Solo Man." *APAM*, Vol. 43, Pt. 3 (1951), pp. 205–90.

Weiner, J. S.: "Nose Shape and Climate." *AJPA*, Vol. 12, No. 4 (1954), pp. 1–4.

Weinert, H.: "Der Urmenschenschädel von Steinheim." *ZfMuA*, Vol. 35 (1936), pp. 463–518.

———: "Uber die neuen Vor-und Frühmenschenfunde aus Afrika, Java, China und Frankreich." *ZfMuA*, Vol. 42 (1950), pp. 113–48.

———: "Zwei neue Urmenschenfunde." *ZfMuA*, Vol. 43, No. 3 (1952), pp. 265–75.

———, Bauermeister, W., and Remane, A.: "*Africanthropus njaraensis* Beschreibung und Phyletische Einordnung des ersten Affenmenschen aus Ostafrika." *ZfMuA*, Vol. 38 (1940), pp. 252–308.

Wells, L. H.: "The Status of the Bushman as Revealed by a Study of Endocranial Casts." *SAJS*, Vol. 34 (1937), pp. 365–98.

———: "Photographs with Note: The Border Cave Skull." *AJPA*, Vol. 8, No. 2 (1950), pp. 241–3.

———: "The Fossil Human Skull from Singa." *BMFM*, No. 2 (1951), pp. 29–42.

Wheeler, M.: *Early India and Pakistan*. New York: Frederick A. Praeger; 1959.

Wiegers, F., Weidenreich, F., and Schuster, E.: *Der Schädelfund von Weimar-Ehringsdorf*. Jena: G. Fischer; 1928.

Wiener, A. S., and Gordon, E. B.: "The Blood Groups of Chimpanzees, ABO Groups and M-N Types." *AJPA*, Vol. 18, No. 4 (1960), pp. 301–11.

Wijeskera, N. D.: *The People of Ceylon*. Colombo: Gunasena; 1949.

Wilber, C. G.: "Physiological Regulations and the Origins of Human Types." *HB*, Vol. 29, No. 4 (1957), pp. 329–36.

Woo, J-K: "Dryopithecus Teeth from Keiyuan, Yunnan Province." *VP*, Vol. 1, No. 1 (1957), pp. 25–32.

———: "New Materials of Dryopithecus from Keiyuan." *VP*, Vol. 2, No. 1 (1958), pp. 38–42.

———: "Fossil Human Parietal Bone and Femur from Ordos, Inner Mongolia." *VP*, Vol. 2, No. 4 (1958), pp. 208–12.

———: "Human Fossils Found in Liukiang, Kwangsi, China." *VP*, Vol. 3, No. 3 (1959), pp. 109–18.

———: "Fossil Human Skull of Early Paleanthropic Stage Found at Mapa, Shaoquan, Kwangtung Province." *VP*, Vol. 3, No. 4 (1959), pp. 176–82.

——— and Chao, T-K.: "New Discovery of Sinanthropus Mandible from Choukoutien." *VP*, Vol. 3, No. 4 (1959), pp. 169–72.

Woo, T. L., and Morant, G. M.: "A Biometric Study of the Flatness of the Facial Skeleton in Man." *Biometrika*, Vol. 26 (1934), pp. 196–250.

Woodward, A. S.: "A Fossil Skull of an Ancestral Bushman from the Anglo-Egyptian Sudan." *Antiquity*, Vol. 12, No. 46 (1938), pp. 190–3.

Wormington, H. M.: *Ancient Man in North America*, Fourth edition. Denver: Denver Museum of Natural History, Popular Series No. 4; 1957.

Wright, S.: "On the Role of Directed and Random Changes in Gene Frequency in Genetics of Populations." *Evolution*, Vol. 2, No. 4 (1948), pp. 279–94.

Wunderly, J.: "The Keilor Skull, Anatomical Description." *MNMM*, No. 13 (1943), pp. 57–70.

Wymer, J.: "A Further Fragment of the Swanscombe Skull." *Nature*, Vol. 176, No. 4479 (1955), pp. 426–7.

Wyndham, C. H., and Morrison, J. F.: "Heat Regulation of MaSarwa (Bushmen)." Vol. 178, No. 4538 (1956), pp. 869–70.

——: "Adjustment to Cold of Bushman in the Kalahari Desert." *JAP*, Vol. 13, No. 2 (1958), pp. 219–25.

Yeager, C. H., Painter, T. S., and Yerkes, R. M.: "The Chromosomes of the Chimpanzee." *Science*, Vol. 91, No. 2351 (1940), pp. 74–5.

Yearsley, M.: "Pathology of the Left Temporal Bone," in Pycraft, W. P., ed.: *Rhodesian Man and Associated Remains*, pp. 59–63.

Yerkes, R. M.: *Chimp Intelligence and its Vocal Expressions*. Baltimore: Williams and Wilkins; 1925.

Yoshimura, H., and Iida, T.: "Studies on the Reactivity of Skin Vessels to Extreme Cold, Part II, Factors Governing the Individual Difference of the Reactivity, or the Resistance Against Frostbite." *JJP*, Vol. 1 (1950–1), pp. 177–85.

Young, W. J., Merz, T., Ferguson-Smith, M. A., and Johnston, A. W.: "Chromosome Numbers of the Chimpanzee, *Pan troglodytes*." *Science*, Vol. 131, No 3414 (1960), pp. 1672–3.

Zapfe, H.: "Die Pliopithecus-Funde aus der Spaltenfüllung von Neudorf an der March (Czechoslovakia)." *VGBV*, Sonderheft C (1952). (Reprinted in the *Yearbook of Physical Anthropology*, New York, 1951, pp. 55–9.)

——: "Results of Research on the Skeleton of *Pliopithecus* (*Epipliopithecus*) *vindobonensis*." Paper read at the Annual Meeting of the American Association of Physical Anthropology, Cambridge, Mass., April 12, 1958.

Zeuner, F.: *Dating the Past*. London: Methuen & Co.; 1952.

NOTICES

Discovery of Fossil Skeletons of Small People in a Cave on the Island of Flores, Indonesia, in 1955. *SD*, Oct. 1960, pp. 62–3; *TI*, Vol. 7, No. 8 (1960).

Chronology of Cenozoic Era given by J. L. Kulp. *NYT*, March 5, 1960.

GLOSSARY

ACETABULUM   The hip socket.

ACHONDROPLASTIC   A form of dwarfing in which the extremities are shortened and thickened.

ACROCENTRIC   See telocentric.

ADAPIDAE   Fossil ancestors of the lemurs and lorises.

ADDUCTION   A drawing together, as the adduction of the great toe toward the other toes in human evolution.

ADDUCTOR MAGNUS   A large muscle extending from the pelvis to the *linea aspera* of the femur. It is important in locomotion.

ALLELES   Alternate genes situated on a single locus of a chromosome.

ALLOMETRY (allometric)   The principle according to which the proportions of related animals change as their sizes change.

ALLOPATRIC   Inhabiting different regions.

ALVEOLAR   Pertaining to the tooth-bearing part of the upper jaw.

ANAGENESIS   The evolution of one species out of another by succession: phyletic evolution.

ANAPTOMORPHS (*Anaptomorphidae*)   Fossil tarsiers.

ANASTOMOSIS   A connecting link between two arteries which ensures blood flow to the vascular territories of both if one is cut.

ANORTHOCLASE   A feldspar.

ANNULUS   A bony ring around the ear hole in certain mammals.

ANTEROPOSTERIOR   Fore and aft.

ANTICLINAL (vertebra)   In jumping primates, the vertebra that marks the midpoint between the front and rear muscles of the back on a pronograde animal.

APOCRINE (gland)   A kind of sweat gland.

APONEUROSES   Tendinous sheaths.

ARCHAEOZOIC   The oldest of the five geological eras.

ARGON-POTASSIUM METHOD, or Argon-40 method. A method of geological dating based on measuring the amount of argon trapped in a potassium atom. See page 313.

ASTERION   The point on the surface of the skull where the lambdoid, parietomastoid, and occipitomastoid sutures meet.

ASTRAGULUS   The ankle bone.

ATELIOTIC   A kind of dwarfing in which the bodily proportions remain normal with due allowance for allometry.

ATERIAN   A North African flint industry characterized by bifacial pressure flaking and tanged points.

ATLAS (vertebra)   The second cervical.

AURIGNACIAN   A European Upper Paleolithic flint industry.

AUSTRALOID   One of the five subspecies of living man, including the native peoples of Australia, New Guinea, and Melanesia; the Negroid dwarfs of Indonesia and South Asia; and certain aboriginal tribes of India.

AUSTRALOPITHECINES   All Lower Pleistocene hominids that are not *Homo*.

AXILLA   Armpit.

BASAL CONGLOMERATES   The conglomerate (puddingstone) which often occurs at the base of beds deposited on a surface that was exposed and eroded before the deposition of the new series.

BASION   The point at the forward lip of the *foramen magnum* on the sagittal line.

BIASTERIONIC   The breadth of the skull on the chord between the left and right asterion (q.v.).

BICONDYLAR (diameter)   The chord between the two condyles of the mandible, usually taken between the outer borders of the condyles.

BICRISTAL DIAMETER   The distance between the crests of the ilia of the two pelvic bones.

BIGONIAL DIAMETER   The length of the chord between the two gonial angles of the mandible.

BIZYGOMATIC DIAMETER   The maximum face breadth measured from one zygomatic arch to the other.

BILOPHODONTISM   A feature of the molar teeth of Old World monkeys. Each molar has two pairs of cusps, one forward and the other to the rear, each pair being joined by a ridge to form a loph.

BIOGEOGRAPHY   The geography of living things, including both plants and animals.

BOLAS STONES   Stones tied together with thongs so that when thrown at an animal or bird they will spread in flight and entangle the victim.

BOREAL   Pertaining to the northerly regions; e.g., boreal forest.

BRACHIAL   Pertaining to the upper arm; e.g., the brachial plexus of nerves.

BRACHIATE   To move through the forest by swinging with the arms from branch to branch, as an ape does.

BRACHYCEPHALIC   Round- or short-headed.

BRACHYCRANY   Of a skull: short or round.

BRANCHING (evolution by)   The evolution of one or more sister species at the same time through environmental adaptation: kladogenesis.

BRECCIA   A cave deposit containing angular stone and bone objects that have been naturally cemented.

BREGMA   The point at or near the top of the skull where the frontal and parietal sutures meet.

BUCCAL   On the cheek, or outer, side of the teeth.

BULLA (tympani)   A hollow, thin-walled, bony prominence of rounded form situated just below the opening of the ear and forming part of the tympanic bone.

BURIN   A graver or narrow chisel, particularly of flint.

CALCANEUS   The heel bone.

CALOTTE   A small, caplike fragment of a brain case.

CALVA   A fragmentary brain case, usually lacking the base.

CALVARIUM   The brain case, without the face.

CAPITATUM (*os capitatum*)   A wrist bone.

CAPOID   One of the five subspecies of man, including the Bushmen and Hottentots.

CARABELLI'S CUSP   An accessory cusp on the lingual side of an upper molar tooth.

CARPAL (bones)   Wrist bones.

CAROTID   An artery supplying blood to the brain.

CATARRHINES   Old World monkeys, apes, and hominids.

CAUCASOID   One of the five subspecies of living man, including most Europeans, North Africans, Near Easterners, inhabitants of India and Pakistan, and overseas settlers from these regions.

CENOZOIC   The present geological era, including the Tertiary and Quaternary.

CENTROMERE   The point where the two coiled strands of a chromosome are attached; in cell division it acts as the focus of separation.

CEREBELLUM   A three-lobed and finely fissured section of the brain situated below the posterior portion of the cerebral hemispheres. Among its functions are the regulation of posture and the maintenance of bodily equilibrium.

CINGULUM   A collarlike rim of enamel about the base of the crown of any tooth except the incisors.

CLACTONIAN   A European Lower Paleolithic flake industry.

CLASS   The third of seven levels in the Linnean taxonomy; e.g., Mammalia.

CLAVICLE   Collarbone.

CLINE, CLINAL   A gradual progression in the dimensions, form, or color of an anatomical feature from one geographic region to another.

CONDYLES   Raised articular surfaces on which bones move, as the occipital condyles at the base of the skull, and the condyles of the lower jaw.

CONGOID   One of the five subspecies of living men, including the African Negroes and Pygmies.

CORACOID PROCESS   The forward peak of the ascending ramus of the mandible to which the temporal muscles are attached.

CORTEX   The outer layer of the lobes of the forebrain; the "gray matter."

CRETACEOUS   The third and last epoch of the Mezozoic Era.

CRÔ-MAGNON   A site in the Dordogne region of France in which a skeleton so named was found. That skeleton. A supposed race.

CROMERIAN   A Lower Pleistocene interglacial period between Günz and Mindel.

CUBOID   A tarsal bone.

CUNEIFORMS   Three tarsal bones.

CYNODONT, CYNODONTISM   Being "dog-toothed." Having a normal-sized pulp cavity: the opposite of taurodontism (q.v.).

CYTOGENETICS   The study of heredity in terms of the anatomy and physiology of cells.

DECIDUOUS TEETH   The milk teeth.

DELTOID   A muscle of the shoulder and upper arm.

DIASTEMA   A gap between two teeth.

DIGASTRIC FOSSAE   Grooves on the inner and under side of the lower jaw to which the digastric muscles are attached.

DIMORPHISM (sexual)   Marked differentiation in size and form between the sexes.

DIPLOE   The cancellous bony tissue between the inner and outer tables of the skull.

DIPLOID   Of cell nuclei: having pairs of chromosomes; e.g., 46 in man. The opposite of haploid (q.v.).

DISTAL   Away from the center; e.g., the hand is distal to the arm.

DJETIS   A late Lower Pleistocene fossil-bearing deposit found in Java.

DOLERITE   A dark igneous rock.

DONAU   A local Central European Lower Pleistocene glaciation.

DORSAL   On the back side.

DRYOPITHECINES   A group of fossil hominoids probably ancestral to living apes and men.

ELSTER   The first European continental icecap, corresponding to the Mindel of the Alpine series.

ECOLOGY   The study of the mutual relations between organisms and their environment.

EOCENE   The second of five divisions of the Tertiary epoch.

EOLITHS   Early stone "implements" which may have been of natural origin.

EPOCH (geological)   A division of a period (q.v.).

ERA (geological)   Any of the five primary divisions of geologic time.

ESTIVATE   To sleep in the hot season—the opposite of hibernate.

ETHIOPIAN REGION   Africa south of the Sahara, and Southern Arabia.

EURYPHAGOUS, EURYPHAGY   Wide-feeding, eating many kinds of food.

EXFOLIATE   To peel off through weathering (of granite).

EXOSTOSIS   A bony excrescence.

FAMILY   The fifth of seven levels in the Linnean taxonomy; e.g., Hominidae, which has two subfamilies, Australopithecinae and Homininae.

FELDSPAR   Any of a related group of crystalline minerals.

FEMUR   Thigh bone.

FIBULA   The thinner and outer of the two shin bones.

FLAKE (implement)   A stone implement made from a flake that has been struck off a core.

FORAMEN   A hole in a bone.

FORAMEN MAGNUM   The opening at the base of the skull through which the spinal cord passes.

FOSSA   A depression or concavity in a bone.

FOVEA   An indented area in the center of the retina.

FRENUM   A connecting fold of membrane in the mouth. One connects the lips and gums at the median line, and another binds the tongue to the floor of the oral cavity.

GAMBLIAN   The last (either third or fourth) pluvial period of the Pleistocene in East Africa.

GENERAL ADAPTATION   Genetic adaptation to interspecific and intra-specific competition; e.g., increased intelligence.

GENETIC DRIFT (the Sewall Wright effect)   A type of evolution postulated by Sewall Wright in which the genetic composition of a population changes by chance because the population is too small to constitute a valid statistical sample.

GENIOGLOSSAL   A pair of muscles that participate in controlling the movements of the tongue.

GENUS   The sixth of seven levels in the Linnean taxonomy; e.g., *Homo*.

GEOGRAPHICAL RACE   A subspecies; a major division of a species, presumably of some antiquity.

GERONTOMORPHIC, GERONTOMORPHY   Having the characteristics of old age, as contrasted with pedomorphic (q.v.).

GIBBERELLIC ACID   A substance involved in the growth of plants.

GLABELLA   The central and most prominent point on the brow ridges.

GLABELLARE   An ill-defined point on the sagittal arc of the frontal bone just above glabella, marking the junction of the glabellan prominence and the curve of the frontal bone.

GLACIAL   An interval of cold climate with mountain glaciers, continental icecaps, or both.

GLENOID CAVITY   The socket in which the mandibular condyle rests.

GLOTTOCHRONOLOGY   The science of determining how long ago two related languages separated.

GLUTEUS MAXIMUS   A massive muscle of the pelvis and thigh which forms the buttock. It is important in walking and particularly in raising the body upward.

GLUTEUS MEDIUS   A powerful muscle of the pelvis and thigh. In walking it throws the body toward the line of gravity when the opposite leg is off the ground.

GLUTEUS MINIMUS   A muscle of the pelvic and thigh underlying the *gluteus medius* and performing more or less the same function.

GONIAL ANGLE   The lower rear corner of the mandible.

GÖTTWEIG   The interstadial between Würm I and Würm II.

GRADE   In this book, an evolutionary level or status through which one or more phyletic lines of animals (or plants) may pass.

GÜNZ   The first of four Alpine glaciations in Europe; believed to have been divided into two peaks, Günz I and Günz II.

HAPLOID   The condition of a sperm cell or unfertilized egg which has only one pair of chromosomes; e.g., in man, 23, which is half the number present in fertilized eggs and in somatic cells.

HAPTOGLOBINS   "Proteins [in the blood serum which are] concerned with the binding [together] of hemoglobin from aged and broken down red blood cells" (C. Stern: *Principles of Human Genetics*, p. 53).

HEMOGLOBIN   "Complex molecules [in the red blood cells] that are composed of the colored, iron-containing heme and a colorless protein, globin" (Stern: *Principles*, p. 53).

HOLOTYPE   The first specimen of a species to be found, named, and described.

HOMINIDS   Australopithecines and men.

HOMINOIDS   Apes, Australopithecines, and men.

HOMO ERECTUS   The extinct species of man from which the living races of *Homo sapiens* evolved.

HOMO SAPIENS   The living species of man and some of our fossil ancestors.

HUMERUS   The upper arm bone.

HYLOBATIDAE, HYLOBATIDS   Gibbons and siamangs.

HYOID BONE   A U-shaped bone at the base of the tongue; to it are attached muscles used in swallowing and speaking.

HYPOPHYSIS   The pituitary gland.

HYPOTHALAMUS   A small subchamber at the upper end of the brain stem which has many functions concerned with emotions and automatic controls of physiological activities.

ILIUM   The uppermost and largest of the three pelvic bones which fuse to form the *os coxae*.

INCA (bones)   Supernumerary bones at lambda.

INFRAORBITAL FORAMEN   A foramen in the zygomatic bone under each orbit.

INION   A projection in the sagittal line of the occipital bone, usually at or below the hindmost point of that bone. It serves as an anchor for some of the neck muscles.

INTERGLACIAL   An interval of warm climate between two glaciations.

INTERPLUVIAL   In tropical regions, a geological time interval separating two pluvials.

INTERSTADIAL   A cool interval between two maxima of a single glaciation.

ISCHIUM (ischial)   The lowermost and hindmost of the three pelvic bones which fuse to constitute the *os coxae*.

ISCHIAL CALLOSITY   A patch of tough, bare skin covering the tuberosity of the ischium in Old World monkeys and some apes.

ISCHIAL TUBEROSITY   A downward extension of the ischium, covered in some primates by an ischial callosity (q.v.).

JURASSIC   The second of the three epochs of the Mesozoic Era.

KARYOTYPE   The chromosomes of an animal arranged by pairs in order of length.

KINGDOM   The first of seven levels in the Linnean taxonomy; e.g., the animal and vegetable kingdoms.

KITCHEN-MIDDEN   An open-air archaeological site, usually Mesolithic, and usually containing bivalve shells.

KLADOGENESIS   Evolution by branching (q.v.).

LABIOLINGUAL DIAMETER   The transverse diameter of a tooth, from cheekside to tongueside.

LAGOMORPHS   Hares and rabbits.

LAMBDA   The point where the two parietal bones and the occipital bone meet.

LANUGO   Fetal hair.

LATERITE   A porous reddish clay formed by the decomposition of certain rocks in tropical regions.

LEVALLOISIAN   A technique of striking flakes ready for use from a prepared core. A flint-tool industry based on this technique.

LINE   In this book, an evolutionary sequence of species passing through two or more grades.

LINEA ASPERA   A raised ridge on the back of the femur.

LOCAL RACE   A minor taxonomic division of a species of lesser magnitude than a subspecies (geographical race).

LOPH   In the molar teeth of Old World monkeys, a pair of cusps joined by a ridge. There are generally two pairs to a tooth, one fore and one aft.

LUMBAR   The region of the back between the rib cage and the pelvis; e.g., lumbar vertebrae.

MALAR   The *os zygomaticum*, or cheek bone.

MANDIBLE   Lower jaw.

MANO (American Indian)   The upper grindstone, held in the hand and rubbed against the metate, or nether grindstone.

MANUBRIUM   The lower segment of the breast bone.

MARL   A crumbly deposit of clay mixed with calcium carbonate.

MASSETER   One of a pair of muscles which take part in the raising and grinding motions of the lower jaw.

MASTOID PROCESS   A hollow protuberance on the temporal bone behind the ear hole.

MAXILLA   The upper jaw bone.

AUDITORY MEATUS   The ear hole.

MEDULLA   (OBLONGATA)   The lowest or posterior part of the brain, which merges into the spinal cord.

MEIOSIS   A process by which a sperm or egg cell divides twice in succession, the second division reducing the nucleus from the diploid (q.v.) to the haploid (q.v.) state.

MELANIN   Pigment granules.

MENTAL FORAMEN   A hole in the outer surface of the lower jaw.

MENINGEAL ARTERIES   Arteries that feed blood to the meningeal covering of the brain.

MESIAL   Toward the center.

MESIODISTAL DIAMETER   Of the crowns of teeth: the length as measured along the curve of the dental arc.

MESIOLABIAL   Of the crowns of teeth: forward and outward.

MESOZOIC   The fourth of the five geological eras.

METACARPALS   The five bones of the hand lying between the wrist bones (carpals) and the finger bones (phalanges).

METACENTRIC   Of a chromosome: having the centromere more or less in the middle.

METATARSALS   The five bones of the foot lying between the tarsals and the toe bones (phalanges).

METATE   An American Indian millstone, the larger or nether stone.

METOPIC SUTURE   A suture between the two frontal bones which usually closes in infancy.

MICROLITH   A small flint implement struck from a small blade core.

MIDDEN   An ancient refuse heap, usually composed largely of mollusc shells.

MID-PHALANGEAL   Pertaining to the middle section of a finger or toe.

MINDEL   The second of four Alpine glaciations of the Pleistocene.

MIOCENE   The fourth of five epochs of the Tertiary period.

MONGOLOID   One of the five subspecies of living man, including principally the peoples of East and Southeast Asia and most of Indonesia, and the Polynesians, Micronesians, and American Indians.

MONOTREME   An egg-laying mammal of Australia.

MONOTYPIC   Of a species: having no geographical races.

MORPHOLOGY   The study of the form and structure of animals and plants.

MOSAIC   A kind of geographical distribution in which many races live close together.

MOUSTERIAN   A Middle Paleolithic flake industry of Europe and Western Asia.

MULLER   A stone used for pounding or grinding.

MULTITUBERCULATES   An extinct order of mammals that flourished during the early Cenozoic.

NASION   The point where the two nasal bones and the frontal bone meet.

NAVICULAR   A wrist bone.

NEANTHROPIC   Referring to morphologically modern types of man.

NEARCTIC REGION   North America and parts of Central America (see Map 2).

NEOTENY   The persistence into adult life of fetal or infantile characteristics.

NEOTROPICAL REGION   South America and parts of Central America (see Map 2).

NEURONE   A nerve cell, including its processes.

NONTONAL (language)   A language in which tones have no semantic meaning, other than for emphasis or questioning.

NOTOPURO   Upper Pleistocene fossil-bearing beds in Java.

NUCHAL   Pertaining to the neck.

OBELION, OBELIONIC   The point on the interparietal (sagittal) suture of the skull between the two parietal foramina.

OCCIPUT, OCCIPITAL BONE   The hindmost bone of the skull.

OCCIPITAL CREST   A crest of bone running horizontally across the occiput in some apes and some hominids.

OCCLUSAL   Pertaining to the occlusion of the teeth when the jaws are closed.

ODONTOLOGY   The study of teeth.

OLECRANON PROCESS   The projection at the proximal end of the ulna: the "funny bone."

OLIGOCENE   The third of five divisions of the Tertiary epoch.

ONTOGENY   The growth and development of an individual organism.

OPISTHION   The rearmost point on the sagittal line of the skull when in the eye-ear plane.

ORDER   The fourth of seven levels in the Linnean taxonomy; e.g., Primates.

ORIENTAL REGION   The Old World tropics from India to Wallace's Line and South China (see Map 2).

ORTHOGNATHOUS   Having jaws that do not protrude: the opposite of prognathous.

OS CAPITATUM   A wrist bone.

OS COXAE   The pelvic bone, consisting of three fused bones, the ilium, ischium and pubis.

OS LUNATUM   A wrist bone.

PACHYOSTOSIS   Thickening of a bone.

PALEARCTIC REGION   Europe, North Africa, and all of Asia except that forming part of the Oriental region (q.v.). See Map 2.

PALEOCENE   The earliest of the five divisions of the Tertiary epoch.

PALEOLITHIC   The stone-age industries of the Pleistocene and their time span.

PALEOZOIC   The second of the four geological eras.

PARIETAL   One of a pair of bones comprising the major part of the skull vault, bordered in front by the frontal bone and behind by the occipital bone.

PATELLA   The kneecap.

PEDOMORPHIC, PEDOMORPHY   Infantile or childlike in the adult form.

PELAGE   The over-all hair covering or fur of an animal.

PERIOD (geological)   A division of an era (q.v.).

PERONEAL   Pertaining to the fibula, as the peroneal artery.

PHALANGES   Finger and toe bones.

PHENOTYPE   What you are: the product of heredity and environment.

PHRATRY   A division of a tribe or other breeding isolate.

PHYLETIC EVOLUTION   Evolution by succession by which one species evolves out of another.

PHYLOGENY   The evolution of a line (q.v.).

PHYLUM   The second of seven levels in the Linnean taxonomy; e.g., the Chordata-Vertebrata is a sub-phylum.

PHYTOGEOGRAPHY   The geography of plants; the counterpart to zoogeography (q.v.).

PILASTER (femur)   A bracing ridge on the back of the shaft of the thigh bone.

PINJOR   A Lower Pleistocene fossil-bearing geological formation in the Siwalik Hills of India, laid down during the first of four Himalayan glaciations.

PLATYRRHINES   New World monkeys.

PLATYSMA   A broad, thin sheet of muscle covering much of the face in primitive mammals; from parts of it are derived the muscles of facial expression in man.

PLEISTOCENE   The earlier and longer of the two epochs of the Quaternary period; it began about one million years ago and is believed to have ended ten thousand years ago.

PLEXUS   A network of blood vessels or nerves.

PLIOCENE   The fifth and final epoch of the Tertiary period.

PLUVIAL   Rainy. In Africa pluvial periods are believed to have corresponded in a general way to periods of glaciation in northerly regions.

POLYTYPIC   Of a species: having two or more genetically distinct geographical races or subspecies.

POLYANDROUS   Pertaining to a system of mating in which a woman may have two or more husbands.

POLYGYNOUS   Pertaining to a system of mating in which a man may have two or more wives.

POLYMORPHIC   Genetically variable.

PONGID   Pertaining to apes.

PONTIAN   A geological time span between about 16 and 10 million years ago, variously attributed to the Upper Miocene and the Lower Pliocene.

PORION   A point on the upper border of the ear hole.

PREMOLAR CONE   A protuberance in the center of an upper premolar found sometimes in the teeth of Mongoloids.

PROGNATHISM   Protrusion of the jaws.

PRONOGRADE   Walking on all fours.

PROSIMIAN   Any primitive primate included among the tree shrews, lemurs, lorises, and tarsiers.

PROTEROZOIC   The second of the five geological eras.

PROTOANTHROPIC   The first of three grades of human evolution according to the scheme of S. Sergi.

PTERYGOIDS   Two pairs of muscles, the internal and the external, concerned with the motions of the lower jaw.

PURINE   A crystalline compound ($C_2H_4N_4$), the parent of other compounds of the uric acid group.

QUATERNARY   The present geological period, including the Pleistocene and Recent epochs.

RACE   A general term referring to genetically distinct divisions of a species.

RADIUS   The shorter and more mobile of the two bones of the forearm; the one on the outer side when the palm of the hand is facing forward or upward.

RAMI (ascending)   The paired branches of the rear portions of the lower jaw which rise upwards to articulate with the cranium.

RETE MIRABILE   A network of blood vessels concerned with heat transfer between veins and arteries.

RHESUS   An obsolete name for the primate genus *Macaca;* a system of blood groups named after the Rhesus monkey, *Macaca mulata.*

RHINIAL   The name of the third index of facial flatness.

RISS   The third of the four Alpine glaciations of the Pleistocene epoch.

SAALE   The second Continental icecap in Northern Europe, corresponding to the Riss Alpine glaciation.

SACRUM   A bone of composite origin connecting the two pelvic bones, the fifth lumbar vertebra, and the coccyx.

SAGITTAL CREST   A crest running along the sagittal (interparietal) suture in some apes and Australopithecines whose two sets of temporal muscles are or were so large that they met at the top of the skull and needed additional area for attachment.

SAHUL SHELF   A region of shallow water off the northwest coast of Australia which reaches New Guinea; it was dry land during parts of the Pleistocene.

SANMENIAN   Geological deposits in Northern China: the lower Sanmenian is Lower Pleistocene and the Upper Sanmenian is Middle Pleistocene.

SAVANNAH   Tropical or semitropical grassland dotted with trees.

SCAPHOID   Keel-shaped: a wrist bone.

SCAPULA   Shoulder blade.

SCLERA   The fibrous outer capsule of the eye, including the transparent cornea.

SECTORIAL   Of canine and incisor teeth: shearing.

SELLA TURCICA   The hypophysial fossa, a depression in the base of the skull in which the pituitary or hypophysial gland is seated.

SERVAL CAT (*Felis Serval*)   A long-legged African wildcat.

SESAMOIDS   Generally rounded or platelike bones found in tendons overlying joints. The patella or kneecap is a large sesamoid bone.

SHAMAN   A medico-religious specialist among primitive peoples.

SHOVEL INCISORS   Incisor teeth that are concave on the inside.

SICKLING   A heritable deformation of the red corpuscles which inhibits oxygen transfer but is believed to produce immunity to some forms of malaria.

SIMOTIC   The second of the four indices of facial flatness.

SINANTHROPUS   A group of fossil men found at Choukoutien in North China.

SOMATIC CELLS   Body cells, as opposed to sperm and egg cells.

SPECIAL ADAPTATION   Genetic adaptation to some special environmental factor; e.g., cold, heat, drought, or special foods.

SPECIES   The seventh of the seven levels in the Linnean taxonomy, and the basic unit of the Linnean system; e.g., *Homo sapiens*.

SPHENOID   A bone in the lower and forward part of the skull. It consists of a body and two pairs of wings and articulates with every other bone of the brain case as well as with the palatine and zygomatic bones and the vomer.

SQUAMOUS   Pertaining to the upper or scalelike part of the temporal bone which articulates with the parietal at the squamous suture.

STADIAL   One of the maxima of a glaciation which had two or more peaks.

STEATOPYGIA   The condition of having large deposits of fat on the buttocks.

STEGODON   A genus of extinct Asiatic elephants.

STENOPHAGOUS, STENOPHAGY   Having a specialized diet.

STERNUM   The breast bone.

STRATIGRAPHY, STRATIGRAPHIC   The study of superimposed layers (strata) in archaeology.

SUBFAMILY   See family.

SUBPHYLUM   See phylum.

SUBSPECIES   A major division of a species, constituting a geographical race.

SUBTENSE   In an isosceles triangle, a line that divides it into two right-angle triangles of equal area.

SUBTERMINAL   Of a chromosome: having its centromere located between its middle and one end.

SUCCESSION (evolution by)   See anagenesis, phyletic evolution.

SUNDA SEA, SHELF   A body of shallow water lying between parts of Indonesia and Southeast Asia. During parts of the Pleistocene this area was above water.

SUPERSTERNALE   A point at the top of the sternum or breast bone used in the anthropometry of the living.

SUPINATOR RIDGE OR CREST   A ridge on the inside of the ulna which gives attachment to the supinator muscle, which rotates the forearm.

SUSTENTACULUM TALI   A projection on the inner side of the calcaneum or heel bone for articulation with a facet of the head of the talus, or ankle bone.

SUTURE   The line of union between any two bones of the skull.

SYLVIAN FISSURE   Also called the lateral sulcus. The most conspicuous fissure of the brain, situated between the temporal lobe and the fronto-parietal region.

SYMBIOSIS   Of two or more species: living together to the mutual advantage of both or all species; e.g., a bird that sits on a rhinoceros and eats his ticks.

SYMPATRIC   Of species: occupying the same territory.

SYMPHISION   An anthropometric landmark at the upper and outer border of the pubic symphysis.

PUBIC SYMPHISIS   The junction of the two pubic bones that are separated by the interpubic disc.

TAIGA   A Russian term for boreal forest.

TALUS   The ankle bone, which articulates with the tibia, fibula, calcaneum, and navicular. In walking each talus bears in turn the entire weight of the body.

TARSAL BONES OR TARSUS   The talus, calcaneum, navicular, cuboid, and the three cuneiforms.

TATROT   An Early Lower Pleistocene level in the Siwalik Hills of Northern India, and its fauna.

TAURONDONTISM   Being "bull-toothed." A condition of the teeth, particularly the molars, in which the fusion of the roots neotenously takes place low down and results in a large pulp cavity. The opposite condition is cynodontism (q.v.).

TAXONOMY   The science of classifying animals and plants; systematics.

TEKTITE   A small, glassy nodule from outer space.

TELOCENTRIC   Of a chromosome: having the centromere at one end; acrocentric.

TEMPORAL BONE   A paired bone forming part of the base and lateral wall of the skull. It is formed from four separate bones in the fetus, representing the petrous portion and mastoids, the styloid process, the squamous part, and the tympanic part.

TERES MINOR   A muscle attached to the axillary border of the scapula and the upper part of the humerus, which participates in rotating the humerus laterally.

TERTIARY   The first of the two periods of the Cenozoic Era.

TIGLIAN   A cool interglacial interval of the Lower Pleistocene in Western Europe preceding Günz I.

TONAL (language)   A language, like Chinese, in which changes of musical tone have semantic meaning.

TORUS   A bony ridge, particularly the supraorbital torus, which is a continuous brow ridge.

TRAPEZIUM   A wrist bone at the base of the first (thumb) metacarpal.

TRAPEZOID   A wrist bone at the base of the first (index) finger metacarpal.

TRAVERTINE   Calcium carbonate deposited by water of springs and streams holding lime in solution.

TRIASSIC   The first period of the Mesozoic Era.

TRINIL   Fossil-bearing Middle Pleistocene beds in Java overlying the Djetis Beds and underlying the Notopuro Beds.

TROCHANTER   At the upper and outer side of the femur, just distal of the neck, is a large prominence, the greater trochanter, to which are attached the *gluteus minimus* and *gluteus medius* muscles. The lesser trochanter, lower and on the inner side, is the attachment for the psoas major and iliacus muscles. A few femora have a third trochanter.

TROCHLEA   A front-to-back rounded groove at the distal end of the humerus which articulates with the ulna.

TYMPANIC PLATE   A curved plate on the temporal bone which lies in front of the mandibular fossa and with which the condyle of the mandible articulates in rotary chewing.

ULNA   The longer and less mobile of the two bones of the forearm; the one on the inner side when the palm of the hand is facing forward or upward.

UNGULATES   Hoofed mammals.

VENAE COMITES   Veins which run parallel to each other on either side of certain arteries and which may be joined by anastomoses (q.v.) just as arteries may.

VILLAFRANCHIAN   The earliest part of the Lower Pleistocene.

VOLAR   Referring to the palm of the hand or sole of the foot.

VOMER   A median bone which forms the posteroinferior portion of the nasal septum. It lies below and behind the septal cartilage.

WAAGENON   A subspecies in a phyletic evolutionary sense, and not a geographical subspecies.

WALLACEA   The islands between Wallace's Line and the boundary of the Australian Region. Their fauna is of mixed Oriental and Australian species. (See Map 3.)

WALLACE'S LINE   A line between Bali and Lombok, and points north and east, which divides the Oriental fauna from that of Wallacea. (See Map 3.)

WEBER'S LINE   The line of faunal balance between Wallace's Line and the boundary of the Australian Region. (See Map 3.)

WEICHSEL   The third and final continental European icecap, corresponding in general to the Würm (q.v.).

WÜRM   The fourth and last of the Alpine glaciations of the Pleistocene epoch.

ZOOGEOGRAPHY   The geography of animals; the counterpart to phytogeography (q.v.).

ZYGOMATIC   A paired bone of the face which forms part of the lower and outer borders of the orbit and parts of its floor. It articulates particularly with the sphenoid temporal and maxillary bones.

ADDENDA

New Information up to October 1, 1969

References are to pages in text.

p. 79. The Tell Ubeidiya remains date from a later time than was previously thought.

p. 91. Traces of fire have also been found at Vértesszöllös, Hungary, geologically dated at about 400,000 years.

p. 183. Recent field studies show that the three great apes do not live in simple harems. The orangs move about in small groups of two to four individuals, and some old males are solitary. The chimpanzees live in fluctuating bands of a dozen or so, mating promiscuously. Gorillas feed in bands centered around a dominant male with several adult females, but may also include a few young males and sexually nonparticipant older ones.

pp. 205–206. *Kenyapithecus* is now considered an African form of *Ramapithecus*.

chap. 7. In 1965, at Kanapoi, in southern Turkanaland, Kenya, Bryan Patterson found a piece of humerus, including its elbow joint, which was dated by the argon-potassium method at 2,500,-000 years. Essentially human, it indicates a complete liberation of the upper limbs from use in locomotion. B. Patterson and W. W. Howells: *Science*, Vol. 156 (1967), p. 64.

In 1967 and 1968, three expeditions to the Omo Valley, in southwestern Ethiopia near the Kenya border, found Australopithecine remains between 2 and 4 million years old. R. Leakey, *Nature*, Vol. 222 (1969), pp. 1117 ff; F. C. Howell, *Nature*, Vol. 223

(1969), pp. 1234 ff.; and "News and Views," *Nature*, Vol. 223 (1969), pp. 1119–20.

pp. 219–20. *Proconsul* is no longer considered an ancestor of man.

pp. 278–87. The Olduvai child has been named *Homo habilis* and is now tentatively regarded as an ancestor of man. P. V. Tobias has most recently (1969) called it *Australopithecus/Homo habilis*. Its teeth closely resemble those of *Meganthropus* of Java, a mandible probably of the same species as the skull of *Pithecanthropus 4*. Both are older than the newly discovered specimens of *H. habilis* that run to the top of Bed I in Olduvai, with no advance in brain size. Even if *H. habilis* is indeed an ancestor, the transition to *Homo erectus* need not have taken place in Africa.

pp. 287–94. *Zinjanthropus* has now been renamed *Australopithecus boisei*, but some workers consider it to be a race of *Australopithecus robustus*. It was apparently older in Olduvai than in South Africa, and older still in the Omo Valley.

p. 297. The Tchad specimen, named *Tchadanthropus*, is now given a more recent date than that first assigned it, and placed closer to *Homo erectus* than to *Australopithecus*.

pp. 297–8. Cf. addendum for p. 79.

pp. 430–431. A new fossil skull found in China, called *Sinanthropus lantianensis*, is older than *Sinanthropus pekinensis* and has a cranial capacity of about 780 cc.

p. 437. Simpson's reference to *Eoanthropus* antedated the discovery that that specimen was a hoax.

p. 487. In 1965 a human occipital bone was found at Vértesszöllös in Hungary, dated at about 400,000 years, and indicating a cranial capacity approaching 1500 cc., well within the middle of the *sapiens* range.

pp. 508–11. The Krapina remains are now believed to date from about 30,000 B.C. or later.

pp. 557–8. The Starosel'e skull has also been updated.

INDEX

Abbevillian industry, 329
ABO blood groups, 173, 193
absorption, concept of, 34
Acheulian industry, 329, 330, 488, 496, 501, 521, 555, 567, 592, 596
achondroplasia, 114–15, 653
acrocentric (telocentric) chromosome, 178, 179
Adapidae, 191
adaptation(s): to crowding, 106–12; environmental, *see* environmental adaptation; general, 28; physiological, *see* physiological adaptation; social, evolution through, 72–118 *passim*; special, 28; unique, of *Homo*, 118
adaptive threshold, 305
Afalou-Bou-Rhummel remains, 605, 607, 608, 609, 633
Afghanistan, 330, 482, 484, 526, 559, 577, 578
Africa, 52, 53, 189, 220, 222, 225, 588; apes of, 140, 141, 144–8; area of, 42; *Atlanthropus* in, 11; Bushmen in, *see* Bushmen; as cradle of mankind, 656; dwarf bush bay (loris) in, 113; Eurasia connected to, 42, 43, 46, 190; and exchange of animals with South Asia, 56; fire as late arrival in, 332; Fort Ternan primate in, 205–6; fossil men in, sites of, 590–609, 612–13; geological events in, 32; human evolution in, 609–10; land mass of, 42, 43, 46; *Limnopithecus* in, 196–7, 198; *Mesopithecus* in, 195; monkeys in, 135, 136–8, 139–40; Negroes in, *see* Negroes; *Pliopithecus* in, 198; pluvial periods in, during Pleisto-

Africa (*continued*)
cene, 315; Pygmies in, *see* Pygmies; tools in, Lower Pleistocene, 227–30, 333; Watusi in, 13, 636; *see also* Central Africa, East Africa, North Africa, South Africa, West Africa
Africanthropus njarasensis, 627
Agache, R., 228, 230
Age of Mammals, 50
agriculture, as ecological grade, 307
Aïn Hanech (Hanash), 226, 228, 229, 298
Ainu, 3, 57, 476–7; and facial flatness, 366, 367; hair of, 476; skulls of, 474, 477; stature of, 456; teeth of, 355, 357, 516; *torus mandibularis* of, 451; transportation used by, 473
Aitape brain case, 399, 406, 410
Alakaluf Indians, 64, 65, 69, 477, 547
Alaska, 318
Alaskan Indians, 63, 65
Aleut language, 5
Algeria, 217, 226, 344, 441, 452, 592, 604, 605, 607
alleles, 36
Allen's rule, 60
allometry, 25–6, 259
allopatric species, 14
Alouattinae, 132, 133
Alpine race, 19
Alpo-Himalayan system, 189
Alps, 309, 527, 548, 553
amino acids, urinary, in primates, 173
Amphipithecus, 193
anagenesis (succession), 27, 28, 106 *ff.*, 111

A NOTE ABOUT THE AUTHOR

CARLETON STEVENS COON, Research Curator of General Anthropology at the University Museum of the University of Pennsylvania, Honorary Curator of Anthropology at the Peabody Museum, Salem, Massachusetts, as well as Research Associate in General Ethnology of the Peabody Museum of Harvard, was born in Wakefield, Massachusetts. He was educated at Phillips Academy at Andover and obtained his B.A., M.A., and Ph.D. from Harvard University, where he also taught before going on to the University of Pennsylvania. Dividing his time between teaching and field work, he has traveled extensively in Africa, Asia, and Europe. He arranged the famous Hall of Man exhibit at the University Museum, and was a regular panel member on the Peabody Award-winning television program *What in the World?* Dr. Coon is past president of the American Association of Physical Anthropologists, and is the leading authority on race. Among his books are *Caravan: The Story of the Middle East* (1951, 1958); *The Story of Man* (1954, revised editions 1962, 1969); and *The Seven Caves* (1957). Dr. Coon has two sons and six grandchildren, and lives with his wife, the former Lisa Dougherty, in Gloucester, Massachusetts.

October 1969

A NOTE ON THE TYPE

THE TEXT of this book is set in CALEDONIA, a Linotype face designed by W. A. Dwiggins (1880–1956), the man responsible for so much that is good in contemporary book design and typography. Caledonia belongs to the family of printing types called "modern face" by printers—a term used to mark the change in style of type-letters that occurred about 1800. Caledonia borders on the general design of Scotch Modern but is more freely drawn than that letter.

Printed and bound by
The Book Press, Brattleboro, Vermont.
Typography and binding design
based on originals by
W. A. DWIGGINS